D1091498

The *Winning* *Tradition*

A History of Kentucky Wildcat Basketball

SECOND EDITION

Bert Nelli and Steve Nelli

THE UNIVERSITY PRESS OF KENTUCKY

For Bill Nelli

Publication of this volume was made possible in part
by a grant from the National Endowment for the Humanities.

Copyright © 1998 by Humbert S. Nelli and H. Steven Nelli
Published by The University Press of Kentucky.
Scholarly publisher for the Commonwealth,
serving Bellarmine College, Berea College, Centre
College of Kentucky, Eastern Kentucky University,
The Filson Club Historical Society, Georgetown College,
Kentucky Historical Society, Kentucky State University,
Morehead State University, Murray State University,
Northern Kentucky University, Transylvania University,
University of Kentucky, University of Louisville,
and Western Kentucky University.
All rights reserved

Editorial and Sales Offices: The University Press of Kentucky
663 South Limestone Street, Lexington, Kentucky 40508-4008

98 99 00 01 02   5 4 3 2 1

Library of Congress Cataloging-in-Publication Data

Nelli, Humbert S., 1930-
    The winning tradition : a history of Kentucky Wildcat basketball / Bert Nelli and
Steve Nelli. — 2nd ed.
        p.   cm.
    Includes bibliographical references (p.   ) and index.
    ISBN 0-8131-2087-X (cloth)
    1. University of Kentucky—Basketball—History.   I. Nelli, Steve, 1962–   .
II. Title.
GV885.43.U53N45   1998
796.323'63'09726947—dc21   98-3788

This book is printed on acid-free recycled paper meeting
the requirements of the American National Standard
for Permanence of Paper for Printed Library Materials.

Manufactured by World Color in Versailles, Kentucky

Page i, Wayne Turner firing from three-point range as South Carolina guard Melvin Watson
looks on helplessly. Like Watson, the Gamecocks were ineffective against the Wildcat assault
as UK won the March 8, 1998, SEC tournament championship, 86-54.

Page ii, A triumphant Orlando (Tubby) Smith is carried off the floor
of San Antonio's Alamodome after winning the 1998 NCAA national title.

Opposite, A high-flying Jeff Sheppard shoots a layup over Utah's Mike Doleac (51) and Alex Jensen (50)
as Kentucky overcomes a ten-point halftime deficit to win the 1998 NCAA championship game, 78-69.

Page vi, A casually dressed Rick Pitino at a UK practice.
The usually Armani-clad Wildcat coach was widely noted for his sartorial spendor.

Contents

Tables

Preface

This book originally appeared in 1984. The fourteen years since have certainly been eventful. They have contained, for the basketball program and its legion of supporters, elements of tragedy as well as glory. The period has witnessed the retirement of Joe B. Hall; the unexpectedly short tenure of Eddie Sutton; the retirement of University of Kentucky President Otis A. Singletary and his replacement by David Roselle, who in turn left Lexington for the University of Delaware; a major NCAA penalty of the basketball program; and the replacement of Athletics Director Cliff Hagan with C.M. Newton, who in turn recruited Rick Pitino as head coach in Sutton's place. Pitino remained in Lexington for eight seasons, during which he returned the Big Blue to college basketball glory and prominence and then, at the peak of his success, electrified Wildcat fans with his sudden (but long anticipated and dreaded) departure for the head coaching position with the Boston Celtics of the National Basketball Association. The Cats are now launched into yet another new era, that of Tubby Smith. On the basis of his first season in Lexington it promises to be another period of success for Kentucky basketball.

The University of Kentucky Wildcats are one of the nation's premier college basketball programs as well as one of the major unifying forces in the state. It has not always been so. Originally basketball at UK was little more than a form of recreation to help students pass the long winter months.

In its early years, college basketball was a women's as well as a men's game. At the University of Kentucky, in fact, women played the game and enjoyed success in 1902, a year before the first men's team was organized. Women's basketball at UK merits full treatment in its own right, and such a study should be written. But it is men's college basketball that has captured the loyalty of Kentuckians.

Adolph Rupp, who coached the team from 1930 to 1972, was obviously a major factor in the development of the Wildcat tradition, but he was not the only one. The tradition, in fact, was already firmly in place and developing strongly by the time the Baron arrived in Lexington. An even more significant fact is that the "Rupp system," much of which was used by Joe B. Hall, originated not with Rupp but with his predecessor, John Mauer, and was based on the system Mauer had learned as a player for the University of Illinois Fighting Illini. Wildcat basketball owed a great deal to the "Illinois connection." Whenever the Wildcats needed a basketball coach in the late teens and the 1920s, they generally looked to the Illini for help. Even Rupp, who came to UK from a high school coaching job in Illinois, needed a strong recommendation from the Illini head coach to obtain the Wildcat coaching position.

Many myths and inaccuracies have grown through the years about University of Kentucky basketball, especially about the Rupp era. This study attempts to separate the facts from the myths. Interestingly, the truth is every bit as fascinating as the myths. The book also examines the role of Joe B. Hall in continuing the program he inherited from Rupp. Hall's accomplishments

Opposite, the much-awaited "Battle of the Bluegrass" saw the first regular-season meeting in over sixty years between two of college basketball's premier teams, the UK Wildcats and the U of L Cardinals. Here, forward Kenny Walker leaps over two Louisville defenders as UK drives to a 65-44 victory at Rupp Arena on November 26, 1983. Center Melvin Turpin is at right.

were often obscured by his stormy relations with the press, but his achievements were many and significant.

This volume examines important events as well as personalities in Wildcat history. These include the 1921 SIAA championship game in Atlanta, the Madison Square Garden appearance of LeRoy Edwards and his teammates in 1935, the Wildcat NIT and NCAA championships, and, on the negative side, the 1951 basketball scandal and UK's exclusively white recruitment policies prior to 1969 and the profound changes that have taken place in the decades since, the "hundred-dollar handshake" scandal of 1985, and the far more serious Emery package scandal of 1988.

Without the knowledge, recollections, and materials provided by several people, this book would not have been possible. The authors profited greatly from discussions with University of Kentucky coaches and players from present and past squads. Jack Givens, with whom we have spent hours discussing Wildcat basketball in the years since 1978, gave permission to use material from his unpublished autobiography. Scrapbooks and photographs were made available by Helen Blake Schu, widow of the 1940s star Wilbur Schu, by Louise Dorsey, sister of 1920s star Bill King, and by former players Basil Hayden, Sam Ridgeway, Aggie Sale, Paul McBrayer, James Sharpe, Red Hagan, Lee Huber, Linville Puckett, Don Mills, Lou Tsioropoulos, Dick Parsons, and Jack Givens. Former UK students Steve Woodruff, Bruce Thomas, Bill Meader, and Scott Peters shared memories and perspectives. Sincere thanks to all of these persons.

The following people helped immeasurably in the preparation of this study: Joyce Baxter, Administrative Assistant, UK Media Relations, who provided aid over the years; Liz Demoran of the UK Alumni Association; Frank Stanger of UK Library Special Collections; Brooks Downing, UK Assistant Media Relations Director; photographer David Coyle; Elizabeth Nelli, who keyed multiple rough drafts of the manuscript with unfailing good humor; and Michael and Stephanie Nelli (ages six and eight), without whose constant attention this revised edition would have been completed earlier.

We especially appreciate the assistance provided by Duane Bolin of Murray State University, particularly his invaluable contributions in the early stages of the revised and updated second edition.

This book is dedicated to Bill Nelli: Native Kentuckian, UK graduate, and Wildcat fan.

Photo Credits

All photos in this book were supplied by the Media Relations Office of the University of Kentucky Athletics Department, with the following exceptions:

Mrs. Louise Dorsey, p. 20
Joe B. Hall, p. 94
Basil Hayden, p. 18
Paul McBrayer, pp. 26, 27, 46 left, 57
Russell Rice, *The Wildcat Legacy,* p. 7 top
Mrs. Wilbur Schu, pp. 41, 62, 63
University of Kentucky Alumni Association, pp. ii, 68, 111
University of Kentucky Memorial Coliseum Sports Dedication (1950), p. 64
University of Kentucky yearbooks: 1903 *Blue and White,* p. 6; 1904 *Echoes,* p. 12; and the following issues of the *Kentuckian:* 1911, p. 11; 1912, p. 16; 1923, p. 17; 1924, p. 22; 1925, p. 25 left; 1926, p. 23; 1927, p. 25 center; 1929, p. 25 right; 1931, p. 37; 1936, p. 32; 1939, p. 40; 1941, pp. 54, 55; 1945, p. 43
David Coyle, pp. i, ii, v, vi, xii, 149, 172-246
Joseph Rey Au, p. 218
Breck Smither, pp. 220, 226, 232
Gary Landers, p. 230
Matt Barton, p. 244 bottom

Opposite, Melvin Turpin stretches his 6'11" frame to block a shot during UK's 86-67 victory over Purdue on December 28, 1983. Dicky Beal stands by for his share of the action.

1

The Tradition

Reporter Ed Ashford of the *Lexington Herald* called it "the shot that was heard around the basketball world." Ashford was describing the dramatic end of a game between the University of Kentucky Wildcats and the visiting Georgia Tech Yellow Jackets, then a member of the Southeastern Conference (SEC), on January 8, 1955. Fresh from a loss just two nights before to little Sewanee, Tech was the weakest team on the UK schedule. The Wildcats were more concerned with a game two days hence against powerful DePaul, as Coach Adolph Rupp ruefully admitted later, than with the rival at hand.

UK controlled most of the game but never held a comfortable lead and, with twelve seconds left, found itself with only a one-point lead and the ball. At that point Tech guard Joe Helms stole the ball and dribbled down court. The 5'9" Helms, the smallest man on the court, pulled up and hit a jump shot from about twelve feet out. Kentucky still had time for a set shot and a rebound but both tries bounced off the front of the rim and the game ended. Wildcat fans could not believe what their eyes were seeing. Most of the fans at Memorial Coliseum that January night remained rooted to their seats, stunned. They waited, as one fan recalled in a 1981 interview, for the public address announcer or one of the referees to inform them that the timekeeper had made a mistake and UK had one more chance. Small wonder. The Wildcats of that era seldom lost, especially at home. In fact, reporter Ashford observed, "it was the first time most of the fans in the gym ever had seen a Kentucky team beaten." The defeat was the first for the

Wildcats on their own court since January 2, 1943, in a total of 129 games—an overall national record which still stands. It also was the first loss at home to a Southeastern Conference team since 1939, some sixteen years before, when Tennessee took a 30-29 decision. In addition it ended an overall thirty-two-game winning streak spread over two seasons.

Kentucky native Lake Kelly was a member of the Georgia Tech team. Kelly vividly and enthusiastically recalled that night. "My parents were sure we would be whipped. They were so convinced that they made sure they were off visiting my sister in Louisiana that day." Kelly and his Tech teammates shared this feeling. They would have preferred to be anywhere but Lexington. The Tech players had no illusions about their chances against the Wildcats. "All through the game we kept wondering when UK was going to break it open. They led through the whole game but never seemed to be able to move away from us. Then with about two minutes left we called time out and by then we realized we actually could win the game. I'll never forget," Kelly continues, "how the Coliseum was when the game ended. Those 12,000 fans just sat there not saying anything for about a half an hour they were so shocked."

The press and basketball fans across the nation shared the amazement of UK partisans. A "startled" *New York Times* columnist described how Tech "with a closing-second goal, ended Kentucky's dominance of Dixie opponents" and dulled the luster of UK's ranking as "the nation's number one college basketball power." The *Los Angeles Times* noted that "Tech accomplished what a

Southeastern Conference school has been trying to do for nearly sixteen years." The *Kansas City Star* echoed Tech coach John "Whack" Hyder's sentiment at game's end: "What is there to say but 'wow.'" Cliff Hagan, a Wildcat basketball great and later UK's athletics director, recalled how he learned of the defeat. Hagan was at the time a second lieutenant stationed at Andrews Air Force Base outside Washington, D.C. During the basketball season he played on the base basketball team, leading them to two World-Wide Air Force championships and winning All-Service honors both years he was in the service. On the morning of January 9, 1955, Hagan's team was on another base preparing for a game later that day. He remembered he was on his way to breakfast when the team's sports information officer, who was travelling with the squad, came running toward him excitedly waving a newspaper. " 'You won't believe what happened last night,' I remember him saying, and he was right, I didn't believe it at first. It was just something that didn't happen to UK at home and especially to a team like Georgia Tech, which had such a poor record that year."

That was not the end of UK's humiliation. On January 31, 1955, the Wildcats again played Georgia Tech, this time in Atlanta. Lake Kelly recalled that before the game he had a brief talk with one of his friends on the UK team.

"Rupp is furious with us," the friend confided. "He has been pushing us hard in practice all week. If we lose this one Rupp will kill us." "They were so tensed up and afraid of ol' Adolph," Kelly notes, "that they lost to us again, and by an even wider margin than they did in Lexington." Ironically, the two losses to Georgia Tech were the only regular-season defeats UK suffered that year.

Through the decades since 1903, when the first organized team played, UK basketball has evolved into a tradition of excellence and huge success. It is a tradition of which Kentuckians obviously are proud. UK is, one observer noted, "the only school anyone cares about." Coach Joe B. Hall once observed proudly that "People throughout Kentucky really care about their basketball." In fact, he continued, "businessmen tell me that business goes up or down depending on whether or not the Wildcats win."

Some people have likened what UK creates in its fans to a fever—Big Blue Fever. Thus on November 25, 1997, the *Herald-Leader* reported that approximately one thousand fans joined the Cats in Hawaii for the Maui Classic, more than for any other school. To Coach Smith, this "sea of blue" was a valuable intangible. When players "see that support, adrenaline gets pumping. It can be demoralizing for the opponent. I've been on the other end. I know."

This page: The agony of defeat shows in the faces of the cheerleaders as UK bows to Florida State (73-54) in the NCAA Mideast Regionals on March 18, 1972—Adolph Rupp's last game.

Opposite page: Top, Wildcat basketball's top fan, Albert B. "Happy" Chandler, former governor, senator, and baseball commissioner, at a 1970 game in Memorial Coliseum. *Below,* UK students wildly cheer the Cats on to victory over the University of Louisville Cardinals on November 26, 1983.

"UK basketball is like a magnet," former Wildcat ballplayer and assistant coach Dick Parsons observed in a January 1983 interview, "that not only draws Kentuckians but also many individuals who didn't grow up in the state but who have developed a love for the Wildcats. There are any number of people who live out of state who loyally follow UK." One example that came to Parsons's mind was "a gentleman we called 'Tombstone Johnny.'" The man owned a tombstone business in Iowa. Apparently he developed an interest in Kentucky basketball by listening to the games on radio. Then he began to attend some of the games when UK played in the Midwest. "We would see him at Iowa and other places on the road. Eventually he made a trip or two to Lexington and just this last fall he called to tell us that he had moved to Lexington. And all this developed," Parsons concluded, "from listening to broadcasts of UK basketball. He became a Wildcat fan, he sent his son here to school, and finally he even came here to live."

Ned Jennings, a former UK starting center (1958/59-1960/61), found the appeal of Wildcat basketball to be very powerful in Eastern Kentucky. "I travel in the mountains in my work," Jennings stated in an interview, "and it is unbelievable what I run into up there. You find people who have been fans for forty years and have never seen a game but they listen to the radio and write down everything that happens." Jennings has learned from experience that the fans often remember more about the team's accomplishments than the players themselves. "You say something," he noted, "and they will pull the book out and flip through it and tell you whether you are right or wrong. You just can't believe it. It just grew over the years and got to be a way of life."

Central Kentuckians are just as ardent in their support as other citizens of the commonwealth. One local Wildcat supporter, real estate developer Dudley Webb, built a hotel in downtown Lexington in order to bolster UK's bid for the NCAA championship finals in 1985. As Webb stated in a "CBS Reports" segment on college basketball which aired on network television on January 20, 1983, "At the time the NCAA search committee was looking at Lexington they weren't sure there were enough rooms here to support the tournament, so at that time we [Dudley and his brother and partner, Donald] committed to build the hotel project. Sixty million dollars to attract the tournament."

A dream of Kentucky and many out-of-state youngsters for generations has been to wear the blue and white uniforms of UK. When the Inez Indians, from the hills of Eastern Kentucky, won the state high school basketball championship at Lexington's Memorial Coliseum in March 1954, Inez star Bill Cassady's dream came true. After the game UK Assistant Coach Harry Lancaster visited the Indians' dressing room and amid the shouting and romping asked Cassady, "Would you like to play at the University of Kentucky?" The youngster's heart nearly stopped beating as he quietly replied, "Yes, that's what I've always wanted to do." "Would you sign a grant-in-aid?" asked Lancaster. "Yes, I'd like to," Cassady replied happily.

It would be satisfying to be able to report that Cassady went on to fame and glory at UK. Unhappily, he did not. His experience was an example of the dark side of Wildcat basketball. For Cassady, college basketball became a dream gone sour. During his varsity career (1955/56-1957/58) he was a seldom-used substitute. This experience was not, according to a former teammate, because of his lack of size or talent. Cassady was one of several players who were beaten down by Rupp's methods of motivation. As one player recalled, "Practice was all business. Games were a relief because he couldn't kill you in public." Rupp was a tough taskmaster who "seldom praised you. . . . You can make some guys mad and they play harder but others quit or just turn off inside." Cassady was one of several talented athletes who were unable or unwilling to deal with the psychological pressures applied by Adolph Rupp. UK basketball has had other negative aspects, such as the point shaving scandal of 1951 and in the 1980s the hundred-dollar handshake and Emery package scandals. Fans and supporters generally prefer to forget or ignore the dark side, but it is just as much a part of the history of UK basketball as the brighter side, and must be examined.

Despite these negative aspects, Kentucky has become "the biggest and best [basketball dynasty] in the country," as former Marquette coach Al McGuire wrote in *Inside Sports* (December 1981). Since the first game in 1903—which, ironically, was a loss to Georgetown College—the Wildcats have won 1,720 games and lost only 529. During those 95 seasons the home record has been 935 games won and 142 games lost. Team championships include the SEC, won or shared 39 times; two National Invitational Tournament (NIT) crowns; and the National Collegiate Athletic Association (NCAA) seven times, in 1948, 1949, 1951, 1958, 1978, 1996, and 1998. Individual recognition and awards have come as well. The university has produced 37 All-Americans, chosen 54 times, the first one in 1921. Adolph Rupp, who led UK to its first four NCAA championships, completed his 42-season career in 1972

Opposite: Rick Robey jumps center at the start of the UK-Tennessee game on February 15, 1978, at Rupp Arena. The Wildcats won 90-77 on their way to the SEC and NCAA Championships. Other UK players shown are Jack Givens (21) and Mike Phillips (55).

with 876 victories, 190 defeats, and a winning percentage of .822, making him one of the most successful, if not the most successful, coaches in college basketball history.

The Wildcats' first home court, called simply "the Gymnasium," was located in the north wing of Barker Hall. The wing was two stories in height. The basement contained baths, lockers, wash stands, closets, and a swimming pool, while the gymnasium proper was on the second floor. It was equipped, noted the *1909-11 Biennial Report* of the university, "with the best apparatus that could be procured." Unfortunately for the basketball team, the Gymnasium was also used for physical education classes until 1909. In that year, according to the 1910 *Kentuckian*, Buell Armory (which is located in the south wing of Barker Hall) "was floored and there was ample time for practice" in the gym.

The Gymnasium, later to be known as the Ladies' Gym, accommodated at most 650 spectators for basketball games. But, as Sam Ridgeway, who played on the 1921 championship team, remembers, "For important games the fans would be lined up to try to get into the place. They couldn't all get in, of course, but you could hear them outside. And there was someone out there with a megaphone relaying what was going on inside. It was pretty much like it is today but on a smaller scale." For the fans who were lucky enough to get in, there was limited seating. A small bleacher section was set up at one end of the court behind the goal but most of the spectators had to stand along courtside or behind the other goal or along a track above the court. A few, Basil Hayden recalls, even hung from rafters. George Buchheit, UK basketball coach from 1919 to 1924, recalled in a June 1953 visit to Lexington that "once the spectators got in that old gym we played in there was hardly room to play the game. And I remember the poles that held up the running track that ran around the top of the gym. We always had to dodge those things."

Within twenty years of its construction in 1902 the Gymnasium was outmoded and the university, responding to a "public clamor for a better court," in the early 1920s completed plans for a new gymnasium to be built for what seemed at the time the outlandish sum of $92,000. In 1924 when Alumni Gym was built, with its then unheard-of seating capacity of 2,800, complaints were raised that too much money was being spent for a building that was simply too large for college basketball. Critics feared that the "spacious" arena might turn out to be a white elephant. While most of the spectators had had to stand in the old Barker Hall gym, in the new structure they sat on rows of benches.

Fans at the first few games played at Alumni Gym commented that the appearance was more that of a football field than of the basketball courts they were accustomed to at the time. Yet long before Alumni Gym was abandoned in favor of a newer structure, it was obvious

UK's first basketball home court, called simply "The Gymnasium." Located in Barker Hall, it was later renamed the Ladies' Gym. It lacked bleachers, and fans stood to see the games—apparently no deterrent.

The tip-off in UK's last regular-season game in Alumni Gym, the Wildcats' second home. The "biggest and best gymnasium in the South" at the time of its construction in 1924, it seated 2,800.

The Wildcats' home for a quarter century was 11,500-seat Memorial Coliseum. "The house that Rupp built" was dedicated in 1950.

that UK basketball had outgrown what once had been "the biggest and best gymnasium in the South." Its replacement, the 11,500-seat Memorial Coliseum, the "House that Rupp Built," was dedicated in 1950. The new building, which cost approximately $4 million to construct and which soon became known as the "Classic Arena in the South," was a multipurpose structure. In addition to being the Wildcats' home basketball court, the auditorium hosted concerts, lectures, public meetings, and other programs. It boasted a large swimming pool and a complete plant for physical education as well as a host of offices for the athletics staff.

UK's home basketball games had been sold out each season since the 1930s. This tradition continued during the twenty-six seasons the Wildcats played at Memorial Coliseum and has continued at Rupp Arena, even though that structure has twice the seating capacity of the Coliseum.

When 23,000-seat Rupp Arena was opened in 1976 some skeptics expressed doubt that it would be possible to fill the building. They were wrong. The UK Athletics Department has no difficulty disposing each year of the 16,000 season tickets. Most of the rest of the tickets go to students on an individual game, first-come, first-served basis. But this policy does not begin to satisfy the demand for tickets. As *Lexington Herald* reporter Andy Mead observed in 1980, "There simply are more people who want to watch the game in person than there is space available." Cliff Hagan maintained that he could fill the university's football stadium for a Wildcat basketball game. As a result of the heavy demand, then UK Vice President Ray Horseback noted in 1984, "It definitely is a status symbol to be seen at a UK game." It has been this way for decades.

The UK basketball program is the envy of the collegiate basketball world. When he was a member of the Atlanta Hawks, Jack Givens found that UK had "the reputation around the NBA of being the number one school in the country. Players feel it's even better than UCLA because of Rupp Arena, which . . . is sold out for every game, and because just about the whole state seems to support the team."

Many rival coaches and players consider Wildcat fans to be among the most knowledgeable in the country because they understand the nuances of the sport. They are generally more interested and informed, Givens discovered, than the typical NBA fan. "In most pro cities," he noted, "people don't go to games because they love basketball; they go because it's something to do, and they might just as soon go to a movie, or a play, or a rock

UK's home court since 1976 is 23,000-seat Rupp Arena. Despite its size, many fans still can't get seats. Here, UK defeats Alabama 85-70 on February 26, 1977.

For many young Kentuckians who grow up listening to games on the radio or seeing them on TV, getting tickets to a game is a dream come true. Here, Phil Grawemeyer signs autographs for young fans in 1955.

caster Denny Trease observed in an interview that "In Kentucky, where there is not much to do, basketball has become a way of life." Oscar Combs, founder and long-time publisher of the Lexington-based publication *The Cats' Pause*, agreed: "UK basketball is the one positive attraction all Kentuckians can identify with."

There is a certain tidiness and seeming logic to this argument, but it just doesn't hold together. Kentucky is not, for example, the only rural state in the Union, but in few states if any is a college sport as important as University of Kentucky basketball is in this state. Indiana, for example, like its next-door neighbor, is essentially a rural state. The citizens of both states have long carried on a torrid love affair with basketball. But, sportswriter Mike Fields observes, "Ask a Hoosier why he thinks Indiana is No. 1 in basketball heritage. While Bobby Knight and IU will be paid their due homage, the high school game will earn the most reverential mention." By contrast, ask a Kentuckian why the Bluegrass state is "the world's basketball wonderland, and his litany of love likely will begin and end" with the University of Kentucky. Bill Harrell, who has coached both in Kentucky, at Shelby County High School and Morehead State University, and in Indiana, where his Muncie Central High Bearcats twice won the state cham-

The UK Wildcats with Cawood Ledford, longtime "voice of the Wildcats"—the man who, until his retirement in 1992, transmitted the tradition to the state and to much of the nation.

concert." Kentucky is a sharp contrast. "The people who follow UK live or die basketball. If UK loses a game it's like a death in a family. Pro basketball doesn't seem to affect as many people as deeply as college basketball does in Kentucky." Linville Puckett, a star guard on the 1954/55 UK team, verified this fact when he quit the team because of a dispute with Coach Adolph Rupp over discipline. "Basketball at Kentucky isn't regarded as a game," Puckett observed, "but as a matter of life and death, with resemblance of one going to war."

Many observers believe Wildcat basketball is so special and important because of the essentially rural nature of the state, which, in the words of former *Lexington Herald-Leader* publisher Creed Black, makes it "the only game in town." In a large city like Philadelphia, Black's former home, sports fans "can spread their enthusiasm and attendance among professional football, baseball, basketball, hockey, and soccer teams" as well as a range of college teams and sports. "Here it's the Wildcats or else." Former Lexington television sports-

The Tradition 9

pionship, confirms that in Indiana "people still turn out for high school basketball. Even if IU is playing, people are going to fill up the gym to see the Bearcats. I don't think that happens in Kentucky when UK is playing."

Emphasis on ruralness also ignores the fact that Kentucky has a major city, Louisville, which has had pro teams in a number of sports as well as a college basketball power, the University of Louisville. Even though the various pro and college teams in Louisville have won championships, they have been unable to hold the fancy of many Louisvillians, much less win the support of people in Eastern, Central, and Western Kentucky. Sportswriter Pete Axthelm's observation that basketball is a city game must be revised for Kentucky. In the commonwealth, basketball is a small-town and rural as well as a city game.

The special position UK basketball occupies in the state did not just happen. It evolved over several decades through the operation of a variety of factors. One, and not the least important by any means, has been the contribution made by radio announcers, including Claude Sullivan and Cawood Ledford—and, today, Ralph Hacker—who since the late 1930s have transmitted "the tradition" from one end of the state to the other and from one generation of fans to another. Billy Reed described Ledford in a 1981 *Sports Illustrated* article as "the link between Adolph Rupp and Joe B. Hall, between Kentucky's storied past and its stirring present." During his tenure, Ledford and the Wildcats built a radio network with 125 stations in Kentucky, Indiana, Ohio, Tennessee, West Virginia, and Florida. One survey found that UK games could be heard in forty states as well as Canada and the Bahamas. As a result, Al McGuire wrote in *Inside Sports,* "the kids in Kentucky start listening to the games on the radio when they are still being burped on their father's shoulder." Terry Mobley, a former UK player and now director of the university's Development-Central Office, made this point in a December 1982 interview. A native of Harrodsburg, Mobley recalled that he was an ardent fan of the Big Blue at least by the time he was five years old. By then, he noted, he was "old enough to listen to the games on radio. The Wildcats are just a part of my heritage," he stated proudly.

Although Ledford and his fellow broadcasters are marvelous talents, the vital ingredients in the growth and maintenance of the UK dynasty have been the athletes and their coaches. In the final analysis the role of certain individuals and certain key events has been of central importance in creating and nurturing the tradition. The first major figure was All-American Basil Hayden, and the first event was the championship game of the Southern Intercollegiate Athletic Association Tournament in Atlanta on March 1, 1921. That championship was the first of a number of milestones in UK basketball history.

Opposite, the nickname "Wildcats" was first used during the 1909 football season, and the Wildcat crest made its first appearance in the 1911 *Kentuckian.*

PART I

Origins of the Tradition

UNIVERSITAS
KENTUCKIENSIS

FELIS
CATUS

2

UK's First Championship Season

Basketball was invented in Springfield, Massachusetts, in 1891 in response to a recognized need for a new sport to fill the athletic void that existed during the winter season. Football was the sport of autumn and baseball filled the needs of athletic youngsters in the spring and summer. Gymnastics, marching drills, and calisthenics were popular in Europe but did not seem well-adapted to American needs or interests.

In December 1891 James Naismith, a young gym instructor at the International Training School of the Young Men's Christian Association at Springfield (now Springfield College) solved the problem. He tacked peach baskets to the lower rails of ten-foot-high balconies at each end of the school's gym, wrote up and distributed a short list of rules, tossed out a soccer ball, and let the contest begin. One of Naismith's most important decisions was to use a soccer ball instead of a football because he wanted to avoid tackling or extremely rough play in his new game. As Naismith noted in his autobiography, if a player "can't run with the ball, we don't have to tackle!" By using a soccer ball the emphasis would be on passing rather than tackling. Although the game was eventually made less violent than football, during its early decades the sport was a far from gentle pastime. In fact, it was a very rough and tough game.

Theodore Roosevelt, while president of the United States, was concerned about the increasing violence and the growing number of injuries in college basketball as well as football. Larry Fox noted in his *Illustrated History of Basketball* that in 1909 Harvard University's president Charles Eliot "called for an end to basketball, which he said had become 'even more brutal than football.'" Others echoed these sentiments. Efforts made in the following years to bring the young sport under control met with limited success. One of the reasons for the brutality was the large number of football players who flocked to the new winter sport as a way to stay in shape and to enjoy a little violent activity during the long winter days. A measure of the savagery of the game in these early years is clearly shown in an interview conducted by former UK Sports Information Director Russell Rice with early Wildcat basketball player Thomas G. Bryant. Bryant, who played from 1905 to 1907, recalled that "we didn't play for championships but for bloody noses." Commenting on a 1907 game with Transylvania, whose players "came onto the floor wearing football pads," Bryant noted that "I've still got a tender ankle that I inherited when J. Franklin Wallace, a 6'3 1/2" 250-pound football tackle stepped on it during the game. He poked me with a left jab, and I came back with a haymaker to the face."

Opposite, the earliest known photo of a UK men's basketball team, showing the 1904 starting five and their manager (there was as yet no coach). Standing, left to right: guards R.H. Arnett and J. White Guyn, center Joe Coons, and forwards C.P. St. John (captain) and H.J. Wurtele. Seated: manager Leander E. Andrus.

In those days, Bryant concluded, "a good fight was the expected thing."

Until the 1930s, even at the University of Kentucky, games were low-scoring, slow-moving, defensive battles and on occasion brutal slugfests. Basil Hayden, UK's first All-American, noted some of the reasons that even the excellent 1921 team—which won the first championship tournament held in the South (and perhaps in the nation)—averaged only thirty-six points while holding rivals to nineteen points per game in a fourteen-game season, including four tournament games. One reason for the low scores was the way players shot. No one, Hayden recalls, shot the ball one-handed. Long set shots as well as free throws generally were taken underhanded, from the knees. Close-in shots were usually taken from the waist or chest. Even a layup was a two-handed shot although a few daring players shot a layup hook if they felt the two-hander would be blocked. Hayden tapped rebounds one-handed but he was unusual. Nearly all shots taken by all players were two-handers, and since few teams set screens, shots could be easily blocked.

Games were slow moving, with the emphasis generally on defense. There was no ten-second line, so a team could hold the ball at midcourt or in the defensive half of the court if it wanted to do so. A center jump followed each basket made. Nevertheless, the clock continued to run. It also continued to run when a foul shot was taken, when violations were called, and when the ball was passed in from out of bounds. The clock was turned off only when a team called a time-out, which happened infrequently. Because the clock continued to run and teams had to move the ball around a lot to get open shots, far fewer shots were taken in a typical game than are taken now.

The most important reason for the low scores, however, was that the games were so rough. It took a lot of contact, Hayden recalls, before the single game referee would call a foul. "Generally the referees back then didn't really know the rules and you practically had to be knocked into the seats before they would call a foul." No one called a foul, he also noted, for touching a man on the arm or even the back when he was shooting which, of course, would throw the shot off. And when it came to rebounding, there was fierce action under the basket. In the battle for position to get rebounds players pushed and shoved and held. One of the techniques Hayden and other players used was to put one hand on an opponent's back, push him down while jumping, "and go up above him and push the rebound back into the basket with the other hand."

The game Naismith presented to the sports world on that winter day in 1891 was offered at the right time and the ideal place. The Springfield YMCA school was a training facility for YMCA general secretaries and physical education instructors. Sports historian Neil Isaacs has noted that the school's graduates "not only went to posts all over the country, taking their Springfield routines with them, but also returned to the school like former seminarians seeking guidance from the seat of their order. Besides, they all kept abreast of what was going on at Springfield by means of *The Triangle,* a monthly newsletter."

Collegians lagged behind YMCAs in the spread of basketball. The first known intercollegiate game took place on February 9, 1895, when the Minnesota State School of Agriculture defeated Hamline by a score of 9-3 and claimed the championship of Minnesota. The first game between eastern colleges was a March 23, 1895, match between Haverford and Temple, which Haverford won by two points, 6-4. Other contests followed between college squads in the Midwest and East, but the first game involving five-man teams is believed to have been a March 20, 1897, contest between Yale and Pennsylvania. Yale won, 32-10.

Soon after the introduction of basketball in Springfield the new sport was offered in YMCAs in Kentucky. By the turn of the century collegians in the state were playing informal games as well as exhibition contests. The first recorded men's intercollegiate basketball game at the University of Kentucky (then known as Kentucky State College) took place on February 6, 1903, against nearby Georgetown College. The girls' basketball team, it should be noted, began play in 1902 and, according to the 1904 yearbook, was "successful from the start."

For what was to become the nation's most successful basketball program, it was an inauspicious beginning. On that winter afternoon the recently organized Kentucky State team, composed largely of football players, was no match for a Georgetown squad that had been playing for months. At the end of the first half the score stood at 7-1 in favor of Georgetown. "During the latter part of the game," the *Lexington Herald* reported on February 7, "State College weakened appreciably" and suffered a 15-6 defeat.

The State team, at the time called "the Cadets" because of the strong ROTC program, played two other games in 1903, both again on their home court. In that first season they defeated the Lexington YMCA team but lost to Kentucky University (now Transylvania University). State's name was changed in the following years

Table 1. UK Basketball Team Record, 1903-1911/12

Season	Won	Lost
1903	1	2
1904	1	4
1905	1	4
1906	4	9
1907	3	6
1907/08	5	6
1908/09	5	4
1909/10	4	8
1910/11	5	6
1911/12	9	0
Total	38	49

as its status and size grew. It became Kentucky State University in 1908 and the University of Kentucky in 1917. But until the 1920s the fortunes of its basketball team were mixed.

University of Kentucky basketball began "on a shoe-string," as *Lexington Leader* reporter Larry Shropshire noted in 1950. The team was "a one-basketball outfit, and the ball used for all practices and games was furnished by the players, who chipped in a quarter or a half-dollar apiece to buy the heavy little balloon." It cost three dollars to buy the ball and, as Thomas Bryant, an original team member, recalled, "if something had happened to that ball, we couldn't have played."

During its first five years of competition Kentucky won only ten of thirty-five games, but the situation began to improve in the 1907/08 season when the team achieved a record of five victories and six defeats. The next year Kentucky had its first winning season, and just three years later it reached the pinnacle of an unbeaten season. It was, the *Kentuckian* exulted, "one glorious march from start to finish. Not only were we undefeated, but during the entire season not once was an opposing team even in the lead."

One reason for the change of fortunes was the appointment of an effective coach in 1909. In that year E.R. Sweetland, already the school's football coach, assumed the additional duties of basketball coach. The year 1909 was a landmark in UK sports history for another reason. Commenting on a 6-2 football victory over the University of Illinois on October 3, 1909, First Lieutenant Philip Corbusier, commandant and professor of Military Science and Tactics at UK, declared before a chapel audience of students that the football team had

"fought like wildcats." The press soon picked up on Corbusier's term and one of the university's oldest traditions was born. Quickly replacing the previously favored "Cadets," "Wildcats" has remained ever since that day the favored nickname for University of Kentucky athletic teams.

In the wake of the successful 1911/12 basketball season the *Kentuckian* heaped lavish praise on Sweetland "for his most successful season" and outlined his methods and achievements. "He filled the boys with confidence, trained and instructed them, as only he can, and, as is his invariable custom, turned out a championship team."

Prior to the appointment of Sweetland, Kentucky had no basketball coach. Instead the team practiced on its own and all responsibilities were handled by a manager. W.B. Wendt, manager in 1906, recalled later that he was "a one-man operation. I made the schedule, printed the tickets, collected money, paid the bills, was in charge of the team on the road, and sometimes swept the floor." Although the appointment of Sweetland changed that situation, the course of UK basketball in the following years was not an unbroken string of successes. Kentucky had losing seasons in 1916/17 and 1918/19. In 1919/20, just the year before they captured the SIAA championship, they lost seven of twelve games under new coach George C. Buchheit. Despite their poor record the foundations were being carefully laid for the Wildcats' first landmark season.

Buchheit (sometimes spelled Bucheit or Buckheit) was the first of three important coaches in the short period from 1919 to 1930 who would move to Kentucky from Illinois. The others were John Mauer and Adolph Rupp. Together, the three transformed the style of play and the fortunes of basketball at the University of Kentucky. In fact, of the five men who coached at UK during the 1920s, four—Buchheit, C.O. Applegran, Ray Eklund, and John Mauer—were University of Illinois alumni. The exception was Basil Hayden, a Kentucky basketball All-American, who coached at his alma mater in 1926/27. Adolph Rupp, who graduated from the University of Kansas in 1923, came to Kentucky in 1930 after a very successful coaching career at Freeport High School in northeastern Illinois, but even he owed his hiring in large part to a recommendation from University of Illinois basketball coach Craig Ruby. This simply emphasized the fact that during the 1920s the Illinois connection was firmly established. The connection developed primarily because of the success of the Illinois football team and its great coach, Robert "Bob" Zuppke (1913-40), as well as the close proximity of Illinois.

The starting five of UK's undefeated 1912 team. Standing, left to right: forward Brinkley Barnett, guard Roscoe Preston, center (and captain) W.C. Harrison, forward D.W. Hart, and guard J.H. Gaiser. Kneeling: team manager Giles Meadors.

Until the early 1930s Kentucky's basketball coaches, including Rupp, also served as assistant football coaches. Thus talent on the football field was often at least as important in choosing a basketball coach as ability on the hardwood. Illinois was a national football power from Zuppke's arrival in Urbana in 1913 through the 1920s, and it enjoyed undefeated seasons in 1914, 1915, 1923, and 1927. Within the Big Ten the Illini won or shared the conference championship in 1914, 1915, 1918, 1919, 1923, 1927, and 1928. University of Illinois basketball teams were not nearly so successful. Ralph Jones, basketball coach from 1913 to 1920, won the conference title in 1915 and shared it with Minnesota two years later. Under Frank Winters (1921-22) and J. Craig Ruby (1923-36) the Illini shared in only two more Big Ten championships—in 1924 with Wisconsin and Chicago, and in 1935 with Purdue and Wisconsin.

Most of UK's football head coaches and assistant coaches, as well as athletic directors, during the late teens and twenties were University of Illinois graduates. Both Buchheit and Mauer had been stars in football as well as basketball at Illinois and they were to coach both sports at UK. Mauer admitted years later that his "pri-mary interest was football" and not his highly successful basketball teams. Even Adolph Rupp served as an assistant football coach during his first years in Lexington. Only after his success on the hardwood was a proven fact was Rupp free to concentrate on basketball and drop his other chores, which included coaching the wrestling team as well as freshman football.

Buchheit was a young man when he arrived at UK in 1919, having just graduated from Illinois, where he played football under Bob Zuppke and basketball under Ralph Jones. Buchheit brought to his new job the style of basketball play he had learned at Illinois. The *Lexington Herald* on February 24, 1921, called it "Buchheit's system," although Hayden, his star player and most famous product, referred to it as the "Illinois system." Actually this was a Big Ten style of play which all the teams of the conference used but which appears to have been developed first by Wisconsin coach Walter E. Meanwell in the years after 1912. Under both the Buchheit and the Illinois systems one man remained under each goal while the other three players roamed the floor. Buchheit altered the system he learned from Jones in one major respect—although both emphasized

defense, Illinois played a zone defense, while UK employed an aggressive and tenacious man-to-man defense.

All teams of the era emphasized an offense that stressed passing because the ball was seldom if ever dribbled. Not until the 1928/29 season were limitations on dribbling finally removed. Buchheit used what Sam Ridgeway has called a zig-zag or figure-eight offense. Following a defensive rebound or after UK won the center tip the three men on the floor would bring the ball upcourt, one passing it to a teammate and quickly turning back toward the middle of the court and then receiving a pass from the third teammate, who was now running toward him. This, Ridgeway says, "seemed to hypnotize opponents," who apparently had never seen the offense before or had not figured out an effective defense against it. While opponents were confused by the movements of the UK players the ball was passed in to the center, who was stationed under the basket for an easy shot. Should this strategy fail, a set shot was taken from outside, and the center and the other two floor players took up rebounding positions under the basket. According to Hayden, there were no set plays. One player, a standing or back guard, remained under the defensive goal, although he might move up to midcourt or even occasionally to the offensive end of the court to take a long set shot.

Buchheit introduced his system in the 1919/20 season with limited success, winning only five of twelve decisions. But the following year he found three new players who, along with holdovers Basil Hayden and Bobby Lavin, fitted his needs and nearly brought UK a perfect season. All were native Kentuckians and all had been playing basketball for years. Hayden, for example, began playing at the YMCA in Paris, his hometown, while in sixth grade.

Each player on the 1921 team had a job to do, or to use a modern term, each was a role player. Hayden, the team captain, Bill King, the other forward, and guard Bobby Lavin handled the ball. King was a fine goal shooter and when the team faced a zone he generally was the man who took the long outside shots. In the years prior to 1924, when a player was fouled he was not required to take the foul shots. Any player could be designated to take these shots and, for the Wildcats, King was generally that player. Lavin, who had played basketball at Paris High School with Hayden and who was the quarterback on the UK football team, was a ball handler and strong defensive player. He also helped with the offensive rebounding. The team's center, Paul Adkins, stayed under or near the offensive goal. At 6'2" Adkins

George Buchheit, UK basketball and assistant football coach from 1919/20 through 1923/24.

was a big man for the time and generally controlled the center jump which followed each goal. Adkins was an adequate rebounder but an effective goal shooter. The finest athlete was Basil Hayden, an excellent all-around player. Although an accurate shooter, he emphasized passing, rebounding, and defense. Hayden was 5'11" tall but could easily place his entire hand above the basket on a vertical leap. On defense he and other team members emphasized ball stealing as well as strong rebounding. "It's sort of devastating to a team you're playing against," Hayden chuckled in an interview, "if you get in there and get the ball when they're running in one direction and you take it away and go in the other direction." The heart of the defense and the man Hayden feels should have been named All-American was Sam Ridgeway. A strapping 6'1" sophomore, Ridgeway was a shot-blocker and an excellent defensive rebounder. "The other team didn't shoot at the basket but once," Hayden laughingly recalls, "and if they missed they didn't get it back to try again because Ridgeway was there and got it."

The accomplishments of the 1921 team were astonishing when one notes that the starting lineup was com-

posed of two first-year players (freshmen were not eligible), Ridgeway and King, and three juniors, Adkins (who played his first two years at Cumberland College), Lavin, and Hayden. It was not only a young team but in a very real sense a squad of "student athletes." Buchheit recognized the talents of this group of young men and welded them into the first great basketball team in Kentucky, and Southern, history. Buchheit was ideally suited to deal with the players of the era. Ridgeway, Hayden, and the others loved basketball but they attended UK for academics rather than athletics. Ridgeway, for example, wanted to study engineering and at the time UK was the only school in the state with an engineering program. Hayden first attended Transylvania but transferred to UK at the end of his freshman year because he wanted to take an industrial chemistry course which was not offered at Transylvania.

As good as Hayden and the others were, they were not actively recruited. Neither Kentucky nor any other school offered athletic scholarships. Anyone who wanted to try out for the UK team could. In the 1920/21 season approximately thirty-five young men responded to a notice Buchheit placed on the bulletin board. Twelve made it through the cuts, and eight were on the travelling team. All were native Kentuckians. The starters were Hayden and Lavin from Paris, Ridgeway from Shepherdsville, Adkins from Williamsburg, and King from

Lexington. The three substitutes who completed the travelling team were forward William L. Poynz of Covington, center James E. Wilhelm of Paducah, and Lexington native Gilbert K. Smith, who played guard. It was, as Ridgeway has observed, not only "a group of native Kentuckians but a real team of students." And the big, quiet, sincere, painfully shy Buchheit, just a few years older than his players, was perfectly suited to his team. He was as much a friend and teacher as a leader. Ridgeway recalled that Buchheit "was the kind of man you wanted to play for, to give your best for. He was the type that, without him asking, you would want to go out and play your heart out for." They probably would not have responded as well to a hard-driving, highly success-oriented coach. Adolph Rupp, whose personality and methods were ideally suited to UK's needs and interests in the 1930s, '40s, and '50s, probably would have been far less successful in 1921.

After a mediocre record of five won, seven lost in 1919/20, Buchheit's second season was a succession of victories marred only by a 29-27 loss to traditional rival Centre and capped by the SIAA tournament, which was, in Sam Ridgeway's words, "UK's first great success." The Southern Conference was composed of teams from all parts of the South, teams that now are members of the Southeastern Conference, the Southern Conference, and the Atlantic Coast Conference, as well as some that are

The 1916 Paris High School basketball team with two future UK stars, Basil Hayden (front row, second from left) and Bobby Lavin (front row, second from right). Besides playing basketball, Lavin was the starting quarterback on the UK football team.

now independents. Fifteen Conference teams were invited to participate in the 1921 tournament. In addition to Kentucky they were Auburn, Alabama, Furman, University of South Carolina, Clemson, Newberry, Birmingham-Southern, Tulane, University of Tennessee, Mercer, Millsaps, Mississippi A&M (now Mississippi State), Georgia Tech, and Georgia.

The teams converged on Atlanta in late February 1921 from all parts of the South for the first basketball tournament ever held in the region. Although Kentucky with its regular-season record of nine wins in ten games was one of the dark horses, the undefeated Georgia Bulldogs were the overwhelming favorites. This preference changed after the Wildcats' resounding 50-28 first-round mauling of a Tulane team the *Atlanta Constitution* on February 26 noted "had a record for achievement that was expected to make them a formidable factor in the final results of the tournament." Georgia also scored an impressive first-round victory over Newberry, but "the prognosticators are not talking Georgia and nothing but Georgia. They are talking Kentucky State [UK] a lot and generally they are speaking in bated breath." Kentucky's rangy and fast players, the "dazzling" passing, and the teamwork impressed all observers. King, Hayden, and Adkins were judged "three of the most scintillating goal shooters imaginable, while the defense seems almost as good as the attack." The talk of the throngs that gathered in the Atlanta hotel lobbies was Kentucky's "bewildering" and "peculiar attack," that is, its play off the center jump. On the jump, which followed each goal, Buchheit reversed the positions of his forwards and guards. When the ball was tossed up, the forwards, Hayden and King, would run past the center circle toward the offensive basket while Ridgeway and Lavin would move in the opposite direction to take up positions guarding the defensive end of the court. Because this play was new to the teams UK played and because of Adkins's height, the Wildcats generally controlled the tip and often converted it into a quick and easy basket. Basil Hayden recalled that no one was able to figure out how to defend against UK's "baffling" attack.

The Wildcats followed up the Tulane win with equally impressive victories over Mercer (49-24) and Mississippi A&M (28-13). The championship game was played on the evening of March 1 and, in what *Constitution* writer Fuzzy Woodruff termed a "'Frank Merriwell' finish," the Kentuckians defeated the University of Georgia team. (Merriwell was a fictional hero of the day who won baseball, football, and basketball games dra-

matically in the final second of action.) "More red-blooded stuff was crowded into one brief minute last night," Woodruff wrote, "than comes to most men in a span of life." With less than a minute left to play in the hard-fought game, Georgia led by only two points, 19-17. Then Georgia made a serious mistake. Throughout the game they had concentrated on containing Basil Hayden because they recognized, Woodruff wrote, that "the Kentucky captain, a blond Apollo, a Kentucky thoroughbred, if one ever stepped on the turf, has been the thorn in the side of Kentucky's opponents." Suddenly, with approximately forty-five seconds to go, Hayden was free beneath the basket for "the merest fraction of a split second." The ball was quickly passed to him. It "hardly pauses in Hayden's hands. His shot is fast, but accurate. It drops through the basket without hesitating" to tie the score.

Kentucky controlled the center jump which followed the score, quickly moved down the court, and got the ball to Adkins, their center and "the surest goal shooter in the tourney." As time ran out, Georgia captain "Buck" Cheeves desperately threw himself at Adkins, who was set under the basket to shoot. The referee's whistle sounded and was followed by the timer's signal that playing time had expired. With the game on the line, Bill King, although only a first-year player, without hesitation and without consulting his coach or teammates headed to the foul line. "King is coolness personified," Woodruff noted. "He hasn't been particularly good on foul shots all night and Georgia has hopes, though it fears for the worst." And indeed their worst fears were realized. "The ball leaves his hands and King's eyes do not even follow it to the basket." After bouncing dramatically on the rim the ball fell through the net and the game was over. "Talk about your finishes," the Atlanta sportswriter concluded, "there never was such a one in reality" and all that could compare in the realm of fiction was "a Frank Merriwell finish." In interviews conducted sixty years later both Basil Hayden and Sam Ridgeway remembered the events in minute detail, as though they had just transpired. It was truly the stuff that boyhood dreams of glory are made of. Both also recalled the tumultuous reception they received on the team's return to Lexington.

Fans of the "Wildcat Five" had closely followed the fortunes of their team through each of their four SIAA tournament games. There was no radio or television coverage, of course, but fans in Lexington received up-to-the-minute reports during each game by telegraph. "A crowd of several hundred students, alumni, and root-

Coach George Buchheit poses with the 1921 Wildcats, "Champions of the South." Front row, left to right: Sam Ridgeway, Paul Adkins, Basil Hayden (captain), Bill King, and Bobby Lavin. Back row: Buchheit, Jim Wilhelm, Bill Poynz, Gilbert Smith, and Athletics Director S.A. "Daddy" Boles.

ers of the University of Kentucky jammed every corner of the lobby and mezzanine floor of the Phoenix Hotel" to listen to the action in the championship game, a *Lexington Herald* reporter wrote the following day. They "whooped and 'hollered' in glee" as the telegrams recording the Wildcats' progress "were megaphoned from the mezzanine floor, and when the final wire came in and the news was shouted 'Final score, Kentucky 20, Georgia 19,' the lid flew off with a bang and bedlam ruled." As soon as the game ended plans were immediately made for a huge reception, banquet, and dance the following evening when the team arrived back in Lexington.

From the beginning, UK's participation in the tournament was occasion for a continuous round of cutting class, dances, and other forms of celebration which cul-

minated in "a paroxysm of joy," the *Lexington Herald* noted in its March 3 issue, "in the greatest homecoming reception ever accorded any athletic team in Kentucky." A huge crowd of students and fans had trooped down to the Southern Station the previous evening to meet the northbound train and welcome home the "eight modest Wildcats" and their quiet, shy coach. Despite a driving rainstorm, the crowd waited happily and patiently for the train's arrival, then it "followed the conquering heroes back to town and for two solid hours" in a scene to be repeated in future years to celebrate other championships Wildcat supporters "kept up a continuous outpouring of praise and tribute to the team that swept everything before it in its 'march through Georgia.'"

Coach Buchheit and his "Wonder Team" were "Champions of the South."

3

The Illinois Connection

The year 1921 was a glorious one for University of Kentucky basketball. "The student body of the University," observed the 1922 *Kentuckian*, "became an aggregation of hero worshippers, and the Blue and White quintet became the acme of things basketball." The future seemed very bright for the "Champions of the South." The glory quickly faded and the Wildcats were unable to defend their hard-earned title in 1922 or for many years thereafter, but this did not in any way decrease fan interest or support.

The magnificent "Merriwell finish" to the 1921 campaign should have provided the momentum for another highly successful season in 1922. Every member of the "Wonder Team" returned and there was every indication "that Kentucky would have a path paved with roses and leading right up to another victory in the tournament at Atlanta." Even before play began, however, the Wildcats' chances were dealt devastating blows when both Basil Hayden and Sam Ridgeway were incapacitated. Hayden, the heart of the team's offense, suffered a serious knee injury high jumping for the track team, while Ridgeway, who played a similar role on the defensive end of the court, fought a year-long bout with diphtheria and never again played basketball for UK. Although Hayden did return to the team during the season, he was not fully recovered from his injury and his running and rebounding were severely limited. The leaper who the previous season had routinely touched the rim of the basket was now barely able to jump. The memory of the 1922 season still makes the proud Hayden wince.

Forward Bill King, center Paul Adkins, and Bobby

Lavin, the running guard and team captain, returned, but without the vital cogs of the championship squad the 1922 team suffered through a lackluster season with only nine wins and five losses. They returned to the SIAA tournament in late February but lost to Mercer by thirteen points (35-22) in the second round.

Hayden graduated in 1922 and, after a brief but far from satisfying career coaching at Kentucky Wesleyan and at his alma mater, went on to become a banker and community leader in his hometown of Paris. In his last two years of college Ridgeway, who had been a star in baseball as well as basketball, completed the requirements for his degree in engineering and participated in campus activities, especially singing with the glee club. During his senior year Ridgeway gained a fuller understanding of the importance of Wildcat basketball, even in this early period, when the glee club sang in various parts of the state. Ridgeway found himself billed as the featured attraction but not, as he recalls, because of his singing voice. "I remember that we put on a concert at Paducah, for example, and I found that I was featured in all the advertising and the newspaper writings because I had played on the championship team, even though I hadn't played in a game since, and that was at least a year and a half later."

Although basketball was important it obviously was not as crucial in the early 1920s as today. That Ridgeway, an athlete with definite All-American potential, could choose not to continue playing, and that coach and fans would not try to pressure him to use the remainder of his eligibility is, in the context of modern college bas-

ketball, all but unthinkable. Lovell "Cowboy" Underwood, a star on Kentucky's 1923/24 to 1926/27 teams, recalled in an interview that "professional basketball wasn't important at all in those days and we didn't think about signing big contracts when we finished school, so we played the game just for the fun we could have." As to the quality of the athletic performance, Underwood firmly believes that it has vastly improved since his playing days. "With the exception of Basil Hayden," he stated bluntly, "the players of my era did not compare in any respect with the players of today."

Even in the 1920s, of course, Wildcat basketball fans loved their team and did not forget their heroes, as Ridgeway discovered in his travels with the university glee club. Already the foundations of the UK tradition were firmly in place. Nevertheless, there were times during the decade when an observer might wonder which direction the Blue and White was going to take. While the team was moderately successful in 1921/22 their record the following season was a disaster, with only three victories and ten defeats. In 1923/24, Buchheit's last as coach, the university bounced back to win thirteen of sixteen games. After the season, Buchheit was asked to remain as coach but decided to move on to Trinity College (soon to become Duke University). His

place was taken by C.O. Applegran, another former University of Illinois athlete.

Applegran's one year as coach began with an exciting 28-23 victory over the University of Cincinnati on December 13, 1924, the first game played at Alumni Gym. Reviewing the season the 1925 *Kentuckian* noted that in the wake of that season-opening victory "predictions for a championship were rife." The high hopes were not to be realized, unfortunately. "At times the Blue and White would rise to great heights and display its real skill and strength" but from the third game "to the end of the season, the Wildcat quintet played a rather mediocre brand of ball." Nevertheless, at the end of the season UK was invited to the SIAA tournament in Atlanta, where they won a narrow victory over Mississippi A&M but lost their second game, to the University of Georgia. The season ended with a respectable but not outstanding record of thirteen victories and eight defeats.

In 1925/26 under Ray Eklund, UK's third basketball coach in three seasons, the Wildcats lost only three of eighteen decisions and produced the university's second All-American in guard Burgess Carey, a tall, husky, powerful defensive specialist. James McFarland, the 1926 team captain, reminisced about Carey in a May 1983 interview: "He was just a great defensive player. He was

The 1923/24 Wildcats, George Buchheit's last UK team. Front row (starting five), left to right: James McFarland, Bill King, A.T. Rice (captain), Bill Milward, and Lovell "Cowboy" Underwood. Athletics Director "Daddy" Boles is at left.

big and tough and strong. It was awful tough to get past him. He would just slam into guys and if somehow they were able to get a shot off he would just reach up and knock it off the backboard." As the team's back or defensive guard, Carey seldom went beyond midcourt and did not shoot the ball. He did not need to. UK had an excellent group of players including, in addition to McFarland, Will Milward, Cowboy Underwood, and sophomore star Paul Jenkins. This group, the 1926 *Kentuckian* enthused, was the greatest team that has worn the Blue and White since the Southern Champions of 1921." This was fortunate because something, if only memories, was needed to soften the pain and frustration of the following season.

The 1927 squad compiled the worst record of any team in UK history, with only three victories and thirteen defeats. Among the opponents who whipped the Blue and White during that painful year were in-state rivals Kentucky Wesleyan and Georgetown, as well as Indiana and Vanderbilt, and Cincinnati and Tennessee, which won two games each. Although the varsity team was woefully short on experience and talent the Wildcats were blessed with an excellent group of freshmen. UK's problems in 1927 were greatly complicated when Coach Eklund resigned just before the start of the season, apparently because he did not want to be saddled with a losing record. Former UK star Basil Hayden responded to the university's desperate call for help and took over the team just a week before it was to play its first game. "I wasn't able to get much coaching in," Hayden has noted. Besides that, "All the talent had graduated except for one player [Paul Jenkins, the team captain] so there wasn't much to work with and there wasn't much chance to develop anything." Although he went into coaching after graduation from college, Hayden soon decided that he was not "the coaching type" and took a job in Richmond as an insurance agent. He had been away from basketball for two years and was out of touch with the game when UK began its frantic search for a coach to replace Eklund. Hayden and his players tried hard and UK fans, for their part, hoped that tradition and enthusiasm would compensate for a lack of talent or depth, but the result was a foregone conclusion. The season began with a 48-10 loss at home to the University of Cincinnati. Although the team did not lose that badly again, the Cincinnati game, as Hayden ruefully recalls, "sort of set the tone for the whole season."

In all the annals of UK basketball Basil Hayden's experience as coach was undoubtedly the most unfortunate. A genuinely decent person, he did not deserve

Burgess Carey, a powerfully built guard, was team captain in 1925/26 and UK's second All-American.

the dubious distinction of being the most unsuccessful coach in the university's history. That this was not due to a lack of ability on his part is demonstrated by his previous record as a winning coach at Kentucky Wesleyan and at Clark County High School. Despite the unsuccessful 1927 season Hayden could have remained at UK but decided that he just "wasn't suited for coaching."

If 1927 represented the low point in Wildcat basketball history, UK's fortunes immediately improved. Moving up to the varsity in 1928 was the most talented collection of freshmen that the school had attracted up to that time, and to mold them into a unit was an able new coach, John Mauer. The starting lineup in 1928 consisted of one veteran, forward Paul Jenkins, and four sophomores. Joining Jenkins, who was for the second straight season the team captain, were Lawrence McGinnis at the other forward position and Stanley Milward at center, while the guards were Cecil "Pisgah" Combs and Paul McBrayer. Ervine Jeffries, still another sophomore, replaced McGinnis on the starting five at midseason. Jeffries was, according to the 1928 *Kentuckian*, a "clever and sensational forward," but his athletic talent was apparently not matched by an interest in academics. A starter and a star on the freshman squad, Jeffries had left school at the end of the academic year only to return in January 1928, thus missing all preseason practice sessions. He left school permanently at the end of his sophomore year after signing a professional baseball contract.

Like all of his predecessors with the exception of Basil Hayden, Mauer was hired to coach football as well as basketball. Both Mauer and his fellow University of Illinois alumnus, George Buchheit, had been collegiate stars in basketball and football. During his career with the Illini, Mauer played in the backfield with "Red" Grange, one of the greatest and most widely publicized players in college football history. In basketball Mauer was an All-Conference forward. He was also a very good student. In 1926, his senior year at Illinois, Mauer received the Conference Medal of Honor, an award bestowed each year since 1914 at each Big Ten institution on "the student demonstrating proficiency in scholarship and athletics."

A quiet, strong-willed, intelligent man, Mauer was an ideal choice to return UK to the prominence and success it had enjoyed under Buchheit. According to Paul McBrayer, whose entire varsity career was spent under Mauer, the Illinois graduate's greatest strength was as a teacher. McBrayer, an assistant coach for nine years (1934-43) under Adolph Rupp and later a successful

coach in his own right at Eastern Kentucky University, believed that "basketball coaching is teaching and selling the game and selling your knowledge to the players. It is getting across to the players that when you tell them to do something that, by God, that is the best way to do it. That if it wasn't, you wouldn't be telling them. And John Mauer did that." In addition, Mauer was a fine person who had a genuine interest in the welfare of each of his players. "He wanted us to get an education. He wanted us to play each ball game up to the hilt. He wanted us to bring out the best in ourselves in every way, and he led by example. His life was such that you could admire and respect him."

In addition to his personal qualities Mauer brought an updated Illinois system to his new job. Before he could teach that system, however, he quickly discovered that he had to work with the players on the fundamentals of the game. Twenty players came out on October 12, 1928, for Mauer's first preseason practice. (Team captain Paul Jenkins headed a group of six who were excused from practice until after Thanksgiving because they were members of the football team.) Reporter Bill Reep in the October 15, 1928, issue of the student newspaper, the *Kentucky Kernel*, related that Mauer "was somewhat surprised" by the performance of his recruits during practice "when he discovered how little the men seemed to know concerning the fundamentals of the game." The players quickly discovered that their new coach's "style of play is very much different from that [to] which they were accustomed." Mauer quickly concluded, according to Reep, that "there is a lot of work yet to be done."

Paul McBrayer remembered that first practice session: "He started that practice as though the players had never seen a basketball or a basketball game in their lives. He gave a long speech in which he told us in detail what he wanted. As I've said, he was a fine teacher. He would correct mistakes on the spot, when they happened." Mauer turned his attention first to shooting. "We quickly found out that we didn't know how to shoot the ball right. With practice, though, we got it right." The basic shot was a two-handed set shot from the waist. No one shot the ball one-handed. To attempt such a shot at Kentucky or any other college in the country would have resulted in banishment from the squad.

By the end of the first week of preseason practice the *Kentucky Kernel* reported that Mauer was continuing to work his players hard "in order that he can have a team that can play the game and know it from 'A to Z.'" The players showed a willingness to work hard to cor-

Three of UK's basketball coaches during the 1920s: *left,* C.O. Applegran, 1924/25 season, the first to coach in Alumni Gym; *center,* Ray Eklund, 1926/27 season; *right,* John Mauer, 1927/28 through 1929/30. Mauer introduced much of what became known under Adolph Rupp as the "UK System." All three, along with George Buchheit, were University of Illinois graduates.

rect their mistakes and to learn "the new system that Coach Mauer is teaching." Mauer continued to concentrate his attention on fundamentals, "such as the bounce pass, two man offense, dribbling, pivoting, crisscross, and the double pass." Players also spent time on "the art of long and short shots. Coach Mauer has one particular method of shooting these shots and the men are trying hard to follow the example that he has offered."

During the preseason the team generally practiced five days a week. Each session was three hours long and Mauer believed in using the time to the fullest. He worked the players hard and in accordance with a plan designed for each day of practice. "So much time was devoted to one thing, so much to the next, and so on," McBrayer recalled. "Then, as we got more experienced in his system, we were able to concentrate on certain things." Practice always started with a thirty-minute period devoted to shooting. Each player had his own ball and worked on the shots he would take in games. After the players were loosened up Mauer would work on the offense. "This was broken down into a series of drills. This way we would work on passing, cutting, screening, rebounding and so forth. First we would work each drill with two players, then three, then four, and finally, the whole team. The drills were very important. Every time there was a mistake, anywhere, it was pointed out and corrected." The same meticulous attention was devoted to the defense. Half-court situations were set up to teach each man his role in the overall team defense. Like Buchheit before him and Rupp after him Mauer used a man-to-man defense. He drilled his team on how to play against various zones but never used a zone defense himself. Most of Mauer's practices ended with a full-court scrimmage under game conditions and with referees. Early in the season some of the scrimmages would be run without interruptions to point out mistakes in order to work on player conditioning. On other days every time a mistake was made play would be stopped "and it would be corrected on the spot." Later in the season, at least one day a week some time would be spent dealing with specific game situations. For example, "You've got thirteen seconds to play. You've got a one point lead. They've got the ball." Another: "You've got thirteen seconds to play. You've got a one point lead and the ball." Every day time was devoted to free throw shooting under game conditions, defense against the full-court press and zone defenses, and other fine points, until it was second nature.

Members of John Mauer's first UK team. *Clockwise from upper left,* Paul McBrayer, Paul Jenkins (captain), Cecil "Pisgah" Combs, and Lawrence "Big" McGinnis.

To Mauer practice was of vital importance. He believed that basketball was a game of habits and that the habits developed in practice were carried over into games. The starting team was determined by performance in practice. As McBrayer recalled, Mauer's philosophy was that "you do well in the game what you do well in practice. If you don't work on something in practice you probably won't do it well under game conditions. Things don't just happen. You have to prepare, and practice is where and when you prepare."

The "Mauermen," as UK was known during Mauer's tenure as coach, were a squad of complete players. There were no specialists. Everyone was expected to be, or to practice hard to become, proficient at both ends of the court. On defense the Wildcats employed, according to the 1930 *Kentuckian,* an "unpenetrable man-to-man" which "was dependent on the speed and agility of these stars who performed like 'ten-second men.'" The emphasis was on team play but if an individual did not do his job he was out of the game. Two-time All-American Carey Spicer, who played under both Mauer and Rupp, recalled in an interview the long hours the former devoted to defense. "Mauer was a good teacher of man-to-man defense and he worked us hard on it. You didn't dare cross your feet on defense. You learned to move them fast, you know, none of that crossing over. He didn't like that," Spicer chuckled. "He wanted you to be able to move with that offensive man." Defensive assignments, it should be noted, were different in this era than today. Lawrence McGinnis, a starting player through most of his career at UK, noted in an interview that "in those days guards guarded forwards and forwards were assigned to guards. That way the good defensive players guarded the good offensive men." This was the way the game had been played from the early days of basketball but, along with many other aspects of the offense and the defense, it would be changed in the middle and late 1930s.

Team play was the hallmark of the offense as well as the defense but everyone was able to shoot, pass, and dribble. Unlike the basketball teams of the 1990s there was no playmaking guard, shooting guard, small forward, or power forward. Instead both forwards were expected to be strong rebounders as well as good shoot-

Far left, Ervine Jeffries, a star of Mauer's 1927/28 team. Jeffries quit school to pursue a career in baseball. *Left,* center Stanley Milward, who played on all three of Mauer's teams.

The 1929/30 team, John Mauer's last at UK. Front row, left to right: manager Leonard Weakley, Stanley Milward, Cecil Combs, Paul McBrayer, Lawrence "Big" McGinnis, and Carey Spicer. Middle row: Mauer, Jake Bronston, Ercel Little, Bill Trott, and George Yates. Back row: Hays Owens, Larry Crump, Milton Cavana, Bill Kleiser, and Louis "Little" McGinnis.

ers, with a range from the corners on in to the basket. Both guards were expected to be able to run the offense. Both came downcourt with the ball and either could initiate the offense, but they were expected to maintain a balance. That is, the ball was to be moved around the court from one guard to the other and in to the center as well as to the forwards until someone was open for a good shot. And whoever was open was expected to take the shot. Under the Mauer system of play, the *Kentucky Kernel* noted, there was little danger that one or two men would dominate the team scoring "because in his method the scoring plays are so arranged that they will give each man an equal chance to contribute to the scoring."

Mauer "startled the entire South," the 1930 *Kentuckian* observed, with "a slow-breaking offense" built around a "complicated short-pass game." A major reason for the success of this offensive was the use of the

outside screen, the first time it was seen in the South. This innovation and other aspects of the offense Mauer brought with him from Illinois demoralized opponents. "It was a joy," McBrayer reminisced, "to play when the other teams weren't familiar with what you were doing."

Another major innovation Mauer introduced to UK and southern basketball, Carey Spicer noted, was the bounce pass. This was, in the terminology of the time, the "submarine attack" and was the heart of the Wildcats' patterned offense. Contrary to general belief, UK players could fast break but, in Spicer's words, "we weren't encouraged to do so." Lawrence McGinnis estimated that Mauer's teams used the fast break about 30 percent of the time.

Mauer was blessed, from his first year with the Big Blue, with an excellent group of ballplayers. All were native Kentuckians, most from Lexington or nearby

towns. None of them was on scholarship but this was not for lack of athletic talent. College teams of the era simply did not actively recruit high school players and did not offer athletic grants. Basketball players and other athletes were still considered to be students and thus were expected to support themselves, either with money supplied by parents or by working part- or full-time. "A lot of us," McBrayer related, "had to work our way through college. We did hard manual labor every summer."

Unlike players of the present day, athletes of McBrayer's era did not have and perhaps did not need elaborate conditioning programs to remain in shape during the off seasons. Ditch digging and other physical labor did the trick for them. Whether for this reason or some other, the Mauermen were a strapping, powerful group of young men, many over six feet in height. The starting team in both 1929 and 1930 was composed of Carey Spicer (6'1") and "Pisgah" Combs (6'4") at forward (Combs had played at guard in 1928); Stanley Milward (6'5") at center; and Lawrence McGinnis (6') and Paul McBrayer (6'4") at guard. McGinnis, who had played at forward in 1928, was team captain in 1929, an honor that went to McBrayer in 1930. All the starting players weighed between 180 and 205 pounds. It was a big team for the era but occasionally Kentucky came up against opponents who were bigger, among them Creighton with a 6'7" pivotman. But few teams of the era exceeded the Wildcats in their combination of size, talent, technique, and discipline. The first two were there from the beginning. The technique and discipline, however, took time and hard work to develop. The team had the same nucleus through all three years Mauer coached at Kentucky and thus the improvement came from experience and maturity.

A game which probably epitomized the Mauer system, philosophy, and style of play was a January 12, 1929, meeting with Notre Dame at South Bend, Indiana. The hallmark of Mauer-led teams was a disciplined, deliberate continuity offense and a gluelike man-to-man defense resulting in a low-scoring, hard-fought game. All these variables were in evidence in the Notre Dame game. In it, the *Courier-Journal* reported on January 13, the Wildcats "played a beautiful, defensive game, time after time taking the ball after the Irish missed a toss and converting it to their own use and seldom allowing Notre Dame to take a shot within the danger zone."

McBrayer regarded the Notre Dame game as "perhaps our best victory" during his playing career at UK. "Notre Dame had a fine team and in George Keogan

Table 2. Record of John Mauer-Coached Teams

Season	Won	Lost	Percentage	Points	
				UK	Opponent
1927/28	12	6	.666	630	505
1928/29	12	5	.706	496	411
1929/30	16	3	.842	599	408
Total	40	14	.741	1,725	1,324

probably the best coach in the country, although he was overshadowed by football coach Knute Rockne. Probably the most interesting to a modern fan," he laughed, "was the score, which was 19-16, and we didn't freeze the ball. In those days there was no ten-second line or three-second zone and the ball was brought back and tossed up after every basket." It was, McBrayer sighed, "a completely different game, but the fans at the time found it exciting."

During Mauer's career as UK coach, the Wildcats won a total of forty games and lost only fourteen for a winning percentage of .741. Mauer's final season was more successful by one victory than that of his successor, Adolph Rupp, the following year.

The college basketball season was considerably shorter in the 1920s and into the 1930s than it has been in the decades since World War II. The Mauermen, for example, only played fifteen regular-season games in 1928 and 1929, and sixteen in 1930. In each of Mauer's three years play began in mid-December at Alumni Gym with a resounding victory. Each year the Cats were invited to the Southern Conference Tournament in Atlanta, which extended the season to the end of February or the beginning of March. In 1928 UK played three tournament games, in 1929 two, and in 1930 three. Regular-season rivals included Georgetown, Berea, and Kentucky Wesleyan. In fact, UK did not drop these schools from its schedule until the beginning of the 1940s, and even played a Berea team composed of servicemen twice during World War II. Nevertheless, by World War II UK had left its less talented and less successful former instate rivals behind and had entered the "big time." That, however, was still in the future.

Also in the future were the spacious arenas. Most of the gyms in which UK played during the late twenties, McBrayer recalled, "were miserable places." Even the City Auditorium in Atlanta, where the SIAA (1921-24), Southern Conference (1925-32), and SEC (1933-34) tournaments were held, was less than adequate. McBrayer related an incident that "shows the conditions

Table 3. Opening-Game Record, 1927-1929

		Score	
Opening Game	Opponent	UK	Opponent
December 16, 1927	Clemson	33	17
December 15, 1928	Eastern (Ky.) Normal	35	10
December 14, 1929	Georgetown	46	9

under which we played a lot of times. The floor in the City Auditorium was slanted. To compensate for that they put green lumber on wooden horses to make the floor level." Not only did this make running and dribbling difficult because of the many soft spots in the floor but "on one occasion while we were playing down there Lawrence McGinnis [who later was Cliff Hagan's high school coach in Owensboro] went up and got a rebound and when he came down he went right through the floor!"

Despite all the problems, "Kentucky and her stalwart stars" were, according to the 1930 *Kentuckian* "a sensation wherever they played." If the Big Blue's deliberate style of play was not exciting, that certainly did not keep people away from the games. On the contrary, the Wildcats not only performed before "S.R.O. houses" in Lexington but were "always the same drawing card on foreign floors, playing to capacity crowds on every trip."

Mauer compiled a glittering record during his career at UK, returned the basketball program to the level it had enjoyed under Buchheit, and laid a solid foundation for the even greater achievements of his successor, Adolph Rupp. The only prize to elude Mauer was the big one, the Southern Conference championship. In both 1929 and 1930 UK was universally acknowledged to have the best talent of any team in the tournament but each year they fell short. In 1929 North Carolina State defeated Duke by a 44-35 score, while the following year the Duke Blue Devils again lost the championship game, this time to Alabama by seven points, 31-24.

"Morgan Blake, Ed Danforth, and other famous Southern sportswriters," the 1929 *Kentuckian* sadly noted, agreed on a basic reason for this failure. Although "the class of the South," the Big Blue was "also a team which was incapable of rising to great heights in tournament play. The Wildcat team plays orthodox basketball, and previous tournaments have proven the fact that an unconscious flip and run [or run and gun] game fits best in the excitement and strain of a long tournament." Another major factor, however, was also involved. Because of his personality Mauer was unable to whip up his players' emotions for the big games. Even McBrayer acknowledged that "Mauer was not a great inspirational talker." Louis McGinnis also noted in an interview that while "Mauer was a very fine person who was dedicated to his boys he did have some difficulties with the press."

When Mauer decided, after the 1930 season, to accept a coaching job at Miami University of Ohio, UK hired a man who was his opposite in personality and in ability to communicate with the press and the alumni. Louis McGinnis summed up the essential difference between the two coaches in a few well-chosen words: "Mauer spent more time coaching than in public relations, which probably hurt him, in contrast to Rupp who did things the other way."

Mauer was far more than a mere footnote to Adolph Rupp, however. He became as successful a coach at Miami, Army, Tennessee, and Florida, as he had been at Kentucky. Looking back on his career at UK, the *Kentucky Kernel* in 1930 proclaimed Mauer "the Moses of Kentucky basketball." Unfortunately he took the Wildcats only part way to the promised land. It was left to Adolph Rupp to complete the journey. But it would not be a ride without cost to Rupp and the university or to some of his players.

Opposite, Adolph Rupp with four of his "runts" at the start of the 1965/66 season. Left to right: Pat Riley, Tom Kron, Rupp, Louie Dampier, and Larry Conley. The fifth starter, not shown, was Thad Jaracz.

PART II

Adolph Rupp and the Wildcat Tradition

4

The Baron Arrives

Adolph Rupp. The name conjures up a multitude of fond, proud, and pleasant memories in the minds of the Wildcat faithful. Adolph Rupp, the "Baron of the Bluegrass," the venerable "Man in the Brown Suit," who coached at the University of Kentucky from 1930 to 1972. The Baron's 876 wins was a record that lasted for twenty-five years until North Carolina's Dean Smith moved ahead during the 1996/97 season.

In the process of winning more than eight of every ten games during his forty-two years at Kentucky (876-190), Rupp-directed teams captured eighteen Southeastern Conference championships, one National Invitational Tournament Crown (when that was a very prestigious tournament), and four National Collegiate Athletic Association titles. Rupp produced some of the most memorable teams in the annals of collegiate sports, including the "Fabulous Five," the "Fiddlin' Five," and "Rupp's Runts." There were, of course, some unhappy, even bitter, memories, such as the shocking loss to Texas Western (now the University of Texas at El Paso) in the 1966 NCAA finals, and the sordid point shaving scandals of the early 1950s. But to UK fans and probably to the sporting public in general, Rupp's achievements far outnumbered his failures and failings.

Within a decade of his arrival at UK, Adolph Rupp had become a bona fide living legend and, as usually happens in such a situation, the past was reinterpreted and rewritten to conform to the larger-than-life image he projected. The glittering success of Rupp's teams seemed, to the Wildcat faithful, to dwarf any previous achievements. Rupp came to be hailed as a miracle worker.

One of the early revisionists was Joe Creason. Later to become a sportswriter and then a very popular columnist with the *Louisville Courier-Journal,* Creason in the late 1930s was a UK undergraduate and the sports editor of both the *Kernel* and the *Kentuckian.* In 1939 he wrote the basketball section of the *Kentuckian.* Reviewing the Wildcats' achievements during Rupp's tenure at the university, Creason maintained that "in the days B.R. (Before Rupp) basketball and Chinese checkers held about the same athletic rating at Kentucky. Not enough customers attended the games to furnish sides for a fast game of two-eyed cat. The teams were groping along with mediocre success, playing the slow-breaking, listless game that is so characteristic of Southern basketball. . . . Thus it came to pass," Creason concluded, "that since the eventful day in 1931 when fate sent Kentucky the softspoken Adolph Rupp, the Wildcats were lifted from the mire of middle class mediocrity to the peak as one of the nation's annual cage powers." The only things Creason had completely right were the use of a slow-breaking offense by the pre-Rupp Wildcats and that the Big Blue was, by the late 1930s, a major basketball power. Everything else was either a half-truth or an inaccuracy. Even the chronology was wrong. Creason believed that Rupp began coaching at the University in 1931 and had just finished his eighth season; he actually began in 1930. This lack of factual accuracy is not, however, the important point about Creason's article. What it signified was that the rewriting of UK basketball history had begun in earnest. It would continue in the following years and would gain additional embel-

lishments. As Creason acknowledged several years later to Thomas D. Clark, the UK history department chairman and his close friend, he had played an important early role in the formation and development of the Rupp legend.

There were other contributors. In the 1941 *Kentuckian*, sportswriter Fred Hill maintained that "before Adolph Rupp shucked his huge frame into the driver's seat of Kentucky's basketball chariot, . . . the net game in the Bluegrass made rather erratic reading. The Wildcats were a sometimes good, sometimes bad team which most of the time did well to break a little more than even." Not only was "Affable Adolph" a great basketball coach but "it would be safe to say [he] has never produced a bad team in any sport." As befitting a legendary figure, "up at Marshalltown, Illinois [actually Iowa], he built a state championship wrestling team from a book, without ever before having seen a wrestling match!"

The Baron's dynamic personality and his ability to win SEC championships obviously were vital ingredients in the near deification of the Kansan even in the years before the late forties and fifties, when he won four NCAA championships. But there was another key factor in the revision of UK basketball history that took place in the late thirties and early forties. This was the hiring by the University of Tennessee of former Wildcat coach John Mauer in 1939. Mauer not only coached Tennessee but led the Vols to SEC championships over the Big Blue in 1941 and 1943, and to a second-place finish to UK in 1939 and 1945. These were, it should be noted, the only exceptions to UK's dominance over the conference between 1939 and 1953. In addition, Mauer's teams administered regular-season defeats in 1940, 1942, and 1945.

Tennessee had been a major UK rival since at least the late 1920s, but with Mauer's presence the rivalry took on a new and deeper meaning. His success in bringing the conference championship to Big Orange Country radically changed the attitude of UK fans toward him. In addition, Mauer played a role in the success of Tennessee's great football squads of the late thirties and early forties through his services as chief scout for coach Robert Neyland. What this meant was that Mauer was a thorn in the side of University of Kentucky athletics not in one but in two major sports. His contributions in football notwithstanding, what made Mauer's presence at Tennessee so threatening was the success of his basketball teams and the danger this seemed to pose to the continuation of UK's control over the only conference sport it dominated. As a result, Wildcat partisans had great difficulty even mentioning John Mauer's name, much less acknowledging his current success at Tennes-

see or his previous contributions to UK basketball. For example, when Mauer's basketball Vols defeated the Cats for the SEC title in 1941, the school yearbook not only attempted to downplay the three-point defeat but also ignored the Tennessee coach and his previous connection with UK. A notable exception was the gleeful reaction to a 53-29 trouncing that the Vols suffered at the hands of the UK team on February 13, 1943: "It was the worst defeat that Johnny Mauer took since handling the reins at Knoxville."

It is clear that at least part of the reason why Mauer's important contributions to Wildcat basketball have been underrated and his role in the development of the University of Kentucky (or Rupp) style of play has generally gone unrecognized was his later success as coach at arch rival Tennessee. Nevertheless, the process of downgrading Mauer and his work at UK actually began with Rupp's hiring, if not before. The Lexington and Louisville press and the campus newspaper reported the hiring of the Kansan with approval and observed that, in contrast to the deliberate style of play advocated by his predecessor, Rupp coached a relatively new but popular style called the fast break. The *Kentucky Kernel* on May 23, 1930, noted that with Rupp's arrival, "Kentucky will bid farewell to its well-known 'submarine' and delayed offense employed by Coach Mauer. Coach Rupp is an advocate of the fastbreak system which is the most popular system used in basketball at present." Actually, as players who were on both Mauer's last team and Rupp's first at UK have pointed out in interviews, differences between the two styles of play were not as great as the press made them out to be, although the contrast in personalities certainly was. In fact, press criticism of the Mauer system is ironic because that system was adopted in toto by Rupp.

Although Mauer was a very able and successful coach who was admired, even loved, by his players, his dour, introverted personality and his inability or unwillingness to communicate with the press made him unpopular with sportswriters and, through them, with UK fans. Public and press alike were pleased with his departure and enthusiastic about the outgoing and dynamic newcomer, Adolph Rupp. The writings of contemporary sportswriters had a lasting effect. The tendency to contrast the Rupp style in his early years at Kentucky with that of his predecessor has continued to the present. In 1976 Dave Kindred, at the time a sportswriter for the *Courier-Journal*, published his imaginative examination of the high school, college, and pro game in the state, *Basketball: The Dream Game in Kentucky.* In it Kindred claimed that "Rupp's teams from the beginning were

models of simplicity and fire. They took hold of the ball and ran. That doesn't seem much of an analysis of a system whose artful practitioners gained national fame, but then basketball is a simple game." Even Neil Isaacs in *All the Moves,* an excellent history of college basketball, stated that Rupp "brought fast-breaking ideas to Lexington, where Johnny Mauer had been teaching a deliberate, ball-control game."

Actually there was a great deal more continuity than is generally realized. As Louis McGinnis, who played for both Mauer and Rupp, pointed out in an interview, "There was no reason for Rupp to make a lot of changes. Don't forget that we were very successful the previous year and that Mauer was an excellent teacher and we were strong in the fundamentals." Essentially what Rupp did was to turn the players loose but within the system Mauer had brought to Lexington in 1927 and had developed in his three years as coach of the Big Blue.

As an All-American under both Mauer and Rupp, as well as captain of Rupp's first team, and later as a personal friend of both men, Carey Spicer had a unique vantage point from which to observe the transition from Mauer to Rupp. Spicer noted in an interview that "we had the good fundamentals from Mauer, and Adolph let us use our own natural ability along with the set offense we learned under Mauer. We could use more variations which made for higher scores but we used practically the same offense we had under Mauer." Spicer had been chosen team captain by Mauer and continued in that capacity when Rupp arrived. "As captain under Mauer I had the playbook with all the plays and all the variations. So when Adolph came, and this was before the football season began, he called me to his office and sort of picked my brain about the type offense we had used," Spicer recalled. "I told him I had this playbook of John's and he said, 'Would you mind if I look at it?'" Spicer soon joined the football team, on which he was one of the backfield stars. When, after the football season ended, he reported for basketball practice (which had been in progress for about three weeks) he found that "we were using all the same plays and, in fact, all the same numbers as we had under Mauer. But," he hastened to add, "Adolph encouraged us to use more variations and to use our own natural ability." Thus the plays UK used under Rupp (as well as his successor, Joe Hall) were basically the same as those used under Mauer, but, Spicer noted, "with improved variations."

Fans and sportswriters have misunderstood two things: Mauer's UK teams did make use of the fast break when the opportunity presented itself, but the cautious Mauer did not encourage his players to run, while Rupp did encourage them to run, and at every opportunity. As Spicer observed about Rupp's first season at UK, "We started out with a set offense but with more fast breaking than under Mauer. Where Mauer permitted a fast break but discouraged it, Rupp not only permitted it but encouraged it." But Rupp did not, also contrary to general opinion, favor a racehorse or run-and-gun style of basketball. By contrast, Ward "Piggy" Lambert, one of the originators of fast break basketball, and his Purdue Boilermakers (as Isaacs noted in *All the Moves*) "specialized in quick breaking whenever the ball changed hands." Rupp, instead, preferred and coached a set offense, the guard around offense, with an emphasis on short passing and as little dribbling as possible, and the use of screens, or, as they were called at the time, blocks, as Mauer had before him. Rupp made use of the outside screen and the bounce pass, two innovations Mauer had introduced to UK and southern basketball.

The contrast between the UK offense and the fast break was made clear by famed *New York Times* reporter Arthur Daley in his description of the Wildcats' January 5, 1935, meeting with the New York University Violets at Madison Square Garden. "The Violets displayed a brand of play that is indigenous to the East. It was one of the fast-break, the quick-cut for the basket and a short flick in. Kentucky, on the other hand, demonstrated something quite new to metropolitan court circles. The Southerners," Daley observed, "employ a slow, deliberate style of offense that is built around thirteen set plays."

By the middle and late 1930s the Kentucky system would be refined with the addition of the inside screen and the second guard around. Nevertheless, in Rupp's first year in Lexington, in McGinnis's words, "we did things pretty much the way we had the year before." There were several reasons for this. Among others, the UK players knew the style and liked it, and it was a proven success. In addition, Rupp was already familiar with it from having coached high school basketball in Illinois for five years. The system Mauer taught, it must be recalled, was essentially what he had learned as a player at the University of Illinois. This system was also used by most Illinois high school teams in the late twenties. Thus Rupp had already adjusted to much of what Mauer taught before he came to Lexington. Rupp had also adjusted to the use of more running in his offense, but this innovation was gaining popularity among high school coaches in Illinois and elsewhere.

The style Rupp used at Kentucky, it must be emphasized, was not the one he had learned as a college player at the University of Kansas. This is evident from

a February 23, 1932, *Lexington Herald* account of the Wildcats' preparations for an upcoming Southern Conference Tournament game in Atlanta against Tulane University. The Green Wave was coached by George Rody, who had been a college teammate of Rupp. "Tulane uses a style of play that greatly resembles the old Kansas style which Rupp played," sportswriter Vernon Rooks observed. By contrast, "Rupp's style falls in the 'outlaw' class, being entirely different from the Kansas system and originated by Rupp." Note that already Mauer's contributions were being ignored and the Rupp legend was forming. It is ironic that the system Rupp employed at the University of Kentucky owed more to John Mauer and to the University of Illinois than to the man for whom Rupp had played at the University of Kansas, Dr. Forest C. "Phog" Allen.

Although Rupp did not originate his system, as Lexington and Louisville sportswriters mistakenly believed, one vital ingredient of his great success was the inner fire that drove him to demand the best that he and his players could offer. Rupp's players performed to the best of their ability at all times and in every game or they did not play. Buddy Parker, who played for UK from 1945 to 1947, stated in an interview that "Coach Rupp instilled in us to be winners or we didn't last. If he taught us anything it was that there wasn't much place for second best. He did not like to lose."

Rupp maintained a constant, steady pressure on his teams all season, every season. It is not difficult for a coach to get his players up for a big game. Rupp's teams performed at their peak not only against good and great teams but also against opponents known to be inferior. And it should be noted that Rupp scheduled a lot of weak teams over the years. Nevertheless, he was able to maintain his players at a high level of intensity even for these "patsies." This is probably the most difficult task for a coach, and Rupp was a master of the art. For Rupp, as many of his former players have noted in interviews, basketball was not a game—it was a life-or-death proposition. Rupp formed this attitude toward work during his childhood years in Kansas.

Adolph Frederick Rupp was born on September 2, 1901, on a farm near Halstead, Kansas, the fourth of six children born to Austro-German immigrants Heinrich and Anna Lichti Rupp. His father died of cancer when Adolph was only nine years old, leaving a widow to tend the farm and raise the children. The result, former UK Sports Information director Russell Rice observed, was a "story of hardships, dawn-to-dusk toil in the fields, and a close family relationship that resulted from the battle for survival on the prairie." The humble beginnings, the solid grounding in the work ethic, and the harshness of life molded young Adolph's character. Rupp the man became, as *New York Daily News* reporter Phil Pepe once observed, a "strong-willed individual who has never been afraid to voice his opinion, even if it is a minority and unpopular one."

At a very early age Rupp became interested in basketball, and the young sport became a major factor in directing the future course of his life. He became a star high school player, averaging nineteen points a game, which for that era was phenomenal. Rupp attended the University of Kansas, but his star did not shine as brightly in college as it had in high school. Rupp recalled in an interview that he usually entered games only "when things were pretty well settled, one way or another." In fact, he ended his college career without having scored a point in varsity competition.

During Rupp's years at Kansas he played basketball for Phog Allen, one of the great college coaches and fine teachers of the sport. Interestingly, Allen was assisted at the time by Dr. James Naismith, the inventor of basketball. Thus Rupp learned basketball from two of the sport's legends. During Rupp's college career Kansas won the Missouri Conference championship in 1922 and 1923 (going undefeated the latter year) and the national championship in 1922.

Following graduation in 1923, Rupp, with a degree in economics, searched unsuccessfully for a job in business. Rupp then returned to Kansas as a graduate student but left after just one semester to accept a high school teaching and coaching job at Burr Oak, Kansas. After a year and a half, he left for Marshalltown, Iowa, High School, where he coached for a year. In 1925 he moved to Freeport, Illinois, High School. During his five years there his basketball teams won more than 80 percent of their games. In 1929 Freeport won eighteen games, lost five, and took third place in the state tournament. The next season the team won twenty games and lost four, losing in the sectional meet after winning the district championship.

In addition to his activities on the basketball court Rupp was hard at work in the classroom. To advance himself in the teaching profession he spent four summers at Columbia University's Teachers College in New York and earned a Master of Arts degree in education. As it developed, Rupp had little professional need of the M.A. because his high school teaching career came to an end in 1930. But Rupp could not foresee this in the late 1920s, and it was to his credit that he devoted the time, effort, and thought to preparing himself as thoroughly as he could for his future. It is also significant

Rupp (second from left) with other members of UK's football coaching staff for the 1930/31 season. Elmer "Baldy" Gilb (center) was Rupp's assistant basketball coach during the mid-1940s. Head football coach Harry Gamage (third from right) and Bernie Shiveley (second from right) both came to UK from the University of Illinois. Shiveley was UK athletics director from the 1940s through the late 1960s.

that in pursuing a graduate degree Rupp chose the best and most prestigious school of education in the nation.

Rupp's career as high school coach and teacher came to an end when, after the 1930 basketball season, John Mauer resigned his position as coach at the University of Kentucky. When news of the opening circulated in coaching circles the university was inundated, according to the *Courier-Journal*, with seventy-one applications, among them one from Adolph Rupp. In addition to being, in the words of the *Lexington Herald*, a "graduate of the Kansas School of Basketball" and a disciple of Phog Allen, Rupp had another major point in his favor: a strong letter of recommendation for the job from University of Illinois coach Craig Ruby. Thus once again the Illinois connection was the deciding factor in filling the basketball coaching position at the University of Kentucky.

On May 21, 1930, UK Athletics Director S.A. "Daddy" Boles telephoned Rupp long distance to make a formal offer, which Rupp accepted. As formalized by a Board of Trustees meeting on May 31, 1930, Rupp was ap-

pointed "as instructor in Physical Education, to have charge of varsity basketball and to assist in other sports." The "other sports" included football and track. Rupp received a two-year contract which paid $2,800 for 1930/31 and $3,000 for 1931/32. By contrast, instructors in academic departments received about $1,500 to $1,700 per year. By 1935 Rupp's salary had been increased to $4,250 for each of the following two seasons to serve as, according to Board of Trustee minutes, "head basketball coach and assistant in other sports."

Fans, students, and players were wildly enthusiastic about Rupp and what they thought was his new offense from the very beginning of his tenure at UK. When Rupp called his first practice, the *Kentucky Kernel* reported on October 17, 1930, he found himself "confronted with forty-six aspiring and perspiring candidates for the varsity five," and this record number did not include a number of fine athletes still playing on the varsity football team. Rupp was not only a shrewd and innovative coach and a good judge of talent; he was also blessed with excellent timing and a large helping of good luck. His ar-

rival in Kentucky coincided with the beginning of the decade that witnessed what sports historians Jack W. Berryman and Stephen H. Hardy termed "the first rush of national interest" in college basketball. By the end of the decade UK was a nationally recognized basketball power and Rupp had taken his place among the elite of college coaches.

Rupp's good luck was evident from the beginning of his career in Lexington. Because four of the five starters from the 1929/30 team had graduated and the Wildcats faced a tough schedule in 1930/31, sportswriters and other experts painted a gloomy picture, predicting that Rupp would be fortunate to have a winning season. These predictions removed a great deal of the outside pressure in Rupp's first season at UK. Although the fact was generally unrecognized at the time, Mauer had bequeathed to his successor the nucleus of an excellent team with talented players who were thoroughly grounded in the fundamentals of basketball. Among them were All-American Carey Spicer, Louis McGinnis, and George Yates, three excellent front-court players. In addition, Mauer's last group of recruits included Ellis Johnson and Forest "Aggie" Sale, two future All-Americans who became sophomores in 1930. Johnson had been a member of the 1928 national championship team while at Ashland High School, and at UK became one of the school's greatest all-around athletes. He was a three-year starter on the varsity basketball and football squads, and he also played baseball and competed on the university's track team. Aggie Sale,

who had played high school ball at Kavanaugh in Lawrenceburg, possessed good speed and agility for a big man, was a better than average shot, and was a great rebounder. Paul McBrayer, also a Lawrenceburg native, recalled that "Aggie was a little ahead of his time as an offensive player." Harry Lancaster, who played against Rupp and UK while an undergraduate at Georgetown College and later served for many years as his assistant coach, related in his *Adolph Rupp as I Knew Him* that "years later, Adolph was to tell me several times that Aggie might have been the best player he ever coached."

Although the success of his first season at Kentucky was based on the talented and well-coached players he inherited from Mauer, Rupp quickly demonstrated that he knew both how to adapt these athletes to his own personality and style and how to recruit other excellent players. McBrayer and other authorities agree, in fact, that the key to Rupp's success was his talent as a recruiter. Recruiting was in its infancy in the early 1930s and, at least in part because of the lack of available funds, Rupp confined his attention to players in Kentucky and Indiana. He made excellent use of the Kentucky high school basketball tournament, which was held in Lexington, and the Indiana high school tournament, to scout potential recruits. He also relied on letters from alumni and interested friends of the university to alert him to talented but unknown or overlooked players. Rupp's first foray outside the Kentuckiana area was the enrollment of New York native Bernie Opper at the Lexington campus in 1936. Yet, as Opper noted in a 1980 interview at

Adolph Rupp with the 1930/31 basketball team, his first at UK. Front row: Ercel Little, George Yates, Carey Spicer (captain), Forest Sale, and Milton Cavana. Middle row: George Skinner, Allan Lavin, Bill Trott, Jake Bronston, Louis McGinnis, and Cecil Bell. Back row: Rupp, William Congleton, Bill Kleiser, Ellis Johnson, Charles Worthington, Darrell Darby, and manager Morris Levin.

38

his home in Los Angeles, the arrival of this future All-American guard had nothing to do with Rupp's recruiting efforts. Opper was a standout high school and amateur basketball player in New York in the early thirties and was offered a scholarship to play at Long Island University, one of the powerhouse teams of the day, but turned it down. "I saw Kentucky play in the Garden [Madison Square Garden]," Opper recalled. "Adolph came there with LeRoy Edwards [UK's star center] in January 1935 and I decided I wanted to leave New York, which was unusual in those days because everybody wanted to play there. Anyway, I wrote a letter to Adolph and told him what I had done and gave him the names of some coaches, like Nat Holman at City College, who could tell him about me. So he wrote back and said come on down and we'll see what we can do for you about a scholarship. So I went and he got me a scholarship." Such was recruiting in the 1930s.

Rupp exercised an iron discipline over his team. He made his position and expectations clear from the very beginning of his career at UK. The *Kernel* on October 17, 1930, reported Rupp's first speech to his team: "I want it understood that there will be no loafers on this team. Every man has got to play ball or get off; that's final." The Baron, as he came to be known, drove his players hard in practice in an effort to cut down on technical errors. He concentrated on basic offensive plays, a tenacious man-to-man defense and, above all, shooting. If a player could not consistently hit the basket he did not last long with the team. Rupp was not a teacher in the sense that Mauer had been. Mauer revelled in instructing his players in the fundamentals of the game—in dribbling, passing, shooting, and the finer points of defense. Rupp, on the other hand, fully expected his players to know the basics of basketball when they arrived at UK. If they were not proficient in the fundamentals or could not learn them quickly, Rupp wasted no time on them. Since many of the Wildcat recruits were deficient in at least some of the fundamentals, it fell upon Rupp's assistants to correct the shortcomings. Rupp was fortunate to find, or shrewd enough to choose, a succession of assistant coaches who were themselves thoroughly grounded in fundamentals and who were excellent teachers. In addition to helping coach the varsity, Rupp's assistant also directed the work of the freshman squad. It was during the freshman practices, which generally were held after the varsity workouts and lasted from about 7:00 to 10:00 at night, that most of the instruction in basics took place.

During a varsity practice, one former assistant recalled, the silence in Alumni Hall and later in Memorial Coliseum was almost deafening. As Rupp himself said: "Why should boys constantly chatter in a class in basketball any more than they do in a class in English? Why should they whistle and sing? If you let 'em talk and wisecrack around, they don't concentrate. I tell the boys if they want to talk, we've got a student union for visiting purposes. And if they want to whistle, well there's a music academy, too."

Rupp was extremely demanding of his players and would not tolerate mistakes. He did not play favorites, especially in his first two decades of coaching at UK, and when one of the players erred during practice Rupp would reprimand him with such sarcastic comments as: "Go back up in the stands and read your press clipping!" or "Boy, will you pass that ball to someone who knows what to do with it!" or "Some day I'm going to write a book on how not to play basketball, and I'm going to devote the first two hundred pages to you!" His thirst for perfection was demonstrated in the first varsity scrimmage against the freshman squad on December 11, 1930. The varsity won 75-21 but Rupp was annoyed because, as the *Lexington Herald* reported the next day, "thirty-one shots at the basket are too many for a freshman team to have in a scrimmage with the varsity." The Baron was somewhat happier two days later when the varsity trounced the freshmen 75-9 and allowed only six shots in the first forty-five minutes of action. He hoped that the real games would turn out the same way, and the opening contest against Georgetown College almost did.

On December 18, Rupp and "the Kentucky Wildcats introduced their new fast-break offense to the Lexington basketball fans in a convincing manner . . . by downing the Georgetown Tigers 67 to 19." Rupp used his entire squad of seventeen players in the process of running up this "overwhelming score." The press enthusiastically reported the positive response of UK partisans to the team's new style of play, which was, reporter Totsy Rose of the *Kernel* concluded, "a great deal more interesting to watch than the system used last year by Coach Mauer." Rose failed to recognize that in most respects it was the same system. The Wildcats were led in scoring by Aggie Sale (nineteen points), Louis McGinnis (sixteen), and Carey Spicer (eight), while George Yates, a substitute center, contributed ten points. Georgetown was led by sophomore guard Harry Lancaster, who scored ten of his team's nineteen points. Lancaster and Georgetown faced the Wildcats in opening-day contests in each of the following two seasons and suffered crushing defeats in each game.

Three action shots from the 1938/39 season, taken in
Alumni Gym. The UK team is in white. Even then the fans
turned out in droves.

Kentucky followed the Georgetown rout with nine
victories in a row. After two consecutive losses, to Georgia and Clemson, the Blue and White ended the regular
season with wins over Georgia Tech and Vanderbilt and
headed to Atlanta for the Southern Conference Tournament. There they defeated North Carolina State, Duke,
and Florida on the way to a March 3 showdown with
Maryland for the conference championship. Although
the Wildcats lost by a score of 29-27, UK fans were well
satisfied with the season record of fifteen wins and only
three defeats. Memories of John Mauer quickly faded.

Contributing greatly to the speed and ease with which
Rupp supplanted his predecessor in the hearts of Wildcat
partisans was the contrasting manner in which the two
men dealt with the press. While Mauer generally antago-
nized the press, Rupp went out of his way to maintain
cordial relations by helping sportswriters meet their
never-ending need for amusing and quotable statements
and by displaying his unique and fascinating personality.
One of the things that endeared him to sportswriters,
and through them an adoring public, was his variety of
widely publicized superstitions. During Rupp's very first
season at UK one sportswriter described a pregame ex-
pedition the new coach had taken with his players: "We
saw, among other things, a black cat. Rupp yelled 'Boys,
it's in the bag!' and proceeded to chase down to the spot
where the black cat had crossed over, and follow in the
footsteps of the cat. Of course, he was referring to the
Washington & Lee game" which took place the next day,
February 6, and which UK won 23-18.

Rupp's most famous and long-lasting superstition
was his brown suit tradition. All through his forty-two
seasons as UK coach he wore a brown suit, brown tie,
brown shoes, and brown socks to every Kentucky game.
According to Rupp, this tradition dated back to his
coaching days at Freeport High School when he got a
new blue suit to replace the old brown one he had been
wearing. The first time he wore the new suit his team was
badly beaten. Rupp took this as an omen and returned to
wearing his old brown suit. Soon after his arrival at Kentucky he had his players believing in the superstition.
Thus when the Wildcats faced Vanderbilt on January
21, 1931, in their first away game of the season, the team
got off to a bad start and played a poor first half. At
halftime Rupp asked guard Jake Bronston, according to
an article in the *Kernel*, "What were you thinking of when
you were going bad out there in the first half?" Bronston
quickly replied, "I was thinking if you had those brown
socks on." Rupp had the brown socks on and UK went

on to win the game 42-37. The press and Big Blue fans loved stories like this one, and Rupp provided a never-ending supply of them.

These were not simply stories or creations for press consumption. According to several former players, Rupp firmly believed in his superstitions. For example, Buddy Parker noted, "Coach Rupp's routine was always the same. Just like the brown suit the practices were always done exactly the same way. He always rode in the same place on the bus, just behind the driver, and before a game he always came out on the floor at a certain time and the same way. He never changed his routine." Dick Parsons, whose experience with Rupp was both as a player (1959-61) and as an assistant coach, elaborated on the superstitions in an interview. "He had a routine when he went to the locker room before the game and at halftime that must have been the same for at least thirty years. He did exactly the same thing every game. I can still see him," Parsons reminisced, "take his coat off and hang it in the first locker in Memorial Coliseum. He would go to the sink and wash his hands and come back and appear before the team. When he left the locker room he never entered the playing area until the UK Fight Song was completed." Among Rupp's other superstitions, according to Parsons, were "black cats, collecting bobby pins wherever he could find them, and he always had buckeyes in his pocket. And these were only a few of them."

Kentucky fans flocked to Alumni Gym to watch Rupp, brown suit and all, and their blue-and-white-clad heroes perform their on-court magic game after game and season after season. At a typical game "the building was jammed to overflowing and many fans had to be turned away. The student body is so large that there are only about 1,000 seats available to the other supporters." From the first season of Adolph Rupp's reign, Alumni Gym was generally filled to overflowing. The Kentucky-Washington & Lee game played on February 6, 1931, drew more than 4,000 of the faithful, while a contest with Georgia Tech three days later reportedly attracted nearly 5,000 Big Blue enthusiasts. One player from this era recalled in an interview "many games in Alumni Gym where there never was anybody ever sat down from the time they came into the building until they left."

Opponents quickly came to dread the zealous Wildcat fans, the innovative and acid-tongued Adolph Rupp, and the multitalented UK players. The Big Blue's set offense and effective use of the fast break and its aggressive man-to-man defense struck fear in the hearts of

Adolph Rupp in the mid-1940s, as he stood on the threshold of his most successful seasons.

opposition coaches and forced many to change their strategy. To try to run with UK was generally futile because few teams, especially those in the SEC, had the talent or depth to keep up with the Wildcats in a running game. As a result many teams used a stall in an effort to slow the tempo of the game so that, even if they were unable to win, they could at least narrow the margin of defeat. This tactic enraged Rupp, who believed it was unfair and detrimental to the future of the sport for an opposing team to be permitted to slow the game down just because their players were less talented than Kentucky's. At annual coaches' meetings and at coaching clinics he lobbied vigorously for changes in the rules. In Chicago in 1932 an effort was made to eliminate the stall. Although many coaches agreed on the need to eliminate the stall and speed up the game, they rejected a proposal to do so submitted by James Naismith, the founder of the game. It would have required the offensive team to shoot the ball within a thirty-second period after inbounding it. This suggestion was innovative. Colleges

did not begin to experiment with it until the 1980s, some thirty years after the shot clock concept was adopted by the National Basketball Association. Rupp played an important role in the passage of a compromise, the ten-second rule, at the 1932 conference. This rule, which is still in effect, allows the offense only ten seconds to move the ball from the back to the front court. If the players are not successful they lose possession of the ball. This strategy was ineffective in combatting the stall because, as Neil Isaacs observed, "the burden of tempo remains on the defense, as Naismith continued to point out as long as he lived."

The ten-second rule, although inadequate, was a beginning. Rupp also played a prominent role in the introduction of the three-second rule at the same 1932 meeting and its permanent adoption in 1936. That rule and the elimination of the center jump after each basket, also in 1936, fell short of the intended objective of reducing the influence of the tall player, but they did help speed up the game, which was Rupp's principal intention. Rupp was also among several coaches over the years who suggested and supported an NCAA-conducted basketball tournament to choose a national champion. Thus while in New York City in January 1935 for a game at Madison Square Garden against New York University, Rupp proposed that the leading college teams from each section of the country meet in a central location, preferably Chicago, to decide the national championship. According to the *New York Times* of January 6, 1935, Rupp stated that "such a tournament would put an end to conflicting claims to so-called national championships." In addition, "it would tend to further interest in this sport throughout the country" and would encourage "a more uniform code of rules interpretation." The first tournament was held in 1939 and, as Tev Laudeman has observed, it eventually did for college basketball what the World Series did for baseball. It provided "a goal and a stimulus for participants, and a focal point of interest for fans." During his career Rupp's teams won the NCAA tournament four times.

Rupp was never close to any of his players while they were team members, nor did he generally indicate a desire for their friendship. In fact, Rupp was a very private person with a small circle of close friends. Even his longtime assistant Harry Lancaster was forced to admit in his reminiscence *Adolph Rupp as I Knew Him* that he came "as close as Adolph would ever let anyone get to him. I don't think he ever had a truly close friend in his life, nor do I think he wanted one."

In his job as coach, winning was all-important to Rupp. He often told his players, "If it matters not whether you win or lose, why do they keep score?" Because he hated "quitters," Rupp constantly tested each athlete's character by probing for physical, mental, and emotional weaknesses. He had little interest in being liked or admired by his players and insisted on maintaining a distance from them. The distance and the relationship he desired to establish with his players were emphasized by the starched khakis he and Lancaster wore at each practice. His players were treated like army recruits, while he and Lancaster, recalled former players Dan Chandler and Vernon Hatton in *Rupp from Both Ends of the Bench*, "resembled Army sergeants in all respects." The relationship changed after the players left Rupp's "army" with honorable discharges. Many, but not all, came to appreciate what Rupp had done for them. Some, like a former player who was quoted in the December 23, 1977, issue of the *Christian Science Monitor*, neither forgot nor forgave: "He made the rules and we obeyed them. There was no joking, no laughing, no singing, no whistling, no horseplay, no breaks in practice, and certainly no questioning his rules. He had us so wrapped up in basketball and winning that we didn't have time for anything else." Lou Tsioropoulos, a star forward on some of UK's greatest teams, believed Rupp behaved as he did for a definite reason—the Baron knew what he wanted in his players and was constantly testing them to see if they measured up. "Basically what he wanted were players who could concentrate, who were assertive, and who could take charge. The ones who were a little sensitive and who couldn't take his criticism didn't make it. He didn't want players who would fall apart at a crucial point in a game."

Bobby Watson, a teammate of Tsioropoulos in 1951 and 1952 and a strong admirer of Rupp, observed in an interview that "the people who got to play liked and respected him. If you didn't get to play much, though, he could make it kind of tough for you. If you weren't a starter you weren't much in his eyes." Not all of the starters admired Rupp, however, and not all of the reserves hated him. Many if not most of Rupp's pre-World War II players with whom I spoke, both starters and reserves, had negative feelings about the Baron. But members of the Rupp teams of the fifties and sixties often were reluctant to depreciate a man they all regarded as "a legend," although some spoke frankly of their feelings when I switched off my tape recorder. One who was willing to speak for the record was Ned Jennings, a 6'8" starting center on two of Rupp's teams of the early 1960s. A very honest and straightforward man, Jennings stated frankly, "I disagree with his methods. He was a very tough individual who very seldom praised you. This may work with

some players but it doesn't with others." Jennings especially regretted the way Rupp beat down some very talented players who could not or would not adjust to his personality or system.

Another perspective was offered by Dan Chandler, who spent four years in the 1950s on the UK bench and never won a letter. He admitted that "many of his boys resent him for their first few years" but "after they graduate, most of them probably come to realize what a fantastic job he has done using them and others, year after year, molding them into that winning tradition." Chandler concluded that the Baron "gets immature boys, turns them into tough winners, and sends them out into life with pride and a solid accomplishment behind them."

Dan Issel, a two-time college All-American and pro star with the Denver Nuggets, who probably enjoyed the closest relationship with Rupp of any of his players, was even more laudatory. In a preface to Tev Laudeman's *The Rupp Years*, Issel expressed the appreciation and gratitude he felt for having been "fortunate enough to have played under Adolph Rupp." What he learned at UK provided the solid foundation, he maintained, for whatever success he enjoyed in professional basketball. "I will remember Adolph Rupp as a warm, compassionate man, but also as a man who would not tolerate mediocrity. He was demanding, but he recognized and appreciated a total effort."

Issel elaborated on his views during a June 30, 1983, interview. "One thing I would be willing to bet about the interviews you have had with former UK players," he began, "was that you didn't come across many who were wishy-washy about Coach Rupp. There seem to be two distinct groups: one is composed of players who hated him and couldn't stand him and the other of those who loved him. I'm certainly in that group over there because everything I have today is directly or indirectly because I came to Kentucky and played for Coach Rupp." Issel then made a very important point. "You have to keep in mind that there are two different types of players: ones that respond when you pat them on the back and others that respond when you kick them in the behind. I was one that needed the kick. Coach Rupp and Coach Lancaster had the philosophy that you kick everybody and if there was a player who needed the pat on the back why he would have to either change his ways or go down the road." For himself, Issel emphasized, Rupp was the ideal coach. "Coach Rupp made me a much better player than I would have been if I hadn't come here. I respected what he did. Then after I graduated and got to know Coach Rupp well, I found that he was not the harsh, gruff man he portrayed in practices

A tense moment in the 1944/45 season.

and on the basketball court. He wasn't like that at all." Issel emphasized that not everyone had the close and pleasant relationship with Rupp that he had enjoyed. He contrasted his own experience with that of another player from Illinois. Guard Greg Starrick, who was an excellent prospect, arrived at UK the year after Issel but never played a varsity game for the Big Blue. Starrick had compiled an excellent record while in high school, with a three-year average of 26.8 points per game and a single-game high of seventy points. Following his senior season he had been not only a unanimous All-State selection in Illinois but a *Parade Magazine* first team All-American. Starrick was the type, Issel noted, "who needed a pat on the back and they just drove him off."

One fact emerges from the interviews with former players. Whether they came to admire and respect Rupp or continued to hate and resent him, he was ever in the thoughts of his "boys." For better or worse, playing for the Baron clearly was an experience that changed a person.

Rupp enjoyed great success throughout his forty-two-year career at UK. The most glittering achievements came in the late forties and early fifties. But the system which produced the "Fabulous Five" and the Spivey-Hagan-Ramsey teams was formed during the 1930s and the war years.

5

Rupp's Formative Era

During Adolph Rupp's first five seasons at the University of Kentucky his teams compiled a phenomenal record of eighty-five victories and only eleven defeats for a winning percentage of .885. The team won one SEC championship, in 1933, and shared the title in 1935. In the last half of the decade the winning percentage tailed off somewhat, to .745, as UK lost twenty-six of 102 contests for an average of slightly more than five defeats a year. Although the roster each season was studded with All-SEC players, the overall quality of the teams during these five seasons was not up to that of the previous squads. Despite the relative decline in athletic talent and the less impressive won-lost record, Wildcat fans did not complain but were, if anything, even more enthusiastic in their support of the Big Blue. The Cats rewarded that support with three SEC championships in the five-year period: 1937, 1939, and 1940. Rupp and UK were picking up momentum and not even a worldwide war, which the United States entered in 1941, could loosen the Big Blue's hold over its conference. By the early forties the presence of the UK team in the SEC title game was almost a foregone conclusion. Only John Mauer and his Vols prevented a clean sweep of the championship, and in the two seasons Tennessee won, 1941 and 1943, the Wildcats came in second.

Kentucky's dominance of the SEC and its status as one of college basketball's major powers was an established fact. To many it seemed preordained. It was not. It was based on a number of factors and although Adolph Rupp was one of them, if not the most important, he was not the only one. Rupp's achievements were built on a solid base—the work of his predecessors, es-

pecially John Mauer. Rupp added his own unique personality and a new and popular style of play. Ralph Carlisle, who was an All-Southeastern Conference forward on UK's 1936 and 1937 teams, observed in a December 1982 interview that Rupp "had a leadership aura about him. Even before he became known as a great coach and an important man he had a quality about him you just can't describe. He was amazing," Carlisle continued. "He could walk into a room filled with people he didn't know and who didn't know him and in no time at all he was the center of everything. He always seemed to have something to say that was appropriate for the moment," noted Carlisle (who is himself regarded by many people as an excellent speaker and a dynamic personality), "and he always seemed to be able to draw the attention that he wanted to draw. He just knew how to do it. Now, that's not a bad quality, is it?"

Two Rupp assistant coaches of the era merit special mention for their contributions to the program. Both Paul McBrayer, 1934-43, and Harry Lancaster, who assumed the position in 1946, played important roles in training players in the fundamentals of the game, helping with recruiting and scouting, and serving as buffer between the players and an increasingly autocratic and irascible Rupp. According to several players from the thirties and early forties, McBrayer, along with Blanton Collier, was responsible for many of the patterns, plays, and variations that UK teams used under Rupp and Joe Hall and contributed the minute details of the tenacious man-to-man defense he learned from John Mauer in the late twenties. When he became assistant coach, Lancaster, who had played for Collier while at Paris High

School, helped perfect the superbly synchronized and coordinated offense (he fully developed the fast break's potential) and the sticky defense that distinguished the UK teams of the late forties and fifties.

It was to Rupp's credit that he permitted assistants the latitude to develop their role fully and to contribute to the program. Rupp was a highly intelligent man. In addition, he had a genius for picking other people's brains and for absorbing new ideas and adapting them to his own use so they became his ideas. Like their coach, Wildcat teams adapted to changing situations. Although Rupp and his players loved the fast break, UK basically employed a guard-oriented patterned offense. Even the fast break was carefully planned and coordinated. The first pass, for example, was to go upcourt. It was never to go to the side because that slowed the break.

Rupp's use of the fast break was an important element not only in the success of his teams but also in their public appeal. Most of the Southern teams of the era employed one variation or another of a slow-down offense. Many did so because they could not compete with UK at its own game. They did not have enough quality players and either did not or could not recruit them.

Although basketball scholarships, according to Aggie Sale, were being awarded by 1932 (not 1935, as some books have reported), most SEC teams in the thirties and early forties carried as few as two or three scholarship players. Most team members were on football scholarships.

There was also a dearth of first-rate coaches. Quite simply, basketball was not considered as important at other conference schools as it was at UK. Many of the coaches were assistants on football teams who were pressed into duty to direct the basketball squads. Even in the late forties, noted Wallace "Wah Wah" Jones in an interview, "at some schools one assistant football coach would take the job this year and another assistant would take it the next year. Rupp's success eventually forced them to take basketball more seriously." Even Mauer, at both Kentucky and Tennessee, divided his attention between basketball and football. No other basketball coach in the SEC, as several former Wildcats noted in interviews, took the sport as seriously or concentrated as completely on his job as Rupp. Rupp also was fortunate in that, when the SEC was formed in 1933, Maryland, North Carolina, Duke, and North Carolina State did not join the new league. All had been members of the Southern Conference and would have been formidable rivals. Instead, other than UK, the teams that helped form the SEC were oriented toward football more than basketball.

The final ingredient in UK's success was the players themselves. The Big Blue was blessed throughout the thirties and early forties with a steady stream of talented athletes, more than any other SEC rival of the era was able to assemble. Although some of the UK players during this formative era were outstanding, there was not the profusion of "blue-chip" athletes that would distinguish Wildcat teams during the decade commencing in 1943/44. Nearly all of the early UK players were Kentucky natives, many of them from the Bluegrass area. With few exceptions the out-of-staters were from nearby sections of Indiana and Ohio.

Strangely enough, considering the success he would soon enjoy in the SEC, during his first two seasons in Lexington Rupp was unable to improve on the record of his predecessor, John Mauer, in the Southern Conference Tournament. In 1931, following a 12-2 regular season, the Cats were invited to the Southern Conference Tournament in Atlanta, where they swept to easy victories over North Carolina State, Duke, and Florida, only to fall in the finals to Maryland in the final seconds of play. In that March 3, 1931, contest UK made only two field goals and three foul shots in the entire first half. Incredibly, the Cats took twenty-one shots before they sank their first goal. Holding the Big Blue "to two field goals in one half of a game," Ralph McGill (at the time a sportswriter) marveled in the March 4 issue of the *Atlanta Constitution,* "is perhaps the greatest guarding feat in the eleven years of tournament history." Kentucky rallied in the second half and held a 27-25 lead with only forty seconds to go in the game. That was when Maryland's star guard, Lewis Berger, "broke out in a tremendous one-man attack that won the game 29-27.... The uprising of Lewis Berger," wrote Ed Danforth in the same issue of the *Constitution,* "was the greatest single exploit the eleven years of the Southern conference basketball tournament has produced." Louis McGinnis, who played forward on the 1931 UK team and was the leading scorer in the conference tournament, recalled in an interview that a little known factor in the defeat was Maryland's use of a zone defense. "I think that was the first time that Rupp ran into the zone defense. We weren't prepared for it and we couldn't work our offense against it and our guards weren't hitting over it. The zone was a deciding factor in the game." Although they did not win the tournament the Wildcats placed three men on the All-Southern team, the first time they had accomplished that feat. The three were McGinnis, referred to in the press as "the diminutive forward," cen-

ter George Yates, who played "masterful basketball" despite an illness, and team captain and forward Carey Spicer, who also made All-American for the second time. Guard Jake Bronston made second team All-Southern. Guard Ellis Johnson, a starter during most of the regular season, suffered an ankle sprain in midseason and did not play in the tournament, while Aggie Sale was hampered by a painful hip injury which limited his playing time through most of the season.

Kentucky's style of play that year, both offense and defense, was similar to what it had been the previous season under John Mauer. The players were used to the Mauer system and Rupp, as a new coach fresh from the high school ranks, was smart enough not to try to introduce a new system. Instead, with Carey Spicer's copy of the Mauer playbook as guide, Rupp retained the same plays and even the same play numbers. Thus the number six play in 1929/30 was still number six in 1930/31 and, in fact, until the end of Rupp's career. Rupp even held three-hour daily practices, as his predecessor had.

By the fifties the Baron's highly organized and intense practices were generally concentrated into a period of no more than an hour and a half. Rupp, it must be emphasized, was a quieter, more modest person that first year than he would be later in his career. Or so his early players maintain.

Louis McGinnis noted that "we just sort of carried on with what we had been doing and worked the fast break in as we always did when we got the chance." Mauer's slow break, McGinnis observed, was what is now referred to as a deliberate offense. During Rupp's first season, "there was still a lot of screening and passing to open things up for a close in or a layup shot. That is, we just took our time to get a good shot and then we took it. If a fast break was available we took it." A difference, however, was that Mauer did not encourage his players to take advantage of a fast break opportunity and Rupp did. The players could be more innovative under Rupp. He permitted them much more freedom within a structured system than Mauer had.

Three All-Southern members of Rupp's first team at UK, in 1930/31: *left to right,* Louis "Little" McGinnis, who played forward; Carey Spicer, team captain and All-American selection; and George Yates, who played center and was voted All-Southern for his performance in the 1931 Southern Conference tournament. All three were also on Mauer's last team.

Rupp's second UK team (1931/32) boasted three future All-Americans: Forest "Aggie" Sale, John DeMoisey, and Ellis Johnson. Front row, left to right: Cecil Bell, Ercel Little, Gordon George, Harvey Mattingly, Evan Settle, Bill Kleiser. Middle row: Bill Davis, C.D. Blair, Darrell Darby, Johnson, Howard Kreuter, Charles Worthington. Back row: assistant coach Leonard Miller, James Hughes, DeMoisey, Sale, George Skinner, Rupp.

The season following Rupp's arrival (1931/32) was the first in which the conference permitted the awarding of athletic scholarships to members of the basketball team. Before then the only assistance the university provided was in helping players find jobs in Lexington. With the money they earned the boys paid for room and board which, Aggie Sale noted in an interview, could be found for as little as four dollars a week. "You could get a meal at a rooming house on Upper Street for twenty-five cents and it was just as good as what you can find now for seven or eight dollars."

UK again had a very successful regular season in 1931/32 but also once again fell short in the tournament. After an injury-plagued sophomore season, Sale and guard Ellis Johnson came into their own. They, along with fellow juniors Darrell Darby and Howard "Dutch" Kreuter at forward, senior Charles Worthington at guard, and sophomore John "Frenchy" DeMoisey, a starter at forward until he was sidelined for five games by academic problems, rolled to a fourteen-victory regular

season record that was marred only by a final game loss by one point to Vanderbilt. UK entered the conference tournament as co-favorites with Maryland. Led by Sale with twenty-one points, Darby with seventeen, and reserve forward DeMoisey with six points, the Wildcats crushed Tulane on February 26 by twenty points (50-30) in their first tournament game, only to fall short by one point the next afternoon to North Carolina. The Maryland "Old Liners," as the team was called, fared even worse than UK. In their first-round game the overconfident Maryland squad, one reporter observed, "stood around like craven images, no doubt thinking Florida would be paralyzed by the Old Liners' mighty presence."

With the formation of the Southeastern Conference, UK's luck in tournament play soon changed. As *Atlanta Constitution* sportswriter Ralph McGill observed in the aftermath of the 1933 SEC championship game, "What Kentucky needed, it seems, was to get out of the Southern conference." The Wildcats fielded a veteran team with Sale and DeMoisey alternating at center and one

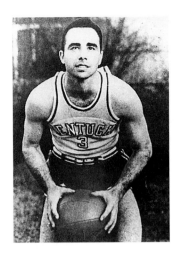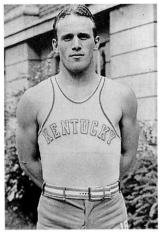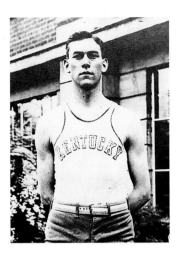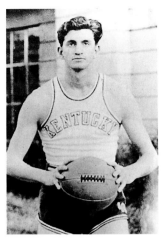

Among the stars of the powerful 1932/33 team were *(left to right)* Bill "Racehorse" Davis, Ellis Johnson, Forest "Aggie" Sale, and John "Frenchy" DeMoisey. Davis and Johnson were all-around athletes, starring in football as well as basketball; Johnson, an All-American guard in 1933, was also outstanding in baseball and track. Rupp later said that Sale, who was college player of the year in 1933, may have been the best player he ever coached.

forward and with Darrell Darby at the other forward. George Yates, an All-Conference performer in 1930/31, did not play the following season and was a little-used substitute at center in 1932/33. The guards were Ellis Johnson and Bill "Racehorse" Davis, the latter the only sophomore on the starting team. Johnson and Davis were excellent ball handlers and passers who could sink the outside set shot when necessary, but most of the scoring was handled by the forwards and center. Sale and DeMoisey, both of whom measured around 6'5" in height, complemented each other beautifully. Sale was much the better leaper; he generally jumped center (remember that a center jump followed each basket) and handled most of the rebounding but also could shoot a two-handed set shot. DeMoisey, who was not as mobile as Sale, usually stationed himself on or near the foul line (there was no three-second area at the time) and took his favorite shot, a turn-around half hook or, as Sale described it, a "flip" shot.

The Wildcats lost three regular-season games—to Ohio State, Creighton, and South Carolina—but reached their peak in the SEC tournament. On four successive days, February 25 through 28, the "Ruppmen" roared to overwhelming victories over Mississippi, Florida, LSU, and Mississippi State. The closest game of the four was that against LSU, which UK won by only thirteen points, 51-38. In the championship game the Big Blue led at halftime by a score of 29-7 but substituted freely in the second half and finished the game with a 46-27 victory and the title.

DeMoisey, Sale, and Johnson were chosen to the All-Conference team. Ralph McGill thought this was ridiculous. His choices were DeMoisey, Darby, Sale, Johnson, and Davis, all of Kentucky. "There were other great players," McGill admitted, "but the all-conference *team* is Kentucky's." The captain of the UK squad, Aggie Sale, was, McGill bubbled, "redoubtable, versatile, clever, skilled, capable, brilliant, scintillating, dazzling and otherwise dominating." McGill obviously was not alone in this opinion. In addition to All-American honors, Sale was chosen by the Helms Athletic Foundation as the college basketball player of the year. UK was chosen the team of the year.

In 1933/34 the Ruppmen won all fifteen regular-season games and outscored their opponents by an almost two-to-one margin, 656 points to 340. DeMoisey and Davis were joined on the starting team by junior forwards Dave Lawrence and Jack Tucker and Milerd "Andy" Anderson, a sophomore guard. The squad travelled to Atlanta with high hopes of repeating as SEC champions, but their hopes were quickly dashed. Although DeMoisey and Davis were named to the tournament first team, UK was eliminated in the first round by Florida (38-32).

Going into the game the lightly regarded Florida Gators were given little chance of beating the undefeated Wildcats, who were the top-seeded team in the tournament. Instead, the Gators accomplished what reporter Bert Prather, writing in the February 25, 1934, issue of the *Courier-Journal,* termed "one of the biggest upsets in the history of Southern basketball." Unfortunately for

UK, "the Gators were charged up to the sky for the encounter," were as fast as the Wildcats, and "proved superior" in playing defense. If all this was not bad enough, UK's offensive star, DeMoisey, had a poor game and got in foul trouble early in the second half. The Wildcats were probably lucky to lose by only six points.

The tournament format was dropped in 1935 (though it was reinstated the following year) and UK shared the championship with LSU. The departure of 1934 All-American Frenchy DeMoisey and the decision of Bill Davis not to return for the 1934/35 season were hardly felt. The three returning starters—Lawrence, Tucker, and Anderson—were joined by two members of the undefeated 1933/34 freshman team, Warfield Donohue and LeRoy "Cowboy" Edwards. Another member of that group, Ralph Carlisle, who would be an All-Conference forward in 1936 and 1937, was a substitute in 1934/35.

The Rupp system began to take definite shape in the 1934/35 season with the arrival of Edwards, Donohue, and Carlisle and the hiring of former Wildcat All-American Paul McBrayer as assistant coach. McBrayer would bring an attention to detail, a passion for hard work, and a number of innovative ideas to the program, among them the inside screen and the second guard around, the latter originally used by Blanton Collier at Paris High School. (Years later, Collier would become a head football coach, first at Kentucky and then with the Cleveland Browns of the National Football League.)

The Edwards-led team of 1934/35 set a trend and a standard for future UK teams that would not be matched until the late forties. Although only a sophomore and just 6'5" in height, Edwards was the prototype of the modern center. As McBrayer recalled, "He had a lot better moves around the basket than most centers did at that time, he was much stronger in the upper body and he had a good touch for the basket in close." Teammate David Lawrence also marveled at Edwards's strength and shooting ability. In an interview, Lawrence noted that the big center had "a good close-in jump shot, an excellent hook shot with either hand, and could rebound above the basket."

The 1934/35 season was the only one Edwards played at UK, but because of him it was memorable. He was named All-SEC and All-American and the Helms

Outstanding members of the 1934/35 team included LeRoy Edwards (25), voted All-American and college player of the year in his only varsity season; and Ralph Carlisle (14), an All-SEC selection at forward in both 1936 and 1937.

LeRoy "Cowboy" Edwards, a scoring and rebounding sensation whose single varsity season (1934/35) was memorable. Edwards was All-SEC, All-American, and college player of the year.

Foundation Player of the Year—and he was only a sophomore. Unfortunately for the Wildcats and their faithful fans, his was a spirit more akin to that of the "do-your-own-thing" sixties than the Depression thirties. Edwards returned to his hometown, Indianapolis, at the end of the school year, never to return to the University of Kentucky. The following season he played basketball on a semipro team and in 1937 became a professional when he joined the Oshkosh (Wisconsin) All-Stars, one of the premier teams of that era. Edwards was a great player, and one can only guess what he would have accomplished if he had remained at UK and completed his eligibility.

During 1934/35 the Wildcats won nineteen games,

lost only two, and finished the season as co-champions of the SEC. One of the losses, to New York University, was in a sense a triumph rather than a defeat. As Tev Laudeman has noted, "It broke Kentucky out of the mold of being just a good southern team." It had a number of other important results as well, including the favorable attention it brought Rupp and the team in the *Times* and other New York papers, and the important part it played in helping to promote intersectional play as well as highlight the differences in officiating between the East, the South, and the Midwest. When, after the game, Rupp complained bitterly that what had transpired in the contest bordered on a steal, many sportswriters agreed with him.

The NYU game was part of a doubleheader, the second one ever played at Madison Square Garden. According to one newspaper account it "was so exciting that the capacity crowd of 16,539 fans nearly went wild." The two teams offered contrasting styles. While the Violent Violets employed a fast break offense, the Wildcats used set plays, quick short passes, and the setting of screens. The screens, or blocks, were an integral part of the UK offense. Unfortunately referees in the East considered them illegal because most were moving picks. Every time the Cats set a screen the referee called a foul. (There was, Lawrence explained, only one referee and NYU chose him.) Edwards had three fouls within a few minutes after the start of the game. At the time four personal fouls brought expulsion from a game. Edwards lasted until the last minute of the game but played much more cautiously than normal and scored only one field goal. His game and that of his teammates were thrown off during most of the first half by the rough play of the NYU players, especially their center, Irving Turjesen. One reporter described it as verging on "warfare."

Although Turjesen scored only one point in the contest, his pushing, shoving, and jabbing effectively neutralized Edwards. The referee was much more indulgent of the NYU tactics than of UK's use of the moving screen. The Wildcats seemed bewildered during the early going by the NYU fast break, the rough play, and the referee's interpretation of the rules. Nevertheless, they fought back from an early 4-0 deficit to take the lead for the first time after more than twelve minutes of the first half had elapsed. It remained a close and rough game thereafter, but the Big Blue held the lead through nearly all of the second half. Then, with a minute left to play, the Violent Violets' captain, Sidney Gross, sank a field goal to tie the score at 22 all. The Wildcats controlled the following center tap and set up their offense for a game-winning basket, but at this critical juncture

Edwards was called for setting an illegal block. Gross stepped to the foul line for the Violets. Arthur Daley, in the January 6, 1935, *New York Times,* described the dramatic moment: "The ball teetered on the front edge of the rim with agonizing uncertainty and then toppled through the net to give the New York University quintet its twenty-second successive victory over a two-year span in Madison Square Garden." Although nearly a minute still remained in the game after the successful free throw, the Wildcats were faced with an impossible task. Without Edwards, who had fouled out, the Cats were unable to control the center tap. The Violets took possession of the ball, the *Lexington Leader* reported ruefully, "and iced the game by freezing it during the remaining seconds."

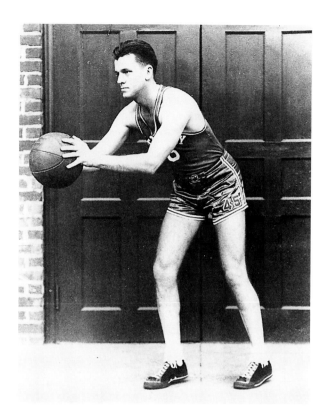

Although Edwards was held to only six points in the NYU game, he scored the phenomenal total, for that era, of 343 points for the entire season. By contrast, Carey Spicer's team-leading total for the 1930/31 season had been 190 points, and Aggie Sale had managed to tally 194 points in 1931/32. Edwards scored more than twenty points each in six of UK's twenty-one games during the 1934/35 campaign, with a season high thirty-six-point performance against a very good Creighton University team on February 22. This is impressive when one notes that UK rivals were able to score twenty or more points only eleven times during the season.

Big Blue fans looked forward to 1935/36 with high expectations. They were to be disappointed, of course, because Edwards did not return. The big center was ahead of his time in many respects, including the belief that college basketball should bear immediate financial rewards for players as well as coaches and sponsoring institutions. According to former UK players, Edwards made monetary and other demands of Rupp and the university that they could not or would not meet.

Although guards Anderson and Donohue were back, the entire starting front line was lost because forwards Lawrence and Tucker had departed through graduation. Junior Ralph Carlisle and sophomore Joe "Red" Hagan quickly moved into the starting forward positions and proved to be at least the equal of their predecessors, with Carlisle winning All-SEC honors in both 1936 and 1937. But filling Edwards's shoes proved an impossible task, not only in 1936 but for several years to come. Compounding the problem in 1936 was the fact that Rupp had arranged a very demanding sched-

Top: Warfield Donohue, who played guard from 1934/35 through 1936/37. *Bottom:* Louisville native David Lawrence, an All-SEC forward in 1934/35.

ule. In addition to tough SEC rivals Tennessee, Alabama, and Vanderbilt, the Wildcats faced intersectional powers Notre Dame, New York University, Michigan State, Butler, and Creighton. And, recalled Ralph Carlisle, UK just did not have the talent that season.

Carlisle, who blossomed as a star in 1936, contrasted the games in Madison Square Garden with and without Edwards. In 1935 "we could have beaten NYU if they hadn't held Edwards all night long. Oh, it was terrible. The things Rupp said after the game didn't really go far enough because it was just highway robbery." The next year was a different matter entirely. "We went up there to New York and we just got beat and that's all there was to that. They won 41 to 28. That year they were just a better team than we were. We just plain didn't have much." In the opinion of Tev Laudeman that situation lasted into the early 1940s. During those years (1936-43), wrote Laudeman in *The Rupp Years,* "hard times came to Adolph Rupp." To a certain extent, it must be emphasized, this was relative. It was in comparison to the achievements of the pre-1936 period and what the Wildcats were to accomplish after 1943. And these eight so-called lean seasons at any other SEC school would have been glory years. The Big Blue not only won the league championship four of the eight years but placed nine players on the All-SEC team (three of them made the first team in two different seasons), and two players were All-American selections. The All-SEC performers were Ralph Carlisle, forward, 1936 and 1937; Warfield Donohue, guard, 1937; Bernie Opper, guard, 1938 and 1939; Mickey Rouse, guard, 1940; Marvin Akers, forward, 1941, and guard, 1943; Lee Huber, guard, 1941; Ermal Allen, forward, 1942; and Melvin Brewer, center, 1943. The All-Americans were Opper and Huber. Some of the others, especially Carlisle, might have made the honor teams if UK's won-lost record had been better. Although UK had some good centers, among them Melvin Brewer, what was lacking during this era was an outstanding player in the pivot who, like Edwards, and after 1945, Alex Groza, could dominate a game.

Several players of that era give a great deal of credit for what UK achieved to Assistant Coach Paul McBrayer. Bernie Opper recalled in an interview that McBrayer "was very, very influential. He was an excellent teacher of defensive and offensive basketball and rebounding. Mac was a strong believer in defense and he put us through the paces. He just loved to see somebody shut somebody out." In those years, Opper noted, "if you

Like other Rupp teams of the period, the 1938/39 SEC champion Wildcats were stronger at guard positions than in the front court. Front row, left to right: Rupp, Lee Huber, Waller White, Harry Denham, Keith Farnsley, Bernie Opper, Elmo Head, Layton Rouse, Donald Orme, and assistant coach McBrayer. Back row: trainer Frank Mann, James Goodman, Fred Curtis, Homer Thompson, Marion Cluggish, Stanley Cluggish, Carl Staker, Rogers Nelson, and manager J.B. Faulconer.

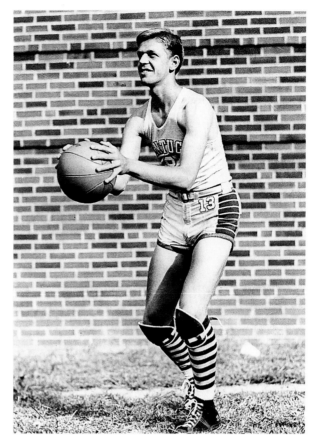

Three outstanding players of the late 1930s. *Above left,*
Bernie Opper, star guard and Rupp's first recruit from the
New York area, All-SEC in 1938 and 1939 and All-American
in 1939. *Above,* Lee Huber, two-time All-American guard
(1940 and 1941), who came to UK on a tennis scholarship.
Left, Ermal Allen, a small but fierce and rugged competitor
who was an All-SEC forward in 1941, as well as a star
halfback on the football team.

scored in double figures it was phenomenal. In the year I made All-American I think I averaged four or five points a game. If a team scored forty points that was good. Just a few years before LIU was being advertised as a point a minute team. That is, they scored forty points a game!"

Ken Rollins, who was team captain and starting guard in 1946/47 and 1947/48, was a sophomore starter on the 1942/43 team. In an interview Rollins recalled that McBrayer was "a very vital participant in coaching tactics and had complete charge of the freshmen." He worked with the freshmen "on all of the basic fundamentals of basketball. You would have thought that we had never been taught anything before, but that's good. Don't take anything for granted." Freshmen were also run through all of the drills and plays that the varsity used in preparation for their moving up. "When it came to the varsity," Rollins continued, "Coach McBrayer was at one end of the floor and Coach Rupp at the other and during practice we caught it at both ends. Coach McBrayer had what appeared to me to be a lot of authority. Coach Rupp listened an awful lot to what Coach McBrayer was saying and suggesting." In sum, McBrayer "contributed to everything that was done."

Former star forward Red Hagan recalled in an interview that during his varsity career (1936-38) "at least two-thirds of the team looked to Mac for everything they did. I know I did and I think the others did too. Mac didn't want it that way but it just was because just about everyone on the team felt Adolph was not very knowledgeable about basketball." It was only later, "when Adolph became more successful, that his word almost became law on the team, and I guess even the campus."

Ed Lander, who played at UK during the early forties and served as a scout later in the decade, also reminisced about Rupp and McBrayer in a January 1983 interview. Lander knew Rupp from around the age of thirteen when the Rupps moved into a house across the street from where the Lander family lived. While still in high school, in 1937 or 1938, Lander started watching UK practices. In 1940 he entered the university as a freshman. Over a period of several years he developed an admiration for Paul McBrayer. In the Kentucky system "Mac did all the teaching and he was superb at teaching the mechanics of the game. He really made us better players than our talents warranted." (Several other players made this same point.) But McBrayer's contributions went far beyond that in both the late thirties and the early forties. "Mac coached all phases of the game. Any time something needed to be explained or corrected or something new was put in, he did it. Before and during the games Rupp said the inspirational things and Mac explained what we were supposed to do. After the war Harry Lancaster took over what Mac had done, which was pretty much the actual preparation for the game and the coaching during the game." Rupp's approach, Lander noted, was specific and direct. "It was to go out and do it. For him the important thing was the end result, to win. He knew how to win. He wasn't that interested though, in the basics, in teaching. But he was smart enough to get Mac and then Lancaster who were."

Tom Parker, who was a co-captain and forward on Rupp's last team, in 1972, made essentially the same point in an interview. "Coach Rupp had a unique abil-

ity to attract good people. Not only athletes but assistant coaches." While Parker was at UK Rupp's assistants were Lancaster, who became athletics director in 1968, Joe Hall, and Dick Parsons. In Parker's view Lancaster was a major contributor to UK's success. "Not to take anything away from Coach Rupp, those four NCAA championships he won, you can give Coach Lancaster half the credit." Parker considers Rupp to have been "a master tactician, a General Patton-type," and a master psychologist and motivator. But "when it came down to a specific play or to needing a basket or something specific done Coach Lancaster was the one that did the job. And then after he left the coaching ranks and took the AD job Coach Hall filled that need."

Ed Lander offered specific examples of McBrayer's contributions. "He put in a back block system and I remember a play he put in after a defensive free throw. Actually, in basketball you can only block [or set picks] two ways, inside or outside, but he was constantly refining variations on those two types of blocks. He also taught us how to handle things in ball control situations like at the end of the game when we had a small lead. He taught that more than forty years ago and it is identical to the way [Indiana University head coach] Bobby Knight teaches it now." Lander remembered observing McBrayer develop his techniques at the practices he attended while still a high school student. The system McBrayer taught "was really, as I understand it, a refinement of the basic offense Mac learned from Johnny Mauer when he coached at Kentucky. And it, in turn, was the system Rupp continued to use during the rest of his career."

McBrayer entered the service in 1943 expecting to return to his position as assistant coach after the end of the war. In this hope he was to be bitterly disappointed because Rupp hired Harry Lancaster. Lancaster, who had played for Georgetown in Rupp's first game as UK coach, had worked as an instructor in the UK Physical Education Department before being called into the Navy in 1944. In his book *Adolph Rupp as I Knew Him* Lancaster recalled that "Rupp had told me after McBrayer went into the service that he did not want Mac back after the war. I got the idea that Adolph thought Mac was after his job." Although it cannot be proved, another possibility is that Rupp felt he no longer needed McBrayer. A successful program was under way with a style of play that was pleasing fans and winning games and league titles. Effective drills, plays, plans, and procedures were now in place. Obviously McBrayer had played a major role in standardizing and rationalizing the system but, looked at in a cold-blooded way, he was no longer essential to its continued functioning. Another former Mauer player, Elmer "Baldy" Gilb, filled Rupp's needs from 1944 to 1946 and helped guide the Cats to an NIT championship in 1946. A UK assistant football coach at the time, Gilb was not, he explained in an interview, interested in a full-time basketball assistant coaching position, so Harry Lancaster was awarded the job in the spring of 1946.

Lancaster resembled McBrayer in many respects and filled much the same function as his predecessor, but he also differed in several important ways. Unlike McBrayer he did not have a connection with the University of Kentucky prior to Rupp's arrival nor did he have a power

The 1940/41 season inaugurated Rupp's second decade. *Far left,* Milt Ticco shoots against West Virginia in the season opener, which UK won 46-34. *Center,* Marvin Akers helps boost UK to victory over Tennessee, 37-28, on February 15. *Near left,* Mel Brewer (15) tips off against perennial power Notre Dame. UK lost 48-37. Rupp's Wildcats didn't beat Notre Dame until 1943.

base of his own either in the university or in Lexington. While Lancaster had been a star in both basketball and football at Georgetown College he had not been an All-American as McBrayer had. As a player, it might be noted, McBrayer's record overshadowed Rupp's own accomplishments. Contrary to some later reports, Rupp had been a substitute and not a starter on the 1923 University of Kansas national championship team. Neither did Lancaster have a direct connection with John Mauer, as McBrayer did. With McBrayer's departure, a key link with Mauer, the source of much if not most of the Kentucky style of play was severed and the system became fully the "Rupp system."

Nearly everyone who was connected with Rupp acknowledges that he had a giant ego, and having to share credit for the success of the Big Blue could not have been pleasant for him. What was worse, in the words of Red Hagan, a star forward from 1936 to 1938 and later a successful coach, "Knowledgeable fans and all the players knew Mac was really running the team. During a time-out at least three-quarters of the players turned to McBrayer to find out what to do." In the post-World War II period all ideas had to emanate from Rupp. One did not sell him an idea either, related one player who after graduation served for several years as a scout and recruiter. "You had to implant the idea in his mind so it was his idea and not yours. You had to turn it around so it came from him. Coach Lancaster was a master of that."

Ironically, it is extremely doubtful that any of Rupp's apparent worries about his status were justified. Except in the aftermath of the basketball scandals of 1951,

Rupp's position was never in jeopardy nor his high standing in the coaching profession in doubt. Even during the relatively lean years of the late thirties and early forties Rupp's reputation was constantly on the rise nationally. As for the local situation, it is doubtful that the majority of students or other fans were greatly concerned about who the assistant coach was so long as the head coach was Adolph Rupp. The question of who contributed what to the program was also of far less significance to them than whether or not the Cats won. In this they reflected the attitude of the Baron. As more than one player has observed, Rupp knew how to win and how to produce a pleasing product. The 1941 *Kentuckian* quoted what it claimed to be Rupp's motto: "Always a good show." Whether or not Rupp had a formal motto, it did epitomize the Baron's wide appeal.

The passion of the Kentucky basketball faithful for their Big Blue team and especially for its head coach did not cool in the early forties despite the war. If anything it became even more ardent.

The first phase of Rupp's career came to an end in 1943. During this era the Wildcats became the dominant basketball power in the Southeast. However, as one former player has noted, "Our record when we went across the river [that is, to the Midwest and the East] was just so-so because in terms of scholarships and emphasis on basketball they were probably ahead of Kentucky. We really didn't fare too well." UK gained some important intersectional victories and savored some memorable moments but there were also many bitter defeats.

An event that provided Adolph Rupp's greatest thrill

The 1942/43 Wildcats, Paul McBrayer's last team as assistant coach. Front row, left to right: Carl Althaus, Bill Turley, Bob Atherton, Ed Fish, and Tom Moseley. Middle row: Rupp, trainer Frank Mann, Wilbur Schu, Clyde Parker, Mulford Davis, Kenny Rollins, Bill Barlow, William Hamm, and McBrayer. Back row: Milt Ticco, manager Bob Landrum, Marvin Akers, Melvin Brewer, Jim Weber, Hoyt Moore, Ed Lander, E.S. Penick, and Paul Noel.

Paul McBrayer, an All-American guard while a player, served as UK's assistant basketball coach from 1934 through 1943, when he went off to war. Rupp did not rehire him at war's end and McBrayer became the highly successful head coach of the Eastern Kentucky Colonels, a position he held until his retirement.

in all the years his teams played at Alumni Gym took place on February 14, 1938. UK was playing a fine Marquette squad that had beaten Notre Dame and several other powerful teams. It was a game the Wildcats were not expected to win but they were holding their own. With only twelve seconds to play the score was tied at 33 and UK had the ball out of bounds. The ball was put in play and after a couple of passes it was in the hands of forward Red Hagan. With only six seconds remaining, Hagan sank a two-hand shot from beyond midcourt and UK won 35-33. The crowd went wild and A.B. "Happy" Chandler, then governor, immediately sent for a hammer and nail. Rushing from the stands Chandler went to the spot where Hagan had taken his shot. There, forty-eight feet, two and a quarter inches from the basket, Chandler drove a nail to immortalize the occasion.

During that same 1937/38 season the Big Blue gained one of its most important intersectional victories of the era—a decisive 40-29 win over the Pittsburgh Panthers in the Sugar Bowl Tournament. Actually it was not a tournament because only two teams were invited to New Orleans for the contest, which took place on December 29, 1937. The game was intended to bring together a team regarded by the Sugar Bowl Committee as the strongest in the North and the most powerful squad in Dixie. In 1937 Pitt, with an unbeaten record, appeared to be a worthy representative for the North. Pitt coach Doc Carlson was one of the famous coaches of the time, but he still used the old figure eight offense, and that proved easy for UK to handle. The figure eight involved continual movement of the ball and was intended to free a man for an easy layup. Carlson did not permit his players, Bernie Opper remembered, to shoot the ball from beyond the free throw line. "If they tried Carlson would pull them right out." Opper described what Pitt tried to do. "Every time they ran the figure eight the man I was guarding moved out so they would set up a play. So I saw in the first quarter that he kept moving and moving out. One time," Opper chuckled, "when he moved out instead of going with him I stopped in the middle and broke up the crisscross. They didn't know what to do. There I was picking off passes and they were still running that same pattern."

The Wildcats followed up their important victory over Pitt with a disastrous "trip across the river" on which they lost three games in a row to Michigan State (43-38), Detroit (34-26), and Notre Dame (47-37). For several years playing Notre Dame was a painful experience for Rupp. Before his arrival, UK under the direction of John Mauer had played the Fighting Irish only once, winning a 19-16 decision at South Bend in 1929. Rupp scheduled Notre Dame, a nationally recognized power, for the first time during the 1935/36 season. When the Baron made the arrangements he thought LeRoy Edwards would be on his team. The two schools met on February 10, 1936, and the Wildcats were badly outclassed, losing by the score of 41-20. Even with Edwards in the lineup the Big Blue would have had problems because Notre Dame was a perennial national power with excellent players and one of the truly great coaches of the era, George Keogan. As Wildcat All-American Lee Huber recalled in an interview, "Notre Dame was the biggest rival we had. The three years I played at UK, they beat us every year." The Big Blue, in fact, lost seven straight regular-season games to the Irish until 1943, when Rupp gained his first decision over a Keogan-coached team.

By the end of the 1942/43 season Rupp's team had won a total of 214 games and lost only fifty-seven. The Baron reigned supreme in the Southeast. The following decade would witness UK's emergence as one of the major basketball powers in the nation.

6

Wildcat Basketball's Golden Decade

The "glory years" of Kentucky basketball spanned the period from 1943/44 to 1953/54. Although this covered eleven seasons, UK played only ten of them. The Wildcats were under an NCAA suspension in 1952/53 and did not compete on the intercollegiate level, play being limited to four intrasquad games. During this era the Big Blue scaled the heights of glory with championships in both the NIT (1946) and the NCAA tournament (1948, 1949, and 1951), as well as capturing the SEC championship in each of the ten seasons the Cats competed in the conference. Unfortunately, in the aftermath of the point shaving scandal of 1951, the program also plumbed the depths of humiliation.

When the UK squad assembled for practice in preparation for the 1943/44 season not even the most loyal of Big Blue fans would have dreamed that the Wildcats were embarking on the most successful decade in the university's basketball history. This was the height of World War II, when able-bodied young men were needed for military service. Some universities were fortunate enough to have the use of army or navy trainees. UK was not. Rupp had to make do with military rejects and youngsters who had not yet reached the draft age of eighteen. As a result, the team he assembled may have been one of Adolph Rupp's most important. In the belief that the shortage of experienced players rendered the building of a competitive squad impossible, Rupp and Athletics Director Bernie Shiveley seriously considered dropping basketball for the 1943/44 season, if not

until the end of hostilities. Rupp admitted to a reporter in January 1944 that the youngsters "surprised me as much as anyone. They're just a bunch of kids who showed up for basketball practice last fall when we decided for sure to have a team."

The team's veterans were two sophomores, forward Wilbur Schu and guard Tom Moseley. The other fifteen players were freshmen. It appeared that the most that could be expected was to suit up a team. No one anticipated a representative team, much less a squad that would lose only one regular-season contest, win the SEC championship, and place third in the NIT in New York. Variously referred to as "the beardless wonders," "the freshmen," and "the Wildkittens," the 1944 aggregation was one of the top teams in the nation and lent great luster to the coaching reputation of Adolph Rupp.

Although the "Wildkittens" of 1944 boasted some excellent individual talents, the secret of the squad's success was that it functioned so effectively as a unit. The "beardless wonders" hustled and scrapped all season long and achieved some things no previous UK team had, including the first victory over Indiana University, the first win over Big Ten champion Ohio State in Columbus, and the first victory in New York's Madison Square Garden, a 44-38 win over St. John's, which had been NIT champion in both 1943 and 1944. They also defeated Notre Dame for only the second time in Rupp's tenure at UK and whipped an excellent University of

Cliff Hagan goes in for a layup during his record-setting performance against Temple on December 5, 1953. His fifty-one-point single-game score was unbroken until 1970. He was UK's athletics director from 1975 to 1989.

Illinois team 51-40 in Lexington on February 7, thus avenging the only loss of the regular campaign. At season's end three freshmen won spots on the SEC first team, center Bob "Tank" Brannum and guards Jack Parkinson and Jack Tingle. Wilbur Schu placed on the second team while fellow sophomore Tom Moseley and freshman Rudy Yessin won honorable mention. Brannum later was named an All-American.

The "Wildkittens" capped the season with their first appearance in the NIT, the premier tournament of the era. Only eight teams were invited to the tournament, and UK only had to win three games to capture the championship. They got off to an auspicious start with a 46-38 trouncing of a fine Utah squad but were upset two days later by St. John's, a team they had beaten during the regular season. The "beardless wonders" met Oklahoma A&M (now Oklahoma State University) and seven-footer Bob Kurland in the consolation game, while St. John's played DePaul and its giant center George Mikan for the championship. UK and St. John's neutralized the play of the big men with excellent team play and won their March 26 contests. In fact, although Kurland stood under the basket and batted away shot after UK shot (goaltending was legal then) the kittens soundly thrashed the Aggies, 45-29. Ironically, the Idaho "Blitz Kids," because of their early elimination in the

Above, Bob Brannum, All-SEC and All-American during his freshman year in 1944, was unable to break into the starting lineup when he returned from the service in 1946, and transferred to Michigan State.

Right, members of the 1943/44 "Wildkittens," all freshmen except for Wilbur Schu and Tom Moseley. Their 19-2 season brought UK its sixth SEC championship and first appearance in the NIT. Front row, left to right: Nathaniel Buis, Rudy Yessin, Jack Parkinson, Buddy Parker, and Moseley. Back row: manager Allan Abramson, Schu, Truitt DeMoisey, Bob Brannum, George Vulich, Jack Tingle, and Rupp.

NIT, were free to accept an NCAA bid when Southwest Conference co-champion Arkansas withdrew from the tournament following the injury of two starters in an auto accident. An all-civilian squad which averaged just 18.5 years in age, Utah became the Cinderella team of the tournament and emerged as the NCAA champions of 1944.

The following season, 1944/45, UK performed brilliantly again for a group of fuzzy-faced seventeen-year-olds and military rejects. Back from the 1944 team were Jack Tingle and Wilbur Schu at forward and Jack Parkinson at guard. Each was an All-SEC performer during the previous campaign. Gone was All-SEC and All-American center Bob Brannum, who had left for the service, but his departure was hardly felt, at least during the first part of the season. Taking Brannum's place was Martin's Ferry, Ohio, native Alex Groza. Although only an eighteen-year-old freshman, Groza already displayed "the perfect basketball hands," the "great team spirit," and the "uncanny ability at hitting the basket" that would later mark his play as a member of the "Fabulous Five." Although the 6'7" pivotman played only in UK's first eleven games of the campaign, he scored enough points to lead the team in scoring for the entire season.

When Groza left for military service the Wildcats had a perfect record. This included victories over such strong teams as Indiana, Wyoming, Temple, Long Island, Michigan State, and Ohio State. The most satisfying triumph for Groza was that over Ohio State on December 23, 1944, at Alumni Gym. Groza noted in a May 1983 interview that he had wanted to attend his home state university but the interest was all one-sided. To defeat Ohio State would thus be sweet revenge, especially since the Buckeyes also boasted a great center, Arnie Risen, who would later star as a professional player. Ironically, the 6'8" Risen was a Kentucky native from Williamstown. The two teams entered the game undefeated, and the Buckeyes were defending Big Ten champions. It was, in other words, a *big* game. The two teams and their marvelous centers exchanged baskets throughout the contest. The score was tied at the end of regulation time but UK pulled ahead in the five-minute overtime to prevail by five points, 53-48. Groza finished with sixteen points, followed by Tingle and Parkinson with fifteen each. The only Ohio State players in double figures were Risen and forward Don Grate, each with fourteen points.

Following Groza's departure Kentucky suffered its only regular-season losses to Tennessee, Notre Dame, and Michigan State. The Wildcats recovered by the end of the regular season, swept to the championship of the SEC tournament, but lost in the first round of the NCAA to Ohio State, a team they had defeated during the regular season while Groza was still in the lineup. It is not beyond the realm of possibility that the Big Blue, with Groza in the lineup for the entire season, would have gone undefeated and perhaps even won the NCAA. This is not meant to denigrate his replacement, Kenton "Dutch" Campbell. The 6'4" freshman was talented enough to be voted first team All-SEC center in 1945. Nevertheless, Campbell simply was not in the same class as Groza, who after the war was a three-time All-American, Helms Foundation Player of the Year, and one of the greatest pivotmen in the history of college basketball.

The foundations of the great post-World War II University of Kentucky teams were laid in the 1943/44 and 1944/45 seasons. The latter campaign was the first in which the Big Blue won twenty or more games, now the yardstick of a successful season. Rupp, whose position as one of the nation's foremost coaches was already securely established, emerged from the triumphs of these two seasons as a veritable miracle worker because of the great performances of his all-civilian teams in victories over such intersectional powers as Notre Dame, Indiana, Illinois, Ohio State, St. John's, Long Island University, Utah, and Oklahoma A&M. All this, however, was but a prelude to what was soon to come.

In the 1945/46 season Rupp had back the nucleus of the fine 1944 and 1945 teams—senior Wilbur Schu and juniors Jack Tingle and Jack Parkinson, as well as Kenton Campbell, who had won All-SEC honors in 1945 as a freshman. Despite their earlier accomplishments Campbell lost his center position to a freshman, Wallace "Wah Wah" Jones, while Schu was forced to share his forward position with yet another freshman, Joe Holland. Still another freshman, Ralph Beard, walked (or rather ran) into a starting guard position. Jones arrived at the Lexington campus as the greatest high school player in the nation, but Beard was not far behind in either publicity or talent. At UK both Beard and Jones quickly proved that they fully deserved all the superlatives showered upon them. The powerful rebounding of Jones and the speed of Beard made the Wildcat fast break sizzle. The Big Blue completely dominated the SEC and finished the season with twenty-eight victories and only two defeats. The Wildcats overpowered their opponents in the conference tournament in Louisville and placed four players on the All-SEC first team (Tingle, Jones, Beard, and Parkinson) and their fifth starter, Schu, on the second team. Parkinson, an excellent shooter both

from outside and on drives to the basket, also won a spot on postseason All-American teams.

The Big Blue capped the 1945/46 season by winning the NIT championship, an achievement that previously eluded Rupp and his Wildcats. UK entered the tournament as heavy favorites and swept to an easy 77-53 triumph over Arizona in its first-round test. That proved to be the Wildcats' only breather. The West Virginia Mountaineers fought the Big Blue on even terms in the semifinals. The score was tied fourteen times before UK broke the game open with about two and a half minutes left and scored eight straight points to take a 59-51 decision.

The championship game against the Rhode Island Rams and their magnificent star Ernie Calverley was an even tougher game. The score was tied twelve times in this contest, the last time with only forty seconds to play. At that point, with the score knotted at 45, Calverley fouled Ralph Beard. Beard recalled in an interview that he was scared to death as he stepped to the free throw line with Madison Square Garden's 18,000 fans screaming for him to miss. The Rams, who had entered the

tourney as 20-1 underdogs, had quickly become the Cinderella team and the darlings of the Garden crowd and the New York press. The Rhode Island dream ended as Beard sank his free throw (at the time one free throw was awarded for a nonshooting foul) and UK took the lead, 46-45. The Rams tried desperately, but unsuccessfully, to score in the final few seconds. This was one of Rupp's biggest victories. The NIT was not only the first national tournament, dating from 1938, it also had the most prestige—at least until the basketball scandals tarnished it, along with Madison Square Garden and New York City basketball in general. Until then the Garden was the "Mecca of Basketball," and it was especially sweet for the Wildcats to gain a major victory there.

Rupp lost only three lettermen from the NIT championship team, and such was the quality of the 1946/47 team that their departure was hardly felt. Departing through graduation were part-time starting forward Wilbur Schu and reserve guard William Sturgill, while junior guard Jack Parkinson was called up for military service. It was unfortunate for Parkinson—who had been team captain, leading scorer, and an All-American

Tension and exhaustion are evident on the faces of Rupp and his 1945/46 starting five, a team that bagged the SEC trophy and UK's first NIT championship. Left to right, Wilbur Schu, Wallace "Wah Wah" Jones, Ralph Beard, Jack Parkinson (captain), Jack Tingle, and Rupp.

in 1946—that he had to depart for a year of duty in the army because when he returned for the 1947/48 season he could not even crack the starting lineup, much less become a star on the "Fabulous Five" team.

Amazingly, Parkinson was one of three All-Americans who languished on the Wildcat bench during the 1947 and 1948 campaigns. The others were Kansas native Tank Brannum, who had won All-American honors at center for UK as a freshman in 1944, and West Virginian Jim Jordan, who was named All-American in both 1945 and 1946 while a naval trainee at North Carolina. Jordan, who played at guard, arrived in Lexington as a freshman with four full years of varsity eligibility still available, while Brannum still had three more years. Brannum, Jordan, and Parkinson obviously were not lacking in talent. Their misfortune was simply that in 1946/47 and 1947/48 Rupp had players who were even more richly blessed with playing ability than these former All-Americans.

If UK and Adolph Rupp had a problem in those seasons it was an overabundance of talented athletes. Rupp had nineteen players on his team roster in 1946/47 and eighteen the following season. By 1948/49 the squad was down to a more manageable twelve players. The prospect of playing for the great Rupp attracted these and many more quality athletes to Lexington. Some of the players had started at the university before or during the war only to have their careers interrupted by military service. Among these were Cliff Barker, Ken Rollins, Mulford "Muff" Davis, John Stough, and Jack Parkinson. The others were either recruited by Rupp or were attracted by his reputation. Once again Rupp's luck came to the fore. Before the 1945/46 season the United States Army asked him for a favor—to develop a sports and recreation program for soldiers in Europe. While he was overseas, noted Buddy Parker in an interview, Rupp sold the UK program to some of the fine athletes he came across. Among these were Dale Barnstable and Jim Line, both of whom were All-ETO (European Theater of Operations) players. Both later contributed greatly to the UK program. So many out-of-state players arrived, in fact, that in the 1947/48 season, for the first time in the history of UK basketball, native-born Kentuckians constituted a minority, six of eighteen players on the Wildcat roster. This continued in 1948/49 when only four of twelve varsity players were from Kentucky. Among the four were seldom-used sophomore guards Joe Hall of Cynthiana and Garland "Spec" Townes of Hazard.

In the years from 1945 to 1948 the university came

Wilbur Schu rebounds a missed shot in a 1946 game against LSU. "Wah Wah" Jones is no. 41.

to resemble a revolving door for basketball talent. Wave after wave of talented ballplayers arrived only to learn that for one reason or another they did not quite measure up to Rupp's standards, and sooner or later they departed. Players transferred from UK who possessed the ability not only to start but to star on other college teams. Thus Frenchy DeMoisey's younger brother Truitt and Deward Compton, both of whom played either center or forward, transferred to the University of Louisville, while former All-American center Bob Brannum and richly talented guard Albert Cummins (who languished on the UK third team) moved to Michigan State. After graduation Tank Brannum went on to star in the NBA for six years, four of them with the Boston Celtics.

One of Adolph Rupp's basic rules throughout his career was to decide on a starting lineup and stay with it. He generally substituted as little as possible. During the immediate postwar years, Buddy Parker observed, Rupp did bend this rule, but only in games where the

Wildcats badly outclassed their opponents. In those contests Rupp "would suit up part of the team at halftime. The boys who played the first part of the game would shower and change into street clothes and be up in the stands with their girlfriends. I don't reckon," Parker laughed, "that's ever been done at any other college in the country." Parker noted that UK had three teams with enough ability "to have probably beaten ninety-five percent of the teams in the SEC." In fact, "some of the scrimmages between the first and second teams were better played and more competitive than most of the conference games we played." It was indeed an embarrassment of riches, but UK fans did not complain.

To help him mold the magnificent groups of athletes who flocked to UK in the postwar years into championship teams Rupp had the services of Elmer "Baldy" Gilb through the 1945/46 season. Gilb, however, preferred football to basketball coaching and decided not to continue as Rupp's assistant. The Baron's prewar assistant coach, Paul McBrayer, had gone off to military duty in 1943 but with his discharge from the service was once again available. Unfortunately for McBrayer, who loved the university, Rupp had apparently long before determined not to ask him to return to the staff. Several interviewers maintained that although he was approaching the pinnacle of his success Rupp was apparently in constant fear that his job and his reputation were in jeopardy. This was perhaps a carryover from the insecure years of his youth in Kansas. Whatever the reasons, several former players have observed that Rupp found it extremely difficult to bear other people receiving publicity he felt should be his. And the Baron was well aware that many people, including some sportswriters, held McBrayer's coaching ability in high regard. Obviously Rupp could not accept the idea of having McBrayer back as assistant coach and thus as rival for control of the team and of publicity.

With McBrayer out it was necessary to find someone else to serve as assistant. According to Lee Huber, a pre-World War II UK All-American, he was tapped for the job. In an interview Huber related the process by which Rupp had Andy Anderson sound him out before the 1946/47 season. Rupp did not conduct the negotiations personally or directly, Huber noted, "because he wouldn't risk being turned down." Huber was not interested in the job, and Rupp turned to physical education instructor Harry Lancaster, a personal friend who had proved his worth to the basketball program on a number of scouting trips for the team. This was a fortunate choice because Lancaster complemented Rupp's talents and personality so perfectly. Lancaster served as assistant coach until 1968, when he accepted the position of athletics director at the university.

The UK record in the post-World War II era was truly spectacular. During the four seasons from 1945/46 through 1948/49, the Cats won 130 of 140 games played, for an average of 32.5 victories a season. The record was only slightly less impressive over the next four seasons the Big Blue played, as the Wildcats won 111 games and lost only ten, for an average of nearly twenty-eight victories a season. The Blue and White captured the SEC championship every one of those eight seasons. UK also won the NIT championship in 1946 and the NCAA in 1948, 1949, and 1951.

In the opinion of Harry Lancaster, UK could have won at least five straight NCAA championships. In an interview he pointed out that "we won the conference in 1950 but the representative from our district, the Athletic Director at Virginia, didn't invite us to participate in the NCAA and at the time you had to be invited. Instead of us, he invited a team from his own conference." Lancaster noted how ridiculous the situation was. "Here we were, defending champions two years running, and we weren't invited. So we skipped that year but we came

Harry Lancaster, who played against UK in Rupp's first game as coach, became the Wildcats' assistant coach following World War II. In 1968 he was named athletics director, making him Rupp's boss.

back in 1951 and won it and we might have even won it in 1952 but Spivey was lost to us because of the scandal." The Cats did not play a schedule in 1952/53 but returned the following season with a vengeance. They posted a perfect 25-0 season record and the conference championship in 1953/54 but did not participate in the NCAA tournament because the team's three best players—Hagan, Ramsey, and Tsioropoulos—were ineligible, as they were graduate students. (The rule has since been changed.)

Of all the achievement-filled seasons during this period probably the greatest was 1947/48, the season of UK's most famous team, the "Fabulous Five." The Wildcats not only posted a 36-3 record and held the conference title and their first NCAA championship, but also provided half of the U.S. Olympic basketball team which went on to win a gold medal at the Olympic Games in London.

The starting five were Wah Wah Jones and Cliff Barker at the forwards, Alex Groza at center, and Ralph Beard and Ken Rollins at guards. Rollins, a senior, was team captain for the second straight season. In an interview Rollins noted that although this group did not come together as a starting team until the 1947/48 season, World War II was responsible for the "Fabulous Five." The twenty-six-year-old Barker, Rollins, age twenty-four, and Groza, who was twenty-one, were exservicemen, as were the majority of the team's substitutes. The result was, as Rollins noted, an excellent mixture of maturity and youth. Thus Barker started at UK "in 1939, played just part of his freshman year, fell in love, went home, got married, and joined the Air Force. I started in 1941, played my freshman and sophomore years, and got drafted into the Navy. Groza," Rollins continued, "arrived in '44, played part of a year, and was drafted. Then in 1945 along came some great talent straight out of high school in the persons of Beard and Jones. Then you have us all coming together after the end of the war" when Groza, Barker, and Rollins returned to UK in time for the 1946/47 season. "It took us a full year to get everything together," Rollins stated, "for us to be comfortable together and get that chemistry."

The great success achieved by the 1947/48 team, Rollins believed, was a combination of a number of factors, including speed, size (for the era), unselfishness, good shooters, and a certain chemistry. It must also be remembered that all the players were hard workers. "None of us was ever lazy or ever slacked off" either in practice or in games. "Another thing we had," Rollins continued, "was the killer instinct. I get so disturbed with teams that get fifteen or so point leads at halftime and

Kenny Rollins started at guard in 1942/43 but his career was interrupted by military service. He returned to star on the 1946/47 and 1947/48 teams.

fritter it away in the second half. Brother, if we got twenty on a ball club that was just the beginning," he maintained, slapping the desk to emphasize his point. "We weren't satisfied. We wanted twenty more and more often than not we got them. No mercy! None whatsoever. We never had compassion for anyone," he laughed.

Rollins, Jones, Groza, Beard, and Harry Lancaster in interviews discussed the contributions of each member of the starting five to the team's success in the 1947/48 season. They noted that every successful team needs at least one player who is willing to sacrifice his personal glory for the success of the squad and who is also willing to take a leadership role. The 1948 team was especially fortunate because it had not one but two such players. Both Barker at forward and Rollins at guard got as much pleasure from making a good pass as from scor-

ing a basket. Rollins was, in Lancaster's words, "our coach on the floor." Groza, Beard, and Jones did most of the scoring but Rollins also was a good if not great shooter. He had an excellent long set shot and a jump shot from around the foul line. Rollins also scored points on the fast break. Barker, on the other hand, was not a scorer. He had been an excellent shooter before the war but had lost his touch during the fifteen months he spent in a Nazi prisoner-of-war camp. Most of the points he made were on rebounds or fast breaks, although he did occasionally hit a jumper from eight or ten feet out. Amazingly, considering his poor shooting touch, Barker hit the longest field goal in Wildcat history, a 63' 7 1/2" missile unleashed against Vanderbilt on February 26, 1949, at Alumni Gym. Barker characteristically downplayed the shot during an interview in November 1983, claiming that it was just luck and not very important anyway. Barker's major contributions to the team were excellent defense, strong rebounding, and great ball-handling. He was often the trigger on the fast break because of his strong defensive rebounding and his ability to get the ball out quickly on the break once he had the

rebound. His passing was legendary. As one of his team-mates observed, "He could do just about anything with a basketball except shoot it."

The team's chief offensive weapon was the center, Alex Groza. He was very quick and fast for a big man and often got downcourt on the fast break. He had good hands and an excellent scoring touch. All he needed, a teammate recalled, was "a little operating room." Therefore the team constantly worked on ways to get him open because "once you got him the ball, that was it. He was an excellent faker and he had a variety of shots and was a great rebounder." His chief attribute, though, was a combination of floor balance and court sense.

The 6'4" Jones, also a football and baseball star, was a powerful rebounder who was especially effective on the offensive boards. He had an excellent two-hand shot from above his head which he took from the corner and from around the foul line. Beard had a variety of shots including a long two-hand set shot and a one-hand jump shot from medium range. If guarded too closely, the 5'10" Beard, who was extremely fast and had great quickness, could get by his man for a layup. Like the other

Ralph Beard's jump shot against Georgia Tech in the 1948 SEC championship helped UK to a 54-43 victory. "Wah Wah" Jones is no. 27, Alex Groza is no. 15.

The 1948 NCAA champions, probably UK's greatest team. Front row, left to right: Rupp, Johnny Stough, Ralph Beard, Kenny Rollins (captain), Cliff Barker, Dale Barnstable, and assistant coach Harry Lancaster. Back row: manager Humzey Yessin, Garland Townes, Jim Jordan, Joe Holland, Alex Groza, Wallace Jones, Jim Line, Roger Day, and trainer Wilbert "Bud" Berger.

guard, Ken Rollins, Beard scored many of his points on the fast break.

Harry Lancaster reminisced about the "Fabulous Five" and their fast break. "They were a beautiful team," he observed. "They had the finest fast break I have ever seen, before or since. It was just magnificent the way Groza got the ball off the board." When Groza or Barker got the rebound "he would hit Jones around the head of the circle. He would hit Rollins at about midcourt, and Rollins would hit Beard going under the basket. Beard and Rollins were just so quick." Lancaster also noted that when the "Fabulous Five" ran the fast break "the ball might touch the court once or twice but never more. None of this dribble, dribble, dribble. It was bing, bing and in it went." Lancaster closed his discussion of the "Fabulous Five" with the observation that "Rupp would never admit it but that was the best team we had man for man."

Only Rollins was lost from the great 1948 team. Dale Barnstable, a 6'3" junior from Antioch, Illinois, took Rollins's place in the starting lineup. At the beginning of the 1948/49 season Barnstable played at guard, but it did not take long to see that a better passer was needed. The happy solution was to move Barnstable to forward and shift the team's best passer, Cliff Barker, to guard. The result was another glitteringly successful season. The Cats won thirty-two games and lost only two en route to a second straight NCAA championship. Beard and Groza won All-American honors for the third season in a row and were joined on the honor teams in their senior season by forward Wah Wah Jones. In 1949 Alex Groza became the third UK star to be named the Helms Foundation Basketball Player of the Year. Two years later another Wildcat center, Bill Spivey, became Player of the Year.

Spivey, UK's first seven-footer, joined the varsity in the 1949/50 season and led an inexperienced team composed largely of sophomores to a very respectable 25-5 record and yet another conference championship. After being snubbed by the NCAA, the two-time defending national champions accepted an invitation to play in the NIT. It quickly became evident that this was a mistake because they met a City College of New York team that administered the worst drubbing Rupp had ever suffered. What made the defeat even more humiliating at the time was that the CCNY team entered the tournament with a deceptively lackluster 17-5 regular-season record. In the wake of the basketball scandal which began to break in the summer of 1951, evidence was uncovered that the squad had shaved points in games throughout the 1949/50 season. CCNY did not begin to play up to its potential until tournament time, when it won not only the NIT but the NCAA championship. No other team in college basketball history has ever matched this accomplishment, although UK and other teams of the era tried.

The Wildcats achieved another thirty-win season (32-2) and an NCAA championship in 1950/51. Along

Three-time All-American Alex Groza scores against Georgia on his way to a record-setting thirty-eight-point game total on February 21, 1949. UK downed the Bulldogs 95-40.

with Spivey, who was named All-American and College Player of the Year while still a junior, UK had a talented squad that included senior Walt Hirsch and junior Shelby Linville at forward and junior Bobby Watson and sophomore Frank Ramsey at guard. Reserves included future college coaches Guy Strong and C.M. Newton as well as Lucian "Skippy" Whitaker, Lou Tsioropoulos, and Cliff Hagan, who became a sophomore and joined the varsity at midseason.

The 1950/51 season shines brightly in Bill Spivey's memory, especially a December 16 game at Memorial Coliseum with Kansas in which he outduelled another great center, Clyde Lovellette. In an interview Spivey recalled it as "my best game at UK. The press from coast to coast was playing it up and Rupp was really anxious to win because he had played for the Kansas coach, Phog Allen." By the time the game started "I was really psyched up because of the press and because of clippings Rupp had been pasting on my locker saying how good Lovellette was." UK crushed Kansas 68-39 and Spivey assured himself the Player of the Year award by completely outclassing one of his major rivals for the honor. Spivey was so emotionally charged up that at one point in the game he treated Wildcat fans to their first view of a dunk during a game. Dunking was legal at the time but Rupp did not permit it during games, although he did in practice. "I stole the ball from Lovellette under the basket and it took me only about three bounces of the ball to get to the other end and I went up and slammed it through the basket. I just couldn't help it." Spivey laughed. "I was so fired up I even beat the guards downcourt. The fans went crazy. They went absolutely wild."

The 1950/51 team was one of the most successful in Wildcat history but fans were expecting even more the following season. And their expectations were justified. With Bill Spivey in the lineup the 1951/52 team had the potential to be one of the greatest college basketball squads in history. Even without him it was excellent. With the 7' Spivey at center the team would have boasted 6'4" junior Cliff Hagan and 6'5" senior Shelby Linville at forward, and 6'3" junior Frank Ramsey and 5'10 1/2" senior (and team captain) Bobby Watson at the guard positions. Among the sixteen available reserves were 6'5" junior Lou Tsioropoulos at forward and center, and 6' senior Skippy Whitaker and 6'1" sophomore Bill Evans, who played at both forward and guard. This aggregation possessed talent, size, and depth. It could have become, as Spivey noted, an even better team than the "Fabulous Five."

Unfortunately, injury to Spivey and the basketball scandal intervened. Spivey injured his knee prior to the start of the season, and before he was ready to return to action he was implicated in the fast-spreading scandal. Although Spivey was never convicted of wrongdoing he never played in another game for the Wildcats. His place in the lineup was taken by Cliff Hagan who, although only 6'4" tall, had good jumping ability and an awesome hook shot. UK lost only three of thirty-two games, but one of the defeats was to St. John's in the Eastern Regional of the NCAA by a 64-57 score. The loss was especially painful because the Cats had smashed the same St. John's team by forty-one points (81-40) in a regular-season meeting. Spivey might have made a difference in the tournament game but he was under investigation by law enforcement authorities in New York City.

The existence of corruption in college basketball was first publicized in 1945 when five Brooklyn College players were expelled from school after admitting they had accepted bribes to lose a game. The extent of the point shaving and game fixing did not become evident, however, until 1951 when Manhattan College star Junius Kellogg reported to the District Attorney's office that he had received an offer of $1,000 to control the point spread in a game. Although the scandal centered on New York area teams and Madison Square Garden games, investigations disclosed the fact that between 1947 and 1950 fixers had tampered with at least eighty-six games in twenty-three cities and seventeen states. Authorities named thirty-three players as having participated in the fixes, and there were rumors that many more were involved.

As the revelations began to appear in the press Adolph Rupp made what soon proved to be an unfortunate statement. In an interview in Lincoln, Nebraska, on August 15 he maintained that "the gamblers couldn't get to our boys with a ten-foot pole." The team, he continued, was under "constant and absolutely complete supervision while on the road." Furthermore, the Baron bragged, "nowhere was that supervision more complete than in New York." New York authorities soon demonstrated that gamblers had indeed been able to "get to" some of UK's players, and with money rather than poles. The press and New York sportswriters in particular gleefully turned Rupp's words against him. Larry Fox pointed out in his *Illustrated History of Basketball* that when "the scandal 'hit in the family,' Rupp no longer urged leniency for players who 'only' shaved points." In this unfolding drama Rupp did not perform with distinction.

In the fall of 1951 Ralph Beard, Alex Groza, and Dale Barnstable were taken into custody and admitted

Bill Spivey, UK's 7' center, dominates Kansas star center Clyde Lovellette in the Wildcats' resounding 68-39 defeat of Rupp's alma mater on December 16, 1950.

sharing $2,000 in bribe money to shave points in a 1949 NIT game against Loyola. The Wildcats were ten-point favorites going into the game but suffered a stunning 67-56 defeat and elimination in the opening round of the tournament. Soon Jim Line, a star of the 1950 team, Walt Hirsch, team captain and star forward in 1951, and Bill Spivey were implicated. All but Spivey admitted accepting money and when they came to trial received suspended sentences. Spivey, who adamantly proclaimed his innocence, was indicted for perjury but was found innocent.

Beard, Groza, and Barnstable appeared before Judge Saul S. Streit of the Court of General Session in New York on April 29, 1952, to hear their sentences. As with the athletes of other universities who appeared before him and admitted their guilt, Judge Streit was relatively lenient. But the judge was not as understanding in his

Wildcat captain and forward Walt Hirsch fights for a loose ball in a January 8, 1951, game against DePaul during UK's first season in Memorial Coliseum. The Cats won 63-55.

dealings with gamblers, universities, coaches, and alumni. In an earlier trial when passing sentence on the game fixers Judge Streit maintained that "the responsibility for the sports scandal must be shared not only by the crooked fixers and corrupt players, but also by the college administrations, coaches and alumni groups who participate in this evil system of commercialism and overemphasis."

As the school with the most successful basketball program in the nation the University of Kentucky came under particularly close scrutiny and, in Judge Streit's opinion, was found wanting. The judge, in a sixty-seven-page opinion delivered on April 29, 1952, found the university to be "the acme of commercialization and overemphasis." The magistrate complained that "intercollegiate basketball and football at the University of Kentucky have become highly systematized, professionalized and commercialized." He also found "covert subsidization of players, ruthless exploitation of athletes, cribbing at examinations, 'illegal' recruiting, a reckless disregard of their physical welfare, matriculation of unqualified athletes by the coach, alumni, and townspeople, and the most flagrant abuse of the 'athletic scholarship.'"

Judge Streit was particularly critical of Adolph Rupp

who, in his view, "failed in his duty to observe the amateur rules, to build character and protect the morals and health of his charges." After their experience with Rupp, Beard and the other players were "ripe for plucking by the Fixers."

Judge Streit also decried Rupp's relationship with Lexington bookmaker Ed Curd. As Russell Rice noted in *Big Blue Machine*, Curd was "the undisputed 'king' of Lexington bookmakers at the time" as well as "a nationally known gambling figure who operated in comparative security above the Mayfair Bar on Lexington's Main Street. He was friendly with the 'right' persons, made his contributions to charity—Rupp had gone to Curd's home to solicit for the local children's hospital—and operated a 340-acre farm near Lexington. His name was mentioned at least twice in the Senate Crime Committee investigation as Lexington's betting commissioner."

In testimony before the court Rupp admitted knowing Curd (misspelled "Kurd" in the court records) and agreed that it was "general knowledge" that Curd was a bookie who operated a bookmaking establishment in Lexington. Rupp further acknowledged that Curd had on at least two occasions joined the Baron and others of the

Kentucky travelling contingent at meals at New York's Copacabana night club and had travelled on the train to at least one game with the team. The Baron denied the allegation of some of his players that he frequently telephoned Curd to learn the point spread on UK games.

The university and its president, Herman L. Donovan, defended Rupp and refused to dismiss him even when it became evident that such action would spare the team punishment by the SEC and the NCAA. On August 11, 1952, the Executive Committee of the SEC announced its findings and decision. The punishment meted out was harsher than the university had feared. The Wildcats were barred for one season from conference play and participation in postseason tournaments. Three months after the league ruling, the NCAA asked all member schools not to schedule UK during the 1952/53 season.

A few days after the NCAA announcement President Donovan informed UK alumni that he had ordered an internal investigation of Rupp, which had produced a report that exonerated the basketball coach of any wrongdoing. "From all we could learn," Donovan maintained, "Coach Rupp is an honorable man who did not knowingly violate the athletic rules." The announcement pleased Big Blue fans but not, apparently, the university's football coach, Paul "Bear" Bryant.

The Bear, who had arrived in Lexington in 1946, brought UK its first success and national prominence in football, but felt that he and his program were not fully appreciated on campus or in the state. (Bryant's immediate predecessors as head coach were A.D. Kirwan, later a UK history professor and university president, and Athletics Director Bernie Shiveley, who also assumed the duties of football coach in 1945.) Both Rupp and

The 1950/51 SEC and NCAA champion Wildcats. Front row, left to right: Lindle Castle, Lucian Whitaker, Bobby Watson, Guy Strong, and Charles Riddle. Middle row: Rupp, Cliff Hagan, C.M. Newton, Walt Hirsch (captain), Paul Lansaw, Dwight Price, and assistant coach Lancaster. Back row: Frank Ramsey, Shelby Linville, Bill Spivey, Roger Layne, Lou Tsioropoulos, and Read Morgan.

Bryant were coaching geniuses, both had enormous egos, and both needed a large stage on which to perform. It proved impossible for them to coexist on the same campus. Supposedly Bryant was under the impression that Donovan would dismiss Rupp and was angry to learn instead that the Baron had received a vote of confidence. Thus instead of forcing Rupp's departure from the university, the basketball scandal precipitated Bryant's departure.

For Rupp, who always feared failure, the entire affair must have been a humiliating and debilitating experience. Gerry Calvert, who played on UK's varsity from 1953/54 through 1956/57 and who later became Rupp's attorney and good friend, maintained in an interview that the Baron's problems with his eyes and with diabetes began much earlier than most people realized and that the pressure on Rupp during the various investigations had a great and adverse effect on his health.

If the scandal was a traumatic experience for Rupp, it was devastating for the players involved. The very

promising professional basketball careers of Alex Groza and Ralph Beard were cut short by the scandal, while Bill Spivey, who had the potential to be one of the greatest of all pro players, never got an opportunity to play in the NBA. In the 1949/50 season Groza and Beard, together with former "Fabulous Five" teammates Cliff Barker and Wah Wah Jones, began their careers as players and part owners of the Indianapolis Olympians, a new franchise in the newly formed NBA. The Olympians finished their first season as Western Division Leaders (the league was made up of three divisions). Although the Olympians were defeated in the second round of the playoffs, the season was a success both on the court and at the ticket office. Groza and Beard quickly emerged as two of the league's brightest stars. At the end of the 1949/50 season both were among the league's top ten scorers and Groza, with a 23.4 points per game average, finished second to the Minneapolis Lakers' great center George Mikan and his 27.4 average. Beard and Groza played just one more season before

Five stars of the 1953/54 Wildcat squad, UK's first undefeated team since 1911/12, pose with a beauty queen. Left to right: Phil Grawemeyer, Bill Evans, Lou Tsioropoulos, and co-captains Cliff Hagan and Frank Ramsey.

the scandal broke. Claiming it was necessary to protect the reputation of the young league, Commissioner Maurice Podoloff declared the two players "ineligible for life" and forced them to sell their shares in the Olympians for a fraction of the real worth. Spivey's fate was equally tragic. Even though he was never found guilty of wrongdoing, Spivey was banned for life from playing in the NBA even before he had a chance to play his first pro game.

Rupp and the university were penalized for one year; Groza, Beard, and the other players paid for their mistakes with their careers. Each was successful in picking up the pieces of his life, but the full potential of every one for an athletic career went unfulfilled.

During the 1952/53 season the Wildcats were prohibited from intercollegiate play but not from practice or intrasquad scrimmages. Rupp and Lancaster used the season, as Laudeman noted in *The Rupp Years*, "to polish up the team's offense and defense without the pressure of preparing for a particular game." The team also held four public scrimmages which attracted a total of nearly 35,000 spectators. The smallest turnout was on the worst night of the entire winter when 6,500 fans braved the cold and the icy streets to attend a scrimmage between a squad composed of varsity players and the freshmen. The spectators learned at these scrimmages that UK would be loaded with talent when the 1953/54 season rolled around.

Led by the "Big Three"—Cliff Hagan, Frank Ramsey, and Lou Tsioropoulos—the Wildcats returned to the basketball wars with a convincing 86-59 drubbing of Temple University before more than 13,000 screaming fans at the Coliseum on December 5, 1953. Hagan, in particular, had a sensational game as he broke the SEC single-game scoring record with fifty-one points. Although he was only 6'4", the hook-shooting Hagan performed brilliantly at center throughout the season. He had one of the smoothest and most effective hook shots in the history of the game and was an excellent rebounder. While Hagan was small for a college center, Ramsey at 6'3" was taller than most guards in the 1950s. In addition to size Ramsey was fast, aggressive under the boards, and a good but not great outside shooter.

His points usually came from driving layups, rebounds, or the fast break. Few opponents were able to stop him when he moved to the basket. He was also an excellent defensive player. Both Hagan and Ramsey were named All-Americans for the second time. According to teammate Phil Grawemeyer, the 6'5" Tsioropoulos, who made the All-SEC second team in 1954, was the team workhorse. "A lot of people didn't realize it," Grawemeyer observed, "but he was a good shooter. He didn't get much of a chance to show what he could do because we needed other things he could do more." Among other things Tsioropoulos "was an excellent rebounder and a terrific defensive man. If we needed it he could even guard a guard. He was fast, he was strong, and he was tough."

The Wildcats swept through the regular season undefeated and whipped LSU in a playoff to determine the league champion and representative to the NCAA tournament. The Cats declined an invitation, however, when the NCAA declared Hagan, Ramsey, and Tsioropoulos ineligible to participate in the tournament because they were no longer undergraduates. It is indeed ironic, as Hagan noted in an interview, that "we were penalized for the year we were forced to sit out and that was for something we had not been involved in. If we had taken five years to graduate we wouldn't have had a problem. So we were penalized for trying to do the right thing. Isn't that something?"

Thus UK's "Golden Decade" ended on a bittersweet note. The Big Blue crowned an era of brilliant basketball performance with a perfect regular-season record, a rare achievement indeed. What happened off the court proved once again to be the Wildcats' undoing. For the second season in a row the lingering effects of the scandal denied UK's three best players the opportunity to compete for the national championship even though there was no suspicion of personal involvement on their part.

In the four years from 1948 through 1951 Adolph Rupp made college basketball history when his teams won the NCAA tournament an unprecedented three times. The Baron would win only one more national championship in the remainder of his long career, and that triumph would appear, even to Rupp, to be something of a fluke.

7

The Afterglow

During Adolph Rupp's last eighteen seasons as head coach (1954/55-1971/72) the Wildcats compiled a record of 384-107 for a winning percentage of .782. Although no longer perennial SEC champions, the Big Blue won the conference title outright nine of the eighteen seasons and shared it in another two. Interestingly, UK not only participated in NCAA postseason play each of the eleven seasons it won or shared the conference title but also represented the SEC three other times: in 1956 when Alabama refused an invitation because it might have to play against teams containing black players, and in 1959 and 1961 when Mississippi State declined for the same reason. Thus UK appeared in fourteen of the eighteen NCAA tournaments played between 1955 and 1972 but did not approach the glittering record of success achieved by Big Blue squads of the late forties and early fifties. Only twice during these years were the Wildcats able to get beyond the regionals. In 1958 the "Fiddlin' Five" won the national championship and in 1966 "Rupp's Runts" were runners-up.

Lack of greater success in postseason play as well as with regular-season conference and intersectional foes was a source of frustration for the aging Rupp. All through his career, but particularly during his last two decades of coaching at UK, Rupp exhibited great concern about records and reputation. In an interview, Ned Jennings noted that when he played at UK (1957-61) the Baron made the team very conscious of the fact that "he had never been beaten on TV, never been below .500, never lost an opening game, anything that was a first." Jennings recalled a December 28, 1959, game against

Ohio State and its sophomore stars Jerry Lucas, John Havlicek, and Mel Nowell. "They had us down pretty good at the half. Nobody had ever scored 100 points on us on UK's floor and that was his main concern at halftime. 'Just slow the game down,' he said. Well, we wound up beating them [96-93] but his big worry was that someone would set a record against him."

Despite his many records and achievements, Rupp was in some ways a tragic figure during the last part of his career. These years were filled with physical pain and an increasing sense of professional frustration, in large part because of the spectacular success of John Wooden and the UCLA Bruins.

Prior to Wooden's amazing achievements in the sixties and seventies only Rupp and UK had won as many as four NCAA titles and only UK, Oklahoma A&M, San Francisco, and Cincinnati had won two in a row. The Baron wanted very badly to be the first coach to capture five titles. Instead, this honor went to Wooden, the "Wizard of Westwood." Wooden's Bruins did not stop with five NCAA championships, however. In the twelve years between 1964 and 1975 the Bruins won ten NCAA titles. In addition, UCLA set a collegiate record of eighty-seven straight victories, and three of Wooden's squads completed undefeated seasons—two during the career of Lew Alcindor (later Kareem Abdul-Jabbar) and one during that of Bill Walton. To Larry Fox this was "a dynasty unmatched and unapproached in college basketball" history. In fact, Fox maintained, Wooden's achievement far exceeded that of pro basketball's best—Red Auerbach's eight straight and eleven of thirteen NBA

championships with the Boston Celtics. "Wooden had to keep his streak going with a continuously changing cast: no player could remain more than three seasons. With small teams, big teams, shooting teams, defensive teams, Wooden kept on winning."

To a man as jealous of his achievements and reputation as was Adolph Rupp, John Wooden's outstanding success during the twilight years of the Baron's career was undoubtedly a source of frustration and bitterness. In addition, Rupp during this period suffered greatly from physical ailments. "In fact," Harry Lancaster observed in an interview, Rupp "didn't coach the last fifteen years he was here. He was out of it as soon as the game started." Responsibility for directing the team during the game, as several knowledgeable people have noted, fell to Lancaster, who apparently was always able to maintain a level head, even during the most tension-packed moments of a contest. Rupp "was a sick man," Lancaster continued. "He had back problems. He had had his spinal column fused and that bothered him . . . . Then he wound up as a diabetic and had a hole in one foot that wouldn't heal. Rupp suffered a lot of pain." During Rupp's later years, according to Lancaster, "there was drinking and it was noticeable on his Sunday night [television] program."

In addition to various health problems, Rupp had another major concern: the increasing importance during the late fifties and the sixties of the black athlete. During the fifties Wilt Chamberlain, with his intimidating dunk shot, and the defensive genius Bill Russell helped revolutionize the college game. On offense the use of the jump shot and the dunk permitted play to move closer to the basket than in the era of the two-hand shot from the chest. This change, in turn, placed increased emphasis on defense, especially on the use of a variety of zones. It was difficult for Rupp to adjust to the new style of play. As one former player theorized, the Baron "didn't really understand zones because he had seldom been forced to play against a zone." Rupp and Harry Lancaster did finally make use of the zone in the mid-sixties, but with great reluctance.

With his devastating zone press, John Wooden demonstrated that he recognized and accepted the growing importance of the defensive game. Wooden also made excellent use of black players to develop the UCLA dynasty, among them Walt Hazzard, Lucius Allen, Curtis Rowe, Sidney Wicks, Henry Bibby, and perhaps the greatest college player in basketball history, Kareem Abdul-Jabbar.

There is some disagreement about Rupp's real attitude toward blacks. Black students at UK during the mid-sixties charged that Rupp was a racist who had no intention of recruiting or coaching black players. Bill Russell, a star player and later a playing coach with the Boston Celtics of the NBA, agreed. In his autobiography *Second Wind: The Memoirs of an Opinionated Man*, Russell wrote of Rupp: "I know many players who had been coached by him at the University of Kentucky, I'd met him myself, and nothing I ever saw or heard of him contradicted my impression that he was one of the more devout racists in sports. He was known for the delight he took in making nasty remarks about niggers and Jews, and for his determination never to have black players at the University of Kentucky." Rupp apologists, on the other hand, maintained that the Baron was indifferent to race. His only interest was an athlete's playing ability and he would have recruited blacks if the conference had permitted him to do so. On Rupp's behalf it should be said that he did schedule games with intersectional rivals that had black players. UK played away games against blacks as early as the 1940s. The first black to play on UK's home court, according to Bobby Watson, was St. John's University's Sollie Walker. The Wildcats had played the St. John's Redmen several times at Madison Square Garden, but the December 17, 1951, game at Memorial Coliseum was the Redmen's first visit to Kentucky. It was not a pleasant experience for the visitors—St. John's was thoroughly whipped, 81-40.

Competing against an occasional black in intersectional play was not the same, though, as actually recruiting blacks. The excuse that Rupp did not recruit blacks because the SEC would not permit it is spurious. On the contrary, Harry Lancaster recalled in a 1983 interview, "There was no regulation within the SEC or even here at UK against recruiting blacks. In fact, when John Oswald was president here [1963-68] he drove Adolph crazy telling him to recruit blacks." Lancaster noted that "Adolph always used the excuse that he didn't want to recruit one and have him sitting on the bench. Oswald would answer, 'You've got whites sitting on the bench and you don't seem to object to that. What's the difference if a black sits on the bench?' Adolph would come back from talking with Oswald and say, 'That son of a bitch is going to drive me crazy. He's unreasonable. He's unreasonable.'"

By the 1960s the Baron was a dominant figure not only in the League but nationally. Throughout his career he had been an innovator who was not afraid to take chances. Yet instead of pioneering within his conference, Rupp waited until Vanderbilt, a private university, integrated the SEC before he signed his first black, Tom Payne of Louisville, to a scholarship. With great

reluctance one is led to the conclusion that Rupp did not recruit blacks earlier because he did not want to.

In a sense Rupp was a captive of the great success he had enjoyed during his "Golden Decade" from 1943/44 to 1953/54. During that period the Baron was freed from the need to recruit star players actively. Although he did often engage in personal recruitment, he seldom needed to because excellent ballplayers were eager to come to him. In addition, the method of recruitment was different in the forties than later. Instead of having to go to the players, coaches were permitted to bring high school seniors to the college campus for tryouts. As Ken Rollins, Cliff Hagan, and other stars of the era noted in interviews, Rupp brought droves of players to Lexington for tryouts. Rollins, for example, was brought in with forty-nine other athletes for a week of workouts. Only three of this group were offered scholarships. Other groups worked out in the weeks before and after the Rollins contingent. By all accounts Rupp and his assistants, McBrayer and Lancaster, were masters of this type of recruitment. In the aftermath of the basketball scandals of 1951, campus workouts were prohibited. By the late fifties droves of outstandingly talented players were no longer knocking at Rupp's door begging to be permitted to play at UK. In addition, quality athletes tended increasingly to be blacks.

The changing environment was evident as early as the 1954/55 season when Rupp searched for a replacement at center for All-American Cliff Hagan. Dissatisfied with the players coming up to the varsity from the freshman team and with the reserve centers returning from the undefeated 1953/54 squad, Rupp turned to the junior college ranks for help. At Lon Morris Junior College in Jacksonville, Texas, the Baron found and recruited Bob Burrow, the nation's leading junior college scorer and the JC "Player of the Year" for 1954. The 6'7" Burrow possessed a variety of shots, was a powerful rebounder, and more than held his own on defense. The Texan was named to the All-SEC team in both 1955 and 1956 and was an All-American in the latter year. Rupp was so pleased with Burrow that he turned often to junior colleges in the following years with results that were sometimes, but not always, worthwhile. For example, while Adrian Smith became a starting guard on the 1958 NCAA championship team and guards Bennie Coffman and Sid Cohen made important contributions in the 1958/59 and 1959/60 seasons, the highly talented and eagerly awaited Vince Del Negro, a center and forward, and Doug Pendygraft, a guard, proved to be bitter disappointments in 1960/61. In large part because of their experience with Del Negro and Pendygraft, and although

UK during the early sixties was in desperate need of quality players, Rupp and Lancaster discontinued recruiting in the junior colleges.

Cotton Nash, a three-time All-American (1962-64), ruefully recalled UK's recruiting problem during the early sixties. In an interview Nash noted that for lack of taller players he had to play at center, although he believed he would have been more effective at a forward position. "I'm just sorry Rupp didn't [actively recruit] because I spent four years there at 6'5" and he couldn't find anyone bigger than me to bring in to play center and let me get out there at forward. I didn't want to play center," Nash emphasized. "I'd have preferred not to play there. The only thing I've regretted was that he didn't go out and recruit some bigger guys to go with us little guys." During his senior season, 1963/64, the Wildcats' front line consisted of sophomore Larry Conley and senior Ted Deeken, both 6'3," at forward and the 6'5" Nash at center. The backcourt consisted of Terry Mobley and Randy Embry. "We had to emphasize the fast break because we were always outmanned physically. Then toward the end of my last year we even put in a zone defense. UK teams had always been strictly man-to-man on defense before that."

The early 1960s was a traumatic period for ardent fans of the Big Blue. In fact, during the six seasons from 1959/60 through 1964/65 their team won only one SEC championship (1963/64), shared another (1961/62), and lost an average of eight and a half games a year, a previously unimaginable figure. By ordinary standards UK's record during this six-year period was a good one, a total of 112 victories and a winning percentage of .717. But Wildcat fans had come to expect something more than "good." Little did they realize that the worst was yet to come. After a rebound in 1965/66 which boasted a 32-2 season record, an SEC championship, and second place in the NCAA tournament, the 1966/67 season brought disaster—a 13-13 season. This was the nadir of Adolph Rupp's long and illustrious career. For the first time fans and sportswriters seriously suggested that the game had passed by the Man in the Brown Suit, and that he should consider retirement. Instead, the Baron coached five more seasons and proved that he could return UK to a position of dominance within the SEC, winning or sharing the championship each of the five seasons. Success in the NCAA tournament, however, still proved to be an elusive goal.

Although it was not recognized at the time, the downward slide had begun in the 1954/55 season. On the eve of the season everyone connected with UK basketball, from coaches to fans, expected the seemingly

endless successes of the preceding decade to continue. The Wildcats compiled an excellent 22-2 record, but the two losses, both to Georgia Tech, may have been harbingers of future problems within the SEC. That, at any rate, is the opinion of Phil Grawemeyer, who was a starting forward on the 1954/55 team. "I believe that was the beginning of a change in the SEC," Grawemeyer stated in an interview. Other schools began to feel that it was possible to beat UK and they devoted greater attention and more resources to basketball. "Not all of them, mind you, but different ones at different times developed strong teams. Through that period after I was in school Mississippi State, Vanderbilt, LSU, Tennessee, Alabama, and Auburn had some good years. The SEC developed to the point where no team had a guarantee it would win the title."

Fans seemed to have ample reason to be confident of UK's chances in 1954/55 because Rupp had another strong team, at least during the early part of the season. The starting five consisted of 6'6" Jerry Bird and 6'8" Phil Grawemeyer at the forwards, 6'7" Bob Burrow at center, and 6' 1" Bill Evans and 6' Linville Puckett at guards. It was a well-balanced team with one of the tallest front lines in the country, and with shooting ability and strong rebounders. The Wildcats seemed to have all the ingredients for a second consecutive undefeated

season. The first loss to Georgia Tech dashed that dream. The second defeat, also at the hands of the Yellow Jackets, was the prelude to an attempted Wildcat rebellion. Following the Tech game in Atlanta the UK team returned to Lexington. Since Rupp had not scheduled a practice the next day, a Sunday, most of the players decided among themselves to take a break and go home. Unfortunately for them, Rupp got wind of their plans, sent someone to check the players' rooms, and called a practice for Sunday. Somehow the players found out about the change and got back to campus in time.

In a 1983 interview, Linville Puckett described the succeeding events. He had not left town because "the girl I was dating, who is now my wife," lived in Lexington. Puckett recalled that on Sunday afternoon he was at the Jack Cook Service Station just down the street from the Coliseum and Stoll Field. Cook's was a meeting place for members of the basketball and football teams. "Well," Puckett reminisced, "I was sitting there at the service station and the players came in and told me that Adolph had found out they had left town, and would I say I had left town, too. So I agreed to say I had gone home." The players had heard that Rupp planned to take some of their privileges away and they agreed that if he did so they would quit the team as a group. They went to the Coliseum for the meeting called by Rupp. After

The 1954/55 starting five plus one. Left to right: Gayle Rose (first reserve guard), Jerry Bird, Bob Burrow, Rupp, Phil Grawemeyer, Bill Evans (captain), and Linville Puckett. The photo was taken before Rupp and Puckett had their run-in.

asking each player if he had gone home, Rupp announced that he was going to take away their movie passes and $15-a-month laundry allowance for a specified length of time.

Puckett had been asked to serve as the players' spokesman because he had never been afraid to express his views. After Rupp's announcement, Puckett immediately responded, "'If you need mine for that long you can keep them for the rest of the year.' That kind of shocked him," Puckett noted, "and he went on down the row and every one of them said the same thing. They all agreed that if Rupp was going to do what he said, we would quit. So we did quit. We went outside the Coliseum. Everybody but Bill Evans." Evans, the team captain, was married and had not been involved in any of the plans.

Outside the coliseum the players discussed what had happened and agreed that "if Rupp would let us keep our movie passes and our $15 a month for laundry, we would stay on the team. They [Rupp and Lancaster] sent Evans out to tell us all to come back in. So we went in." Rupp did not, as most accounts of the events claim, attend this second meeting with the team. "Adolph went to his office," recalled Puckett, "and had Harry and Bill Evans speak to us. Harry told us what a mistake we were making if we quit the team, so all of them agreed to go in and practice except me. Old hardheaded me went the other way." Puckett is convinced that everything would have blown over and Rupp would have welcomed him back to the team if the incident had not received widespread publicity. He understood that "the team manager worked for the *Courier-Journal* and quick as he saw what went on he went and called the paper and told them what had happened. When that hit the paper there wasn't anything more that could be done. Happy Chandler got Harry to speak to Adolph, but Adolph said it was all there in the papers and he would look bad if he took me back." Even though the rest of the players returned to the team, they "didn't get to keep their passes and laundry money." According to Puckett, Rupp followed through on his threat to withhold these from players who had quit the team, even temporarily.

Puckett and teammate Billy Bibb transferred to Kentucky Wesleyan, where they joined two other former Wildcats, Logan Gipe and Pete Grigsby. With this nucleus the Owensboro team nearly pulled an upset over Louisville and did defeat Coach Ed Diddle's Western Kentucky Hilltoppers. "It was the first time that Wesleyan beat them in Bowling Green in thirty-nine years," Puckett related.

At UK, reserve Gayle Rose moved into the starting

Wildcat captain Phil Grawemeyer, plagued by injuries during the 1955/56 season, wears a protective headpiece in a December 10 game against Temple.

lineup, but Puckett's departure had an impact felt especially during postseason play. According to Phil Grawemeyer, "The team really missed Puckett because he was a terrific passer. No one else we had was as good." Combined with the loss of two other starters, Puckett's departure was to prove disastrous when UK got into the NCAA regionals.

Grawemeyer was the second player lost to the team. During a close contest with DePaul in Chicago (which UK eventually won 76-72), he fell and broke a leg while driving toward the basket. This was Grawemeyer's second serious injury of the season. Before the season started he had suffered a fractured skull in practice and wore a special headgear through much of the season. At the time he broke his leg, he was averaging thirteen points and thirteen rebounds per game. Despite a slim build he was a strong rebounder, had excellent speed, an accurate jump shot from long range, and a hook shot from around the foul circle. His place in the starting lineup was taken by 6'4" sophomore John Brewer, who

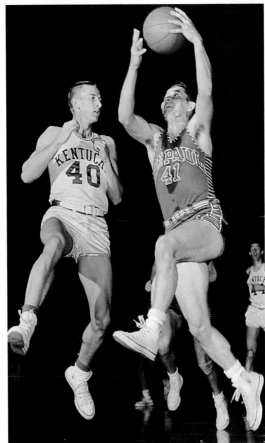

The Wildcat way to victory. *Left,* Bob Burrow guards a Vanderbilt player on February 20, 1956. Vernon Hatton *(center)* and Gerry Calvert *(right)* battle DePaul for a Kentucky victory on December 12, 1955.

showed great promise but could not match Grawemeyer's contributions on defense or under the basket. Nevertheless, the Wildcats with Brewer in the starting lineup closed out the regular season with four straight victories over conference foes. For the NCAA regionals UK was to lose yet another regular. Bill Evans, the team leader and an All-SEC performer, was ineligible for postseason play because he was a graduate student. Sophomore Gerry Calvert became a starter at guard and performed well. With only two of the original starting five, UK went down to defeat in the opening round of the Eastern Regionals at Evanston, Illinois.

The 1954/55 team worked so hard and overcame so much adversity that it was dubbed the "Desire Kids." The following season Rupp had regulars Grawemeyer, Burrow, and Bird back for their senior seasons. They were joined in the starting lineup by junior Gerry Calvert and sophomore Vernon Hatton at the guards. Burrow won All-SEC and All-American honors, while Hatton performed so effectively he was selected SEC "Sophomore of the Year." With this blend of experience and youth the Wildcats should have had an excellent year. Instead, they experienced their worst season since 1942.

Team captain Phil Grawemeyer recalled that "nothing seemed to go as it had the year before. We had the players but we just couldn't get it all together and clicking right. I guess coaches see it all the time but can't do anything about it." UK lost its opening game at home, an almost unheard of event. As if this disaster was not enough, the Wildcats also lost the UK Invitational Tournament for the first time since it was inaugurated in the 1951/52 season. Another first UK did not find pleasant was its loss of the SEC championship to Alabama—for the first time since 1942/43. Because Alabama declined an invitation to the NCAA tournament, the Big Blue made its annual appearance in the postseason event but with less than satisfying results. The Wildcats had the misfortune to meet the Iowa Hawkeyes in the finals of the Eastern Regionals on the Hawkeyes' home court. "I guess I learned then how other teams felt when they came into the Coliseum," Grawemeyer laughed, "because I knew there had to be some Kentucky fans there but you couldn't hear them. It was all Iowa and those fans just roared." It was, Grawemeyer summed up, "just one of those years."

With the graduation of the excellent front line of

Grawemeyer, Burrow, and Bird, little was expected of the 1956/57 squad. With Vernon Hatton and team captain Gerry Calvert returning, there was strength at guard but the front line was a question mark. The freshman team had produced only one player of note—but what a player! Stoop-shouldered, slow-moving, and frail-looking off the basketball court, 6'4" Johnny Cox was a whirlwind on it. A native of Letcher County in the Eastern Kentucky mountains, Cox was a star from the beginning of his varsity career. He had an accurate one-handed jump shot from medium range and a devastating hook shot with either hand from closer in, and was an effective rebounder. Cox had an excellent sophomore year, which he capped by being named to the All-SEC team.

Even with Johnny Cox in the lineup, the Wildcat front line lacked the overall height, scoring punch, and rebounding skill of the previous season. Rupp found it necessary to use at least six different starting lineups during the 1956/57 season in order to squeeze the most out of the available material. Hatton was injured for a month in midseason and was never, during the remainder of the season, up to the level of performance he had shown in the previous campaign. This put even more

pressure on Cox to score. The Wildcats confounded the experts who freely predicted that "this could be the weakest Kentucky team in the past fifteen years." They finished the season with a 23-5 record, won their eighteenth SEC title, and appeared once again in the NCAA tournament. The Big Blue actually was favored to sweep the Midwest Regionals because they were to be played at Memorial Coliseum, but the anticipated easy time did not materialize and UK was blitzed by Michigan State, 80-68.

Undoubtedly the high point of Adolph Rupp's last eighteen years as a college coach was UK's victory over Seattle University and its great star Elgin Baylor in the finals of the NCAA tournament on March 22, 1958. This victory, which fulfilled the Baron's vow in the aftermath of the gambling scandal to win another national title and return himself and UK to the top of the college basketball world, also was one of the great, albeit pleasant, surprises of Rupp's long career.

Entering the 1957/58 season, UK boasted a veteran team composed largely of seniors. Rupp quickly became disillusioned about the team's chances as it lost three early season games, including a UK Invitational Tour-

Few held out much hope for the 1957/58 team at the beginning of the season. They emerged as NCAA champs. Front row, left to right: Rupp, Adrian Smith, John Crigler, Ed Beck, Don Mills, Johnny Cox, Vernon Hatton, and assistant coach Lancaster. Back row: student manager Jay Atkerson, Earl Adkins, Bill Smith, Phil Johnson, Bill Cassady, Lincoln Collinsworth, and Harold Ross.

nament contest with West Virginia. "We've got fiddlers, that's all," Rupp confided to the press. "They're pretty good fiddlers; be right entertaining at a barn dance. But I'll tell you, you need violinists to play in Carnegie Hall. We don't have any violinists." By that, said Phil Johnson in an interview, Rupp meant that UK no longer had the type of player that had characterized the team during the golden era.

The success of the 1958 team, noted Harry Lancaster, was entirely unexpected. Compared to UK's previous NCAA championship squads, "we had no real ability at all but we had everybody doing the thing he could do best." Despite, or perhaps because of, the lack of individual talents this was a well-balanced team on which each player had a role he understood and accepted. Ed Beck was a fine rebounder and a very effective defensive center. "He couldn't score," Lancaster stated, "but if he could cut that high-scoring center on the other team down from twenty-five or thirty points to eight or nine, which was about Ed's average, why it leveled things down beautifully." The other starters were John Cox and John Crigler at the forwards and Vernon Hatton and Adrian Smith at the guards. Together they constituted the "Fiddlin' Five." Cox was an excellent shot, especially from the outside, and Hatton thrived on pressure, as he proved several times during his career as a Wildcat. Smith was an underrated player while at UK but he proved his ability during a long and successful career in the NBA with the Cincinnati Royals.

To Lancaster, "the unknown and unsung player on the team" was John Crigler. "He had no particular abilities but he was the only true driver we had. Cox had a fine jump shot but he wasn't fast and didn't drive well to the basket." Thus it is surprising that in the title game of the NCAA tournament the Seattle coach, John Castellani, assigned his All-American forward Elgin Baylor to guard Crigler. "We couldn't believe our good luck," Lancaster recalled with a chuckle. "We had Crigler drive on Baylor and almost immediately we had three fouls on him. He was in foul trouble the rest of the game." UK won by the surprisingly wide margin of twelve points, 84-72.

Rupp's fourth NCAA championship was certainly not a fluke. As Tev Laudeman noted in *The Rupp Years*, three of UK's six defeats in the 1958 season were by only one point, and the Cats played "the toughest schedule in the school's history up to that time. Almost every nonconference opponent was a veteran team, on the way to winning a conference championship or finishing high in the race." The "Fiddlin' Five" squad was helped by a factor Laudeman did not mention—geography. The

NCAA tournament field at the time contained only twenty-four teams, so UK had to play only four games to win the championship, and all four were played in the state of Kentucky before highly vocal and supportive Wildcat fans. The first two games, against Miami of Ohio and Notre Dame, were played at Memorial Coliseum in Lexington, while the tournament finals were played only eighty miles away in Louisville, where the Big Blue always enjoyed ardent support.

Full and effective use of the home court and home fan advantage also underlines the fact that the "Fiddlin' Five" were a team of opportunists. Most certainly it was not a great team, but it was a successful one. Several other teams during Rupp's last years had better individual talents and more successful regular-season records, but for one reason or another each fell short in the NCAA tournament. The very next year, in fact, with All-American Johnny Cox and All-SEC Bill Lickert leading the way, UK compiled an excellent 23-2 regular-season record. Amazingly, this was only good enough for second place in the final conference standings behind Coach James "Babe" McCarthy and his Mississippi State Bulldogs.

Rupp with Johnny Cox, the lone returning starter from the "Fiddlin' Five" championship team, show off a warm-up jacket listing UK's four NCAA titles, at the time an unprecedented accomplishment.

Table 4. Record of Adolph Rupp-Coached Teams, Selected Years, 1961/62-1970-71

Season	Regular Season		NCAA	
	Won	Lost	Won	Lost
1961/62	22	2	1	1
1963/64	21	4	0	2
1965/66	24	1	3	1
1967/68	21	4	3	1
1968/69	22	4	1	1
1969/70	25	1	1	1
1970/71	22	4	0	2

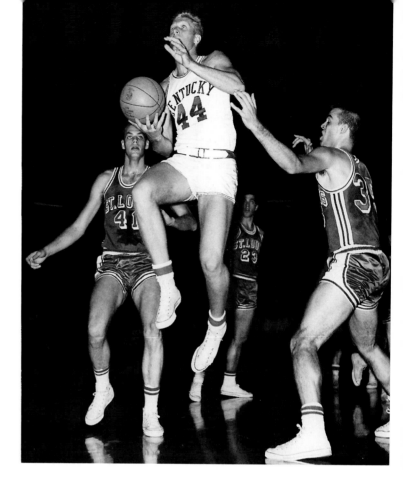

Three-time All-American Cotton Nash (1962, 1963, 1964) goes in for a layup despite close guarding by two St. Louis defenders. UK emerged the victors (86-77) in this December 11, 1961, contest.

Fortunately for the Big Blue, the Bulldogs refused to participate in the NCAA tournament because they would have had to play teams with blacks on them. UK eagerly departed for Evanston, Illinois, where it met the University of Louisville in the opening round of the Mideast Regionals. Although the Cardinals had a lackluster 17-10 record, in their contest with the Wildcats they played a half-court pressing defense that UK could not solve, and crushed the Cats 76-61. "We had them down by seventeen points in the first half," recalled Don Mills, "but they started using that press. It was the first time we faced the press in a game all season. For some reason we didn't work on defending the press in practice, either. Then our shooting turned cold and when they started coming back the Evanston crowd got behind them and that was a big help for them, too. But the press was probably the big factor."

It was difficult to live down the defeat, Dick Parsons related in an interview. Although only a sophomore, Parsons was a starting guard on the 1958/59 team. "I'll never forget what Coach Rupp said after the game: 'By God,' he said, 'I'll tell you one thing, you'll never forget this game.' And we haven't," noted Parsons ruefully. "No one will let us forget."

The UK Wildcats compiled good regular-season records and won or shared conference titles in 1961/62, 1963/64, 1965/66, and 1967/68 through 1970/71. With one exception, the Big Blue ended each season in the NCAA regionals.

The exception was the 1965/66 season, when "Rupp's Runts," with no starter taller than 6'5," nearly won a fifth NCAA championship for the Baron. In an interview published in the June 27, 1982, *Courier-Journal,* Pat Riley recalled that the Runts "started out as a

team that people didn't have a whole lot of faith in. . . . We were very small and we had lost a lot of our top players. So we started out in the preseason as a team that wouldn't be one of the contenders." During the previous season the Wildcats had struggled to a miserable 15-10 record. The 1964/65 team had contained three effective seniors—Randy Embry, Terry Mobley, and John Adams—and four of the stars of the following season—juniors Larry Conley and Tom Kron and sophomores Pat Riley and Louie Dampier. Little wonder UK fans were caught unaware by the stunning achievements of the team. "But once we started to play," Riley observed, "it was like a snowball going downhill, we began to believe that we were a great team."

"Rupp's Runts" may not have been a great team overall, but they were, in the opinion of Harry Lancaster, "one of the finest that we ever had for moving the basketball." Lancaster also noted, in a 1980 interview, that "they were so intelligent and even though small they were very quick." Riley freely acknowledged the vital

contributions of Larry Conley and Tom Kron. He believed the contributions "were never chronicled the way they should have been. They literally sacrificed themselves for the team. Louie Dampier and I were parasites off what they did." Although scoring stars in high school, Conley and Kron decided that with so many good shooters on the team they could contribute more to the success of the Wildcats as playmakers and passers than as scorers. "They were the reasons," Riley continued, that he and Dampier were named All-Americans, "though I didn't fully appreciate it until I was in the pros. It's easy to shoot the ball and not have a whole lot of other responsibilities." Conley and Kron, he emphasized, "did what it took to win." The fifth member of the starting team, and the only sophomore, was Thad Jaracz. Although only 6'5" Jaracz played center and contributed a good shooting touch from close to the basket as well as speed and quickness. Spelling Jaracz when UK needed more size in the pivot was another sophomore, 6'8" Cliff Berger.

With Jaracz in the starting lineup, "Rupp's Runts" averaged 6'3" in height, with Riley and Conley (both 6'3") at the forwards, and Dampier (6') and Kron (6'5") at the guards. Jim LeMaster was a sophomore guard on the Runts' team. In an interview, LeMaster maintained that the principal ingredients in the team's success "were quickness and teamwork. There was just an excellent chemistry on that team. Everybody, the whole team, just worked so well together. And all the players were just so unselfish." LeMaster also noted that all the starters and most of the reserves were good shooters but for the good of the team each was a role player. Kron was the playmaker as well as the defensive star of the team; when UK played the one-three-one zone, he played the point. Conley had a fine touch but concentrated on passing, at which he was excellent. The best shooters on the squad, according to LeMaster, were Dampier and Riley, while Riley and Jaracz were the best rebounders. The only player with leaping ability was Riley. "We got our rebounds with team defense and blocking out. That is, with good fundamentals."

Like Riley, LeMaster emphasized that before the season not much was expected of the 1965/66 team, but "once we started playing everything seemed to jell." Because of their lack of size the Runts emphasized the fast break and were so effective that they had a perfect record until the final week of the regular season. The only loss came in the next-to-last game of the season against Tennessee in Knoxville. Ironically, UK at home had trimmed the Vols just the week before by fourteen points.

In the NCAA regionals played in Iowa City the Cats

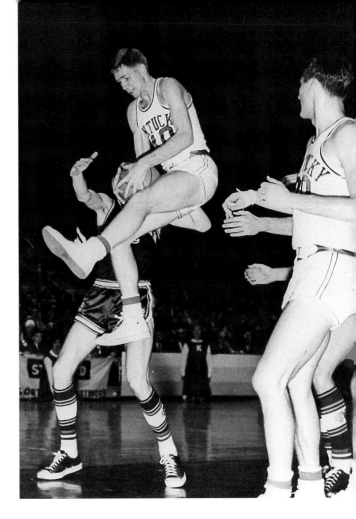

Larry Conley, one of the unsung heroes of "Rupp's Runts" in 1965/66. He and guard Tom Kron sacrificed their own records for the good of the team.

faced two tall and talented teams and defeated both. In the first game, on March 11, 1966, UK played Dayton with its 6'11" center, Henry Finkel, who later would play with the perennial NBA champion Boston Celtics. The next day the Wildcats outplayed All-American Cazzie Russell and the Michigan Wolverines. The following weekend the Big Blue travelled to College Park, Maryland, for the NCAA finals. UK faced the Duke Blue Devils, the second-ranked team in the nation, in a March 18 contest that many rate one of the best played and most exciting college games ever. Although Kron and Conley were weakened by flu, the Cats outplayed the Blue Devils and won by four points, 83-79. It was an important victory, but there was still one more game to play, against lightly regarded Texas Western (now the University of Texas, El Paso).

Harry Lancaster admitted in an interview that "when we beat Duke on Friday night we thought we

had it won." The Cats watched Texas Western defeat Utah and, according to LeMaster, were not impressed. At that time the semifinal and final games were played on successive days, and UK was drained emotionally from the Duke game, which it had regarded as the more important contest. Physical weakness also affected the players. Joining flu-sufferers Kron and Conley on the ailing list was Pat Riley, who turned up on game day, March 18, with a badly infected foot which apparently was treated incorrectly. Despite the physical problems, the Wildcats still seemed to have too much talent and experience for Texas Western, the underdog, to overcome. Almost no one thought the Texas team had any chance of defeating the mighty Wildcats with their proud tradition and experienced coaches.

Once the game started, the Big Blue found that their rivals were neither intimidated by the pressure nor overwhelmed by press clippings. After about five minutes of play in the first half, and with the score tied at 9, Texas Western guard Bobby Joe Hill twice stole the ball from UK dribblers at midcourt. Texas Western was never behind after that. The steals, although they had a devastating effect on the Cats, were not the only reason for the upset. Riley, for example, related that he "can still see 'Big Daddy'

Lattin dunking over our one-three-one zone and Neville Shed stuffing home a thunder dunk." UK lost 72-65.

UK partisans emphasize the role of overconfidence and illness in the game's outcome, but these are probably not the most important reasons. *Courier-Journal* sports editor Billy Reed's emphasis on the role of race seems to be more accurate. In a March 2, 1982, article, Reed observed, "In retrospect, that was a historic game. It told everyone, in case the point had been missed, that the game had changed, never to be the same again. The five black starters for Texas Western were too quick for Rupp's all-white team." According to Reed, the only consolation that could be found was the statement of an unidentified sports editor at the annual team banquet that "at least we're still the best white team in the country." Reed hastened to add that "the statement offended the sensibilities not only of anti-racists, but of UK followers who understood the lesson of the Texas Western game." Perhaps that lesson was learned, but one thing the game results did not change during the remainder of Rupp's tenure was recruiting. At that time the coaching staff included one of the finest recruiters in the college game, Joe B. Hall, who had joined the staff that season with the primary responsibility for recruiting. During Rupp's last years at UK, Hall recruited several talented players but, with the exception of Tom Payne, all were white. The responsibility for this exclusive attitude obviously was not Hall's. As he had proved before joining the Wildcat staff and again while UK head coach, Hall was concerned about talent rather than color.

The Wildcats' biggest need during the 1960s probably was a dominating center. Ironically the state produced two during the decade but neither one attended UK. Both were black. Wes Unseld, twice named an All-American at the University of Louisville, was a high school senior in 1964. One can only wonder about how great the 1966 UK team would have been with Unseld at center, and whether the 1967 season would have turned out differently. Later in the decade 7' Jim McDaniels led Western Kentucky to a three-year record of sixty-five wins, nineteen losses, two Ohio Valley Conference championships, and a third-place finish in the 1971 NCAA tournament. UK was Western's victim in the opening game of the 1971 Mideast regionals in Athens, Georgia, the first time the two ever met. All five of Western's starters were native Kentuckians and all were black.

Forward Pat Riley's gesture epitomizes the frustration of the Cats as they go down to a 72-65 defeat in the 1966 NCAA tournament against an all-black team from Texas Western.

Louie Dampier evades two Illinois defenders, while Thad Jaracz (55) awaits a possible rebound. Illinois won the December 5, 1966, game 98-97 in overtime.

If 1966, with its glittering won-lost record and second-place finish in the NCAA, was a pleasant surprise for the Wildcat faithful, the following season was a crushing disappointment. Despite the presence of Riley and Dampier, UK limped to a 13-13 record, the worst in Rupp's long career. But help was on the way. In 1966, his first season as recruiter, Joe Hall signed a large and talented group of players to scholarships. Led by 6'8" Dan Issel, 6'4" Mike Casey, and 6'4" Mike Pratt, Coach Harry Lancaster's freshman team stormed to an 18-2 record. The frosh were so talented and successful that they attracted more fan interest and support than the varsity team.

For the varsity, 1966/67 was a long and miserable

season made more difficult by an injury to Pat Riley and a run-in between Rupp and starting guard Bob Tallent. Because of back problems growing out of a water skiing accident suffered in the summer of 1966, Riley, who had been a superb rebounder and prolific scorer during the preceding season, was below par the entire season. Tallent, a fine outside shooter with excellent range, was faulted by Rupp for making too many mistakes and for not being the ballhandler and playmaker that his predecessor Tommy Kron had been. In his own way, Rupp made Tallent, the team, the media, and through them the UK fans fully aware of his feelings. In a February 13 game against Tennessee in Knoxville, the drama came to an unfortunate but perhaps inevitable conclusion. During the contest, in which UK was badly outplayed and lost 76-57, Tallent made a mistake and was immediately pulled from the game. When he reached the bench, the junior guard and Rupp "exchanged bitter words." In the locker room after the conclusion of the game the two exchanged more words. When the team returned to Lexington, Rupp had the equipment manager inform Tallent that his services would no longer be needed. The Baron then informed the press that, among other things, Tallent could not play well under game pressure. Probably because of the team's poor season performance, this behavior by Rupp was widely criticized. The university newspaper suggested that perhaps it was Rupp who was "choking," while UK President Oswald reprimanded the coach for his treatment of Tallent.

At the end of the season UK not only had a 13-13 record but its performance within the SEC was a disaster. The Cats won only eight of eighteen conference games and tied for fifth place in the final standings. Hated Tennessee won the SEC championship. Furthermore, the Vols as well as Vanderbilt and Florida swept their two-game series with the Wildcats. During the season UK was routed by Cornell (92-77), Florida (89-72), Tennessee (76-57), Alabama (81-71), Auburn (60-49), and Vanderbilt (110-94).

Serious suggestions were advanced that it might be time for the Man in the Brown Suit to consider retiring. The sixty-six-year-old Rupp, of course, would hear none of it. He was well aware that Hall had collected an excellent crop of players. It was not beyond the realm of possibility that the Issel-Casey-Pratt group could bring Rupp his fifth NCAA title before they completed their eligibility at UK, especially if Hall continued to stock the UK team with choice athletes. And Hall certainly fulfilled that responsibility. In the 1968/69 season forward Larry Steele, a future NBA star, and guard Bob McCowan joined the varsity. The next season brought

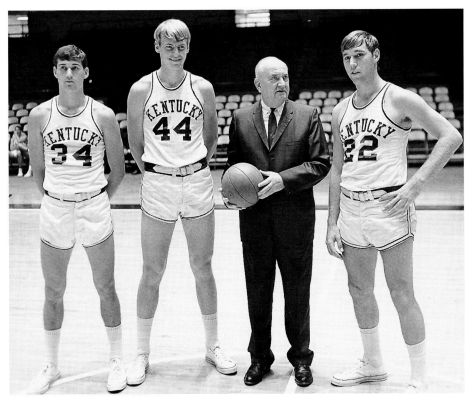

Part of Rupp's refusal to retire after the disastrous 1966/67 season was the large crop of talented players garnered by Joe Hall's recruiting efforts, and the hope of a fifth NCAA championship. *Left,* Rupp with (left to right) Mike Casey, Dan Issel, and Mike Pratt, all signed by Hall in his first year as recruiter. *Below,* more of Hall's recruits in a December 5, 1970, win against Michigan: Tom Parker (12), Tom Payne (54), Larry Steele (25), and Mike Casey (34). Payne was UK's first black player.

forwards Randy Noll and Tom Parker, the latter with his deadly left-handed outside jump shot, and two tall and talented guards, Stan Key and Kent Hollenbeck, along with 6'8 1/2" center Mark Soderberg. In 1970/71 began the varsity careers of 6'11" Jim Andrews and 7' Tom Payne as well as two powerful forwards, Dan Perry and Larry Stamper.

Unfortunately for the team's hopes, injuries and defections depleted the Wildcat ranks. While Issel, Casey, and Pratt started together at UK, they did not finish together. Casey, a fiery competitor and excellent offensive player, suffered a broken leg in an auto accident during the summer between his junior and senior years and had to sit out the 1969/70 season. Although he returned to the starting lineup the following season, he was unable to regain the quickness and speed that had distinguished his play and made him a virtual one-man fast break before the accident.

The 1969/70 UK team was talented. The usual starting lineup was Pratt and Steele at the forwards, Issel at center, and senior Terry Mills and junior Jim Dinwiddie at guards. Reserves included forwards Tom Parker and Randy Noll, center Mark Soderberg, and guards Bob McCowan, Bill Busey, Stan Key, and Kent Hollenbeck. The Cats compiled a 25-1 regular-season record but lost to Jacksonville and its 7' center Artis Gilmore by a score of 106-100 in the NCAA regionals. It is fascinating to contemplate (as Issel did in a June 1983 interview) the possible results if Casey, a great clutch performer, had

Above, Dan Issel, who played from 1967/68 through 1969/70, holds the men's career scoring record for UK. Here he shoots against the LSU Tigers.

Right, Stan Key (30) dribbles and Mike Pratt (22) watches as UK trounces Georgia 116-86 on February 16, 1970.

been available and in top condition. But Casey, of course, was not available. One of the hazards of big-time athletics is injury. A number of other key performers were lost for varying periods during this and other seasons because of injuries. Obviously the purpose of dependable reserves is to fill in for injured regulars. Hence a serious drain on UK was the loss of several talented reserve players, including Noll and Soderberg, who transferred to other schools. One other player, Tom Payne, made himself available for the NBA draft after only one varsity season at UK and was drafted by the Atlanta Hawks.

During the 1969/70 season Issel broke the UK career scoring record set by Cotton Nash in 1964. Before the season began, Issel recalled in an interview, Rupp promised that he would do everything he could to help break Nash's record if Issel would participate in the conditioning program that Assistant Coach Joe Hall had introduced at UK. The grueling program was very unpopular with the team, and Issel's cooperation was essential to head off a rebellion. This story has been recounted before, but the aftermath of his record-setting performance at Oxford, Mississippi, on February 7, 1970, has not. During the season Rupp had been true to his word and had left Issel in games even after the outcome was decided in favor of UK. Finally, in the February 7 game against the University of Mississippi, which the Wildcats won 120-85, Issel broke the UK single-game record as well as the career record. "After the game," Issel related, "Coach Rupp came up to me and said: 'I was

Above, high-flying Larry Steele helped UK whip Michigan 104-93 on December 5, 1970. Steele went on to a long and successful career in the NBA. *Left,* Ronnie Lyons executes a layup hook, a shot made necessary by his 5'9" height, to boost UK to an 85-69 victory over Marquette on March 16, 1972. This was the last victory of Adolph Rupp's career.

kind of sorry to see you break [Cliff] Hagan's record but I'm glad you beat Nash's record.'" Apparently Rupp felt this way because the independent-minded Nash had been outspoken in expressing opinions to and about the Baron. Because Nash was so crucial to the team's success Rupp had been unable to retaliate at the time. Issel's single-game record of 53 points still stands, but a member of the UK Lady Cats team, Valerie Still, now holds the school career mark. She scored 2,763 points in 119 games (from 1978/79 to 1982/83), while Issel scored 2,138 in 83 contests. It might be noted, however, that while Issel's record was set in three seasons of varsity competition, Still played four varsity seasons.

During his last four years as coach, Rupp suffered from a variety of serious physical ailments. In February 1971 he checked into the University Medical Center for treatment of an ulcerated foot which had been bothering him for more than a year. When he returned to the team he had to sit with his foot resting on a stool. Rupp was back in time for the final game of the season at the Coliseum against arch rival Tennessee. It was not a crucial game. The title had been decided five days before at Auburn when the Wildcats scored a nineteen-point victory over the Tigers (102-83). Nevertheless, the Tennessee game, which UK won 84-78, was a "welcome back" for Coach Rupp and a tune-up for the upcoming NCAA regionals in Athens, Georgia. At the regionals, despite the presence of 7' Tom Payne and 6'11" Jim Andrews as well as sharpshooting Tom Parker and Larry Steele, the Wildcats were no match for an excellent Western Kentucky team. They suffered a humiliating twenty-four-point defeat. The next night, in the consolation game of the regionals, the Blue and White were routed for the second straight game, 91-74, by Coach Al McGuire's Marquette Warriors. Tom Parker recalled that this, his junior season, was a very difficult time because "although we had a lot of talent and had a winning year, we never really got it all together. That was the year Coach Rupp

was fighting to keep his job and a lot of the things that occurred off the floor had an effect on the way the team performed."

When the Wildcat squad assembled the following October for preseason practice, it was still uncertain whether this would be Rupp's final campaign as coach. The uncertainty persisted throughout the season although university regulations specified seventy as retirement age. Rupp made it very clear that he did not want to retire and applied pressure through the media as well as friends on the Athletics Board to obtain an exemption.

Although no one could be certain at the time that it would be the Baron's "last hurrah," former players, including Tom Parker and Jim Andrews, recalled it as a special experience. "Every place we went during my senior year," Parker related, "people gave him a standing ovation. In a way it helped UK because out of respect for Coach Rupp the crowds were a little more mellow than in other years. It was really good to see that at Auburn, Florida, and even Tennessee because it showed they respected the man for what he had done."

At the end of the season Rupp's fate was still in doubt. The UK administration was still waiting, as it had all season, for the Baron to take the initiative and announce his retirement. Rupp refused to do so. Finally, nine days after UK's elimination in the NCAA regionals, the Athletics Board met and voted not to waive the mandatory retirement rule. Rupp was forced into retirement. He received the news with bitterness.

As Tev Laudeman observed in the conclusion to *The Rupp Years*, the Man in the Brown Suit was gone "but he had left a mark of excellence on basketball which could never be erased."

UK President Otis Singletary congratulates Adolph Rupp on the achievements of his long and distinguished career in a ceremony marking the Baron of Basketball's retirement, March 6, 1972.

Opposite, Joe Hall and Leonard Hamilton confer mid-game with Truman Claytor and Dwight Anderson

PART III

Joe Hall: Keeper of the Flame

8

The Passing of the Torch

Joe B. Hall signed on as head basketball coach at UK in 1972. While here he became one of the most successful coaches in the country. Hall's teams averaged more than twenty-two victories a season, won or shared the SEC championship eight times, won the NIT in 1976, and were runners-up in the NCAA tournament in 1975 and national champions in 1978. Yet it was not unusual for callers-in to Hall's radio show to demand of him, as one did, "Why don't you just forget your lame excuses and admit you can't coach." Nor was it unusual for newspapers to contain letters from fans similar to one printed in the January 26, 1983, *Herald-Leader*. After describing Hall's numerous shortcomings as a coach and a molder of young men the writer bitterly concluded: "As far as I am concerned, the only real mistake Adolph Rupp ever made was convincing Hall to stay at Kentucky when he might otherwise have gone to St. Louis to build his dynasty. If Joe Hall really cares about the University of Kentucky he will step aside after this year and give the school the chance it needs to be great again."

Like comedian Rodney Dangerfield, Hall often "gets no respect." Yet Hall told reporter Mark Bradley (*Lexington Leader*, February 19, 1982), "I don't care what people say about me as long as they keep the Kentucky program in perspective." Hall's mission, Bradley observed, was "to guard the flame" of UK's basketball tradition, and that means the program. "The important thing to me," Hall often stated, "is the program, that's Number 1." The program, reporter Bradley maintained, was "bigger than any player, any coach. Bigger than the ghost of Adolph Rupp,

than the flesh of Joe B. Hall. The Program. Joe Hall says it lovingly, as a priest might speak of The Lord."

A native of Cynthiana in north central Kentucky, where he was born in 1928, Joe Beasman Hall absorbed the Wildcat tradition as he grew up. In a 1980 interview Hall recalled that he and his brother "never missed the radio broadcasts of the UK games" and that he still had some of the statistics he compiled while listening. Hall attended Cynthiana High School, earning three letters each in basketball and football and captaining both teams in his senior year. One of the greatest thrills of his life was being invited by Adolph Rupp to try out for a place on the UK squad and being chosen from a group of approximately 150 for a scholarship. Unfortunately for Hall this was the era of the "Fabulous Five," a group he still regards as the greatest team of its era, just as he considers John Wooden's UCLA squads the greatest teams of their era. With little chance to play at UK, Hall transferred after his sophomore season, and with Rupp's help, to Sewanee. After completing his eligibility Hall returned to UK to finish his degree.

Hall's coaching career began in 1956 at Shepherdsville High School in Bullitt County as both basketball and football coach. During his second season the basketball squad compiled a 22-6 record and went to the district finals, winning conference "Coach of the Year" honors for Hall. On the strength of this record Hall was offered, and accepted, a position as assistant coach at Regis College, a small Jesuit institution in Denver. After only one season he was named head coach and athletic

Victory is sweet as the Wildcats hoist Coach Joe Hall aloft after winning the University of Kentucky Invitational Tournament trophy on December 21, 1974.

director, and in his five seasons as head coach at Regis he built a powerhouse. Although nominally operating on the small-college level, Hall's teams defeated such schools as Arizona State, Oklahoma State, Oklahoma City, Air Force Academy, Denver, Colorado State, Creighton, Idaho State, and Montana State. Just as he was gaining national prominence for Regis the school's leaders decided to deemphasize basketball by cutting financial support and reducing the number of athletic scholarships awarded. To remain at Regis under these circumstances would have meant professional suicide so Hall moved on, accepting a head coaching position at Central Missouri State College. In his one season there Hall's team had a 19-6 record, won the conference championship, and represented the league in the NCAA tournament.

During the years Hall coached at Regis and Central Missouri he kept in contact with Rupp, and in 1965 accepted an offer to return to his alma mater as an assistant coach with the primary responsibility of recruiting. "Of course, Coach Rupp wanted me for recruiting purposes once before," Hall recalled at a later date, "and I told him I wasn't interested in being on the road all the time. That was while I was at Regis. When I turned him down, I told him if he ever needed a full-time coaching assistant, to call me. Well," Hall continued,

"this time he said if I would take the job that I would be a regular assistant and the whole staff would be involved in recruiting."

Whether or not Rupp and Lancaster participated in the recruiting, the major burden fell on Hall's shoulders, and he performed these duties so effectively that in a short time he earned a reputation as a master recruiter. In his first season on the job Hall collected an excellent group of high school stars from Kentucky, Illinois, Ohio, Alabama, and Tennessee. In addition to Dan Issel the new Wildcats included Kentucky's "Mr. Basketball," Mike Casey; Mike Pratt, one of Ohio's top scorers; Randy Pool, Tennessee's top high school prospect; and Travis Butler, widely regarded as "Alabama's top schoolboy cager in history"; as well as Bill Busey, Jim Dinwiddie, Terry Mills, Benny Spears, and Mort Fraley from Kentucky. In the following years Hall continued to find and sign for UK an excellent collection of prospects, including Larry Steele, Greg Starrick, Bob McCowan, Larry Stamper, Jim Andrews, Ronnie Lyons, Tom Payne, Tom Parker, Randy Noll, Stan Key, Mark Soderberg, and Kent Hollenbeck.

Although he was earning a reputation around the nation as an outstanding prospect for a head coaching position, Hall was, according to Russell Rice, a frustrated and insecure man. A dedicated family man, "Hall's worst

In 1948, Joe Hall was a sophomore and in his only varsity season of Wildcat play. Here, Adolph Rupp poses with his eventual successor and Hall's teammates, left to right: Garland Townes, Walt Hirsch, Joe Hall, Bob Henne, and Roger Day.

A crew-cut Joe Hall, then an assistant coach and principal recruiter for the Cats, signs Stan Key to an athletic scholarship. Key starred at guard for UK from 1969/70 through 1971/72 and was co-captain of Rupp's last team.

fears came to roost as he found himself more and more on the road in search of basketball players," Rice maintained in his *Big Blue Machine.* "In addition there was an element of frustration in a job that seemed to hold no future for him." Although Rupp was nearing the mandatory retirement age of seventy, "the Baron showed no signs of accepting retirement unless it was forced on him. It was generally assumed that Harry Lancaster would become head coach when and if Rupp retired." All this changed, however, when Athletic Director Bernie Shiveley died in December 1967 and Lancaster eventually was named his successor. "Joe was suddenly first in line to succeed Rupp. The problem," Rice noted, "was that Joe had no guarantee that he would even be on the UK basketball staff after Rupp retired." Hall sought assurance that he would be named Rupp's successor but received "nothing concrete," and on April 2, 1969, he forced UK's hand by accepting the head coaching position at St. Louis University.

What happened next is open to dispute. Rupp later claimed that Hall asked if he could have his old job back.

According to Hall, Rupp asked through an intermediary that the two meet one more time to discuss the situation. Hall told Oscar Combs (*Kentucky Basketball: A New Beginning*) that he had agreed to the meeting because he "wanted to hear just what Coach Rupp had to say. He told me," Hall recalled, "if I would return to UK that he would personally endorse me for the head job when he retired. Before, no one had assured me of that. Other UK officials also promised me their support. That's when I decided to return." Whatever the real reason, just a week after accepting the coaching position at St. Louis, Hall was back on the job at the University of Kentucky.

If Hall thought this settled the question of Rupp's retirement he was wrong. The Baron had no intention of bowing out gracefully and in his last three years on the job did everything he could to postpone the dreaded retirement. Rupp supporters, led by former basketball star Dan Issel, urged university officials to waive the mandatory age limit and permit Rupp to coach as long as he wanted. Others, including many former players, argued that it was time for Rupp to step aside. "For one of the few times in history," Oscar Combs noted, "Kentucky fans divided and chose sides."

Further complicating the situation in 1972, Rupp's last season at UK, was the presence of one of the greatest freshman groups in Wildcat history. The "Super Kittens," recruited by Hall, included Kevin Grevey, Jimmy Dan Conner, Mike Flynn, Bob Guyette, Steve Lochmueller, Jerry Hale, and G.J. Smith. Under Hall's direction the freshman team (freshmen were not permitted to play varsity ball at the time) compiled a perfect 22-0 record, and the Kentucky faithful talked seriously of another NCAA championship. If the Wildcats were to win their fifth national title, Rupp adherents argued, the honor should go to Uncle Adolph. Because of all he had done over the years for the university, Rupp deserved the privilege of coaching the "Super Kittens."

Two days before the end of the 1972 regular season the Baron made a final public bid for sympathy. "If they force me to retire," Rupp told a newspaper reporter, "then they might as well take me out to the Lexington Cemetery." The UK administration did not budge. Later that spring the Athletics Board announced the mandatory retirement of Adolph Rupp and the hiring of Joe B. Hall. Rupp refused to attend the ceremony celebrating Hall's promotion. Instead he reportedly stalked from his office, announcing curtly that he was "going to the farm."

The Rupp era was ended, but comparisons between the Baron of the Bluegrass and his successor have continued, generally to the disadvantage of Hall. The main

reason for this, claimed Cawood Ledford in an interview published in the June 7, 1983, *Lexington Herald-Leader,* was the difference in personality between the two men. "There couldn't be two men more different," maintained Ledford, who knew both Rupp and Hall well. "Adolph was always on stage, you know. He was one of the great colorful characters I've known in my life." Yet ironically Rupp was not the person he appeared to be in public. "He just wasn't a real warm person, really," Ledford recalled. "I don't think he had a close friend. . . . I don't think anyone outside his family got to know him very well."

Other knowledgeable people made similar observations about Rupp. Former UK Sports Information Director Russell Rice noted in his book *Joe B. Hall: My Own Kentucky Home* that "although a camera or microphone would turn Rupp on automatically, he would try to avoid the limelight in his private life." Despite, or perhaps because of, his aversion to the masses in his private life, people tended to gravitate toward Rupp. By contrast, Rice noted, Hall gravitated to people. Rice considered Hall "the mainstream type; when he is dining in a restaurant, he talks to the waitresses, the busboys, the folks seated at the next table." In his daily life Hall, Rice continued, "touches an amazing number of people in all walks of life, but he seems to enjoy most those types that he encounters in the small groceries or on the farms during his hunting and fishing trips." Cawood Ledford

also noted that Hall was much more socially inclined than the Baron. As a result Ledford grew to know Hall much better than he ever did Rupp. His personal friendship with Hall made it difficult for Ledford to understand or explain the contrast between Rupp's cordial and close relations with the press and Hall's, which were adversarial and often strained.

The fact is that both Rupp and Hall wanted the same thing, a favorable press, and both tried to control treatment of the UK basketball program and of themselves in the newspapers. Rupp was successful. Hall's efforts boomeranged and merely increased suspicions on both sides. In contrast to Hall, who often seemed heavy-handed and blunt in his demand for favorable copy, Rupp's control of the press was subtle and indirect but very effective. Unlike his successor the Baron instinctively knew how to manipulate the press and later radio and television. With an offhand joke or a colorful quote he was able to present himself in a favorable light as a warm and likeable person while providing reporters with what they in turn desperately needed—interesting stories that would appeal to readers or viewers. Hall, a much more bland personality, was unable or unwilling to do this. Even Ledford admitted that Hall seemed to "have the knack of saying the wrong thing sometimes" and then of compounding his problems by reacting angrily when his statements and actions were reported in the press.

Billy Reed, at the time the *Courier-Journal's* sports

Hall put his players through their paces in the UK strength and conditioning program.

editor and one of Hall's fiercest critics, in a January 29, 1981, article compared UK's basketball program as directed by Hall to a totalitarian state. "Inside the Program," Reed maintained, "Hall rules supreme. He decides everything. . . . A bunker mentality, an us-against-them kind of thing, prevails within The Program. 'Them,' of course, includes rival coaches, recruiters and referees. It also includes the press, particularly the print media. Inside The Program," asserted Reed, "the press is distrusted, even despised." At UK, he concluded, "The Program is all-powerful and all-pervasive" and in fact "has become virtually autonomous, with only the barest of ties to the rest of the athletic department." Although this was an extreme and emotional attack, even Russell Rice admitted that Hall monitored his players so closely that they nicknamed him "Papa Bear" after he fell asleep on Kevin Grevey's bed while waiting into the wee hours of the morning for his star forward to return to his room.

Hall wanted to know everything about his players and, Rice noted, generally did. He kept in close personal touch with the players, had them to his house for meals, took them fishing, let them help with work around his farm, kept a close check on their academic progress, and set up classes on how to deal with the media. This was in sharp contrast to Rupp, who remained aloof from his players and left discipline, class attendance, and anything else that was needed to others. In the Rupp era, Hall recalled, "you showed up for practice on October 15 and that was the first time you would see Coach Rupp. You stayed at a distance and he kept his distance. It left you with a fear and respect for him. You never got to a point where you felt comfortable around Coach Rupp." Hall wanted to change that atmosphere.

Players and coaches who worked with Hall have tended to disagree with the essentially negative assessment by sportswriters. Although Dan Issel revered the memory of Adolph Rupp, he stated in a June 1983 interview that he believed Joe Hall was "becoming a legend in his own right."

Former UK Assistant Coach Joe Dean discussed Hall and the UK program before he left Lexington in late July 1983 to assume his duties as head coach at Birmingham Southern College. In a wide-ranging discussion, Dean maintained that "working with Coach Hall for the last six years has been a tremendous learning experience for me. I feel he is not only a great basketball coach

An off-court workout. Kyle Macy and Rick Robey help Hall hang tobacco on his Harrison County farm in the fall of 1977.

but also a fine person. He really cares about his people and does everything he can to help them. Most people outside the program don't understand that." Hall is, Dean continued, "a down-home, sincere, honest person who cares about one thing and that is the success of University of Kentucky basketball. I honestly don't think he receives the credit he deserves for the job he has done during the last eleven years as UK head coach. When he was hired I doubt there were many people who expected him to last eleven years but he has. I hope," Dean concluded, "that Coach Hall can continue to coach here as long as he wants and that he wins at least another national championship along the way." While Hall was the one who decided on his retirement date, a second NCAA title proved elusive.

Even critics admitted Hall's great recruiting skills, but they faulted him for not getting the best and the most from the talented players he brought to the UK campus. This is ironic because not only did Hall have a winning percentage of nearly .750 (297 wins and 100 losses) but his teams won or shared the SEC championship eight of the thirteen seasons he was at UK.

Unfortunately for Hall this period witnessed the emergence of the SEC as one of the strongest conferences in the nation. No longer was the SEC the football conference which Rupp could so easily dominate. Those days "when Kentucky made a monkey out of the other conference opponents are over," Jock Sutherland wrote in a January 20, 1983, *Herald-Leader* article. "All of the other SEC schools have built beautiful arenas, and the basketball program is now important to all of the conference teams." Another indication of the increased strength of the SEC, Sutherland noted, was its record against nonconference foes during the 1982/83 season. Through January 16, 1983, conference teams had a 27-17 record against non-SEC teams. Alabama had an 8-0 record, including a twenty-three-point victory over powerful Georgetown, before the conference season began but only a 1-5 record in its first six SEC games. Later in the season Alabama took time out from its regular succession of drubbings at the hands of conference foes to play and soundly defeat UCLA, which at the time was ranked number one in the nation. Georgia, another conference doormat in the 1983 season, caught fire in the SEC and later the NCAA tournament and was one of the Final Four teams in the playoff for the national championship. One SEC coach familiar with the parity in the conference expressed amazement to a Lexington reporter during the 1980 season at the lack of appreciation for Hall's accomplishments. "I don't know why," he began, Hall "has his detractors here in Lexington, be-

cause the man has done a job that's the envy of practically every school in the country, not only in recruiting and promoting, but in coaching. Kentucky may get knocked" by other coaches, he continued, "but it's just envy. . . . Joe does a very good job with his talent."

Hall, for his part, knew when he inherited the Rupp throne in 1972 that for him it would be a hot seat unless he won soon, won often, and won big. Unfortunately, Hall did not begin his tenure the way Big Blue fans wanted and expected—that is, with an NCAA championship in his first season as head coach. All his team did was compile a 20-8 record and win the SEC championship. But this team boasted the "Super Kittens" who were supposed to bring UK its fifth national title. Jim Andrews, who was the starting center and team captain, recalled that "after they went 22-0 as freshmen everybody assumed they were going to go out the next year and win the title. But it isn't that easy." Steve Lochmueller, one of the "Super Kittens," reminisced about his sophomore season in a February 1983 interview. "It was really a pressure-filled year. Not only for us but more especially for Coach Hall and his staff because here they were following a legend. If we didn't succeed in some fashion," he noted, "it would be easy for people to say that Coach Hall doesn't have it like Coach Rupp did, that the players just don't do as well as they did under Coach Rupp." Fellow "Super Kitten" Bob Guyette emphasized the same point. "Coach Hall had a lot of pressure on him. It was a very intense year. In fact, the first couple of years were tough, until 1975 when we got to the finals of the NCAA. That took some of the pressure off Coach Hall."

The usual starting lineup in the 1972/73 season consisted of sophomores Kevin Grevey and Jimmy Dan Conner at the forwards, senior Jim Andrews at center, and sophomore Mike Flynn and junior Ronnie Lyons at guards, although sophomore Bob Guyette started several games at forward and Conner often switched to guard when the Wildcats needed a big guard. With his height and good scoring touch Andrews was vitally important to the team's success. The 6'11" Ohio native had come a long way from his sophomore season when he was a backup center, along with 6'8 1/2" junior Mark Soderberg, to fellow sophomore Tom Payne. The 7' Payne, who was UK's first black player, left after the end of the season to play pro ball. Soderberg also departed, leaving Andrews to carry the load at center. Although Andrews was the team's leading scorer in 1973, with an average of 20.1 points per game, the Big Blue also depended heavily on the contributions of sophomore starters Grevey, Conner, and Flynn, who combined for an average of nearly forty points a game, as well as the solid

bench strength provided by sophomores Guyette and Lochmueller.

The "Super Kittens" were a multitalented group and they knew it. When the season started, Jim Andrews noted in a January 1983 interview, "they figured all the teams we played would be afraid of us. We started the season with a great game against Michigan State, up there. Just beat the tar out of them." Unfortunately, he continued, "the sophs were young, inexperienced kids. They didn't know enough yet to keep their mouths shut. 'We can't wait until Iowa comes in here,' they told reporters. 'We're just going to tear Iowa up.' Well, it didn't work out that way. Iowa just whipped us. And then we played Indiana and North Carolina and they beat us. Well the kids learned some valuable early lessons."

After suffering these early season shocks the Wildcats rebounded with two easy victories to capture the UK Invitational Tournament and followed that up with victories over intersectional rivals Kansas and Notre Dame to end December. In January the Blue and White entered the important part of the season, the eighteen-game home-and-home schedule against the other teams of the SEC. This second season did not get off to a good start. In the period between January 6 and February 3 UK lost four conference games. Perennial nemesis Tennessee beat the Big Blue in an exciting 65-64 contest in Knoxville while Vanderbilt swept the season series with a one-point victory in Nashville and an impressive seven-point win in Lexington. Perhaps the most difficult defeat for the Wildcats to accept, Steve Lochmueller noted, was a 61-58 decision to lightly regarded Mississippi. It was UK's first loss to Ole Miss in forty-five years, and Coach Cob Jarvis proudly proclaimed it the greatest victory in Reb basketball history.

On February 3, 1973, with four conference defeats and only five victories on their record, the highly touted Wildcats looked very vulnerable but showed great character by fighting back in February and winning seven straight games. With two games left on the regular schedule UK, which a month before appeared to be out of the race, was in a position to win the league championship. With the title on the line the Big Blue turned a pressure-packed away game against Auburn on March 3 into a 91-79 rout.

Everything came down to the final game of the season, a home contest with Tennessee which would decide the SEC championship. The day before the game, students began camping on the sidewalk in front of Memorial Coliseum to assure themselves of good seats. At game time the Coliseum was packed to overflowing, with an estimated crowd of 13,000. The Vols, led by their

Jim Andrews sinks Tennessee with his last-second shot on January 22, 1973. UK won 72-70 and Hall ended his first season as head coach with the SEC championship, but the fans blamed him for not bagging the NCAA title.

7' center, Len Kosmalski, led 65-61 with 11:07 left in the game. Then Kevin Grevey took over. He hit four jump shots in a row to put UK ahead 69-67. Grevey finished the game with a total of twenty-eight points to pace the Big Blue to an 86-81 victory and give Hall the SEC championship in his first season as head coach.

The Wildcats departed for the Mideast Regionals in Nashville with high hopes. In the opening round they faced Ohio Valley Conference champion Austin Peay and its scoring sensation "Fly" Williams. Austin Peay was coached by Lake Kelly and Leonard Hamilton, both later members of the Wildcat coaching staff. UK had much more trouble with their small but quick rivals than Big Blue fans had anticipated, but finally prevailed in overtime, 106-100. This set up a return match with Big Ten champion Indiana, winner of a regular-season contest between the two teams.

The young Wildcats impressed Indiana coach Bobby Knight with their sticky defense and tenacious play but again lost to the Hoosiers, 72-65. Jim Andrews finished his varsity career in spectacular fashion, scoring twenty-three points, pulling down ten rebounds, and rejecting

Steve Lochmueller shoots a hookshot during the 1973/74 season.

"for the losses and the pressure from the fans and the press for our poor record. There was just a lot of pressure on Coach Hall and on us. We fought like crazy all season but we just couldn't quite make it. It was not an enjoyable experience." The major problem, both Guyette and Coach Hall believe, was a lack of size and muscle. Hall stated that with 6'3" Conner at forward, 6'8" Guyette at center, 5'9" Ronnie Lyons at guard, and 6'6" Steve Lochmueller as backup center, "there was no way we could match some opponents physically. We were just too small a team."

The 1973/74 season got off to a typical good UK start with a resounding 81-68 victory over Miami of Ohio in the opening game, but immediately after that everything fell apart. The Wildcats lost the next three games by decisive margins to Kansas (71-63), Indiana (77-68), and North Carolina (101-84). In the Indiana game, played in Louisville, the Big Blue actually led by five points at halftime but during the intermission Indiana coach Bobby Knight decided on an adjustment in personnel that other UK rivals during the season would also make. In the second half 6'5" substitute guard John Laskowski was placed in the lineup against UK's 5'9" Ronnie Lyons. Laskowski took his shorter opponent inside with devastating effect. Although he had scored only six points in the Hoosiers' previous two games against the Wildcats, Laskowski hit eleven of fifteen shots and led the Indiana squad to a nine-point victory. Hall's worries about lack of team size were borne out in this and numerous other games during the season.

UK bounced back from its three-game losing streak to win the next three games against Iowa (88-80), Dartmouth (102-77), and Stanford (78-77). The latter two were UKIT contests. The Blue and White finished the intersectional schedule on a losing note, however, when they met Notre Dame at Freedom Hall in Louisville on December 29. With 6'9" center John Shumate contributing twenty-five points and fourteen rebounds, the Fighting Irish destroyed UK, 94-79. Thus the intersectional schedule ended with four victories and four defeats. Hopes for a better fate against SEC rivals were immediately dashed when, on January 5, 1974, the Wildcats travelled to Baton Rouge to play LSU. Eddie Palubinskas, Collis Temple, and Glenn Hansen combined for seventy-four points to lead the Tigers to a 95-84 victory. The Wildcats staggered through the remainder of the SEC campaign winning nine games but losing the same number.

Joe Hall, his staff, and members of the team departed almost gratefully in May on a month-long exhibition tour of Tahiti and Australia. Both Hall and the

six Indiana shots. The Wildcat players and fans were broken-hearted. After trailing through most of the game the Big Blue fought its way back and finally, with 7:35 left, gained the lead 61-59. Then disaster struck. UK took four successive shots that banged around the rim but refused to fall in. "If they had only gone in," Hall lamented after the game. "They were good shots, but they just wouldn't drop. After our comeback, it was kind of a disappointment." The Wildcats consoled themselves with the thought that with a little luck they would have gained a place in the NCAA Final Four.

If their sophomore season ended on a disheartening note for the "Super Kittens," their entire junior season was a disaster. Despite the great expectations of coaches, players, fans, and the press, the Big Blue limped to a 13-13 season record, matching Rupp's 1967 mark. Not since 1927, when the season totals were 3-13, had UK had a worse record. Bob Guyette ruefully noted in an interview that his junior season stands out in his mind

players maintained in interviews that this trip, on which the Wildcats played a total of nineteen games in twenty-six days, was one of two major factors responsible for the team's turnabout in 1974/75. The other key was the arrival of an excellent group of freshmen who provided the combination of size and depth that had been lacking in the previous two seasons.

Bob Guyette maintained that the State Department-sponsored Australian tour was very important in helping the team make a turnaround from the disastrous 1973/74 season. "The chance to be together and to play a lot of games under adverse conditions really helped us the next season," Guyette stated. After playing one game in Tahiti, against the National team, the UK squad flew to Australia for a series of contests all across the country. "We travelled by car," Guyette continued, "six of us to a station wagon plus luggage. We would drive all day and arrive in the town where we were scheduled to play just in time to suit up for the game. We would stay the night in private homes and then be off early the next morning for the next game. So," he concluded,

"playing the games while we were so tired helped us get ready for our final season."

If the Australian trip was an unqualified success, so was the vitally important job of recruiting. Before departing on the foreign trip Hall put the finishing touches on a recruiting campaign that yielded a group that rivaled the famous "Super Kittens," both in numbers and in quality. Realizing that the team's major weakness was lack of size and bulk in the front line, Hall signed three 6'10" centers—Rick Robey, 235 pounds, from New Orleans; Mike Phillips, 240 pounds, from Manchester High School in Ohio; and Dan Hall, 220 pounds, from Kentucky's Betsy Lane. Hall also recruited two of the most talented players ever to come out of central Kentucky: 6'4" forward Jack Givens from Bryan Station High School, and Henry Clay High School product James Lee, a 6'5" forward. In Lexington high school circles they were known respectively as "Mr. Silk" and "Mr. Steel."

The signing of Givens and Lee to basketball scholarships underlined a radical and basic change that was taking place in UK recruiting. By the 1974/75 season

Jimmy Dan Conner's hustling brand of ball helped the Cats to an NCAA runner-up spot in 1974/75. Here he dribbles around a Northwestern player in the season opener, which UK won 97-70.

Above, Reggie Warford, Hall's first black recruit as head coach, helped UK drub Mississippi State 112-79 on February 1, 1975. Warford was a major factor in the Cats' conquest of the 1976 NIT title.

the racial composition of the Wildcat squad was completely and permanently changed. In only three seasons as coach, Joe Hall accomplished something Rupp had found almost impossible to do, recruit blacks. In his first season Hall signed one black, guard Reggie Warford, a hard-working and intelligent player. The following season two talented guards, Larry Johnson and Merion Haskins, joined the team, and in 1974 Hall added forwards Givens and Lee. By the following season, when Warford was a senior and Hall was in his fourth year as head coach, the transformation was complete. With the addition of guards Dwane Casey and Truman Claytor in the 1975/76 season, the Wildcats had a team composed of seven blacks and six whites.

By his senior year Warford, who during his freshman season had been the lone and often lonely black on the squad, would jokingly remark as he walked

through the locker room: "Man, it sure was different when I first came here." Years later, Warford related to D.G. FitzMaurice (*Lexington Herald,* May 24, 1979) some of the experiences he had had as a freshman on the otherwise all-white Wildcats. The tone of the year was perhaps set during the first week of practice when, Warford recalled, one of the players "called me to his room. I was a freshman, and I thought I should go, so I did. This guy and two other players were sitting around a table chewing tobacco and playing Rook. I figured they wanted another player, and even though I didn't know how to play Rook, I was going to fake it. Instead," Warford said, "this guy looks up, and in a very soft voice, tells me he doesn't like colored boys and for me to stay out of his way. I told him that was fine with me, and today we get along all right." Warford's four years at UK were, FitzMaurice observed, "one bizarre incident after another." Through them all Warford managed to retain his sense of humor, but it must have been a trying experience for the young man. As FitzMaurice noted, "Warford, certainly not the most gifted guard to wear the basketball Wildcats' blue and white, nevertheless conducted himself with style and grace during his career at Kentucky despite circum-

Below, the coaching staff in action during a time-out. Dick Parsons kneels to Hall's right, while Leonard Hamilton leans over Parsons.

stances that at times would have distressed a man of lesser character."

Although Hall may be open to criticism on other points, where recruiting is concerned it is clear that he was color-blind. He wanted players with athletic talent, regardless of color. Even more important to him than talent, however, was what he regarded as a good attitude and willingness and ability to fit into the UK system and to abide by Hall's standards of behavior. With regard to the use of narcotics, for example, Hall maintained "If any of my players smoke pot, they're gone. For good. No suspension. Gone." No compromise with permissiveness. "Life's too short to be putting up with illegal behavior," Hall pointed out. "I'd get out of coaching first." From all indications, Hall stuck to his principles.

In 1975 UK had a superabundance of talent with the Givens-Robey group joining the Grevey-Conner contingent. The team was an excellent combination of size, speed, shooting ability, rebounding, solid man-to-man defense, and depth. Hall and his assistant coaches—Dick Parsons, Leonard Hamilton, and Lynn Nance—used the talent very effectively. The usual starting lineup consisted of Grevey and Guyette at forwards, Robey, the only nonsenior, at center, and Conner and Mike Flynn at guards. Grevey, a two-time All-American and three-time All-SEC selection, and Conner carried most of the scoring load while Guyette, at power forward, and Robey, who was also the third leading scorer on the team, handled the rebounding. Playmaking duties fell to Flynn, who had to sacrifice his own scoring for the good of the team. UK's strong bench included forwards Givens and Lee, 6'10" center Mike Phillips, and speedy sophomore Larry Johnson and senior Jerry Hale at guards.

Although the team got off to a good start with victories over Northwestern and Miami of Ohio, in the next game, against Indiana in Bloomington, the Wildcats seemed to return to the losing ways of the previous season. The game was a humiliating experience for the Big Blue not only because of the score, 98-74, but because of the manner in which the Hoosier center, Kent Benson, initiated UK's freshman pivotmen, Rick Robey and Mike Phillips, to the rough and tumble of big-time college basketball. Knight's offense involved a lot of movement and setting of picks, moving picks, to free players for open shots at the basket. Benson was particularly vigorous in setting picks, and UK's players responded with elbows or forearms to the face or chest. The Wildcats complained bitterly because the referees seemed to ignore Indiana's illegal picks but called penalties on UK players trying to fight through the picks.

Finally, with just a couple of minutes left in the game and the Hoosiers enjoying a commanding lead, an incident took place that seemed to add the final measure of humiliation. It was precipitated by a foul called against Indiana substitute Steve Ahlfield for charging into UK's Jerry Hale. IU coach Bobby Knight became particularly incensed over the call, feeling that too many fouls were being called against the Hoosiers, a view which Hall, of course, did not share. Knight walked in front of the Wildcat bench to talk to the official, and Hall left the bench to join in the argument. As the UK coach turned away Knight cuffed him on the back of the head. Although Knight immediately claimed it was a playful gesture, the Wildcat bench interpreted it as a symbol of contempt. Assistant Coach Lynn Nance, who had once been a member of the FBI and knew some karate, started to take off his coat and go after Knight but was restrained. Eventually everyone calmed down and the game was permitted to continue and—finally and mercifully—to end.

The Big Blue would not forget the valuable lessons learned in Bloomington. Hall maintained later that it

Tempers still flare on the court. Here, Indiana coach Bobby Knight (right) has just hit (or patted) Hall on the back of the head during a December 7, 1974, game, and Assistant Coach Lynn Nance has to be restrained by Hall. To add to the insult, Indiana trounced the Cats 98-74.

Jack Givens (21) and Mike Phillips (55) fight a Washington State player for a rebound in the 1974 UKIT.

was "a pivotal game. It woke us up to the physical type of play that we were going to face throughout the season and the fact that we had to give the same kind of effort if we were to win." In the early stages of the following game, against powerful North Carolina in Louisville, there were no signs that the lesson had been learned. Hall acknowledged that "going into the next game, against North Carolina, we were still a little stunned from the loss to Indiana. It took about fifteen minutes for us to find out where we were and what style of ball we were to play the rest of the season." With the Blue and White down 31-16, Hall called time-out and employed a tactic to wake the team up that he would put to good use under similar circumstances in the future. He benched four starters. When they finally were permitted to return to the contest they responded with inspired play. Guard Jimmy Dan Conner, in particular, played like a man possessed. He finished the game with thirty-five points and led the Wildcats to a 90-78 vic-

tory over an excellent Tar Heel team that included Phil Ford, Mitch Kupchek, and Walt Davis, all future stars in the NBA.

The Wildcats followed up the North Carolina victory with impressive wins over Washington State and Oklahoma State to take the UKIT championship, as well as traditional rivals Kansas and Notre Dame. The average margin of victory in the four games was twenty-five points, with Kansas going down in a thirty-seven-point defeat, 100-63. What a stunning reversal from the previous season, when the Big Blue had had a difficult time against intersectional foes. UK was not to have as easy a time in its SEC schedule as against intersectional foes (after the loss to Indiana) but, as Guyette has noted, "Our senior year seemed overall to be the reverse of the previous season when so much was expected of us and we just didn't deliver. In 1975 not as much was expected of us but we got better and better as the season progressed." Jack Givens, who was a freshman reserve in 1975, observed in an unpublished autobiography that "success in basketball is a strange thing. It seems to build on itself. It only takes one or two good games to get things going right. The momentum carries over into practice and you have some great practices and you're even more up for the next game." Except for occasional lapses which Hall did not accept with good grace, that was the story of 1975. UK lost only three regular games after the Indiana defeat and all were to SEC opponents—to Auburn, Tennessee, and Florida. Although the Wildcats defeated Alabama both times they played, the Tide was in the race for the conference title all season. In fact, the championship wasn't decided until March 8, the final day of the regular season.

UK was in Starkville for an evening game against Mississippi State, while the Alabama-Auburn game was the SEC game of the week on television that afternoon. It would take a combination of a UK victory and an Alabama defeat for the Big Blue to tie the Tide for the conference championship. Against all odds that is exactly what happened. The Wildcats thoroughly dominated their game to win by thirty-eight points, 118-80, to set the stage for Hall's second appearance in the NCAA in three years. The UK team was placed in the Mideast Regionals, where it would face Marquette and Indiana, two of the top squads in the nation, as well as Central Michigan, which featured two future NBA stars, Dan Roundfield and Rory Sparrow. The Wildcats disposed of Marquette by twenty-two points, 76-54, at Tuscaloosa on March 15, and Central Michigan by seventeen points, 90-73, on March 20 at Dayton. This set the stage for a return match with Knight and the Hoosiers for the re-

gional championship and a trip to the Final Four in San Diego. It was, Jack Givens maintained, "probably the best college game I've ever seen or been involved in, even though I didn't play that much."

Indiana entered the game as the number one team in the nation and the odds-on favorite to win the national championship. The Hoosiers had suffered a serious blow late in the season when forward Scott May, the team's leading scorer, broke a wrist. Indiana was so strong and so deep that despite the loss of May the Hoosiers were able to finish the regular season undefeated. With a special cast to protect his wrist May started the UK game but did not play up to his usual brilliant standards. Nevertheless, the two teams were evenly matched and the game was hard fought. The Wildcats had learned in the first Indiana game how to play tough, aggressive, and physical basketball and how to make effective use of a deep and talented bench. They had learned their lesson so well that reporter Robert Marcus of the *Chicago Tribune* dubbed them the "Slaughterhouse Five." In analyzing the game, which the Big Blue won 92-90, Marcus wrote: "The Kentucky Wildcats played like five guys who make their living sledge hammering steers in a stockyard Saturday to earn their greatest basketball victory in a decade."

After the game came another thrill for Givens and his teammates. The squad boarded a bus for the return trip to Lexington. "A police escort met the bus as it crossed the Ohio River," he recalled, "and we rolled down the interstate at about seventy miles per hour to the

Above, 6'9" power forward Bob Guyette scores against Mississippi State en route to the 1975 NCAA finals in San Diego.

Left, Mike Flynn displays his fastbreak technique for fans at Memorial Coliseum.

Coliseum. We were leading a long caravan of supporters. For miles behind us cars with their lights on were honking their horns. People were standing on the expressway overpasses with signs, waving at us. You'd look over in a field," he continued, "and a farmer and his family who had watched the game on TV or listened on the radio would be standing with a big homemade sign waving at us. It was great. Of all my experiences, I'll probably remember that one longer than any of them." When the team arrived in Lexington and the bus pulled up in front of the Coliseum "it seemed there were a million people there. All the seats were filled and the floor was packed with people. They were chanting 'San Diego here we come.'"

After that game, Givens noted, the Wildcats' playing went downhill. The tension of the Indiana game and "the fact that we were up so high made it seem like an NCAA final game. We wanted to beat Indiana so badly and got up so high for the game that it was hard to get up again after that. The seniors especially seemed to be flat or emotionally exhausted after the Indiana game."

An additional problem was that the finals were played in San Diego, far from friends and fans. None of the Wildcats had been to California, and playing basketball almost seemed like a secondary consideration. "We had a great time sightseeing," Givens recalled. "We

went to Sea World and to the zoo and Easter morning we had an Easter egg hunt outside the hotel where we were staying." The coaching staff and the freshmen would learn from the mistakes made in 1975. When they returned to the NCAA finals in 1978 they would be all business.

The Big Blue played poorly in the semifinal game against Syracuse, but because of a sparkling performance from reserve forward Jack Givens UK proved too strong for the easterners and won by sixteen points. In the other semifinal game perennial national champion UCLA met the Louisville Cardinals, whose coach, Denny Crum, had played and later coached under John Wooden. UCLA won an exciting and hard-fought contest in overtime, 75-74, to set up a meeting between UK, winner of four NCAA titles, and UCLA, national champions nine of the previous eleven seasons. In addition to whatever advantage UCLA might enjoy from its phenomenal success in NCAA tournament competition, the Bruins would be playing close to home and would have the full and vocal support of their fans. As if all this was not enough, Wooden announced his retirement on the day before the championship game.

The effect of Wooden's announcement was electrifying and immediate, as the Bruins' coach undoubtedly had anticipated. The UK coaches and players realized

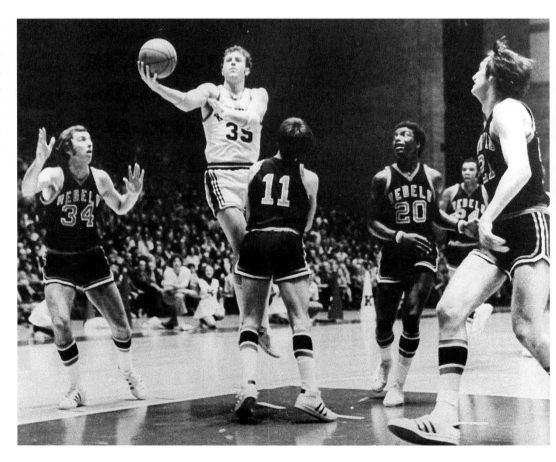

Kevin Grevey shovels an underhanded layup with his right hand as he shoots against the entire Mississippi starting lineup. Grevey, a southpaw, had a left-handed outside jump shot with tremendous range.

the psychological impact the announcement would have on the UCLA players and supporters but, as Bob Guyette noted, there was little they could do about it. As game time approached it was clear that Wooden's words were having the desired effect on his players and, when the game got under way, on the fans. The announcement may also have had an effect on the referees because, Guyette maintained, "Wooden did get away with some things, like walking out on the floor and some other things, that were out of character for him, I thought. For example, he got up and scolded the officials a few times." Givens also believes the referees were affected "because they made some calls in critical situations differently than they would have under other circumstances." And still, Guyette noted, "it was a close game."

The Wildcats finally lost 92-85 but, as Hall later stated, there could be no doubt "about the tremendous effort our players gave, and after we viewed the game on film we saw what a tremendous game they played, and we can only say that UCLA played a better game. They had a great motivation to win, and it was one of the finest games that we had seen them play that season."

The Wildcats returned to Lexington and a rousing welcome from the faithful at the Coliseum. The "Super Kittens" had grown up. They had vindicated themselves and Hall in the eyes of UK's legion of fans. The pressure on Hall was not ended, however. In the view of many of the Wildcat faithful he had not won "the big game." It would now be up to Givens, Robey, and associates to carry the banner of the Blue and White forces to the promised land and bring UK its first national championship in nearly twenty years—not an easy goal.

Mike Flynn firing a short jump shot in UK's 92-90 victory over Indiana in the NCAA Mideast Regional final played March 22, 1976, in Dayton. Kevin Grevey (35) positions himself for a possible rebound. This win avenged Kentucky's December 7, 1974, regular-season loss to IU.

9

Return to Glory

If the 1975 team began UK's return to its former glory, the 1978 squad completed the journey. The road was not an easy one to travel. In fact, through much of the 1975/76 season it appeared that the Wildcats were trapped in a living replay of the 1973/74 debacle. After the first twenty games the won-lost record was 10-10. The conference record to that date, February 14, was even worse. The Big Blue was able to win only five games while dropping seven. There appeared to be little hope for improvement in the six remaining SEC contests.

Through graduation UK had lost the nucleus of the 1975 NCAA runners-up and was left with an untested group of underclassmen. Gone from the team were four of the five starters from the 1975 team—Grevey, Guyette, Conner, and Flynn—plus valuable reserves G.J. Smith and Jerry Hale.

The only senior on the 1976 squad was guard Reggie Warford, who had not played enough in the previous three seasons to qualify for a single varsity letter. Fortunately for the Big Blue, when he finally got a chance to play Warford proved to be a pleasant surprise. Along with junior Larry Johnson, Warford would provide the Wildcats with strong play at guard, especially late in the season and during tournament play. Taking over Grevey's forward slot and scoring load was Jack Givens. The Lexington native's leadership qualities were recognized when he was chosen team captain, even though at the time he was only a sophomore. Rick Robey, the only returning starter from the 1975 team, was moved from center to power forward. The New Orleanian averaged 15.6 points

per game but because of injuries played in only twelve games, including four SEC contests. In Robey's absence fellow sophomore James Lee moved into the starting lineup. At center was still another sophomore, Mike Phillips.

A potentially excellent recruiting crop was ruined when a New Jersey high school sensation, Bill Willoughby, decided, after accepting a scholarship, to forgo college in order to enter the NBA draft. Another promising recruit, guard Pat Foschi, enrolled at UK but left school before the basketball season started, while Bob Fowler, a jumping jack 6'4" forward, was at the university for just one season before transferring to Iowa State. The only freshmen who remained the entire four seasons were guards Truman Claytor and Dwane Casey.

The 1976 season began on a sour note. The Big Blue travelled to Evanston, Illinois, for their opening game against the Northwestern University Wildcats only to lose by twelve points, 89-77. UK also lost the next game, to the North Carolina Tar Heels in Charlotte, but evened their record with victories over Miami of Ohio and Kansas. The Wildcats went down to their third defeat of the season when they met the Indiana Hoosiers in Louisville on December 15. Led by All-Americans Scott May and Kent Benson, the Hoosiers were on their way to an undefeated season and the NCAA championship but were pushed to the limit by a scrappy Wildcat team before finally prevailing in overtime, 77-68. The Blue and White completed their intersectional schedule on a positive note with victories over Georgia Tech and Oregon

Rick Robey, James Lee, and Jack Givens savor the ultimate victory, the NCAA championship, on March 27, 1978—the end of a long, tough season for the Cats.

State to win the UK Invitational Tournament, and the traditional late December meeting with the Notre Dame Fighting Irish in Louisville. With their intersectional schedule finally behind them, recalled Truman Claytor in an interview, the Wildcats turned with high hopes to the conference race. But their hopes were to be dashed immediately as they opened their SEC schedule with three straight losses—to Mississippi State, Alabama, and Tennessee. To add to UK's problems Rick Robey suffered a thigh bruise during the first conference game, with Mississippi State, and a knee sprain two nights later against Alabama. After missing the next three games Robey returned to the lineup for two games but reinjured the knee in practice and was sidelined for the rest of the season.

On February 14, with the SEC season two-thirds completed and disaster seemingly in the offing, the Wildcats suddenly changed direction and ended the regular season with six straight conference victories. Jack Givens recalled the frustrations of his sophomore season, "It appeared that we were going nowhere but we kept on trying and working and it paid off. We won our last six conference games and in the next to the last game we beat Alabama, the league champs that year, in a nationally televised game from the Coliseum. That victory got us an invitation to the NIT in New York and we felt lucky to be invited." Even with the strong finish the Big Blue could do no better than tie for fourth place in the conference. Givens was right. UK was lucky to be invited to the NIT.

The ten-day trip to New York for the NIT was UK's first appearance in the "Big Apple" since the basketball scandal of the early fifties. According to Claytor, Lee, Givens, and Dwane Casey, the players were frequently asked how it felt to be the first UK team to appear in Madison Square Garden in twenty-six years. The Wildcat players' response was succinct and to the point: "That was long before our time and we don't think much about it."

The Big Blue peaked at just the right time. To win the tournament UK had to play and win four games in nine days. In close and exciting games they defeated Niagara, Kansas State, Providence, and, for the title, the University of North Carolina at Charlotte. The strong

A preseason photo of the 1976/77 Wildcats shows the team's changing racial composition. Seated, left to right, Mike Phillips and Rick Robey. Standing, Kyle Macy (a redshirt who did not play that season), Jay Shidler, Tim Stephens, James Lee, LaVon Williams, Jack Givens, Merion Haskins, Larry Johnson, Dwane Casey, and Truman Claytor.

UNC Charlotte team was coached by Lee Rose, previously of Lexington's Transylvania University, and led by future NBA star Cedric "Cornbread" Maxwell. Powered by a fourteen-point performance by Reggie Warford in his final appearance in a Wildcat uniform, UK overcame second-half foul trouble and another outstanding game from Maxwell, who was voted the most valuable player in the tournament, to win 71-67.

With the season-ending ten-game winning streak and the NIT championship, the Wildcats converted a potentially disastrous season into a memorable one. In another respect 1976 was a milestone in UK basketball annals: for the first time a majority of both the starting players and the reserves were black. The ratio was in stark contrast to the situation just a couple of years before, when UK had a bad reputation among blacks. Jack Givens, a highly recruited senior at Lexington's Bryan Station High School, recalled that in 1974 "some blacks, especially some older people, would come up to me and tell me I shouldn't go to UK. They would tell me that UK didn't like blacks, that I wouldn't get to play, that they would have me locked up, amazing things like that." Typical of Kentucky blacks, Givens had never followed Wildcat basketball so "I didn't really notice that UK didn't have any black starters until people started pointing it out. UK only had one black player, Reggie Warford, on the varsity and he was sitting on the bench. There were two other blacks, Larry Johnson and Merion Haskins, on the freshman team."

Fortunately for the Wildcats, when Givens talked with Warford, Johnson, and Haskins "they told me they really liked UK, that everything was great." Givens acknowledged that if Adolph Rupp had still been coach he probably would not have attended UK, in large part because he doubted Rupp would have been interested in him. But Joe Hall and Dick Parsons made a very favorable impression on Givens and his mother, and they seemed to be genuinely interested in the "Goose" and his well-being. The UK coaching staff impressed James Lee and the other blacks they recruited in the same positive way, and they continued to attract blue-chip white athletes, as well. Two other master recruiters joined the UK staff, Leonard Hamilton in 1974 and Joe Dean in 1977.

In the 1976/77 season everyone from the NIT championship team returned except Reggie Warford, and the Wildcats had another excellent group of freshman recruits. Joining the squad were sharpshooters Jay Shidler and Tim Stephens and rugged rebounder LaVon Williams. Shidler, who arrived at UK with bleached hair and was promptly nicknamed "White Lightning" by an adoring public, had an excellent long-range jump shot and

The 1976/77 squad tries to relax and loosen up before a game.

played hustling defense. The Lawrenceville, Illinois, native became a starting guard as a freshman, scoring in double figures in twelve games and registering a game and career high of twenty points against Indiana. Stephens's contributions were limited because of injuries in 1977 and 1978, and he decided to transfer from UK after his sophomore season. Williams also served as a substitute in 1977 and 1978 but became a starting forward in his junior and senior seasons with the Wildcats. In addition to the freshmen, Purdue transfer Kyle Macy arrived on the Lexington campus. Although he was ineligible to play in 1976/77, it was obvious that Macy, who had been Purdue's third leading scorer as a freshman with a single-game high of thirty-eight points against Minnesota, would be a valuable addition to the team in 1977/78.

With a young and inexperienced team UK had played inspired ball in the last third of the 1975/76 season and capped a dazzling comeback with the NIT

championship. After the Big Blue won the NIT on March 21, 1976, Joe Hall told his team, as Jack Givens reported, that "some people would say and write that it was a great ending but that they were wrong because, as he put it, 'the NIT championship is only the beginning for you.'"

UK's prospects for the 1976/77 season appeared to be excellent. The Cats had an experienced and deep squad with juniors Jack Givens, Rick Robey, and Mike Phillips and senior playmaker Larry Johnson. Joining them in the starting lineup was the sensational freshman prospect Jay Shidler. Hall also made full and effective use of his talented reserves, who included James Lee, LaVon Williams, Truman Claytor, Merion Haskins, and Dwane Casey.

The Big Blue won twenty-six games and lost only four, but each of the four defeats was crucial. The first, to Utah, cost the Wildcats the championship in their invitational tournament. In the grueling eighteen-game conference schedule UK suffered only two defeats, both at the hands of Tennessee, who tied the Cats for the SEC championship. By virtue of holding the series edge the Vols won the right to represent the conference in the Mideast Regionals at Baton Rouge, with the regional finals at Rupp Arena in Lexington, while UK was placed in the East Regionals with games first in Philadelphia and then in College Park, Maryland.

After impressive victories over Princeton and Virginia Military Institute the Big Blue met North Carolina in the regional finals for the opportunity to move on to the finals of the national championship. The Cats fell behind early in the game but worked their way back to trail by only one point, 71-70, with 1:32 left in the game. That was as close as they came, as the Tar Heels pulled away to win 79-72. UK hit five more field goals than North Carolina but lost the game at the free throw line. Because they were behind through most of the game the Wildcats were forced to commit fouls, and the Tar Heels cashed in on thirty-three of their thirty-six free throws, while UK, with only eighteen free throws, converted on sixteen of them. In an interview Kyle Macy recalled the North Carolina contest as "one of those games where they [the Wildcats] just never got the big break or they could have won the championship that year because it was an outstanding team."

In analyzing the season Hall blamed midseason disciplinary problems for the Wildcats' falling short of his and the team's goal of an NCAA title in 1977. In December, on the eve of the UKIT, Hall had suspended Mike Phillips, Jay Shidler, and Truman Claytor for a curfew violation. Without them the Wildcats struggled before pulling away from a weak Bowling Green team. In the tournament finals, however, they had problems with Utah, a disciplined and balanced squad, and fell by two points, 70-68. Looking back on the events Hall was convinced that the incident created a division within the team. "I don't think we ever completely recovered from that," Hall maintained. He was determined not to let anything similar happen the next season.

Adding a sense of urgency to this determination was the anticipated impact of penalties imposed by the NCAA on the UK football and basketball programs. In December 1976 the NCAA, college sports' governing body, announced the results of an investigation of UK. The report documented violations of the NCAA code by UK recruiters, staff members, and alumni. Although most of the violations had been committed by or in the interests of the football team, the basketball program was also penalized. The football team was prohibited from appearing on NCAA telecasts and postseason bowl

Senior Larry Johnson was playmaker for the Cats in 1976/77.

games for one year, although it was permitted to appear in an already scheduled Peach Bowl Game in Atlanta. In addition, the number of recruits UK was allowed to sign was limited for the next two years to twenty-five in football and three in basketball. Because recruitment is the lifeblood of a successful college athletic program, such a restriction could adversely affect Wildcat basketball and football for years to come. Thus pressure to win in 1977/78 started early.

The football team responded with a glittering 10-1 season. Pressure was intense on Hall and the basketball team to win not only the conference title but the national championship. Indeed, nothing less than an NCAA title would satisfy sportswriters and fans. The specter of possible failure haunted Hall during the entire season. Although the Big Blue was ranked number one for all but two weeks, Hall criticized, cursed, and chastised his squad throughout the season and even suggested, after a loss to LSU in February, that they might be immortalized in Wildcat annals as the "Folding Five" or the "Quitting Quintet."

After UK completed the season with a victory over Duke in the finals of the NCAA to win their first national championship in twenty years, *Sports Illustrated* reporter Larry Keith observed that "it was never easy for Kentucky. There was never any time to sit and smile. From the very first game this season, the Wildcats were haunted by their tradition, pressured by their opponents and driven mercilessly by their coach. All the joys of winning had to wait until they had won it all."

Jack Givens recalled that "the pressure of my senior season [1977/78] actually started during my junior year right after we lost to North Carolina in the East Regionals of the NCAA at College Park, Maryland." After that defeat "we moved to dedicate ourselves to win it all the next year. We worked hard all summer and looked forward with great excitement and anticipation to the coming season but we knew we had lost two quality people in Larry Johnson and Merion Haskins. We knew we had our work cut out for us."

Even with the graduation of Johnson (a vastly underrated player) and Haskins, UK appeared to have a deep and talented squad. Returning were four starters from the 1977 team plus all of the top reserves, including forward James Lee, who was good enough to start and even star on most college teams. At UK he was the first reserve off the bench. The front court starters were the sharpshooting 6'4" left-hander Jack Givens and two powerful 6'10" inside players, Rick Robey and Mike Phillips. Back at one guard position was crowd favorite

Jay Shidler demonstrates the style that earned him the nickname "White Lightning" during his sensational freshman season, 1976/77.

Jay Shidler, who had started twenty-eight of UK's thirty games as a freshman. Shidler's main problem had been a lack of consistency, which he hoped to improve in his sophomore season. But on the second day of practice he broke a bone in his right foot and was sidelined for five weeks. In Shidler's absence junior Truman Claytor got an opportunity to display his talents as a shooter, ball handler, and defensive player. By the time Shidler was ready to return to action Claytor had won a starting guard position. This replacement meant that the Illinois native was relegated to a reserve role because the other guard, the playmaker, was Kyle Macy.

For Shidler or anyone else to displace Macy was unthinkable. Even before Macy played his first varsity game for the Wildcats, Hall was lavish in his predictions of greatness for the young man. During Macy's redshirt

Reserve guard Dwane Casey (20), besides playing solid man-to-man defense, made invaluable contributions to team morale in the 1977/78 championship season. He later became a UK assistant coach.

6'10" forward-center Scott Courts, and 6'8" forward Fred Cowan. Givens, Claytor, and Shidler provided excellent outside shooting and, along with reserve guard Dwane Casey, solid man-to-man defense.

Casey was acknowledged by his teammates to be one of the keys to UK's success in 1978. Jack Givens maintained that Casey was "one of the most important people on the team that year. . . . Everyday in practice and every minute he was in a game he showed more heart and desire than any guy I have ever seen. Considering the limited amount of time he got to play he could have complained and caused dissension. Instead he was always the happiest and most optimistic member of the team."

Co-captains Jack Givens and Rick Robey were team leaders. Macy put all these talents together and contributed some of his own. He became UK's floor leader on both offense and defense. In addition he possessed an accurate jump shot and was probably the best free throw shooter on the team as well as a smart, if not very quick, defensive player. As Macy noted in an interview, the year he spent as a redshirt was invaluable because it provided an opportunity to observe. He wasn't "thrown right into the fire. I had that year to learn the program and get to know the other players, the coaching philosophy, and to build up my motivation."

Both Macy and Joe Hall agreed that another important ingredient in Macy's excellent play in 1977/78 was the strength and endurance he gained during his redshirt year. In fact, all of the players for the 1978 team that were interviewed gave a full measure of credit to the conditioning program for UK's outstanding success that season. Even Dan Issel credited the conditioning program, which Hall introduced when he joined the UK coaching staff in the mid-1960s, with helping to improve his play during his four years at UK (1966/67-1969/70).

The formal preseason conditioning program began shortly after the start of classes in the fall semester and continued until basketball practices started on October 15. Players were also expected, but not required, to follow a strict regimen throughout the summer and also to play informal basketball games two or three nights a week at Alumni Gym. The conditioning program included work on the running track as well as in the weight room. Pat Etcheberry, who was strength coach for the football and basketball teams and former track and cross country coach, said that "the basketball program stresses development of the lower body more than the upper body as well as work to develop and maintain flexibility." The result, if the player worked to the limit of his

season, 1976/77, Hall maintained that "we have not had a guard with the leadership qualities of Macy. The closest was Jimmy Dan Conner, who had the leadership but not the skills Macy has. Kyle is an excellent outside shooter, passer, penetrator. He's a quarterback, a coach on the floor." Heady praise indeed for a college sophomore with just one year of varsity playing experience at Purdue, but it was fully justified. Seldom has a college player lived up to his advance billing as rapidly or as completely as Kyle Macy did. The 6'3" guard from Peru, Indiana, was the final ingredient in Joe Hall's formula for success. The Wildcats had an abundance of size and strength. In addition to Robey, Phillips, and Lee, Hall could call on 6'6" sophomore forward LaVon Williams and three freshman giants: 6'10" center Chuck Aleksinas,

capabilities (and Etcheberry was famous for making sure he did), was a strong, agile athlete with great endurance.

Following very successful conditioning and practice sessions, the 1977/78 basketball season began with a solid thumping of a touring Russian team in an exhibition on November 11 in Memorial Coliseum. In that contest the "Fysical Five," as the 1978 team came to be called, handled a big, strong, and talented Soviet squad with ease and cruised to a thirty-four-point victory, 109-75.

During the regular season, which began with a 110-86 victory over Southern Methodist, the Big Blue suffered only two losses, neither to an intersectional foe. The Wildcats defeated SMU, Indiana, Kansas, South Carolina, Portland State, St. John's, Iowa, Notre Dame, Nevada Las Vegas, and sixteen of eighteen SEC opponents. After the December 12 game against South Carolina at Rupp Arena, which UK won by nineteen points, 84-65, Gamecock coach Frank McGuire marveled that the Wildcats "were like a pro team, with the kinds of bodies they've got out there."

Hot-shooting Truman Claytor won a starting position as guard when Shidler was injured before the start of the 1977/78 season.

UK's only losses were away games against conference foes Alabama and LSU. The memory of those games remains fresh in Jack Givens's mind. "We were undefeated at the time, and the press and our fans expected us to continue that way. Alabama had a good team but no one expected us to lose, even though we hadn't played well the previous few games." He noted that Hall "warned us before the game that Bama was playing well and that we would get killed if we didn't play a great game. To say that we played badly would be an understatement. Alabama played with more enthusiasm, more desire, more pride, more heart, more everything than we did and whipped us by a score of 78 to 62." Hall was furious. He blasted the team, especially the stars, in the press, singling out Givens, who he knew could take the criticism and would understand the motivation, which was to blast the team out of its sense of complacency. "He said I played scared and with no heart," Givens recalled. "He threatened to remove me from the starting lineup. And those were the nice things he said about me."

The Wildcats returned home after the Alabama loss and, with the faithful roaring their approval, defeated Georgia, Florida, and Auburn by wide margins. The "Fysical Five" seemed to be back to playing their game. Then the Big Blue travelled to Baton Rouge to play the LSU Tigers on February 11. As Givens observed, "everything fell apart again." UK lost its second conference game by one point, 95-94, in overtime. "What made it so bad," the Goose noted, "was that their entire starting team fouled out in regulation time to only two of our starters. So in the overtime period it was our first team against their second team. Once again Coach Hall ripped us apart in the press and I came in for my share of the criticism. As a team he referred to us as the 'Quitting Quintet' and the 'Folding Five.'"

The Wildcats played at Mississippi State two days later and, although they won by twelve points, did not play particularly well. Things did not get back to normal until the following weekend when UK, now at home, thoroughly outclassed Tennessee to win by thirteen points. "This was an especially sweet victory," recalled Givens, "because not only was Tennessee our most hated rival but they had beaten us five straight times over the preceding three seasons. As if by magic the Alabama and LSU games were all but forgotten. Instead of the excessive criticism from the sportswriters and the fans there was excessive praise." The rest of the season was clear sailing for the Wildcats, but the NCAA tournament brought new crises.

As the top-ranked team in the nation, according to all the polls, UK was seeded number one in the Mideast Regionals. In their very first tournament game, a March 11 encounter with Florida State in Knoxville, the Big Blue found themselves in serious trouble. Throughout the season quick teams like Alabama had given the Wildcats problems and Florida State was a much quicker and more talented squad than Alabama. At halftime Florida State was ahead by seven points and Hall was furious. "He lectured us on all the things we were doing wrong and predicted that if things continued the same way in the second half we would end up the same as we did at Alabama." And that, noted Givens, would be a bitter fate. "He finally told us that if we were going to lose we would lose with people who wanted to play and who wanted to win. So at the start of the second half he put in Dwane Casey, LaVon Williams, and Fred Cowan. For the first time in three years I wasn't starting a second half. The move totally surprised everyone, players, media, fans." It also surprised Coach Hugh Durham and his Florida State Seminoles. Givens continued:

Fortunately for Hall the move worked, because if it hadn't the second guessers would have been all over him and the Adolph Rupp diehards would have been after his scalp. At any rate, Dwane and the others came out playing as though there was no tomorrow and, since one loss eliminates you in the NCAA, there was no tomorrow for us. They played great defense, fought like demons for rebounds, and dove for loose balls and they had Florida State completely off balance. If they hadn't gotten tired and could have shot better I might never have returned to the game. But I did get back in. When Rick [Robey], Truman [Claytor], and I reentered the game we played inspired basketball and UK won. Coach Hall's move was a real gutsy one and in the end he looked great because it proved to be the turning point in the game. I think the decision exemplified the way Coach Hall handled pressure all season. His job was to win games but he intended to do it his way. He was going to make his own decisions regardless of whether or not the fans, the press, or even his own players agreed. If his career at UK was to come to an end he was going to go down fighting.

Givens confessed to having "a great deal of respect and admiration for Coach Hall."

The Wildcats came back in the second half of the Florida State game to win by nine points, 85-76, but they still had four more games to play to win the national championship. The next opponent, Miami of Ohio, was no match for UK's size, skill, and experience and fell 91-69. The regional finals, against the Michigan State Spartans and their freshman sensation, "Magic" Johnson, was another matter, but the Cats were able to make adjustments and win the game. In a May 1983 interview Kyle Macy recalled that "Michigan State was in a zone that was giving us a lot of trouble in the first half. As we came out of the locker room at the end of the half, Coach

James Lee, a powerful forward, moves downcourt on a fast break against Arkansas in the semifinals of the 1978 NCAA tournament. UK won 64-59 in a tougher game than the final one against Duke.

Hamilton stopped Coach Hall and suggested trying an offense that he had in mind." Hall agreed to the plan and "called Rick Robey and me over and explained what he wanted us to do. Basically what it involved was for Rick to come up and set a pick on the zone, which is a little unusual. Fortunately," Macy laughed, "it worked." Robey's picks freed Macy for outside jump shots. "I would either hit the shot or be fouled and hit the free throws." Hamilton's offensive adjustment and Macy's shooting skill brought the Wildcats back in the second half, and UK eked out a three-point victory, 52-49.

The Michigan State game underlined a point Macy made about the Wildcats' success in 1978. "I've always felt a major reason we won the championship that year was because we had the ability to adjust to every situation. If a team tried to stop Jack or Rick inside we had other players in the starting lineup or on the bench who could pick up the slack. There wasn't any one thing a team could do to stop our offense. And at the same time we did play pretty good defense."

By defeating Michigan State the Big Blue won the Mideast Regionals and qualified for the finals in St. Louis. In their first game, against an excellent Arkansas Razorback team, the Cats had still another chance to show their adaptability. "I'd say the Arkansas game was really the toughest game of the entire tournament," Macy stated. "That was because they presented some problems as far as matchups were concerned. They were a little shorter team than we were and quicker, and they had some outstanding shooters in Sidney Moncrief, Ron Brewer, and Melvin Delph. I think we did a good job of keeping our composure," he maintained, "and not making too many unforced errors, and then, with about a minute to play, made a big play when we had a run out with Jack [Givens] against their press." Givens also recalled the Arkansas contest as the "best game of the five we played in the whole tournament. Arkansas had a much better team than Duke. In fact, they were definitely one of the best teams we played all season."

The UK players had no doubts about winning the championship game against Duke. "We went into the Duke game prepared for anything they were going to do," noted Givens. "We were so excited and fired up about playing that we didn't even need Coach Hall to get us prepared. Everybody's attitude was just great." Kyle Macy pointed out that "before the game we had a team meeting, even before the coaches got there, and everybody just looked at each other and said: 'Hey, we've worked this hard to get here, let's just go out and do it.'" The Cats were a serious and dedicated band of veterans

in 1978. As freshmen in San Diego for the 1975 NCAA finals they had learned, in Givens's words, "that there was plenty of time for partying and having a good time after it's all over. So when we went to St. Louis my senior year we were strictly business. We went to St. Louis to win. We knew the only way we were going to be satisfied was to win."

In the Duke game the Wildcats were powered by one of the outstanding individual efforts in the history of the NCAA championship game. As the April 3, 1978, issue of *Sports Illustrated* proclaimed in recounting UK's success: "The Goose was Golden." Jack Givens scored forty-one points in leading the Big Blue to a 94-88 victory over the outclassed Blue Devils. The smooth-shooting southpaw's point total was just three short of Bill Walton's record for the championship game. Givens is still amazed by his performance. "In fact," he noted, "when the game started out, I think I missed a couple or three shots. I certainly didn't expect to get the shots I did. I took twenty-seven shots from the field in that game and hit eighteen. I hadn't taken that many shots in any other game my four years at UK but the shots were there against Duke. We were a lot quicker than Duke was and I got a lot of points on fast breaks but I got a lot more against their zone."

"Inexplicably," *Sports Illustrated* reported, "the Blue Devils did not come out of their zone defense until it was too late, and Givens just kept pouring in sweet jumpers, along with a selection of tips, layins and free throws." According to James Lee, this lack of strategy simply reflected the fact that Duke was a young and inexperienced team. "We would never have permitted a player to get so many open shots right in the middle of our zone," observed Lee. "After he hit a couple, we would have made an adjustment in our zone. The Duke players just didn't know what to do and, being a veteran team, we took full advantage of their mistakes. What most people didn't realize, and still don't realize," he emphasized, "is how versatile a team we were. We were able to adjust to any style of play or any situation. It was a real pleasure to be on that team."

Hall recounted after the game that "when we saw how open Duke was leaving the middle, we junked our game plan and just tried to get it to Jack." Characteristically, Givens saved his best performance for his most important game as a Wildcat. Also characteristically, he maintained that he played "a better all-around game [against Arkansas] than I did against Duke."

After twenty years in the wilderness UK was again college basketball's national champion. In the euphoria following the Duke game even then *Courier-Journal*

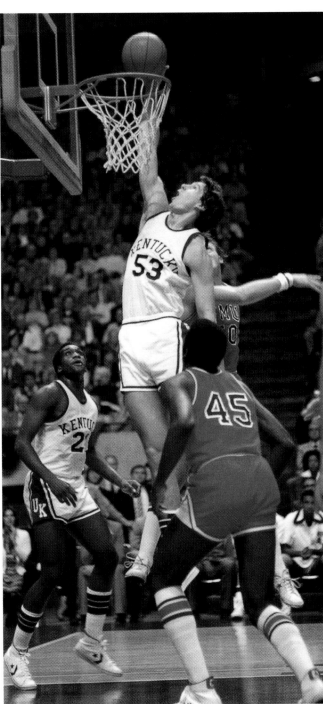

Above, Mike Phillips sinks the ball as the Cats run away from the Runnin' Rebels of the University of Nevada Las Vegas, 92-70, on March 4, 1978.

Right, the Wildcats roared off to a fast start for the 1977/78 season as they corralled the SMU Mustangs in the season opener. Rick Robey lays it in. Jack Givens is ready in case of a rebound.

Above, Truman Claytor prepares to sink two from long range against the Duke Blue Devils in the 1978 NCAA championship game in St. Louis. Two keys to winning the championship were reserve forward James Lee *(below left),* shown here driving against the University of Nevada Las Vegas on March 4, and stellar playmaker Kyle Macy *(below right),* the Cats' "coach on the floor."

The sweet taste of victory. *Left,* "The Goose Was Golden!" Jack Givens shoots for two of his forty-one points against the Duke University Blue Devils in the NCAA finals, his last—and best—Wildcat performance. *Below,* Rick Robey's victory roar says it all. *Bottom,* the Wildcat faithful, awaiting the team's return from St. Louis, revel in UK's first NCAA championship in twenty years.

sports editor Billy Reed found words of praise to shower on Hall. "Invariably," Reed maintained in a special post-tournament issue, Hall "doesn't get nearly as much credit or attention as slick-talking, media-oriented coaches such as Digger Phelps of Notre Dame. . . . Hall has earned the right to be respected by the press, the public and his peers. That, and the right to a little peace of mind." This was only a temporary truce, however. An end to hostilities was not in the offing—either from the press or from Hall.

With the victory over Duke in the 1978 national championship game, UK regained the glory of the Rupp era, but that enviable situation lasted only a short time. The NCAA-imposed restrictions on the number of basketball scholarships had an immediate impact on UK's basketball fortunes. Only because of the brilliant play of Kyle Macy and freshman Dwight Anderson, an all-out effort by the other members of the team, and a fine coaching job by Hall and his staff, were the Wildcats able to stave off potential disaster in 1979. Nevertheless, victory in the 1978 NCAA tournament marked a major turning point in the coaching career of Joe B. Hall.

Following the 1978 season Hall and Ernst Jokl, a retired UK professor of physical education and a widely respected authority on sports medicine, collected statistics from the 1948, 1958, 1968, and 1978 seasons to compare physiques and performance of the current national champions with earlier Wildcat teams (Tables 5 and 6). Not only did the Wildcat teams of 1958, 1968, and 1978 have higher scoring averages than the 1948

Table 5. UK Team Records, Selected Years, 1947/48-1977/78

Season	Average Points Scored Per Game		No. of Games UK Scored 100 Points
	UK	Opponent	UK
1947/48	69.0	44.0	0
1957/58	74.5	62.6	0
1967/68	88.9	77.9	7
1977/78	84.2	69.8	6

NCAA champions, but so did UK's opponents in 1968 and 1978. Neither the "Fabulous Five" nor the "Fiddlin' Five" were able to score 100 points in a game. The high scoring Issel-Casey-Pratt group, which ranked fourth in the nation in 1968, totaled 100 or more points seven times during the season, while the 1978 team, which had a reputation for playing a more deliberate, ball-control game, scored 100 points six times. The 1968 and 1978 teams not only scored more points than their predecessors but were also more accurate, both from the field and from the free throw line. Although fans and even sportswriters tend to believe that the Wildcats were better in the "good old days" of Rupp than under Joe Hall, the evidence seems to prove otherwise. In size and shooting ability, even on free throws, the 1978 team was superior to the other squads examined.

Table 6. Comparison of UK Players, Selected Years, 1947/48-1977/78

	Starters					Substitutes			
	1947/48	1957/58	1967/68	1977/78		1947/48	1957/58	1967/68	1977/78
Height	6' 2 1/6"	6' 3 1/3"	6' 4 3/4"	6' 5 1/2"		6' 1 1/2"	6' 3 1/2"	6' 4 1/3"	6' 5 1/6"
Weight	192.0	183.8	209.2	206.6		177.9	188.2	196.0	206.1
Field goal percentage	33.47	37.88	46.51	55.97		27.54	34.05	48.87	49.55
Free throw percentage	63.08	75.22	70.76	77.86		61.59	67.47	70.58	70.86

10

Building a New Tradition

For Joe Hall and his Wildcats the 1978/79 season was a series of problems, including injuries and defections. Finally, in the SEC tournament, exhaustion and lack of players—UK was down to seven experienced players for the championship game—caught up with the Big Blue to prevent a Cinderella finish to a frustrating season. Nevertheless, at least one rabid UK supporter was hopeful. At the end of the season Oscar Combs, who in 1976 had sold off his two weekly Eastern Kentucky newspapers and moved to Lexington to launch *The Cats' Pause,* a weekly sports magazine devoted to UK sports, published a book entitled *Kentucky Basketball: A New Beginning.* The optimism reflected in the subtitle seemed fully justified. Hall, finally freed after two seasons of NCAA-imposed restrictions on recruitment, had signed five of the top high school seniors in the country to scholarships—Sam Bowie, Dirk Minniefield, Derrick Hord, Charles Hurt, and Tom Heitz—while a sixth, Melvin Turpin, had announced that after a year in prep school to improve his academic record he also would enroll at UK.

Bo Lanter, who walked on as a redshirt at UK in 1978/79 after an excellent season at Midwestern State University at Wichita Falls, Texas, stated in an interview that "if someone had told me when I transferred that I was going to be at Kentucky four years and that we would not win a national championship, I would have told him he was crazy. There were no doubts in my mind. After all," he pointed out, "we were coming off a national championship and that means good recruiting. Then [for the 1979/80 season] we signed four superstars in Bowie, Minniefield, Hord, and Hurt. Matter of fact, I

was counting on two or three [championship] rings before I got out of school." Although UK would not win another NCAA title during the Hall era, a new tradition was being built, one that was racially integrated.

The venerable Wildcat tradition was safe and secure in the hands of Joe B. Hall, and now it had become a tradition for black Kentuckians as well as for whites. Toward the end of Hall's coaching tenure a UK signee was quoted in the press as saying that to play for the Blue and White was "a dream come true." This black athlete was happy to join the Wildcat tradition, but for him it was not the tradition of Beard and Groza, Hagan and Ramsey, or Nash and Issel, but of Givens and Minniefield, two black stars from Lexington. As he put it, "Playing at UK is something I've always wanted to do. I've grown up watching Jack Givens and Dirk Minniefield play at UK, and I really look up to them." This attitude is a welcome and healthy change from the racially exclusive tradition of the Rupp era.

The Wildcats began the 1978/79 season with six black and six white players. Among the three freshmen recruits on the squad was 6'3" guard Dwight Anderson of Dayton, Ohio, one of the most exciting and talented players in UK basketball history. Although he remained less than a season and a half, his stay was memorable. Anderson was a multitalented player who possessed blinding speed, lightning quickness, uncanny moves, and outstanding leaping ability. In only his seventh game as a member of the Big Blue, against a strong Notre Dame team on national television, Anderson scored seventeen second-half points to lead the Wildcats from a twelve-

Although he played less than two seasons at UK, flashy and versatile Dwight Anderson (*above*) left an indelible imprint on Wildcat basketball. *Below*, he and Hall are interviewed on national television after his brilliant performance against Notre Dame, December 30, 1978.

point deficit, with only eight minutes left in the game, to an 81-76 win. His play was so outstanding that NBC color man and former Marquette coach Al McGuire was moved to proclaim on the air: "A new star was born tonight in college basketball." And Anderson, the game's Most Valuable Player, was not even playing his normal position of guard. Because UK was so shorthanded throughout the season, Anderson had to play at forward. Although just a substitute in UK's first thirteen games, and forced to play opponents several inches taller, "Dwight Lightning" finished the season as the team's second leading scorer.

From the beginning of the 1979 season the Wildcats lacked depth and size, the cumulative effect of the recruiting restrictions imposed in 1977. In 1977/78 the Big Blue had added 6'8" forward Fred Cowan and 6'10" centers Chuck Aleksinas and Scott Courts as well as walk-on guard Chris Gettelfinger. The 1978/79 season brought the arrival of 6'7" forward Clarence Tillman, 6'6" Chuck Verderber, Dwight Anderson, and walk-on Bo Lanter. Of the six scholarship players recruited during those two seasons only two—Cowan and Verderber—completed their careers at UK. Courts departed the team at the end of his freshman season, leaving the 6'10" 258-pound Aleksinas as UK's biggest player. Aleksinas became dissatisfied with the Wildcat style of play, unfortunately, and quit the team in January 1979. In a June 1983 reunion of the 1978 NCAA championship team, Aleksinas admitted he had made a mistake in quitting and regretted his decision. But that admission did not help the 1979 team. Neither did it help that another member of the championship team, 6'3" junior forward Tim Stephens left the squad at the beginning of January 1979. With the departure of Stephens and Aleksinas, UK was left with only ten scholarship players and without a natural center. With a front court consisting of 6'3" 175-pounder Dwight Anderson, 6'7" 220-pound LaVon Williams, and 6'8" 210-pound Fred Cowan, and with 6'3" 188-pound Kyle Macy and 6'1" 180-pound Truman Claytor at the guards, the Cats could not be mistaken for the "Fysical Five," but they were quick and rugged.

The 1978/79 team had a poor regular-season record by UK standards, winning sixteen and losing ten, including eight losses to SEC rivals. The Wildcats were saved by the fact that the conference had returned to the postseason tournament format for the first time since 1952. With the flashy and often brilliant Anderson, streak-shooting Claytor, and smart, steady Macy leading the way, the Big Blue upended Mississippi, Alabama, and LSU in SEC tournament play to qualify for the championship game and an automatic bid to the

NCAA tournament. Unfortunately for the Cats, Anderson, who had averaged twenty points in the previous eight games, suffered a fractured wrist in the first minute of the LSU game and was lost for the championship game against Tennessee.

Joe Dean considered the UK-Alabama game, which the Wildcats won 101-100, to be "one of the greatest games I have ever seen. We were shorthanded, we were playing Bama in Birmingham, and their star, Reggie King, had a great game but we still won because Claytor, Macy, and Anderson were just absolutely incredible that night shooting the ball. Then, against LSU," Dean's story continued, "Anderson broke his wrist and we had to play with a makeshift lineup." With only seven experienced players, plus the seldom used Lanter and Gettelfinger, the Big Blue were simply outmanned by Tennessee. They did force the game into overtime before finally falling, 75-69. "It was tough to lose to the Vols," Dean acknowledged, "but our players were just so worn out."

UK's late-season heroics brought an invitation to participate in the NIT, but without the spectacular Anderson to ignite them the exhausted Wildcats ran out of miracles. Although they played their first tournament game before their wildly cheering fans at Rupp Arena, the Big Blue lost in overtime to Clemson of the Atlantic Coast Conference by one point, 68-67.

Considering the variety of problems UK faced during the season, 1979 has to be reckoned a successful season. The four seasons that followed were in many respects less satisfying.

Before the start of the 1979/80 season, yet another highly touted player, forward Clarence Tillman, quit the team and school, leaving only six returning lettermen. Before the end of December, Anderson also would depart and, as in 1978/79, the Wildcats would again be short on experience. Hall never explained the real reasons for Anderson's departure, but in a February 13, 1980, *Courier-Journal* article, Billy Reed claimed that a rift between the coach and his enormously talented but undisciplined star was inevitable. "It wasn't that I doubted Anderson's ability," Reed maintained. "It was just that, judging by what I had seen and heard of Anderson, I didn't think he would be unselfish enough to fit into Hall's disciplined, team-oriented system." In 1979 UK had been "so thin," especially after Chuck Aleksinas quit the team, that "Hall had to sit there and let him [Anderson] do things. He had no choice." In 1980 the situation was different. With five excellent freshman prospects joining the team, Hall was less dependent on the highly individualistic Anderson. The basic problem, in Reed's opinion, was that Hall and Anderson "defined

LaVon Williams puts up a rebound against LaSalle on December 2, 1978. Chuck Aleksinas (50) quit the team in midseason, and forward Fred Cowan (right) moved to center.

'fun' differently. To Hall, fun means success through hard work, sacrifice, discipline and selflessness. To Anderson fun means success through doing your own thing both on and off the floor."

Conversations with former UK players underscore the point that Hall subscribed to essentially the same theories of motivation as Adolph Rupp did. Like his predecessor, Hall believed there were two types of players—those who had to be driven hard to perform their best and those who needed encouragement and special treatment. Like Rupp, Hall preferred the former type and insisted that players with sensitive egos either adjust to his hard-driving style of coaching or leave. Over

More fast and furious Wildcat action. *Above left,* Melvin Turpin muscles the ball in over an Alabama defender. *Right,* Derrick Hord leaps high against Georgia while Charles Hurt (44) moves into position for a possible rebound.

the years many talented players left while many others who decided to stick it out at UK simply shriveled up inside and never played up to their abilities. Players and journalists I talked with agreed that Derrick Hord was a player who needed encouragement and sensitive treatment. But as sportswriter Mark Bradley of the *Herald-Leader* observed in an interview, that was not Hall's style.

Derrick Hord was one of five very talented high school stars who arrived on the Lexington campus at the start of the 1979/80 season. With recruiting restrictions finally removed by the NCAA, Joe Hall enjoyed a bountiful harvest. In addition to the smooth-shooting Hord, who was generally considered the best basketball player ever from the state of Tennessee, Hall signed to national letters of intent 7'1" Sam Bowie, outstanding guard prospect Dirk Minniefield, and high school All-American forwards Charles Hurt and Tom Heitz. The Wildcats just missed signing the most highly regarded of all the college prospects, 7'4" Ralph Sampson, when he chose the University of Virginia over UK, his other final choice, in or-

der to be closer to his family. Even without Sampson, the future looked bright for Hall and the Big Blue.

In the following seasons, Hall added several more blue-chip athletes to the UK roster. The 1980/81 season brought, in addition to 6'11" center Melvin Turpin, Indiana's high school "Mr. Basketball," Jim Master, a guard with an excellent shooting touch; 6'9" forward Bret Bearup from Long Island; and 5'11" Dicky Beal, a lightning-quick guard with exceptional jumping ability. Forward Troy McKinley and guard Mike Ballenger arrived for the 1981/82 season and were joined the following season by forwards Kenny Walker, Georgia high school player of the year, and Todd May, Kentucky's "Mr. Basketball," as well as Indiana's "Mr. Basketball," guard Roger Harden. Ballenger and May subsequently left UK, Ballenger to Western Kentucky while May transferred during his freshman season to Wake Forest and later moved to Pikeville College. In the spring of 1983, Hall signed four more excellent prospects—6'7 1/2" forward Winston Bennett of Louisville Male High School,

Kentucky's "Mr. Basketball"; 6'3" guard James Blackmon of Marion, Indiana; 6'3" Laurel County guard Paul Andrews; and Vince Sanford, a 6'5" swingman from Lexington's Lafayette High School.

A new method of recruiting emerged in the late 1970s and early 1980s, and Hall was fully as effective in its practice as Adolph Rupp was in the system used in the 1940s. Although recruiters still spent a great deal of time travelling around the country watching high school games and visiting prospects and their families, the key to locating and capturing the top players, the "Blue Chippers," to use Al McGuire's very descriptive term, was the summer basketball camp. While most summer camps stressed instruction in the fundamentals of basketball, the more prestigious ones, like Five-Star, Sportsworld's Superstar, and B/C Basketball Camp, offered competition, pure and simple. In the July 17, 1983, issue of the *Herald-Leader,* sportswriter Mike Fields reported on a visit to the B/C camp, located in Rensselaer, Indiana. Director Bill Cronauer, who along with partner Bill Bolton ran B/C, touted B/C as a "superstars" camp which stressed "saturation basketball" from morning until evening for a solid week. The Rensselaer camp attracted more than 460 young hopefuls, each paying $220 to attend. Part of the attraction was the opportunity to test one's talent against high-level competition. Undoubtedly of much greater importance is the presence of more than 300 college coaches. "One observer," Fields noted, "compared the

B/C Camp to a horse sale, right down to the players wearing hip numbers as identification. The college coaches, strictly prohibited by NCAA rules from making any contact with campers, are the buyers in the scenario," the reporter continued. "They consult player catalogs, which are sold at the door for $10 a clip. The coaches don't bid on the players, but they do evaluate them and decide whether to ante up scholarships." The college coaches, Fields learned, certainly benefitted from this congregation of basketball talent. Instead of spending months crisscrossing the nation in search of prospects, the coaches could book a motel room in Rensselaer for a week and evaluate hundreds of kids." Bolton and Cronauer also held two camps in Milledgeville, Georgia, and one in Bowie, Maryland. In a given summer they would attract about 1,300 players and almost as many coaches.

Incoming UK freshman forward Winston Bennett underscored the importance of summer camps for high school players in a July 1983 interview, acknowledging that he gained "a lot of valuable experience from the summer camps." Tagged a can't-miss prospect while still a ninth grader, the 6'7 1/2" Louisville native maintained that "the opportunity to play against some of the best players in the United States really helped me a lot to improve my game. When you go up against guys who are bigger and stronger than you are it makes you either get stronger or learn techniques to overcome their advantages."

The summer basketball camp has become an important scouting and recruiting method. Here, Jack Givens instructs campers in UK's Seaton Center.

Chuck Verderber's rebound helped UK to an 86-80 victory over Notre Dame on December 29, 1979.

In addition to the camps run by talent scouts like Bolton and Cronauer, many coaches, including Joe Hall, offered their own camps. The Joe B. Hall Wildcat Basketball Summer Camp attracted the cream of the high school basketball crop. This offered Hall and his staff a marvelous opportunity to observe the best talent available competing against one another every day for a week. In many respects this was an even more valuable opportunity to judge ability than the tryouts Rupp used so effectively in the 1940s to build his great teams.

The camps were not, and still are not, the end-all of recruiting, but they are invaluable for pinpointing the most likely prospects for intensive recruiting before the start of their senior year in high school. As Leonard

Hamilton noted in an interview, "Recruiting is a year-round job," but the various summer camps are crucial "for evaluating talent." This is still true.

The UK coaching staff did an excellent job of "evaluating talent" in preparation for the 1979/80 season. Going into the season the Big Blue appeared to have the same mixture of talented and battle-tested veterans and brilliant freshmen that propelled the 1975 team to the NCAA finals. The Wildcats started the season with six returning lettermen (the seventh, sophomore Clarence Tillman, left school in October), five freshmen, and walk-on guards Chris Gettelfinger and Bo Lanter, who won scholarships through hard work and solid performance in practice and occasional game appearances. The veterans included forwards Fred Cowan, Chuck Verderber, and LaVon Williams and guards Kyle Macy, Jay Shidler, and Dwight Anderson. Macy was the brains of the team while Anderson was the catalyst.

Unfortunately Anderson also proved to be a disruptive influence. Before the December 29 game with Notre Dame, Anderson, Sam Bowie, and Dirk Minniefield were caught violating team rules and were disciplined. According to a team press release, Anderson decided to leave the team for, as Hall put it, "personal reasons," while Bowie, who although only a freshman was the team's starting center, and Minniefield, a substitute guard at the time, were suspended for the Notre Dame game "for violation of well-established training rules." The coaching staff never divulged the real reasons for Anderson's departure, despite heavy pressure from D.G. FitzMaurice of the *Herald-Leader,* Billy Reed, and other sportswriters. In an article in the December 30 *Herald-Leader* FitzMaurice maintained that as "Richard Nixon had his Watergate" so too did Joe Hall "have a Wildcatgate on his hands." The reason for the accusation was Hall's refusal to confirm or deny a report made by Lexington television sports director Tom Hammond that Anderson was discovered with a "controlled substance, a narcotic," that is, marijuana, in his possession. "It is time," FitzMaurice stated with indignation, "for Joe Hall to level with the fans, and to quit playing cute word games with the press. It's time for Coach Hall to set the record straight. It's time for the complete truth to emerge. Anything less is an insult to Kentucky fans everywhere."

Hall did not respond, however, and the campaign to pressure him into "setting the record straight" eventually died because it finally became clear that Hall would not budge. The incident had the unfortunate result of increasing the already existing antagonism between the press and UK's coaching staff. Hall, for his

part, felt the press should concentrate on the team's on-court performance which, considering the lack of experienced players, was surprisingly good in 1980. After Anderson's departure in December 1979, UK was down to five scholarship players. Through much of the rest of the season the Big Blue started two freshmen—Bowie and Minniefield—along with veterans Cowan, Williams, and Macy.

After a season-opening loss to Duke in overtime, 82-76, in the 1979 Hall of Fame Game in Springfield, Massachusetts, the Wildcats played brilliant ball throughout December, culminating an eleven-game winning streak with an 86-80 victory over Notre Dame on December 29 in Louisville. In the nationally televised game the Cats, playing without the suspended Anderson, Bowie, and Minniefield, defeated a strong Fighting Irish team that entered the contest with a 6-0 record and a number three ranking in the national polls. The Big Blue faltered in January—the "January Swoon," as the press termed what seemed to be an annual occurrence for Hall's teams—losing three of ten conference matches. UK rebounded in February to win nine straight games and the regular-season SEC championship for the thirty-second time in the league's history. The Cats were knocked out of the SEC tournament in Birmingham by an inspired LSU team but, as regular-season champions, were placed in the NCAA Mideast Regionals with games scheduled for Bowling Green and Lexington. With the advantage of playing before the home crowds the Big Blue seemed a shoo-in as regional champions. After a strong performance against Florida State the Cats returned home to Rupp Arena for a return match with Duke. But even with the full support of their loyal fans, the Big Blue had no more luck in this game than in the Hall of Fame game. Once again UK lost, this time by one point, 55-54, when Macy missed a long jump shot at the buzzer. "It was," Bo Lanter maintains, "the only key shot I can recall Kyle missing in the time I was at UK. You could always depend on Kyle to hit the pressure shot or free throw. Even on that one [Duke guard] Vince Taylor admitted after the game that he had hit Kyle." With the loss to Duke, Kyle Macy's brilliant career at UK came to an end. Macy noted in an interview "with a break here or there we could have won the Duke game and made it to the Final Four, and with a young team. Even with the loss, though, it was a very good season."

With Macy gone, a lot of responsibility fell to Dirk Minniefield in the 1980/81 season, especially since his running mate through much of the season was converted forward Derrick Hord. Backups included very promising freshman prospects Jim Master and Dicky Beal as

Jim Master demonstrates his impeccable free throw technique.

well as junior Bo Lanter and senior Chris Gettelfinger. Hord never did fully adjust to the guard position and the following season was moved back to forward, his natural position. Hord's conversion to guard was made necessary in part by the lack of experienced players at that position. Another factor was the abundance of talent available at forward where, in addition to starters Fred Cowan, a senior, and sophomore Charles Hurt, the Cats had team captain Chuck Verderber and 6'9" freshman Bret Bearup. At center UK had even more talent available with Sam Bowie, who would become an All-American that season as a sophomore, and freshman Melvin Turpin, who proved to be a capable backup.

The Big Blue lost only four regular-season games in 1980/81, but three of these defeats were to SEC teams, thus denying UK its thirty-third SEC championship, at least for a year. The Wildcats were nevertheless invited to the NCAA Mideast Regionals at Tuscaloosa, where they played small, quick Alabama-Birmingham for the second time in the season. The Big Blue had defeated Alabama-Birmingham in the championship game of the UKIT at Rupp Arena in December, but in the return match UK fell short by seven points, 69-62. The ground-

New York native Bret Bearup scores as the Cats top Indiana on December 3, 1983. James Blackmon is no. 10.

work for a very successful 1981/82 season, and even for an NCAA title, seemed to be laid, however. UK would lose only Fred Cowan and Chris Gettelfinger through graduation. Back would be UK's most experienced team since the 1978 national champions. But then disaster struck.

Before the start of the 1981/82 season Joe Hall announced that All-American and twice All-SEC center Sam Bowie was suffering from a small, incomplete fracture of his left tibia, or shin bone. Bowie missed the entire season, a loss that dealt a crippling blow to UK's title hopes. In an interview Bo Lanter maintained that "when you have a player like Bowie you have a franchise. I feel it was a big step for the UK program to get a player like Bowie. So his loss was a very serious blow. For one thing not having him in the middle hurt

Minniefield. With Bowie out, Dirk, even though he is a great athlete, just had to do too much. "

Dirk Minniefield also stressed Bowie's importance. "When we lost Sam," he stated in an interview, "we definitely lost our inside punch because all of a sudden we were a team without a proven inside player. Now Melvin [Turpin], who had little playing experience, had to step in and try to take over. This meant the guards had to make a big adjustment. I had to take on more of a scoring load early in the season, but once Melvin got settled in we went more to an inside-oriented style of play." The Wildcats had to adjust to the loss of Bowie, and to a great extent they did.

UK's resilience and overall talent is evident from the fact that the team did not fold, despite the unexpected loss of its leading scorer and rebounder and the heart of its man-to-man defense. Bowie's place in the starting lineup was taken by untried sophomore Melvin Turpin, who led the team in rebounding and blocked shots and was third in scoring. The team's leading scorer in 1982 was Derrick Hord, who returned to his familiar forward position. Senior Chuck Verderber usually started at the other forward position although Charles Hurt started eight games and was generally the first player off the bench in the other games. Dirk Minniefield, the team's assist leader, returned as playmaking guard while sophomore Jim Master, an outstanding outside shooter, started twenty-nine of UK's thirty games in 1981/82. The Big Blue proved to have a deep and talented bench even without Bret Bearup, a 6'9" 230-pound power forward who chose to redshirt in 1982 after playing in twenty-six of UK's twenty-eight games in his freshman season. In addition to Hurt, reserves included Tom Heitz, who had redshirted in 1981, and freshman Troy McKinley in the front court, while speedy sophomore Dicky Beal, freshman Mike Ballenger, and senior Bo Lanter contributed at guard.

UK completed the 1981/82 season with an overall record of 22-8, including 13-5 in regular SEC play and 2-1 in the postseason conference tournament. The SEC co-champion Wildcats travelled to Nashville and an all but assured NCAA tournament confrontation with the University of Louisville, a game the media had for months been clamoring for. Even the *Sporting News* on December 5, 1981, featured a cover story on "The Bitter Fight for Kentucky" between UK and the Louisville Cardinals and an eagerly anticipated "Louisville-Kentucky matchup in March." The NCAA selection committee obliged by placing the Wildcats and Cardinals in the same regional.

All that stood in the way of "the game" was for the

Big Blue to defeat lightly regarded Ohio Valley champion Middle Tennessee. But instead of going on to meet Louisville for the championship of Kentucky and advancing to the NCAA Final Four, the Wildcats suffered a humiliating 50-44 defeat. Derrick Hord admitted in an interview that "I'd be lying if I said we weren't looking ahead but we didn't take Middle Tennessee for granted. It was just one of those nights where we couldn't do anything right and they couldn't do anything wrong. They were really pumped up because they wanted to knock off Kentucky and we couldn't get our shots to fall. I know I was something like two for sixteen and normally I'm a 50 percent shooter. So they outscored us and that's the name of the game." Middle Tennessee was a small, quick team and Bo Lanter noted that UK adjusted its game to combat Middle Tennessee's quickness "rather than having them adjust to our height." Lanter compared the Middle Tennessee game with the 1981 NCAA tournament loss to Alabama-Birmingham. "Alabama-Birmingham had a better team than we thought they had and they played extremely well against us and I give them a lot of credit. I also give Middle Tennessee credit but I just feel like the loss to Middle Tennessee was more of a fluke than the one to Alabama-Birmingham was. We just plain old didn't play them," he acknowledged. "We made a lot of mistakes, stupid mistakes. It really

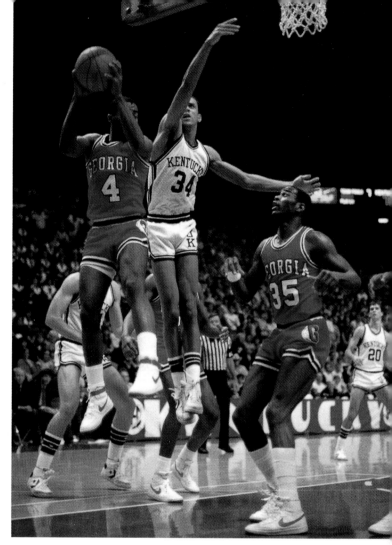

Above, Kenny Walker plays rock-ribbed defense against Georgia, while guard Jim Master waits in the background.

Left, Dicky Beal (5'11") lays the ball up as UK closes its 1983/84 regular season with a victory over LSU. Beal's inspired playing sparked the Cats to the SEC championship.

killed me because it was my last game at UK. I wanted a national championship so bad and that was the end. I'll never forget the feeling that night. I was so upset I cried like a baby after the game." For departing seniors Lanter and Verderber that was the end of their dream of winning a national championship. For the returning members of the team, the 1982/83 season would prove equally frustrating.

UK had a winning season in 1982/83, won the SEC championship, and played in the NCAA tournament. By normal standards that should qualify as a successful season. But for Wildcat fans and for the press it was *not* a successful season for two reasons: the Big Blue lost to

The 1982/83 season was disappointing for many, including senior Derrick Hord, who came under intense criticism from Hall and the local press when his game began to deteriorate at midseason.

Louisville and that defeat knocked the team out of contention for UK's sixth NCAA championship. Without exception, the players and coaches interviewed saw the 1982/83 season in a more favorable light. They felt the team overcame problems and adversities to end the season on a positive note. Dirk Minniefield maintained that what stood out in his mind about his senior year was "the way the team put aside all the outside distractions, the newspapers and all, and came together and played great down the stretch. I thought that by the end of the year we got to be a total team. All things considered," Minniefield observed, "we went pretty far. In fact, we probably went a lot farther than some people thought we could go." To Minniefield, the Louisville game "was great from all aspects. I think that once the game started we were more than they expected. They came back and beat us but that's what you expect a great team to do."

For Derrick Hord, 1982/83 was "an up-and-down season." "Jim [Master], Melvin [Turpin], and Dirk [Minniefield] and the rest of the guys really looked great," Hord acknowledged in a July 1983 interview. During the previous season the Bristol, Tennessee, native had led the Cats in scoring with a 16.3 points per game average. At the end of that season Hord was named All-SEC and honorable mention All-American. On the basis of his tremendous potential and his performance in 1981/82, a lot was expected of him in his senior year. Ironically, Hord "had the best opening season since I got here," but for reasons

he cannot fully understand his play soon became inconsistent. "There I was, averaging nearly seventeen points and getting about thirty minutes a game" during the preceding season "and I came into the latter part of the season this year and the coaches are looking around me to put somebody else in. They don't want to put me in. It does something to your confidence. It's a learning experience anyway," he noted grimly.

When Hord's game started falling apart, Hall added to his inner anguish by ripping him apart in practice, during and after games, and in the press. Although the player recognized that an integral part of Hall's coaching philosophy was picking on his players, especially seniors who seemed not to be performing up to their potential, in order to force them to play better, it apparently had the opposite effect on Hord. A very intelligent, thoughtful, and sensitive young man, Hord reacted by withdrawing even further within himself. He acknowledged that during the season "a lot of people" had told him that he let "a lot of things bother me that I probably should have ignored but," he noted, "that's the way I am. I'm usually a sensitive person in that respect and I like to perform for somebody who thinks I can do the job. If I go into the game and feel that they don't think I can do the job then I'm thinking, Why did they put me in?" In addition, he continued, Kenny Walker "was having a great freshman year and he [Hall] knew that he could put Kenny in and Kenny would excite the crowd and get the team going while I'm kind of a silent player. In my junior year I'd go out there and people wouldn't know I was there. I'd usually get the job done pretty well without a lot of excitement." What this meant was that when things went wrong for Hord, Hall apparently felt there was no reason for keeping him in the game.

Hord emphasized that he understood Hall's motivation in openly criticizing his play and that of others on the team. He maintained that "all of us really knew that it wasn't personal." But the treatment accorded coaches and players in the media, especially in the local press, was something he could not comprehend. "The Louisville papers like to jump on Coach Hall but the Lexington papers jump on everybody. 'Piranha Press,' that's what I call them. They build you up to break you down. Not all the reporters though, just a couple." Apparently other members of the team felt the same way because, Hord maintained, "there was a time" during the middle of the season "when we just didn't go in and talk with the press." It would begin early in the season, he went on. "They'd start talking 'January slump' in October when we had press conferences. They'd bring on a lot of stuff. I know that is part of the game, but

nowhere else in our conference do they write stories like they do here."

Despite the problems, Hord stated emphatically that if he had it to do all over he definitely would come to UK. "I would probably do things a lot differently but it has been a great experience."

Derrick Hord undoubtedly received and accepted more blame than he deserved for UK's failure to fulfill its promise during the four years he was on the team. The major problem with the team in that period, maintained Jack Givens in an August 1983 interview, was a lack of consistency, especially after the loss of Sam Bowie. "All the guys looked super in some games," Givens noted, "but in others they wouldn't be looking for their shots. It only takes a few bad games to get your confidence down and you start wondering whether you can do it at all." Givens, who observed the team at close range as a television commentator for UK home games, continued his description. "It seemed as though each member of the team was waiting for someone else to come out and do things. After Sam, who was their leader, was lost they never did establish another leader. No one else played as consistently, both on offense and defense, as Sam did." Givens thought Dicky Beal "might have become the leader if he had stayed healthy. When he was in the game you could see the difference in the team. Everyone was more alert and involved with Dicky in there."

Others, including sportswriters and some players, believed that the loss of Assistant Coach Dick Parsons after the 1980 season was a major factor in UK's problems in the following years. Parsons left because of a change in NCAA regulations which reduced the size of coaching staffs. Hall wanted all of his coaches to help with recruiting, something Parsons reportedly no longer enjoyed. *Courier-Journal* veteran sportswriter Earl Cox regarded the departure of Parsons as a great loss for the Wildcat program. "The little guy with the quiet demeanor," Cox wrote on January 18, 1983, "had a strong influence on Hall. He was the one who tugged at Hall's coat to keep him away from referees. He was the one who soothed players' feelings after tongue-lashings by Hall. Joe listened to Dicky's suggestions. They were a team, on and off the floor, fishing buddies even." One of the players with whom I talked also lamented the loss of Parsons. "We all hated to see Coach Parsons go," he maintained. "Coach Parsons was close to the players and we all liked him a lot. He also played an important part in the preparation for games and coaching during the games. We've all missed him since he left."

The Wildcats finished the 1982/83 season with a 23-8 record. Six of the losses were suffered within the tough

Joe Hall, Dirk Minniefield, Derrick Hord, and Charles Hurt in Lexington's Triangle Park.

and highly competitive SEC. The Big Blue avenged an early season loss to Indiana with a 64-59 victory in the semifinals of the NCAA Mideast Regionals in Knoxville to set up the long-awaited confrontation with Louisville on March 26. The eagerly anticipated "Dream Game" was the first meeting between the two schools in twenty-four years. Although UK lost in overtime, 80-68, it was a more hotly contested and well-played game than the final score might indicate. Jack Givens also acknowledged that the Wildcats played a much stronger game than he had expected. "I really expected Louisville to win by about eight in regulation time. I thought the Louisville forwards would pretty much have their own way but Derrick started out hot and Charles [Hurt] had a good game. I felt Kenny would give UK strength coming off the bench, and I expected Melvin to have a great game. And he did. Jim Master played just super. He had a much better all around game than I expected.

You just can't do anything about an overtime period if you start off bad. That five-minute overtime period feels awful short when you get four or five points behind right away. But I thought UK overall played a good game."

Minniefield and the other players had good feelings about the Louisville game. "I knew they had a great team," Minniefield said about the Cardinals, "but I think we were more than they expected. I don't feel Louisville expected us to play as well as we did." In an interview with Billy Reed printed in the July 20, 1983, *Courier-Journal,* Jim Master recalled that by the Louisville game UK had developed into "a great team" that was "only a play or two from going to the Final Four. That's the first year we've done that since I've been at Kentucky. It was positive—very positive." Sportswriters also expressed great enthusiasm over the game. Noting that the final score was deceiving, one reporter observed that "the

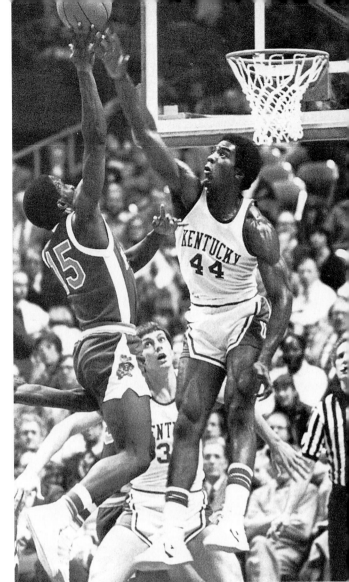

Right, Charles Hurt, a high school All-American, was a top-notch rebounder and a defensive player who never showed his good shooting touch while at UK. Behind him is Tom Heitz (33). *Below,* Fred Cowan dodges the Vanderbilt defense.

game had everything, steals, dunks, comebacks; it was truly a basketball fan's 'Dream Game.'"

In the aftermath of the March 26 "Dream Game," Louisville and Lexington sportswriters continued their demands for an annual meeting between the two schools. Joe Hall, for his part, maintained his adamant opposition to regular-season games with state schools. Cliff Hagan, as UK athletics director, had fully supported Hall's position on this issue. But as university officials, trustees, a growing number of fans, and even the governor indicated a growing interest in—or at least, a willingness to discuss—the possibility of a UK-U of L series, Hagan altered his position. According to reporter Jerry Tipton in an April 3, 1983, *Herald-Leader* article, "Hagan and others in the UK hierarchy" who supported Hall and his policy in the past had by this time "lessened that support." Hagan's position, as quoted by

Tipton, now was that "if the coach wants to play, we'll play." According to Hagan, "It's always the coaches who decide whom they want to play, where they want to play and if they're going to play." Referring specifically to Hall, he said, "He's continuing a practice. If he wanted to change it, I'm sure we'd change it." Thus very clearly the point was made that a major, perhaps the only, stumbling block remaining in the way of the series was Joe B. Hall.

Just a couple of days later the UK Board of Trustees underlined Hall's growing isolation on the issue by voting that the Athletics Board formally consider a request for the Wildcat basketball team to schedule games with other state schools, especially the University of Louisville. The Athletics Board met on April 14. On the eve of the meeting Hall reiterated his position in an exclusive front-page article published in the university newspaper, the *Kentucky Kernel*. According *to Kernel* sports editor Mickey Patterson, the UK coach maintained that the policy he inherited was "evidently initiated for a reason." In addition, Hall went on, "the policy or tradition of not playing state schools has been very good to the University of Kentucky." Among other things, it has confirmed UK's status within the state "with border-to-border support," has made and maintained the Wildcats "as a national power," and has even brought "international prominence." If, Hall continued, "I felt that we would be benefitted by playing state schools I would have scheduled them a long time ago, but from where I sit it's

never been explained to me how it would help our program here at Kentucky to play state schools, and all the arguments for playing games have not been arguments that would be beneficial to the University of Kentucky." Hall blamed "the state's media" for misinforming the public about the need for and benefits to be gained from playing U of L and other state schools. "I think it's a crusade by the *Courier-Journal*," Hall bluntly stated, "to bring about a schedule between Louisville and Kentucky." Furthermore, "I think it's definitely a desire of the University of Louisville to be on our schedule and our local [Lexington] press has picked it up as a way to sell newspapers, and I think once the fire dies down, the interest will die down." That prediction proved almost immediately to be inaccurate.

The day after Hall's interview appeared in the *Kernel*, the Athletics Board convened to discuss the question and Hall made a final bid for support. When the meeting opened he handed each board member a copy of a printed statement opposing the proposal before the body. He then spoke to the board, asking the members to ignore "external pressures that are not in the best interest of the University of Kentucky and its basketball program" and allow him to maintain the practice started by his predecessor, Adolph Rupp, "of not playing state schools during the regular season." Hall then left the meeting to allow board members to analyze the proposal and his statement.

Joe Hall and his staff plot strategy during a 1983/84 game: left to right, Lake Kelly, Hall, Leonard Hamilton, and Jim Hatfield.

After a spirited and wide-ranging debate the board voted 12-6 to ask Hagan and Hall to make an exception to long-standing practice and "ascertain if mutually acceptable terms and conditions" existed for a UK-U of L game. The resolution directed the negotiators to be sure that "such negotiations should not only be mutually acceptable to the parties but also should result in no financial loss to either program."

After nearly two months of negotiations between Hagan and U of L Athletics Director Bill Olsen the fans got their wish. Hagan and Olsen finally agreed on a four-year pact which would alternate games between Lexington and Louisville, with the first game at Rupp Arena.

Entering the 1983/84 season, UK possessed a team that was awesome, at least on paper. Sam Bowie, "the franchise," was back after two seasons of injuries and was joined in the front court by Kenny Walker, Bret Bearup, Tom Heitz, Troy McKinley, and freshman Winston Bennett. Melvin Turpin, a potential All-American, was back at center for his senior season, while the guards included sharpshooting Jim Master, Dicky Beal, and Roger Harden, as well as freshmen James Blackmon and Paul Andrews.

Helping to coach this group were associate coach and master recruiter Leonard Hamilton and two newcomers, Lake Kelly and Jim Hatfield. Both Kelly and Hatfield brought to their new jobs considerable experience as head coaches on the major college level, Kelly at Austin Peay and Oral Roberts, and Hatfield at Mississippi State, Southwestern Louisiana, and Hardin-Simmons, where he also served as athletics director. According to sportswriter Jerry Tipton, Hall was pleased with his coaches, both old and new. Writing in the December 1, 1983, *Herald-Leader*, Tipton maintained that "Hall has gone on record as saying this year's staff is the best he has worked with." Although all the coaches made contributions in practice, during games, and in recruiting, there was a division of labor. Kelly was assigned primary responsibility for overseeing defense, and Hatfield concentrated on the UK offense and helped with recruiting, while Hamilton continued to add to his reputation as one of college basketball's outstanding recruiters. There was no question, however, that Hall was boss. As Kelly emphasized to Tipton, Hall is "the hammer. He makes it [the program] go."

The Wildcats were a talented and deep squad, one apparently capable of getting to the NCAA championship game in Seattle, but only if a number of questions could be resolved. The most important was whether Sam Bowie and Dicky Beal, the keys to a successful season,

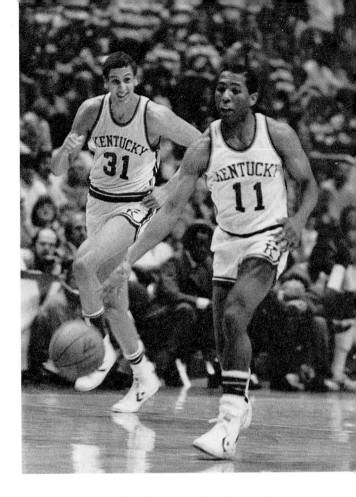

The prospect of reaching the 1984 NCAA finals in Seattle depended heavily on whether Sam Bowie (31) and Dicky Beal (11) could snap back from serious injuries. Bowie had been sidelined for two seasons with a shinbone stress fracture; Beal had had knee surgery.

could come back from serious injuries. Bowie, the former All-American, had not played for two seasons because of a stress fracture of his left shinbone, while Beal had undergone three arthroscopic knee operations as well as enduring an assortment of other injuries during his first three years at UK. At the beginning of the 1983/84 season Beal was still in pain from the latest surgery, and serious doubts were expressed by Hall and others as to whether he would ever again play for UK.

Discussing his problems at a November 24 press conference, just three days before the Wildcats would open the regular season against Louisville, Joe Hall ruefully observed: "I'm optimistic about the future but concerned about the present." The concern was based in large part on the play of Bowie and Beal in UK's 73-55 victory over the Netherlands National Team in an exhibition game in Rupp Arena on November 22. Bowie had appeared to be confused, tentative, and tired through much of that con-

test, while Beal, whom Hall was counting on to start at point guard, was able to play only four minutes.

Adding to Hall's worries were the back spasms that sophomore forward Kenny Walker began to suffer toward the end of the exhibition game. This ailment continued to plague Walker in the following weeks, hampering his practice time and limiting his performance during games, while various therapies were tried. Doctors finally settled on the use of stretching exercises and whirlpool treatments. The reason for this approach, Hall reported to the press on December 9, was that "the doctors think his muscles are so tight that they never relax. They're like rocks." This diagnosis evidently was correct because soon after the treatments were begun Walker returned to full effectiveness. Bowie and Beal also finally overcame the effects of their injuries and inactivity, and by the last third of the season the Wildcats were at full strength.

At the beginning of the season, however, with serious questions about the health and effectiveness of three of UK's five starters, the Wildcat bench became increasingly important. There was good reserve strength on the front line, with 6'9" senior Tom Heitz, 6'9" junior Bret Bearup, and 6'6" junior Troy McKinley available, along with highly touted freshman Winston Bennett, a powerfully built 6'7" Louisville native. The backcourt replacements were less numerous but might prove to be talented. In the absence of Dicky Beal, who had started only eight games during his first three years at UK, the Big Blue would have to depend on sophomore Roger Harden to direct the offense. The only other guards on the squad were untested freshmen James Blackmon and Paul Andrews. Help arrived in midseason when 5'5" (some claimed he was really 5'2") Lexington native Leroy Byrd, a transfer from the University of Nevada at Las Vegas, joined the team in time to take part in a 64-40 blowout of a strong Georgia team on January 29, 1984, at Rupp Arena. The shortage of players at guard never really became a problem. Harden filled in admirably for Beal at point guard while the quick and multitalented Blackmon contributed at both point guard and shooting guard throughout the season.

The season opener, a November 26 game with Louisville, was billed as "the Battle of the Blue Grass." It more than lived up to its billing—at least for Wildcat partisans, for whom it was a glorious evening. A UK victory was generally anticipated, but the margin of victory, twenty-one points, was not. With Harden starting his first college game and Bowie his first since the 1980/81 season, the Big Blue began the game tight and uncertain but quickly recovered their composure. UK led by

as many as three points four times early in the game (the last time at 12-9) but, as *Herald-Leader* sportswriter Jerry Tipton observed, "Louisville seemed to come unglued because of Kentucky's defensive pressure." The Cardinals seemed confused by Hall's decision to play man-to-man defense from the opening tipoff. Turpin and Bowie, the "Twin Towers," intimidated the Cards inside, while veteran guards Lancaster Gordon and Milt Wagner, U of L's top scorers, were unable to hit their outside shots. But the game's turning point came near the end of the first half when James Blackmon, playing in his first college game, came up with two steals in the space of ten seconds and converted both into baskets. Such plays were supposed to be a U of L, not a UK, trademark. The Cards never got over the shock. During the second half the Cats led by as many as twenty-nine points, and during his postgame press conference Hall expressed his pleasure at the ease with which UK had won the contest.

With the victory over Louisville the Wildcats em-

Freshman guard James Blackmon (10) stunned the U of L Cardinals with two quick steals near the end of the first half. Louisville never recovered, and the Cats went on to win "the Battle of the Blue Grass" 65-44 on November 26, 1983. Jim Master is no. 20.

barked on what their supporters and the press expected to be the "Road to Seattle" and a sixth NCAA title. The euphoria of the Louisville victory lasted a week—until UK's December 3 meeting with an inexperienced and supposedly outmanned Indiana Hoosier team. Coach Bobby Knight's strategy exposed the Wildcats' lack of team quickness (especially in Beal's absence) and questionable outside game. Even Jim Master, the team's most dependable outside shooter, had trouble hitting his twenty-footers when guarded closely. UK entered the game as seventeen-point favorites, but the Hoosiers, led by freshmen Marty Simmons and Steve Alford and junior Uwe Blab, a 7'2" native of West Germany, fought their taller and more experienced opponents to a standstill throughout the first half, which ended with IU ahead 32-31.

Indiana continued to frustrate the Cats in the second half until, with seven minutes left in the game, Hall turned to freshman guard James Blackmon, who proved to make the difference, as he would in UK's December 24 meeting with Illinois. In the closing minutes of both games the Big Blue cleared one side and let the Marion, Indiana, native go one-on-one. The result in both games was victory for the Wildcats. After the Indiana game, Hall confided to the press that "Blackmon was super. He was the only guy we had who played." Blackmon's offensive play began to tail off in January but he made valuable contributions in a number of early season games and his speed and quickness helped to break the press throughout the season.

UK swept through its December intersectional schedule with victories over Kansas, Wyoming, Brigham Young (to capture the UK Invitational Tournament championship), Cincinnati, Illinois, and Purdue, for a perfect 8-0 record and high hopes and great expectations for the upcoming SEC schedule. The Wildcats

Kenny Walker battles for a rebound in the November 26, 1983, UK-U of L game. UK's 65-44 victory avenged the Cats' defeat by the Cardinals at the close of the previous season.

A triumphant trio of Wildcats celebrate UK's win over U of L at Rupp Arena. Left to right, Jim Master, Melvin Turpin, and Sam Bowie. For Bowie it was the first regular-season game in two years.

started off the "second season," against conference opponents, with another strong showing by Blackmon in his first starting assignment for UK against Mississippi. The Big Blue won the January 2 game at Rupp Arena, 68-55, without Jim Master who, along with Troy McKinley, had violated a team curfew and been benched by Hall.

Master returned to the starting lineup in the next game, against LSU in Baton Rouge on January 7, but he soon seemed to lose his shooting eye, hitting four of ten shots against LSU, four of twelve against Mississippi State, and one of five against Auburn, and missing all four shots taken in the January 22 game against Houston. Although Master began to regain his touch in February, he was unable to regain the shooting form of his previous seasons, and UK's overall play suffered as a result. No one else on the team seemed able to hit the outside jumper consistently to loosen up an opponent's defense and open up the inside for Walker and the "Twin Towers." Fortunately Turpin's shooting throughout the season, with the exception of games against Auburn and Georgetown, was exceptional. In UK's 96-80 trouncing of LSU, for example, Turpin hit fifteen of seventeen field goal attempts as well as five free throws, for a total of thirty-five points. In the words of D.G. FitzMaurice, Turpin "played like an All-Cosmos pick, or maybe better."

Early in the season Bowie shot poorly but compensated with excellent passing, strong rebounding, and solid man-to-man defense. As the season progressed he also regained his shooting eye, and while he never returned to the All-American form of his sophomore season, he did come close. Although Kenny Walker had to play in the long shadow of the "Twin Towers," he was a consistent and valuable contributor on both offense and defense and was clearly a star of the future.

Going into their January 13 meeting with Auburn the Wildcats were riding a thirteen-game winning streak. To many they seemed destined to complete the season with a perfect record as well as the national championship. Although Hall warned that such statements were premature, few listened, especially when it became known that some members of the team had stated, within earshot of the press, that the 1983/84 squad was probably the greatest team in college basketball history. Reality, in the chubby but hugely talented body of Charles Barkley, rudely interrupted such dreams and returned the Cats and their followers to reality. FitzMaurice observed in the January 14 *Herald-Leader* that "it took a 272 pound wrecking ball, but the Twin Towers were finally razed here [at Auburn] last night."

Still recovering from a back injury that limited his play early in the season, Barkley did not even start for the Tigers against UK. Coming off the bench, the "Round Mound of Rebound" (one of Barkley's many nicknames) played thirty minutes, scored twenty-one points, and grabbed ten rebounds as Auburn pulled an 82-63 upset to replace UK atop the SEC standings. The stunning nineteen-point defeat was devastating for the Cats, but the worst was to come four days later in Gainesville, when lightly regarded Florida outclassed the Big Blue and won 69-57. The Gators employed a game plan that was being used increasingly against UK. Florida sagged in on defense and forced the Wildcats to take, and hit, the outside shot. The result, sportswriter Bill Weronka wrote in the *Courier-Journal,* was that "the Gators sagged and so did UK's outside shooting, just as it has the last three games. And this time the inside game wasn't any help."

Bruised and demoralized by the road trip to Auburn and Gainesville, the Wildcats returned home, where they rebounded to win all four games convincingly. They roared past Vanderbilt, 67-46; Houston, 74-67; Georgia, 64-40; and Tennessee, 93-74. The Big Blue appeared to have regained their momentum. The victory over Houston was especially sweet. The January 22 game, played on "Super Sunday" on national television

Point guard Roger Harden bounces the ball past a Purdue defender on December 28, 1983. Harden was starting guard through much of the 1983/84 season until Dicky Beal recovered from surgery and returned to play.

Freshman Winston Bennett goes up on a shot as UK downs Houston 74-67 on January 22, 1984. Melvin Turpin (54) was another powerhouse in the game.

inspired game and handed the visitors their third defeat of the season, all to SEC teams. UK bounced back two nights later to whip Mississippi State 77-58, but with only seven regular-season games left (all with SEC opponents) the Blue and White seemed to be in serious trouble once again.

It was obvious that something had to change to get UK back to the level of intensity and performance that had marked their play in December. Lending a note of urgency was the fact that their next game was against the Auburn Tigers and their powerful but agile center, Charles Barkley, and high-scoring forward Chuck Person. The Tigers entered the February 11 game at Rupp Arena atop the SEC standings, one game ahead of UK. Barkley played his usual strong game against Turpin, but Dicky Beal and Winston Bennett came off the bench to score seventeen points each and lead the Big Blue to an 84-64 runaway victory. Two nights later Beal again came off the bench to ignite the Cats to a hard-fought win over the tough Florida Gators, 67-65. The final ingredient was ready to be added to the UK starting team.

On February 19 against Vanderbilt in Nashville, Dicky Beal finally overcame the various injuries that had plagued him during his UK career and became the starting point guard. Later in the season Sam Bowie explained in simple but direct terms Beal's importance to the team: "Dicky puts us in another gear." Beal's style of play blended well with the usual starters—Bowie, Walker, Turpin, and Master—as well as Bennett and Blackmon, the Cats' principal substitutes. Benefitting especially from Beal's move into the starting lineup was Blackmon, who had been called on during the season to play both the point and shooting guard positions. Explaining the effect on Blackmon's play, Hall noted that "It takes a lot of pressure off him, not having the ballhandling responsibilities and not having to guard the other team's quick player." With Beal handling the ball, UK's fast break became a more potent weapon and the team was seldom bothered by the full-court press. The outside shooting also improved, in part because Bowie finally regained his shooting eye and also because Beal began to display a touch that had not been evident during his first three years of college play.

The Wildcats won four of their last five regular-season games and, with hot-shooting Sam Bowie leading the way, wrapped up their thirty-fifth SEC title with a nineteen-point victory (76-57) over Mississippi at Rupp Arena on March 1. The regular-season finale two nights later against LSU, which at the time was ranked second in the conference standings, was important only as an

just before pro football's championship game, represented a meeting between college basketball's number three ranked team (UK) and number four ranked Houston. It was also billed as a meeting of the giants—the Cougars' All-American Hakeem "the Dream" Olajuwon and UK's "Twin Towers." On this day the Wildcats had too many towers for Houston to handle.

After this strong home stand it appeared that Hall had the team back on track to win the SEC title and build the needed momentum for the league and national championships. With January and its annual slump past, UK took to the road on February 4 for a game against an Alabama team which, up to this point, had not played up to expectations. But the Tide on this day played an

opportunity for the fans to bid farewell to the departing seniors and for the Cats to build momentum for postseason competition. In both respects the evening was a success. For the Wildcat faithful it was a golden moment. They had an opportunity to relive happy memories as the five seniors—Beal, Bowie, Heitz, Master, and Turpin—were introduced, along with their parents, before the game, and then to cheer as the entire team participated in the dismemberment of a strong LSU Tiger team, 90-68.

For the first time since the revival of the SEC tournament in 1979, UK entered the postseason competition on a positive note and, for the first time in that period, won the tournament. Building on a late-season emphasis on fundamentals in practice as well as the momentum from the impressive victory over LSU, the Wildcats, led by red-hot shooting Melvin Turpin, whipped Georgia in their first tournament game, 92-79. In that contest Turpin tied the SEC tournament single-game scoring record with forty-two points and

Above, Turpin gets physical with Auburn's "Round Mound of Rebound," Charles Barkley, in a February 11, 1984, meeting. The Cats won 84-64, after losing to Auburn less than a month before. When the teams met in the SEC finals in March, UK slipped past the Tigers 51-49 with a last-second basket by Kenny Walker *(left),* a vital member of UK's brilliant front-court trio. Here, Walker contributes to the Cats' 90-68 rout of LSU on March 3, 1984.

Dicky Beal goes up for a shot against U of L in the 1984 Mideast Regionals. Beal led the Cats to a 72-67 victory in a game that was much closer than their season opener.

broke the field goal record with eighteen two-pointers. (Both records had been set by UK's Cliff Hagan in 1952.) In addition, the Wildcat center pulled down sixteen rebounds, one short of the tournament record set by Alabama's Bobby Lee Hurt in 1983. The Big Blue had a tougher time against their next opponent, Alabama, but with Dicky Beal hitting two pressure-packed free throws with three seconds to play, UK won 48-46 to set up a confrontation with Auburn for the tournament title. Despite excellent performances by Charles Barkley and Chuck Person, the Wildcats won that game at the buzzer as a last-second jump shot by Kenny Walker bounced around the rim and finally fell in. The final score was 51-49, and with the victory UK was assured of being placed in the Mideast Regionals of the NCAA, where,

assuming they won, two of their three games would be played at Rupp Arena.

The Wildcats began their quest for the NCAA title (a record-setting twenty-ninth appearance) on March 17 in Birmingham against the Cougars of Brigham Young, the first of three opponents they had defeated during the regular season that they would face in the Mideast Regionals. The others were Louisville and Illinois. In their earlier meeting, in the UKIT, Brigham Young had proved a tough and tenacious opponent until UK's superior size, speed, and strength wore the Cougars down and the Big Blue broke the game open in the second half to win by thirty-four points. Hall was determined not to give BYU a chance to dictate the pace of the game this time. With Beal leading the charge the Wildcats roared to an early 15-4 lead before BYU's use of a karate defense slowed the pace. UK adapted easily and coasted to a 93-68 victory. It was, Hall admitted in a postgame interview, "the type of game you'd like to open a tournament with." Following the surprisingly easy win over BYU the Cats returned to Lexington to prepare for a March 22 meeting at Rupp Arena with the Louisville Cardinals, UK's opponent in the opening game of the regular season.

In the days before the rematch, the Louisville players expressed their pleasure at getting a chance to redeem their pride. And redeem it they did. The game was not decided until the final thirteen seconds of play. The Cardinals got excellent performances from their guards—Lancaster Gordon with twenty-five points and Milt Wagner with twenty-three—but "time and again," Billy Reed wrote in the March 23 *Courier-Journal*, "it was the senior from Covington [Dicky Beal] who rallied the Cats when they seemed in danger of faltering." Joe Hall agreed that Beal, the shortest player on the floor, was the key: "Beal just did a super job down the stretch orchestrating for us, both offensively and defensively."

UK turned from its hard-earned 72-67 victory over the Cards to prepare for the regional championship game on March 24 against Illinois, winner in a mild upset over a strong Maryland team. Playing a bruising physical game, the underdog Illini took away the Wildcat fast break and, at least in the first half, their inside game as well. Bowie was scoreless in the first half, which was not surprising because he never got a chance to shoot the ball. Fortunately he came alive in the second half to score eleven points and grab ten of his game-high fourteen rebounds. Living up to their nickname, the Fighting Illini refused to wilt and the game was not decided until Beal, the tournament's Most Valuable Player, scored five points in the final forty-three seconds of play. The Wildcats had a

54-51 victory and their first appearance in the Final Four since 1978. But Seattle, where the 1984 NCAA finals were played, proved to be a far less satisfying experience than St. Louis had been in 1978.

The Big Blue entered what was to be their final game of the season as slight underdogs, playing against the powerful Georgetown Hoyas and their great 7' center, Patrick Ewing. The Hoyas came into their March 31 confrontation with UK with Final Four experience, having lost in the final seconds of the 1982 championship game to North Carolina, when Ewing was a freshman. Despite their inexperience in Final Four competition, the Wildcats jumped off to a quick lead in the first half. When the shot-blocking Ewing, the centerpiece of Georgetown's intimidating pressure defense, picked up two fouls in the first seven minutes of play and his third with 8:52 remaining in the first half, UK appeared to be in a commanding position. The Big Blue led throughout the game's first twenty minutes, enjoying as much as a twelve-point lead (27-15) and ending the half with a 29-22 advantage.

This lead melted in the second half as UK had dry shooting spells of truly incredible proportions. The Cats scored not a point in the first ten minutes of the second half and only two in the first sixteen minutes. The starters took twenty-one shots in the half and did not score a single point from the field, although they did hit three free throws. As a team, UK connected on only three of thirty-three shots in the second half for a shooting percentage of 9.1. The halftime lead disappeared and the game ended with the Wildcats on the short end of a 53-40 final score.

In a season packed with achievements, UK had the misfortune to save its worst performance for last. After the debacle, Hall, the players, and Big Blue fans groped for an explanation. How could this happen to a team as talented as the Cats? In the final analysis it is probably impossible to explain UK's second-half shooting, but some reasons can be identified.

For one thing, at halftime Hoyas coach John Thompson made key personnel switches on defense. He put intense and aggressive 6'9" freshman forward Michael Graham on 6'11" Turpin and assigned Ewing to guard 7'1" Bowie. Bowie played away from the basket and did not drive to the hoop, which saved Ewing from committing additional fouls. These defensive adjustments, as well as guard Gene Smith's tenacious dogging of Dicky Beal out front, played a part in UK's poor shooting percentage in the second half, but they are only part of the story. As Jerry Tipton, who covered the Cats throughout the season, observed in the April 1 *Herald-Leader,* "Kentucky

got pretty much the same shots it had shot en route to a 29-4 season record. Melvin Turpin got his favorite turn-around jumpers in the lane. Jim Master was taking those perimeter jumpers. Sam Bowie got shots from fifteen feet. Dicky Beal popped from the top of the key and drove to the basket. None of it went in the basket." *Kernel* sportswriter Mickey Patterson fully agreed, concluding that it all added up to "a freak happening, an oddity beyond comparison."

Jack Givens, who was in Seattle for the game, had a different view. In an interview Givens observed that in the second half UK "came out wanting to protect that lead and not wanting to make any mistakes. They just played too tentatively, and when you play that way you are in hot water because the Hoyas are a loose, self-confident team. Kentucky was playing that way in the first half. Just running and playing their game. They missed those shots early in the second half and they thought too much. They started thinking about the shots instead of just shooting them. They became hesitant and it was like no one wanted to shoot—except Winston Bennett." While the game was still in progress CBS television analyst Billy Packer offered a similar explanation for the

UK earned its first trip to the NCAA Final Four since 1978 with a victory over the Fighting Illini. Here Bret Bearup guards against an Illini shot.

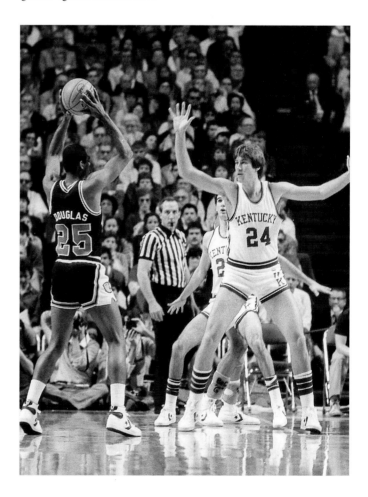

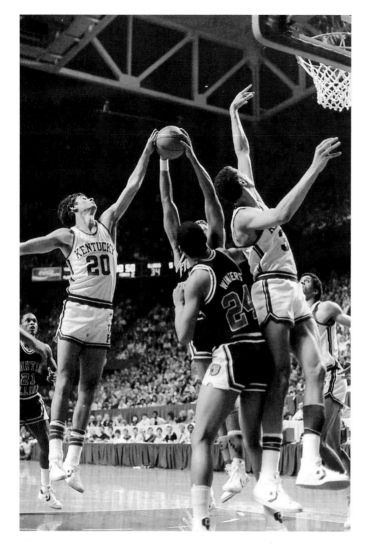

Jim Master and Sam Bowie fight for a rebound against Illinois in the 1984 NCAA Regional. It was to be their last victory. A week later the Wildcats fell to the Georgetown Hoyas in the Final Four.

physically dominate an opponent the way the 1978 team often did, and I think that came back to haunt them in the Georgetown game when they had them down in the first half and they had Ewing in foul trouble." What is ironic, he concluded, "is that Georgetown didn't play that well in the second half. If the Cats had just hit 30 percent [of their shots] in the second half they could have won—or at least come really close." To be both fair and accurate, UK did dominate some teams late in the season, among them Georgia in the SEC tournament and BYU in the Mideast Regionals.

A week after the game, and after viewing game film, Joe Hall had this explanation on his final television show of the season: "In the first half we played tremendous basketball. Georgetown, being down at halftime, came out and they were unbelievable. They really got physical inside with us. I wouldn't say they intimidated us. I'd say they just physically took us out of the game with their inside play." Hall emphasized the role referees can play in determining a game's outcome. "I'm not talking about bad calls or good calls. I'm talking about the style of play they allow to exist. And they just allowed it to be a very physical game. I think Georgetown had the type athletes that could benefit from that type game more than we could. They just rooted us out inside. They put a lot of pressure on us defensively and we got almost shell shocked. Offensively we got excellent shots," Hall acknowledged, "but we were trying so hard they just wouldn't fall."

Each of the theories has some validity, but a more comprehensive explanation combines elements from various theories, though from a somewhat different perspective. For example, the referees probably did let Georgetown play their type of game and that certainly was not to UK's advantage, especially in the second half. But this underlines the fact that the 1984 Wildcats were not a physical team, in contrast to the 1978 NCAA champions, with their "karate defense." More important, the 1984 squad was not one that could adapt to a different style of play as well as the 1978 team could.

Perhaps of equal importance, the 1984 team lacked experience in Final Four competition. As members of the 1978 team emphasized in interviews, a Final Four game is like no other college basketball contest. No other college game, regular or tournament, is as pressure-packed. Joe Hall had been to the Final Four twice before and knew what was needed to win the national championship, but it is one thing for a coach to tell a team and another for the players to fully understand what he is saying. Georgetown, on the other hand, had been there before. Several of the key Hoya players had participated

complete reversal in UK's fortunes. The Wildcats, Packer theorized late in the game, "might have felt like they had the big lead and relaxed a little bit at halftime and just never could get it back in stride."

Another former UK player offered still another perspective. According to this view UK's play in the second half of the Georgetown game was simply another example of a persistent late-season problem—the Wildcats' inability to "put an opponent away when they had him on the ropes." The Cats "lacked the killer instinct. They just never did really dominate an opponent late in the season the way they did on occasion early in the season. When they had a team down they just never did put them away," he stated emphatically. "They never did

in the 1982 championship game. They knew from experience the pressure involved and the price that has to be paid. From losing in their earlier effort, they were even more determined this time.

Georgetown's experience—and UK's lack of experience—were evident at the end of the first half and the beginning of the second half. In the last three minutes of the first half Georgetown cut the UK lead from twelve points to seven and began to change the game's pattern. Thus the second half merely continued a pattern that had begun to develop in the first. Stated another way, the Wildcats did not score a point in the last 3:06 of the first half. Combine that with the first 2:52 of the second half, when the Hoyas went ahead for good on a Ewing tip-in, 30-29, and the momentum had been completely reversed in Georgetown's favor. During that six minutes the Hoyas established the superiority of their punishing, physical style of play, at least for that day, and the confidence of the UK starters was severely shaken. Stated bluntly, UK just did not exhibit the "killer instinct" that Georgetown did.

For many fans, the problem in the Georgetown game was not the loss but the *way* it was lost. The Wildcats did not suffer an ordinary defeat, fighting all the way to a close finish. They were humiliated. And to attempt to explain that is what makes an analysis of the game so difficult, but also so fascinating.

Whatever the reason or reasons, the "Year of the Twin Towers" (as one popular poster described the 1983/84 season) ended on a less than satisfying note. Hope was renewed, however, as the Wildcats entered Hall's thirteenth and, although it was not known at the time, final season as UK's head coach. Ever the attraction of sports, a new season brought with it new possibilities as well as new challenges. Seemingly the slate was wiped clean with the departure of four starters. Gone from the richly talented 1983/84 squad were the leading scorer (Melvin Turpin), the leading rebounder (Sam Bowie), the leading free throw shooter (Jim Master), and the team's playmaker (Dicky Beal), along with reserve Tom Heitz. The UK media guide for 1984/85 used such terms as "rebuilding," "question mark year," "young," "inexperienced," "hard to predict," and "[with] freshmen playing key roles" to describe the upcoming season. Any attempt to dampen fan expectations was, as usual, futile. Both supporters and the press recognized that, although it was a rebuilding year, Hall possessed some excellent building blocks.

Returning from the Final Four team were Kenny Walker, Winston Bennett, James Blackmon, Roger

James Blackmon (10) and Winston Bennett (25) in a December 4, 1984, game against SMU at Rupp Arena.

Harden, Bret Bearup, Troy McKinley, Paul Andrews, and Leroy Byrd. In addition, the Wildcats had yet another bumper crop of recruits: Richard "Master Blaster" Madison, a 6'7" three-sport phenom from Memphis; Ed Davender, a 6'2" guard from Brooklyn, New York; 6'8" forward-center Cedric Jenkins of Dawson, Georgia; Todd Ziegler, a 6'7" forward from Louisville; and California native Robert Lock, a 6'10" center.

As late as August 1984 it also appeared that Hall's first international recruit, 7'4" West German Gunther Behnke, would join the other newcomers. In a four-page spread in the *Courier-Journal* devoted to Behnke, sports-

writer Rick Bozich asserted it was Kentucky's love affair with basketball that drew the young German. Bozich also observed, however, that "Germans have strange ideas about basketball and education. They believe Universities exist for improving the mind instead of the body." Unfortunately, when Behnke arrived in Lexington he apparently found basketball and education to be in conflict rather than in happy harmony. Before the end of his first month in Kentucky, Behnke had changed his mind and returned to Germany. In retrospect, surmised *Herald-Leader* sports columnist D.G. FitzMaurice, Behnke, the "man-child," was "confused and dismayed by all the hoopla that accompanied" Wildcat basketball.

A great deal had been expected of Behnke, and his early departure placed a heavier burden on junior Kenny Walker. Indeed, the 1984/85 team would be built around Walker, a preseason All-American pick who as a sophomore had been the Wildcats' second leading scorer, third leading rebounder, and the team leader in minutes played. It was Walker who had hit the last-second shot to defeat Auburn in the championship game of the 1984 SEC tournament. And it was Walker who would carry the 1984/85 team on his wiry, muscular frame. Starting all thirty-one contests, Walker held or shared high scoring honors in twenty-eight games, and led the Wildcats in rebounding twenty-six times. With impressive totals of 22.9 points per game and 10.2 rebounds per game, the junior from

Roberta, Georgia, became the first player since 1977 to lead the SEC in both scoring and rebounding. While Walker performed at a very high level throughout the season, his teammates did not, a fact which helped explain the Wildcats' inconsistent performance.

Kentucky's season got off to a dismal 1-4 start before the December 21-22 UKIT. The Cats won the season opener against Toledo (63-54), but then lost to Purdue and Southern Methodist University, as well as to a mediocre Indiana team (by the embarrassing score of 81 to 68) and to Louisville (71-64). Kentucky's prospects for a winning season changed however when, due largely to Walker's ever-improving play, the Wildcats concluded a string of seven consecutive victories, two in the UKIT (against East Tennessee State, with freshman Ed Davender contributing twenty-seven points, and against Cincinnati in the championship) followed by defeats of the Danny Manning-led Kansas Jayhawks (92-89), Auburn, North Carolina State, Vanderbilt, and Mississippi.

Although the streak raised UK's record to a respectable 8-4, prospects reversed again when the Wildcats travelled to Tuscaloosa for a January 12 matchup against a fine Alabama team. The Tide prevailed 60-58 when Walker's sixteen-footer missed with two seconds left in the contest. "I can't make all of them," Walker lamented after the game. "It felt good when I let it go. When it started rolling around the rim, I thought it might roll in." While Walker scored twenty-five points, Bret Bearup and Winston Bennett, the other frontline starters, managed only seven points between them. FitzMaurice remarked in his postgame column that "the University of Kenwalky, er, Kentucky, lost by a bucket. . . . Walker had his usual brilliant outing . . . but his shoulders were sagging as he fired UK's last salvo."

Although Kentucky followed the Alabama loss with a one-point win against Mississippi State (58-57) on January 16 at Rupp Arena, a win that temporarily gave the Wildcats sole possession of first place in the SEC, the January slump set in with the next three contests. Kentucky lost to Florida on January 19, to Georgia four days later, and then to Tennessee on January 27.

As always, the loss to Tennessee was particularly galling. FitzMaurice did not mince words in expressing the frustration of Kentucky's fans: "There's death; there's taxes; and there's Kentucky losing to Tennessee in the Stokely Athletics Center." After the loss, Hall asserted in his weekly press conference that he "was impressed with our club in late December and early January. I definitely

Guard Ed Davender dribbles the ball upcourt under the watchful eyes of Joe Hall, Leonard Hamilton, and Jim Hatfield.

felt we were playing over our heads, but it was possible to do that with effort. They were playing with superhuman effort to exceed their abilities. Now, we're playing a little under our abilities." Hall attributed the loss to Tennessee to poor defense and observed that the defeat was "kind of a bottoming out" for the team.

The coach's renewed emphasis on defense following the loss to Tennessee had the desired effect as the Cats eventually emerged from their January doldrums. By mid-February, after five straight SEC wins (against LSU, Auburn in overtime, Vanderbilt, Mississippi, and Alabama), Kentucky was again at the top of the league standings.

The victory over powerful Alabama on February 15 in Rupp Arena, after an early season defeat, was especially satisfying and came despite continued dismal shooting by the Wildcat guards. A cynical FitzMaurice lamented in the *Herald-Leader,* "You could put Kentucky's guards in a rowboat, float them out in the middle of mythical Lake Lexington, hand them an anvil, tell them to throw it overboard, and chances are, they'd miss the water." Despite the guards' five for twenty-six shooting from the floor, Walker's solid nineteen-point, eight-rebound performance ensured the victory.

The Alabama win proved to be the high point of Kentucky's 1984/85 season. Although the Wildcats managed a road win over Florida on February 20 and a satisfying home victory over Tennessee on February 28, these wins were sandwiched between regular-season losses to Mississippi State, Georgia, and LSU. The roller-coaster final month of the regular season and an SEC tournament loss in Birmingham to Florida did not produce the desired momentum as the team entered NCAA tournament play for a record thirtieth time. They came with a mediocre record of 16 and 12. Indeed, the NCAA selection came as a surprise to the coach and players, a surprise that worked to the team's advantage, according to Hall. The coach later asserted that the players had thought about the tournament all year, but "the possibility of getting in was remote. When they did get a bid, it fired them up." As always, some programs felt slighted when the selection committee's choices were announced. Florida, for example, had a better record and had beaten the Cats twice, including a victory in the SEC tourney, but Kentucky's reputation, along with a tough preconference schedule, proved to be deciding factors.

If others outside the Kentucky program disagreed with the Wildcats' invitation, the surprised but grateful Kentucky squad silenced any critics with hard-fought wins in Salt Lake City over the University of Washington and its star, Detlef Schrempf (66-58), and over the

Running Rebels of UNLV (64-61). In these games Kenny Walker cemented his claim to All-American status with high point totals of twenty-nine and twenty-three, but it was the much-maligned guard trio of Roger Harden, Ed Davender, and James Blackmon who won praise following the UNLV victory. The three guards combined for twenty-five points and nine assists against a Las Vegas defense that was, as one writer put it, "quicker than a card dealer's hands."

The UNLV win sent the Wildcats to a surprising spot among the NCAA's final sixteen in the West Regional semifinal showdown against the St. John's Redmen in Denver. Despite growing fan expectations for a return to the Final Four—to be played in Lexington—UK was soundly defeated by the powerful and balanced Redmen. Featuring 7' center Bill Wennington, sophomore power forward Walter Berry, sophomore guard Mark Jackson, and two-time All-American swingman Chris Mullin, St. John's raised its record to 30-3 and went on to a West Regional finals win over North Carolina State and a Final Four berth.

Against Kentucky, Mullin scored thirty points to lead the New Yorkers. He insisted after the game that he was "pretty wide open all night. They were probably the easiest shots I got all year. It was nice out there not getting bumped around and double-teamed. It was like being out of jail for a night." In addition to his scoring spree, Mullin also assisted in the Redmen's victory when he inadvertently poked Kenny Walker in the right eye with 11:16 remaining in the contest. Despite the swollen eye, Walker again led the Wildcats with twenty-three points on ten of fourteen shooting from the field and three of three from the foul line. The defeat ended the Wildcats' brief "Cinderella ride" in the tournament, and the team finished the season with a record of 18-13.

Despite the up and down regular season, the Cats' strong showing in the tournament ensured that Kentucky's reputation as an NCAA power was not diminished. In fact, it was that very reputation that had ensured a thirtieth NCAA appearance. It was also that reputation that brought the 1985 Final Four to Lexington. Although the Wildcats were absent from the Final Four field, and although big city boosters had expressed doubts about the city's small size and lack of accommodations, the tournament proved to be a boon to the local economy, and the media exposure provided still another advantage for Kentucky's future recruiting efforts.

Those recruiting efforts would be conducted under different leadership, however, for the 1984/85 season proved to be the end of an era. About twenty minutes

after the loss to St. John's, Joe B. Hall announced his retirement as UK coach. Conscious of the tradition begun by John Mauer and Adolph Rupp, Hall wore a brown coat, for the only time in his coaching career, in honor of his predecessor. Conscious as well, perhaps, of his own coaching journey, the announcement was made in Denver, where Hall had begun his college head coaching career at Regis College. Hall's overall head coaching record, including earlier stints at Regis and Central Missouri State, was 373-156. In his thirteen seasons as Kentucky's head coach (1972-1985), Hall's record was 297-100 and included eight SEC championships, a National Invitational Tournament championship in 1976, three trips to the NCAA's Final Four, and an NCAA national championship in 1978. His winning percentage of .748 placed Joe B. behind Adolph Rupp's percentage of .882, but slightly ahead of Rupp's predecessor, John Mauer, at .740.

Hall remarked that "twenty years of service is about all anyone could ask of life.... I've done what I like to do where I most wanted to do it." Stating that he had decided to retire the previous summer, Hall read from a prepared statement without tears or apparent emotion: "The satisfaction I have experienced makes it a little easier to say." Hall's satisfaction came from his success in upholding the famed UK tradition. And that success did not come easily. In a January 9, 1985, "Cover Story" for *USA Today,* Hall intimated that the "only truly successful season at Kentucky ends with a national championship. And it helps if you go undefeated, too." While he obviously did not go undefeated, his consistent success over thirteen seasons, capped by an 18-13 final season in which Hall guided an underdog squad to the Sweet Sixteen of the NCAA tournament, demonstrated to many of the faithful that Rupp's successor could indeed coach.

Kentucky athletic director and former UK star Cliff Hagan noted that Hall had "not only carried on the Kentucky tradition, he has enhanced it." Liz H. Demoran, editor of *The Open Door,* a publication of the University of Kentucky National Alumni Association, wrote that Hall's ability to win consistently was remarkable, that "Hall was a buffer, staving off the arrival of today's modern equity that new rules, better developed high school athletes and big bucks behind numerous programs throughout the country have helped to achieve."

More than a buffer, Hall was indeed "keeper of the flame," but at the same time he was the chief architect of a new Kentucky tradition. In addition to his remarkable success in the era of post-UCLA dominance and the new parity in NCAA basketball, Hall dismantled the Kentucky program's reliance on white athletes alone. And symboli-

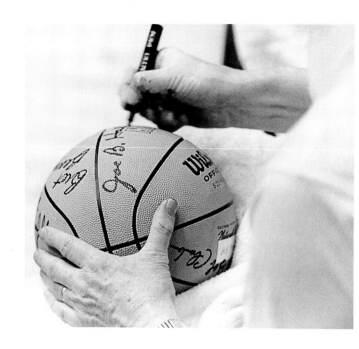

A UK ritual: Signing basketballs for legions of fans.

cally significant, it was under Hall that the team's home court was moved to cavernous Rupp Arena, the 24,000-seat iron and steel boxlike structure that marked the transition of Kentucky basketball into the modern era.

When Adolph Rupp retired, the conventional wisdom was that his successor would face an impossible task: replacing a legend. While Hall did not become a legend, he crafted a highly successful record in his own right. Furthermore, he chose his own retirement date— no small achievement. The general belief that it would be wiser to be the man who succeeded the man who replaced Rupp did not prove accurate. As it turned out, the coach who replaced Rupp did very well for himself and for the Wildcats' basketball program. It was the coach who replaced Hall who faced the program's most serious problems since the point shaving scandal of 1951. While Rupp was able to weather that storm and even go on to win another national championship, Joe Hall's successor was not to be as fortunate.

Opposite: Antoine Walker and Cameron Mills celebrate UK's 83-63 rout of Wake Forest in the Midwest Regional final on the way to the 1995/96 national championship.

PART IV

The Fall and Rise of Wildcat Basketball

11

*The Sutton Era,
Short but Not Sweet*

When Joe B. Hall stepped aside following the 1984/85 season, he left a program unequaled by any other college sports team both in its success and in its importance to its fans. In Alabama, Nebraska, Oklahoma, and Texas, football came close. North Carolina, UCLA, and Kansas had college basketball programs that were proven winners. Kentucky basketball, however, was an unparalleled tradition, a program followed and worshipped by millions of Kentuckians, many of whom had never finished high school. The Wildcats were a way of life, an opportunity for every citizen of the Commonwealth to identify with a winner, to be a part of the best that there was in the world.

Kentucky needed a steward for its program. It needed a coach who could be a winner. It needed a coach who could bleed blue. In contrast to Adolph Rupp's lingering presence following his forced retirement, Joe B. Hall's graceful exit facilitated a smooth search process for the Wildcats' next head coach. Coveted and pursued by big-name coaches throughout the country, the UK job and its peculiar challenge promised pressure, to be sure, but also power and prestige. Television commentator and former Marquette coach Al McGuire emphasized the mystique that comes along with being the leader of the Wildcat program: "My genuine opinion of the Kentucky basketball program is that there is only one and it is top drawer, Park Avenue, and that all other

basketball programs in the country think they are, but they are not. . . . At Kentucky, basketball is a type of religion, such a fanatical obsession that they expect to be national champions each year, and they live and die with each ball game. . . . I even think there are times when the horses kinda bend down a little to the roundball."

On March 24, 1985, the *Herald-Leader* reported university president Otis A. Singletary's promise to Kentucky's players that "the best [coach] in the country" would be secured. For those millions who shared McGuire's assessment of the "top drawer" quality of the UK program, Singletary's goal seemed both reasonable and easily attainable. The UK president attempted to reassure the Wildcat faithful: "I don't think we'll have any trouble getting candidates. We have no friends to reward, no enemies to punish." When asked about the screening process, Singletary added, tongue-in-cheek, "We'll need a large body of water to see if they can walk across it."

Joe Hall also met with reporters for an "informal talk." Although Hall joked that "he might set up a desk and have a secretary at Rupp Arena during the Final Four to handle the expected flood of coaches seeking his recommendation," he assured reporters that, unlike his predecessor, he would not attempt to play a role in the search process. "My involvement," he said, "will be absolutely none and that's on a voluntary basis."

Despite the team's dismal 13-19 record, Eddie Sutton worked as hard as ever during his last season at Kentucky, 1988/89. Sutton and the team suffered through the Big Blue's first losing season since 1926/27, when UK went 3-13.

The five-man ad hoc committee appointed by Singletary to recommend a new coach faced no dearth of possibilities. The probable front-runners for the UK coaching position were said to include Gene Bartow of Alabama-Birmingham, Bobby Cremins of Georgia Tech, and Eddie Sutton of Arkansas. Other candidates prominently mentioned ranged from former UK players (C.M. Newton, Pat Riley, and Dan Issel) and assistant coaches (Dickie Parsons and Gale Catlett) to established head coaches like Gene Keady, Lute Olson, and Sonny Smith.

As the underdog Villanova Wildcats of Rollie Massimino were in the process of winning a thrilling 66-64 victory over Georgetown in the April 1 championship game of the NCAA tournament at Rupp Arena, many coaches and fans in Lexington for the contest were finding the coaching situation for the UK Wildcats to be as interesting as the game. Some candidates seemed to make the coaching search a priority. Among those jockeying for position at the Final Four were Lute Olson of Arizona and Eddie Sutton of Arkansas.

Lee Rose, the coach at South Florida who had already taken the University of North Carolina-Charlotte and Purdue to the Final Four (and who had roots in Lexington through his prior tenure as coach at Transylvania College, now Transylvania University), Gene Bartow, who had led UCLA and Memphis State to the Final Four before starting a new program at UAB, and Lute Olson were all granted interviews with the search committee. The front-runner appeared to be Olson, but

on March 31 the Arizona coach withdrew his name from consideration after failing to come to terms with UK Athletics Director Cliff Hagan. The *Herald-Leader* reported that "the press gathered at [Lexington socialite] Anita Madden's party that night waiting for . . . Hagan to arrive with the news of Olson's hiring." Hagan arrived at the party with different news, informing the gathering, "We have no coach."

Only two days later, on April 2, Hagan and UK officially named Eddie Sutton as Joe B. Hall's replacement. According to Alexander Wolff and Armen Keteyian, writers for *Sports Illustrated* and authors of the controversial book *Raw Recruits*, Sutton "had politicked vigorously around town that week, schmoozing with the Kentucky muckamucks, hoping to get consideration for the UK coaching vacancy." It is rumored that during the semifinal game between Villanova and Memphis State on March 30, Sutton asked Joe Dean, Converse representative and later athletic director at LSU, why he had been unable to get an interview. Dean knew that Kentucky's president and athletic director were very hesitant about considering the Razorbacks' coach. Wolff and Keteyian reported that "there was just something about him—even his permed hair—that gave the UK people pause. Indeed, Dean knew how Hagan had reacted when Sutton's name was first broached in a Denver hotel suite the night Joe Hall resigned. 'I'm not hiring any coach,' Hagan had said, 'with a damn Afro.'" Despite the athletic director's early sentiments, Dean promised that he

President Otis Singletary, second from right, introduces new basketball coach Eddie Sutton. Sutton's wife, Patsy, is at right. Athletics Director Cliff Hagan is at left.

would try to persuade UK officials to grant him an interview. Dean's actions led not only to an interview, but to a job offer. Eddie Sutton would be Joe B. Hall's successor. While Wildcat fans could easily argue with Hagan's selection criterion relating to Sutton's hair style, they would ultimately rue the day that he second-guessed his gut feeling and decided to hire the Razorbacks' coach. Eddie Sutton's legacy is all the more painful because for a time he appeared to be the perfect coaching choice.

After he was officially named as the new Kentucky coach by the UK Athletics Association Board of Directors, Sutton was introduced to the media on April 2. Describing the position as "the number one job in America," Sutton declared that "this was the only job I would have left the University of Arkansas for." Sutton assured reporters, "I just happened to be here" for the NCAA tournament and corresponding coaches' convention in Lexington. He was elated when he was contacted about the job: "Believe me, I would have crawled all the way to Lexington. . . . I told Cliff, 'I didn't think you'd ever call.'" Without finding it necessary to crawl, Sutton had so captivated the search committee that Hagan had extended the job offer less than two hours after a ninety-minute interview at Lexington's Hyatt Regency Hotel.

The new coach came to Lexington with impeccable basketball credentials. At Arkansas, Sutton had amassed a record of 260-75 from 1974 through 1985, an average of 23.6 victories a season. At Barnhill Arena, the Razorbacks' home court in Fayetteville, Sutton-led teams had lost only eight times in 129 contests. He had won national coach of the year honors twice (1977 and 1978) and had been named the top coach of the Southwest Conference four times.

Sutton was a disciple of Henry Iba. He first played for the legendary coach at Oklahoma State, then served as his graduate assistant. "Fast Eddie," as he would later be called, began his head coaching career at Tulsa Central High School, where he posted a 119-51 record from 1960 to 1967. Sutton then started the basketball program at Southern Idaho Junior College, where his record was a sterling 83-14 over three seasons (1967/68 to 1969/70). Building his programs on what he called "the three Ds—dedication, discipline, and defense," Sutton moved on to a five-year stint at Creighton, where his teams went 82-50, before leaving for Arkansas in 1974. Sutton's established reputation for winning and proven coaching skills made his selection more than acceptable to Wildcat fans. In addition, the up-tempo style played by his squads at Arkansas gave UK followers hope that Wildcat games would become even more exciting to watch. Of course, Wildcat fans expected him to win at least as often as Joe B. Hall had done with his more methodical, deliberate coaching style. Hall invited the new coach to speak at the team banquet on April 11 as a way to introduce him to the squad. In a press release, Hall stated, "I couldn't be happier. In stepping down, I didn't want to let the program down, but with Eddie, I see nothing but great days ahead. . . . With the naming of Eddie Sutton, this is a great day for Kentucky basketball." That seemed an accurate statement at the time.

Kentucky's players expressed similar satisfaction with the selection. As soon as Sutton was named coach, Kenny Walker quelled rumors of an early departure to the NBA by stating that he would remain at UK for his senior season. Roger Harden expressed his admiration for Sutton's success in developing sound guard play and playing a looser style of basketball than Hall with the comment that Sutton "doesn't just speak of the fast break, he runs it. It didn't really matter to me who got the job, but he will certainly work in my mind."

Abe Lemons, former coach of the Texas Longhorns and rival of Sutton during his Arkansas years, praised the new Wildcat coach while simultaneously expressing his shock that Sutton had taken the job. In the April 13 edition of *The Cats' Pause*, Lemons said: "It surprised me. I don't know what happened to him. I thought he had found a home [at Arkansas]. He knows his business. I think the University of Kentucky got a good coach." Lemons explained that his surprise rested on his understanding of the tremendous pressure that is part of being the head coach at UK: "He didn't catch a lot of flack at Arkansas. At Kentucky you get a lot of flack. He needs to go see some John Wayne films and toughen up."

The early days of the coaching transition appeared to go smoothly, as Joe Hall carried through on his promise not to interfere, and Sutton formed his own coaching staff. Sutton shrewdly retained master recruiter Leonard Hamilton as an assistant coach. In addition to the popular and very successful Hamilton, Sutton chose James Dickey, his assistant for four years at Arkansas, and Doug Barnes, a former head coach at the University of Arkansas at Monticello, an NAIA school. Both Dickey and Barnes were familiar with the Sutton system, and many members of the local press and fans eagerly awaited the unveiling of the new Wildcat style.

The Sutton style would be a welcome return to the fast-breaking, guard-oriented glory days of Rupp's Runts and the Fiddlin' Five. Kentucky fans had become a little

Eddie Sutton, James Dickey, and Wayne Breeden considering game strategy.

bored with Hall's dependence on the power game, as well as with the development of strong, disciplined post players such as the "Twin Tower" combinations of Rick Robey and Mike Phillips, and Sam Bowie and Melvin Turpin. Sutton's system intoxicated Kentucky fans with images of Kentucky players equaling the style and accomplishments of such star guards as Sidney Moncrief, Ron Brewer, and Marvin Delph, who had played under the coach at Arkansas. Wildcat fans were more excited about the upcoming season than they had been in years. It held out realistic hopes for both a national championship and an exciting playing style.

While Sutton had avoided controversy about his staff selections and playing style, Abe Lemons quickly turned out to be a prophet: Eddie Sutton would have to "toughen up" quickly. Looking back on Sutton's first few months in Lexington, sportswriter Jerry Tipton listed a couple of controversies that marked the "bumpy road" of the coaching transition. Tipton reported that Sutton was "linked with the open New Jersey Nets job" in the NBA. Sutton denied real interest in the position, saying that "the Nets contacted him first." The Nets, however, countered that Sutton telephoned first and that his interest in the job was genuine. Following this rumor came

Sutton's decision to break with UK tradition and have his teams wear Nike athletic shoes, the shoes worn by his Razorback teams, rather than Converse, which had been the shoe of choice for Rupp and Hall. It was all the more ironic because Converse representative Joe Dean had helped Sutton get the UK job in the first place.

These minor controversies over the Nets and shoes became forgotten when, on October 27, 1985, the *Herald-Leader* published the first in a series of articles called "Playing Above the Rules," which described violations of NCAA rules by Kentucky and other universities. The appearance of the first article, entitled "Boosters' Cash, Gifts Lined Pockets of UK Players," written by Jeffrey Marx and Michael York, had the impact of a bomb blast across the Commonwealth. Before his first game as head coach at UK, Eddie Sutton was forced to address controversies that had originated while he was still coach at Arkansas.

As Sutton prepared his squad for a November 14 exhibition home opener against the Czechoslovakian national team, speculation swirled that Joe B. Hall's resignation had been precipitated by concerns over press investigations into several irregularities in the Wildcat basketball program. A November 11 *Sports Illustrated* article, "Blowing a Fuse Over the News" by Alexander Wolff and Robert Sullivan, revealed that "the *Herald-Leader* was not alone in evincing interest in Hall's tenure at Kentucky. Three months before Hall resigned, it became known that the university was looking into his handling of his personal allotment of 323 season tickets, which had a value in his final season of at least $24,000."

Wolff and Sullivan admitted that the "probe turned up no evidence that any of Hall's tickets were sold for more than face value," the same conclusion reached by reporter Richard Whitt of the *Courier-Journal*. Even before the *Herald-Leader* and *Sports Illustrated* ran their stories, the *Courier-Journal* had caught wind of the potentially explosive story and thoroughly investigated it. As Whitt stated in a November 1985 interview, "I'm the one that first investigated it and I found that there was no story." After its Louisville rival dropped the story of alleged ticket abuse, the *Herald-Leader* picked it up and also found that it led nowhere. Instead of simply dropping the story, however, *Herald-Leader* reporters Marx and York developed another angle, which came to be known as "the hundred-dollar handshake scandal." Faced with angry phone calls, a bomb threat, and hundreds of subscription cancellations following publication of the series, *Herald-Leader* editor John S. Carroll attempted to answer critics' concerns over his decision to publish the story. Carroll asserted in an editorial that

instead of acting out of any desire to do harm to the UK basketball program, "we launched the investigation simply to avoid being beaten on a big story by a competitor." Although the *Courier-Journal* appeared to have concluded that "there was no story," rumors at the time of an impending investigation by that newspaper supposedly prompted the *Herald-Leader* investigation. According to Carroll's editorial, interviews with UK fans and players about the tickets revealed "other abuses in the program." Thus, Carroll maintained, "it was fear of defeat—rather than a quest for glory—that prompted the *Herald-Leader* to pursue this story."

Regardless of their origin, the articles made waves in the Bluegrass and across the nation. Specifically, Marx and York accused Wildcat boosters in their October 27, 1985, article of showering UK players with cash. "For years, ordinary fans have rewarded University of Kentucky basketball players with a loyalty that is nationally known. What is less known is that a small group of boosters has been giving the players something extra: a steady stream of cash." In addition to interviewing former UK players about selling game tickets, a practice forbidden by the NCAA after August 1, 1980, the reporters focused on gifts given to players in the form of cash, clothes, free meals, and payments for speeches and public appearances. Of the thirty-three Wildcats who played for Kentucky between 1972 and 1985 who were interviewed by Marx and York, the authors claimed that "thirty-one said they knew of improper activities while they were playing and 26 said they participated."

The second installment of the series appeared the next day and focused on accusations of recruiting violations at other universities. This article cited schools such as the University of Pittsburgh (and the activities of former Wildcat Reggie Warford as assistant coach) and the University of Georgia for recruiting violations. Significantly, neither article cited the University of Kentucky basketball program for recruiting violations in recent years.

The series won the 1986 Pulitzer Prize for investigative reporting. It also created widespread and varied reactions from fans, coaches, and the press. For their part, Kentucky fans were generally outraged that the local paper had hurt their beloved program. Follow-up stories and comments appeared in newspapers across the country. While Wildcat fans blasted the *Herald-Leader* for its audacity, Ray Meyer, the venerable coach of DePaul University, commented in the *Chicago Daily News*, "Boy, I want to vomit when I read that stuff. . . . Twenty-six players, and they're admitting that things like

that went on. Then all those wins at Kentucky don't mean a damn thing." The controversy even made it into the pages of the *Chronicle of Higher Education*. Ironically, the controversy did little to damage Joe B. Hall's reputation, despite the fact that the alleged violations occurred during his tenure.

For their part, many of the former players interviewed for the *Herald-Leader* series insisted to *Sports Illustrated* reporters that "they had been misquoted or quoted out of context." One unnamed Wildcat player angrily assured *SI* "I was never offered any money." The NCAA found only one player interviewed for the series willing to stand by his statement as printed by the paper. David Berst, the NCAA director of enforcement, lamented, "We simply may not ever know the right answer or the truth of the matter." In a statement that would come back to haunt him, Eddie Sutton asserted in the 1985/86 *Kentucky Basketball Facts Book*, "Winning at all costs is our biggest problem. Some institutions have put so much pressure on a coach that he resorts to violating NCAA rules in order to win."

While the attention of the media was fixed on the scandal, Sutton and the Kentucky team prepared for the 1985/86 basketball season. Preseason practice was already under way when the scandal series began. Even with the shadow of scandal continuing to hang over the program, the Wildcats had an extremely successful season. The team was led by returning All-American senior forward Kenny "Sky" Walker, who was coming off of a season where he had averaged 22.9 points and 10.2 rebounds per game. Four other players who started a significant number of games the previous year also returned: junior forward Winston Bennett (7.2 points and 5.3 rebounds per game), and guards Ed Davender (8.5/1.5), Roger Harden (5.3/1.5), and James Blackmon (5.4/1.4). The only starter lost from the eighteen-win season of 1984/85 was center Bret Bearup. The 1985/86 UK squad featured several young players who would vie to replace Bearup's size in the lineup, including sophomores Robert Lock (6'10") and Cedric Jenkins (6'9"). However, since the Cats were switching to the three-guard offense, their roles would be to come in off the bench and provide size and depth. Others returning included guards Leroy Byrd and Paul Andrews, along with forwards Richard Madison and Todd Ziegler.

The only first-year player on the team was 6'7" forward Irving Thomas, a Miami, Florida, native who had averaged 18.6 points and 14.5 rebounds per game in high school. Thomas was highly recruited after leading his high school team to a 28-1 record and the 4A Florida

state title. He chose Kentucky over Georgetown, UCLA, North Carolina State, and Florida.

The media quickly noted that while the team did not possess exceptional quickness or size, it did have experience. It also seemed to have a more relaxed, optimistic, and confident attitude than the previous year's squad. As early as October 16 *Herald-Leader* sportswriter Jerry Tipton claimed that the "'New' Cats" were "oozing confidence." Early in the first season of the "Sutton Era" at UK, all was happiness, jokes, and positive feelings within the program. Only eleven days before the scandal stories were published, the *Herald-Leader*'s John McGill wrote that a "secure Sutton [is] likely to avoid the perils of pressure at UK." Later events highlighted the irony of these early predictions.

The 1985/86 campaign finally got under way on November 14 with a home exhibition against the Czechoslovakian national team, which UK won easily. The regular-season schedule began seven days later, on November 22, with another home game, against Northwestern State of Louisiana, before the Cats ventured off to Hawaii to play Chaminade University and the University of Hawaii. Kentucky then returned for a December 3 home game against Cincinnati. The Wildcats easily won these games by wide margins, beating Northwestern State (77-58), Chaminade (89-57), Hawaii (98-65), and Cincinnati (84-54).

The first real test for Eddie Sutton and his new system occurred at Rupp Arena against Bobby Knight's Indiana Hoosiers. Knight's 1984/85 team had been a disappointment, going 19-14 and failing to make the NCAA tournament. Nevertheless, IU had finished second in the postseason NIT in New York and featured returning Olympic team and All-American guard Steve Alford. The Hoosiers had also beaten Kentucky by thirteen points in Bloomington the previous year. Alford, a member of the United States' 1984 gold medal Olympic basketball team, was not, however, allowed to play in the Kentucky game. He was hit with a one-game suspension by the NCAA's eligibility committee the Friday before the game for violating an NCAA rule by allowing his picture to be used in a calendar sold by a sorority in a charity fund-raising effort.

Following the game, Bobby Knight pointed out the irony of the squeaky-clean Alford being suspended while Kentucky remained intact despite being under NCAA scrutiny. "I thought it was a tremendous irony," the press quoted Knight as saying, "with all the garbage that's gone on in Kentucky over the years, that this happens prior to that particular basketball game." UK Athletics Director Cliff Hagan refrained from engaging in a battle of words with Knight, saying only, "I can't comment about anything that Bobby Knight says about anything." Apparently it was now becoming fashionable to bash the UK basketball program, something that Adolph Rupp (were he alive) would never have believed.

Even with Alford out, the Hoosiers gave the Wildcats a tough game, with UK pulling out a 63-58 victory that ran its record to five and zero. Kentucky, after hitting just eleven of twenty-seven shots in the first half, made eleven of nineteen attempts to hold on to the game. Ed Davender led the Cats with twenty-two points, with Kenny Walker adding sixteen points and three rebounds in what, for him, was a subpar game.

The Big Blue suffered its first loss of the season on December 14 at the University of Kansas Allen Field House against the Danny Manning-led Jayhawks. Manning scored twenty-two points and played a strong all-around game. Even more critical to Wildcat fans than the loss of the game was an injury to Kenny Walker's eye early in the second half. The injury took him out of the game after only twelve points and four rebounds. Without Walker, Kansas was able to widen its eight-point halftime lead to the final seventeen-point victory margin, despite Kentucky's hitting twenty-four of twenty-seven free throws. The Wildcats returned home to host the UKIT with a 5-1 record. Crucial for Kentucky's hopes for a strong season was Walker's quick recovery from the eye injury. As it turned out, there was little reason to worry.

Kentucky easily won the UKIT, beating East Carolina and Pepperdine by a combined total of sixty-eight points. Walker scored nineteen against the Pirates, and followed that up with twenty-one against the Pepperdine Waves, easing Wildcat fans' concerns about his vision. Winston Bennett continued his solid play in the tournament, scoring twenty-three points and grabbing sixteen rebounds in the two games. While Kentucky played a three-guard offense (Blackmon, Davender, and Harden), with Walker and Bennett being the post men, the Cats received solid performances from their backup big men throughout most of the young season. Against Northwestern State, Cedric Jenkins scored eight points in nineteen minutes. Versus Chaminade, it was Rob Lock going four for four in twelve minutes, totaling eight points. Against Cincinnati, Todd Ziegler scored six points in eight minutes. Against Pepperdine, Rob Lock scored twelve points and grabbed two rebounds in just five minutes of action. Although Kentucky relied on Kenny Walker and the three-guard offense, it seemed to be getting decent contributions from different players

when necessary. This combination would enable the Cats to enjoy one of their most surprising and entertaining seasons in many years, although in the end the inability of the bench to contribute in a crucial NCAA tournament game would be a major factor in ending the Wildcats' season.

Following the UK victory over Pepperdine, the *Herald-Leader*'s John McGill compared the current team to Rupp's Runts of 1965/66. "Now this is not to say," McGill observed, "that Eddie Sutton's first bunch are up to the overall skill level of the Runts, nor that they might make it to the title game of the NCAA Tournament like the Runts did. But they are clearly cast in the same mold." This was quite a comparison to make so early in the season. Yet McGill's bold statement probably turned out to be more accurate than most Wildcat fans could have imagined or hoped.

Next came the game the entire state had been awaiting. On December 28, a thin, overachieving Kentucky squad met a very solid and deep Louisville team. The Cardinals, who would go on to win the national championship at the NCAA tournament later that season in Dallas, featured a crop of players, mainly between 6'4" and 6'7", who were all excellent athletes. U of L also had a superb freshman center in 6'9" Pervis Ellison, who teamed with returning stars Herbert Crook, Mark McSwain, Jeff Hall, Billy Thompson, and Milt Wagner to form a very talented unit. In addition, Louisville boasted another top freshman, forward Tony Kimbro. Thompson, who had averaged 15.1 points and 8.4 rebounds per game during the Cards' disappointing 19-18 season the year before, was a potential All-American. The size, depth, and jumping ability of the Cardinals' front line gave Kenny Walker problems during the game. He could manage only eleven points on five for thirteen shooting, but did manage to grab fourteen rebounds. Winston Bennett, who grew up in Louisville, was a major factor in the 69-64 UK victory at Rupp Arena, scor-

Kenny Walker appears to be taking on the entire Kansas team. Walker suffered an eye injury during the December 14, 1985, loss to the Jayhawks.

ing twenty-three points and garnering seven boards. Richard "Master Blaster" Madison also played a key role, using his athletic ability to score ten points and help contain the Cards on the defensive end of the court. Louisville's Billy Thompson was noticeably quiet during the game, taking only six shots and scoring just eight points due to the Cats' tremendous defensive pressure.

Two days after the U of L game, the Wildcats closed out their nonconference schedule with a 93-55 romp over Virginia Military Institute on December 30. With eighteen points, Walker led the Cats in scoring for the seventh time in ten games as Kentucky raised its record to nine wins and only one loss. Sutton and the Wildcats opened the SEC season with an 80-71 road win at Vanderbilt to raise the team's record to 10-1. Then, on January 4, 1986—just as Big Blue fans began to envision a regular season with only one defeat—came a 60 to 56 loss at Auburn. The Tigers opened up sixteen-point leads during both halves, handling Kentucky's defensive pressure extremely well. Again Walker led the Cats with twenty-two points and six rebounds, but that was not enough, as Kentucky shot just 40.3 percent from the floor and attempted only eight free throws (hitting six), compared to sixteen (twelve successful) for Auburn. After being consistent during much of the season, Winston Bennett made only two of eleven shots, finishing with as many fouls as points (four) and grabbing only five rebounds in twenty-eight minutes of play. Chuck Person, an All-American college player who would go on to a successful professional career, was not to be denied, hitting for twenty-four points and grabbing nine rebounds for the Tigers.

The Wildcats rolled through the next eight conference games, even avenging their loss to Auburn with an 81-71 home court victory on January 31. Only a close two-point win at LSU on January 29 and a five-point win at home against Georgia on January 23 gave UK fans any reason to feel concerned. Walker led the Cats in scoring in five of those eight games, and almost matched his season high of thirty-three points (scored against Hawaii) with thirty-one in the seventeen-point victory over Mississippi on January 8. Bennett continued his solid play, leading the team in rebounds in four of those games and topping the scoring column twice, including twenty-six at home against Tennessee.

On February 2, 1986, Kentucky took the floor at Reynolds Coliseum in a midseason nonconference game against North Carolina State. Against a talented Wolfpack team that included future NBA players Nate McMillan, Bennie Bolton, Chucky Brown, Charles Shackleford, Chris Washburn, and Vincent Del Negro (son of the former Wildcat player), Kentucky blew a five-point halftime lead and lost 54-51. By sagging inside to stop Kenny Walker and Winston Bennett, Jim Valvano's squad forced Kentucky's guards to try to beat them from outside. Shackleford, at 6'9", and the 6'11" Washburn scored sixteen points each and helped contain Walker at the defensive end of the court. Although Ed Davender led the team with sixteen points, it came on just five for fourteen shooting. Walker was held to ten points, and Bennett hit just five of eighteen shots in scoring twelve points. Although Kentucky outrebounded the much larger State squad 34-28, it could not overcome its poor 32.8 percent shooting performance.

The next Wildcat opponent, the Vanderbilt Commodores, studied the defense utilized by the Wolfpack and came out ready to do battle with the 18 and 3 Cats on February 5 at Rupp Arena. UK was able to notch its ninth straight SEC victory with a 73-65 win behind a season best twenty-two-point, seven-rebound, four-assist effort from James Blackmon and sixteen points from Winston Bennett, but the Cats faithful were beginning to worry about Walker. The All-American forward was held to only sixteen points by the outmanned Commodores. Walker was able to take only six shots from the floor during the entire contest, as the Vandy defense sagged every time he touched the ball, committing enough fouls (twenty-nine during the course of the game) to send him to the line for sixteen free throws. Walker was becoming frustrated since, despite Blackmon's strong performance, opponents were collapsing inside on him. Walker, who had been wearing protective goggles since the eye injury at Kansas, found the inside pressure made it difficult to maneuver. Although UK was 19-3, its star player was being rendered ineffective. In order to get Walker the ball more often in situations where he could score, Sutton began changing his offense. Ironically, as Walker explained, "We're in the process of putting in the old offense under Coach Hall, and it takes awhile for it to come back."

Although the Cats may have seemed disorganized as they changed their playing style in midseason, the results did not change. They kept on winning. The team reeled off ten more consecutive SEC victories, and Walker seemed to return to form, scoring thirty-two on February 27 at Tennessee in a narrow 62-60 victory. Jerry Tipton explained UK's victory over Tennessee, writing, "How did UK do it? The Wildcats did it the old-fashioned way. They earned it by going to Kenny Walker repeatedly." In other words, they had successfully returned

to the old Hall-era offense. This was UK's first victory in eight years at Stokely Athletics Center, and only the second in fourteen seasons, as the Cats had been jinxed playing in Knoxville. The ten wins included seven to close out the regular season and three victories to win the SEC tournament championship. Kentucky won the regular-season SEC crown with a 17-1 record, including 9-0 at home.

In the SEC tournament played at Rupp Arena, the UK team disposed of Ole Miss by twenty-six points, LSU by three, and Alabama by eleven. The Wildcats joined the 1984/85 team as the only squads to that point to win both the SEC regular and tournament crowns in the same season. Kenny Walker and Winston Bennett shone during the tournament, leading the Cats to victory and on to the NCAA tournament with a glittering 29-3 record. Roger Harden, however, was the only Wildcat named to the All-SEC tournament team after scoring thirty-four points and handing out fourteen assists in the three games.

Kentucky opened the NCAA tournament at the Charlotte Coliseum against Davidson from the Southern Conference. Because Davidson was located only a few miles north of Charlotte, this was, in effect, a home game for them. In the tournament for the first time since 1970, Davidson jumped to an early lead and led 18-13 before UK called time-out with 12:28 to go in the half. After regrouping, Kentucky rallied past the spirited Davidson squad to gain a 38-26 halftime lead. The Cats' superior talent and size eventually won out as Kentucky outrebounded Davidson 39-19 in capturing a 75-55 victory. Kenny Walker scored twenty points in the contest, making him the third player in Wildcat history to top 2,000 points for a career. The victory raised UK's record to 30-3, the sixth thirty-win season in school history.

The next opponent in Charlotte was the always dangerous Hilltoppers from Western Kentucky University, led by star player Kannard Johnson. It seemed as though the Cats would easily dispose of the squad from Bowling Green. Kentucky opened up a twelve-point halftime lead and led by sixteen points midway through the second half. The pesky Hilltoppers, however, made the Big Blue earn the victory. The key shot for the Cats was a long jumper by Roger Harden, the only shot he hit all day, which silenced a Western rally after the Hilltoppers had cut the lead to 63-59. Johnson led WKU with twenty points and grabbed six rebounds. The star of the game, however, was Kentucky's All-American. Kenny Walker scored thirty-two points and set a school record by making all eleven of his shots from the floor. Walker also

moved into a tie with Jack Givens for second place on the all-time UK scoring list, with 2,038 points. Walker was only 100 points shy of the legendary Dan Issel's all-time record of 2,138 points. If the Cats could make it to the finals, Walker might be able to challenge Issel's record.

Kentucky faced two SEC opponents in the next two rounds of the tournament. This schedule probably was a handicap, since it meant that Kentucky would have to beat Alabama and LSU four times each during the season in order to make it to the Final Four in Dallas. Alabama and Kentucky squared off on March 20 at the Omni in Atlanta. Alabama was led by star forwards Derrick McKey and Buck Johnson, both of whom went on to have successful NBA careers. UK opened up a slight 32-28 lead at the half and was able to increase the final margin by one, to 68-63. The Cats' largest lead in the second half of this tense affair was nine points, and with Kenny Walker saddled with four fouls and playing the entire forty minutes, the outcome was in doubt right down to the final horn. Walker led a balanced UK scoring attack by netting twenty-two points, followed by Bennett (fourteen), Davender (thirteen), and Blackmon (eleven). Cedric Jenkins played a very strong twenty-three minutes, helping Walker and Bennett (who played thirty-nine minutes of the contest) control the powerful Crimson Tide forwards. Jenkins scored six points, had four rebounds, and fouled out in a spirited effort. Johnson and McKey played the entire game for Alabama, scoring sixteen and twelve points respectively and grabbing nine and twelve rebounds.

Kentucky's dream season ended after forty minutes of its thirty-sixth game, when the Wildcats succumbed to the balanced play of LSU's starting five, four of whom scored in double figures. The Tigers were led by John Williams, a muscular 6'8" 240-pound power forward, who scored sixteen points. The Cats led by one at the half against Dale Brown's large and powerful team. LSU took the lead for good with 2:31 to go in the game and went ahead 55-53. Although Kenny Walker hit eight of eleven shots and scored twenty points, it was not enough in what proved to be his final game in the Blue and White. There would be no Final Four in Dallas for the Wildcats. Walker ended his college playing years fifty-eight points short of Issel's scoring record, but his had been, nevertheless, a spectacular career.

Ironically, one of the key reasons for Kentucky's failure to beat LSU for a fourth time in the NCAA tournament was the lack of bench play. All season long, Eddie Sutton had worked on developing Cedric Jenkins, Richard Madison, and Rob Lock, largely so that they could

play important minutes against teams like LSU that possessed a lot of size and depth. Madison did not even play against the Tigers, and Jenkins (two points) and Lock (zero points) were ineffective in limited action. The Wildcats did not have any of the bench strength they had worked all season to develop. Quite simply, the Cats' starters wore down after playing 178 of 200 minutes of the game at the Omni.

Still, when the season began with a new coach and a small, three-guard lineup, only the most die-hard of Cats fans could have hoped for a 32-4 record and a trip to the regional finals of the NCAA tournament. Kentucky finished the regular season ranked third and fourth in the nation by the AP and UPI respectively. Eddie Sutton was named national "Coach of the Year" by the AP and the National Association of Basketball Coaches. Kenny Walker was named a consensus first-team All-American, scoring 20.0 points and grabbing 7.7 rebounds per game. Walker also averaged a team high 34.8 minutes per contest and hit 58.2 percent of his shots from the floor. Although his statistics were not up to his junior season numbers, Walker had overcome defenses that keyed on his every move and had led his team through a spectacular season despite being poked in the eye against Kansas and having to wear goggles most of the year. Walker was named first team All-SEC and SEC "Player of the Year" by the AP, while Winston Bennett and Roger Harden made the second and third teams respectively. Ed Davender and James Blackmon had solid seasons as well. Walker (who finished fourth overall), Bennett, and Davender all finished in the top twenty in the SEC in scoring. Harden finished third in assists at 6.4 per game, while Davender was sixth in steals at 1.6 per contest. As a team, the Cats had succeeded in doing what Eddie Sutton wanted: they had led the SEC in scoring defense, giving up only 61.2 points per game. This was over five points per game better than Auburn, the next best defensive team.

While the players were disappointed that they would not be joining the Final Four in Dallas, they still were proud of the team's accomplishments. Jerry Tipton wrote, "There were precious few tears in Kentucky's locker room Saturday evening." Still, the players had begun to believe that this squad was a team of destiny, and the fact that the season was over was hard for them to comprehend. Roger Harden was quoted as saying, "You never stop believing until the buzzer goes off." And Kenny Walker said, "It hasn't sunk in yet. I didn't plan for it being over yet." Walker continued, "It's a big disappointment, but not a disgrace." Wildcat fans surely felt the same way.

The first Sutton team had one more opportunity to play together. In June the Wildcats took off on a seventeen-day, seven-game tour of Japan and Hong Kong, where they won five of six games in the Kirin World Basketball Games against national teams from Japan, Czechoslovakia, and Finland. In addition, UK defeated the South China team in Hong Kong before leaving for home. Coach Sutton called the tour "extremely successful." He explained to the fans that playing a series of international games with a three-point line would be beneficial to the team, since the 1986/87 season would be the first in which the line would be a part of all college games. Sutton turned out to be a prophet, as the 1986/87 Wildcats quickly fell in love with the three-point shot.

Eddie Sutton was riding high. Despite the early season controversies, he had led an overachieving squad to a 32-4 record in 1985/86 and was honored for his coaching. In addition, he had scored a major recruiting coup by signing Owensboro High School All-American Rex Chapman, a 6'5" guard, to a national letter of intent. Chapman was "Mr. Basketball" in Kentucky and was considered by some to be the top guard prospect in the nation. Terry Mills, a powerful 6'10" forward from Romulus, Michigan, was the other prize recruit that Sutton coveted. After signing only Irving Thomas the prior season, the Cats were short on young, talented players, particularly big ones. Mills would fill that void nicely. John McGill quoted Sutton on this subject after Chapman's signing. McGill wrote, "Sutton must have felt as if he were in a nightmare—and the worst centered on recruiting. UK got only one player, Irving Thomas, out of the last crop, which made this season's signing so crucial. Sprinkle in an investigation, and the nightmare begins." While Mills did not sign with UK, instead going with the University of Michigan, the signing of Chapman, whose father had played one season in Lexington, and the successful 1985/86 season were feathers in Sutton's cap. Still, with the loss of Kenny Walker to graduation (and a first round draft choice of the NBA New York Knicks) and the ongoing probe into the UK basketball program, the nightmare that McGill mentioned continued to haunt Sutton and the Wildcats.

In addition to Chapman, UK also signed Derrick Miller, a 6'6" guard from Savannah, Georgia. Miller was generally considered only a step or two below Chapman, earning Georgia's Class A "Player of the Year" honor and being named third team All-American by *Parade Magazine*. The Big Blue began the 1986/87 season expecting to be led by seniors James Blackmon and Winston Bennett, junior Ed Davender, and freshman-to-be Chapman. Juniors Rob Lock, Richard Madison, and

Cedric Jenkins would be expected to step up and help Bennett in the middle, thus replacing Kenny Walker by committee. Miller was to provide depth at the small forward and shooting guard spots.

Eddie Sutton was now settled in, and it was felt that Rex Chapman would help ease the loss of Kenny Walker. In addition, the scandal stories had faded for the time being into the background. Both the university and NCAA were quietly investigating possible violations, but no results appeared imminent. Hopes for the season were high across the state, based largely on the success of the previous year's team, the arrival of "King Rex," and fans' faith in Eddie Sutton's coaching abilities. These hopes were probably excessive. An October Jerry Tipton article titled "Sutton Trying to Temper Hopes for Era of Rex" reported how an overflow crowd of 12,000 attended a fifteen-minute scrimmage and had very high expectations for Chapman and the team. John McGill reported the next month that Sutton had told the team several weeks previously they "had the least talent of any Kentucky team in history." Silence followed Sutton's lecture, a silence which, according to McGill, suggested an "ominous ring of truth." The Wildcats' schedule was tough, and the undersized squad had to rely on several inexperienced players. The challenge was made even more difficult when Winston Bennett was forced to redshirt and miss the entire campaign due to preseason knee surgery. This made the coaching job by Sutton during the season all the more impressive, since despite the injury to the team's best inside player and the ongoing NCAA investigation, he guided the inexperienced UK squad to the NCAA tournament.

Although the Wildcats had a winning record in 1986/87, the difficulties that would face them during the entire season became painfully obvious in the very first game, against Austin Peay. On November 29, 1986, Kentucky opened at Rupp Arena against the Governors in what fans and media assumed would be the traditional easy "tune-up" game. Kentucky started three guards (Chapman, Blackmon, and Davender), along with forward Richard Madison (6'7") and center Rob Lock (6'11"). Instead of a tune-up, the contest was pressure packed and came down to the very last seconds. Austin Peay held a one-point lead with only thirty-nine seconds left to play, but the Wildcats, thanks to a jumper by sophomore Irving Thomas and a free throw by Paul Andrews, were able to squeak through to a 71-69 win.

Despite Rex Chapman's successful eighteen-point introduction to UK fans, the Wildcats had barely overcome a patsy team. Although the Big Blue was ranked eleventh in the nation by the AP going into the game

and was playing at home against an unranked opponent, Eddie Sutton's reaction after the game underlined his low expectations for the squad. After the game, Sutton was quoted as saying, "We're happy to win. I'm afraid that's the way it will be all season." He went on to say, "We had no inside game whatsoever." The coach was correct: Kentucky was outrebounded by the smaller opponent 38-27 and scored only one basket all game off a post-up move.

Kentucky followed the Austin Peay game with another victory, albeit a 66-60 fight, against the Red Raiders of Texas Tech. Chapman struggled, scoring only four points, but Ed Davender followed up his twenty-point opening game performance with a twenty-three-point showing. Next came the December 6 meeting with Bobby Knight's Indiana squad at Assembly Hall in Bloomington. The Hoosiers this time had Steve Alford eligible for the game, and he proved to be the difference. Alford scored twenty-six points and handed out six assists in the Hoosiers' 71-66 victory. Chapman equaled Alford's point total, but this time it was Davender who had an off night, scoring only six points. Kentucky followed this loss with three straight wins, including an 81-69 victory over Boston University to capture the UKIT. However, controversy continued to follow the Wildcat program during this period. On December 17, forward Todd Ziegler had a shoplifting charge dismissed after completing community service requirements.

Despite their struggles, the Wildcats had a 5-1 record as they prepared to take on the defending national champion University of Louisville Cardinals at Freedom Hall on December 27. Kentucky hit eleven of seventeen three-pointers in the game, including five by Rex Chapman (who scored twenty-six points) and easily defeated a talented U of L team. Richard Madison grabbed seventeen rebounds, and the combination of Madison, Rob Lock, and Irving Thomas played tremendous interior defense, holding Cardinal stars Pervis Ellison and Herbert Crook to four and six points, respectively. As Kentucky prepared to start SEC play, fans and the media jumped on the UK bandwagon. The Wildcats had taken a game that had been hyped as a colossal battle and embarrassed the defending champions by a score of 85 to 51.

Two days later, on December 29, the *Atlanta Journal* carried an article by Mark Bradley titled "Rex Chapman: The Extraordinary Kentucky Freshman." Bradley's article started with, "I have seen basketball's future, and its name is Rex Chapman. Some look upon him and see Jerry West reincarnate, others a smaller, swifter Larry

Bird. I see an original, a wondrous creature who cuts across ethnic convention." A day earlier John McGill wrote that Rex Chapman "turned in an epic performance. He may not be a legend yet, but he's clearly building up the portfolio." *Sports Illustrated* writer Curry Kirkpatrick went even further, making these comparisons: "Jerry West throwing in textbook-form three-point bombs without looking? (Once Chapman let loose from *five*-point territory.) Larry Bird half-court bounce passing and three-quarter-court hook passing on the break? Michael Jordan hotdog dunking and fake-and-pullback dribbling over and around his taller elders? Oscar Robertson absolutely *controlling* the contest?"

The press and many fans gave every indication of believing that Chapman would not only replace Kenny Walker as the star that would lead the Wildcats to postseason success, but would also become one of the greatest players in college basketball history. Kentucky fans and the media, including the national press, seemed to be spinning out of control. It is probable that much of the adulation for Chapman was due to his good looks, his aggressive, slashing, jumping style, and, in Kentucky at least, his local origin. Indeed, Chapman was a very talented player, but to compare him with Jerry West, Larry Bird, Michael Jordan, or Oscar Robertson at this point in his career was not only ridiculously premature, but also unfair to Chapman himself. The excessive hype about Chapman and his three-point shot would prove to be Kentucky's downfall.

It is a very rare team indeed that can succeed game after game relying almost exclusively on outside shooting, especially when it exhibits a largely nonexistent inside presence. This point was indicated by McGill when he praised Chapman and the Wildcats on their reliance on the three-pointer, although the writer probably did not understand the negative connotations of what he said at the time. McGill wrote about how UK hit eleven of seventeen three-pointers and quoted Derrick Miller as saying, "You make the three-point shot, and everyone gets quiet. That's what makes the game fun." Kirkpatrick continued in his January 5, 1987, *Sports Illustrated* article with an even more extreme version of what the three-point shot would mean to Chapman and Kentucky: "Seldom has an athlete merged a persona with a moment and created sheer magic—Joe Namath and the Super Bowl, Billie Jean King and Sex Tennis come to mind—as Chapman seems to have done with the three-point shot. If he had arrived last year he would be just another fabulous phenom. This way he's seriously approaching manger material."

As good as Chapman was—and he was *very* good—there was no way that either he or the rest of the Kentucky team, with its small size and just slightly above average level of talent, could live up to such unrealistic and unfair expectations. The press had turned Chapman into an overhyped player. It is a seemingly annual tradition for the Lexington press to take players like Todd May, Derrick Hord, Jay Shidler, and Dwight Anderson and, following one or two strong performances, anoint them as stars. Inevitably the players cannot live up to such hype. They either end up labeled as disappointments (like Hord and Shidler) or they transfer to escape the pressure (like May and Anderson). Chapman's situation was different. He was producing, he was playing very well. He would be an excellent, maybe even a great player if given the time and room to develop his skills and maturity. But the better he played, the more unrealistic the expectations for Rex, "the Boy King," became. Something would have to give at some point unless he could be given the time and encouragement needed for him to truly develop into a player as talented and skilled as West, Jordan, Bird, or Robertson.

The bandwagon became somewhat lighter following season game number eight, a 69-65 loss to Georgia at Rupp Arena on December 30. The Bulldogs controlled the game throughout, taking a 36-29 halftime lead, and shot 58 percent from the floor on the way to victory. Kentucky hit just nine of twenty-eight three-pointers, many of them after UK was already far behind. What fans may now have begun to realize was that although the small, thin Wildcat squad could live by the three and have tremendous performances, as against Louisville, it could also die by the three, as it did in this game against Georgia.

Kentucky was able to gain a 63-60 upset road victory over Auburn. The Tigers, led by Chris Morris, entered the game ranked as high as fifth in the nation and looked ready to feed upon the reeling Wildcat squad. Instead, Rex Chapman hit six three-pointers on his way to a game high twenty-four points, and UK was able to hold onto its lead despite a furious Auburn comeback late in the game.

On January 7, however, the Wildcats' season continued its roller-coaster ride. Eddie Sutton's team, now back in Rupp and ranked ninth in the country by the AP, played an unranked Alabama team led by Derrick McKey. This was a squad that Kentucky had defeated four times the previous year. Unfortunately, this time around Kenny Walker and Winston Bennett were not present to control the athletic Crimson Tide big men.

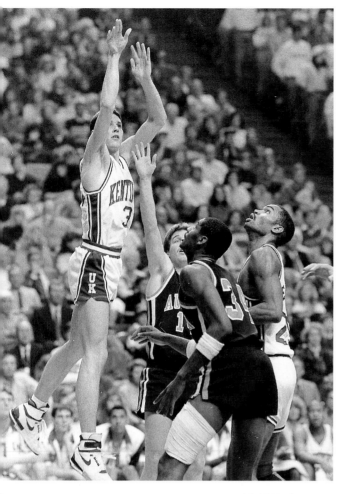

Four views of Rex Chapman in action: *(Left)* "King Rex" shoots during the January 9, 1988, loss to Auburn. Winston Bennett is at right. *(Above)* "The Boy King" at the free throw line. *(Bottom left)* Shooting over the Indiana Hoosiers. *(Bottom right)* Chapman again firing away from long range as Coach Eddie Sutton looks on.

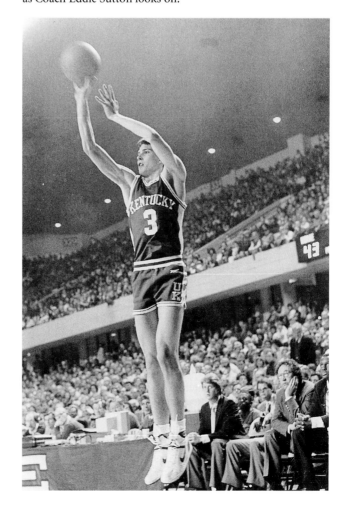

McKey scored twenty-five points and grabbed nine rebounds to help Wimp Sanderson's squad dominate the glass by a 32-23 count. Richard Madison and freshman Derrick Miller were the only Wildcats to play solid games, both scoring in double digits and rebounding effectively. Kentucky's starting guard trio of Chapman, Davender, and James Blackmon hit a combined five of twenty-three shots and passed out only nine assists combined. The fourteen-point loss was, to that point, the worst ever suffered by the Cats at Rupp Arena, tying a loss to Alabama in 1980.

The results against their next opponent, Tennessee, were equally unsatisfying. On January 10, the Wildcats were humbled in Knoxville by a 75-68 score, dropping UK's SEC record to 1-3. In the process, the Volunteers outrebounded their visitors by a sizable 34-22 count. As Tennessee guard Dyron Nix pointed out afterward, "We had control of the game all the way." Thus, despite hitting six of eleven three-pointers and getting twenty-nine points from Ed Davender, the Wildcats could not outclass the Volunteers, who had lost four of their eleven games leading up to the contest. John McGill did a little tongue-in-cheek the day after the game, writing, "Urgent Mailgrams found on the Stokely Athletic Center Floor:

*ATTN: CEDRIC JENKINS. HELP! STRESS FRACTURE IN FOOT NOTHING COMPARED TO DISTRESS FRACTURE IN UK TEAM. HEAL QUICKLY. DESPERATELY YOURS, CONFUSED IN LEX."

McGill had a similar "mailgram" for Mike Scott, a 6'11" center who was not yet eligible to play that season.

It was becoming obvious that despite strong, although somewhat inconsistent, guard play, Kentucky could not win consistently without a bigger contribution from its front line. As Tennessee's Tony White (who scored thirty-two points) pointed out in the same article, "Last year I was driving around Ed (Davender) 'cause I had him beat, but Kenny Walker would be sitting right there in my face." In addition, as McGill noted, "Because there's no consistent scoring threat inside, UK's long shots are finding no breathing room. And it's beginning to catch up." He, like Eddie Sutton and the Wildcats, had begun to understand the limitations of the three-pointer when there was nothing else to complement it.

Kentucky rebounded with a 57-49 win in Starkville against Mississippi State on January 12, raising its record to 8-4 overall and 2-3 in the SEC. The Wildcats then evened their SEC record with a home victory, 67-62 against Florida. Against the Gators, UK won by hitting

52 percent of its shots and out-rebounding a very talented Florida team that included 7' Dwayne Schintzius by a remarkable 49-33 margin. Center Rob Lock garnered thirteen rebounds, and Cedric Jenkins answered McGill's call with six rebounds in eleven minutes. Kentucky, it appeared, had righted the ship once again and found most of the ingredients necessary to be a consistent winner in tournament play. However, the team hit only fifteen of thirty-one free throws, continuing its poor showing in that area.

On January 18 everything crashed down around the Wildcats at Rupp Arena. Dale Brown's Tigers embarrassed Kentucky by a score of 76-41. Even worse, Sutton's charges were outscored 51-20 after trailing by just four points at halftime. It was the worst UK loss since the 1950 squad lost 89-50 to City College of New York in the NIT, the worst home court loss since Cincinnati won 48-10 in 1926. It was the worst Rupp Arena loss ever. Kentucky made only 25 percent of its shots, was outrebounded by nine, and had just eight assists compared to twenty-six turnovers. If there was a silver lining for the Wildcats, it was the twelve of fourteen free throws successfully made. Sutton first called the loss to LSU his most embarrassing loss in his thirty years of coaching, then simply referred to it as a fluke. Regardless, the Wildcats' weaknesses were being exploited to their fullest and every coach in America now knew how to play against this UK squad. Unless Sutton could learn from and adapt to what his opponents were doing, the Wildcats would have but a brief visit to March Madness in 1987.

On January 21 Kentucky won 71-65 on the road against Vanderbilt, the eleventh consecutive win for the Wildcats against the Commodores. Next, with a record at this point of ten wins and five losses, UK took on the Midshipmen of the United States Naval Academy and their star center (and future NBA great) David Robinson. Although Robinson dominated the game from an individual standpoint, scoring forty-five points and grabbing fourteen rebounds, the Cats put together a team effort that included four players scoring in double figures to win the game 80-69. On January 29 the inconsistent squad from Lexington travelled to Oxford to play Ole Miss. Kentucky's "season of dubious distinction" continued. Mississippi's eleven-game losing streak against the Wildcats ended when they beat UK 76-65. The major problems again appeared to be free throws (nine for sixteen), rebounding (outrebounded by six), and shooting (37.5 percent from three-point range and 44.6 percent overall). Sutton had not found a way to control games from the bench.

It was clear that Kentucky lacked the inside players to compete on a consistent basis, and Rex Chapman, at least at this point in his career, was a very good player but not able to dominate a game by himself. To win, the Wildcats had to perform as a team; against strong opponents UK needed the other team to play a subpar game. Big Blue fans, the media, and Coach Sutton were not accustomed to such conditions.

Kentucky won against Mississippi State on January 31. Probably the biggest news, though, as reported the next day by Jerry Tipton, was speculation that several of the Wildcats were jealous of Chapman or disliked him for other reasons and wanted to "beat him up." Chapman dismissed the stories as untrue rumors, but these rumors typified the season: inconsistent basketball and embarrassing off-court distractions.

Possibly because of the public airing of these distractions, Kentucky played its most consistent and solid basketball of the season during the first eleven days of February. On February 7, the Wildcats trailed Alabama by six with just 1:23 to play, but won 70-69 on an Ed Davender shot with twelve seconds remaining. Four days later, the Wildcats trailed Tennessee by ten with 1:13 left, but won 91-84 in overtime.

Kentucky closed the season as inconsistently as it had begun. Although the Big Blue finished the regular season on March 1 with a 75-74 squeaker over a very

Ed Davender and Eddie Sutton discuss strategy.

talented Oklahoma team, they had dropped three of the five games played between the Tennessee and Oklahoma victories. And all the losses had been to conference rivals: by eighteen to Florida on February 14, by thirteen to LSU on February 21, and by eight to Georgia on February 28. Rex Chapman and Ed Davender continued to play well throughout the later part of the season, although both were inconsistent at times. Following a shaky start, Richard Madison had become UK's lone consistent rebounding force, leading the team in rebounding in ten of the last thirteen regular-season games.

The Big Blue entered the SEC tournament paired against a talented but also inconsistent Auburn team that it had already beaten twice. Both the 18-9 Wildcats and the 16-11 Tigers believed they needed to win the game to make the NCAA field, although Auburn probably needed the victory more. It showed. Auburn got the decision, 79-72. Kentucky went just five for nineteen from the three-point arc, and hit only eleven of twenty-four free throws. Chapman and Davender each scored seventeen points and played solidly, but they alone were not enough. The Lexington squad was still able to back into the NCAA tournament, as it was given an at-large bid and a relatively high eighth seed in the Southeast Regional.

The Chapman saga continued in the days leading up to the NCAA tournament, with the *Courier-Journal*'s Jim Terhune publishing a story on the controversies and situations that Chapman had faced thus far during the season. Included were rumors of the prejudice Chapman faced because he dated black women, poor relationships with other players on the team, and the pressures of dealing with "rock star-style idolatry." In other words, UK's most talented player—Davender was probably the most consistent—was distracted on the eve of tournament play.

Kentucky returned to Atlanta to open its Southeast Regional run against the ninth seeded Ohio State Buckeyes. Ohio State had finished the regular season with three straight losses en route to a 19-12 record. As Rob Lock pointed out, "They struggled, we struggled." If the Big Blue won, it would probably have to face a powerful Georgetown squad, but the Wildcats first had to beat the Buckeyes. Ed Davender admitted prior to the game that "Georgetown's a little bit in everybody's mind." Despite its history of inconsistency and its marginal talent, Kentucky appeared to be looking ahead past Ohio State to the Georgetown game as though the Cats were certain to beat the Buckeyes. That was a serious mistake.

Ohio State stretched a two-point halftime lead into

a 91-77 victory in the March 13 meeting. Dennis Hopson led the Buckeyes with thirty-two points, and Rex Chapman hit just four of sixteen shots on his way to a thirteen-point performance. Kentucky made only eight of twenty-three three-point shots and was outrebounded by nine. Ed Davender scored twenty-three points, joining Rob Lock (fourteen points) as the only Wildcats to play well. UK's season was over at 18-10, and, as Jerry Tipton wrote, "Winston Bennett was supposed to power this team, but his knee went bad. A foot problem forced Cedric Jenkins out, and he never recovered. Help was on the way in the blocky form of Mike Scott, but that didn't work out, either. No wonder Kentucky fell in love with a shot that was guaranteed to produce frustration as well as a shooter's fantasy." In other words, Kentucky—which at one point was down to just seven active scholarship players—had lived and then died by the three-point shot. It was all the Wildcats had.

Although the comparisons to Michael Jordan and Jerry West had become less frequent, Rex Chapman was named to the second team All-SEC squad following the season, and Sutton believed that this was just the beginning for his star. Sutton was quoted as saying, "He's just a freshman. He's still going to be a fine basketball player." While this was high praise for a first-year player, it was a long, long way from the early season hype. Davender made third team All-SEC. Chapman had averaged 16 points per game, Davender was next at 15.1 points, with no other Wildcat making double figures. Richard Madison led the team with 7.4 rebounds per game.

The disappointment began to fade only days after the season ended as Sutton, the players, the fans, and the media began to look forward to the 1987/88 season. Chapman would return a year older and, all anticipated, a more consistent player. Winston Bennett was expected back to help shoulder the load. In addition, Kentucky signed six top freshmen, including two high school All-American power players: 6'11" center/power forward LeRon Ellis from California and 6'6" swingman Eric Manuel from Georgia. Other freshmen included Sean Sutton, a point guard from Lexington's Henry Clay High School and the coach's son, forward Reggie Hanson, a Proposition 48 player, forward Johnathon Davis, and two 6'7" freshman forwards from Eastern Kentucky, Deron Feldhaus and John Pelphrey. Davis, Feldhaus, and Pelphrey would redshirt and thus sit out the upcoming season. Since the only starter lost would be James Blackmon, the future for UK basketball seemed bright.

The Blue and White opened the 1987/88 season with ten consecutive victories, including wins over outstanding Indiana and Louisville squads. Four different players led the Wildcats in both scoring and rebounding in those opening ten victories, displaying a balance and depth that had been lacking in the previous season. During this period, Sutton revived the comparisons of Chapman with Jerry West. The coach said in a Jerry Tipton article: "He reminds me of Jerry West. I hesitate to say that because Jerry West was probably one of the top 15 players of all time." The remark was indeed unfair to Chapman, who was not as uniquely talented nor as fundamentally solid a college basketball player; comparing their professional careers would be even more of a distortion, since Chapman has bounced around the NBA while West was a perennial All-Star. While Chapman was undeniably talented, such comparisons created unfair pressure and expectations each time he appeared on the basketball court. West recognized what was happening, and in the same article he tried to temper the comparisons: "I always look at it as a form of flattery to me. But I don't understand why people do that in the first place. It's best to let him be Rex Chapman." Kentucky fans, however, believed the hype. As Tipton wrote following West's comments, "Sorry, Rex. Sorry, Jerry. After some dipsy-do creation or picture perfect jumper, it's all but impossible to resist."

On January 9, 1988, the Cats lost to Auburn by one point, 53-52, at Rupp Arena, bringing their record to ten wins and one loss. Winston Bennett scored twenty points and grabbed ten rebounds, demonstrating just how invaluable he might have been the previous year. The Wildcats rebounded with convincing victories over two of their nemeses of recent years, Alabama (63-55) and Tennessee (83-65), before losing 58-56 to Florida at Rupp Arena on January 20. Richard Madison's three-point try bounced off the rim in the game's closing seconds, sealing the defeat. Kentucky was held to 28.1 percent field goal shooting, and only its proficiency at the free throw line (where UK hit twenty-one free throws compared to Florida's four) kept the Wildcats in the game. The size of Dwayne Schintzius and the speed of future pro star Vernon Maxwell, combined with off nights for Rex Chapman (five for nineteen from the field) and Ed Davender (seven points), proved too much for the Blue and White to overcome.

After savoring the defeat of Dale Brown's LSU team in Baton Rouge on January 23, Wildcat fans suffered through an 83-66 loss to Vanderbilt on January 27 in Nashville. Although this was a solid Commodore squad led by future NBA player Will Purdue, the size of the loss surprised UK and its fans. By now 13-3, the Wild-

cats' next opponent was Notre Dame on January 17 at Freedom Hall. Digger Phelps' Fighting Irish, led by All-American guard David Rivers, were en route to an NCAA tournament appearance and a twenty-win season. Freshman LeRon Ellis started his first game for the Wildcats, replacing Cedric Jenkins, who had not rebounded, scored, or defended physically enough for Sutton's liking. Ellis scored fourteen points to help lead Kentucky to a 78-69 victory. Ed Davender contributed twenty-three points, continuing to prove that he was easily the team's most underrated player. Not only were his scoring, passing, and defensive skills important, but so were the intangibles he offered. While Chapman and Bennett were probably more physically talented, more often than not it was Davender who rose to the occasion against talented opponents like David Rivers to key Kentucky's big-game victories.

Kentucky followed the Notre Dame victory with wins over Ole Miss, Mississippi State, Auburn, and Alabama before losing back-to-back games to Tennessee and Florida. The Wildcats then reeled off seven straight regular- and postseason victories against SEC competition, culminating with a 62-57 victory over Georgia to win the SEC tournament. Rex Chapman returned after missing several games because of a back injury to help earn the victory over Georgia in the championship game. But according to Georgia coach Hugh Durham following the game, Manuel was the real key to the Cats' recent run of successes. "I really think Kentucky is in a position that they can challenge for the national championship," Durham maintained. "When [Eric] Manuel went into the lineup it made them better at two positions. It moved Winston Bennett to strong forward. That's a plus there. . . . It's a different Kentucky team, in our opinion, with Winston Bennett and Eric Manuel at those spots." Sutton, who inserted Manuel into the starting lineup when the Cats played Syracuse on February 28, agreed with Durham. The team was stronger with Manuel in the lineup replacing LeRon Ellis.

With a starting lineup of Bennett, Chapman, Davender, Lock, and Manuel, UK entered NCAA tournament play eager to improve on the disappointing performance of the previous season. As Durham had pointed out, Kentucky was a legitimate contender for the national title, and the Big Blue opened the tournament in Cincinnati with victories over Southern University and Maryland. All five Kentucky starters, led by Davender and Chapman with twenty-three each, scored in double figures against the strong Maryland squad. The Wildcats outrebounded the Terrapins and shot thir-

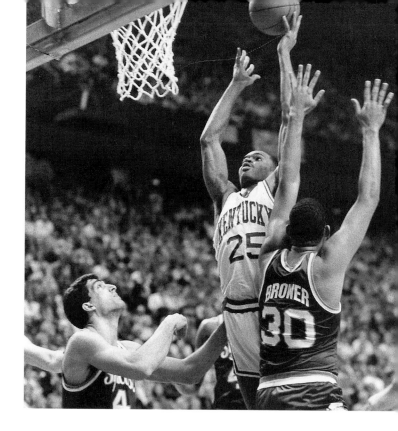

Winston Bennett contributing two points to UK's 62-58 victory over Syracuse on February 28, 1988. At left is Orangeman center and future NBA player Rony Seikaly.

teen more free throws. Winston Bennett, who had seventeen points, twelve rebounds, and made a key defensive play near the end of the game, was a "hero all day." Unfortunately, the season ended with an 80-74 loss to Villanova in the Southeast Regional finals in Birmingham despite thirty points from Rex Chapman. Rollie Massimino's Villanova Wildcats opened up an eleven-point halftime lead and held on for the victory. While Kentucky finished 27-6, the loss to Villanova was a disappointment for the UK Wildcats and their fans. Worse, sanctions later imposed by the NCAA forced the deletion of all three tournament games from Wildcat records.

The pain of the loss to Villanova on March 24, however, was nothing compared to events that began to unfold a week later. On March 30 an Emery Worldwide envelope was sent from UK assistant coach and master recruiter Dwane Casey to Claude Mills, the father of prep standout Chris Mills. According to an April 25 *Sports Illustrated* article by Alexander Wolff:

The next morning [March 31], Eric Osborn, an employee at Emery Worldwide's distribution center near Los Angeles In-

ternational Airport, was sorting dozens of packages when he noticed that the envelope in question had come open. The label identified the sender as Dwane Casey, who's an assistant basketball coach at the University of Kentucky. The package was addressed to Claude Mills, the father of Chris Mills, a Kentucky signee who may be the finest high school basketball player ever to come out of LA. Osborn noticed a videocassette sticking out of the package. Then he noticed something else: 20 $50 bills.

Casey acknowledged sending the package and tape, and Chris Mills admitted signing for it. Both, however, denied that the envelope contained any money.

The *Sports Illustrated* article implied that Mills was, indeed, being paid off by the university: "In February 1987, when Keteyian [another *SI* reporter] visited the one-bedroom apartment that the elder Mills shares with Chris and another son, Tracey, the living room was furnished with a couch, a table, and several basketball trophies. The Millses now have new furniture. In November, around the time of the early signing date for basketball recruits, Chris began driving a 1984 Datsun 300ZX."

The main focus of the Emery Package investigation, Chris Mills later transferred to Arizona and went on to play in the NBA.

Both Claude Mills and Casey denied any payoff. Casey and his attorney alleged that it was a conspiracy by UCLA backers to discredit UK and solidify its lock on local talent. However, the NCAA was now digging seriously. Only four weeks earlier it had released a report on its findings regarding the violations reported in the *Herald-Leader* "hundred-dollar handshake" series. While the NCAA had reprimanded the Wildcats following that investigation, no serious penalties had been meted out. The NCAA's prior investigation now appeared to have been inept, the NCAA itself looked ridiculous, and the likelihood of serious sanctions against UK increased dramatically.

Following release of the NCAA findings into the "hundred-dollar handshake" allegations in early March 1988, the *Herald-Leader* ran an editorial entitled "A Sad Day for Truth at UK." In the editorial, the newspaper claimed that "UK conducted its investigations with a wink and a smile. The results made it impossible for the NCAA to conduct a thorough investigation of its own." John S. Carroll, editor of the *Herald-Leader*, found it ironic that, less than one month after the NCAA had stated it found no reason to place serious penalties on the Wildcats because of the university's deception and the deception of its boosters, UK found itself in the middle of another scandal. Carroll alleged that the school had stonewalled the NCAA and that the school's boosters had bullied players into recanting their stories; furthermore, neither the university nor its fans seemed to feel a collective guilt.

While these improprieties upset Carroll sufficiently to cause him to write about them, his editorials simply led to a flood of cancelled subscriptions to the newspaper. Big Blue fans did not share his embarrassment. Rather, they objected to any attacks on Wildcat basketball.

On April 20 Billy Reed published an article in the *Herald-Leader* in which he wrote, "You've heard the party line, maybe even adhered to it. Everybody's against UK. Jealous of the Cats. Wants to bring The Program down. . . . But for dispassionate observers, the obvious conclusion is that nothing much has changed in Lexington over the decades. Coaches, players and fans have come and gone, but the *mentality* has remained the same." Reed made this comment in comparing the 1988 scandals to the 1951 case where a New York judge denounced Adolph Rupp and the "UK atmosphere" that led to repeated violations of amateur rules. Nothing, according to Reed, had changed except the individual participants.

The Program, as Reed called it, was now in turmoil. On April 29 the NCAA began a formal investigation of

the Mills situation. *Sports Illustrated* pointed out that "it was the third time in the last 12 years that the NCAA has looked into similar allegations involving Wildcat basketball players or recruits." In addition, shortly thereafter a former Indiana player, Rick Calloway, claimed that Shawn Kemp, who committed to Kentucky before deciding to forgo college for the NBA, after failing to meet Proposition 48 guidelines, was "looking for a handout" when he went to Bloomington on a recruiting trip. This Associated Press story appeared in the *Herald-Leader*, and by implication—since Calloway claimed that Kemp was incredulous that IU would not offer him anything—suggested (although it did not state directly) that UK had made offers to Kemp. Kemp denied all allegations. To add to the confusion and stories, "King Rex" decided to turn professional, skipping his final two years of play for the Wildcats.

In a May 14 article in the *Herald-Leader*, Billy Reed listed three major reasons he believed led to Chapman's decision to turn professional: lack of privacy and vicious reports about his private life, disappointment with Eddie Sutton as a coach, and the Chris Mills situation, which did, in fact, lead to serious NCAA sanctions. There is no question that Chapman's privacy had been invaded as a result of all the attention he received, and the possibility of playing for a team facing NCAA sanctions certainly could have helped shape his decision. The point about Sutton, however, is the most interesting, since Chapman chose UK over Louisville at least in part because of the coach and his reputation for developing guards who went on to the NBA. Reed maintained that conflict developed between player and coach "when Sutton began questioning Rex's shot selection and preaching a patterned offense."

Without realizing it, Reed might have touched on a fourth reason that drove Chapman away from the Wildcats when he continued, "Had he stayed for the full term at UK, championship or not, he was destined to go down as no worse than another Cotton Nash—a three-time consensus All-American. . . . Had Chapman ever been turned completely loose, maybe he could have been another Nash. Or another Jerry West. Or maybe even another Pistol Pete Maravich." Such offhanded statements had to take their toll on Chapman, adding immeasurably to the pressure he faced. It appears that Chapman was not, in fact, as talented as Maravich, West, or Nash; he was a fine player who had averaged 17.6 points per game during his years as a Wildcat (in comparison with Nash, who had averaged 22.6 points and 12.3 rebounds per game during his career in Lexington). Chapman had toiled for a modestly talented squad for two years, play-

ing for a coach for whom he had lost respect, in a situation where he might lose television exposure to NBA scouts should Kentucky receive heavy NCAA penalties for recruiting violations, in a city where his every move was observed and discussed and where his play was constantly compared to that of others.

Jerry West had been right—Chapman should have been left alone to be himself. Had he been permitted to develop, comparisons to Nash might have been appropriate by the end of Chapman's senior season. In the end, his decision was probably an easy one to make: professional basketball for the expansion Charlotte Hornets (who drafted him in the first round) in place of the madhouse that he would have had to face the next season in the Bluegrass.

Kentucky was about to enter the 1988/89 season without its best players from the previous year, as Chapman, Davender, Lock, and Bennett had left. Its best recruit, Chris Mills, reportedly was considering not enrolling at UK because of the controversy. The elder Mills was quoted as saying, "I don't even want Chris to go to Kentucky. I really don't." Don McLean, another prep standout who had also been interested in UK, chose UCLA over the Wildcats following the NCAA investigation into the Mills accusations. Shawn Kemp elected to jump to the NBA. Sean Woods, another Kentucky recruit and Proposition 48 casualty, enrolled at the Lexington campus but would be ineligible to play during his first year at the university.

It was clear that Eddie Sutton's days were now numbered. His final UK team did include Chris Mills. It did not, however, number Eric Manuel, who sat out the season after the NCAA began investigating allegations that he had cheated on his American College Test (ACT), a national college entrance examination. The NCAA pointed to the dramatic improvement on the ACT Manuel took in Lexington, where he scored 23, after having previously failed twice to make scores even close to that level on the equivalent Scholastic Aptitude Test (SAT) taken in Macon, Georgia. The NCAA report that banned him from playing college basketball for a member school alleged that 211 of 219 questions were answered identically to the person seated next to Manuel, and the NCAA accepted this fact as proof that he had cheated. Manuel denied cheating, but the university chose not to appeal on his behalf. After the NCAA revoked his eligibility to play, Manuel responded, "I don't feel like I've let anybody down, because I didn't do anything wrong. If anything, [Kentucky] let me down."

The Wildcats were not yet on probation. Eddie Sutton and his squad were coming off a 27-6 season.

Eric Manuel passing the ball during his brief career in Lexington. He was the only player to suffer sanctions in the wake of the Emery Package investigation. The NCAA accused Manuel of cheating on his ACT test, and he was banned from playing at any NCAA institution.

The 1988/89 team, however, had lost a load of talent from the previous year's squad, and it was difficult for the remaining players to focus on basketball given the events swirling about them. Kentucky went 13-19, its first losing season since 1927. It lost to Vanderbilt in the first round of the SEC tournament to end the season. It was, in short, a terrible year both on and off the court. The Mills investigation dominated media and fan attention, and basketball took second place. Following the season, Sutton resigned in disgrace from the Kentucky position. Despite his overall record at UK of eighty-eight wins and thirty-nine losses, Sutton left as a loser. The Wildcat basketball program had also been transformed into a loser, at least for the time being.

Mills transferred to Arizona following the season. Ironically, even though the evidence presented in Wolff and Keteyian's *Raw Recruits* suggests that both Sutton and Mills played important roles in the sordid affair, both went on to very successful careers. Following a year off from coaching, Sutton took over the head coaching job at Oklahoma State, even guiding the team to the Final Four of the NCAA tournament a couple of years later. Mills had a very successful career at Arizona and went on to the NBA. Eric Manuel, on the other hand, was prohibited from ever again playing NCAA basketball and ended up performing for an NAIA school. He never made it to the NBA.

Only months before the 1988/89 season was to begin, Kentucky had boasted a squad of Chapman, Kemp, Manuel, Mills, Ellis, Woods, and Miller, potentially the most potent and deep lineup in college basketball that season, or most other seasons for that matter. Now, UK's very forgettable starting lineup most of the season was Reggie Hanson, Derrick Miller, LeRon Ellis, Sean Sutton, and Chris Mills. Although Ellis (sixteen points per game) and Mills (14.3 points per game) played well, the team was not especially competitive, being badly beaten by traditional rivals Indiana (by twenty-three points) and Louisville (twenty-two points), as well as by squads such as Vanderbilt (thirty points) that the Wildcats had generally outscored. Still, Eddie Sutton believed following the season that his team, even with such limited talent, could have been successful were it not for the distractions that surrounded them. "We would have won twenty games last year," the coach maintained, "but every day the kids would pick up the paper and read something about the investigation. These are nineteen- and twenty-year-old kids. After a while, it really gets to them."

Some UK players transferred rather than spend their college careers playing for a team going on probation. Mills had to leave or lose his eligibility by remaining with the Wildcats. He was joined by LeRon Ellis and Sean Sutton. Sutton apparently wanted to return to the team the next year, but allegedly was rebuffed by the new coaching staff.

Athletics Director Cliff Hagan also departed, to be

LeRon Ellis shooting a free throw during the disastrous 1988/89 season. Ellis would transfer to Syracuse before the start of the next season.

replaced by C.M. Newton, who had a reputation for being squeaky clean. Even so, it seemed that the world considered the UK basketball program to be dirty, and no amount of denial from within could change this perception. As Billy Reed pointed out in his April 20, 1988, article in the *Herald-Leader*, "Say what you will about Indiana, Louisville, North Carolina, Kansas, Georgetown, or any other perennially Top Ten program, but they generally manage to avoid the various sorts of scandals and gaffes that have plagued UK for almost four decades." While the coach and his star players could jump ship relatively unscathed and go on to build successful futures, the program at the University of Kentucky was left to wither. Things looked bad, very bad, for the Wildcats.

The NCAA placed Kentucky's basketball program on probation for three years, including a two-year ban from postseason play, a loss of scholarships, and a one-year ban from televised play; the university forfeited revenues from the 1988 NCAA tournament (as well as its three victories) because of Manuel's participation.

Former Wildcat player C.M. Newton was appointed UK's athletics director on April 1, 1989, following a thirty-two-year career as coach at Transylvania, Alabama, and Vanderbilt.

In addition, Chris Mills was declared ineligible to play for the Big Blue, although he could and did transfer and retain eligibility, while Manuel was banned from ever again playing basketball for any NCAA member institution.

According to an article that appeared in the *Honolulu Star-Bulletin* on May 19, 1989, "Steve Morgan, the NCAA's associate executive director in charge of enforcement, said the committee 'very seriously considered' further sanctions against The Program." The death penalty, where a school has to drop the sport, was rumored to be a possible NCAA response, according to some accounts. In the end, it appears that UK's cooperation with the investigation was cited by the NCAA as a reason for leniency. David Berst, the director of enforcement for the NCAA, expressed the belief that Kentucky was actually rewarded for its cooperation with the investigation. Berst praised UK's "dramatic change in attitude." Ironically, the very actions taken by President David Roselle which so impressed Berst and the NCAA angered many of the Wildcat faithful, who believed that the president should have fought to the end to defend the basketball program against all charges.

The NCAA sanctions were widely seen as a deterrent to attracting a new and effective head coach as well as quality recruits. As the Sutton era came to a close, UK began the quest for a coach who could simultaneously clean up the program, create public excitement in a meagerly talented team going on probation, and ultimately return the school to its glory days as an NCAA champion. The university had its work cut out. For the first time, several high profile coaches that Kentucky identified as candidates indicated that they were not interested in the position. The Kentucky Wildcat basketball program was in crisis.

12

Pitino and the Road Back to the Top

The search for a new head coach following Eddie Sutton's resignation on March 19, 1989, lacked some of the intrigue and possibilities associated with the hiring of the two previous UK basketball coaches. Many coaches who might normally have been very interested instead shied away from taking over a program depleted of star players and going on NCAA probation. Despite the paucity of marquee names in the applications, Athletics Director C.M. Newton was unfazed, as he seemed to know exactly the coach he wanted to hire for the position. And that person, Rick Pitino, was very interested in the job. Pitino was still under contract to the NBA New York Knicks when he began expressing interest in UK. The New York-born Pitino had taken Providence University to the NCAA Final Four in 1986/87 before jumping ship to coach his hometown professional team. But was Pitino the logical choice to restore UK's image, bring back pride to Bluegrass basketball, and run a squeaky-clean program? Pitino was a dapper New York Italian who coached a star-laden NBA team in the most media-hyped market in the country. He favored fine Italian food and bright lights, a far cry from the country cooking and television blackouts that conventional wisdom said he would face in the backwaters of Kentucky.

In Newton's eyes, however, Pitino met the Wildcats' needs. "I knew hiring the right man would be important," Newton recalled in a 1991 interview. "After I studied his success at other places and got eyeball to eyeball with Rick, I knew he was the one. . . . I'm convinced we have the best coach in the nation." As a high-profile professional coach, Pitino could add luster to UK's tarnished image as well as attract players wanting to play for the "Knicks Coach." In addition, Pitino favored an even more up-tempo style of play than Sutton, and thus might be able to quickly rekindle fan support for and interest in a team that lacked talent. Still, although he led the Knicks to a career regular-season record of ninety wins and seventy-four losses during his two seasons as coach, and a berth in the 1988/89 NBA playoffs, Pitino had yet to prove himself the "winner" that UK fans expected in their next coach. Pitino would learn that just making the NCAA Final Four, as his Providence team had done, is not enough to satisfy the Wildcat faithful. After an initial grace period, Pitino would be expected to "win it all."

The lead article in the *Herald-Leader* on May 25, 1989, was devoted to speculation about whether or not Pitino would decide to relocate to Lexington. Jerry Tipton's article discussed the various factors weighing on Pitino in making his decision. C.M. Newton was quoted as recognizing that Pitino faced a difficult decision in "whether to leave one of the premier professional basketball positions, one that he has built into championship caliber, to rebuild the Kentucky basketball program." In this same article, Pitino lamented leaving Providence to coach in the NBA and stated his desire to return to college coaching. Tipton quoted Pitino as saying, "I've always said I'm a college coach on borrowed time." Indeed, the *New York Times* recalled that Pitino had often said while coaching the Knicks that "he planned to go back to college coaching. He never set a timetable for the return, however."

The surprising factor was that Pitino decided to leave

New York just after signing a two-year contract extension to the three-year deal signed with the Knicks in July 1987. Nevertheless, the Knicks let him out of his contract, probably because of the strained relationship between Pitino and his boss with the Knicks, Al Bianchi. Thus *New York Times* sportswriter George Vecsey noted in his May 31, 1989, column that "there was something cold about Pitino's relationship with Bianchi, the Knicks' general manager, who may not have wanted to hire Pitino in the first place."

In the aftermath of his dismissal as Knicks' general manager in March 1991, Bianchi presented his side of the story. In an April 8, 1991, *New York Times* interview prior to his departure from the city, Bianchi recalled that Pitino "kept saying, 'Well, I might have stayed if not for Al.' The fact is he was here to make a quick hit. The one thing I remember him saying was: 'You can't trust those guys upstairs. Get what you can while you can.'" In the same article, Pitino maintained that "there was a basic mistrust both ways, from the start" between the two men.

Strangely enough, the one issue that potentially could have made Kentucky cautious about Pitino, given the university's probationary status, did not become a major factor in his hiring. The University of Hawaii had been found guilty of recruiting violations during the 1974/75 season, when Pitino was a graduate assistant, and during the 1975/76 campaign, when he was an assistant coach. "The NCAA Committee on Infractions," the *Honolulu Star-Bulletin* noted in a May 23, 1989, article, "said Pitino broke eight rules, including arranging free airline transportation for Hawaii players to the mainland, using basketball tickets to buy cars and helping players receive free meals at McDonalds." Pitino vehemently denied "any mistakes" while in Hawaii. "I was a graduate assistant [actually he was an assistant coach during his second year at the University of Hawaii]. I didn't make any mistakes. I don't care what anybody says."

The Hawaii head coach at the time of the violations, Bruce O'Neil, when informed of Pitino's comments, was quoted in the May 23 *Honolulu Advertiser* as saying, "If Rick is smart, he wouldn't bring that kind of stuff up. . . . Rick's got to be real careful. He's always had trouble with loyalties. He talks about stabbing people in the back. That can go both ways." Pitino let the matter drop, as did the University of Kentucky.

It seemed logical, however, that the NCAA scrutiny of the Hawaii program during Pitino's tenure would work against him, given UK's need to rebuild its image in the wake of Sutton's departure. Pitino, for his part, addressed the issue in a Jerry Tipton article: "Mother Teresa can't coach basketball. I feel I'm close to that. I'm as ethical as you can find in a basketball coach because of my good ego. The good ego is anybody who has to cheat in order to win deflates his ability as a basketball coach. Certainly that's nothing I would do. I'm one of those people who thinks he can win just by all the old-fashioned methods."

For his part, UK President David Roselle "seemed to dismiss them [the allegations of Pitino's violations at Hawaii] as a hindrance in a news release yesterday," according to Tipton. Pitino related in his book *Full-Court Pressure* that C.M. Newton "told me the president was not concerned about the Hawaii incident." Pitino recalled Newton saying, "'He's totally comfortable with what you stand for.'" It thus appears that even while placing "a premium on compliance with NCAA rules as a criterion," UK officials focused even more on finding a winning coach. And the signing of Pitino was vital to the resurgence of the Wildcats, as Oscar Combs bluntly stated in the June 24 *Cats' Pause*: "Perhaps it's not fair to say Kentucky could not bounce back had Pitino refused UK's offer, but I'll go ahead and say it anyway."

Pitino proved Newton, Roselle, and Combs right. No major recruiting- or other basketball-related scandals touched the Wildcats under him. In addition, he proved many of his naysayers wrong both by lasting in Lexington as long as he did, by winning the 1996 NCAA championship, and by being NCAA runner-up in 1997. All this success seemed far away, even out of reach, before the New Yorker arrived in town to start his first season. Initial concerns probably began to disappear for many Wildcat fans upon Pitino's arrival, as he quickly won over the allegiance of Kentuckians with his energetic style and tremendous coaching skills. In addition, Pitino became a one-man PR department, bringing fame and fortune to the university and himself through national and regional advertising contracts and snappy quotes for sportswriters. Pitino also proved to be an effective recruiter, bringing good and even above-average talent to the Bluegrass, even while the program struggled under the shadow of NCAA restrictions. Most importantly, he won.

Pitino won regular-season games and regular-season SEC titles, SEC tournaments, and NCAA tournament games. Finally in 1996 he won the NCAA championship, and then in overtime in 1997 with an injury-depleted squad he fell just short of repeating that accomplishment. That he did all this in such a short time is amazing. One has only to look back on the condition of the Wildcat program when the New Yorker took over to recognize the distance that UK and Pitino travelled together. Pitino

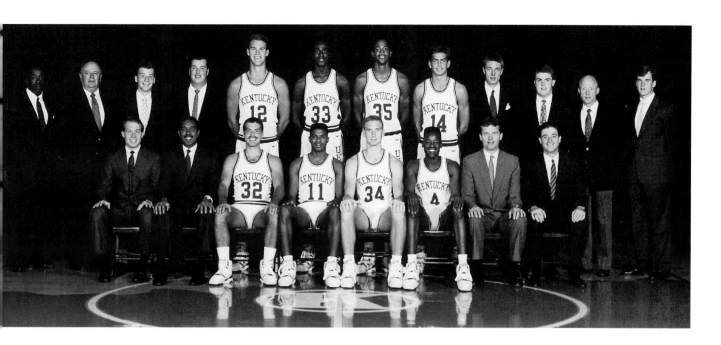

The 1989/90 Kentucky basketball team, coaches, and major support personnel. Seated, left to right: Herb Sendek, Tubby Smith, Richie Farmer, Sean Woods, John Pelphrey, Derrick Miller, Ralph Willard, and Rick Pitino. Standing, left to right: Ray Oliver, Bill Keightley, Jeff Morrow, Robbie Gayheart, Deron Feldhaus, Johnathon Davis, Reggie Hanson, Jeff Brassow, David Deaton, Spencer Tatum, Walt McCombs, and Billy Donovan.

led the 1989/90 team to a 14-14 record, a remarkable achievement in the wake of Sutton's disastrous final season, the exodus of several stars, the lack of size and talent, and the distractions remaining from the various scandals.

With the 1989/90 team, Pitino had several solid players to work with, but no real star. *Chicago Tribune* columnist Skip Myslenski put it bluntly, if ungraciously: Pitino had, Myslenski wrote, "a group of eight scholarship players who were short on talent and low on confidence." Not only were they "small and slow," but "together they were as anonymous as all those sources scurrying around Washington."

Derrick Miller, Reggie Hanson, Deron Feldhaus, John Pelphrey, Sean Woods, and Richie Farmer were the team's key players. At 6'7", Feldhaus and Pelphrey provided the team's "size." In addition, this squad was neither particularly quick nor full of deadly outside shooters. One thing the team did possess, and in abundance, was heart.

Hanson, Feldhaus, Pelphrey, and Farmer were Kentucky natives. For them, playing for the Big Blue was a dream come true. Pitino demanded that his players give him 110 percent and this squad, the "Bombinos," responded. It was, if nothing else, an exciting season for players and fans alike. Despite losing by fifty-five points to Kansas, losing to Louisville, and having Southwest-

ern Louisiana win the UKIT, it was by most measures a successful season. The team earned the nickname "Pitino's Bombinos" because of their youth, their enthusiasm, and their emphasis on three-point shooting. Lexington sportswriter John McGill seems to have been the first to use the term. On December 6, 1989, after UK bombed Tennessee Tech 111-75, he wrote, "Pitino's Bambinos? No, call them Pitino's BOM-binos."

Because of the lack of talent available, Pitino later admitted, "we needed a gimmick the first season and the three-point offense gave us one." Playing Pitino's up-tempo style with full-court pressure defense and an emphasis on long-range shooting on offense, and possessing superbly conditioned bodies from a grueling preseason conditioning program, the Wildcats were able to score over 100 points in eight of their twenty-eight games, providing fans with plenty of excitement. The Pitino style also enabled the Wildcats to beat teams with superior talent. Kentucky defeated Alabama (which finished 26-9), Georgia (20-9), LSU (23-9), Tennessee (16-14), and Vanderbilt (21-14). In fact, entering its final two games, UK sported a 14-12 record, with a chance to attain a seemingly impossible 16-12 mark. That was not to be. Losses to Ole Miss and Notre Dame spoiled this possibility. Still, 14 and 14 was remarkable under the circumstances, and for the first time in history the entire state (except possibly Pitino himself) was happy, or

at least relieved, that the Wildcats had attained mediocrity. Miller led the team in scoring with an average of 19.1 points per game, while Hanson was the key to its balance, averaging 16.4 points and 7.1 rebounds per game and playing solid defense. Pelphrey and Feldhaus also averaged in double digits in points and were key rebounders for this undermanned and overachieving squad.

In Pitino's words, the team was "special," not only because of the style of play, "but special because they went through fatigue. They treated fatigue with laughter. They fought right through that and became outstanding basketball people." As had become abundantly clear even in preseason practices, the team lacked almost every tangible basketball asset, including depth, experience, size, speed, rebounding, and pure shooters. What it possessed in full measure was heart. What it attained, with only eight scholarship players, none taller than 6'7", was a respectable fourth place finish in the SEC race. Pitino was named SEC Coach of the Year by UPI and National Coach of the Year by *Basketball Times*. These achievements provided quite a contrast to the prevailing wisdom expressed prior to the 1989/90 season and summed up by the *Atlanta Journal and Constitution*'s Tony Barnhart when he warned Pitino that "a bleak situation waits at Kentucky." As matters unfolded, what awaited Pitino was not a bleak situation but rather a rare opportunity.

For UK fans, the 1990/91 season brought great promise for a continued, and perhaps accelerated, return to the ranks of the basketball elite. Pitino's coaching ability had been proven in abundance to players and fans

the prior season, the new style of play seemed well suited to the returning lettermen, and Pitino's first recruiting class included a big catch. Returning were senior Reggie Hanson (16.4 ppg/7.1 rpg) and juniors Richie Farmer (7 ppg), Deron Feldhaus (14.4 ppg), John Pelphrey (13.0 ppg) and Sean Woods (9.1 ppg). Pitino's recruits included Gimel Martinez, a McDonald's All-American center/forward from Miami. The "big catch," however, was Jamal Mashburn, a 6'8" power forward from New York. Mashburn averaged 23.3 points and nine rebounds per game as a high school senior and was considered to be one of the top dozen high school players in the nation by almost every pundit. Although Kentucky failed to land Eric Montross, a seven-footer from Indiana who instead chose to play for Dean Smith at the University of North Carolina, adding Mashburn to the Wildcat lineup gave the team a dimension it had lacked, a potential "star." For Pitino, adding Mashburn did more than provide one talented player, it helped open the New York area to UK recruiters.

When the *Herald-Leader* ran its college basketball preview in the November 18, 1990, issue, John McGill's top twenty-five featured UNLV (the defending national champions) at number one and the Kentucky Wildcats at number twenty-five. A report on the Cats in that same edition predicted that UK would challenge for the conference title (although it was ineligible for any championships or postseason play due to NCAA penalties) and that UK would improve not more than "three or four games over last season's 14-14 mark." The paper listed UK's strengths as including "depth, experience in Pitino's system, leadership." Weaknesses were identified as lack

John Pelphrey, Reggie Hanson, Jeff Brassow, and Deron Feldhaus relaxing on the bench during the 1990/91 season, Rick Pitino's second as Wildcat coach.

of size, limited outside shooting, and a "questionable" point guard backup to Sean Woods. While Kentucky had landed a splendid point guard replacement for the future in University of Missouri transfer Travis Ford, he would not be able to begin utilizing his remaining three years of eligibility until the 1991/92 season.

Pitino began exhibiting his well-honed motivational skills early in the season. His first objective appeared to be to build up large expectations for Mashburn, and then dare the player to live up to his star billing. Thus Pitino predicted to the press that Jamal Mashburn would become one of the school's greatest basketball players. In doing so, Pitino expressed little concern about the praise going to the freshman's head. He wanted Mashburn to think of himself as being great. "Everything I say—most of the time—is calculated," the coach acknowledged. "It is with Jamal. I want him to think he's great because he lacks that a little bit." In fact, stated Michael Bradley in the *Sporting News*, "When Mashburn arrived at Kentucky, Pitino could see he was lacking in confidence. It even came out in the psychological tests Kentucky gives its players. 'He did not totally believe he was a great player,' Pitino says."

Pitino also utilized the press to motivate John Pelphrey, complaining publicly about the player's lack of foot speed and perimeter defensive ability while simultaneously commending Jeff Brassow's work ethic. The coach proved his ability to manage even the slightest details and to make "calculated" statements for an advantage when he took the Lexington Center Corporation to task for not having a floor in Rupp Arena that he could utilize for recruiting purposes. "As an aide to recruiting, UK must get a floor at Rupp that makes sense," Pitino said. "In a world that's making millions and millions of dollars from televised basketball, we can't come up with a decent floor in the greatest state in the world for basketball." The coach almost succeeded in getting a new paint job for his court during the season, managing to find a painter who was a loyal fan willing to donate his time and a Lexington paint store to donate the materials. Scheduling difficulties, however, forced a postponement of the refurbishing until the next season. Still, one had to take notice. Not only was Pitino aware of everything taking place on the floor with his team, but also of what the floor itself could bring to the team through free on-the-air advertising of the Wildcat program.

Mashburn began living up to Pitino's lofty expectations during preseason practice and averaged 28.1 points and 12.7 rebounds per game in intrasquad matches. In

UK's "Monster Mash," Jamal Mashburn, firing a jump shot over a Florida defender. Mashburn was Pitino's first important recruit at Kentucky.

Kentucky's opening win over the University of Pennsylvania, Mashburn played well, scoring twelve points and grabbing four rebounds. Gimel Martinez also had a solid debut, scoring ten points in the 85-62 home court victory. The Cats opened the season with four straight victories. Most impressive was the revenge they gained against the University of Kansas on December 8. Kansas had whipped Kentucky 150-95 the previous season. This time around, the Wildcats defeated the Jayhawks by an 88-71 score. The key to the game was Sean Woods, who scored twenty-five points, handed out eight assists, and grabbed six rebounds. Kansas guard Adonis Jordan ruefully observed, "I think it was payback time for them."

Pitino had motivated his team before the game by building Kansas coach Roy Williams into a villain for running up the score the previous year. His motivational strategy appeared to pay off handsomely.

The first loss of the season came in the next game, and in a heartbreaking fashion for the Wildcats. Kentucky led tenth-ranked North Carolina most of the game, but was outscored down the stretch by the Tar Heels. Losing this game by an 84-81 score in Chapel Hill was a heartbreaker for the Wildcats. Rick Pitino described the loss as "very difficult," "a very bitter pill," and "a shame." This was one of very few "bitter pills" that Pitino, the players, and Wildcat fans had to swallow during the season, as the Cats finished with a 22-6 record and a number nine ranking in the final AP poll.

As early as January 1991, Billy Reed pointed out that the best story in college basketball "is taking place right here, right now, at the University of Kentucky. The job being done by Coach Rick Pitino and his Wildcats is marvelous, wondrous and nothing short of downright miraculous. When Pitino was hired," Reed went on, "he was given an unusual seven-year contract because, said Athletics Director C.M. Newton, the program would need at least two years to recover from the hardships created by the NCAA probation." Instead, the Wildcats achieved a top ten ranking and would have been regular-season SEC champions in Pitino's second year in Lexington, except that they were declared ineligible to hold the crown. Following the Wildcats' season-ending 114-93 victory over Auburn in Rupp Arena on March 2, 1991, Pitino rejected the SEC ruling and laid claim to the unofficial title with the best record in the league. Championships, the coach told the crowd, should be won or lost on the court. Then cheerleaders brought out an eighteen-foot-high banner proclaiming Kentucky number one in the SEC, and C.M. Newton announced that in a few days there would be a parade for the team. "Then we're coming back to the [Memorial] Coliseum and have the dad gummest pep rally you've ever seen." There followed a victory parade in downtown Lexington to celebrate the nonexistent title. Pitino was named Associated Press SEC Coach of the Year and received his second straight National Coach of the Year award, this time from the *Sporting News*.

The Wildcats utilized great coaching and balanced play to achieve their surprising top ten finish. Five players averaged between 10.1 and 14.4 points per game. Kentucky was now well ahead of the three-year program that Pitino had laid out for the team when he arrived in Lexington:

Year One, 1989/90
Establish his style of play
Growth, conditioning, and seasoning of young players
Win over the fans

Year Two, 1990/91
Continued seasoning and conditioning of players
Good recruiting class
Finish in upper division of SEC

Year Three, 1991/92
Challenge for SEC championship
Play in NCAA tournament

Kentucky fans began looking forward with high expectations to the 1991/92 season, as the Cats would be off probation and eligible for postseason play with the nucleus of the team returning. In addition, Jamal Mashburn would be a year older, while Travis Ford would be eligible to play point guard and provide yet another three-point shooting threat.

In order to increase Wildcat chances for continued success in upcoming games, Pitino had another idea: drop two traditional and powerful rivals. John McGill lamented Pitino's decision to draw "a red line through Kansas and North Carolina, schools with tradition as rich as Kentucky's and schools the majority of UK fans deserve, and surely want, to see." For their parts, both Kansas and North Carolina appeared to want to continue their rivalries with UK. According to McGill, however, among Pitino's arguments for changing the Wildcat schedule were: "UK needs to tailor its schedule to areas it plans to recruit heavily, and that means games against Eastern schools and trips to big-city talent pools like New York and Chicago" and "UK is in a rebuilding process and thus needs a less demanding schedule to have a good chance of getting in the NCAA Tournament next year."

While McGill poked legitimate holes in both arguments, Pitino was in charge and the coach seemed to believe that the scheduling changes would help him win more games and attract better talent. Since that was his belief, the changes were made. Rivalries and nostalgia meant little to a new coach driven to win a championship. Given Pitino's results, the end probably justified the means so far as Wildcat fans were concerned. Still, many true fans of basketball had to be saddened by the loss of classic confrontations between perennial powers Kentucky, Kansas, and North Carolina.

Pitino's second argument, that of needing a less demanding schedule, seems amusing in retrospect, given the achievements he realized with the 1991/92 squad. Making the tournament was never in question. Rather,

how far the Wildcats could advance in their first year of eligibility for postseason play was really the only issue.

Three highly touted recruits for the 1992/93 season, who would eventually be keys to winning a national championship, attended Midnight Madness at Memorial Coliseum as part of their recruiting travels: Walter McCarty, Tony Delk, and Jared Prickett. Another future Wildcat, Rodrick Rhodes, also attended. However, the main focus at this event was on the current squad, not possible recruits. With Mashburn, Pelphrey, Martinez, Woods, Farmer, and Feldhaus returning, the Wildcats were considered to be one of the top half dozen teams in the nation going into the season. These amazingly high expectations were, in large part, a tribute to Pitino's coaching ability.

Wildcat newcomers for the 1991/92 season would supply little immediate help. Incoming recruits included first-year forwards Aminu Timberlake and Andre Riddick, as well as guard Chris Harrison. Junior college transfer Dale Brown, who ultimately developed into a defensive stopper and generally solid all-around player, also joined the squad, along with sophomore Travis Ford.

The marginal quality of Pitino's recruits (aside from Mashburn) to this point in his tenure at UK led *Herald-Leader* sportswriter Jerry Tipton to suggest on July 13, 1991, that "the lone chink in Rick Pitino's armor" was his inability to recognize top-notch talent when recruiting. The transfer of Carlos Toomer following the season later appeared to confirm this perspective. When recruiting pundit Bob Gibbons said in the fall of 1989 that Pitino made a mistake signing Toomer, the coach angrily retorted, "Bob Gibbons is not my guru.... Carlos Toomer is a big-time point guard." As it turned out, Gibbons had been correct in his assessment.

Compared to his other talents, Pitino seemed at that point in his career at UK to display less ability to evaluate young talent for recruiting. At the same time, he obviously got more out of the solid players that he signed than just about any other coach in the country got out of McDonald's High School All-Americans. And getting the most out of the players on his 1991/92 squad was what Pitino set out to do. He had only one star, Mashburn. That, in retrospect, was sufficient.

Before the season got into full swing, Pitino diverted attention from the relevant talent level of his squad to his own promotional activities. *Sports Illustrated* and the *Herald-Leader* ran articles on Pitino's move into the advertising world. These articles made much of Pitino's commercialism: he had opened his own Italian restaurant, Bravo Pitino; endorsed a model of the Ford Explorer bearing his signature; licensed his picture to a local shirt maker; and endorsed a long distance telephone company, a hotel, a potato chip, and a clothier.

Pitino also got into a heated dispute with Channel 27 in Lexington when it aired a story suggesting that he would leave the Wildcats in the near future. Pitino was upset at the television station because he believed that the story would harm his recruiting efforts if players thought he planned to leave UK after they had committed to the school. Although he later claimed that he had acted in jest, the coach went so far as to threaten to pull his regular Wildcat basketball show from the station. At the time, some critics believed that the motivation for Pitino was personal leverage and the ability to gain some editorial control over the station and its reporting. Indeed, many people at the time expected Pitino soon to leave Lexington and return to the NBA, either to New York or to Los Angeles. The coach, however, honored his pledge to his players and remained with the squad despite all those "hot" rumors. And when he did eventually depart, it was not to one of the two main media centers but to Boston.

While desire for profit was probably Pitino's major reason for the rush into commercialism, it is possible that the coach felt this publicity could divert some attention from the pressures facing his squad in the upcoming season. That the team faced so much pressure to begin with, however, was partially due to Pitino himself, even through he blamed the media. As UK entered the season, it had a dream matchup ready to take place. Kentucky was invited to compete in the Preseason NIT. The opening game would be played at Rupp Arena against the University of Pittsburgh. The Cats then would travel to New York to face (if both teams won their initial game) Eddie Sutton's Oklahoma State squad. This scenario seemed to be written for Pitino: his team could gain instant television exposure and get great publicity in the New York recruiting hotbed, and he could be the "good" that had triumphed over the "evil" in basketball that Eddie Sutton had represented because of his troubles in Lexington.

While the script was great, it played out differently on the court. Pittsburgh crushed UK 85-67. Questions about the talent and playing ability of the Kentucky squad began to be heard. Some considered the Wildcats to be overrated, and Pitino's star dropped down closer to earth, at least temporarily. According to Jerry Tipton, Pitino blamed "talk of the Final Four and high national ranking for lulling his team into a false sense of secu-

rity." However, Pitino was as guilty as the media. He had, in fact, made numerous statements before the beginning of the season that took for granted the team's playing in New York, including plans for giving away tickets in a promotional event to see the Big Blue perform in the Big Apple. The loss to Pittsburgh served as a wake-up call for both the team and the coach.

Kentucky quickly recovered from the shocking defeat in the Preseason NIT and had a great year, particularly in light of the distance the team had travelled since Pitino's arrival. Aside from a slump in late January and early February, when the Wildcats lost three of four games and fell to number nineteen in the AP poll—a steep decline from their preseason number four ranking—UK had a very steady season. Even during the slump, which dropped the Cats to 15-5 and 5-3 in the SEC, Pitino presented a very calm front to the public, going so far as to proclaim to the press: "I'm pleased with our record!" Whether Pitino was simply being honest or, again, was saying things for a purpose, one can only guess, but he added, "We are limited in some areas. . . . I can't ask any more of a basketball team than ours." The pressure was diffused, and the Wildcats responded by finishing the season strongly and then going on to win the SEC tournament championship with an 80-54 thrashing of Alabama.

The NCAA tournament was a welcome sight for Pitino and the team, but probably even more so for the legions of loyal fans. After all, the Cats had been absent from the event since 1988. Kentucky entered the tournament ranked in the top ten, on a roll, and with its sights set on nothing less than a national championship. Amazingly enough, the Cats nearly succeeded. Everything else during the season—the great regular-season record, conference tournament title, everything—faded in comparison with Kentucky's final game of the season. In fact, for UK fans and true basketball fans everywhere, the 1991/ 92 season will be long remembered as featuring one of the greatest college games of all time. Kentucky reached the final eight with victories over Old Dominion, Iowa State, and Massachusetts (Pitino's alma mater) and faced defending national champion Duke on March 28 in the East Regional championship in Philadelphia. The winner was to go on to the Final Four.

The Wildcats brought a 29-6 record to the game and had not lost since March 5, when Florida whipped them 79-63 in Gainesville to drop the team's record at the time to 22-6. Duke, on the other hand, was 31-2 and had been ranked as the top team in the country since winning the NCAA crown the year before. Kentucky appeared to be badly overmatched. Only Mashburn on the Wildcat squad was equal in talent to the lineup Duke put on the floor for this contest, which included National Player of the Year Christian Laettner, All-American point guard Bobby Hurley, and future NBA superstar Grant Hill, as well as Thomas Hill, Brian Davis, and Antonio Lang. Furthermore, Duke coach Mike Krzyzewski was considered to be one of the top coaches in the country. Unlike University of Massachusetts coach John Calipari (who had taken away his team's momentum by getting a technical foul for leaving the coaches' box with 5:47 left to play and his team trailing Kentucky by only two points after slicing nineteen points from UK's earlier lead), Krzyzewski was one of the handful of coaches in the country every bit the equal of Pitino in motivational skills, coaching ability, and preparation. For one of the few times in the Pitino era, the Wildcats did not possess a solid edge because of their coaching staff.

Kentucky got off to a good start in the game by hitting shots from behind the three-point line, including John Pelphrey's two consecutive three-pointers, and built up a 20-12 lead. The Blue Devils, however, fought back and led by five points at halftime. The Wildcats accomplished their solid first half performance and maintained contact with Duke by utilizing a 2-3 zone instead of their trademark pressure man-to-man defense. Kentucky had two objectives: staying out of foul trouble and getting in better rebounding position against the taller and stronger Duke squad. The zone helped them accomplish both objectives for a while. Foul trouble was critical, and—as Pitino had feared—would influence the outcome of the contest.

Unfortunately for the Wildcats, the second half brought more fouls and a growing deficit. The Big Blue fell behind by twelve (67-55) with just over eleven minutes to play when Bobby Hurley hit a three-point shot over Travis Ford. Less than a minute later, however, Duke called a time-out, as the Wildcats had cut the lead to 67-60 and were back in the game. Kentucky battled back, even having the opportunity to win the game in regulation play, and forced overtime against the highly favored Duke team. The Blue Devils seemed genuinely surprised that the smaller, slower, less-talented but gritty squad from Lexington could stay in this important contest. "Throughout the game we thought we'd make our run and just blow them out," Duke's Brian Davis said later. "They kept coming back."

Kentucky's ability to hold its own was all the more remarkable given the fact that two players, Jamal Mashburn and Gimel Martinez, fouled out of the game

Sean Woods' key shot against Duke with 2.1 seconds left in overtime in the 1992 NCAA East Regional final. Unfortunately for the Cats, Christian Laettner responded immediately with a game-winning sixteen footer at the buzzer for an incredible Duke victory, 104-103.

and Pelphrey, Woods, and Brown finished with four fouls each. Mashburn, who scored twenty-eight points, fouled out with only fourteen seconds remaining in overtime, and his departure was crucial. Duke lost only Brian Davis to fouls, although Laettner and Lang ended the game with four fouls each. The Cats did more than continue "coming back"—they went ahead with only 2.1 seconds to play in overtime on a tremendous twisting, turning, baby hook bank shot in traffic by Sean Woods, a shot Christian Laettner later called "incredible."

Victory appeared to belong to the Wildcats. It was unbelievable. This overachieving team in its first year back from probation and made up largely of native Kentuckians who, aside from Mashburn (and perhaps Woods), probably could not even have suited up for Duke seemed about to pull off an upset at least as big as Duke's upset of UNLV the previous year. The apparent victory, however, quickly evaporated. A combination of circumstances—fouls, the loss of Mashburn, poor defensive strategy, luck, and Laettner's skill—enabled Duke to turn imminent defeat into victory. The law of averages prevailed, and Pitino, who had outcoached Krzyzewski for 44 minutes and 57.9 seconds, was himself outcoached in the last crucial seconds of overtime. Kentucky had what it wanted: A lead against the top team in the country. Only 2.1 seconds stood between the Cats and the Final Four.

Instead, Christian Laettner hit a sixteen-footer over Feldhaus and Pelphrey at the buzzer to seal Duke's 104-103 overtime victory. It was the so-called "shot heard 'round the college basketball world." While Laettner called his shot "lucky," and no doubt there was an element of luck along with his skill, some questioned Pitino's defensive alignment of the final, fatal play. Grant Hill was allowed to throw an uncontested inbound pass almost seventy feet to Laettner. Pitino had chosen his defensive alignment, with players clustered around the basket, to minimize the chance of a foul call and a game-ending free throw opportunity for Duke, as well as to protect against the Blue Devils' superiority in height and size; they might have tried for an easy tip-in shot right at the basket. Had Mashburn, who (along with Woods) made the All-Tournament team for the East Regionals, not fouled out only twelve seconds earlier, he would have been available to guard Laettner instead of the smaller and less physical Feldhaus and Pelphrey, and the outcome might have been different. Mashburn, however, was not available. Duke won and went on to win the tournament for a second year in a row. Two great coaches, Pitino and Krzyzewski, had matched wits and alignments right down to the final seconds. The game was a classic.

Of course, Wildcat fans believed that the wrong team emerged victorious from the confrontation. Had the final Laettner shot not gone in, it would have been a storybook victory for the Wildcats and a treat for long-time radio announcer Cawood Ledford, who had already announced his decision to retire following the season. After what proved to mark the end of his long and distinguished broadcasting career, the venerable "Voice of the Wildcats" said, "I always thought the best game I ever saw was when Kentucky beat Indiana in Dayton in

The legendary Cawood Ledford, radio's "Voice of the Wildcats" from 1953 to 1992.

'75, but this one would have topped it, if only the shot hadn't gone in."

Somewhat easing the pain of defeat was that, as Pitino acknowledged in *Full-Court Pressure*, Krzyzewski "was a gracious winner." In the midst of the wild postgame celebration, Pitino wrote, the Duke coach spotted a dejected Richie Farmer, put his arm around the Wildcat guard, and said, "I'm sorry Richie, . . . I'm so sorry." One must hasten to point out that Krzyzewski was not apologizing for his team's victory, nor wishing that UK had won the game. Rather, he was noting that it was unfortunate that one team had to lose such an epic battle. It was his way of saluting the magnificent effort waged by Farmer and the rest of the Wildcats, players and coaches. As Krzyzewski told the CBS sportscasters after the contest: "It wasn't a game that anybody lost. Whoever had the ball last won. We beat a very determined and great basketball team." Clearly the guilt and failure that ended the Sutton era, "Kentucky's Shame" as *Sports Illustrated* had labeled it in 1989, was erased with the "game of games."

Athletics Director C.M. Newton felt so strongly about what the four seniors on the squad—Farmer, Feldhaus, Pelphrey, and Woods—had done that he broke with Wildcat tradition and university policy and had their numbers retired at the team's postseason awards banquet on April 19, citing their "unusual and outstanding contributions" to Kentucky basketball as reason enough for making the exception. "Three years ago," Newton recalled, "our basketball program was devastated. Today, it is back on top, due to four young men who persevered, who weathered the hard times, and brought the good times back to Kentucky basketball. Their contributions to UK basketball cannot be measured in statistics or record books." They had helped save something die-hard UK fans cherished more than anything: Wildcat basketball. These four were seemingly part of an event of almost religious proportions, the salvation of the program. They were, quite simply, the "Unforgettables."

The accomplishments of the 1991/92 team were certainly impressive. They included a 29-7 season record, a Southeastern Conference Eastern Division championship, the SEC tournament championship, and then advancement all the way to the East Regionals final in the NCAA tournament before losing in overtime and by one point to eventual champion Duke in what many have called the greatest college basketball game ever played. All this success came in only three seasons. The team members themselves were well aware of what they had achieved. Steve Nack, of *Sports Illustrated*, quoted John Pelphrey as recalling those heady times. "'It was unimaginable,' says Pelphrey, who went from all-average to All-SEC in two years. 'We won 65 games in three years! The NCAA put us on probation to make us suffer, but we never did really.'"

After such a year, Kentucky Wildcat fans had a lot to look forward to in the upcoming 1992/93 season. While Farmer, Feldhaus, Pelphrey, and Woods would be gone, UK's best player from 1991/92, Jamal Mashburn, would be back. So would Travis Ford, fully recovered from a broken left kneecap suffered in a preseason exhibition game the prior year and now ready to take over the starting point guard slot. The other returning guards were Dale Brown, an excellent three-point shooter and defensive ace; Jeff Brassow, who suffered a severe injury to his right knee only two games into the 1991/92 season and had to sit out the rest of the campaign; the dependable Junior Braddy; and Chris Harrison. Rejoining Mashburn in the front court were 6'8" Gimel Martinez, 6'9" Andre Riddick, and 6'9" Aminu Timberlake. New recruits in 1992/93 were 6'10" former junior college star

Rodney Dent (who, Pitino felt, would be the physical presence the Cats had lacked the previous three seasons); 6'9" Jared Prickett, whom Pitino termed "a bigger, more skilled version of Feldhaus"; guard and high school scoring phenom Tony Delk; Todd Svoboda, a 6'9" center who joined the team as a walk-on for his last year of eligibility after an impressive playing career at Northern Kentucky University; and Rodrick Rhodes, who was felt at the time to be in a class by himself and a worthy successor to Jamal Mashburn.

Jersey City, New Jersey, product Rodrick Rhodes arrived in Lexington as one of the nation's top five prep players and a consensus high school All-American who had been more heavily recruited than Mashburn while in high school. He was regarded as UK's plum recruit. The 1992/93 *University of Kentucky Basketball Guide* stated that "when Pitino talks about Rhodes he smiles." Pitino went on to describe the new sensation: "He's a slasher, extremely quick. He could be the quickest person on the team. He's very strong, has great leaping ability, and is extremely explosive." Conspicuously missing from that assessment, however, was mention of outside shooting ability, a lack which proved to be one of his major flaws. Another was attitude. Thus, while in 1992 in *Full-Court Pressure* Pitino had described Rhodes as "such a good kid," by October 15, 1996, when the *New York Times* published an article by Tom Friend, the Rhodes-induced smile was apparently a thing of the past. Friend quoted Pitino as saying, "We used to break huddles saying, 'One, two, three, hard work,' but Rodrick would say, 'One, two, three, work is hard.'" Friend observed that "Mashburn was everything that Rhodes was not. Mashburn was a tireless worker, did not taunt, took the smart shots, and had the offense run through him." What Rhodes also did not have was "Mashburn's three-point shot or his stoicism, both a must to be Pitino's pet." After relations between the two cooled, Rhodes described Pitino as thinking of himself as "the God of coaches." But all that, and much more, came in the future. At the beginning of the 1992/93 season, the Bluegrass was still calm.

Jamal Mashburn was again UK's star player in 1992/93, performing more consistently and regularly rising to the occasion in big games. Mashburn averaged twenty-one points and over eight rebounds per game. Travis Ford came on strong during the season, as the 5'9" junior point guard averaged 13.6 points and 4.9 as-

(Top) Rick Pitino watches closely as Rodrick Rhodes attempts a jump shot. Rhodes was a multi-talented player, but Pitino learned quickly that outside shooting was not one of the talents. *(Bottom)* Rodney Dent jamming the ball against Florida State pressure.

sists per game. He also shot nearly 53 percent from behind the three-point arc and hit over 88 percent of his
free throw opportunities. The Wildcats were receiving
solid center play as well during the year, although it was
by committee and not through any single big man playing consistently during the season. The trio of Andre
Riddick, Gimel Martinez, and newcomer Rodney Dent
(Pitino's designated "enforcer") gave the Wildcats good
strength and depth in the middle.

Jared Prickett was perhaps UK's third most important player—behind Mashburn and Ford—by the end
of the season, starting in nine of the Cats' last ten games.
That Prickett and not Rodrick Rhodes was playing such
an important role for the Wildcats was both surprising
and, to some extent, disappointing. While Prickett played
solid basketball, Rhodes seemed able to play at a higher
level that only Mashburn was capable of matching.
Rhodes was the team's star-in-waiting and was expected
to take much of the scoring and rebounding pressure
off Mashburn. *The Cats' Pause Official 1993/94 Kentucky
Basketball Yearbook* put it this way: "Will the real Rodrick
Rhodes please stand up? At the start of last season,
Rhodes burst onto the scene by scoring 27 points against
Georgia Tech and 20 at Louisville in big December show-
downs. By the end of the year, Rhodes was languishing
on the bench" as the eighth or ninth man.

Rhodes's season was not as terrible as this assessment
suggests. He played in thirty-three of UK's thirty-four
games, and started in nineteen. He scored in double figures thirteen times, earned MVP honors of the ECAC
Holiday Festival in New York City, and was named to
the All-SEC Freshman Team. Thus there were high
points during the season, such as a shot he hit with three
seconds left to give the Wildcats an 80-78 win over Auburn on Seniors Day, February 27, 1993. Unfortunately,
there were very low points as well, such as his performance in the Cats' season-ending loss to Michigan,
where Rhodes contributed but one point and one rebound in fourteen minutes of play. It was, indeed, an
up-and-down freshman year, and not what was expected
from the player that recruiting guru Bob Gibbons had
ranked second on his list of the top 500 prep seniors.

Like Rhodes, the Wildcats also started the 1992/93
season with a bang, winning their first eleven games and
rising to a number one ranking in the AP and CNN/
USA Today polls before losing by sixteen points at
Vanderbilt on January 13. Unlike Rhodes, however, the
team did not cool off much after the hot start, losing
only twice more during the regular season: at Arkansas
on February 10 and at Tennessee on February 24. The

Rick Pitino engages forward Jared Prickett in deep
discussion.

Wildcats then swept through the SEC tournament at
Rupp Arena. Led by Travis Ford's sharpshooting and
Andre Riddick's SEC tournament record nine blocked
shots, Kentucky blew Tennessee out by a 101-40 score
in the opening game and followed that with an eleven-
point victory over Arkansas and then a seventeen-point
win over LSU for the conference title. Ford took tournament Most Valuable Player honors.

On the eve of the NCAA tournament, Kentucky was
ranked second in the nation—behind Coach Bobby
Knight and the Indiana University squad that the Wildcats had beaten 81-78 on January 3—and was seeded
first in the Southeast Regionals bracket of the tournament. UK opened the tournament in Nashville against
sixteenth-seeded Rider College and won convincingly,
96-52. Mashburn, Riddick, and Martinez led a balanced
scoring attack against the outmanned squad from New
Jersey. The Wildcats followed up the Rider victory with
equally lopsided wins over solid Utah (83-62) and Wake
Forest (103-69) squads to reach the final game of the
Southeast Regionals. Playing in Charlotte, Kentucky

faced off against a small but quick Florida State team that featured future NBA players Bob Sura, Sam Cassell, and Charlie Ward to determine who would represent the region in the Final Four. Kentucky led 54-46 at halftime on its way to a convincing 106-81 victory. Jared Prickett scored twenty-four points to offset Mashburn's subpar performance (just twelve points on five for twelve shooting) and carried UK to victory and its April 3, 1993, date in New Orleans with a multitalented Michigan squad. The Wildcats had won their four games in the regionals by an average of thirty-one points.

The 1992/93 Kentucky squad moved another step closer to Pitino's goal of a national championship by reaching the Final Four. Their foe in the semifinal round was the University of Michigan and its "Fab Five" squad of freshman stars. Just as had happened in the previous season's tournament loss, Mashburn again fouled out in overtime, this time with 3:23 still left to play. At that point UK was leading 76-72. Mashburn left with thirty-six points and six rebounds to his credit. Talking with the press after the game, Jared Prickett recalled that losing Mashburn "made all the difference" in the outcome. Mashburn, Prickett continued, "was the best player on the floor at the time. You couldn't stop him, and so losing him really hurt us." Michigan's Juwan Howard agreed: "Kentucky had no other options to go to besides Ford, and we kept the ball away from him."

The result was that the Wildcats, without Mashburn, were outscored nine to two. Increasing UK's problems was that—paralleling Martinez's fouling out against Duke the year before—another inside force against Michigan was lost when Kentucky's leading rebounder in the contest, Jared Prickett, fouled out only twenty-four seconds into the overtime period. Compounding this accumulation of unfortunate circumstances, the Cats had lost the services of Dale Brown with 6:13 left in regulation time. Brown, who scored sixteen points and played his usual solid defense, was forced to leave the game with a separated shoulder from diving after a loose ball. Until he suffered the injury, Brown was living up to his reputation as a big game player. He had sixteen points, including four three-pointers. The injury forced Pitino to use a freshman, Tony Delk, down the stretch. The Wildcats lost by 81-78 to the superbly talented Wolverine squad, which featured future NBA stars Chris Webber, Jalen Rose, and Juwan Howard.

Kentucky finished the season with a record of 30-4. Pitino became the tenth college coach in history to guide two different schools to the Final Four.

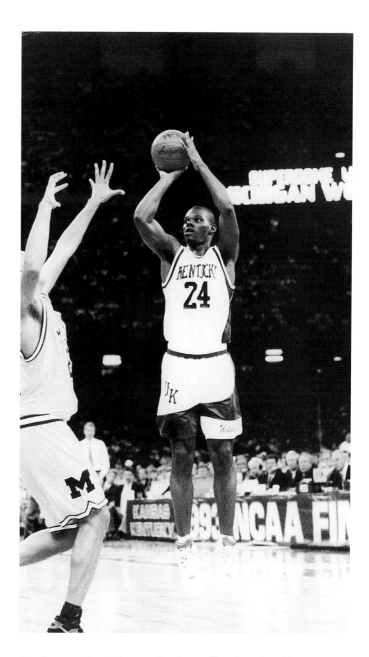

For the second straight year the Cats suffer a heartbreaking overtime loss in the NCAA tournament. Jamal Mashburn (shooting here) and his mates fell just short in the Final Four against Michigan's freshman "Fab Five," 81-78.

Following Pitino's advice, Mashburn declared himself eligible for the NBA draft and was picked fourth in the first round by the Dallas Mavericks. At least in part because Mashburn was gone, 1993/94 proved to be a frustrating season with Pitino unable to settle on a set lineup. Combinations were changed throughout the sea-

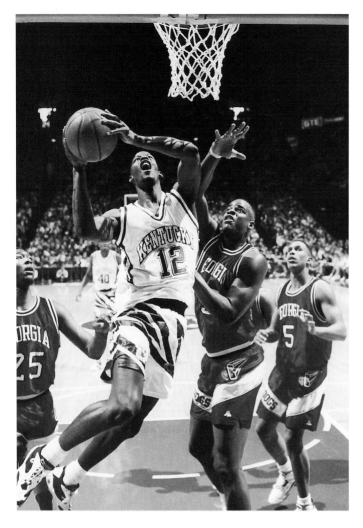

Rodrick Rhodes scores on a layup against Georgia at Rupp Arena.

son, and the team's play was inconsistent. The hope was that Rodrick Rhodes would fill the void left by Mashburn's departure, keeping defenses from keying on Travis Ford's perimeter shooting. While Rhodes's statistics were better than during his freshman year, his performance was still inconsistent. Although he had a scoring average of 14.6 points per game for the season, he ranged from a high of twenty-three points down to a low of zero. Furthermore, in Pitino's view, he still had attitude problems. Finally, after Rhodes had a four-point, two-rebound performance at Georgia on January 8, 1994, Pitino demoted him to the bench the next two games (against Mississippi and Tennessee). When Rhodes finally entered the games, he responded with eighteen points and eight rebounds against Ole Miss and twenty-two points and ten rebounds against the Vols to earn his way back into the starting lineup. In all, he started

twenty-nine of UK's thirty-four games. He missed one of the Cats' games because of suspension—but more on that later. Relations between Rhodes and Pitino, which had been fine when the player first arrived on the Lexington campus, apparently reached a critical point when Rhodes received a technical foul for "taunting" against Georgia. By this point, Pitino later acknowledged, he was fed up with the temperamental sophomore.

Rhodes hardly helped his own cause with another costly technical, this time against Arkansas at Rupp Arena, which opened the way for a Razorback victory. As if the technicals, along with his inconsistent play, were not enough, he capped it all with an abysmal performance against Marquette in the NCAA regional. In that contest—which marked the end of the Wildcat season—Rhodes went zero for nine from the floor, no free throws attempted, and had three rebounds; in the same game, substitute guard Jeff Brassow got nine rebounds and even Travis Ford grabbed four.

What became increasingly clear during the 1993/94 season, both to opponents and to the UK coaches, was that Rhodes was unable to rise to Mashburn's level of play; as a result, rivals were able to control Ford more effectively, making him work for shots instead of allowing him to set up for uncontested three-point opportunities as he had done the previous season. Ford's scoring average dropped to 11.3 points per game from 13.6. Sophomore Tony Delk, however, picked up the slack and led the team in scoring with 16.6 points per game. Although also a perimeter shooter and relatively small at 6'1", Delk was extremely athletic and able to get his shots off against strong defensive pressure. Jared Prickett and Andre Riddick rounded out the starting five for much of the season, although Rodney Dent was the starting center at the beginning of the year. Unfortunately, Dent suffered a season-ending injury in the eleventh game. This loss would have a serious effect on the Cats' hopes to advance further in the NCAA tournament than they had the previous two seasons. Pitino had a worthy replacement but could not use him. Mark Pope, a 6'9" forward/center transfer from the University of Washington, the "Freshman of the Year" in the Pac-10 Conference, and a force on both offense and defense, had two years of eligibility left with UK. They would not, however, begin until the 1994/95 season.

In the meantime, Riddick played center, with help from Prickett and returning senior Gimel Martinez. The other front court player available was 6'9" sophomore Walter McCarty, who had sat out the 1992/93 campaign because of Proposition 48 restrictions. McCarty was a

superbly talented player who could score inside and from the three-point line; however, he lacked bulk and game experience. Early in the season Pitino pointed out that "Walter is physically not ready, and, mentally, he hasn't played college ball, so he's going to need a good year [to adjust]." The Kentucky coach vowed to ease McCarty, whom he [and others] saw as an impact player, into college ball and not to throw him into the fray as he had Rhodes. "We can bring [McCarty] along the right way instead of the incorrect way we brought along Rhodes last year," Pitino stated. "When I say incorrect, I mean we put him in a position where he had so many ups and downs, and it's unfortunate that he had to go through that type of season." Nevertheless, McCarty played in all thirty-four UK games and started ten, tied with Travis

Sophomore Tony Delk, here looking over the defense, led the team in scoring with 16.6 points per game during the 1993/94 season.

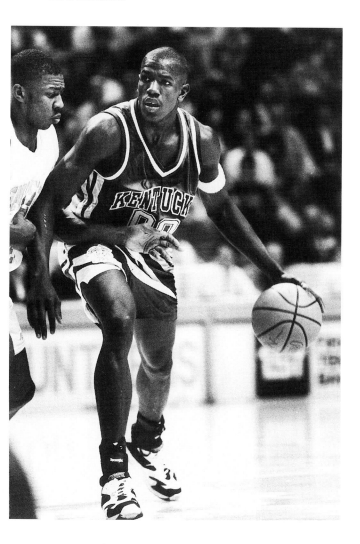

Ford for second best three-point percentage (38.0) on the team, and was Player of the Game against Ole Miss and LSU. Backcourt reserves were senior Jeff Brassow, freshmen Jeff Sheppard and Anthony Epps, and junior Chris Harrison.

Kentucky had started the 1993/94 season on November 27 with a 78-70 victory over Louisville at Rupp Arena. Tony Delk burst onto the scene in the opening game of his sophomore season, scoring nineteen points and grabbing ten rebounds. That Delk would be the Wildcats' best player might not have been expected at the end of the prior season, but it was not such a big surprise to Pitino after hearing about Delk's hard work during the off-season. "All of us heard so much about Tony Delk this summer," Rick Pitino said following the U of L game. "This was the first time we've seen it." Delk made it clear that in addition to scoring, he could be a big factor on the boards for the somewhat undersized Wildcats when he grabbed ten rebounds against the Cardinals.

Despite possessing no "star" players (although Delk had begun to show the makings of one), the 1993/94 team members generally played well together and had a surprisingly strong season, with everyone making important contributions. Even Chris Harrison, the last player on the bench, made two crucial three-pointers during the Wildcats' comeback victory at LSU on February 15 and twelve days later against Georgia was Player of the Game with twelve points, two assists, and two steals.

UK followed its season-opening victory over Louisville with another win (Tennessee Tech), a twelve-point defeat by Indiana (96-84), and then nine victories in a row, including a one-point squeaker over a tough Arizona squad, before falling to Georgia in Athens, 94-90. The Cats won the next two handily (Ole Miss, 98-64, and Tennessee, 93-74), with Rodrick Rhodes coming off the bench to make major contributions. Rhodes's performance earned him a place back in the starting lineup, replacing Jared Prickett.

That Rhodes had to regain a starting spot was a testament to his sometimes lackadaisical play and the increasing tension between player and coach. Prickett, on the other hand, had played himself out of the lineup through sluggish performances, which was surprising because Prickett had earned the starting spot a year earlier because of his hustle and rebounding prowess. Now Rhodes and sophomore Walter McCarty (who moved over to the power forward spot with Rhodes starting at small forward) provided the strongest inside play at the forward positions.

The Wildcats passed an NCAA tune-up with a neutral court 67-64 victory over the University of Massachusetts on February 6 in East Rutherford, New Jersey. UMass featured star players Lou Roe and Marcus Camby (both later to play in the NBA), but the smaller Wildcats held their own on the boards, grabbing forty rebounds, the same number as the Minutemen. Prickett, back in the starting lineup again, got fifteen of Kentucky's rebounds to go along with seventeen points. Lou Roe scored twenty-eight points, but centers Riddick and Martinez held Camby to only five points.

The Big Blue had to be concerned even in victory, since Travis Ford shot only two for eleven from the floor and scored ten points. In fact, since late December, Ford's scoring had been cut nearly in half and his accuracy had dropped by 15 percent. The early season injury of center Rodney Dent, who had provided the Wildcats with solid inside play, had resulted in increased pressure on Ford. For his part, Ford emphasized Mashburn's departure to the NBA and the corresponding increase in attention that defenses showed him as the main reasons his shooting percentage had declined from almost 53 percent the prior season to just over 40 percent through the UMass game. Despite not shooting well or scoring as much as before, Ford remained a valuable member of the Cats' squad, playing solid defense, passing well, and providing floor leadership.

Shortly after the UMass game, Pitino became concerned that his team was beginning to rely too much on individual play. When UK lost two straight games to solid Arkansas and Syracuse squads, Pitino resorted to his immense manipulative talents to regain control over his team. After the defeats, the first back-to-back losses the Cats had suffered in more than two seasons, the coach tried to get the squad to rededicate itself to learning and abiding by the Pitino system. For inspiration, he opened a team meeting by writing two words on the blackboard, "The Unforgettables," in order to make the point that "Sean Woods, John Pelphrey, Deron Feldhaus, and Richie Farmer elevated themselves to hero status by executing precisely. Their jerseys hang in Rupp Arena. They are the 'Unforgettables.'" After emphasizing that nickname, Pitino added, "If we don't play well, we'll be 'The Forgettables.'" Pitino was telling, not asking, his talented group of former prep stars, including Rhodes and Delk, to assume more responsibility and focus on the team rather than on their own individual statistics.

His psychology lesson seemed at first to backfire in the next game, on February 15, against LSU in Baton Rouge. The Tigers led 48-32 at halftime, and with fif-teen minutes to go in the game the score was 68-37 in favor of LSU. Then bench warmer Chris Harrison started a UK initiative by hitting two three-pointers, matching his season high with eight points. Whether it was a delayed impact from Pitino's "Forgettables" speech, Harrison's shooting, or something else altogether, Kentucky began a comeback. And what a comeback it was. When it was over, Pitino happily expressed his feeling about the outcome: "I coached about 200 NBA games and I've coached about sixteen years of college and I have never seen a comeback on the road like that in my life. . . . Nothing has ever come close to this."

After a day's reflection on the game and its import, the *Herald-Leader*'s Jerry Tipton wrote (February 17): "Kentucky Coach Rick Pitino saw more than a 31-point deficit on the scoreboard. He saw a successful season teetering toward collapse. At that same moment, Louisiana State Coach Dale Brown saw his mediocre team rising boldly from the brink. A disappointing season might yet be salvaged. Then, one of the greatest comebacks in college basketball history jerked everyone who saw the game through a stomach-clutching 180-degree change of direction. Kentucky's still-difficult-to-believe 99-95 victory Tuesday at LSU radically altered the prospects for each team."

The Wildcats had been sluggish, and in fact their season was on the verge of falling apart. The spectacular comeback win jump-started the squad again. In addition, Walter McCarty had a breakthrough game, coming off the bench to score twenty-three points and grab eight rebounds. That LSU hit only thirteen of twenty-four free throws down the stretch did not hurt the Cats at all. Still, UK had not folded when folding would have seemed perfectly logical. This was a performance to build on. The thirty-one-point deficit was the second most points ever overcome in an NCAA game, just one less than Duke's thirty-two-point comeback against Tulane in 1950.

The victory over LSU helped UK salvage a solid, if not spectacular, season. But it was anything but smooth sailing from then on. Following a 77-69 victory over Vanderbilt (February 19), Pitino suspended Prickett, Ford, and Martinez for cheating. They sat out the team's next game, which was against Tennessee. During the Vanderbilt game, Ford had instructed Walter McCarty (a 51 percent free throw shooter) to shoot free throws for Andre Riddick (a 32 percent shooter). McCarty did and made both shots. Then, later in the game, Martinez (an 80 percent free throw shooter) shot two free throws for Prickett (a 55 percent shooter who had missed all

four of his previous attempts). While Kentucky won and some fans found it funny that the team had tricked the referees, Pitino was not amused. Sportswriter Mark Coomes put the situation starkly in his February 23, 1994, *Louisville Courier-Journal* article: "A flim-flam at the foul line has resulted in one-game suspensions for three University of Kentucky basketball players." In the same issue, fellow *Courier-Journal* sportswriter Rick Bozich applauded Pitino's action and provided a glimpse into the coach's fury: "Integrity takes a daily beating in college sports, so give Pitino credit for reinforcing the notion that what is wrong is wrong. Give him further credit for understanding that his five years of good work trying to change Kentucky's image as cheaters should not be soiled by trying to sneak the wrong guy to the line."

In Pitino's view, the problem was compounded when the players later went on television and joked about the situation. Pitino did not suspend McCarty or Riddick because he believed that neither player knew at the time that a mistake had been made. Despite playing without

Walter McCarty firing a jump shot over the outstretched hand of Auburn's Franklin Williams.

three of their best players, and having to start Chris Harrison, who was averaging less than two points per game, the Wildcats won 77-75 in Knoxville against a weak Tennessee squad. It was a close game, but just winning in Knoxville, where the Cats had won only four times in their previous twenty games, was an accomplishment.

Kentucky's next problem occurred when Pitino suspended Rodrick Rhodes for UK's March 5 SEC tournament opener against Mississippi State for breaking a team rule. The Wildcats won 95-79 without Rhodes, as Delk (twenty-nine points) and Jeff Brassow (nineteen points) picked up the slack. Jerry Tipton observed on March 12 that "the suspension caps what has been a checkered season for Rhodes. Earlier he had been chastised for two costly technical fouls [which contributed to UK's losses to Georgia and eventual national champion Arkansas] and for indiscriminate three-point shooting in the pre-season. He was also benched for poor rebounding in January." In the SEC tournament championship game, Rhodes responded by scoring fifteen points in Kentucky's 73-60 victory over Florida. He did not, however, get a single rebound. The win was ironic because the Gators wound up in the Final Four of the NCAA while UK was quickly eliminated.

Despite finishing with a 26-6 record and winning the SEC tournament title, Kentucky was seeded number three in the NCAA tournament's Southeast Regionals. Pitino, who had expected at least a number two seed, was surprised and upset. Still, Kentucky's seeding probably did not matter. After beating a 19-11 Tennessee State squad in its opening game in St. Petersburg on March 18, Kentucky was two nights later whipped 75-63 by a less talented Marquette team. Marquette's bulky squad exploited Kentucky's "Thin Towers" of Riddick and McCarty. In this game, the Wildcats, who had lived by the three-point shot, died by the three pointer: they hit only ten of thirty-eight, and the season was over. The record, twenty-seven wins against only seven losses, painted an overly positive picture. The 1993/94 Wildcats probably were, indeed, "Forgettables." Cheating at the free throw line; needless and irresponsible fouls; suspensions; a squad that, despite decent size and good depth, was consistently outrebounded during the season—this team did not equal Pitino's previous squads in character, style, or results.

Most importantly, the 1993/94 team lacked a "go-to guy" who could score in critical situations and games. In getting shut out (no points on zero for nine shooting) against Marquette, Rhodes had proved incapable of being that star player. Despite averaging 14.6 points

per game, Rhodes was such a disappointment that Pitino reportedly told the player to transfer if he could not dedicate himself to the team.

Tony Delk, who had led the team in scoring as a sophomore at 16.6 points per game, was probably at least a year away from becoming a "go-to" player in the clutch. The player whom fans had been counting on to carry the 1993/94 squad in key situations, Travis Ford, saw his scoring average fall all the way to 11.3 points per game, and he ended up hitting less than 40 percent of his shots from the field. Although Ford won the "Most Valuable Player" award in the SEC tournament, he had a disappointing season.

After the unsatisfying 1993/94 campaign had ended, new worries emerged to roil the UK faithful: concerns over whether Rick Pitino intended to leave Lexington. The coach did not calm these worries when he was quoted in the press as saying, "I think someday I'll return to the NBA." That day appeared to be in the near future because Pitino was showing a great deal of interest in becoming head coach of the Los Angeles Lakers. This was the third year in a row that Pitino had seriously considered an NBA offer. As he had in previous years, he decided to remain in Kentucky. Interestingly, as reported in the 1994/95 *SEC Basketball Preview*, Pitino called a team meeting to gauge the reaction of his players to the possibility of his leaving for the NBA. According to the magazine, only one player, Rodrick Rhodes, suggested that Pitino should consider the Lakers job.

During the same summer of 1994, Rhodes, like his coach, was giving thought to leaving for the NBA. In fact, Rhodes seemed to be simultaneously considering several options: turn professional, transfer to another school, return to UK to be redshirted for the season, or return to the team as a featured player. The junior forward finally decided to return to the Wildcats. This would prove to be his last year in Kentucky blue and white, for everything fell apart for him during the 1994/95 season.

The continuing "Rhodes saga," as sportswriters characterized it, turned on four contests during the 1994/95 season, games which not only found Rhodes at his very worst, but also were viewed on television. Against Louisville he shot one for nine and grabbed one rebound. Afterward Pitino reportedly told Rhodes that he would never be another Mashburn. Against LSU a big Wildcat deficit at halftime provoked, in the words of Tom Friend (*New York Times*, October 15, 1996) "a locker-room shouting match between Rhodes and Pitino. The coach told him to 'shower, get dressed,' but

Rhodes claimed he was yelling at his teammates, not the coach." Just before the start of the second half, "Pitino found Rhodes crying in the shower and let him partake in the huge Kentucky comeback."

The third fiasco of the season took place in the championship game of the SEC tournament against arch rival Arkansas. In the contest, Rhodes "badly missed two free throws in the final seconds of the tie game, bawled on the bench and was too despondent to play the overtime. Kentucky won, but his tears after the game were seen as a selfish act."

In the fourth and most important game, the Wildcats faced the North Carolina Tar Heels in the final game of the NCAA Southeast Regionals. Rhodes, according to Friend, viewed the contest "as a live-or-die matchup between him and Jerry Stackhouse, and he went two for 10 and zero for six from three-point range for seven points and no rebounds."

The team realized some significant successes: a 28-5 season record, a 14-2 league record, the first Kentucky SEC regular season title since 1986, its fourth straight SEC tournament crown, and advancement to the Elite Eight of the NCAA, just one game shy of the Final Four.

1995 SEC tournament MVP Antoine Walker led UK to its fourth straight tournament championship, 95-93 over Arkansas.

Despite all these achievements, fans felt it had been a disappointing season, and the reason was the initially promising campaign ended before a championship had been attained. Bigger things were expected from this squad of Wildcats—an NCAA title, not the Elite Eight. This was, after all, the type of squad Pitino wanted on the floor. On further consideration, it is probably more accurate to say that rather than a disappointing season, Kentucky had a disappointing end of the season.

All this, however, was in the future. Entering the 1994/95 season the outlook for Kentucky appeared to be quite positive, although the results proved to be something less. Despite the departure of Travis Ford, Jeff Brassow, Gimel Martinez, and Rodney Dent (UK lost an appeal to the NCAA to receive an extra year of eligibility because of Dent's season-ending injury in the previous campaign), the Wildcats were very deep when the 1994/95 campaign began. In addition to numbers, the team had size in the front court with seven players measuring between 6'7" and 6'9": senior Andre Riddick; juniors Walter McCarty, Jared Prickett, Rodrick Rhodes, and Mark Pope; and freshmen Antoine Walker and Scott Padgett. The backcourt was equally deep with junior Tony Delk, senior Chris Harrison, sophomores Anthony Epps and Jeff Sheppard, and freshmen Allen Edwards and Cameron Mills, the last a walk-on. The team was loaded with very good, athletic players who were, for the most part, interchangeable. It was an excellent squad for Pitino's up-tempo style of play.

The Wildcats opened the campaign at home on November 26, 1994, by demolishing Tennessee-Martin by a score of 124-50. The Wildcats also handed Notre Dame its worst home court loss since 1898—a 97-58 rout, with six of the Cats scoring in double figures, led by McCarty's twenty. During the regular season, Kentucky lost only to UCLA, Louisville, Mississippi State, and Arkansas. The Wildcats then won the SEC tournament title for the fourth straight year with a thrilling 95-93 overtime victory against Arkansas. In that game, the Big Blue had trailed Arkansas by nineteen at one point in the first half, by six at halftime, and by nine with only ninety seconds remaining in overtime. Kentucky won despite Rodrick Rhodes's missed free throws with the score tied and only 1.3 seconds remaining in regulation. Kentucky won because reserve point guard Anthony Epps came through when it mattered most, hitting two free throws to put the Wildcats in front, 94-93. Antoine Walker became the first freshman to win the MVP award in the SEC tournament. In overtime, Pitino had relied on Walker at small forward rather than Rhodes. Pitino ob-

served that his Wildcats "were dead three or four times against a great, well-coached basketball team. This is the proudest moment of my coaching life." Given some of the thrills of the Mashburn years and the "Unforgettables," the coach's statement meant a lot. Surely, if the team showed this much heart and had gained such respect from Pitino, it would play tough and win the NCAA championship. Unfortunately, Pitino's pride would soon turn to disappointment.

UK was the number one seed in the Southeast Regionals. In the first game, played in Memphis, the Cats beat sixteen seed Mount St. Mary's by 113-67. Kentucky breezed through games against Tulane (82-60) and a very good Arizona State squad (97-73). In the latter contest, Delk went eleven for eighteen from the floor and scored twenty-six points. Kentucky hit 50 percent (seven of fourteen) from the three-point area and grabbed eight more rebounds than did the Sun Devils. UK, now with twenty-eight wins and four losses, looked unbeatable. Thus far in the NCAA tournament it had an average margin of victory of 30.7 points. All UK now had to do was beat a University of North Carolina squad that had struggled to win over Georgetown in its regional semifinal game (raising its record to twenty-seven wins and five losses). Big Blue fans expected that when the Wildcats overcame North Carolina, they would once again be off to the Final Four, this time in Seattle.

Kentucky and North Carolina were very different teams with very different coaches. The Wildcats possessed no single superstar player, but were loaded with numerous excellent athletes. Cats fans believed their team's pressure defense and depth would wear down the Tar Heels. While possessing star players Jerry Stackhouse and Rasheed Wallace, as well as solid starters Jeff McInnis, Dante Calabria, and Donald Williams, North Carolina had demonstrated little depth during the season. Finally, Pitino was entering his coaching prime, while many believed that UNC's legendary coach Dean Smith was past his.

Instead, the March 25, 1995, meeting between the two squads proved to be a bitterly disappointing experience for the Wildcat faithful. Jerry Tipton described the shock in the next day's *Herald-Leader*: "Kentucky's elimination from the NCAA tournament last night looked more like that coveted trip to the Final Four midway through the first half. Thanks in part to an ugly double-technical involving the starting centers, North Carolina's main man inside [Wallace] left the game with three fouls barely 10 minutes after tip-off. Surely now," the reporter continued, "top-seeded Kentucky would proceed to beat

an already shallow North Carolina team. Instead, the deep and talented Kentucky team lost 74-61 in the Southeast Regional finals."

It was little short of amazing. Wallace played only twenty-four minutes for the Tar Heels; Stackhouse scored eighteen points, but hit only three of nine from the field. Based on the subpar performances of its stars, surely North Carolina stood no chance of beating Pitino's deep and talented Wildcats. Two major factors caused the upset: North Carolina's much maligned bench outscored UK's vaunted reserves twelve to eleven and—more importantly—Kentucky's key players did not step up and perform in this big game. Delk was only seven for twenty-one from the floor in getting his nineteen points. McCarty, with fourteen points, was the only other Wildcat to score more than seven. Rhodes hit only two of ten shots, scored seven points, and had no rebounds. Walker, the freshman who starred against Arkansas in the SEC tournament, picked up more fouls (four) than points (two) in the nine minutes that he played.

Pitino lamented after the game: "We had a great team coming in here, and we're going home as individuals." The *Herald-Leader*'s John Clay quoted Jerry Stackhouse's analysis of his confrontation with Rodrick Rhodes: "I think he kind of got more towards a one-on-one game. It's not a one-on-one battle, it's definitely a team battle. I think if I went down and scored, then he wanted to come down and score. I think that's probably why they took him out in the second half." Unfortunately for the Cats, no one who replaced Rhodes performed any better.

It was Kentucky, not North Carolina, that got rattled and looked tired and increasingly confused as the game wore on. UK took thirty-six three-point attempts, hitting only seven (19 percent). This performance by the Wildcats occurred despite having Wallace on the sidelines for 40 percent of the game. Several Kentucky players seemed to believe that the double-technical called when Wallace elbowed Andre Riddick—and then Riddick responded by choking the Tar Heel center—influenced the game. Instead of calling the technical on Riddick, however, referee Tim Higgins inexplicably (even after watching replays on a TV monitor) called the technical on McCarty, who had acted as a peacemaker. McCarty and other observers expressed disbelief. This technical hurt UK because, only 3:54 into the game, it was already McCarty's second foul. He had scored five points, but Pitino was forced to remove him from the game.

Big Blue fans, however, should not try to make excuses for the Wildcats. Simply put, Kentucky was outplayed. Kentucky was outhustled. Kentucky was outthought. Kentucky hit only 28 percent of its shots (twenty-one for seventy-five) from the floor. The Cats lost despite turning the ball over only twelve times as compared to twenty for North Carolina. How did this happen? *Dallas Morning News* columnist Kevin B. Blackstone wrote on March 26 that the difference was coaching. In a column titled "Slick Pitino Outclassed by True Legend Smith," Blackstone stated: Pitino "may be a good coach, but he turned in as poor a performance from the bench as his players did on the court." The Dallas sportswriter pointed to Pitino's response to the scuffle between Riddick and Wallace. The coach pulled Riddick immediately and let him get cold on the bench. Blackstone also thought that Pitino did a poor job of making sure his team capitalized on Wallace's absence from the court: "Pitino admitted Wallace's foul trouble was a golden opportunity that was missed. He blamed the misfortune on his players, however, rather than himself. Such a sad lament characterized his post-game comments."

Jerry Tipton was less direct. He commented that Kentucky paid for its lack of a "go-to guy," was intimidated by the "psychological warfare" of the Tar Heels, and choked under pressure. While Blackstone and Tipton had several other criticisms of Pitino and the team's performance, suffice it to say that neither the coach nor the players had performed up to their abilities on this spring day in Birmingham. Pitino had now lost all three games he had coached against Smith, and this one had to hurt much more than the others.

The Cats' collapse against North Carolina was eerily reminiscent of the 1983/84 Kentucky squad's collapse against a less talented but also physically imposing Georgetown squad in the Final Four. While North Carolina had the best individual players in Stackhouse and Wallace, Kentucky had more depth and better overall athletic skills. Similarly, Georgetown had Patrick Ewing —by far the best player on the floor that day eleven years earlier—as well as several other solid players, but Kentucky had more to work with in Sam Bowie, Mel Turpin, Derrick Hord, Dicky Beal, Jim Master, Kenny Walker, and a number of other fine players. Against the Hoyas, Kentucky got Ewing in early foul trouble, but settled into taking jump shots and did not take full advantage of Georgetown's vulnerability. This was very similar to the Pitino squad's inability to exploit Rasheed Wallace's foul trouble. Like the 1983/84 squad in the Georgetown game, Kentucky seemed to choke against North Carolina, going ice cold from the floor. Unable to score for

Two well-satisfied Wildcats, Tony Delk and Walter McCarty, relaxing on the bench during the 1994/95 season.

long stretches of time, the Big Blue were intimidated by Ewing's blocking shots (he was called several times for goaltending) and by Michael Graham (called for pushing and shoving). Wallace and Stackhouse did the trick this time around, utilizing their elbows and trash talk to take the Wildcats out of their game. And finally, Joe B. Hall was bested by John Thompson of Georgetown much as Pitino was bested by another legend, Dean Smith.

The question in Lexington now was whether Pitino and his team could recover from their humiliating defeat against North Carolina and make a run for the NCAA crown that Pitino and Wildcat fans so desperately coveted. While Hall had already won a title (1977/78), he retired a year after the embarrassing defeat at the hands of Georgetown without winning another NCAA championship. Could Pitino recover from his devastating and humiliating loss and lead his squad to the championship that had eluded Bluegrass fans for four straight years? He would certainly have the talent on his next squad, but could he—in the words of the *Dallas Morning News*'s Blackstone—take the next step and move from being "slick" to becoming a "legend"?

During the 1994/95 campaign, Tony Delk nearly duplicated his prior year's performance, averaging 16.7 points and 3.3 rebounds per game. Rhodes and McCarty also averaged double figures in points, 12.9 and 10.4 respectively. Mark Pope led the team in rebounding at 6.2, despite playing only twenty-two minutes per game. Kentucky, in putting together its 28-5 season, outscored

opponents 87 to 69 on average. The Wildcats, for the year, hit 46 percent of their shots and held opponents to only 40 percent. That North Carolina hit 49 percent was further proof that UK did not play up to par.

Tony Delk had proved himself to be Kentucky's best player. He would be a senior, and would be expected to become a team leader. Walter McCarty was also beginning to develop into a fine player, making very effective use of his size, quickness, and outside shooting ability. These two rising seniors were being counted on to provide leadership for the Wildcats in the next season, and would have to put their poor performance against the Tar Heels out of their minds as they began preparations for their final season as Wildcats. Sophomore-to-be Antoine Walker, who had averaged 7.8 points and 4.5 rebounds as a freshman, was also expected to step up. Kentucky also had recruited superstar high school swingman Ron Mercer from Oak Hill Academy in Virginia.

It was clear, however, that Rhodes would not be back. Pitino had neither the room nor the inclination to keep his former prize recruit on the deep, talented squad that he had coming in for the new season. The only question was whether Rhodes would turn professional, redshirt, or transfer to another school. Since the NBA was displaying little interest in him, Rhodes announced in August that he was leaving for the University of Southern California. The "Rhodes saga" was finally history, and the Cats could now focus on the future. A few days after the Rhodes press conference, Pitino and the Wildcats left for a five-game exhibition tour through Italy.

13

Two Golden Seasons

The 1995/96 season bore a strong resemblance to 1977/78—"the season without joy." In both years Kentucky had the most talented and deepest squad in the nation. This fact fueled lofty expectations which, from preseason to the Final Four, permitted nothing less than the Holy Grail of college basketball, a national championship. And in both years, if the Wildcats were not successful, the full burden of responsibility for failure would fall on the head coach. Neither excuses nor reference to past successes would suffice. To illustrate the immense pressures weighing on Pitino's shoulders as the 1996 Final Four approached, John Feinstein in the *Wall Street Journal* related an exchange between longtime friends Rick Pitino and Wake Forest head coach Dave Odom shortly after UK had eliminated Wake in the 1996 regional in Minneapolis. "Good luck next week," the Wake Forest coach said. "It should be fun for you to take your team back to your old stomping grounds." The Kentucky coach, "who grew up less than an hour's drive from the New Jersey Meadowlands, last year's Final Four site, laughed. 'If we don't win,' he said, 'I might as well stay right there. I won't have any friends left back in Kentucky.'" Feinstein concluded that Pitino "was joking, sort of."

The same story could have been related about Joe B. Hall as the Final Four approached in 1978. In both years success was achieved, but it was not preordained. Anything could happen during the season and a lot did to distract attention and energies from the task of winning basketball games. The first distraction in 1995/96

occurred before the season even started. In July 1995, former team trainer JoAnn Hauser filed suit in Fayette Circuit Court against Rick Pitino, C.M. Newton, and the UK Athletics Association. Hauser contended, reported Thomas Tolliver (*Herald-Leader*, July 19, 1995), that "she was a victim of sex discrimination because she was moved in May from trainer of the men's team to the same position with the women's team" in order that

A knee injury suffered against Vanderbilt on January 4, 1994, knocked center Rodney Dent out for the remainder of the season. Left to right: Dent, trainer JoAnn Hauser, and Rick Pitino.

Ron Mercer had a lot to smile about during his two-year career at Kentucky, where he helped win an NCAA basketball championship in 1996 and a runner-up spot in 1997. He became a consensus All-American in the latter year.

"Pitino could hire his old friend, Edward 'Fast Eddie' Jamiel, who she said is not as qualified for the job as she is." (The lawsuit slowly dragged its way through the legal system. Finally, on November 10, 1997, two years and four months after the suit was filed and just as the court was scheduled to hear the case, the two sides reached a settlement. In exchange for a payment of $220,000 from UK, Hauser agreed to drop her suit.)

Even the color of the Wildcat uniforms became a burning issue during the season. Team uniforms have been changed frequently in recent years at other schools as well as at Kentucky, at least in part, if not entirely, for marketing reasons. *Herald-Leader* business writer Jaclyn Carfagno put it plainly. "The sale of uniforms, shoes and other merchandise carrying the names of the University of Kentucky and Rick Pitino is part of a web of controversial relationships that has mushroomed along with two other forces: the financial demands on college athletic departments and the marketing potential of athletics merchandise carrying team logos."

A college makes money on the rights to use its logo on merchandise, and the more frequently the merchandise is changed or updated, the more money everybody—except the players—makes. At Kentucky Korner at the Civic Center Shops, Wildcat shorts alone cost $59.95 at that time (February 1996). Tank tops, shoes, T-shirts, denim hats, button-down shirts, and jackets were among other items sold with the UK logo.

Between January 1993 and February 1996, Wildcat uniforms changed six times. The sixth change, however, was more than many Big Blue fans could take. First used in a February 11 game against Arkansas at Rupp Arena, the newly unveiled costumes resembled a hue of blue more closely associated with a hated rival located in the Tar Heel state. In the Sunday afternoon game, played on national television, Billy Packer observed that the shade of blue denim side panels and accents looked more like Carolina powder blue than Kentucky royal blue. The next day fans called radio shows and plugged into the Internet to register their protests. On his weekly "Big Blue Line," Pitino was forced to defend what he called the Cats' new "traditional uniform." Even the director of media relations at North Carolina, Steven Kirschner, was drawn into the burgeoning controversy. Kirschner agreed with Pitino. The uniforms "don't look like Carolina blue to me," he said. Instead, "they look like denim." That was not sufficient to cool the controversy. Newspapers printed editorials attacking the new uniforms and complaints were even aired in the Kentucky State Senate.

In his Sunday, February 18, column, Jerry Tipton re-

Mark Pope, Rick Pitino, Anthony Epps, and the infamous "denim uniforms." Many UK fans objected to the color, which they perceived to be "Carolina Blue."

The 1995/96 Kentucky Wildcats: NCAA National Basketball Champions. Seated, left to right: Delray Brooks, Rick Pitino, Allen Edwards, Derek Anderson, Jeff Sheppard, Tony Delk, Anthony Epps, Cameron Mills, Wayne Turner, Jim O'Brien, and Winston Bennett. Standing, left to right: Bill Keightley, George Barber, Jason Lathrem, Oliver Simmons, Nazr Mohammed, Mark Pope, Walter McCarty, Antoine Walker, Jared Prickett, Ron Mercer, Eddie Jamiel, Layne Kaufman, and Shaun Brown.

ported at great length the reaction of one of the callers to "The Big Blue Line." The caller claimed he had been embarrassed on the line by Pitino. In fact, "the coach's response so angered the man that he called the *Herald-Leader* to voice his objection." And voice it he did, in an irate column-and-a-half interview. A month later, the controversy still raged. Another Sunday edition of the *Herald-Leader* devoted major attention to the uniforms. Most of page one and all of two inside pages of the first section of the newspaper were devoted to the topic. The issue lasted to the end of the season, when that particular uniform was dropped from future UK use. An inordinate amount of newspaper space and radio airtime had been wasted on what was, in the larger context of the season, a side issue.

And what did the Wildcats themselves think of the furor? Mark Pope had an eminently sensible response: "Everybody's trying to make a buck here or there. It doesn't affect us. If it says 'Kentucky,' that's all that matters." Pope's comment, printed in the *Herald-Leader*, should have put things into perspective, but apparently only the UK players themselves could rise above the controversy.

Still another distraction during the season was a series of critical articles that appeared in the national and the big city press, such as one published in *Sports Illustrated*. The cover of the February 26 issue featured a photo of an impassioned Rick Pitino and the caption: "A Man Possessed: Kentucky Basketball Coach Rick Pitino." In the issue's lead article, titled "Full-Court Pressure," author William Nack cited "skeptics [who] sug-

gest that Pitino is merely a rebuilder, the handyman you hire to swing a place around but not the one to finish the job." As the Final Four approached, a number of articles appeared in the major metropolitan dailies and in *USA Today*, all of them questioning the Kentucky coach's ability to win "the Big Game." That Pitino could not and did not ignore the negative press is evident from his reaction to the *Sports Illustrated* article. While not denying the accuracy of the article, Pitino complained to the local press that "it left a lot out," and went on to accuse Nack "of leaving out positive aspects of his rapid rise professionally." Former assistant coaches and Pitino's wife, Joanne, had assured the coach that the magazine ignored or minimized their positive feelings about his many accomplishments. C.M. Newton sent a letter to *Sports Illustrated* questioning the magazine's motives.

A much more serious issue was the large egos and demands for more playing time of several Wildcat players. Pitino had to be concerned over the effect that such individual ambitions would have on team cohesion and morale, and the Wildcats' ability to sustain a high level of intensity over the season. The squad was loaded with size, numbers, and talent. In fact, it was "so rich in talent," according to William Nack in his *Sports Illustrated* article, "that at times it resembles a semipro operation in some covert NBA farm system." Or, as Dick Vitale suggested, UK was so loaded with talent that it could field two Top 25 teams. *ESPN College Basketball* magazine's preseason examination of the college basketball scene expressed serious doubts about UK's ability to win the championship and picked Kansas as its number one

team. "How do you keep a Noah's Ark team—two of everything—happy and cohesive? It is a problem coaches say they love to have, but we think it keeps Kentucky from winning it all this year." The magazine identified team chemistry as Pitino's toughest challenge. There were no doubts expressed about the individual talent of the Wildcat players, but there were certainly doubts about whether the parts would jell as an effective team. Kansas, while it possessed less individual talent, was expected to play as the better team.

Concerns about whether the Cats would become a cohesive squad were indeed justified. Before the season even got under way, several issues made the situation, in Jerry Tipton's words, "seem combustible." Among them, "Rodrick Rhodes' controversial departure and Ron Mercer's neat—too neat?—filling of the void. Walker's Media Day line-in-the-sand declaration about playing time. Walker's on-court disagreement with Jared Prickett during the Italy tour. Talented substitute Allen Edwards openly mulling a transfer." To *Sports Illustrated* college basketball expert Alexander Wolff, "those are the kind of things that sound alarm bells to those of us who are doing the pre-season predicting." As a result of these doubts, *Sports Illustrated* picked Kansas to win the national championship.

As far as talent was concerned, UK was loaded. Returning for their senior season were guard Tony Delk, the team's leading scorer the previous two years; forward Walter McCarty; and forward/center Mark Pope; along with Jared Prickett, Allen Edwards, Scott Padgett, Jeff Sheppard, Antoine Walker, Anthony Epps, and Cameron Mills. Incoming freshmen were 6'7" Ron Mercer, rated the top high school prospect in the country; Wayne Turner, one of the most sought-after point guards in America; 6'8" Oliver Simmons, an All-State forward from Tennessee; and 6'10" Nazr Mohammed, an All-State center from Chicago. Redshirt Derek Anderson, a star at Ohio State who had transferred to UK after his sophomore season, was now eligible to play for the Blue and White in 1995/96.

Rick Pitino, for his part, fully recognized the problems he faced in melding his incredibly talented group of athletes into a cohesive unit. Reviewing the previous season, the 1996/97 *Media Guide* noted that "the critics labeled the Wildcats a puzzle with too many pieces," and quoted Pitino's concern: "Are we going to be one ball and 10 people uniting and coming together to be a great team, or are we going to need three or four basketballs?"

To guarantee that he would need only one basketball, the coach began working during the summer on building a team with the right chemistry. The August tour of Italy with the returning veterans served as a pre-season camp. Pitino tried different players at different positions during the five game tour, and Kentucky emerged from the trip ready to go after the elusive national championship trophy. Despite the doubts expressed by *Sports Illustrated* and ESPN, UK was generally favored from the beginning to achieve its goal, being ranked as the top team in the nation in most pre-season college basketball polls.

Kentucky justified its top ranking in a season-opening 96-84 victory over the University of Maryland in the Hall of Fame Tip-Off Classic on November 24, 1995. The Wildcats' starting lineup included Antoine Walker, Ron Mercer, Mark Pope, Tony Delk, and Derek Anderson. Kentucky, barely ahead 37-35 at halftime, pulled away in the second half with Tony Delk scoring nineteen of his twenty-one points. Mark Pope had the best game of his career, scoring a career-high twenty-six points, grabbing six rebounds, and blocking four shots. Pitino and the team's fans hoped this was a breakout performance for Pope, who had yet to live up to expectations. The next game, a matchup with the fifth-ranked University of Massachusetts Minutemen and their All-American center Marcus Camby, would be the acid test for the high expectations held for both Pope and the team.

The Minutemen, however, featured more than just Camby, as Kentucky would find out during the November 28 game. Most importantly, the Minutemen featured teamwork and selflessness, traits that Pitino was still attempting to instill in his talented squad. All five Minutemen starters scored in double figures against Kentucky, and UMass controlled the game from the outset. After allowing the Minutemen to jump to a 29-10 lead midway through the first half, the Wildcats went on a run, hitting six three-pointers to knot the score at 45-45 at halftime. UMass began the second half by again controlling play, and Kentucky, while it had opportunities, could not use its pressure defense to rattle guards Edgar Padilla and Carmelo Travieso and take control of the game. Still, Camby was the key, scoring thirty-two points, grabbing nine rebounds, and dominating the paint. Mark Pope, who had starred against Maryland's Mario Lucus, barely scored more points (five) than he committed fouls (four).

UMass won by a 92-82 count that night in Auburn Hills, Michigan. While Kentucky lost, several very important keys for understanding the rest of the season emerged from the game. First, while UMass was able to weather Kentucky's pressure, it did so with almost no

help from its bench. The Wildcats' bench outscored the Minutemen's by a 32-0 count. Over a long season, Kentucky's depth would serve it well, while UMass's starters, who played almost the entire game in every game, would become more fatigued, with injuries and fouls much more of a risk for them than for the Wildcats. Second, as UMass coach John Calipari pointed out, the loss could serve a useful purpose for Pitino. Calipari credited a preseason loss for helping his team play well against Kentucky. In the same way, the Cats could benefit from this defeat. "It took a loss to the Converse All-Stars to wake them up," the UMass coach said of his squad. "Rick will use this game to get his team where he wants them to go." Finally, UMass had now beaten UK, and beating a Pitino-led team a second time would be very, very difficult.

Calipari proved to be right. The loss did help the Wildcats. There were serious chemistry problems going into the season, and the defeat at the hands of Massa-

Antoine Walker, a key factor in the Wildcats' winning a national title in 1996.

chusetts presented a golden opportunity to unify the team. "In a sense, the loss was perfect for Pitino," John Feinstein later concluded in the *Wall Street Journal*. "Not only did it give him an excuse to tell his players that they weren't as good as people said they were, it also shifted a large portion of the spotlight to UMass, which remained undefeated until late in the regular season." Pitino later acknowledged that the defeat was a blessing in disguise: "If we win that game, we don't win the national championship," Pitino stated flatly after winning the NCAA title four months later. "That loss taught us more about our team than any win in our schedule." Several valuable lessons were learned: Tony Delk would have to play the shooting guard spot for the team to succeed. Anthony Epps would need to improve his game as the starting point guard. Antoine Walker, who did not start that night, would be vital to the Cats' success. And finally, Derek Anderson would have to get his minutes as he proved to be more explosive than advertised.

Kentucky won its next twenty-seven games, starting on December 2 with an 89-82 victory over the Indiana Hoosiers in Indianapolis before 41,071 fans. Antoine Walker was the key to that game, and probably to the season, despite all the talent and depth that characterized the Wildcats, as Pitino readily acknowledged. "We can't be great unless Antoine makes us great," Pitino observed. "He's a special player." In a March 25, 1996, *USA Today* article, Steve Wieberg wrote: "Pitino has been blunt throughout the [NCAA] tournament. The Wildcats' talent runs almost ridiculously deep. They have an established star in senior All-American Tony Delk. But it's Walker and his ability and inclination to do all the ancillary things, besides score" that would determine UK's fate.

The problem was that Walker arrived in Lexington with the reputation of anything but a team player—in fact, as a freshman with an attitude. *Chicago Tribune* sportswriter Melissa Isaacson recalled in the April 1, 1996, issue that "Walker's reputation as a big talker with an even bigger opinion of himself probably cost him Catholic League Player of the Year and Mr. Basketball of Illinois honors." In his first year with the Wildcats, Walker did not appreciate having to sit on the bench and loudly demanded more playing time. Teammate Anthony Epps recalled that when Walker "was benched last year he didn't always handle it well." Another time, when UK players were asked how they would handle diminished playing time, Walker said: "I don't want to speak for the rest of the guys, but I'm not going to accept it." This attitude began to change during the sum-

mer of 1995, first at the Olympic Festival in Denver where Walker began to mature, to gain an appreciation of the importance of playing defense, and to improve his outside shooting. The process of maturing and improving his skills continued during the August tour of Italy, but even on the eve of the 1995/96 season he was still proclaiming: "No one comes here [UK] to sit on the bench."

The change really seemed to take hold after the Wildcats were manhandled by UMass. At a team meeting held the next day, McGeachy recounted in *Sports Illustrated*, "Walker spoke passionately" and "acknowledged his own selfishness and sophomoric behavior but said he wanted the team to succeed." The newly reformed star added that "the only way a team with seven high school All-Americans and a former Member of the Big Ten all-freshman team could win would be for its members to check their egos at the Rupp Arena doors. Walker complemented his words four days later with a career-high 24 points on 10-of-12 shooting, seven rebounds and three assists in a key win over Indiana."

But all was not clear sailing even after that. Pitino found it expedient to bench Walker for most of the second half of Kentucky's SEC tournament loss to Mississippi State to remind his star how it was necessary for him to play in order for the Cats to win. Walker acknowledged the point, saying, "I wasn't having a particularly great game." From Pitino's perspective, "Walker was thinking too much shoot-and-score and too little about the rest of Kentucky's needs."

What did Pitino expect from Walker? The coach had explained that back on March 12 during an impromptu news conference on the tarmac at Bluegrass Airport upon the team's return from the SEC tournament final. "For us to win the whole thing," Pitino had said, Walker "has to rebound, block shots, dominate the low post. He has to pass and make everybody better. If he doesn't do that, we're not going to win the whole thing." That was a tall order. Fortunately, the lesson seemed to get across in time for the Big Blue to sweep through the NCAA tournament.

Still, between the UMass and Mississippi State losses, a lot of very positive things occurred for Walker and the Wildcats. First, the team finished the SEC regular season undefeated, something that no other SEC team had accomplished since 1956. Also, Pitino and Kentucky developed a strong inside-outside combination in Walker and Delk. Walker became the team's most effective inside force and its only true low-post threat. Delk emerged as SEC Player of the Week for the last week of Decem-

ber in 1995 and, during a four-game span (December 23 to January 3), made forty of sixty-five shots for an average of 27.8 points per game. Jerry Tipton's January 6 *Herald-Leader* article stated that "with so many capable players, Pitino had to help shift the focus toward Delk and Walker. Thus, in contrast to recent UK teams, the Cats run more set plays designed to get specific players shots. Without set plays, 'They wouldn't distinguish who the shooters are,' Pitino said. 'You wouldn't get Tony and Antoine getting most of the shots.'"

The sophomore forward and senior guard, along with senior forward Walter McCarty, were clearly the most talented of this very talented group of Wildcats. This fact was underlined when all three players were chosen in the opening round of the NBA draft following the season. Although Pitino described them as "impact players," it was clear that Pope, Anderson, Epps, Turner, Mercer, and Sheppard were relegated to the status of role players. That so many high school All-Americans (and future NBA draft choices) could be forced to fit into supporting roles was a remarkable tribute to the tremendous talent of the Kentucky squad. Even more amazing, however, was that these players would accept their roles for the benefit of the team. Kentucky's success in transforming from a group of nine stars who all wanted the basketball to a style of play which emphasized three leaders (Delk, McCarty, and Walker) and a supporting cast was a tribute to the characters of the individual players, Pitino's coaching talents, and Pitino's shrewd use of the UMass loss.

Between the Indiana game, which was a hard-fought contest, and the UK loss on March 10 to Mississippi State in the postseason SEC tournament, conference regular-season champion Kentucky had few other games that were even close enough to call "contests." A Joe Posnanski *Cincinnati Post* article on February 15, 1996, discussed how this situation led to a unique type of pressure for the Wildcats. "These UK players and coaches," he wrote, "deal with even larger wants, bigger desires, a deeper hunger. They deal with being the beating heart for a state, the envelope of joys and sorrows, the hopes for many lives which are not quite right." Such was the level of pressure facing the Wildcats from the start of the season. Posnanski noted that nothing was quite good enough. "These Wildcats have won 20 consecutive games, and the fans are upset because the new uniform color is too close to North Carolina blue. At midseason, the Wildcats had lost just one game—that loss to Massachusetts, the currently ranked No. 1 team—they had won all the others by an average of 22 points. In the

A happy band of Wildcats celebrate a solid 83-63 victory over Wake Forest in the Midwest Regional final, which qualified Pitino and the Untouchables for the 1996 Final Four.

Lexington newspaper's midseason report card, the Wildcats were given an A-minus." The *Post* reporter then underlined the absurdity of Kentucky fans' expectations: "After beating Georgia by 13, people wonder what's wrong with UK." He quoted Pitino and several players about how the pressure was not only to win, but to dominate. Kentucky's fans had happily forgotten the humiliation of the Sutton years and apparently had learned very little from that era. Winning, specifically winning the national championship, was all that mattered. UK's winning, Posnanski wrote, added "hopes for many lives" in the Bluegrass State.

The Wildcats beat intrastate opponents Morehead State by sixty-four points and Louisville by twenty-three, and SEC rivals Tennessee by seventeen and forty and Mississippi State by eighteen. Kentucky remained in the top five in the nation in both the AP and CNN/*USA Today* polls throughout the entire season, and the March 10 loss to the Bulldogs simply dropped Pitino's squad from number one to number two in the polls. Still, nothing short of winning it all would suffice for Wildcat fans.

Ironically, the loss to Mississippi State was probably a blessing in disguise for the team—although it infuriated fans—as it helped reduce some of the pressures and expectations. Just before the start of the NCAA tournament, Jerry Tipton wrote that before losing to Mississippi State, Kentucky was beginning to be labeled "the biggest nothing-to-gain, everything-to-lose tournament favorite since UNLV in 1991."

UNLV had rolled through that season undefeated before losing in the Final Four semifinals to eventual champion Duke. Tipton then quoted UNLV's head coach, Jerry Tarkanian (now the head coach at Fresno State University), as saying he did not believe Kentucky would lose in the tournament as his Running Rebels had. In fact, Tarkanian said, "Losing two games will help them. What happened to us is we had some potentially tough games. But in every game that year at some point we led by twenty points. I'd try to get our kids all fired up and tell them how tough it was going to be. They got to the point where they didn't believe me." At least this mistaken sense of invincibility was one problem that

Pitino would now not have to face in preparing his team for the tournament.

Kentucky entered the NCAA tournament with a 28-2 season record, and its only two losses occurred to teams that, like the Wildcats, would reach the Final Four: UMass and Mississippi State. Playing in the Midwest Regionals in Dallas, the top-seeded Wildcats dispatched the number sixteen seed, San Jose State, by a 110-72 count, led by McCarty's twenty-four points. Kentucky then reached the Sweet Sixteen with a convincing 84-60 victory over ninth seed Virginia Tech. The Midwest bracket next moved to the Metrodome in Minneapolis, where the Wildcats picked fourth-seeded Utah apart with their pressure defense. In its 101-70 victory, Kentucky made use of balanced play—twelve Wildcats scored in the game—to beat the Utes' star duo of Keith Van Horn (twenty-three points) and Ben Caton (twenty-two points). The game was never in doubt, with Kentucky leading 56-34 at halftime and forcing twenty-one Utah turnovers against the Wildcats' six.

Many, including Pitino, considered Kentucky's next game, against second-seeded Wake Forest from the ACC, a difficult test for the Wildcats. The winner would advance to the Final Four. Although Wake Forest would be without injured starting point guard Tony Rutland, a major loss against Kentucky's full-court pressure, Pitino still maintained that he considered the Demon Deacons, with their star center and balanced attack, to be a major test for his squad. The UK coach based his estimate on Wake Forest's similarity to the UMass squad that had defeated the Cats. "Very much so," Pitino insisted before the game, "except UMass doesn't take as many threes with four people. For us, Wake Forest is even more difficult to defend than UMass." The Demon Deacons featured All-American center Tim Duncan and also possessed a very solid supporting cast, as Pitino pointed out. These appeared to be the same ingredients UMass (with Camby) and Mississippi State (with Eric Dampier) had used in handing the Wildcats their only two defeats of the season. For those looking forward to a tight contest, the game did not go according to the script. The Wildcats, under Pitino's guidance, had learned and benefitted from the earlier defeats, and Kentucky brought forth exceptional defensive pressure and balanced scoring from its starters to win by a convincing 83-63 count. Even the twenty-point margin of victory was misleading, since Kentucky fully dominated the game, holding Wake Forest to just nineteen first-half points and limiting Duncan to only seven shots and fourteen points. The trip to the Final Four was assured.

The Cats delivered a defensive masterpiece against Wake Forest's 6'10" Duncan, who was believed to be Camby's equal. The Wildcats looked to be well prepared to take on UMass center Marcus Camby by using the same defense that had shut down Duncan and Wake Forest. The earlier losses to center-led UMass and Mississippi State teams had taught the Wildcats several lessons on how to improve their play. Now the Big Blue had the chance to prove themselves again.

Kentucky was making its eleventh trip (its second under Pitino) to the Final Four when it advanced to play in East Rutherford, New Jersey, at the Continental Airlines Arena. UMass coach John Calipari's prediction after the early season meeting with UK—that Pitino would very effectively use the loss to motivate his players to get them "where he wants them to go"—had proven to be accurate. Kentucky had refined its defense following the UMass and Mississippi State losses to become better able to defend against squads with strong inside-outside play. During the week leading up to the game, the press emphasized that UMass had more "close game experience" than Kentucky, and that the experience would be a plus for the Minutemen. Pitino, however, saw things differently. In his view, the Minutemen, who were not particularly deep to begin with, would be more fatigued than his Kentucky squad, which had won only one game all season by six points or less (against Georgia), and thus had been able to rest its stars more often late in games throughout the season.

This time Kentucky won a relatively close game by an 81-74 count. The Wildcats succeeded by containing (but not stopping) Camby and completely shutting down the UMass guards. Yet the victory did not come easily. In contrast to the first game, Kentucky did not let UMass get off to a fast start, and the Wildcats held a 36-28 lead at halftime. Led by Camby, who scored twenty-five points, UMass fought back and made Kentucky earn the victory by hitting twelve of fourteen free throws during the final five minutes. Delk and Walker led the Wildcats in scoring, with twenty and fourteen respectively. Kentucky's bench again dominated the less talented Minutemen reserves, outscoring them twenty-six to ten. While Camby had a strong game, he did not dominate and intimidate the UK team as he had earlier in the season. McCarty became the starting center facing off against Camby, and Pitino was able to utilize Pope off the bench for four hard fouls and rough play against Camby. The Wildcats simply wore Camby, and UMass, down.

The Wake Forest victory had indeed provided Kentucky with a good opportunity to test its strategy for

(Top) Walter McCarty shows his feelings during the UK-Massachusetts 1996 Final Four contest. Kentucky's 81-74 victory avenged a regular-season loss to the Minutemen. (Bottom) Walter McCarty and Antoine Walker control Massachusetts's All-American center Marcus Camby under the basket during UK's Final Four victory. Guard Anthony Epps (25) is at left.

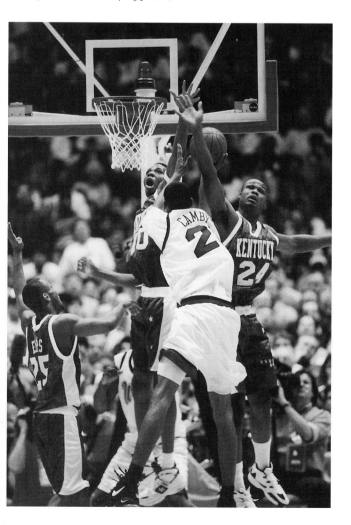

the subsequent meeting with Camby and UMass. And following the contest, Camby acknowledged that he was affected by the pressure Kentucky applied on him. "I probably needed to be a little more aggressive when the double-team came," he said. "They were knocking balls out of my hand and forcing me to take shots I didn't feel comfortable taking." Perhaps more importantly, as Anthony Epps maintained, Kentucky shut down UMass guards Padilla and Travieso. According to Epps, it was the guards, not Camby, who beat Kentucky in the earlier game. This time around, Kentucky shut them down with tremendous pressure defense, just as it had humiliated Wake Forest's guards in their encounter with UK. Furthermore, the Cats remained poised against the Minutemen, despite their lack of close game experience. Reserve center Mark Pope made this point after the game when he said, "You can't blow a team like UMass out." Antoine Walker echoed this point when he said, "We weren't worried [at the end]. It was tight. It was difficult. But we handled it well." In other words, Kentucky had retained its poise and not crumbled when the game got close. UMass coach John Calipari admitted that the game "unfolded the way we wanted it to unfold. But at the end we didn't make the plays, and they did." The Wildcats handled the pressure with "a champion's heart." Now all the Wildcats had to do was win one more game, against a relatively lightly regarded Syracuse Orangemen squad.

The victory over UMass propelled Kentucky to the championship game on April 1, 1996, where it met a surprising Syracuse squad. Syracuse had been ranked fifteenth in the nation at the end of the season and was a number four seed in the West Region. The Orangemen, however, had upset Kansas (ESPN's preseason favorite) in the regional finals to reach the Final Four. Led by power forward John Wallace, who played brilliantly during the tournament, Syracuse beat Mississippi State, ensuring that Kentucky would not have the opportunity to avenge both of its regular-season losses. As a major underdog, and as a team from the Big East conference and nearby New York State, Syracuse was the media darling, seen as a heroic David facing Goliath. Most experts considered Kentucky an overwhelming favorite, but the press, including *USA Today* and the *Chicago Sun Times*, wrote that the Orangemen had a realistic shot at winning. The press also focused on the great pressure weighing on Pitino and the Wildcats, suggesting that this might slow them down against Syracuse, which had already overachieved and thus had nothing to lose. Instead of letting UK bask in a positive light as it was about to redeem itself from the sorry Sutton years, the press did

(Left) Leading Wildcat scorer Tony Delk tallying two of his twenty-four points against Syracuse in the 1996 NCAA title game. Allen Edwards (3) and Ron Mercer (33) position themselves for a rebound. *(Right)* Freshman forward Ron Mercer was a key contributor for UK in the 1996 Final Four. He came off the bench in the title game to hit eight of twelve shots from the floor, including three of four from beyond the three-point line, and twenty points.

all it could to increase the pressure and encourage the plucky Syracuse David to beat the arrogant Kentucky Goliath.

This time, of course, Goliath won, but it was not an easy victory. After taking a 42-33 lead into the locker room at halftime, UK withstood a 16-5 run late in the second half to post a 76-67 victory over the Orangemen and win UK's sixth national title, and first since 1978. John Wallace was magnificent in defeat, scoring twenty-nine points and grabbing ten rebounds, but the Wildcats' athleticism, pressure, and depth were too much to overcome. Tony Delk scored twenty-four points on his way to being named the tournament's MVP, while Ron Mercer added twenty points off the bench. Kentucky won despite being outshot from the floor (50 percent for Syracuse to 38.4 percent for UK) because the Wildcats forced twenty-four turnovers and took twenty-one more shots than Syracuse. The key to the game was Ron Mercer. Syracuse expected Delk and Walker to pose

problems for their zone defense, but Mercer, who averaged only 7.7 points per game during his freshman season, was a surprise to them. Orangemen coach Jim Boeheim said, "Mercer was the one guy that came in and hurt us." Mercer led the Wildcats' bench, which outscored Syracuse's reserves twenty-six to zero.

Following the game, Pitino announced, "The entire state of Kentucky owns our basketball team." What was more important was that Kentucky now owned a champion. This championship Kentucky team was now considered one of the best of all time by some experts. Yet, unlike the all-time great teams to which they were compared, the Wildcats lacked the true superstar that those teams possessed in the mold of Lew Alcindor and Bill Walton (UCLA), Michael Jordan (North Carolina), Magic Johnson (Michigan State), Bill Russell (University of San Francisco), or Scott May (Indiana). *USA Today*'s April 2 cover story quoted Marty Blake, the NBA's director of scouting, as stating, "Top to bottom,

they're the best that I've seen in God knows how long." The story went on to explain that the team's nickname—"Untouchables"—meant "as in untouchable on defense." It was a nickname Pitino had bestowed on the team. Tim Duncan and Marcus Camby, along with almost every other player and coach who had faced Kentucky during the season, would probably agree. Skip Myslenski wrote in the April 3 *Chicago Tribune*, "What was not predictable in this era of so much self-indulgence was this: That all of its talent would work willfully, would stuff their egos in their back pockets, would care not about their individual statistics and operate in unselfish harmony."

This team was "untouchable" because of its defense. In fact, Kentucky won because of its defense, not because of its three-point shooting, as was popularly thought. Kentucky shot only 18.6 three-pointers per game on average during the season. Compared to most teams this was still a high amount, but it was the first time a Pitino-led squad had attempted fewer than 22.6 per game in any season since his arrival in Lexington. Despite the similarities to Pitino's other squads, this team was different from previous ones. It was physically dominating. It was special. This team was a champion.

Pitino had done it. He had lived up to all the lofty expectations that he had helped to create for the Kentucky program and for himself. The "turnaround specialist" had stayed until the end and won it all. Moreover, he had answered his critics and overcome the tremendous pressure facing him and his team. The *Chicago Sun Times*'s Jay Mariotti wrote an article on March 29 titled "Pitino Has Winning Reputation, But Comes Up Short on Rings," in which he boldly stated that "anything but a trophy ceremony Monday at the Meadowlands will be a major bummer." Mariotti happily went on, attempting to rub salt in Pitino's wounds by saying, "As if that isn't enough pressure, Pitino knows a lot of people out there don't like him." *USA Today*'s Steve Wieberg on March 29 quoted Pitino as saying—possibly jokingly—that if he did anything less than win, he should probably "just stay in New Jersey." And Bob Ryan of the *Boston Globe* (March 25) wrote, "Rick Pitino was hired for one reason—to bring a national championship to a constituency for whom college basketball is far bigger than life itself. He now has a team his fans have been waiting for. If he doesn't deliver, he might as well charter a plane for the Seychelles." A *New York Post* headline screeched, "Pitino Is Failure If Cats Lose," which seemed to summarize the view of the big city press.

But Rick Pitino did deliver. He overcame the pressures. He exorcised his personal demons.

Ironically, victory came in Pitino's sixth season. Pitino admitted in Jerry Tipton's December 31, 1995, *Herald-Leader* article—before the championship—"I really felt that I'd stay four or five years." Given all the times that

"How sweet it is!" Rick Pitino and the squad celebrate UK's first NCAA title since 1978 with a 76-67 victory over Syracuse.

Pitino had considered leaving Lexington over the years for various coaching jobs in the NBA, no one, including the staunchest of Big Blue fans, could have expected him to stay on for six seasons. Yet both Pitino and Kentucky fans were now thrilled that he had remained in Lexington for so long. In the same article, Tipton quoted Nolan Richardson, head coach at Arkansas, as saying that the Kentucky job is "the" job in college basketball, financially and otherwise. And Pitino certainly had cashed in over his first five years. Yet winning the championship was what he desperately needed to be acknowledged as truly successful in his chosen profession.

That Pitino could lead Kentucky back so quickly to the top of the college basketball world from the disgraces that the program faced when he took over was quite remarkable. He also did it with players that he had recruited, helping to silence critics who earlier questioned his recruiting judgment. And he did it his way, without stars of the caliber of Michael Jordan or Magic Johnson (except, possibly, for the coach himself), but with teamwork. Pitino had achieved his dream. The question now was, where would he go from there?

USA Today's May 1, 1996, edition included a story about Pitino by Mark Coomes, a *Louisville Courier-Journal* writer. The article described how, just one month after winning it all, Pitino was, surprisingly, largely unchanged. Coomes wrote that "the pursuit of that victory [for the NCAA crown] dominated much of Pitino's adult life but, oddly enough, has changed it precious little. After 24 sleepless hours of celebration, the freshly crowned king of college basketball hunkered down to business as usual, flying off to appearances and recruiting visits as always. 'Outside of feeling great, nothing has changed,' Pitino said. 'All the championship does is make you happy every day.'" A bit of that glee disappeared a few days later when sophomore power forward Antoine Walker announced that he was turning pro. Pitino had tried unsuccessfully to persuade the young athlete to stay at UK for one more season. The player that Pitino called "the straw that stirs our drink" felt he was ready to play for champagne. As it turned out, he was.

It seemed as though after every season Pitino was courting, or being courted by, a professional basketball position. As late as April 21, 1996, Pitino had said publicly that he had no interest in any other coaching position. Scaring Wildcat fans, he again—at least temporarily—changed his mind. This time it was the New Jersey Nets (again) offering Pitino the chance to come back to the New York area and become head coach and general manager. They reportedly offered him $20 mil-

lion over five years. In addition, the Nets were willing to make Pitino a part owner. Following a European golfing trip with Kentucky basketball boosters, Pitino decided to stay in the Bluegrass. While fans will probably never know if Pitino stayed because of a newfound love for Wildcat basketball and Lexington, or if the boosters made financial promises that convinced him to stay, or for some other reason, they still had their coach. That was the most important thing to the faithful, since Pitino had now proven himself to be among the very best in basketball.

Repeating as champions, however, would be very difficult. The team's leading scorer (Tony Delk) and the three best inside players (Antoine Walker, Mark Pope, and Walter McCarty) were now bound for professional basketball. Walker (who had averaged 15.2 points and 8.4 rebounds per game in 1995/96) was the Boston Celtics' lottery pick. Delk was drafted in the first round by the Charlotte Hornets. McCarty was picked up, also in the first round, by the New York Knicks. Pope was drafted in the second by the Indiana Pacers, but went instead to Europe, where he played on a Turkish team. On May 7, 1996, Jerry Tipton wrote that "Antoine Walker's departure to the NBA probably assures that Kentucky won't equal the glories of 1995-96 next season. Kentucky probably won't become the second team since 1955-56 to go unbeaten in Southeastern Conference play. Kentucky probably won't win the national championship." Tipton was correct, but just barely. South Carolina would see to it that his first prediction came true. As to the second prediction, and the more important one for Big Blue fans, the sportswriter almost spoke too soon, as the Wildcats reached the NCAA championship game before finally, and narrowly, going down in defeat.

Kentucky had lost its three leading scorers in Delk (17.8 points per game), Walker (15.3), and McCarty (11.3). Pope had averaged 7.6 points per game and supplied strong interior defense. The cupboard, however, was not exactly bare. Returning would be seniors Derek Anderson, Anthony Epps, Jared Prickett, and Jeff Sheppard (who decided instead to redshirt). Other returnees would include junior guards Allen Edwards and Cameron Mills, as well as sophomores Ron Mercer, Nazr Mohammed, Scott Padgett, Oliver Simmons (who transferred during the season to Florida State after breaking his right foot on November 22), and Wayne Turner. The only significant newcomer was freshman Jamaal Magloire, a 6'10" Canadian import.

Conventional wisdom held that Anderson (at shooting guard) and Mercer (at small forward) could step up

The 1996/97 Kentucky Wildcats, "The Unbelievables," who rose above adversity to come within five points in overtime of capturing a second straight NCAA title. In tribute to the squad, Rick Pitino said, "I never thought I could be more proud of anything than a national championship, but I really am of this squad." Seated, left to right: Delray Brooks, Rick Pitino, Wayne Turner, Derek Anderson, Jeff Sheppard, Anthony Epps, Cameron Mills, Steve Masiello, Jim O'Brien, Winston Bennett. Standing, left to right: Frank Vogel, Simeon Mars, Ron Mercer, Jared Prickett, Jamaal Magloire, Nazr Mohammed, Oliver Simmons, Scott Padgett, Allen Edwards, Eddie Jamiel, Bill Keightley, Shaun Brown.

and replace the loss of Delk and McCarty. As Pitino noted when Walker turned professional, replacing the underclassman would be the much more difficult task. Pitino hoped that Prickett would be the player to help ease the loss of Walker. While the coach knew that Prickett could not totally replace Walker, he did believe that "Jared's fully capable of being an outstanding player." Pitino also discussed Louisville native Scott Padgett, a 6'9" forward who had lost his eligibility until at least December 1996 because of academic problems, as a possible key to replacing Walker's skills. Unfortunately, neither Prickett nor Padgett was a low-post player, one of Walker's many strengths. Unless Magloire or Mohammed could fill that role, Kentucky would become even more dependent on the three-point shot, a risky strategy given the single elimination nature of the NCAA tournament. This team was not as capable of physically dominating its opponents. But it could, as it turned out, outthink them.

With Pitino now safely in Lexington for at least another season and the squad set (even minus three NBA first-round draft picks), Wildcat fans prepared for another exciting—and successful—series of contests. The big question on their minds was asked, and answered, in Jerry Tipton's preseason question and answer article

about the Wildcats. It was: Could Kentucky repeat as national champions? Part of the response included this Pitino quote: "We're not as deep or as experienced or as talented as last year. We're going to lose some games. We can all see that. By the end of the season, this will be a fine team, a fine team capable of winning it all." Few of the experts, however, saw things that way. Kansas was widely regarded as the favorite throughout the year. In fact, television analyst Dick Vitale was already picking Kansas to win the 1997 crown—in the April 3, 1996, edition of *USA Today*—just two days after the Wildcats' victory over Syracuse. Kansas started the season ranked number one in the nation. Kentucky started out as number three.

The 1996/97 season was relatively tranquil compared to the turmoil of some previous campaigns. The tremendous pressure to win had been removed with the championship. And, luckily, with Vitale and other experts almost unanimously picking Kansas to be the top team in the land and the favorite to win the NCAA crown, Kentucky's young and inexperienced players had more time to develop out of the limelight. The consensus seemed to be that Kentucky had enjoyed its moment of glory the previous season and that 1996/97 was finally to be the year for Kansas.

The exodus by most experts from the Kentucky to the Kansas bandwagon picked up speed following Kentucky's first game, a loss to Clemson at the Black Coaches Association Classic in Indianapolis on November 15. Kentucky led 37-31 at halftime before losing to the Tigers in overtime. The biggest difference between the 1996 national champions and the 1997 team became clear in this first game: the current squad was not as effective defensively as the 1996 team. Despite playing forty-five minutes of basketball against a Clemson team with shaky ballhandling skills, Kentucky forced only fifteen turnovers, was outrebounded thirty-three to twenty-one, and allowed the Tigers to hit 55.2 percent of their shots from the field. Jerry Tipton's November 16 article started out, "Any lingering thought of Kentucky as a regal defending champion evaporated here last night." Chuck Culpepper's article in the same edition of the *Herald-Leader* stated that Pitino thought this team had the least amount of talent of any squad since his first two at UK, and that this group was "very delicate." Wildcat fans realized that Pitino was playing an angle with this team; he wanted to toughen them up and motivate them to try to match last year's performance. The press, however, seemed ready to write off Kentucky as being incapable of repeating. They were wrong.

By the end of December, with Kentucky on an eleven game winning streak—including a 74-54 thumping of a solid Louisville squad on December 31—fans and the press had again warmed up to UK and its chances of repeating as champion. Pitino attempted to diffuse the adulation for his squad when he commented that this team lacked the "untouchable" defense of his championship squad. Pitino believed that the prior group was better defensively, more intense, more experienced, and had better inside play.

The coach admitted, however, that in Anderson and Mercer at shooting guard and small forward respectively he had the best wing play since coming to Lexington. He also believed that Epps and Turner provided an edge at point guard over the previous team. The numbers seemed to support the growing comparisons between the two teams. A statistical comparison of the 1996/97 Cats through the first eleven games (before the Louisville win) against the full thirty-six-game statistics from the previous year shows scoring, scoring defense, turnovers forced, and scoring margin were nearly identical in every category. On paper, the team appeared to be the equal of the 1996 squad. Pitino tried to downplay this point with the comment, "Any comparison to last year is unfair. That was the best team I've ever coached."

One of a series of devastating blows suffered by "The Unbelievables" was a season-ending injury (except for two technical foul shots in the NCAA semi-final game) to star Derek Anderson during the January 18, 1997, UK victory over Auburn.

By January 11 Kentucky had run its record to fourteen wins against only the Clemson defeat. But on that day Kentucky travelled to Oxford to face Mississippi. Shockingly, the Cats lost by a 73-69 count. The Rebels built a large lead at the beginning of the second half and held on to win when Anthony Epps threw the ball away with 6.8 seconds remaining and UK trailing 71-69. Prickett led Kentucky with fourteen points, but Mercer had a terrible game, scoring only ten points on four for fifteen shooting and grabbing only four rebounds and no assists. Kentucky's other star and leading scorer (and the leading scorer in the SEC at the time), Derek Anderson, had pulled a back muscle in the previous game victory over Canisius and did not score in ten minutes of action. Unfortunately, Anderson's pulled back muscle was just a precursor of a far more serious injury he was to suffer. In the eighteenth game of the season, a 77-53 victory at Rupp Arena over Auburn, Anderson tore the anterior cruciate ligament in his right knee, ending his season and his Wildcat career. Or so everyone thought. Anderson was able to come back and score in the semifinal NCAA game against Minnesota, making two technical foul shots.

With Anderson injured, many believed UK's chances of upsetting Kansas and repeating as champion were severely damaged, but not over. John Clay wrote in the January 22 *Herald-Leader* that the saddest part was that the former redshirt had unselfishly waited in the wings

until his senior season for his chance to star. Dick Vitale was quoted in the article as saying that Anderson was the team's most complete player on both ends of the court. Clay, however, went on to quote ESPN's Jim O'Connell as saying, "They're still one of the top teams in the country, even without Derek. If any other team would lose a player of that caliber you would see an immediate dropoff. But with Epps and Turner and Edwards, they've got guys who can step in." Clay, however, seemed to disagree, noting that adding Anderson's loss to that of Delk, McCarty, Pope, Walker, and Sheppard would seem to be too much to overcome when Kansas at that time had an unbeaten team that included Jacque Vaughn, Scot Pollard, Raef LaFrentz, Paul Pierce, and Jerod Haase, all returning from the previous year. Too much change for a repeat seemed to be Clay's concern. "Repeating is difficult enough when healthy, after all, and good health is as good a luck as you can get."

Still, Clay's article carried one short quote, one idea that could give hope to the Wildcat faithful. Television analyst and former UK star Larry Conley said, "I think Mercer is capable of taking a team on his back." Those twelve words summarized Kentucky's hopes and chances at the time. No one expected Scott Padgett to step into the lineup after having been little more than a role player during his one year on the squad (1994/95) and develop into a star in his own right. In fact, in Kentucky's first game in the post-Derek Anderson era, Padgett tied with Allen Edwards with a game-high sixteen points in a 58-46 victory over Vanderbilt.

In the twenty-second game of the season, an 82-57 Rupp Arena thrashing of a solid Georgia team, Mercer finally lifted the team onto his back, scoring twenty points to go along with Padgett's twelve. Mohammed and Magloire played an excellent combined game in the post, with each scoring eleven points and the pair grabbing a combined fourteen rebounds. Kentucky was now four and zero without Anderson. With three of the victories coming over NCAA tournament-bound teams (Georgia, Vanderbilt, and Arkansas), UK looked as though it might not miss a beat despite losing its star scorer. Then came the game, on February 4, 1997, when the third-ranked Wildcats travelled to Columbia, South Carolina, to take on the nineteenth-ranked Gamecocks. USC was on a hot streak, having won nine straight SEC games coming into the contest following a disappointing start to the season. The Gamecocks also had tremendous guard play, something that would be even more valuable against the Wildcats, given Anderson's absence. Finally, Kentucky was missing Jared Prickett's

valuable bruising play off of the bench because of an injured ankle. Suiting up only eight players, Kentucky was beaten in overtime by an 84-79 score. Despite the loss, the Cats had a lot to be happy about. They had come back from a 62-51 deficit with just over seven minutes to play, and even had a chance to win in regulation had Ron Mercer's jumper gone in at the buzzer. USC played ten players, and Kentucky was simply worn down by the end of the overtime. Still, Kentucky's rotation (minus the injured Prickett) was beginning to take shape: Mercer, Padgett, Edwards, Mohammed, Epps, Turner, Mills, and Magloire all played well and all were beginning to find their roles on the team. In spite of the loss, things were not looking so bad for the Big Blue.

On February 9, Chuck Culpepper showed just how much winning the national championship the prior year had improved Pitino's relationship with the press, and how much less pressure the press was applying to him and the Wildcats. Even though the loss to South Carolina had taken place only days before, Culpepper wrote a tongue-in-cheek article trying to decide when Pitino had done his best coaching job. Basically, Culpepper

The highly-touted Villanova Wildcats, led by their freshman star forward Tim Thomas (3), were left open-mouthed by Allen Edwards and teammates, as Villanova was blown out 93-56 in Rupp Arena on February 9, 1997.

admitted that Pitino was a tremendous coach who could win with all types of teams and under all circumstances. The article concluded that the coach, in overcoming the loss of Anderson with a good, but not great, team, was doing the best job of his career. Clearly, the pressure was off the Cats. While expectations were still high, Pitino and his team were being given breathing room. This was a luxury Kansas did not enjoy.

Although Kentucky fell to fourth in the national rankings with the loss, it rebounded only five days later to destroy number sixteen Villanova by a 93-56 count at Rupp Arena. Mercer again led the Cats. And, as Thomas George wrote in the February 12 *New York Times*, "It was not until the freshman sensation Tim Thomas and Villanova came to town last Sunday that Mercer got excited. Mercer defended against Thomas mercilessly, limiting him to two-of-seven shooting, nine points, one rebound and six turnovers. Mercer was outstanding: 23 points, 11 rebounds (seven offensive), six assists and two steals." The 6'7" swingman had risen to two challenges in the game: outplaying Thomas and stepping up for the loss of Anderson.

The Cats won their next five games, and their record stood at twenty-seven wins and three losses when they met South Carolina in a rematch, this time in Rupp Arena. Conventional wisdom assumed that UK would win. Af-

Ron Mercer and Derek Anderson savor a UK victory prior to Anderson's January 18, 1997, injury.

ter all, Mercer was now playing not only for another national championship, but also for a top position in the NBA draft. He was carrying the Wildcats to victories in a way and with a style that had not been present while Anderson was playing. Pitino had utilized Anderson's injury, and Mercer's desire to play the next season in the NBA, as a way to motivate his star sophomore into performing at a level that Kentucky fans had not seen in a Wildcat since Mashburn. Furthermore, Eddie Fogler's squad would have to beat Kentucky in Rupp Arena this time, a much more difficult task since UK was undefeated at home thus far in the season. Finally, Pitino was rarely beaten a second time by any team or any coach. This seemed like a good time to go to Las Vegas and bet the house on the Big Blue. As the *1997 Kentucky Wildcat NCAA Tournament Postseason Guide* (prepared by UK Media Relations) wrote about the game, "In a defensive struggle, South Carolina [now rated sixth in the nation] outlasted Kentucky [ranked third], 72-66, earning the top seed for the Southeastern Conference Tournament. USC became the first team to win at UK on Senior Day since 1964, and, in the process, halted the Wildcats' 27-game home winning streak." Mercer scored twenty-five points in defeat, continuing his excellent play. The problem was that no other Wildcat scored in double figures.

In the SEC tournament, Kentucky destroyed Auburn (92-50), Ole Miss (88-70), and Georgia (95-68) to win yet another title, its fifth under Pitino and a record twentieth in its history. Unfortunately, Allen Edwards was injured in the final game of the SEC tournament. He sustained what was diagnosed as "a mild to moderate sprain" of his right ankle, and it was unclear if he could return to close to full form for the NCAAs.

The team entered the NCAA tournament 30-4 (the ninth time UK had won at least thirty games in a season). Mercer joined Raef LaFrentz of Kansas, Tim Duncan of Wake Forest, Danny Fortson of Cincinnati, and Keith Van Horn of Utah on the AP's first team All-American squad. Kentucky finished the pre-NCAA schedule with an average margin of victory of 20.9 points per game, which, while below the 23.4 points per game a year earlier, was still the best in the nation. Although the Wildcats finished the regular season ranked fifth in the nation, the NCAA tournament committee rewarded UK with a number one seeding in the Western Regionals. With Anderson out of the lineup, some observers outside the Commonwealth might have thought that the seeding was too high.

Kentucky opened the tournament with a convincing 92-54 victory over Montana in Salt Lake City on March

13. Turner and Mills led a balanced attack with nineteen points each, while Mercer added sixteen and Prickett fourteen. The Wildcats' next game in Salt Lake City on March 15 was a battle. With Mercer and Turner in early foul trouble and playing just a combined fifteen minutes in the first half, UK was tied at halftime against an eighth-seeded Iowa Hawkeye team. Mercer, despite his goal of playing for a high NBA lottery pick, was outplayed in the contest by Hawkeye star Andre Woolridge and was outscored twenty-nine to ten. However, Iowa lacked Kentucky's depth. Wildcat reserves scored twenty-three points (led by Mohammed with ten and Mills with eleven), compared to only five for Iowa. Prickett and Mills combined to score twenty-six of UK's total of thirty-five first-half points and kept the team in the game. Turner picked up the pace in the second half, but the outcome was still in doubt when Padgett sealed the victory with a jumper with only twenty-eight seconds remaining and Kentucky ahead by only three points. The 75-69 victory was much closer than most had expected. It reinforced the fact that this UK squad was neither as talented nor as dominating as the previous team.

The Cats' next game was on March 20 in San Jose, California, against fourth-seeded St. Joseph's College from Philadelphia. St. Joe's featured a solid three-guard attack and excellent outside shooting reminiscent of South Carolina. Many experts believed that Kentucky was vulnerable to that type of squad. Although Anderson had made a remarkable recovery and claimed to be ready to play, Pitino made the last-minute decision not to play his star—against St. Joe's or anyone else in the tournament—so as to preserve Anderson's knee for a possible NBA career. Pitino's decision, in an era where winning at all costs is expected in college basketball, was a surprising and very commendable decision. The coach placed Anderson's well-being and potential NBA career ahead of UK's winning.

Kentucky was further weakened by the loss of starting swingman Allen Edwards. The Miami native had played one minute against Montana and eighteen against Iowa, scoring only two points and grabbing two rebounds in the latter contest. Only three days after the Iowa game, team physicians altered their diagnosis of Edwards's injury. An X-ray revealed that what had been thought to be a slow-to-heal sprained right ankle was, in fact, a stress fracture on the inside of his ankle. The media pronounced Edwards out for the rest of the year, and Kentucky, now with only eight healthy players, suddenly appeared vulnerable against the eighteenth-ranked team from Philadelphia. The St. Joseph's squad believed they would be able to beat UK's press, and possibly even wear the Cats down in the process. How wrong they were.

As it had all year long, Kentucky found a new star when one was needed. This time, Cameron Mills stepped up and provided nineteen points in only twenty minutes of play off the bench, matching Mercer for team high in scoring in the game. The team got off to a fast start, leading 39-27 at halftime, on its way to a relatively easy 83-68 victory. The only scare came with 8:53 left and the Wildcats firmly in control. Forward Scott Padgett dropped to the floor and did not get up. It turned out to be a mild sprain, however, and Padgett returned to the contest. The faithful had had their only fright of the night.

The 1996/97 squad was unbelievable. They simply refused to accept defeat. It did not seem to matter who was left to play. UK had lost Walker before the season to the NBA, as a lottery selection, and then lost another potential lottery selection when Anderson was injured halfway through the season. It lost a third starter in Edwards, and on top of that Sheppard was redshirted and Simmons had quit the team early in the season. But UK just kept rolling along toward another national title. The Wildcats believed in their coach and in his ability to put them in a position to win.

The Cats' next contest was to be a rematch with the prior season's tournament foe, the Utah Utes. Kentucky had crushed the Utes 101-70 in 1996 and had also rocked Utah 83-62 in the second round of the 1993 Southeast Regionals. Rick Majerus's team, with its All-American forward Keith Van Horn, yearned for an opportunity to redeem itself. This Utah squad was 29-3, was seeded second in the region, and had been ranked in the top ten in the nation almost all year. This appeared to be a better squad than the one that took the floor a year earlier, since almost everyone had returned and the team had added several talented new players. Van Horn was quoted as predicting that his improved Utah team would defeat the injury-damaged and NBA draft–weakened Wildcats. "They are not the team they were last year. And neither are we," Van Horn said. For UK that was definitely true.

Gone from the squad that took the floor against Van Horn and the Utes in 1996 were Delk, McCarty, Walker, Anderson, and Edwards, a fivesome that probably could easily have beaten any team in the 1997 tournament (including Utah and Kentucky). No matter. The result was the same: the Wildcats thoroughly demoralized and destroyed the Utes. Utah, despite Van Horn's protestations to the contrary, looked tentative and afraid of the Wildcats from the beginning, and was never in the contest. The Wildcats held Van Horn to fifteen points and

whipped the Utes by a 72-59 count. Mercer again led the way, this time with twenty-one points in thirty-eight minutes of play. Surprisingly, guard Cameron Mills, who had emerged as a force during the NCAA tournament to the extent that he had been the team's leading scorer during the first three games, was held scoreless in fourteen minutes of action. Of course, Mills had not scored during the Wildcats' first four games of the season, when the team won three, so this was something that Kentucky knew how to overcome. The Cats led 34-24 at halftime and were never threatened after a brief stretch in the second half when Utah came back to tie the score at 43.

Kentucky was now on its way to the Final Four in Indianapolis to face off with another number one seed, Minnesota. The winner of this game would play on March 31 for the national championship. The *Wall Street Journal*, with its computer ranking system "Mad Max," had rated Kentucky, North Carolina, and Arizona first, third, and fifth, respectively, going into the tournament. On Friday, March 28, the day before the Final Four began, Allen Barra and George Ignatin wrote, "In Monday's title match, Max says it's Kentucky over North Carolina by five. But he's rooting for Kentucky vs. Arizona (in which case, Kentucky by 10) because it would be the first title game featuring two teams named the Wildcats. Cool." Kentucky fans generally hoped that North Carolina would defeat Arizona, even though the Arizona Wildcats were the fifth place team from the Pac-10 Conference, and beating them might seem an easier task than defeating the best team from the Atlantic Coast Conference.

Kentucky and its fans relished the opportunity to defeat Dean Smith's squad for two major reasons. First, North Carolina only two years earlier had embarrassed the Wildcats in the NCAA tournament. More important to longtime Big Blue fans, Smith had passed Adolph Rupp during the 1997 tournament as the all-time winningest coach in college basketball history. Revenge would be doubly sweet when Kentucky defeated the Tar Heels. Unfortunately, these fans did not get their wish, as Arizona did indeed best the Tar Heels.

Could Pitino possibly repeat without five of the best players from his previous squad? Well, make that three and a half. Allen Edwards surprised the team and its doctors and returned for the game against the Golden Gophers. Even more surprising was a cameo by Anderson, as he sank two technical foul shots and thus scored two points in the game. But even with Edwards and a touch of Anderson, could the Wildcats defeat the 31-3 Golden Gophers, coached by Kentucky native Clem Haskins? This was a squad deeper than Kentucky, particularly given the injury to Anderson, as well as one that appeared to have the ballhandling talent to neutralize UK's press. After the win over St. Joe's, Scott Padgett had said, "A lot of people don't respect us as much as the usual Kentucky team. They don't think we're the almighty, powerful Kentucky." He knew the difference because during the current season teams "talked trash," while before they had been respectfully silent. While some sportswriters and fans tried to draw parallels to the "Unforgettables," Pitino denied the similarities, saying that the 1991/92 squad was older and more experienced, "like guys coming home from the war." This team was young. It was inexperienced. It was shallow and depleted. Pitino said ruefully, "We've gone from the deepest team to one of the more depleted. That shows you how well I've recruited."

His recruits included a former walk-on, Cameron Mills, credited by Pitino as getting the team to the Final Four. It also included Wayne Turner, a point guard to whom Pitino turned to start after the second loss to South Carolina. While Turner was on the 1996 champion team, he never got off the bench in the final game. Pitino also credited Mercer with stepping up, and, like Mashburn in 1991/92, taking over the starring role despite his youth and inexperience. Pitino said, "This team has accomplished as much as any team I've coached. A walk-on looks like an All-American. The point guard looks like K.J. [former NBA star Kevin Johnson]. Ron Mercer's showing terrific toughness."

Pitino believed going into the Minnesota game that his team had an advantage because of experience, although that edge was very slight: Minnesota did not make the 1996 NCAA tournament, while Kentucky won it. Pitino commented, "If I had my entire team back [the 1996 squad], I'd think it's a little advantage. But I don't have my entire team back. This is basically a new team." Haskins also commented that he did not think experience would make much of a difference. The results of the contest suggested that they may both have been wrong. The pressure of a Final Four game and the Wildcats' press thoroughly stymied and confused the Golden Gophers into a staggering twenty-six turnovers. Minnesota and Kentucky both had nine players play eleven minutes or more during the contest. Yet Kentucky looked much fresher, and its press, which Minnesota had thought it could handle, blanketed the Gophers.

There were probably two keys to the game. First, Minnesota's very fine starting point guard, Eric Harris, had injured a shoulder and was ineffective against UCLA on the way to the Final Four (no points in twenty-three

Co-captain Jared Prickett fighting two Minnesota Golden Gophers for a rebound in the 1997 Final Four game, won by the Cats (78-69).

minutes). Because of Harris's injury, Bobby Jackson, Minnesota's star and the Big Ten Player of the Year, was forced to try to do too much and had an off game, despite scoring twenty-three points. The second factor that favored the Cats was conditioning. In fact, throughout the season opponents acknowledged that Kentucky was the best-conditioned team they faced. UK's strength and conditioning coach, Shaun Brown, was given a lot of credit. It was widely reported that he had whipped Nazr Mohammed into shape, because the player had dropped sixty pounds since enrolling at UK. Kentucky was simply quicker, faster, and had better endurance than Minnesota. The 78-69 Wildcat win on March 29 demonstrated the accuracy of these analyses. Mercer led the Wildcats in scoring with nineteen points, but it was defense that won the game. Unfortunately, Mercer was

forced to play much of the contest in pain, and his physical condition against Arizona only two days later was open to speculation.

Defense. Defense was winning games throughout the 1997 NCAA tournament, just as it had in 1996. Surely this meant that the University of Kentucky Wildcats were destined to become the second team in history to win consecutive NCAA titles more than once. Only UCLA, under the legendary John Wooden, had accomplished this incredible feat. Pitino had proven himself to be one of the best active coaches in the country, if not the very best. Winning the NCAA championship in 1997 would launch him on the way to approaching the Wooden legend. The "Wizard of Westwood's" UCLA teams had won back-to-back NCAA championships in 1964 and 1965, then had gone on to capture seven in a row (from 1967 through 1973), and finally had won their tenth championship in twelve years, this time against Joe Hall's Wildcats (1975), exactly twenty-two years to the day before the 1997 game. Wooden, very much alive, alert, and active at eighty-eight years of age, was there in Indianapolis, Indiana, to watch the Kentucky-Minnesota contest.

Could Pitino take Kentucky's winning tradition and help it achieve the "double double" feat that had been accomplished only by UCLA? Pitino would have the opportunity to do it against another Pac-10 Conference squad, Lute Olson's Arizona Wildcats. Kentucky had a player—Jared Prickett—who had broken Ralph Beard's all-time record for games played as a Wildcat, and the finals would be his 143d game. Also, Prickett, who had missed the 1996 championship season as a medical redshirt, needed to score only eight points against Arizona to reach 1,000 points for his career (he only scored six). Jerry Tipton wrote on March 26 that the obstacles overcome by the Wildcats "might cause the casual observer to wonder if this Kentucky team played or tricked its way to the Final Four."

Pitino answered with an emphatic statement that talent, not luck, not great coaching, got the Wildcats to Indianapolis. Tipton's March 28 article quoted the coach as echoing that idea later: "Very good talent with a big heart playing with a purpose" was what made the team successful. These traits led the team to rebound from Anderson's injury. Padgett, Turner, and (least likely of all) Mills had developed into stars. Mercer, who scored twenty points the year before when coming off the bench against Syracuse, was the only player who had seen action in a championship game. This, seemingly, was a team of destiny. How could Kentucky—which had utilized eleven different starting lineups during the season—return to

the championship game with almost a completely new cast of players and not be destined to win? Surely it would bring another championship, the "double double" championship no less, back to Lexington. All the Wildcats, a number one seed, had to do was beat a number four seed team for the second straight year (Syracuse had been seeded fourth in 1996), and the crown would be returned to Kentucky. A number one seed had won the previous five tournaments. It all seemed to make sense.

Unfortunately for the Big Blue, Arizona came into the frame as another team of destiny—in fact, in retrospect, an even more legitimate team of destiny. Arizona was led by a coach who had twice turned down the opportunity to coach the Kentucky Wildcats. Olson had taken teams with stars like Sean Elliott, Steve Kerr, and Damon Stoudamire to the Final Four, but they never made the final game. How could he, after having such highly ranked squads that could not win, hope to win this year with a 24-9 team that had finished fifth in the Pac-10?

Like Pitino before the 1996 championship, Olson was described as a good coach who simply could not win the big game. Still, despite the early exits his teams often took from NCAA tournaments, Olson excelled at recruiting and developing talented players. Arizona was, surprisingly, the winningest program (by winning percentage) during the 1990s. Arizona had also turned out ten first-round NBA draft choices in the 1990s, tying for the most in this respect. Despite its nine losses during the season and fifth place conference finish, Arizona was a top-notch squad, as the *Wall Street Journal* computer Mad Max pointed out on March 28, 1997. Miles Simon, one of its stars, had missed the first third of the season. Freshman point guard Mike Bibby, described by John Wooden as being even better than his UCLA All-American father Henry, matured throughout the season. Arizona had been behind by ten points in the opening round of the NCAA tournament against South Alabama with only seven minutes remaining, but had erased the pain of recent first-round losses with a come-from-behind victory. Arizona had been given little chance of beating a powerful North Carolina team, but nevertheless it did. Despite being a fourth seed, Arizona was young, talented, and not in the least awed by its Wildcat rivals. More importantly, Arizona was quick and effective at handling the ball. It was the type of team that typically had given Kentucky trouble during the season.

Arizona had beaten two number one seeds, first Kansas and then North Carolina, to make it to the final game. Ironically, Kansas was the third winningest team in college basketball history, while North Carolina was the second. The team that Arizona would face in the finals—Kentucky—was both a number one seed and the winningest program in the history of college basketball. Arizona had the chance to accomplish a feat that had never before been achieved: if it won, it would be by beating three number one seeds. In doing so, it would also be defeating the three winningest programs in history in ascending order of victories. A clash of destinies was about to take place on March 31, 1997.

The game played before more than 47,000 screaming fans in Indianapolis was a classic. Unfortunately for Big Blue fans, the wrong team came out on top of the 84-79 overtime contest. Kentucky looked flat. Billy Packer, who called the game on national television, pointed it out during the game and speculated that the "brutal" victory over Minnesota might be the cause. Ron Mercer, in particular, was off his game, as Arizona's tenacious defense and his collective aches and pains served to limit the All-American to only nine shots and thirteen points. No one on Kentucky's squad could stop the stars on the other team of Wildcats, as Miles Simon (thirty points) and Mike Bibby (nineteen points) seemed to score at will. Padgett and Mills, who had shot so well from three-point land during the tournament (Mills, in fact, was fifteen for twenty-one before his two for six performance in the final game), hit only five of eighteen from behind the arc. As a team, Kentucky was ten for thirty. The thirty shots, half again the number of three-pointers the team had averaged during the season, was a result of the quick, physical Arizona defense forcing them away from the basket.

The lead changed nineteen times during the game, demonstrating just how close the contest really was. Kentucky, probably owing to fatigue, foul trouble, and the quickness of Arizona's three-guard offense, utilized its trademark full-court pressure defense less and less as the game wore on. UK, it appeared, was trying to survive until the end against this fresh and quick opponent, when it probably hoped that its star, Ron Mercer, could figure out a way to pull out a victory. As it happened, Anthony Epps had to hit a difficult, leaning, three-point shot with only 12.1 seconds remaining to tie the game at 74 and send it into overtime. But in the five-minute overtime, Arizona outscored Kentucky ten to five to win. All ten points came from the free throw line. In fact, Arizona shot twenty-four more free throws (forty-one to seventeen) than Kentucky and scored twenty-five more points (thirty-four to nine) from the line. Arizona made only one basket in the final fourteen minutes and twenty-three seconds of play. Foul shots

accounted for all their other points. Made free throws, plus Arizona's ability to break the press and handle UK's pressure defense, were the keys to the game.

In his postgame comments, Pitino cited the foul shooting, not fatigue or the rugged contest against Minnesota, as the key to Arizona's win. The coach added one other comment about what he appeared to believe

Anthony Epps firing away against Arizona in the 1997 NCAA title game. His three-point basket with only thirteen seconds left in regulation sent the hard-fought game into overtime, where UK finally ran out of gas and lost 84-79. Sensational Arizona freshman guard Mike Bibby is behind Epps.

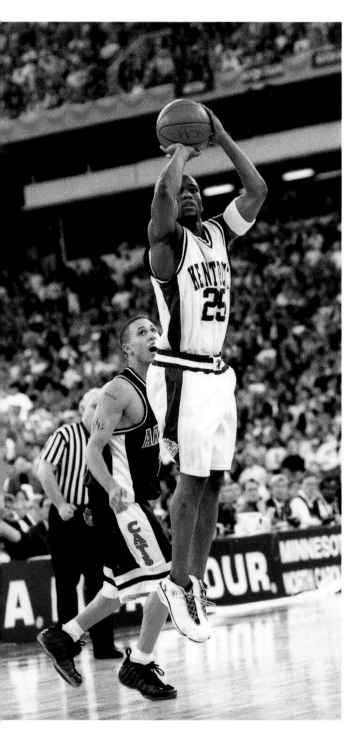

was poor officiating when he stated, "What hurt us more than anything was Wayne Turner's foul trouble. He was the engine that made us go in the post-season." Kentucky, by the end, was running on only one cylinder. Called for twenty-nine personal fouls, Kentucky lost Mercer, Padgett, and Prickett, as well as Turner, to fouls. While Arizona lost valuable inside force A.J. Bramlett to fouls, the impact on the thin Kentucky squad was much more noticeable.

Overtime has not been kind to Pitino and UK in the NCAA tournament. The loss to Arizona in a game which Kentucky guard Anthony Epps called one of the greatest in the history of college basketball was reminiscent of the heartbreaking losses to Michigan and Duke. All were games where UK's star (Mercer this time, Mashburn in the other two) fouled out, but where Kentucky should have won the game anyway. While the matchup between the two Wildcats will most likely not go down in history as the equal of the Duke game with its Christian Laettner shot, it was certainly special. Of course, in a clash of destinies, who could expect anything less?

For the season, Ron Mercer and Derek Anderson led the team in scoring, at 18.1 and 17.1 points per game, respectively. Mercer was a consensus All-American, was drafted third in the NBA lottery, and joined former Wildcat Antoine Walker in Celtic green. Anderson was drafted thirteenth by the Cleveland Cavaliers, and he probably has Rick Pitino to thank for this opportunity, as chancing further injury in the NCAA tournament might have ended his NBA dreams. While no other Wildcat averaged double digits, Padgett, Epps, Edwards, Mohammed, Prickett, Turner, Mills, and Magloire all averaged between 9.6 and 4.9 points per contest. Prickett, at 5.9 rebounds per game, led the Cats in rebounding.

The 1996/97 season, unlike any Pitino season before it, left fans with so many "what-ifs" to ponder that the entire off-season could be spent arguing that Kentucky, not Arizona, deserved to be national champion. (After all, even had Kentucky beaten Duke in 1992, it would still have needed to win two more games for a national title, which was not a certainty by any means.) The result were questions like: "What if Mercer had been at 100 percent effectiveness against Arizona?" "What if four key Kentucky players, versus only one for Arizona, had not fouled out?" "What if the referees had made Arizona earn a victory from the field instead of the free throw line?" "What if UK had made all its free throws?" "What if Antoine Walker had not turned professional after his sophomore season?" "What if Derek Anderson

Rick Pitino can't believe what he is seeing: the amazing and incredible 1996/97 UK Wildcats.

had not gotten hurt?" And the most asked question, "What if Pitino had let Anderson play?"

In his postgame comments, Pitino graciously passed on these opportunities to play "what-if" and commended Olson and his team. In addition to being gracious in defeat, Pitino reminded UK fans what a gallant effort this shrinking, undermanned team had put forth to reach the point where it could lose in overtime for the national title. He said, "God, am I so proud of these guys. I told them if they're down, they're foolish, because they're champions in life. If they feel any remorse at all and say 'What if we made this free throw' or 'what if [something else],' there's no what-ifs. Give Arizona credit. Walk out like champions."

The coach's attitude, particularly given his desire to be considered one of the great coaches of all time, and the degree to which a victory would have moved him further in that direction, was refreshing. Wildcat fans agreed. The *Herald-Leader*'s April 1 story "Cat Fans Still Find Reason to Party" quoted most fans interviewed as being disappointed with the loss, but proud of the team's effort. A crowd estimated by airport officials at between 700 and 800 turned out to welcome the Wildcats when they returned to Lexington.

Following the Cats' 1996 national championship, the team had been treated to a celebration in Rupp Arena. Following the 1997 effort, the team received the same. The media reported that the arena's lower level was filled by at least 12,000 cheering fans who provided a rousing tribute to their champions. Pitino told his team and its fans, "I'm so proud. . . . I never thought I could be more proud of anything than a national championship, but I really am of this squad."

Pitino had always been considered a tremendous coach; the complaint about him was his seeming desire always to search out a greener pasture, no matter what the cost to others. First by winning in 1996, and then by losing in 1997, Pitino proved not only what a great coach he was, but what an effective leader he had become. He had shown in 1995/96 that he could recruit and win with top-notch talent. In 1997 he proved he could take a physically mediocre team (by Kentucky's recent standards) and play into overtime for the national championship. He and his team had performed to the limit of their ability, will, and heart, and just narrowly lost to Arizona. They retained, however, the grace and dignity of champions. Pitino said it all when he anointed them "The Unbelievables." They truly were.

Opposite, Tubby Smith celebrating a national championship to cap his first season as head coach of the Kentucky Wildcats.

PART V

The Tubby Smith Era Begins

14

The Indecipherables

Not one to rest on his laurels, Pitino began looking forward to the 1997/98 season as soon as the 1996/97 season ended. The 1998 Final Four was scheduled to be held in San Antonio. Among Pitino's comments about the coming Final Four were, "We'll take a few days off. Then we'll work to get to San Antonio." He added, "I'm convinced we'll be in San Antonio next year." After the Wildcats' return from Indianapolis, the coach commented to the team and its 12,000-plus cheering fans in Rupp Arena, "Repetition is the key to success as well as good habits. This is a good habit. Let's do it next year."

When the Wildcats returned to the Final Four—in March 1998, sooner than anyone (except the Bluest of Big Blue fans) could reasonably expect—they did so without Rick Pitino. On May 7, 1997, Pitino signed a reported ten-year, $70 million contract to commence a new reclamation job, that of trying to return the woebegone Boston Celtics to their former NBA glory. Thus the Rick Pitino era of Kentucky Wildcat basketball had come to a sudden end. It had, however, been quite a ride.

The end seemed particularly jarring in large part because of the coach's own comments. When rumors about the Celtics surfaced, Pitino emphatically denounced them. John Feinstein on ESPN reported (March 6, 1997) during the middle of the Cats' NCAA run that Pitino would leave UK to coach the Celtics the following season. According to the March 8 *Herald-Leader*, Pitino's immediate reaction was, "I'm not going to answer rumors like that. . . . I've been here eight years now. I think I'm past this stage where I have to (respond). It's been over 13 teams over eight years. So to even com-

ment on it again would be ludicrous." UK's Senior Associate Director of Athletics, Larry Ivy, also dismissed the comment with, "He's going to be at Kentucky until he quits coaching." Less than one month later, Pitino revealed that he had had a "generic conversation" with the Celtics, adding "I don't know what they could offer me that would make sense for me to leave Kentucky." He then asserted, "I really have no desire to leave Kentucky."

In retrospect, perhaps the strangest statement by Pitino regarding his intention to stay at Kentucky was one made in April while he was in Boston to promote his latest motivational book:

I can honestly say I will be back at Kentucky. I have already told that to some of my recruits. I mean that. That's an honest answer. I have videos of Lou Holtz saying he will never leave Notre Dame and then the next thing you know he's announcing he's stepping down. I have a video of John Calipari saying he doesn't have one ounce of interest in pro basketball and the next thing he's in New Jersey saying this is what he always wanted to do. It makes them both look like pathological liars. I'm 100 percent sincere and honest when I say I intend to be back in Kentucky. I have not talked or negotiated with anyone from the Boston Celtics. I had a casual conversation with Larry Bird and that was it.

Given his move to the Celtics shortly thereafter, it would have been wiser for Pitino to have said nothing.

Despite his less than graceful exit, Rick Pitino must be recognized as the savior of the Wildcat basketball program. He stayed eight seasons and brought a national championship to the University of Kentucky. He quickly healed the wounds and cured the ills of the Eddie Sutton

Former walk-on Cameron Mills, an integral part of Kentucky's success in the 1997 and 1998 NCAA tournaments, dribbles the ball upcourt as Coach Smith yells instructions.

era. During his tenure, graduation rates of players improved, no scandals were reported, and his teams won 219 of 269 games, for an .814 winning percentage, which compares favorably with Adolph Rupp's .822. As far as the Big Blue faithful are concerned, he deserves to be remembered as a champion.

On May 6, the day Pitino officially accepted the Boston job, C.M. Newton announced that he would be working from a "short list" of candidates and that he expected the search for a replacement to last less than two weeks. Speculation in the media focused on four current head coaches who had been former Pitino assistants: Tubby Smith at Georgia, Billy Donovan at Florida, Ralph Willard at Pittsburgh, and Herb Sendek at North Carolina State. Ex-Wildcat greats Dan Issel (a former NBA coach) and Pat Riley (a current NBA coach) were also mentioned as potential candidates; although the former expressed some interest, neither appears to have been a serious candidate. From the beginning, attention focused on Tubby Smith, who, after two years as Pitino's assistant (1989-91) had, as head coach, taken squads from both Tulsa and Georgia to NCAA tournament appearances. The 45-year-old Smith had reportedly agreed orally to, but had not yet signed, a two-year extension to his four-year contract as coach of the Bull-

Two proven winners: Rick Pitino and his successor as Wildcat head coach, Tubby Smith.

dogs. One of Smith's sons was a starter on the Georgia team, and another son had expressed his intention to become a walk-on freshman for the Bulldogs.

Newton quickly put an end to speculation when, on May 12, he chose the former Pitino assistant and current Georgia head coach. In fact, according to later reports and an interview with the athletics director, Tubby Smith was Newton's first and only real choice to replace Pitino. Smith, nonetheless, was potentially another Newton gamble. While certainly talented, he would be the first black coach in Wildcat history. African Americans had been playing for the Wildcats for only a little over a quarter century, after all. Kentucky, both the basketball program and the state itself, did not have a long history of being particularly open or friendly toward blacks. Regardless, Newton knew the man he wanted, and he was determined to get him. Smith had a successful record, coached a style of play similar to Pitino, was an effective recruiter, and seemed very capable of handling himself in Lexington.

The newly appointed UK coach tackled the race issue immediately. On his first day, he stated, "It's more important [that] I be competent and [that] I be judged on the content of my character and not the color of my skin." Even so, Smith appeared to recognize the importance of becoming UK's first black head coach. To many, the loss of Rupp's Runts in the 1966 NCAA tournament to a Texas Western squad with five black starters publicized the racism that existed in college sports. Even after that loss, Rupp did not add a black player to his squad for another five years. In those days, Kentucky Wildcat basketball was by whites, for whites. By 1997, times had changed; but had they changed that much?

Maybe so, even in Kentucky. This new outlook was encapsulated by P.G. Peeples, president of the Lexington chapter of the Urban League, who was quoted as saying, "If he wins, he will be accepted." When asked about what would happen to Smith if he lost, Peeples noted that any losing coach would be the target for the wrath of Wildcat fans. He put it in perspective when he pointed out that fans "got angry"—even with Pitino when he won—for changing the color of UK's uniforms; thus in Kentucky, "we're dealing with something that's second to religion." Peeples also pointed out that he himself had rooted for Texas Western in 1966, despite the fact that he was a UK student at the time. Peeples believed that the color Wildcat fans would see when they looked at Tubby Smith in 1997 was Blue and White, not the black or white they might have seen 30 years earlier. While black *Herald-Leader* columnist Merlene Davis on

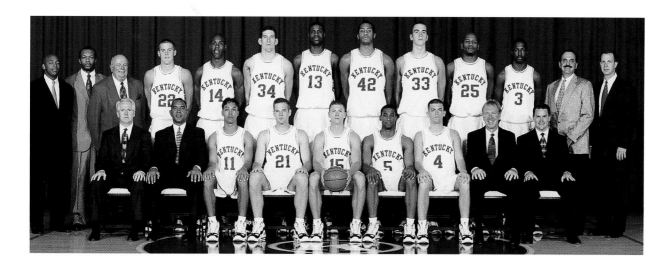

The 1997/98 Wildcats surprised the "experts" to claim the NCAA championship. Seated, left to right: assistant coach Mike Sutton, head coach Tubby Smith, Saul Smith, Cameron Mills, Jeff Sheppard, Wayne Turner, Steve Masiello, assistant coach George Felton, and assistant coach Shawn Finney. Standing, left to right: special assistant Leon Smith, administrative assisstant Simeon Mars, equipment manager Bill Keightley, Ryan Hogan, Heshimu Evans, Scott Padgett, Nazr Mohammed, Jamaal Magloire, Michael Bradley, Myron Anthony, Allen Edwards, trainer Eddie Jamiel, and strength coach Tom Boyd.

May 9, 1997, wrote an open letter to Tubby Smith (which was printed on page one of the Lexington newspaper) entitled "Take My Advice, Kentucky Won't Ever Cozy Up to You," Smith appeared to agree with Peeples' perspective. In fact, Smith was almost immediately nominated to join the largely white Lexington Country Club, a sign that local movers and shakers viewed him as the Wildcat coach, not as an ethnic representative. After all, Kentuckians loved Pitino, a Yankee Italian from New York, because the Wildcats won. Although Smith is an African American, he probably has much more in common with the average Kentuckian than had Pitino. Smith had been raised on a farm in rural Maryland, and was, according to the December 8, 1997, edition of *Sports Illustrated,* "very embraceable." Thus, if the Wildcats consistently won under Smith, there was every reason to believe that the new coach would be both extremely successful and extremely popular in Lexington.

Smith left Georgia—where he had compiled a 45-19 record over two seasons and was about to be paid $605,280 per year—for the Kentucky job and its reported $1.1 million per season total pay package. This made him at the time of his signing the highest-paid coach for any sport in the SEC, with the exception of Steve Spurrier, Florida's highly successful football coach.

Kentucky retained a solid nucleus from its NCAA runner-up squad, including Scott Padgett, Jamaal Magloire, Nazr Mohammed, and Allen Edwards in the front court, while Cameron Mills, Wayne Turner, and the seldom used Steve Masiello returned at guard. In addition, guard Jeff Sheppard, who had been redshirted for the 1996/97 season, was back for his senior year, and 6'6" transfer forward Heshimu Evans, who had sat out in 1996/97, was now eligible to play for the Cats. For a while during the summer it appeared as though Georgia point guard G.G. Smith (Tubby's oldest son) would venture with his father to Lexington, but he finally decided to remain with the Bulldogs. However, Saul Smith, a 6'2" freshman guard and Tubby's middle son, elected to come to UK for his freshman season rather than attend Georgia.

The Big Blue had a solid crop of incoming freshmen. One of Smith's first jobs was to heal any hurt feelings that Pitino's recruits felt over his sudden departure. With this in mind, the new coach quickly contacted David Bradley, Ryan Hogan, and Myron Anthony and attempted to reassure the recruits and their families about his interest in them and his desire to keep them committed to UK. These efforts were appreciated and elicited positive reactions. Perhaps even more important, the returning Wildcat players appeared well satisfied with Smith as Pitino's replacement.

Going into the season, it appeared that the Wildcats' style would not change dramatically under Smith. A former Pitino assistant, Smith would continue to favor an up-tempo, full-court press, shoot-when-open style of basketball. There would, however, be some significant differences in Lexington. First, as guard Wayne Turner said, "You can see the difference. It's more like a college atmosphere than a pro atmosphere." More im-

portantly, unlike Pitino, who had been able to utilize stars like Mashburn, Delk, Walker, McCarty, Anderson, and Mercer, Smith would field a unit of solid, but not individually spectacular, players.

C.M. Newton put the first difference between Smith and Pitino very succinctly: "Tubby's not going to wear Armani. If he does, it's not going to look the same as Rick. He'll have his tie undone or something." Pitino is New York City, Smith is rural Maryland. Although their styles differed greatly off the court, players and fans alike took great comfort in the knowledge that Smith's style on the court would be similar to that of his mentor.

Kentucky fans expected that "Pitinoball" would simply become "Tubbyball." In an October 2, 1997, interview, C.M. Newton pointed out that one of his main search criteria was finding a coach who excelled in the fast break, pressure defense style of play. The athletics director stated that the UK tradition for pressure defense and fast-breaking offense did not originate with Pitino; rather, he believed that Pitino had rekindled memories of some of the best of Rupp's teams. Newton also made clear that finding a coach capable of handling the pressure in Lexington was critical. On both counts, he had Smith in mind.

In an interview the following day, Smith echoed UK's athletics director. The new coach pointed out that his teams at Tulsa and Georgia were among the best defensive teams in their leagues. In Smith's opinion, defense created offense, and he expected that his Wildcat squads would play harassing defense and attempt to push the ball up the court as often and as fast as possible. Kentucky's new coach also observed that his squad would have to utilize teamwork and aggressive play in 1997/98, since 63.3 percent of its point production from the prior season would be missing in the persons of Anderson, Epps, Mercer, and Prickett.

Most teams losing almost two-thirds of their firepower would look at the coming season as a rebuilding year. While Kentucky's talent might not have been up to recent standards when Smith took the helm, fans did not lower their expectations for the Wildcats. Although solid and relatively big at all positions, a couple of major questions and weaknesses would have to be explored as the season moved along. Most importantly, UK had no obvious "go-to guy" as the season began. Many hoped that Jeff Sheppard would become a star player as the season progressed. Could he or anyone else, however, replace Mercer or Anderson? Kentucky boasted four players 6'9" or taller, a luxury that most college teams lacked. Smith hoped that size would translate into a solid

rebounding team. Size, however, could be a double-edged sword. South Carolina and Arizona had exploited a lack of speed and quickness in Kentucky's half-court defense the previous year. Without Mercer and Anderson, questions about team speed would only intensify in the coming campaign. Finally, would the "player friendly" Smith be able to keep the players as focused as Pitino had been able to do?

As the season got under way, two more major concerns arose about the Wildcats. First, Kentucky's shooting, both from the free throw line and the field, was inconsistent and quite average. Second, Kentucky's schedule, both in terms of quality of the teams played and the amount of travel involved, was brutal. While

Coach Tubby Smith exhorting his team to ever greater effort.

the new coach had neither recruited UK's current team nor had much of a hand in preparing the schedule, Smith was faced with surmounting both challenges.

It took only a few games for fans to see that Smith was fully capable of handling the pressures involved in coaching the Wildcats. Nine games into the season, Kentucky had risen from its ninth-place preseason ranking to be ranked fourth in the national polls. This compared very favorably with the third-place ranking at the same point the season before. And, following that ninth game, an 85-71 victory over Georgia Tech, Yellow Jacket coach Bobby Cremins pointed out that "Kentucky changed coaches, but they haven't changed that pressure [defense]. I can see why Tubby was hired. It's sort of like North Carolina [which saw Dean Smith retire just before the start of the basketball season]. The coaches change, but the system doesn't. I couldn't tell if Rick Pitino or Tubby Smith was down there."

Cremins's comment was significant, since Tubby Smith had to overcome some daunting obstacles before facing Georgia Tech. Following two exhibition contests, Kentucky started its first season under Smith with an 88-49 victory at Rupp Arena over Kyle Macy's Morehead State squad. Kentucky scored the first 19 points in the game, and the outcome was never in doubt thereafter. It was the most lopsided opening victory by a UK coach since Adolph Rupp's 1930 squad beat Georgetown College by 48 points. Kentucky shot almost 64 percent from the field. Ominously, however, the Wildcats hit only seven of 16 free throws.

Kentucky's next test came 6,000 miles away, in Maui, Hawaii. UK opened the Maui Invitational against a solid and large George Washington squad. A victory would almost surely lead to a rematch with the Arizona Wildcats. If Kentucky got past Arizona, the third-ranked Duke Blue Devils would likely be their next opponent. To round out the trip, according to Jerry Tipton, UK Senior Associate Director of Athletics Larry Ivy convinced Smith to stop in Phoenix to play Clemson in the first Premier Classic tournament to break up the long trip home and collect $200,000 to help pay for the Maui trip. As if that were not enough, Kentucky would start December with neutral court games against highly ranked Purdue and Indiana squads. The Wildcats would be away from home over a two week period and in several different time zones, playing against five quality opponents. A sweep of the two tournaments along with victories over Purdue and Indiana could position Kentucky as an early season favorite, along with Arizona, Duke, Kansas, and North Carolina, to win the national championship. A series of losses could damage the team's confidence.

Heshimu Evans scoring a fast break basket in the Cats' season-opening 88-49 victory over a badly outmatched Morehead State squad as Jeff Sheppard and Nazr Mohammed observe the dunk.

All in all, Smith and his team answered the early season challenges. Kentucky held George Washington to 34.3 percent shooting from the field and thoroughly dominated the Colonials 70-55. Next up was the long anticipated rematch against Arizona. The headline in the *Herald-Leader* the day after the game said it all: "Cats Overmatched in Rematch." The score was 89 to 74 in favor of Arizona, and the domination was complete, as the lead was not cut below double digits during any of the last 31 minutes and 41 seconds of the game. According to Tubby Smith, "We just couldn't make our shots tonight." There was no question about that, as the Cats hit just 38.8 percent from the field (including only five for 22 from behind the three-point arc) and only 17 of 26 free throws.

The Wildcats now stood at two wins and one loss in the young season, and the next game would be pivotal in building momentum in Smith's first year as coach. While in the Arizona game Kentucky had never led, in the next contest in Maui, against Missouri, the Cats never trailed after the game's first basket. UK pounded the ball inside to Jamaal Magloire, who had 18 points and 17 rebounds in his best outing yet as a Wildcat, and dominated the boards by a 51 to 34 margin, emerging with a 77-55 victory. Although Kentucky still shot poorly from the outside, making just four of 13 three-pointers, its defensive intensity and solid inside play overwhelmed the Tigers. While the Big Blue would have liked to leave Hawaii with a sweep, two wins in the tournament had to be seen as a success.

The stopover in Phoenix on November 29 was also successful. Kentucky defeated a solid, experienced Clemson squad 76-61. Midway through the second half, with the Wildcats trailing by five points, guard Wayne Turner provided a preview of his postseason heroics by making back-to-back steals, hitting a key jump shot, and sparking a 15-2 run. Turner led Kentucky with 17 points, and also added five rebounds and five assists. The team's shooting improved, as the Cats hit almost 54 percent of their shots, including six of 14 from three-point land. It was an impressive performance, and a victory to build on as UK prepared to meet a sixth-ranked Purdue squad that was subbing for Minnesota in the showcase of 1997 NCAA tournament finalist teams in Chicago.

The confident Purdue squad was coming off a narrow 73-69 loss to powerful North Carolina. It featured a capable center in 6'11" Brad Miller, who was averaging 19 points and eight rebounds entering the game, and a deliberate team that normally protected the ball well. Kentucky, and particularly its young centers

Magloire and Mohammed, faced a tough challenge. However, the Wildcats utilized their depth effectively and wore Purdue down, crafting an 89-75 victory. Kentucky's relentless pressure forced 22 Boilermaker turnovers and poor shooting (39 percent from the field). Mohammed, UK's game high scorer, came off the bench to score a career-high 19 points in 18 minutes. Equally important, Mohammed teamed with Jamaal Magloire to bump and bang Miller, limiting him to what was for him a mediocre performance of ten points. After the game, Coach Smith observed, "I thought running both Jamaal and Nazr at him constantly would wear him down." It was a wise decision that worked well for UK.

Against Purdue, Nazr Mohammed played his best game to date as a Wildcat. Against the next opponent, the Hoosiers from Indiana University, he topped even that effort. These back-to-back performances earned him the honor of Southeastern Conference player of the week. Mohammed scored 21 points (tying with Jeff Sheppard for game high) and grabbed 12 rebounds in 25 minutes of action. Kentucky won, although not in its usual fashion. Aside from Sheppard, Mohammed, and Cameron Mills (who scored 12 points), few Wildcats played well, and none scored more than eight points. The remaining Wildcats shot a combined nine of 32 from the field. Still, when A.J. Guyton's game-tying three-point attempt at the buzzer bounced off the rim, Kentucky came away from Indianapolis with a 75-72 victory. Close call or not, the team's record was now six and one, despite the grueling early season schedule.

UK's next game was in Buffalo against Canisius. The Wildcats were guaranteed a healthy $200,000 payday for making the trip to upstate New York to play the under-sized Golden Griffins. Despite a similar early season record (Canisius was four and one), it looked as though the contest would be a mismatch. It was. As expected, the Wildcats dominated the game, winning by an 81-54 margin. In addition to dominating the paint, the Cats got another outstanding performance from Jeff Sheppard, who matched his season and career high with 21 points, on eight for 11 shooting. Big Blue fans now began to hope that Sheppard was ready to become Kentucky's go-to guy. Mohammed also continued his excellent play, scoring 11 points and grabbing six rebounds off the bench in only 14 minutes of action.

Next up for UK was the date in Rupp Arena with twenty-fourth-ranked Georgia Tech. Six Wildcats scored in double figures (and Padgett almost made it seven), led by forward Heshimu Evans's 14-point, ten-rebound performance. In addition, wrote the *Herald-Leader*'s

Chuck Culpepper, the transfer from Manhattan College "lit the spark" that helped carry Kentucky to victory after being behind 35-34 at halftime. This performance proved to be the first indication of what Evans would bring to the Cats as the season progressed: intensity, strong defense, rebounding, and—if needed—scoring. Kentucky's bench outscored the Yellow Jacket reserves by a 30-to-four margin. Depth, along with solid rebounding, continued to be the keys to Kentucky's strong early season showing. In fact, in outrebounding Georgia Tech by a 51 to 34 count, the team continued its streak of outrebounding every opponent to this point during the Smith era.

UK's next game was December 20 against Tulsa, where Smith had coached prior to going to Georgia. The Wildcats, continuing a recent pattern, were lackadaisical in the first half and went to the Rupp Arena locker room behind by one, 29-28. According to Allen Edwards, "Coach Pitino would have been in here screaming, throwing things, threatening people." Smith, instead, used his patented stare to fire up the team. "A lot of people got the stare," commented Scott Padgett, and it worked. The Wildcats outscored Tulsa by 22 points over the next 20 minutes and won the game by a convincing 74 to 53 margin. Mohammed again led a balanced scoring attack, this time totaling 17 points. And Kentucky again outrebounded its opponent, 33 to 30.

UK was already looking forward to its holiday showdown with state rival Louisville. However, the Wildcats first had to face American University. American possessed a losing record and a small squad. This would be a chance for Kentucky, which had struggled in the first half of recent games, to get out to a quick start and practice "putting away" its opponent. Unfortunately, things were not looking good on this front when, with just a couple of minutes remaining in the half, the score was tied at 25. Great pressure defense, however, enabled Kentucky to score the last ten points of the period and jump to a 35-25 halftime lead on the way to a 75-52 victory. Again the Big Blue outrebounded its opponent, although this time only by 30-29, and controlled the pace of the game with its pressure defense, forcing 17 turnovers. Probably more encouraging was that in its last couple of games, the UK squad seemed to be shooting better from both the floor and the free throw line. For the second game in a row, the Wildcats hit over 50 percent of their field goals and 70 percent of their free throws.

Next up was an athletic, if underachieving, Louisville squad. Prospects for a competitive game did not appear promising. Although UK players said they considered Louisville a tough opponent, sportswriters made light of the Cardinals' chances. Billy Reed stated, "U of L and [Denny] Crum have replaced Notre Dame and Digger Phelps as the turkeys on UK's holiday schedule." Louisville entered the game with three wins and six losses, and its record against the Wildcats during the 1990s was only one and six. Furthermore, U of L had a young team that had played a tough schedule. The Cardinals and the Wildcats seemed to have switched roles, with U of L depending on the three-point shot, and the bigger, stronger Kentucky squad muscling the ball inside. Reed predicted another 20-plus point win, although he "hoped" for a terrific game that went down to the "last shot." Reed got more than he hoped.

Following the game Tubby Smith acknowledged that "their game plan was better than ours." The final score at Rupp Arena was 79-76, with Louisville on top at the end of the nip and tuck affair. The game really did come down to the final shot, as Reed had wished, with Scott Padgett missing a three-pointer at the buzzer that would have tied the score.

The bigger, stronger Wildcats outrebounded the

Alex Sanders (44) blocks a shot attempt by Allen Edwards as the underdog Louisville Cardinals pull a shocking 79-76 upset over the heavily favored Wildcats in Rupp Arena.

Cardinals, although that may have been by design on U of L's part. Louisville center Alex Sanders took Magloire and Mohammed outside on offense and outhustled the Wildcat big men on defense. Crum's game plan of making the UK centers move more than they were used to doing, combined with U of L's superior quickness and better outside shooting, helped seal the victory. Louisville hit 12 of 22 three-point shots compared with just five of 23 for Kentucky, something that had not happened in many years in Lexington. Most of the 24,303 fans in attendance were in shock when Padgett's shot did not fall and the Wildcat record dropped to 10-2.

Following the game, Louisville reserve center Troy Jackson said, "The media questioned our players, our coaches, our athletic staff, our recruiting, everything. Everybody said that we sucked, that we're bad, nothing but quitters. We showed you. We showed everybody." Despite the motivation that U of L players got from negative comments about their talent and dedication, the results were still surprising. Most surprising was the ability of the Cardinals' reserves to outscore UK's bench and the lack of defensive pressure that the Wildcat guards were able to apply on U of L's young backcourt.

After the loss to Louisville, Smith decided to turn up the intensity on his squad. He had taken a low-key approach during the early part of the season, and perhaps the players had become too comfortable. Following the U of L game, he told the media, "Now, we're going to be more intense and put more pressure on them to play with an urgency, which I think is important in big games." Also, he said, on offense the Wildcats would run more set plays instead of relying on their motion offense. Allen Edwards applauded the coach's move because "in the motion offense, we had guys running around with no purpose." Smith also decided to make a lineup alteration, starting Mohammed in the pivot in place of Magloire.

All these changes appeared to pay off when UK travelled to Athens, Ohio, on December 30, 1997, to play Ohio University. Kentucky won 95-58, the first time all season the Wildcats had topped the 90-point mark. UK's big men, Mohammed and Magloire, each scored 15 points and dominated the paint as Kentucky outrebounded the smaller Eagles by a 41-28 count. The 11 and two Wildcats had now outrebounded their opponents in every game of the nonconference schedule. Despite the shocking loss to Louisville and the disappointment of not getting revenge against Arizona, Smith's squad had performed at least as well as could have been expected, given the presence of a new head coach, the loss of key players, and the tough schedule.

Next up for the Big Blue was Vanderbilt and the start of the SEC campaign. Smith decided it was time to tinker with the team's defensive schemes. Thus far in the season, the Kentucky squad was among the least effective in the conference in defending against the three-point shot. According to Smith, the chief reason for UK's poor perimeter defense was its ineffective pressing: "We've given up a lot of baskets [on open jumpers] in transition." The coach then went on to state that the Wildcats would press less in SEC games, relying more on their solid half-court defense. Scott Padgett, pointing out a strategic difference between Kentucky's current and previous coach, said that Smith's defensive scheme placed players closer to the basket and relied on double-team traps more often to protect the paint. This made it harder to challenge perimeter shots.

Smith and the Wildcats made their adjustments and kicked off the SEC schedule in Rupp Arena on January 3 against Vanderbilt. Nazr Mohammed's 19 points and 12 rebounds led the team to a remarkable second half comeback victory. What was remarkable was not that Kentucky overcame a six-point halftime deficit to de-

Nazr Mohammed, who arrived in Lexington as an overweight project, emerged in 1997/98 as a dominating presence. The UK center here leads the Cats to a 71-62 victory over Vanderbilt.

feat the Commodores by a 71-62 count—after all, second half come-from-behind victories were becoming (much to Tubby Smith's displeasure) standard fare for the 1997/98 squad—but rather the fact that the Cats grabbed 33 rebounds compared to only seven for Vandy. For the game as a whole, UK outrebounded the Commodores by a remarkable 57-18 margin.

As Jerry Tipton wrote in the January 4 *Herald-Leader,* "The rebounds made moot Vandy's superior shooting (42.6 percent), greater number of three-point baskets (7-6), assists (14-12) and steals (9-7), plus fewer turnovers (14-19)." Tipton pointed out that the Big Blue again had trouble shooting against a zone defense, making just 41.4 percent of their shots. After the game, Smith commented that rebounding was the reason his team was able to win a contest in which it otherwise played poorly. "If we don't rebound the ball, we don't win the ball game, the way we've been shooting."

A newly beardless Scott Padgett scored 13 points and grabbed 14 rebounds as the Wildcats stretched their home winning streak at Rupp Arena to 23 victories over the Commodores. The reason for Padgett's bare face was a directive Smith issued after the Ohio University game to shave off all facial hair. The reason, he maintained, was to make team members "look better. We needed a change. That's why we did it." In jest, Padgett claimed that shaving had triggered a remarkable aerodynamic improvement and added two inches to his vertical jump. Regardless, at the 4:49 mark of the second half of the Vandy game, his 14 rebounds were only one less than the rebounds managed by the entire Commodore team. Something had kindled a fire under the Wildcats to induce such a physically dominating performance against their relatively big and strong opponents. Undoubtedly a major factor in the Commodores' less than sterling performance was that Vanderbilt had played four games in seven nights (including travel to and from Hawaii). Vandy simply could not match the Wildcats' positioning, quickness, or determination on either the offensive or defensive boards. For whatever reason, UK dominated a team whose record prior to the contest (11-2) matched that of the Blue and White.

The team's next game, on January 6 in Athens, Georgia, promised to be a highly personal and emotional one for the Smith family. Not only had Tubby Smith for two years recruited and coached the Georgia players whom the Cats would face, but also his oldest son, G.G., was the Bulldogs' point guard and team leader. And, of course, another son, Saul, was a reserve UK point guard who, when he entered the game, might have to guard

Wildcat freshman guard Saul Smith trying to dribble past his older brother, Georgia Bulldog point guard G.G. Smith. UK won both its games against Georgia, by 90-79 in Athens on January 6 and 85-74 at Rupp Arena (above) on February 22.

his older brother. To the media the contest was the Battle of the Smiths. It was a big enough event for *Sports Illustrated* to dispatch senior writer Alexander Wolff. Despite the media hoopla and national coverage, the game, as Chuck Culpepper acknowledged in its aftermath, was just a game. A typical UK-Georgia game, in fact, with the Cats once again coming out on top, 90-79, to place Kentucky's record against Georgia at 92 victories against only 17 defeats. While the media hype focused on the Smith family, the Big Blue quietly went about its business. Led by Turner (with 20 points) and Edwards (with 19), the Cats outplayed the Georgia squad. If for Tubby Smith it was a bittersweet victory, for the players it was just another game—and another victory—in a grueling and pressure-packed season.

After playing and defeating one Bulldog squad in Athens, UK journeyed to Starkville on January 10 to take on the Bulldogs of Mississippi State. With a 77-71 victory the Big Blue raised its record to 14-2, and 2-0 in the SEC by getting off to one of its better starts of the sea-

son in a game in which it never trailed. Despite this showing, the Wildcats needed late game heroics from Heshimu Evans and Scott Padgett to seal the victory. Kentucky continued its dominance of the glass by outrebounding its opponent by a 39-31 count. Yet this was not the typical UK domination of the paint that fans were used to seeing. Instead, Mississippi State's Tyrone Washington outplayed Kentucky's Mohammed/Magloire combination. Mississippi State's center scored 23 points and had eight rebounds, compared to the UK duo's combined 14 and 11. But Washington was unable to score from the field during the crucial final minutes of the contest. In fact, as Mississippi State coach Richard Williams said of his center, "Late in the game, he asked to come out. We had to take him out because he was exhausted. Two against one, that can wear you out a little, especially when the two are Mohammed and Magloire."

In another respect it was not a typical UK game, for not only were the centers outplayed, but also the Wildcat defense forced only nine turnovers, and the bench did not score until 12:13 remained in the game. Of course, in a pattern that would continue through the end of the season, when it mattered the Big Blue centers wore down the opponent, the defense stopped the Bulldogs from scoring, and the bench, particularly Evans, came up with big plays. Another plus off the bench was freshman point guard Saul Smith's three-point shot with the game tied at 48. It was a big, unexpected basket, and as father and coach Tubby Smith pointed out later, "That was major, because I know what would have happened if he missed it. But for his sake, he made it."

As the squad returned to Lexington to prepare for the next game (against South Carolina), Kentucky—to the evident surprise of numerous nervous fans—retained its standing as one of the top-ranked teams in the nation. In this regard, Chuck Culpepper gave an interesting perspective on the season in his January 11 article: "If this were 1992, everybody would talk about how admirable this team is. How plucky. What a fighter. After all, it has only one likely NBA first-round draft choice (Nazr Mohammed), whereas its two predecessors combined for five. Coming off a two-year symphony that included outrageous matters like a 99-65 win over Indiana, this Kentucky team, by contrast, seems to be running in mud. A plodder. It plays in the bizarre haze of people asking, 'What's wrong?'" In years past if the Wildcats had opened a 25-9 lead over Mississippi State, Culpepper noted, that would have meant "the lights were out," but not in this particular season. In other words,

The famous Tubby Smith stare, which the coach uses effectively to motivate his players, particularly (according to team members) in the locker room during halftime.

this group of Wildcats was not richly talented. Only time would tell if they could jell into a team capable of reaching the goal of every UK squad—an SEC title followed by the national championship. And only time would tell if Smith would be considered the equal of Pitino as coach.

The South Carolina Gamecocks arrived at Rupp Arena on January 13 with fond memories of utilizing superior quickness and outstanding guard play the prior season to defeat the Blue and White twice. In his article leading up to the rematch, Jerry Tipton found an intriguing angle to the game when he pointed out, "When South Carolina swept Kentucky, and Georgia won two of three from South Carolina last season, then UK coach Rick Pitino noted perimeter defense as the key. Whether Georgia's guards or its defensive scheme made the critical difference may be determined tonight in Rupp Arena. Tubby Smith, who came from Georgia to replace Rick Pitino this season, brings his Ball-Line defense to this matchup." Tipton's observation was insightful; was

Smith's somewhat more controlled style of play better suited than Pitino's when playing against a team with more quickness and better ball-handling skills? In this game at least, the answer was a resounding "Yes!"

Smith erased the pain of Pitino's losses to the Gamecocks from UK fans' minds with a dominating 91-70 victory. Kentucky pressed less often, utilized a zone defense, and shot the ball extremely well on its way to the easy win. With this victory, it became clear that Smith was turning the Wildcats into his team by moving slightly away from his predecessor's style of play, which had emphasized 40 minutes of pure—sometimes almost chaotic—full court man-to-man pressure and quick three-point shooting. While Pitino had disdain for the zone defense, Smith willingly profited from it when it made sense to do so. Swingman Allen Edward, who had a career-high 12 assists in the contest, explained: "We pressed a lot more [last year] and they had the quickness to really hurt us. We played zone [this game] and forced them to shoot." UK shot 54 percent from the field, had a season-high 25 steals against only seven turnovers, and utilized superior depth to overcome USC's star guards Melvin Watson and BJ McKie. Scott Padgett pointed out, "Our top eight or nine players can play with just about anybody in the nation. Our players don't get much hype because we have so many. Look at Kansas. Raef LaFrentz and Paul Pierce carry the team. We don't have anybody who has to carry the team. That's the biggest strength of the team. You can't focus on one player." Kentucky played its best game of the season in running its record to 15-2 overall and 4-0 in the SEC. The Big Blue looked cohesive and ready to jell as a team. Alas, this was not to be, at least not quite yet.

Next up for the Wildcats was another home game, this time against the twenty-second-ranked Arkansas Razorbacks. Listening to Tubby Smith following the January 17 contest, one might have thought his sixth-ranked Kentucky team was soundly beaten: "Twenty-two turnovers, you can't be satisfied with that. I thought [Arkansas] took us out of our offense completely. I'm concerned and disappointed." That disappointment came in an 80-77 overtime victory for the Cats. Luckily for UK fans, Arkansas missed a three-point shot at the buzzer that could have sent the contest into a second overtime. Smith's concern probably stemmed from the complete reversal that his team showed compared to its solid domination of an excellent South Carolina squad only four days before. This time around, Kentucky, not its opponent, turned the ball over more than twice as often as it earned an assist (22 versus ten). The Wildcats

shot just two for 19 from behind the three-point arc, an unwelcome return to the poor shooting that had been typical before the win over the Gamecocks. Wayne Turner (16 points), Heshimu Evans (a career-high 20 points in relief of an ineffective Allen Edwards), and Nazr Mohammed (whose tip-in with 29 seconds remaining in regulation sent the game into overtime), were the key players who helped Kentucky overcome one of its most sluggish performances of the year.

Rebounding and Scott Padgett made the difference in the Wildcats' next game, a close and hard-fought 70-67 victory over a mediocre Alabama squad at Freedom Hall in Louisville. Surprisingly, this same Tide team which was so difficult for the Blue and White to vanquish on January 21 had been destroyed 94-40 by arch rival Auburn only three days before. Obviously Alabama more than made up for that disaster against the league-leading Wildcats, but fortunately for UK, the effort fell just short of total success. Kentucky improved its season record to 17-2 and 6-0 in the SEC. "They really hurt us down inside. That was the name of the game," Alabama coach David Hobbs lamented after the contest. Specifically, Hobbs referred to Padgett and Mohammed, who combined to shoot 68 percent from the field and grab 18 rebounds. Tubby Smith claimed to see a silver lining in the team's seeming inability to make quick work of weaker opponents, commenting, "Hopefully this is building some toughness and some confidence that we can win close games." How prophetic that statement proved to be!

As UK prepared to face Tennessee on January 24 in Knoxville, Jerry Tipton wrote, "It might be disappointing, even alarming and potentially costly. But Kentucky's porous three-point defense should not be surprising." In this game, at least, that porous three-point defense would not be tested against the big but poor-shooting Volunteers. Tennessee led briefly by a 17-16 count. Kentucky, however, then went on a 20-point run and opened a 48-30 lead at halftime on the way to an 85-67 victory. The Cats won with dominating inside play and good outside shooting. Three of Tennessee's big men went to the bench in the first half with three fouls each, and the Wildcats dominated the depleted Volunteer interior, outscoring Tennessee 50-15 in the paint and outrebounding them by a 48-30 count. Jeff Sheppard destroyed the Vols in the first half by hitting four of five three-pointers. For the night, UK shot an outstanding 52 percent from the field. Kentucky played a solid, fundamental game, and, as UT player Tony Harris put it, "They killed us with patience. They executed well, and they didn't care who scored."

Cameron Mills shooting his devastating jumper from beyond the three-point line as Tubby Smith and his son Saul (11) look on.

From its solid win in Knoxville, UK moved on to Nashville for its second meeting of the season (on January 27) with Vanderbilt. In a hard-fought and surprisingly close contest, the Big Blue prevailed in the very last second of regulation time by a score of 63-61, on a miracle running ten-foot scoop shot by Nazr Mohammed that banked in at the buzzer. Against the Commodores the big problem for the Cats was rebounding. To this point in the season, the one constant for the Blue and White had been rebounding. The team had outrebounded each of its first 20 opponents, and none more convincingly than Vanderbilt. In Lexington, UK had grabbed 57 rebounds to Vandy's 18. In Nashville, the Commodores won the rebounding battle 37-32, but they still lost the game. How had the Cats prevailed? Scott Padgett echoed Coach Smith: "We're just the type of team that feels if we can stay close, [we] will find a way to win."

Unfortunately, the Cats quickly forgot that they had to stay close in order to "find a way to win." In the very next game, against Florida, UK lost to a team with a less

than sterling 3-4 SEC record going into the February 1 meeting in Rupp Arena. The final score was a shocking 86-78 in favor of the Gators, and the game was really not that close. Even though senior guard Cameron Mills hit a career high 31 points, Florida dominated the boards (outrebounding Kentucky 40 to 30) and the half-court offense. Aside from Mills and a ten-point effort by Padgett, no other Wildcat player was able to reach double figures. Florida rode the strong play of guard Jason Williams, who scored seemingly at will (24 points) and dominated the open floor against the Big Blue. UK attempted to combat Florida's quickness and outside shooting by replacing its big men with smaller, quicker players. Unfortunately, as Tubby Smith noted following the game, "That didn't work." In fact, nothing seemed to work. Florida, for its part, was happy to see Mohammed (two shots from the field in the whole game), Magloire (four shots) and Padgett (also four shots) not patrolling under the basket throughout much of the contest, as the Cats played the Gators' game instead of trying to power the ball inside. It was a lesson that Smith freely acknowledged, and which he took to heart in anticipation of the coming rematch in Gainesville. As a result of the loss, which rankled Wildcat fans and the media, Kentucky's record fell to 19-3, and 8-1 in the SEC.

After the disappointing loss to Florida, the Wildcats looked to rebound against an LSU squad that had a losing record and was generally considered one of the weaker teams in the conference. Even though the February 4 game would be played on their home floor in Baton Rouge, the Tigers were generally expected to be destroyed by a hungry and angry squad of Wildcats. Instead of the anticipated rout, and only because LSU guard Maurice Carter missed an open three-pointer in the final seconds, UK eked out a 63-61 cliffhanger.

Following the game, Wildcat radio commentator Sam Bowie asked Jeff Sheppard the question that was undoubtedly on the minds of all Big Blue fans: "What's wrong?" Sheppard acknowledged his (and his teammates') frustration when he admitted, "If we knew, we'd have found the solution tonight." The Cats gave up eight three-pointers to the Tigers, continuing the poor perimeter defense that had plagued the team but which, fortunately, was remedied as the postseason tournaments approached. UK's centers were again relegated to being largely nonfactors in the game, with Mohammed taking only five shots in scoring a total of only three points in 20 minutes of action, and Magloire scoring only two points. As a team, Kentucky shot poorly (23 for 60 from the field), played lax perimeter defense, and

again failed to dominate the boards (managing a 30-30 tie in the rebounding count).

Tubby Smith spoke for UK fans when he summed up his feelings after the game by saying, "It's the most disappointed I've been all year. I thought they just outhustled us once again." Coach Smith, Sheppard, and the rest of the Cats were now searching desperately for answers as they prepared for their next opponents, the Villanova Wildcats.

Given the disappointing recent performances against Florida and LSU, a nonconference outing appeared to be just what the UK team needed to regain focus and momentum. And so it was. The visiting Big Blue squad outhustled and outthought the Villanova Wildcats in the February 8 contest played in Philadelphia. Kentucky raised its season record to 21-3 with a 79-63 victory, while Villanova fell to 9-12.

Reflecting upon the victory over the weaker Villanova squad, *Herald-Leader* columnist Chuck Culpepper observed: "Lurching toward the end of a decade of Unforgettables, Untouchables and Unbelievables, the Indecipherables yesterday continued to do nothing in particular except win." He added, "If you walk around Kentucky's hometown, you get a combination of snow in your shoes and people telling you these Wildcats are *a so-so 21-3 team* and wondering what is wrong with them." The team was winning, but—as Culpepper lamented—it was not dominating games the way fans and media in the 1990s had come to expect of Wildcat squads.

UK returned to Lexington for its second meeting of the year against Tennessee on February 11. Unlike the game in Knoxville, this one was more closely contested. Kentucky jumped to an early lead, but Tennessee fought its way back to gain a 21-19 advantage with just over six minutes remaining in the first half. The Cats took a 33-30 lead into the locker room at half time, thanks to a late flurry by Jeff Sheppard. The Big Blue opened the second half with a three-pointer and a layup to push the lead to eight points, and stretched the margin to 13 with two minutes remaining, before the Volunteers battled back to cut the final margin to six points at 80 to 74. Mohammed led UK with 21 points and 16 rebounds, heading a balanced attack that saw five Wildcats score in double figures.

Seventh-ranked Kentucky continued to struggle at home, losing to the eighteenth-ranked Mississippi Rebels on Valentine's Day. Ole Miss took an early lead before Kentucky utilized its tremendous defensive pressure and went on an 18-to-one run to take a 24-11 lead. Although the Wildcats had a seemingly comfortable 34-23 lead at halftime, in the second period the team went away from

what had been working for them. In the first half, the Big Blue had forced the ball in to Mohammed, who scored 12 points. After the intermission, not only did Mohammed not score, he did not even have a shot at the basket.

Tubby Smith commented after the game, "We started the second half so flat and I couldn't really tell you why. We just didn't come out of the locker room ready to play." Kentucky's uninspired play and lack of inside attack enabled Ole Miss to win in Lexington for the first time since 1927. The Wildcat faithful watched Ansu Sesay, the Rebels' star power forward, score 14 second-half points in leading his squad to a 73-64 victory. With this loss, UK's record fell to 22-4, and 10-2 in the SEC.

The Big Blue attempted to regroup on the road in its next contest on February 18 against the Gators in Gainesville. The game not only allowed Kentucky an opportunity to redeem itself following its sloppy play against Ole Miss, but also gave the Cats the chance to gain revenge against the only other SEC squad to beat them during the season. Florida, for its part, was without star point guard Jason Williams, who was kicked off the team on February 17 for breaking team and university rules. UK capitalized on Florida's lack of guard play by starting four guards. Smith and Mills made their first starts as Wildcats, alongside regulars Sheppard and Turner. The Gators kept the contest competitive for about ten minutes, but the absence of Williams soon took its toll. Scott Padgett pointed out after the game, "They didn't have that extra guy to penetrate and pitch to give guys open shots." From one point down (13-12), the Cats once again made use of a spurt, this time a 25-6 run, to take control of the contest. Afterwards, Florida's Eddie Shannon was surprisingly honest when he admitted, "We came on the court afraid of Kentucky. When they made the run, we folded instead of regrouping." The result was a 41-24 halftime lead on the way to a 79-54 drubbing of the Gators.

Georgia visited Lexington for UK's Senior Day on February 22 as 24,272 fans came to Rupp Arena to say farewell to seniors Edwards, Mills, and Sheppard. Bulldog point guard G.G. Smith led a surprisingly effective Georgia charge to take a 44-36 lead over the Wildcats. At halftime, Tubby Smith got on Wayne Turner for G.G.'s excellent first half. Following the game, Turner recalled that the coach "called me the worst defensive player he ever coached. Something kind of clicked in my head. I think I'm one of the best defensive players on the team. That got me fired up. Coming into the second half, I thought, I'll show that no one can beat me off the

Wayne Turner driving to the basket against Tennessee pressure as Scott Padgett (34) gets in rebounding position. UK finally won the hard-fought February 11 game, 80-74.

dribble. I'm going to shut G.G. down." The result was that on the very first Bulldog possession of the second half, Kentucky's defensive pressure forced the Georgia point guard to pick up his dribble and drag his foot, forcing a turnover. UK's second half defensive pressure held the Bulldogs to 31 points, and the Wildcats raced away to a relatively easy 85-74 victory. After scoring 12 points in the first half, G.G. Smith added only seven more the rest of the way on four for 11 shooting. As a squad, the Bulldogs hit only 35 percent from the field for the game. UK also dominated the boards, outrebounding Georgia by a whopping 47-20 count, as Mohammed led the way with 11 rebounds to go along with his team-high 16 points. The victory clinched at

least a tie for the Eastern Division regular-season championship for Kentucky and raised its record to 24-4 and 12-2 in the conference.

UK followed up its Georgia victory with an easy 83-58 road win over Auburn. The game was significant for the Wildcats because of Jeff Sheppard's continuing emergence as the team's go-to guy, as he scored 25 points, including five for 11 from behind the arc. In the process, Kentucky also clinched sole possession of the regular-season Eastern Division title.

The Big Blue travelled to Columbia with the intention of spoiling South Carolina's Senior Day celebration by beating the Gamecocks. Wayne Turner described UK's thinking as the game approached: "Everybody that was here last year remembers what [USC] did to us on Senior Day. . . . We just wanted to return the favor for them and make it up to our seniors from last year." The score in the 1997 Rupp Arena contest had been 72-66, with South Carolina on top. This time around, Turner and his teammates were determined to turn the tables and did so in the February 28, 1998, meeting with a solid 69-57 victory. Although UK had already locked up its thirty-ninth regular-season SEC title, and was unlikely to be anything other than a number two seed in the upcoming NCAA tournament, no matter how the regular season and SEC tournament ended, the Wildcats were highly motivated in this game. They had a taste for sweet revenge!

Kentucky physically dominated the quick, good shooting, highly ranked Gamecock squad, and continued the process of rounding into top form in preparation for the start of the SEC and NCAA tournaments. The Big Blue took a 34-29 halftime lead, and with tre-mendous perimeter defense—previously a weakness of this squad—controlled the second half of the game in gaining the victory. Heshimu Evans started his first game at Kentucky in place of Allen Edwards, who had left the team to be with his family following the death of his mother. Evans made the most of his opportunity, scoring a Wildcat career-high 22 points while pulling down 12 rebounds. Furthermore, his athletic play seemed to be just the spark that the rest of the squad needed to reach a top-notch performance level. Gamecock coach Eddie Fogler agreed: "Their zone really bothered us. That's all we worked on for two days, but it's hard to assimilate the size they have and the athleticism they have with Evans out front." In fact, this Kentucky defense with Evans playing the point in the zone held USC to just 32 percent shooting in the second half, the worst performance all season for South Carolina. Jeff Sheppard hit six of ten shots from three-point land, and again led the team in scoring with 24 points. Critical for UK and its chances in the postseason, Sheppard seemed again to confirm his emergence as the go-to player that the squad desperately needed. His clutch shooting, combined with Evans' athleticism and the dominant inside play of Mohammed, Magloire, and Padgett, was making Kentucky a force to be reckoned with.

After nearly an entire season of experimenting, Smith had finally hit pay dirt at exactly the right time. He seemed to have found the key to solving the season-long problem of how to control the strong outside shooting of Wildcat opponents just in time for the postseason tournaments.

15

The Comeback Cats

By the end of the regular season, even the media had come to the realization that this squad was not "indecipherable." Many observers began acknowledging that UK was a team of winners. Like their coach, they accomplished the all-important goal of winning games, but in their own way. What media and fans alike found confusing was that the quiet and low-key Smith did things differently from the brash and flamboyant Pitino.

Two days after the South Carolina game ended the regular season, Billy Reed wrote, "Don't breathe a word of this to Dicky V., Billy P., or any of college basketball's other high-profile pundits, but just about everybody is overlooking a pretty good team that has an excellent shot to make the NCAA Final Four in San Antonio." That team, of course, was Kentucky. Reed pointed out that the Wildcats "looked like a team that was getting its act together at just the right time." Furthermore, he added—and rightly so—that Smith had done one of the best coaching jobs in the country. The SEC tournament, an event the Cats had won every year but one during the 1990s, would be a great chance to test the mettle of a UK squad (and its coach) that seemed to be peaking perfectly for postseason success.

During the SEC tournament, the Lexington media, especially television, started referring to the tourney site as "Catlanta." And Georgia's capital city did indeed prove extremely hospitable to the Big Blue. UK won three league tournament games—for the Conference title— as well as its first two NCAA East Regional contests, all five played in the Georgia Dome, which seemed to take

on the appearance of a UK home court, complete with stands full of screaming Wildcat faithful. Tubby Smith had returned to Georgia in style.

The Cats opened with an 11-point decision over Alabama on March 6. UK led by only two points over the Crimson Tide at halftime. Alabama started the scoring in the second half, tying the score, and even led 54-51 at one point. Seldom-used freshman center Michael Bradley, however, emerged as the Blue and White's secret second half weapon, scoring ten points and grabbing six rebounds. His strong play helped forge an 82-71 victory in the quarterfinal game. In the process, Kentucky set an SEC tournament record with an incredible 53 rebounds, compared to Alabama's 32.

The next day, Jeff Sheppard again helped lead seventh-ranked UK to victory, this time against sixteenth-ranked Arkansas. Sheppard followed up a team-high 17 points against Alabama with another team-high 17 points against the Razorbacks. Unfortunately, after scoring his seventeenth point early in the second half, Sheppard suffered a severe ankle sprain. UK's star guard did not return to the contest, and fans wondered whether he would be able to play on March 8 in the tournament finals. The Wildcats, first with and then without Sheppard, dominated the NCAA tournament-bound Arkansas squad, outrebounding them by a 51-30 margin. UK had a 25-point lead at halftime and finished the game with the same 25-point margin for a 99-74 blowout. Five UK players scored in double figures, and Heshimu Evans turned in a solid performance as a starter with an 11-point, 6-rebound, 5-assist performance. Kentucky now

Tubby Smith waves the spoils of victory after UK's defeat of a surprisingly tough and resilient Stanford Cardinal squad in the NCAA semifinal game. The Comeback Cats had prevailed once again.

moved on to face fifteenth-ranked South Carolina in the tournament finals.

To reach the tournament finals, South Carolina had to beat Mississippi, which had won the Western Division regular-season title. The Gamecocks appeared ready to give Kentucky a battle for the SEC's automatic NCAA tournament bid, but appearances were deceiving. The Wildcats dominated USC as thoroughly as they had the Razorbacks, winning by an 86-56 score. Amazingly, the Cats accomplished this domination of the guard-oriented South Carolina squad without Sheppard, who was nursing his sprained ankle. Wayne Turner and Allen Edwards stood in for the injured Sheppard, scoring 18 and 15 points respectively. More importantly, Kentucky held South Carolina to under 37 percent shooting from the floor and star guards BJ McKie and Melvin Watson managed only 12 and eight points respectively. Holding an opponent to a low shooting percentage, however, was becoming commonplace for the Wildcats. Since the loss to Ole Miss, UK had dramatically stepped up its defensive pressure, limiting its last seven SEC foes to no better than 38.5 percent shooting from the field. In contrast to earlier in the season, the defensive pressure now extended out to the three-point line, where those seven teams hit only 28.8 percent of their shots. The answer to the early season questions and concerns regarding the team seemed to be that Smith and his players had needed time to adjust to each other in order to fashion a system that would work for them.

The Wildcats entered the 1998 NCAA tournament with a 29-4 record, and as SEC regular-season and tournament champions. Jeff Sheppard and Nazr Mohammed led a balanced scoring attack, and the strong late season play of Allen Edwards, Wayne Turner, and Heshimu Evans seemed to increase overall team athleticism. Sheppard, rusty from a redshirt year's inactivity, was finally rounding into top form late in the season. The Georgia native's stepped up play complemented the strong inside game that the Wildcats had developed during the regular campaign in Mohammed, Padgett, and Magloire. Coach Smith had seemingly found the right formula entering the 1998 NCAA tournament. A major question mark was the condition of Sheppard's ankle, as Kentucky's emerging star would be sorely missed if he was unable to play during the tournament. Fortunately for UK, this question mark was quickly removed.

With Sheppard miraculously able to play for a total of 15 minutes despite his injured ankle, the Wildcats dominated their first-round opponent, the South Caro-

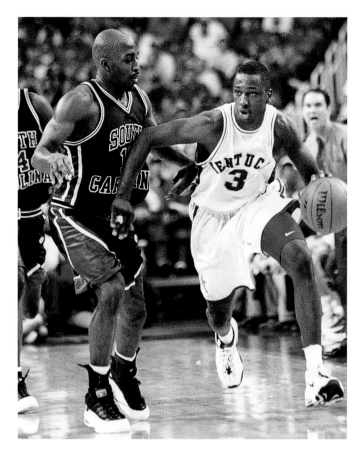

Allen Edwards drives past South Carolina guard Melvin Watson in the SEC tournament title game in Atlanta, which UK won 86-54. Gamecock coach Eddie Fogler is at right.

lina State Bulldogs, in their March 13 meeting. Outmanned and undersized, the Bulldogs went down to defeat by a score of 82-67. Edwards observed that while the South Carolina State squad, led by its 5'10" star Roderick Blakney, made a valiant effort, "they were just a little too small."

Against Saint Louis two days later, Sheppard returned to the starting lineup and led the team in scoring with 18 points, as all five starters (Padgett, Mohammed, Edwards, and Turner being the others) scored in double figures. The Billikens had a reputation for sticky man-to-man defense, and had a scoring star in freshman Larry Hughes. The Wildcats dismantled Saint Louis on both counts and raised their record to 31-4. Hughes scored only 11 points on four for 17 shooting against the Big Blue's helping man-to-man defense. Any question about which team had the better man-to-man defense was ended in the early minutes of the game by Turner and Evans, who drove around their men for easy layups. UK thoroughly dominated Saint Louis, opening up a 46-18 lead on the way to an 88-61 victory. The Cats

held the Billikens to under 20 percent shooting from the field in the first half, and the outcome was not in doubt during the final 20 minutes. In fact, according to Padgett, UK could have booked its passage to St. Petersburg for the NCAA tournament's Southeastern Regional semifinals after opening a 10-0 lead in the first three minutes of the game. Kentucky was now playing as a team—Smith's way—and also seemed to be regaining some of the cocky swagger that it had possessed under Pitino.

The Wildcats' next opponent was UCLA—like the Big Blue, a team with a long tradition of success. Unfortunately for the Bruins, this meeting of the two storied programs in St. Petersburg on March 20 was not one between equals. UCLA earned its spot versus the Wildcats as the result of an 85-82 victory over Michigan. While the win was an impressive effort over the tall, big, and very physical Wolverines, it proved to be a costly victory. Coming down awkwardly from a first-half thunderdunk, 6'1" star point guard Baron Davis suffered a complete tear of the anterior cruciate ligament, a knee injury that meant he would be lost for the rest of the season—which was, as it turned out, one more game.

Against Kentucky, UCLA coach Steve Lavin elected to move 6'5" forward Toby Bailey to guard, with 6'6" freshman reserve Travis Reed starting at forward. It probably would not have mattered who played where, or even if Davis had been healthy enough to compete. The Wildcats entered the game favored to win, and this they did, in an impressive manner, 94-68. UCLA was never able to get its offense into gear. Just 0:44 seconds into the game the score was tied at 2-2. For the Bruins and their fans, that was the high point of the contest; from there it was all downhill. By halftime the deficit was seventeen (40-23); it escalated in the second half. For the game UCLA was held to 29.1 percent, the team's worst shooting performance of the season. The UK defense forced its opponent into committing 19 turnovers, and with 14 blocked shots set an NCAA tournament record. Of that total, centers Mohammed and Magloire each blocked six, with Edwards and Evans accounting for the other two. As usual, Wildcat scoring was well distributed, with five players reaching double figures, led by Scott Padgett's 19 points, and the Cats' bench outscoring the Bruin reserves 26-11. The one battle UCLA won was control of the backboards. Amazingly, the smaller Bruins outrebounded the Big Blue by ten, 51-41, but this achievement did not lead to success where it counted, in the game's final score.

As Kentucky streaked ahead to its final 26-point margin of victory (94-68), attention began to shift to the Wildcats' next opponent. The UCLA romp seemed to serve as a useful tune-up for the upcoming grudge match against the Duke Blue Devils, just two days away.

Twenty years after Jack Givens led a UK team to victory over Duke for the NCAA tournament title, and six years after Christian Laettner's last-second shot broke the hearts of Big Blue fans in an overtime thriller, the Wildcats and the Blue Devils took the court in Florida to determine who would represent the South Regional in the 1998 Final Four in San Antonio.

UCLA forward Kris Johnson puts the ball up against intense pressure from Nazr Mohammed (left), Heshimu Evans (center), and Scott Padgett (behind Johnson). The Bruins were never in the game and lost by 26 points, 94-68.

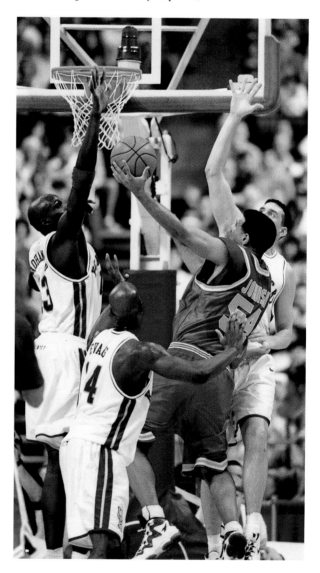

In 1992, Krzyzewski had outcoached Rick Pitino. In 1998, first-year head coach Tubby Smith got the better of the Duke leader, even though throughout most of the contest the Blue Devils dominated the larger, slower Wildcats. Duke opened several big leads in the first half and led by ten points at halftime, 49-39. The Blue Devils widened this margin to 17 points midway through the final half, and UK's chances looked bleak indeed.

During the regular season against Florida in Rupp Arena, Smith had chosen to go to a small lineup to counter the quickness of the Gators, and the results had been disastrous. After watching Mohammed and Magloire get outmaneuvered time after time by Duke's quicker inside players, Smith again gambled that a smaller lineup would work against the Blue Devils. The strategy was gutsy. More importantly, this time it worked.

The Wildcats spread the floor and let Turner parlay his size and quickness by taking Steve Wojciechowski to the basket and either hitting a runner in the lane or passing off to Evans, Sheppard, Edwards, or Padgett for open jumpers. Turner thoroughly dominated the Duke point guard at both ends of the court during several critical minutes of the second half. For some reason, Coach K decided to stay with Wojo despite the obvious mismatch, a mismatch that Tubby Smith used to full advantage.

Along with Turner, other key players for Kentucky were Evans, Padgett, and Sheppard, who hit critical shots, rebounded effectively, and played solid defense. The unsung hero was Heshimu Evans, whose 11 rebounds, fourteen points, and especially his hustle, were essential to the UK victory. The star for Kentucky, however, was Sheppard. The senior guard solidified his late season emergence as the Wildcats' go-to guy, hitting key baskets and free throws on the way to an electrifying 18-point, 11-rebound performance.

Duke, which led by 17 points with 9:33 to play, went suddenly cold, while Kentucky went on one of its patented runs, outscoring the Blue Devils 17-3 in a little more than four minutes. At this critical juncture in the contest, UK's experience made the difference. Duke relied heavily on talented freshmen—Shane Battier, Elton Brand, William Avery, and Chris Burgess—but their relative inexperience began to show in the final minutes of the game.

A key play unfolded on a relatively innocuous scramble for a loose ball with 5:21 left in the game. To retain possession, Duke called timeout. That was the team's last timeout. Smith and UK still had timeouts remaining, but chose not to use them until only 4.5 seconds remained in the game, thus denying the Blue Dev-

Wayne Turner's ability to drive past Duke point guard Steve Wojciechowski was the key to UK's comeback from a 17-point second half deficit.

ils an opportunity to get sufficiently organized to withstand the Wildcats' furious charge. As sportswriter Ron Green of the *Charlotte Observer* pointed out (March 23, 1998), "Without any timeouts, Krzyzewski couldn't orchestrate the final moments like he wanted."

With 2:16 left, Evans batted a missed UK shot back out to Cameron Mills for an open three-pointer, his first basket of the tournament. That basket put the Cats in front for the first time in the game, 80-79. Duke still had chances to win, the last with 4.5 seconds remaining. In 1992, the Blue Devils had thrown a three-quarters court pass to Laettner to maximize use of the clock. This time, Duke was forced to inbound the ball deep in its backcourt to freshman William Avery, who spent valuable time dribbling the ball up the court against UK's solid pressure defense. Avery shot a desperation 35-footer that hit high off the backboard and fell away harmlessly as the buzzer sounded to end the game. Final score: 86-84.

In the midst of the wild team celebration, Jeff Sheppard broke away to shake hands and express his regard for Coach K, who graciously said, "Son, you guys made the big plays. You deserve to win." Later, Sheppard voiced his admiration for the Duke coach. "What Coach K said about us as a team and as players is something I'll

Cats win, Cats win! Allen Edwards (3) and Jeff Sheppard (15) give full vent to their emotions as Shane Battier (31) and William Avery (5) reflect the shock and dejection of the Blue Devil players over the 86-84 final score. The come-from-behind UK victory, decided in the last second of play, wiped out Big Blue bitter memories of Duke's 104-103 overtime victory in the 1992 East Regional final, won on Christian Laettner's so-called "shot heard 'round the basketball world."

never forget. . . . [To] lose that game and say such nice things to us, that's just class." In the March 24, 1998, issue of *USA Today*, Steve Wieberg reported the postgame exchange of courtesies between the Duke coach and several UK players who approached him to pay their respects, concluding: "The NBA might take note: there *is* a place for sportsmanship and dignity in big-time sports."

But now, on to San Antonio. In 1997 Rick Pitino had promised that the Cats would go back to the Final Four in 1998. What Pitino promised, Tubby Smith delivered.

UK's first opponent in Texas was the Stanford Cardinal squad from Palo Alto. At the beginning of the NCAA tournament, the California team was believed to have a good, but not a great, chance of getting to the regionals. Obviously by making it all the way to the Final Four, they surprised the so-called experts. On the basis of the team's strengths and weaknesses, this misreading of Stanford's chances seemed logical. The Cardinal's strengths consisted of size in the front court, with eight players 6'7" or taller; strong rebounding; solid three-point shooting; and good defense. The shortcomings that seemed to negate these considerable assets were lack of athleticism and speed at some positions and problems defending against extremely quick teams. Stanford had been soundly whipped twice by Pac-10 rival and conference champ Arizona, a squad that was generally expected to make it to the NCAA championship game. What the experts failed to sufficiently consider were the intangibles, especially desire, heart, and intelligence, and the fact that Stanford had finished the regular season on a roll, having won eight of its last ten games.

The Cardinal reached the Final Four by defeating the underdog Rhode Island Rams, coached by Jim Harrick, who had guided UCLA to the 1995 national title. The Rams were expected to give Stanford problems, possessing excellent outside shooters and great team speed, although they lacked size. As predicted, they seemed to be more than the West Coast team could handle. With just 2:04 left in the game, Rhode Island led by 11 points and appeared to be in total control, well on its way to the Final Four. And then Cardinal guard Arthur Lee took over. In the final 124 seconds of the contest, Lee scored 13 points and the squad from Palo Alto clawed its way to a 79-77 victory.

Despite this dramatic comeback, Stanford entered its March 28 game against tournament-tested Kentucky as a decided underdog. Rather than behaving like an intimidated squad that was overwhelmed by making the Final Four, the Cardinal team performed as though it firmly believed it belonged in this exclusive company. Indeed, the West Coast team played as though it fully expected to win. It required a determined effort by the Cats, led by the best performance of Jeff Sheppard's college career, to finally defeat Stanford. And victory was not assured until the very final moments of the game, when Peter Sauer missed a contested 75-foot shot taken with just half a second left in overtime, to seal Kentucky's 86-85 win.

Going into the game, UK supposedly enjoyed a huge psychological advantage because of its frequent appearances in the Final Four. In contrast, Stanford's lack of Final Four experience was expected to be a key factor in the contest's first three or four minutes. That is, Stanford was expected to be tentative before it could settle down to try to play its game, and by that time UK would be firmly in control. The only problem with that scenario was that the Cardinal refused to follow it.

The excellent leadership and outside shooting of point-guard Arthur Lee, combined with the ability of their front court to control the boards, allowed the Californians to jump to an 8-0 lead just 2:20 into the game. With 6'8" Mark "Mad Dog" Madsen, 6'7" Peter Sauer (whose knee injury made him questionable even to start), and 7'1" Tim Young combining for 30 of the team's total of 45 rebounds, Stanford became only the fifth opponent all season to outrebound the Wildcats. And because of its control of the boards, the Cardinal was able to dictate tempo and hold the lead throughout the entire first half.

Yet even with rebounding problems and poor shooting (only 38.7 percent in the first half), UK trailed by only five points (37-32) when the teams went to the locker rooms. During the second half, the Wildcats' shooting accuracy improved and Mohammed began to assert himself, getting all 18 of his points after the intermission. Throughout the contest, as his teammates freely acknowledged afterward, Jeff Sheppard carried the team offensively, scoring a career-high 27 points, including four critical three-pointers and the Big Blue's last point in overtime, a free throw.

Despite Kentucky's efforts, Stanford refused to crack. The Cats gained their first lead, 54-53, with 10:04 to go, but the Cardinal fought back and the lead changed hands nine times in the second half. At the end of regulation time the score was tied at 73 and it appeared the game could go either way in overtime. The two sides seemed to be evenly matched and both possessed plenty of fighting spirit. Unfortunately for the Californians, just 0:22 seconds into the extra period, they lost their lead-

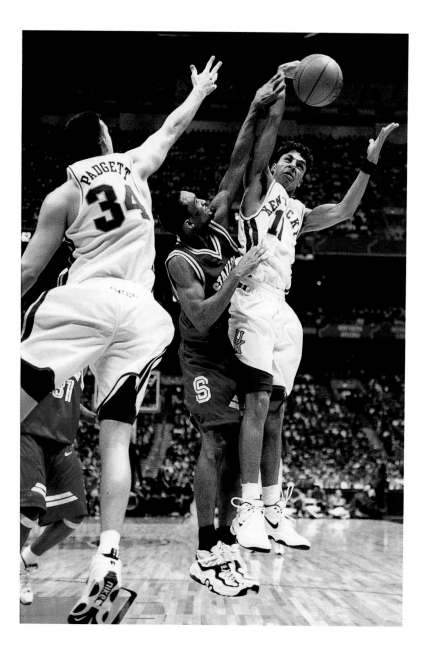

Scott Padgett (left) and Saul Smith battle a Stanford player for a rebound in UK's bitterly contested 86-85 overtime Final Four victory. This was yet another successful comeback effort by the Wildcats, who played with poise and self-confidence.

ing rebounder (with 16) and a dangerous inside scoring threat when center Tim Young committed his fifth foul. Even with Young gone and the injured Sauer sitting on the bench, Stanford refused to give in. Finally, with just 15.4 seconds left in overtime, Madsen fouled out. When Sheppard hit one of two free throws, the Big Blue had what seemed to be an insurmountable four-point lead. Sauer returned to the game, bad knee notwithstanding, and hit a clutch three-pointer with 9.2 seconds to go. Coach Mike Montgomery called the Cardinal's final timeout, which, it turned out, could have been vital for the team just a few seconds later—it was that kind of game—because with 2.5 seconds left, Turner was fouled and missed both free throws. Sauer grabbed

the rebound, but without timeouts and with the clock running out he was forced to start dribbling up court, dogged by defensive pressure from Edwards. With only half a second left, Sauer let fly with a 75-foot prayer, but missed. Tubby and his Comeback Cats had trailed early and come out on top once again.

For the third year in a row, the Wildcats were in the title game. However, the generally anticipated matchup with North Carolina did not materialize when, in the second contest of the day, the Tar Heels were soundly beaten by Utah. UK was now to face its seemingly perennial NCAA opponent, the Utes, this time for the national championship.

When the tournament began in the second week of

March, Coach Rick Majerus led a squad that appeared to be a mystery, perhaps capable of getting to the Sweet Sixteen, but surely no further. Like Stanford, a team it somewhat resembled, Utah was grossly underestimated. Built around All-American forward Keith Van Horn, the Utes had been unable to make it out of the regionals in 1996 and 1997, losing both times to Rick Pitino's Wildcats. Van Horn graduated in 1997 and proved the excellence of his talent in his first NBA campaign. Without Van Horn, Utah was (like the 1997/98 Cats) without the supposedly all-important go-to player. What the Salt Lake City squad possessed—as it always seemed to—was an abundance of big, slow players who were strong rebounders and played solid defense, but were incapable of keeping up with quicker, more athletic opponents. And to get out of the West Regional and into the Final Four, Majerus and his squad would probably have to face the lightning quick and supremely self-confident defending national champions, the Arizona Wildcats, who (conventional wisdom said) would undoubtedly devour them. Instead of conforming to expectations and being destroyed by number one–seeded Arizona, the Utes employed a specially designed triangle and two defense to hold high-scoring guards Mike Bibby and Miles Simon in check and whip Lute Olson and his Wildcats 76-51.

Although Utah appeared to be similar to the squads of previous years, there were vital differences between the 1998 team and its predecessors. These included more self-confident and experienced players who, unlike prior years, firmly believed they could win; excellent team defense, which in the first five NCAA tournament games held opponents to an average of 61.8 points; and by season's end one of the best point guards, possibly the best, in the nation, 6'2" junior Andre Miller. Against Arizona, Miller completely outplayed All-American Mike Bibby and then, in the Final Four, again proved the excellence of his game against North Carolina's Ed Cota.

Against the highly favored Tar Heels, like Arizona a number one seed, the underrated Utes immediately jumped into the lead and never let it go. Carolina was able to cut the margin to two, 57-55, with 2:02 left, but the Utes held on for a 65-59 upset. It was an exhilarating and hard-earned victory. The immediate question then was whether Majerus could devise a game plan in just two days to defeat yet another highly favored and experienced opponent. And after such an exhausting effort against the Tar Heels, could his players rouse themselves for yet another peak performance, this time against the swarming, sharpshooting, shot-blocking UK team that featured so many title game–tested veterans?

Once the game got under way, it quickly became evident that this time Utah would not grab an early lead and dictate the pace of action. Instead, the Utes displayed big game jitters, committing four turnovers and falling behind 8-4 in the first three and a half minutes. After the shaky start, however, the Salt Lake City squad used good shooting and strong rebounding to fight its way back, and late in the half, in the words of *USA Today*'s Steve Wieberg (March 31, 1998), "cranked up what arguably has been the tournament's best defense, and that turned on their running game." With forward Alex Jensen scoring on a couple of fast break baskets and a free throw, they scored ten unanswered points in a one and a half minute span, extending a one-point lead into a 34-23 advantage with 4:36 left in the first half. For the remainder of the period, Kentucky was able to play Utah, even and the Cats retreated to the locker room behind by ten, 41-31.

Bad as it was, it could have been worse for UK, much worse. The Wildcats, who had been able to control the boards against most foes during the season, were being thoroughly dominated by their bigger and stronger opponent. Led by center Mike Doleac, the Utes held a remarkable 24-6 rebounding advantage after the game's first 20 minutes. Of the 24 rebounds, nine were off the offensive boards, an amazing statistic when one considers that Utah missed only 12 shot attempts during the entire period. The team from Salt Lake City hit 57.1 percent of its shots in the first period to 45.2 for the Big Blue, which missed all six of its three-point attempts.

Despite being outrebounded and outshot, UK's quickness, which forced 12 turnovers leading to ten points, kept the Big Blue within ten points by intermission. Andre Miller, who had seemed unflappable against Arizona and North Carolina, turned the ball over six times (including three in the first three minutes) against the defensive pressure applied by Wayne Turner and his teammates.

Clearly Coach Smith needed to change the game's momentum to favor the Wildcats. In the locker room, according to Wayne Turner, the coach said to his squad, "Twenty-four to six on the boards? Are you serious?" This was Smith's way of pointing out to his players the need to toughen up in the remaining 20 minutes, to play a more physical game, and to match Utah's aggressiveness in going after the ball.

When the second half began, the Utes quickly pushed their lead up to 12 points before Kentucky slowly began to chip away. The comeback did not take place early in the period, nor did it come easily. A major ele-

Heshimu Evans played a key role in UK's comeback from a 12-point second half deficit to win the NCAA title, 78-69.

in the second half 18-15. In addition to these and other heroes off the bench, Scott Padgett led the team in scoring with 17 points (and was named game MVP), while Jeff Sheppard added 16 points and was designated the most outstanding player in the Final Four.

For the Utes, who (like their counterparts) were a collection of overachievers, the 78-69 loss was heartbreaking. A 12-point lead early in the second half melted away under intense defensive pressure, and down the stretch Utah missed 11 straight shots. As Coach Rick Majerus later acknowledged, the Wildcats had simply worn down his players. Because of exhaustion—as well as double and triple teaming—Mike Doleac, who totaled 15 points and ten rebounds for the game, missed six shots in the game's crucial final minutes, while Utah's excellent point guard and leading scorer (with 16) Andre Miller failed to convert on two driving layups.

Cameron Mills, shooting over Utah's Drew Hansen, hit two clutch second half three-pointers in the Wildcat victory.

ment in UK's comeback was Smith's composure and his confidence in both his players and his game plan. Despite falling so far behind, Smith continued his season-long practice of frequent substitutions throughout the contest. Thus Heshimu Evans came off the bench early in the second half and rewarded his coach's confidence by hitting a key three-pointer to cut the lead to 47-40. When Utah forward Hanno Möttölä answered with what could have been a momentum-killing three-pointer of his own, Evans promptly responded with another three, followed by a deuce to cut the lead to 50-45. In addition to Evans, who scored ten key points, Cameron Mills contributed eight points, including two clutch threes down the stretch. In fact, UK's bench outscored the Utes' reserves 25-7. Evans, however, was probably the key for the Big Blue, and his contributions were not limited to offense. He played with his usual great emotion, provided solid defense, and pulled down six second-half rebounds. After being so thoroughly dominated by their opponents in the first 20 minutes, the Wildcats outrebounded Utah

Top, The Kentucky bench begins to react to the reality of a seemingly impossible dream coming true: the squad that had been labelled "the worst 21-3 team in the country" was about to win the national title. *Lower right,* Sophomore center Jamaal Magloire made valuable contributions to the Wildcats' success in 1997/98.

As the contest ticked down to the final minutes and seconds and their opponents wilted, the Wildcats seemed to grow stronger and more confident. Cameron Mills proudly pointed out after the game, "We obviously have a lot of depth and talent." *Wall Street Journal* sportswriter Frederick C. Klein observed in his April 1 column: "Kentucky owed its championship to depth and the unflashy labor that goes into a wear-'em-down defense." As the person who had recognized and channelled the team's great potential, Tubby Smith deserved full credit for UK's success. He brought the squad along carefully, held to his beliefs, and neither panicked nor gave in to well-meaning admonitions and advice from fans and the media. Instead, he did things his way. In early February Smith's way seemed to many of the faithful to have produced "the worst 21-3 team in the country," but by the end of March the record was a universally acclaimed 35-4

Tubby Smith and the Wildcats returned to Lexington on March 31, where they were greeted by an estimated 1,000 fans who had congregated at Keeneland across from the airport and then, after a triumphant motorcade along Versailles Road, joined in a celebration downtown. The Big Blue bus carrying the team went

directly into Rupp Arena, where a crowd of approximately 20,000 welcomed their heroes home. As the fans roared their appreciation, Coach Smith introduced his players one by one and described the contributions that each had made to the team's success; then the championship trophy was displayed, followed by raising to the arena rafters the banner denoting UK's seventh NCAA title.

The *Herald-Leader* observed, "The ceremony also served as a coronation for a coach who completed his first year at UK with a championship." Athletics Director C.M. Newton summed up his feelings about Smith by calling him "a better person than he is a coach, and believe me, he's a great coach." During the course of the season, Smith had certainly proved that he was a brilliant leader who could adapt himself and his coaching concepts to the talents of his players rather than stubbornly trying to force them to fit into a rigid system—in this case, "Pitinoball"—as many coaches would have done. As a result, he put his own personal stamp on the team, won the full support (and apparently the love and admiration) of his players, and proved 1997/98 was definitely not, as a local sportswriter had feared, the Year of the Indecipherables. In Coach Smith's words, it was the Year of the Comeback Cats.

Early in the season it became clear that this edition of the Wildcats, unlike the previous two Final Four teams, lacked hugely talented go-to performers. Those players had left for the NBA. What remained was a collection of athletes who, while they had been well trained in fundamentals by Pitino in the past and Smith in the current season, were essentially role players.

The question facing the new coach was, What does one do with a whole team of role players? His answer to that puzzle was to fit those role players into a cohesive unit and emphasize the team concept rather than individual accomplishments. As *USA Today*'s Tom Weir marvelled (March 26), "Kentucky had virtually no one among the Southeastern Conference's individual statistical leaders." Thus everyone was called upon to contribute whatever he could. The result was the creation of a "one-for-all" spirit and a happy team. Scott Padgett observed during the Final Four, "It's a lot looser atmosphere this year" around the Wildcat team. "A lot of [the] time under Coach Pitino," he went on, "you had that fear factor. Sometimes you played tight because you knew that if you made a mistake you were coming right out." Smith, on the other hand, allowed players the opportunity to make up for mistakes. Exuberance, Padgett further noted, was also back in vogue.

Padgett had tried to make these points during the

season, at a time when UK was being dismissed by media and fans as a group of Indecipherables. While this edition of Wildcats did not win artistically, it somehow managed to win. And win. First one player would rise to the challenge, and then in the next game, someone else. While fans and the media noted that the Big Blue exhibited neither form nor finesse, Coach Smith could have pointed out to them that in a basketball game points are not awarded on the basis of appearance. The whole team, Smith recalled after the season, "worked extremely well together. It didn't matter who was on the floor."

In 1997/98 Kentucky was a relaxed and loose squad which came to have supreme confidence in itself and its collective talents. Thus no matter how far behind the Big Blue might find itself—and in the Duke, Stanford, and Utah games that meant double digit deficits—the players believed they could and would come back and

Scott Padgett, guarded by forward Hanno Möttölä, capped an excellent season with an MVP-winning performance against Utah in the 1998 NCAA championship game.

win. In the crucial last three tournament games, that faith was justified.

The national title was a sweet reward for the excellence of Tubby Smith's coaching, but perhaps even more significant in the final analysis was a statement about Smith that Jeff Sheppard made on March 29: "He really does a good job of teaching us the game of basketball but even a better job of teaching us how to be men." According to longtime UK equipment manager Bill Keightley, Smith could teach his players more than basketball because "He's a good person by nature. He wouldn't know how not to be. . . . And these kids love him."

Smith's character and personality also appealed to the general public. As early as UK's late November 1997 trip to the Maui Classic, sportswriter Austin Murphy observed that the new coach, as the sixth of seventeen children raised on a Maryland farm, "has little trouble relating to Kentucky's rural fan base." From conversations with the numerous fans who had accompanied their beloved Cats to Hawaii, Murphy noted in the December 8, 1997, *Sports Illustrated* that while the Big Blue faithful "will always be grateful to Pitino for rescuing their program from probation and then delivering a national title, it's surprising how little they seem to miss him. Pitino, of course, never pretended to be anything but a visitor to the Bluegrass state, cracking wise about Lexington's 'international cuisine' and poking fun at the accents of his homegrown players. He inspired more respect than affection." By contrast, the *SI* writer found, these same fans had already warmed to Smith because, as one of them put it, "Tubby's the salt of the earth." Smith himself said, according to *USA Today* (March 31,

1998), that he did not experience any racism nor receive any hate mail after his team's shocking losses to U of L, Florida, and Mississippi, all on UK's home floor at Rupp Arena.

Interestingly enough, the *Chicago Tribune* on November 30, 1997, printed an article by reporter Rick Morrissey about "the first African-American head coach at the University of Kentucky." Datelined from Lexington, Morrissey's writing related that "in 1985, *Louisville Courier-Journal* columnist Billy Reed [now of the *Herald-Leader*] wrote that there would be a Martian in the White House before Kentucky would hire a black coach." Reed referred, the writer explained, "to the school's record of change." Morrissey also described for *Tribune* readers the belief expressed by columnist Merlene Davis and black UK students that Smith would not be given a fair chance.

Smith himself recognizes and acknowledges that his is probably the toughest college basketball coaching job in the nation. He pointed out that UK is "more than just a basketball program, it's a way of life." Tubby Smith and his Wildcats were deserving champions. Might their success also lay to rest the question of color, to which the *Chicago Tribune* article (among others) alluded? Wendell Barnhouse wrote in the Fort Worth *Star-Telegram* following the game, "Somewhere, one wonders if Adolph Rupp was watching Monday night's game. And if he smiled at the outcome." As the standard-bearer of the Wildcats' winning tradition, Rupp ought to smile. Winning was what counted to the Baron of the Bluegrass. The Comeback Cats and their coach had become a vital part of that tradition.

The Winning Tradition Lives On!

Wildcat Facts

All-Time Leading UK Scorers —Varsity Career

Player (Position)	Years	Points	Games	Ave.
1. Dan Issel (C)	3 (1967/68-1969/70)	2,138	83	25.7
2. Kenny Walker (F)	4 (1983-86)	2,080	132	15.8
3. Jack Givens (F)	4 (1974/75-1977/78)	2,038	123	16.6
4. Tony Delk (G)	4 (1993-96)	1,890	133	14.2
5. Jamal Mashburn (F)	3 (1991-93)	1,843	98	18.8
6. Kevin Grevey (F)	3 (1972/73-1974/75)	1,801	84	21.4
7. Cotton Nash (C-F)	3 (1961/62-1963/64)	1,770	78	22.6
8. Alex Groza (C)	4 (1944/45-1946/47, 1948/49)	1,744	120	14.4
9. Ed Davender (G)	4 (1985-88)	1,637	129	12.7
10. Louie Dampier (G)	3 (1964/65-1966/67)	1,575	80	19.7
11. Mike Casey (G)	3 (1967/68-1968/69, 1970/71)	1,535	82	18.7
12. Ralph Beard (G)	4 (1945/46-1948/49)	1,517	139	10.8
13. Melvin Turpin (C)	4 (1980/81-1983/84)	1,509	123	12.3
14. Cliff Hagan (C)	3 (1950/51-1951/52, 1953/54)	1,475	77	19.2
15. Pat Riley (F)	3 (1964/65-1966/67)	1,464	80	18.3
16. Johnny Cox (F)	3 (1956/57-1958/59)	1,461	84	17.3
17. Kyle Macy (G)	3 (1977/78-1979/80)	1,411	98	14.4
18. Winston Bennett (F)	4 (1984-88)	1,399	133	10.5
19. Rick Robey (F-C)	4 (1974/75-1977/78)	1,395	105	13.3
20. Mike Phillips (C)	4 (1974/75-1977/78)	1,367	120	11.4
21. Mike Pratt (F)	3 (1967/68-1969/70)	1,359	81	16.8
22. Frank Ramsey (G)	3 (1950/51-1951/52, 1953/54)	1,344	91	14.7
23. Jim Andrews (C)	3 (1970/71-1972/73)	1,320	80	16.5
24. Sam Bowie (C-F)	3 (1979/80-1980/81, 1983/84)	1,285	86	14.7
25. Jim Master (G)	4 (1980/81-1983/84)	1,283	121	10.6

Tournaments

(For Dates, Sites, and Scores See All-Time Record Section)

Sugar Bowl Tournament

(Ten Appearances—Five Championships)

1963	Won 2, Lost 0.	Defeated Duke for championship.
1956	Won 2, Lost 0.	Defeated Houston for championship.
1951	Won 1, Lost 1.	Eliminated in finals by St. Louis.
1950	Won 1, Lost 1.	Eliminated in first game by St. Louis. Defeated Syracuse in consolation game.
1949	Won 2, Lost 0.	Defeated Bradley for championship.
1948	Won 1, Lost 1.	Eliminated in finals by St. Louis.
1946	Won 0, Lost 1.	Lost to Oklahoma A&M.
1940	Won 0, Lost 1.	Lost to Indiana.
1939	Won 1, Lost 0.	Defeated Ohio State for championship.
1937	Won 1, Lost 0.	Defeated Pittsburgh for championship.

Southern Intercollegiate Athletic Association (SIAA) Tournament

(Three Appearances—One Championship)

1924	Won 0, Lost 1.	Eliminated in first game by North Carolina.
1922	Won 1, Lost 1.	Eliminated in second game by Mercer.
1921	Won 4, Lost 0.	Defeated Georgia for championship.

Kentucky All-Americans

(37 Players Chosen 54 Times)

Basil Hayden (F) 1921
Burgess Carey (G) 1925
Carey Spicer (F) 1929, '31
Paul McBrayer (G) 1930
Forest Sale (C-F) 1932, '33
Ellis Johnson (G) 1933
John DeMoisey (C) 1934
LeRoy Edwards (C) 1935
Dave Lawrence (F) 1935
Bernard Opper (G) 1939
Lee Huber (G) 1941
Bob Brannum (C) 1944
Jack Parkinson (G) 1946
Jack Tingle (F) 1947
Ralph Beard (G) 1947, '48,* '49*
Alex Groza (C) 1947, '48,⁻ '49*
Wallace Jones (F) 1949⁻
Bill Spivey (C) 1951*
Cliff Hagan (C) 1952,* '54*
Frank Ramsey (G) 1952, '54⁻
Bob Burrow (C) 1956⁻
Vernon Hatton (G) 1958
Johnny Cox (F) 1959*
Cotton Nash (C-F) 1962,⁻ '63,⁻ '64*
Pat Riley (F) 1966
Louie Dampier (G) 1966*, '67⁻
Dan Issel (C) 1969, '70*
Kevin Grevey (F) 1974, '75
Jack Givens (F) 1977, '78
Rick Robey (F-C) 1977, '78
Kyle Macy (G) 1979, '80*
Sam Bowie (C) 1981
Melvin Turpin (C) 1984⁻
Kenny Walker (F) 1985, '86*
Jamal Mashburn (F) 1993*
Tony Delk (G) 1996*
Ron Mercer (G-F) 1997*
*Consensus; ⁻ Second Team Consensus

Olympic Trials Tournament

(One Appearance— Champions College Bracket)

1948   Won 2, Lost 1.
Qualified as NCAA Champion. Defeated Louisville and Baylor for championship College Bracket. (Lost to AAU Champion Phillips Oilers in National Finals.)

Olympic Games

(One Appearance— One World Championship)

1948   Won 8, Lost 0.
Kentucky participated along with the Phillips Oilers as the United States' basketball entry. Defeated France for the championship.

Southeastern Conference (SEC) Tournament

(37 Appearances—21 Championships)*

1998	Won 3, Lost 0.	Defeated S.C. for championship.
1997	Won 3, Lost 0.	Defeated Georgia for championship.
1996	Won 2, Lost 1.	Eliminated in finals by Mississippi State.
1995	Won 3, Lost 0.	Defeated Arkansas for championship.
1994	Won 3, Lost 0.	Defeated Florida for championship.
1993	Won 3, Lost 0.	Defeated LSU for championship.
1992	Won 3, Lost 0.	Defeated Alabama for championship.
1991	Won 0, Lost 0.	Ineligible due to NCAA probation.
1990	Won 0, Lost 0.	Ineligible due to NCAA probation.
1989	Won 0, Lost 1.	Eliminated in quarterfinals by Vanderbilt.
1988	Won 3, Lost 0.	Defeated Georgia for championship; title vacated
1987	Won 0, Lost 1.	Eliminated in quarterfinals by Auburn.
1986	Won 3, Lost 0.	Defeated Alabama for championship.
1985	Won 0, Lost 1.	Eliminated in quarterfinals by Florida.
1984	Won 3, Lost 0.	Defeated Auburn for championship.
1983	Won 0, Lost 1.	Eliminated in quarterfinals by Alabama.
1982	Won 2, Lost 1.	Eliminated in finals by Alabama.
1981	Won 0, Lost 1.	Eliminated in quarterfinals by Vanderbilt.
1980	Won 2, Lost 1.	Eliminated in finals by LSU.
1979	Won 3, Lost 1.	Eliminated in finals by Tennessee.
1952	Won 4, Lost 0.	Defeated LSU for championship.
1951	Won 3, Lost 1.	Eliminated in finals by Vanderbilt.
1950	Won 3, Lost 0.	Defeated Tennessee for championship.
1949	Won 4, Lost 0.	Defeated Tulane for championship.
1948	Won 4, Lost 0.	Defeated Georgia Tech for championship.
1947	Won 4, Lost 0.	Defeated Tulane for championship.
1946	Won 4, Lost 0.	Defeated LSU for championship.
1945	Won 4, Lost 0.	Defeated Tennessee for championship.
1944	Won 3, Lost 0.	Defeated Tulane for championship.
1943	Won 3, Lost 1.	Eliminated in finals by Tennessee.
1942	Won 4, Lost 0.	Defeated Alabama for championship.
1941	Won 3, Lost 1.	Eliminated in finals by Tennessee.
1940	Won 3, Lost 0.	Defeated Georgia for championship.
1939	Won 3, Lost 0.	Defeated Tennessee for championship.
1938	Won 0, Lost 1.	Eliminated in first game by Tulane.
1937	Won 3, Lost 0.	Defeated Tennessee for championship.
1936	Won 1, Lost 1.	Eliminated in second game by Tennessee.
1935		No tournament held.
1934	Won 0, Lost 1.	Eliminated in first game by Florida.
1933	Won 4, Lost 0.	Defeated Mississippi State for championship.

*Tournament resumed in 1979 for first time since 1952.

Southern Conference Tournament

(Seven Appearances—No Championships)*

1932	Won 1, Lost 1.	Eliminated in second game by N. Carolina.
1931	Won 3, Lost 1.	Eliminated in finals by Maryland.
1930	Won 2, Lost 1.	Eliminated in semifinals by Duke.
1929	Won 1, Lost 1.	Eliminated in second game by Georgia.
1928	Won 2, Lost 1.	Eliminated in semifinals by Mississippi.
1926	Won 2, Lost 1.	Eliminated in semifinals by Miss. A&M.
1925	Won 1, Lost 1.	Eliminated in second game by Georgia.

*Kentucky joined Southeastern Conference in 1933.

NCAA Tournament

(39 Appearances—7 Championships)

1998	NATIONAL CHAMPIONS	
	W6, L0.	Defeated Utah for title.
1997	W5, L1.	Eliminated by Arizona in championship game.
1996	NATIONAL CHAMPIONS	
	W6, L0.	Defeated Syracuse for title.
1995	W3, L1.	Eliminated by North Carolina in Southeast Regional Finals.
1994	W1, L1.	Lost to Marquette in Southeast Regional Second Round.
1993	W4, L1.	Eliminated by Michigan in Final Four.
1992	W3, L1.	Eliminated by Duke in East Regional Finals.
1987	W0, L1.	Eliminated by Ohio State in Southeast Regional First Round
1986	W3, L1.	Eliminated by LSU in Southeast Regional Finals.
1985	W2, L1.	Eliminated by St. John's in West Regional Semifinals.
1984	W3, L1.	Lost to Gerogetown in semifinal game.
1983	W2, L1.	Eliminated by Louisville in Mideast Regional Finals.
1982	W0, L1.	Eliminated by Middle Tennessee in Mideast First Round.
1981	W0, L1.	Eliminated by Alabama-Birmingham in Mideast First Round.
1980	W1, L1.	Eliminated by Duke in Mideast Regional Semifinals.
1978	NATIONAL CHAMPIONS	
	W5, L0.	Defeated Duke for title.
1977	W2, L1.	Eliminated by North Carolina in East Regional Finals.
1975	W4, L1.	Lost to UCLA in Championship Game.
1973	W1, L1.	Eliminated by Indiana in Mideast Regional Finals.
1972	W1, L1.	Eliminated by Florida State in Mideast Regional Finals.
1971	W0, L2.	Eliminated by Western Kentucky in Mideast Regional first game.
1970	W1, L1.	Eliminated by Jacksonville in Mideast Regional Finals.
1969	W1, L1.	Eliminated by Marquette in Mideast Regional first game.
1968	W1, L1.	Eliminated by Ohio State in Mideast Regional Finals.
1966	W3, L1.	Lost to Texas Western in championship game.
1964	W0, L2.	Eliminated by Ohio University in Mideast Regional first game.
1962	W1, L1.	Eliminated by Ohio State in Mideast Regional Finals.
1961	W1, L1.	Eliminated by Ohio State in Mideast Regional Finals.
1959	W1, L1.	Eliminated by Louisville in Mideast Regional first round.
1958	NATIONAL CHAMPIONS	
	W4, L0.	Defeated Seattle for title.
1957	W1, L1.	Eliminated by Michigan State in Midwest Regional Finals.
1956	W1, L1.	Eliminated by Iowa in Eastern Regional Finals.
1955	W1, L1.	Eliminated by Marquette in Eastern Regional first round.
1954	Withdrew after winning automatic berth as SEC champion.	
1952	W1, L1.	Eliminated by St. John's in Eastern Regional Finals.
1951	NATIONAL CHAMPIONS	
	W4, L0.	Defeated Kansas State for title.
1949	NATIONAL CHAMPIONS	
	W3, L0.	Defeated Oklahoma A&M for title.
1948	NATIONAL CHAMPIONS	
	W3, L0.	Defeated Baylor for title.
1945	W1, L1.	Eliminated by Ohio State in first round.
1942	W1, L1.	Eliminated by Dartmouth in second game.

Kentucky's All-Time Record

(Losses in boldface; * indicates overtime)

1903—Won 1, Lost 2

Coach: Unnamed
Starters: (J. White Guyn & R.H. Arnett, G; Joe Coons, C; H.J. Wurtele & Lee Andrews, F)

Feb. 6	**Georgetown**	**H**	**6**	**15**
Feb. 18	Lexington YMCA	H	11	10
Feb. 20	**Kentucky U.**	**H**	**2**	**42**
			19	67

1904—Won 1, Lost 4

Coach: Leander E. Andrus, Mgr.
Captain: St. John (Guyn, Arnett, St. John, Wurtele, Coons)

Feb. 4	**Georgetown**	**A**	**11**	**26**
Feb. 11	**Kentucky U.†**	**A**	**5**	**12**
Feb. 13	**Georgetown**	**H**	**10**	**22**
Feb. 26	**Kentucky U.**	**A**	**12**	**14**
Mar. 4	Cincinnati	H	25	21
			63	95

† Kentucky University (Transylvania and Georgetown game at UK was called off because of failure to agree on a referee. State College (University of Kentucky) team was present and agreed to play. The offer was accepted and KU won 12-5.

1905—Won 1, Lost 4

Coach:
Captain: J.M. Coons

Jan. 13	**Georgetown**	**H**	**9**	**14**
Jan. 21	Cincinnati YMCA	H	22	43
Jan. 27	Kentucky U.	H	30	29
Feb. 4	**Kentucky U.**	**H**	**1**	**22**
Feb. 22	**Kentucky U.**	**H**	**23**	**33**
			85	141

1906—Won 5, Lost 9

Coach: W.B. Wendt (Mgr.)
Captain: D.P. Branson (Baer, Donan, Barbee, Wilson, Herman)

Jan. 11	Lexington YMCA¹	H		
Jan. 12	**Miami (Ohio)**	**H**	**10**	**15**
Jan. 19	Central U.	H	15	14
Jan. 20	**Georgetown**	**A**	**9**	**34**
Jan. 26	Central U.	A	17	15
Jan. 27	**Cincinnati**	**H**	**16**	**29**
Feb. 3	**Christ Church, Cin.**	**H**	**24**	**38**
Feb. 9	**Georgetown**	**H**	**22**	**28**
Feb. 12	**New Albany YMCA**	**A**	**12**	**29**
Feb. 13	Vernon College	A	34	1
Feb. 14	Moores Hill	A	32	11
Feb. 15	**Christ Church, Cin.**	**A**	**17**	**54**
Feb. 16	**Cincinnati YMCA**	**A**	**9**	**38**
Feb. 17	**Miami (Ohio)**	**A**	**19**	**29**
			236	348

¹W.B. Wendt on Jan. 9, 1969, verified that State College opened the 1906 season against Kentucky U. in the YMCA. Athletic committees of the two schools had cancelled all games after a fight at a football game in November 1905. Wendt and the Kentucky U. manager agreed to play at the YMCA and list the State College foe as YMCA instead of Kentucky U. State College won but Mr. Wendt didn't remember the score, which he hadn't listed.

1907—Won 3, Lost 6

Coach: A.M. Kirby (Mgr.)
Captain: J.M. Wilson (Shanklin, Baer, Bryant, Barbee)

Jan. 16	**Lexington YMCA**	**H**	**17**	**25**
Jan. 19	Georgetown	H	16	15
Jan. 25	Central U.	H	22	9
Feb. 12	**Central U.**	**A**	**23**	***25**
Feb. 15	Kentucky U.	H	16	14
Feb. 21	**Georgetown**	**A**	**8**	**19**
Mar. 1	**Lexington YMCA**	**A**	**22**	**41**
Mar. 7	**Kentucky U.**	**A**	**5**	**19**
Mar. 9	**Central U.**	**H**	**13**	**15**
			142	182

1907/08—Won 5, Lost 6

Coach: J.S. Chambers (Mgr.)
Captain: Richard Barbee

Jan. 10	**Lexington YMCA**	**A**	**19**	**29**
Jan. 21	Kentucky U.	H	20	15
Jan. 25	**Central U.**	**A**	**21**	**32**
Feb. 4	Kentucky U.	A	20	15
Feb. 8	Louisville Coliseum	H	29	28
Feb. 10	**Georgetown**	**A**	**22**	**30**
Feb. 13	Central U.	H	31	20
Feb. 15	**Lexington YMCA**	**H**	**19**	**23**
Feb. 22	**Louisville Coliseum**	**A**	**18**	**30**
Mar. 3	Georgetown	H	18	13
Mar. 7	**Central U.**	**A**	**10**	**29**
			227	264

1908/09—Won 5, Lost 4

Mgr.: J.S. Chambers
Captain: W.C. Fox

Jan. 9	Lexington High	H	29	9
Jan. 18	**Advent Mem. Club**	**A**	**27**	**41**
Jan. 19	**Cincinnati**	**A**	**25**	**41**
Jan. 27	Central U.	H	24	23
Feb. 6	**Central U.**	**A**	**20**	**35**
Feb. 8	Georgetown	H	43	32
Feb. 15	Cincinnati	A	48	19
Feb. 18	Cincinnati	H	28	23
Feb. 26	**Central U.**	**H**	**20**	**26**
			264	249

1909/10—Won 4, Lost 8

Coach: R.E. Spahr and E.R. Sweetland
Captain: Bill Rodes

Jan. 8	Ky. Wesleyan	A	14	*12
Jan. 22	Georgetown	H	31	11
Jan. 24	**DePauw**	**H**	**11**	**24**
Jan. 28	**Central**	**A**	**17**	**87**
Feb. 4	**Georgetown**	**A**	**16**	**34**
Feb. 7	**Cincinnati**	**A**	**17**	**47**
Feb. 9	**DePauw**	**A**	**16**	**28**
Feb. 10	**Rose Poly Technic**	**A**	**11**	**52**
Feb. 16	Tennessee	H	26	5
Mar. 5	**Central U.**	**H**	**13**	**31**
Mar. 8	Georgetown	H	24	23
Mar. 11	**Central**	**A**	**9**	**51**
			205	405

1910/11—Won 5, Lost 6

Coach: H.J. Iddings
Captain: J.H. Gaiser

Jan. 13	Lexington High	H	29	36
Jan. 20	**Transylvania**	**H**	**18**	**23**
Jan. 27	**Ky. Wesleyan**	**A**	**19**	**25**
Feb. 4	Bethany	H	24	11
Feb. 9	**Ohio Wesleyan**	**A**	**19**	**37**
Feb. 10	**Otterbein**	**A**	**27**	**41**
Feb. 11	**Christ Church, Cin.**	**A**	**21**	**32**
Feb. 17	Georgetown	A	47	22
Feb. 23	Butler	H	21	16
Feb. 27	Transylvania	A	22	19
Mar. 3	Transylvania	H	30	24
			277	286

1911/12—Won 9, Lost 0

Coach: E.R. Sweetland
Captain: W.C. Harrison

Jan. 5	Georgetown	H	38	9
Jan. 12	Central U.	A	32	13
Jan. 19	Miami (Ohio) U.	H	31	14
Jan. 27	Lexington YMCA	H	32	20
Feb. 1	Central U.	H	52	10
Feb. 7	Tennessee	H	27	15
Feb. 22	Vanderbilt	H	28	17
Feb. 23	Vanderbilt	H	22	18
Mar. 1	Georgetown	A	19	18
			281	134

Southern Champions —Leading Scorers—

Brinkley Barnett (Jr. F)	7.1
D.W. Hart (Jr. F)	5.4
W.C. Harrison (Sr. C)	4.0
Jake Gaiser (Sr. F)	3.9
R.C. Preston (So. G)	2.7
H.L. Farmer (Jr. F)	2.2

1912/13—Won 5, Lost 3

Coach: J.J. Tigert
Captain: B. Barnett

Jan. 24	Lexington YMCA	H	25	27
Feb. 8	Cincinnati	H	20	18
Feb. 13	Marietta	H	42	16
Feb. 15	Louisville	H	34	10
Feb. 19	**Vanderbilt**	**H**	**17**	**24**
Feb. 20	Vanderbilt	H	42	29
Feb. 27	Miami (Ohio) U.	H	24	16
Mar. 1	**Christ Church, Cin.**	**H**	**19**	**30**
			223	170

—Leading Scorers—

R.C. Preston (Jr. C)	9.1
Binkley Barnett (Sr. F)	8.4
Ralph Morgan (So. F)	4.0
H.L. Farmer (Sr. F)	3.9
William Tuttle (So. F)	1.0

Kentucky's All-Time Record 249

1913/14—Won 12, Lost 2

Coach: Alpha Brumage
Captain: William Tuttle

Jan. 10	Ashland YMCA	H	28	15
Jan. 17	Louisville YMCA	H	30	21
Jan. 20	Ashland YMCA	A	30	19
Jan. 21	Marshall	A	46	6
Jan. 22	**Virginia U**	**A**	**23**	**39**
Jan. 24	**Va. Military Inst.**	**A**	**18**	**32**
Jan. 31	Louisville YMHA	H	59	12
Feb. 7	Louisville	H	22	17
Feb. 11	Tennessee	H	21	14
Feb. 12	Tennessee	H	20	18
Feb. 21	Cincinnati	H	20	18
Feb. 23	Chattanooga	H	40	7
Feb. 28	Marietta	H	19	17
Mar. 3	Louisville	A	26	13
			402	248

—Leading Scorers—

R.C. Preston (Sr. F) 6.1
Tom Zerfoss[1] (Sr. F) 6.0
Karl Zerfoss (So. G) 4.7
William Tuttle (Jr. F) 3.9
Herschel Scott (Jr. G) 3.2

[1] Only played in first six games.

1914/15—Won 7, Lost 5

Coach: Alpha Brumage
Captain: Ralph Morgan

Jan. 16	Maryville	H	37	17
Jan. 23	Louisville	H	18	14
Jan. 30	St. Andrews	H	32	15
Feb. 4	Maryville	A	23	22
Feb. 5	**Tennessee**	**A**	**21**	**36**
Feb. 6	**Tennessee**	**A**	**22**	**27**
Feb. 12	**Vanderbilt**	**H**	**34**	**39**
Feb. 13	Vanderbilt	H	36	24
Feb. 17	Tennessee	H	22	13
Feb. 18	Tennessee	H	20	18
Feb. 26	**St. Andrews**	**A**	**25**	**50**
Feb. 27	**Louisville**	**A**	**15**	**26**
			305	301

—Leading Scorers—

Ralph Morgan (Sr. F) 8.3
Jim Server (Jr. C) 5.3
William Tuttle (Sr. F) 3.8
Karl Zerfoss (Jr. F) 3.7
Herschel Scott (Sr. G) 2.9

1915/16—Won 8, Lost 6

Coach: James Park
Captain: K.P. Zerfoss

Jan. 14	Cincinnati	A	39	24
Jan. 18	Georgetown	A	29	22
Jan. 31	Georgetown	H	30	22
Feb. 4	**Vanderbilt**	**H**	**25**	**39**
Feb. 5	**Vanderbilt**	**H**	**20**	**23**
Feb. 12	**Louisville**	**H**	**22**	**28**
Feb. 15	Centre	A	38	5
Feb. 19	Cincinnati	H	34	10
Feb. 22	Louisville	A	32	24
Feb. 23	**Tennessee**	**H**	**17**	**28**
Feb. 26	Maryville	H	36	25
Feb. 29	Centre	H	38	14
Mar. 3	**Marietta**	**H**	**22**	**27**
Mar. 4	**Marietta**	**H**	**23**	**27**
			405	318

—Leading Scorers—

Derrill Hart (Sr. F) 13.3
Jim Server (Sr. C) 5.7
Robert Ireland (Jr. F) 5.6
Karl Zerfoss (Sr. F) 3.3
George Gumbert (Sr. G) 2.4

1916/17—Won 4, Lost 6

Coach: W.P. Tuttle
Captain: Robert Y. Ireland

Jan. 17	Centre	H	31	21
Jan. 27	Georgetown	A	19	22
Jan. 30	Rose Poly Technic	H	33	12
Feb. 9	**Tennessee**	**H**	**20**	**23**
Feb. 10	**Tennessee**	**H**	**19**	**22**
Feb. 16	**Centre**	**A**	**24**	**28**
Feb. 21	Georgetown	H	32	18
Mar. 1	Cumberland	A	48	20
Mar. 2	**Tennessee**	**A**	**26**	**27**
Mar. 3	**Tennessee**	**A**	**10**	**30**
			262	223

—Leading Scorers—

C.C. Shrader (Sr. F) 7.1
Robert Ireland (Sr. F) 5.4
"Dutch" Longworth (Sr. C-F) 4.4
Pat Campbell (Jr. F) 4.2
William Rodes (Sr. G) 1.3

1917/18—Won 9, Lost 2, Tie 1

Coach: S.A. Boles
Captain: Patrick Campbell

Jan. 9	Ky. Wesleyan	H	23	13
Jan. 17	**Centre**	**A**	**21**	**29**
Jan. 24	Georgetown	H	22	18
Feb. 7	Tennessee	H	33	26
Feb. 8	Tennessee	H	40	12
Feb. 9	Ky. Wesleyan[1]	A	21	21
Feb. 14	Georgetown	A	25	16
Feb. 21	Centre	H	22	***20
Feb. 28	Cumberland	A	42	21
Mar. 1	Tennessee	A	29	18
Mar. 2	Tennessee	A	32	20
Postseason Game (For State Championship)				
Mar. 9	Centre	N-Lou.	12	24
			322	238

—Leading Scorers—

H.C. Thomas (Jr. C-F) 10.8
Arthur Bastin (Jr. G) 4.0
A.P. Shanklin (Sr. F) 3.5
Pat Campbell (Sr. F) 3.2
Goerge Zerfoss (Jr. F) 2.8

[1] This unique tie game resulted from scorer's error which was not discovered until after the teams' departures. The contest was rescheduled, but never played for unknown reasons.

1918/19—Won 6, Lost 8

Coach: Andrew Gill
Captain: J.A. Dishman

Jan. 13	Ky. Wesleyan	H	46	5
Jan. 18	**Georgetown**	**H**	**30**	**32**
Jan. 25	**Centre**	**A**	**30**	**38**
Jan. 31	**Cincinnati**	**A**	**18**	**28**
Feb. 6	Chattanooga	A	28	25
Feb. 7	**Tennessee**	**A**	**22**	**40**
Feb. 8	Cumberland	A	22	21
Feb. 14	**Vanderbilt**	**H**	**26**	**36**
Feb. 15	**Georgetown**	**A**	**18**	**22**
Feb. 21	Cincinnati	H	34	21
Feb. 22	Ky. Wesleyan	H	18	13
Feb. 24	**Centre**	**H**	**10**	**21**
Feb. 28	Tennessee	H	30	14
Mar. 8	**Miami (Ohio) U.**	**H**	**14**	**38**
			346	354

—Leading Scorers—

H.C. Thomas (Sr. F) 7.1
J.C. Everett (Jr. F) 6.6
Bob Lavin (Fr. G) 5.0
Tony Dishman (Sr. G) 3.3
Ed Parker (Sr. F) 3.3

1919/20—Won 5, Lost 7

Coach: George C. Buchheit
Captain: J.C. Everett

Jan. 17	**Cincinnati**	**A**	**11**	**13**
Jan. 22	Maryville	H	27	13
Jan. 31	Georgetown	H	25	14
Feb. 5	**Tennessee**	**H**	**24**	**29**
Feb. 7	**Tennessee**	**H**	**26**	**27**
Feb. 14	**Centre**	**A**	**15**	**44**
Feb. 17	Georgetown	A	28	16
Feb. 21	Ky. Wesleyan	H	43	13
Feb. 26	**Cumberland**	**A**	**21**	**30**
Feb. 27	**Centre**	**A**	**25**	**28**
Feb. 28	Tennessee	A	34	26
Mar. 6	**Centre**	**A**	**18**	***20**
			297	273

—Leading Scorers—

Basil Hayden (So. F) 10.8
William Blakely (Sr. G) 7.0
J.C. Everett (Sr. C) 5.5
Bob Lavin (So. F) 4.1
Jim Wilhelm (Jr. F) 3.6

1920/21—Won 13, Lost 1

Coach: George C. Buchheit
Captain: Basil Hayden

Jan. 12	Ky. Wesleyan	H	38	13
Jan. 15	Cumberland	H	37	21
Jan. 18	Georgetown	H	38	23
Jan. 21	Chattanooga	H	42	10
Jan. 26	Cincinnati	A	26	19
Jan. 29	Auburn	A	40	25
Feb. 8	**Centre**	**A**	**27**	**29**
Feb. 15	Georgetown	A	56	11
Feb. 18	Centre	H	20	13
Feb. 22	Vanderbilt	H	37	18
SIAA Tournament (Atlanta, Ga.)				
Feb. 25	Tulane		50	28
Feb. 26	Mercer		49	25
Feb. 28	Mississippi A & M		28	13
Mar. 1	Georgia (finals)		20	19
			508	267

—Leading Scorers—

William King (Fr. F) 11.4
Basil Hayden (Jr. F) 9.6
Paul Adkins (Jr. C) 6.5
Bob Lavin (Jr. G) 2.5
Fred Fest (So. C) 1.3

1921/22—Won 10, Lost 6

Coach: George C. Buchheit
Captain: R.E. Lavin

Jan. 14	**Georgetown**	**H**	**17**	**26**
Jan. 17	Louisville	A	38	14
Jan. 18	**Vanderbilt**	**A**	**12**	**22**
Jan. 21	Louisville	H	29	22
Jan. 26	Mississippi A & M	H	28	21
Jan. 27	Marshall	H	34	12
Feb. 4	Centre	A	28	21
Feb. 6	Georgetown	A	26	17
Feb. 8	Washington & Lee	A	21	20
Feb. 9	**Va. Military Inst.**	**A**	**32**	**37**
Feb. 11	**Georgetown U.**	**A**	**23**	**28**
Feb. 13	**Virginia**	**A**	**30**	***32**
Feb. 16	Clemson	H	38	14
Feb. 20	Centre	H	40	23
SIAA Tournament (Atlanta, Ga.)				
Feb. 24	Georgetown		41	21
Feb. 25	**Mercer**		**22**	**35**
			459	365

—Leading Scorers—

Paul Adkins (Sr. C) 8.8
William King (So. F) 8.3
Bob Lavin (Sr. F) 5.2
Basil Hayden (Sr. F) 5.0
William Poynz (Jr. F) 2.9

1922/23—Won 3, Lost 10

Coach: George C. Buchheit
Captain: Fred Fest

Jan. 13	Georgetown	A	24	13
Jan. 20	**Tennessee**	**A**	**26**	**30**
Jan. 22	Chattanooga	H	25	18
Jan. 25	**Alabama**	**H**	**35**	**45**
Jan. 27	**Centre**	**H**	**14**	**21**
Feb. 3	**Georgia**	**H**	**19**	**23**
Feb. 5	**Cincinnati**	**A**	**24**	**33**
Feb. 7	**Centenary**	**H**	**21**	**29**
Feb. 10	**Tennessee**	**H**	**23**	**28**
Feb. 14	**Centre**	**A**	**10**	**17**
Feb. 15	**Clemson**	**H**	**13**	**30**
Feb. 19	**Georgetown**	**H**	**21**	**48**
Feb. 23	Sewanee	H	30	14
			285	349

—Leading Scorers—
Carl Riefkin (Jr. F) 10.2
Fred Fest (Sr. C) 7.2
William Poynz (Sr. G) 3.3
Gilbert Smith (Sr. G) 1.5
W.G. Wilkinson (Sr. F) 1.2

1923/24—Won 13, Lost 3

Coach: G.C. Buchheit
Captain: A.T. Rice

Jan. 1	Vanderbilt	H	33	13
Jan. 8	Mexico YMCA	H	25	14
Jan. 12	Georgetown	A	32	24
Jan. 14	**Mississippi A & M**	**H**	**16**	**17**
Jan. 15	Sewanee	H	50	15
Jan. 18	**Tennessee**	**A**	**13**	**20**
Jan. 19	Chattanooga	A	24	23
Feb. 4	West Virginia	H	24	21
Feb. 9	Centre	A	27	18
Feb. 11	Georgetown	H	39	35
Feb. 13	Clemson	H	38	13
Feb. 14	Virginia	H	29	16
Feb. 19	Virginia Tech	H	36	14
Feb. 21	Centre	H	38	24
Feb. 23	Georgia Tech	H	33	27

SIAA Tournament (Atlanta, Ga.)

Feb. 29	**North Carolina**		**20**	**41**
			477	335

—Leading Scorers—
Jim McFarland (So. F) 9.9
Will Milward (Jr. C) 5.3
Lowell Underwood (So. C) 4.9
Carl Riefkin (Sr. F) 4.3
Bill King (Sr. F) 2.9

ALUMNI GYM ERA (1924-50)

1924/25—Won 13, Lost 8

Coach: C.O. Applegran
Captain: James McFarland

Dec. 13	Cincinnati	H	28	23
Dec. 18	**Indiana**	**H**	**18**	**20**
Dec. 20	**Michigan**	**H**	**11**	**21**
Jan. 3	**Cincinnati**	**A**	**20**	**24**
Jan. 5	**Illinois**	**A**	**26**	**36**
Jan. 6	**Wabash**	**A**	**10**	**57**
Jan. 9	Mississippi	H	26	23
Jan. 10	Georgetown	H	25	17
Jan. 17	Centre	A	33	26
Jan. 30	Washington & Lee	H	28	22
Feb. 2	West Virginia	H	29	19
Feb. 5	**Alabama**	**A**	**15**	**24**
Feb. 6	Georgia Tech	A	18	16
Feb. 7	**Georgia**	**A**	**24**	**28**
Feb. 9	Tennessee	A	35	22
Feb. 12	Tulane	H	29	22
Feb. 14	Georgetown	A	36	21
Feb. 18	Tennessee	H	26	21
Feb. 21	Centre	H	39	10

Southern Conference Tournament (Atlanta, Ga.)

Feb. 27	Mississippi A & M	31	26
Feb. 28	**Georgia**	**31**	**32**
		538	510

—Leading Scorers—
Jim McFarland (Jr. F) 7.1
Lowell Underwood (Jr. F) 6.3
Will Milward (Sr. C) 6.2
Foster Helm (So. F) 3.7
Charles Alberts (Jr. G) 2.5

1925/26—Won 15, Lost 3

Coach: Ray Eklund
Captain: Burgess Carey

Dec. 19	**DePauw**	**H**	**29**	**38**
Jan. 5	**Indiana**	**A**	**23**	**34**
Jan. 9	Berea	H	37	23
Jan. 12	Georgetown	A	36	21
Jan. 16	Georgia Tech	H	25	24
Jan. 21	Centre	H	45	25
Jan. 30	Georgetown	H	25	20
Feb. 1	Alabama	H	27	16
Feb. 4	Centre	A	46	19
Feb. 5	Washington & Lee	H	44	34
Feb. 8	Auburn	H	35	26
Feb. 12	Tennessee	A	51	17
Feb. 15	Georgia	A	22	18
Feb. 18	Tennessee	H	27	21
Feb. 20	Vanderbilt	H	30	20

Southern Conference Tournament (Atlanta, Ga.)

Feb. 26	Va. Military Inst.		32	25
Feb. 27	Georgia		39	34
Mar. 1	**Mississippi A & M**		**26**	**31**
			599	446

—Leading Scorers—
Gayle Mohney (Jr. G) 11.1
Paul Jenkins (So. F) 7.3
Jim McFarland (Sr. F) 5.6
Lowell Underwood (Sr. C) 3.7
Henry Besuden (Sr. C) 2.1

1926/27—Won 3, Lost 13

Coach: Basil Hayden
Captain: Paul Jenkins

Dec. 18	**Cincinnati**	**H**	**10**	**48**
Dec. 21	**Indiana**	**H**	**19**	**38**
Dec. 27	**Cincinnati**	**A**	**22**	**51**
Dec. 31	**Princeton**	**H**	**26**	**30**
Jan. 3	Florida	H	44	36
Jan. 10	**Ky. Wesleyan**	**A**	**24**	**31**
Jan. 15	**Vanderbilt**	**H**	**32**	**48**
Jan. 21	**Tennessee**	**A**	**14**	**19**
Jan. 22	**Georgia Tech**	**A**	**16**	**48**
Jan. 29	Centre	H	27	25
Feb. 1	**Georgetown**	**A**	**19**	**26**
Feb. 4	**Washington & Lee**	**H**	**34**	**36**
Feb. 7	**West Virginia**	**H**	**26**	**44**
Feb. 11	**Mississippi**	**H**	**17**	**37**
Feb. 12	Centre	A	22	16
Feb. 19	**Tennessee**	**H**	**21**	**30**
			373	563

—Leading Scorers—
Paul Jenkins (Jr. F) 6.1
Edwin Knadler (Sr. F) 4.4
Karl Ropke (Sr. F-C) 4.2
Frank Phipps (Jr. F) 3.4
Foster Helm (Sr. C) 2.5

1927/28—Won 12, Lost 6

Coach: John Mauer
Captain: Paul Jenkins

Dec. 16	Clemson	H	33	17
Dec. 20	**Miami (Ohio) U.**	**H**	**31**	**36**
Jan. 4	Berea	H	37	16
Jan. 9	Centre	A	36	25
Jan. 14	Vanderbilt	H	43	23
Jan. 16	Virginia	A	31	28
Jan. 18	**Naval Academy**	**A**	**26**	**32**
Jan. 19	**Maryland**	**A**	**7**	**37**
Jan. 28	Tennessee	H	48	18
Feb. 3	Washington & Lee	H	34	28
Feb. 4	**Indiana**	**A**	**29**	**48**
Feb. 8	Vanderbilt	A	54	29
Feb. 9	Tennessee	A	43	16
Feb. 11	**Georgia Tech**	**H**	**31**	**35**
Feb. 18	Centre	H	30	20

Southern Conference Tournament (Atlanta, Ga.)

Feb 24	South Carolina		56	40
Feb. 25	Georgia		33	16
Feb. 27	**Mississippi**		**28**	**41**
			630	505

—Leading Scorers—
Irvine Jeffries (Sr. G) 11.5
Cecil Combs (So. F) 10.3
Paul McBrayer (So. G-C) 5.5
Hays Owens (So. F) 3.8
Paul Jenkins (Sr. F) 3.3

1928/29—Won 12, Lost 5

Coach: John Mauer
Captain: Lawrence McGinnis

Dec. 15	Eastern Normal	H	35	10
Dec. 21	Miami (Ohio) U.	H	43	***42
Jan. 4	**North Carolina**	**H**	**15**	**25**
Jan. 12	Notre Dame	A	19	16
Jan. 16	**Georgia Tech**	**A**	**19**	**33**
Jan. 17	Tennessee	A	35	29
Jan. 19	Tennessee	H	27	22
Jan. 26	**Alabama**	**H**	**26**	**27**
Feb. 1	Mississippi A & M	A	25	*23
Feb. 2	Mississippi A & M	A	32	14
Feb. 3	**Tulane**	**A**	**22**	**34**
Feb. 8	Washington & Lee	H	31	30
Feb. 13	Centre	H	47	11
Feb. 22	Mississippi	H	35	30
Feb. 23	Mississippi	H	32	24

Southern Conference Tournament (Atlanta, Ga.)

Mar. 1	Tulane		29	15
Mar. 2	**Georgia**		**24**	**26**
			496	411

—Leading Scorers—
Stan Milward (So. C) 6.8
Louis McGinnis (So. F) 5.8
Cecil Combs (Jr. G) 5.8
Carey Spicer (So. F) 5.7
Paul McBrayer (Jr. G) 2.9

1929/30—Won 16, Lost 3

Coach: John Mauer
Captain: Paul McBrayer

Dec. 14	Georgetown	H	46	9
Dec. 20	Miami (Ohio) U.	H	35	20
Dec. 31	Berea	H	29	26
Jan. 3	Clemson	H	31	15
Jan. 10	**Creighton**	**H**	**27**	**28**
Jan. 11	Creighton	H	25	21
Jan. 18	Tennessee	H	23	20
Jan. 24	Mississippi A & M	H	38	17
Jan. 25	Mississippi A & M	H	20	14
Jan. 31	**Tennessee**	**A**	**24**	***29**
Feb. 1	Georgia	A	22	*21
Feb. 3	Clemson	A	34	20
Feb. 8	Georgia Tech	H	39	19
Feb. 14	Georgia	H	36	23
Feb. 18	Ky. Wesleyan	H	32	20
Feb. 22	Washington & Lee	H	28	*26

Southern Conference Tournament (Atlanta, Ga.)

Feb. 28	Maryland	26	21

Mar. 1	Sewanee		44	22
Mar. 3	**Duke**		**32**	**37**
			591	408

—Leading Scorers—

Cecil Combs (Sr. F) 6.6
Carey Spicer (Jr. F) 6.5
Stan Milward (Sr. C) 5.9
Louis McGinnis (So. F) 5.4
Paul McBrayer (Sr. G) 4.8

ADOLPH RUPP ERA

1930/31—Won 15, Lost 3

Coach: Adolph Rupp
Captain: Carey Spicer

Dec. 18	Georgetown	H	67	19
Dec. 27	Marshall	H	42	26
Dec. 31	Berea	H	41	25
Jan. 3	Clemson	H	33	21
Jan. 10	Tennessee	H	31	23
Jan. 16	Chattanooga	H	55	18
Jan. 21	Vanderbilt	A	42	37
Jan. 31	Tennessee	A	36	*32
Feb. 6	Washington & Lee	H	23	18
Feb. 9	Georgia Tech	H	38	34
Feb. 13	**Georgia**	**A**	**16**	**25**
Feb. 14	**Clemson**	**A**	**26**	**29**
Feb. 16	Georgia Tech	A	35	16
Feb. 20	Vanderbilt	H	43	23

Southern Conference Tournament
(Atlanta, Ga.)

Feb. 27	North Carolina State		33	28
Feb. 28	Duke		35	30
Mar. 2	Florida		56	36
Mar. 3	**Maryland (finals)**		**27**	**29**
			679	469

—Leading Scorers—

Carey Spicer (Sr. F) 10.6
Louis McGinnis (Sr. F) 9.6
George Yates (Jr. C) 7.0
Aggie Sale (So. C-F) 5.6
Jake Bronston (Jr. G) 3.9

1931/32—Won 15, Lost 2

Coach: Adolph Rupp
Captain: Ellis Johnson

Dec. 15	Georgetown	H	66	24
Dec. 18	Carnegie Tech	H	36	34
Dec. 23	Berea	H	52	27
Dec. 30	Marshall	H	46	16
Jan. 2	Clemson	H	43	24
Jan. 14	Clemson	A	30	17
Jan. 15	Sewanee	A	30	20
Jan. 16	Tennessee	A	29	28
Jan. 21	Chattanooga	H	51	17
Jan. 30	Washington & Lee	H	48	28
Feb. 3	Vanderbilt	A	61	37
Feb. 6	Duke	H	37	30
Feb. 8	Alabama	H	50	22
Feb. 13	Tennessee	H	41	27
Feb. 20	**Vanderbilt**	**H**	**31**	**32**

Southern Conference Tournament
(Atlanta, Ga.)

Feb. 26	Tulane		50	30
Feb. 27	**North Carolina**		**42**	**43**
			743	456

—Leading Scorers—

Aggie Sale (Jr. F) 13.6
John "Frenchy" DeMoisey (So. C-F) 10.0
Darrell Darby (Jr. F) 8.4
Howard Kreuter (Jr. F) 3.9
Ellis Johnson (Jr. G) 3.6

1932/33—Won 21, Lost 3
SEC Champions (Tournament)

Coach: Adolph Rupp
Captain: Forest Sale

Dec. 9	Alumni	H	52	17
Dec. 12	Georgetown	H	62	21
Dec. 17	Marshall	N1	57	23
Dec. 20	Tulane	H	53	17
Dec. 21	Tulane	H	42	11
Dec. 30	Chicago	A	58	26
Jan. 2	**Ohio State**	**H**	**30**	**46**
Jan. 6	Creighton	A	32	26
Jan. 7	**Creighton**	**A**	**22**	**34**
Jan. 10	South Carolina	H	44	36
Jan. 14	Tennessee	A	42	21
Jan. 16	Clemson	H	67	18
Jan. 28	Tennessee	H	44	23
Jan. 31	Vanderbilt	A	40	29
Feb. 1	Clemson	A	42	32
Feb. 2	**South Carolina**	**A**	**38**	**44**
Feb. 6	Mexico U.	H	81	22
Feb. 11	Georgia Tech	H	45	22
Feb. 13	Alabama	N2	35	21
Feb. 18	Vanderbilt	H	45	28

SEC Tournament (Atlanta, Ga.)

Feb. 24	Mississippi		49	31
Feb. 25	Florida		48	24
Feb. 27	LSU		51	38
Feb. 28	Mississippi State (finals)		46	27
			1125	637

(N1) Ashland, Ky.
(N2) Birmingham, Ala.

—Leading Scorers—

Aggie Sale (Sr. C-F) 13.8
John "Frenchy" DeMoisey (Jr. C-F) 12.0
Bill Davis (Jr. G) 7.0
Darrell Darby (Sr. F) 4.0
Ellis Johnson (Sr. G) 3.8

1933/34—Won 16, Lost 1

Coach: Adolph Rupp
Captain: John DeMoisey

Dec. 5	Alumni	H	53	20
Dec. 9	Georgetown	H	41	12
Dec. 14	Marshall	H	48	26
Dec. 16	Cincinnati	H	31	25
Dec. 21	Tulane	A	32	22
Dec. 22	Tulane	A	42	29
Jan. 12	Sewanee	A	55	16
Jan. 13	Tennessee	A	44	23
Jan. 20	Chattanooga	H	47	20
Jan. 27	Tennessee	H	53	26
Feb. 1	Alabama	N1	33	28
Feb. 3	Vanderbilt	A	48	26
Feb. 8	Alabama	H	26	21
Feb. 10	Georgia Tech	H	49	25
Feb. 15	Sewanee	H	60	15
Feb. 17	Vanderbilt	H	47	27

SEC Tournament (Atlanta, Ga.)

Feb. 24	**Florida**		**32**	**38**
			741	399

(N1) Birmingham, Ala.

—Leading Scorers—

John "Frenchy" DeMoisey (Sr. C) 12.5
Bill Davis (Sr. G) 8.3
Dave Lawrence (Jr. F) 7.9
Garland Lewis (So. C) 4.9
Jack Tucker (Jr. F) 3.0

1934/35—Won 19, Lost 2
SEC Co-Champions

Coach: Adolph Rupp
Captain: Dave Lawrence and Jack Tucker

Dec. 10	Alumni	H	55	8
Dec. 13	Oglethorpe	H	81	12
Dec. 21	Tulane	A	38	9
Dec. 22	Tulane	A	52	12

Jan. 2	Chicago	H	42	16
Jan. 5	**New York U.**	**A**	**22**	**23**
Jan. 14	Chattanooga	H	66	19
Jan. 18	Tulane	H	63	22
Jan. 19	Tulane	H	55	12
Jan. 26	Tennessee	H	48	21
Feb. 1	Alabama	N1	33	26
Feb. 2	Vanderbilt	A	58	22
Feb. 5	Xavier	A	40	27
Feb. 9	Georgia Tech	H	57	30
Feb. 11	Alabama	H	25	16
Feb. 13	**Michigan State**	**A**	**26**	**32**
Feb. 16	Tennessee	A	38	36
Feb. 22	Creighton	H	63	42
Feb. 23	Creighton	H	24	13
Mar. 2	Vanderbilt	H	53	19
Mar. 7	Xavier	H	46	29
			985	446

(N1) Birmingham, Ala.

—Leading Scorers—

Leroy Edwards (So. C) 16.3
Dave Lawrence (Jr. F) 9.1
Garland Lewis (Jr. C-F) 5.8
Jack Tucker (Sr. F) 3.7
Warfield Donohue (So. G) 3.5

1935/36—Won 15, Lost 6

Coach: Adolph Rupp
Captain: Milerd Anderson

Dec. 6	Georgetown	H	42	17
Dec. 17	Berea	H	58	30
Dec. 23	Pittsburgh	H	35	17
Jan. 8	**New York U.**	**A**	**28**	**41**
Jan. 14	Xavier	A	36	32
Jan. 17	Tulane	H	49	24
Jan. 18	Tulane	H	39	21
Jan. 21	Michigan State	H	27	19
Jan. 25	Tennessee	H	40	31
Feb. 1	**Vanderbilt**	**A**	**24**	**33**
Feb. 3	Alabama	A	32	30
Feb. 7	Alabama	H	40	34
Feb. 10	**Notre Dame**	**A**	**20**	**41**
Feb. 11	Butler	A	39	28
Feb. 15	**Tennessee**	**A**	**28**	**39**
Feb. 18	Xavier	H	49	40
Feb. 21	Creighton	H	68	38
Feb. 22	**Creighton**	**H**	**29**	**31**
Feb. 24	Vanderbilt	H	61	41

SEC Tournament (Knoxville, Tenn.)

Feb. 28	Mississippi State		41	39
Feb. 29	**Tennessee**		**28**	**39**
			813	587

—Leading Scorers—

Ralph Carlisle (So. F) 11.5
Joe Hagan (So. F) 8.0
Garland Lewis (Sr. C) 7.5
Warfield Donohue (Jr. G) 3.0
J. Rice Walker (So. C-F) 2.4

1936/37—Won 17, Lost 5
SEC Champions (Tournament)

Coach: Adolph Rupp
Captain: Warfield Donohue

Dec. 9	Georgetown	H	46	21
Dec. 12	Berea	H	70	26
Dec. 15	Xavier	A	34	*28
Dec. 21	Centenary	H	37	19
Jan. 2	Michigan State	H	28	21
Jan. 5	**Notre Dame**	**N1**	**28**	**41**
Jan. 8	Creighton	H	59	36
Jan. 14	**Michigan State**	**A**	**23**	**24**
Jan. 16	Akron U.	N2	32	22
Jan. 23	Tennessee	H	43	26
Jan. 30	Vanderbilt	A	41	26
Feb. 1	Alabama	N3	38	27
Feb. 3	**Tulane**	**A**	**28**	**35**
Feb. 4	Tulane	A	28	25
Feb. 8	Mexico U.	H	58	30

(continued)

Date	Opponent	Site	UK	Opp
Feb. 10	Alabama	H	31	34
Feb. 13	Tennessee	A	24	26
Feb. 20	Vanderbilt	H	51	19
Feb. 22	Xavier	H	23	15
SEC Tournament (Knoxville, Tenn.)				
Feb. 26	Louisiana State		57	37
Feb. 27	Georgia Tech		40	30
Mar. 1	Tennessee (finals)		39	25
			858	593

(N1) Louisville, Ky.
(N2) Cincinnati. Ohio
(N3) Birmingham, Ala.

—Leading Scorers—
Ralph Carlisle (Jr. F) 9.9
Joe Hagan (Jr. F) 7.3
Homer Thompson (So. C) 4.9
Walter Hodge (Sr. G) 3.7
Bernie Opper (So. G) 3.5

1937/38—Won 13, Lost 5
Coach: Adolph Rupp
Captain: J. Rice Walker

Date	Opponent	Site	UK	Opp
Dec. 15	Berea	H	69	35
Dec. 18	Cincinnati	H	38	21
Dec. 22	Centenary	H	35	25
Sugar Bowl Tournament (New Orleans, La.)				
Dec. 29	Pittsburgh (finals)		40	29
Jan. 8	Michigan State	A	38	43
Jan. 10	Detroit	A	26	34
Jan. 15	Notre Dame	A	37	47
Jan. 22	Tennessee	H	52	27
Jan. 29	Vanderbilt	A	42	19
Jan. 31	Alabama	N1	57	31
Feb. 5	Xavier	A	32	39
Feb. 7	Michigan State	H	44	27
Feb. 12	Alabama	H	28	21
Feb. 14	Marquette	H	35	33
Feb. 17	Xavier	H	45	29
Feb. 21	Vanderbilt	H	48	24
Feb. 26	Tennessee	A	29	26
SEC Tournament (Baton Rouge, La.)				
Mar. 3	Tulane		36	38
			731	512

(N1) Birmingham, Ala.

—Leading Scorers—
Joe Hagan (Sr. F) 10.1
Fred Curtis (Jr. F) 6.3
Bernie Opper (Jr. G) 5.6
Homer Thompson (Jr. C) 4.9
Mickey Rouse (So. G) 4.4

1938/39—Won 16, Lost 4
SEC Champions (Tournament)
Coach: Adolph Rupp
Captain: Bernard Opper

Date	Opponent	Site	UK	Opp
Dec. 2	Georgetown	H	39	19
Dec. 10	Ky. Wesleyan	H	57	18
Dec. 17	Cincinnati	H	44	27
Dec. 21	Washington & Lee	H	67	47
Jan. 4	Long Island	A	34	52
Jan. 6	St. Joseph's	A	41	30
Jan. 14	Notre Dame	N1	37	42
Jan. 21	Tennessee	H	29	30
Jan. 28	Alabama	N2	38	41
Jan. 30	Vanderbilt	A	51	37
Feb. 4	Marquette	H	37	31
Feb. 8	Xavier	A	41	31
Feb. 11	Alabama	H	45	27
Feb. 13	Mississippi State	H	39	28
Feb. 18	Tennessee	A	36	**34
Feb. 21	Xavier	H	43	23
Feb. 25	Vanderbilt	H	52	27
SEC Tournament (Knoxville, Tenn.)				
Mar. 2	Mississippi		49	30
Mar. 3	Louisiana State		53	34
Mar. 4	Tennessee (finals)		46	38
			878	646

(N1) Louisville, Ky.
(N2) Birmingham, Ala.

—Leading Scorers—
Fred Curtis (Sr. F) 9.2
Homer Thompson (Sr. C) 6.7
Keith Farnsley (So. F) 6.4
Mickey Rouse (Jr. G) 5.4
Marion Cluggish (Jr. C) 5.3

1939/40—Won 15, Lost 6
SEC Champions (Tournament)
Sugar Bowl Champions
Coach: Adolph Rupp
Captain: Layton Rouse

Date	Opponent	Site	UK	Opp
Dec. 9	Berea	H	74	24
Dec. 16	Cincinnati	H	30	39
Dec. 21	Clemson	A	55	31
Sugar Bowl (New Orleans, La.)				
Dec. 27	Ohio State (finals)		36	30
Jan. 1	Kansas State	H	53	26
Jan. 6	Xavier	A	42	41
Jan. 8	West Virginia	H	47	38
Jan. 13	Notre Dame	A	47	52
Jan. 20	Tennessee	H	35	26
Jan. 27	Alabama	N1	32	36
Jan. 29	Vanderbilt	A	32	40
Feb. 3	Marquette	A	51	45
Feb. 10	Alabama	H	46	18
Feb. 12	Xavier	H	37	29
Feb. 13	Mississippi State	H	45	37
Feb. 17	Tennessee	A	23	27
Feb. 19	Georgia Tech	A	39	44
Feb. 24	Alabama	H	43	38
SEC Tournament (Knoxville, Tenn.)				
Feb. 29	Vanderbilt		44	31
Mar. 1	Tennessee		30	*29
Mar. 2	Georgia (finals)		51	43
			892	724

(N1) Birmingham, Ala.

—Leading Scorers—
Mickey Rouse (Sr. G) 8.3
Keith Farnsley (Jr. F) 7.2
Marion Cluggish (Sr. C) 7.2
Lee Huber (Jr. G) 5.4
Jim King (So. C) 3.9
Carl Combs (Jr. G) 3.9

1940/41—Won 17, Lost 8
Coach: Adolph Rupp
Captain: Lee Huber

Date	Opponent	Site	UK	Opp
Dec. 7	Alumni	H	62	25
Dec. 11	West Virginia	H	46	34
Dec. 13	Maryville	H	53	14
Dec. 18	Nebraska	A	39	40
Dec. 19	Creighton	A	45	54
Dec. 20	Kansas State	A	28	25
Dec. 27	Centenary	H	70	18
Sugar Bowl (New Orleans, La.)				
Dec. 30	Indiana		45	48
Jan. 4	Notre Dame	N1	47	48
Jan. 9	Xavier	A	48	43
Jan. 11	West Virginia	A	43	56
Jan. 18	Tennessee	A	22	32
Jan. 20	Georgia Tech	A	47	37
Jan. 25	Xavier	H	44	49
Feb. 1	Vanderbilt	A	51	50
Feb. 3	Alabama	A	38	36
Feb. 8	Alabama	H	46	38
Feb. 10	Mississippi	H	60	41
Feb. 15	Tennessee	H	37	28
Feb. 17	Georgia Tech	H	60	41
Feb. 24	Vanderbilt	H	58	31
SEC Tournament (Louisville, Ky.)				
Feb. 27	Mississippi		62	52
Feb. 28	Tulane		59	30
Mar. 1	Alabama		39	37
Mar. 1	Tennessee		33	36
			1182	943

(N1) Louisville, Ky.

—Leading Scorers—
Jim King (Jr. C) 6.0
Lee Huber (Sr. G) 5.9
Keith Farnsley (Sr. F) 5.8
Mel Brewer (So. C) 5.1
Milt Ticco (So. C-F) 4.8

1941/42—Won 19, Lost 6
SEC Champions (Tournament)
Coach: Adolph Rupp
Captain: Carl Staker

Date	Opponent	Site	UK	Opp
Dec. 6	Miami (Ohio) U.	H	35	21
Dec. 13	Ohio State	A	41	43
Dec. 16	Nebraska	H	42	27
Dec. 22	South Carolina	H	64	25
Dec. 30	Texas A & M	H	49	29
Jan. 2	Washington & Lee	H	62	32
Jan. 10	Xavier	A	40	39
Jan. 17	Tennessee	A	40	46
Jan. 19	Georgia	A	51	26
Jan. 20	Georgia Tech	A	63	53
Jan. 24	Mexico	H	56	26
Jan. 31	Georgia	H	55	38
Feb. 2	Alabama	A	35	41
Feb. 7	Notre Dame	A	43	46
Feb. 9	Alabama	H	50	34
Feb. 14	Tennessee	A	36	33
Feb. 16	Georgia Tech	H	57	51
Feb. 21	Xavier	H	44	36
SEC Tournament (Louisville, Ky.)				
Feb. 26	Florida		42	36
Feb. 27	Mississippi		59	32
Feb. 28	Auburn		40	31
Feb. 29	Alabama (finals)		36	34
Postseason Game (Louisville, Ky.)				
Mar. 14	Great Lakes Navy		47	58
NCAA Tournament (New Orleans, La.)				
Mar. 20	Illinois		46	44
Mar. 21	Dartmouth		28	47
			1161	928

—Leading Scorers—
Marvin Akers (Jr. G) 7.6
Mel Brewer (Jr. C) 7.0
Milt Ticco (Jr. F) 5.8
Ermal Allen (Sr. F) 4.9
Ken England (Jr. G) 4.9

1942/43—Won 17, Lost 6
Coach: Adolph Rupp
Co-Captains: Marvin Akers and Melvin Brewer

Date	Opponent	Site	UK	Opp
Dec. 12	Cincinnati	H	61	39
Dec. 19	Washington	H	45	38
Dec. 23	Indiana	N1	52	58
Jan. 2	Ohio State	H	40	45
Jan. 4	Ft. Knox	H	64	30
Jan. 9	Xavier	A	43	38
Jan. 16	Tennessee	A	30	28
Jan. 18	Georgia	A	60	28
Jan. 19	Georgia Tech	A	38	36
Jan. 23	Notre Dame	N1	60	55
Jan. 26	Vanderbilt	H	39	38
Jan. 30	Alabama	A	32	41
Feb. 1	Vanderbilt	A	54	43
Feb. 6	Alabama	H	67	41
Feb. 8	Xavier	H	48	36
Feb. 13	Tennessee	H	53	29
Feb. 15	Georgia Tech	H	58	31
Feb. 20	DePaul	A	44	53
SEC Tournament (Louisville, Ky.)				
Feb. 25	Tulane		48	31
Feb. 26	Georgia		59	30
Feb. 27	Mississippi State		52	43
Feb. 27	Tennessee		30	33
Postseason Game (Louisville, Ky.)				
Mar. 6	Great Lakes Navy		39	53
			1116	897

—Leading Scorers—

Milt Ticco (Sr. F)	10.1
Mel Brewer (Sr. C)	8.3
Marvin Akers (Sr. G)	7.1
Mulford Davis (So. F)	7.1
Kenny Rollins (So. G)	5.3

1943/44—Won 19, Lost 2
SEC Champions (Tournament)

Coach: Adolph Rupp
Captain:

Date	Opponent	Site		
Dec. 1	Ft. Knox	H	51	18
Dec. 4	Berea (Naval V-12)	H	54	40
Dec. 11	Indiana	N1	66	41
Dec. 13	Ohio State	A	40	28
Dec. 18	Cincinnati	H	58	30
Dec. 20	**Illinois**	**A**	**41**	**43**
Dec. 28	Carnegie Tech	N2	61	14
Dec. 30	St. John's	A	44	38
Jan. 8	Notre Dame	N1	55	54
Jan. 15	Wright Field	H	61	28
Jan. 31	Ft. Knox A.R.C.	H	76	48
Feb. 4	DePauw	H	38	35
Feb. 7	Illinois	H	51	40
Feb. 12	Cincinnati	A	38	34
Feb. 26	Ohio U.	H	51	35
SEC Tournament (Louisville, Ky.)				
Mar. 2	Georgia		57	29
Mar. 3	Louisiana State		55	28
Mar. 4	Tulane (finals)		62	46
National Invitation Tournament (New York, N.Y.)				
Mar. 20	Utah		46	38
Mar. 22	**St. John's**		**45**	**48**
Mar. 26	Oklahoma A & M (consolation)		45	29
			1095	724

—Leading Scorers—

Bob Brannum (Fr. C)	16.7
Jack Tingle (Fr. F)	8.4
Jack Parkinson (Fr. G)	7.0
Wilbur Schu (So. G)	6.2
Tom Moseley (So. G)	4.2

1944/45—Won 22, Lost 4
SEC Champions (Tournament)

Coach: Adolph Rupp
Captain:

Date	Opponent	Site		
Dec. 2	Ft. Knox	H	56	23
Dec. 4	Berea	H	56	32
Dec. 9	Cincinnati	H	66	24
Dec. 16	Indiana	N1	61	43
Dec. 23	Ohio State	H	53	*48
Dec. 26	Wyoming	N2	50	46
Dec. 30	Temple	A	45	44
Jan. 1	Long Island	A	62	*52
Jan. 6	Ohio U.	H	59	46
Jan. 8	Arkansas State	H	75	6
Jan. 13	Michigan State	H	66	35
Jan. 20	**Tennessee**	**A**	**34**	**35**
Jan. 22	Georgia Tech	A	64	58
Jan. 27	**Notre Dame**	**N1**	**58**	***59**
Jan. 29	Georgia	H	73	37
Feb. 3	Georgia Tech	H	51	32
Feb. 5	**Michigan State**	**A**	**50**	**66**
Feb. 17	Tennessee	H	40	34
Feb. 19	Ohio U.	A	61	38
Feb. 24	Cincinnati	A	65	35
SEC Tournament (Louisville, Ky.)				
Mar. 1	Florida		57	35
Mar. 2	Louisiana State		68	37
Mar. 3	Alabama		52	41
Mar. 3	Tennessee (finals)		39	35
NCAA Tournament (New York, N.Y.)				
Mar. 22	**Ohio State**		**37**	**45**
Mar. 24	Tufts (Consolation)		66	56
			1464	1042

(N1) Louisville, Ky.
(N2) Buffalo, N.Y.

—Leading Scorers—

Alex Groza (Fr. C)	16.5
Jack Tingle (So. F)	11.5
Jack Parkinson (So. G)	10.4
Wilbur Schu (Jr. F)	8.0
Kenton Campbell (Fr. C)	6.3

1945/46—Won 28, Lost 2
NIT Champions
SEC Champions (Tournament)

Coach: Adolph Rupp
Captain: Jack Parkinson

Date	Opponent	Site		
Dec. 1	Ft. Knox	H	59	34
Dec. 7	Western Ontario	H	51	42
Dec. 8	Western Ontario	H	71	28
Dec. 15	Cincinnati	H	67	31
Dec. 18	Arkansas	H	67	42
Dec. 21	Oklahoma	H	43	33
Dec. 29	St. John's	A	73	59
Jan. 1	**Temple**	**A**	**45**	**53**
Jan. 5	Ohio U.	H	57	48
Jan. 7	Ft. Benning	H	81	25
Jan. 12	Michigan State	A	55	44
Jan. 14	Xavier	A	62	36
Jan. 19	Tennessee	A	50	32
Jan. 21	Georgia Tech	A	68	43
Jan. 26	**Notre Dame**	**N1**	**47**	**56**
Jan. 28	Georgia Tech	H	54	26
Feb. 5	Michigan State	H	59	51
Feb. 4	Vanderbilt	A	59	37
Feb. 9	Vanderbilt	N2	64	31
Feb. 16	Tennessee	H	54	34
Feb. 19	Ohio University	A	60	52
Feb. 23	Xavier	H	83	40
SEC Tournament (Louisville, Ky.)				
Feb. 28	Auburn		69	24
Mar. 1	Florida		69	32
Mar. 2	Alabama		59	30
Mar. 2	Louisiana State (finals)		59	36
Postseason Game (Louisville, Ky.)				
Mar. 9	Temple		54	43
National Invitation Tournament (New York, N.Y.)				
Mar. 16	Arizona		77	53
Mar. 18	West Virginia		59	51
Mar. 20	Rhode Island (finals)		46	45
			1821	1194

(N1) Louisville, Ky.
(N2) Paducah, Ky.

—Leading Scorers—

Jack Parkinson (6-0 Jr. G)	11.3
Wallace Jones (6-4 Fr. F)	9.7
Ralph Beard (5-10 Fr. G)	9.3
Jack Tingle (6-3 Jr. F)	9.2
Wilbur Schu (6-4 Sr. F)	7.7

1946/47—Won 34, Lost 3
SEC Champions (Tournament)

Coach: Adolph Rupp
Captain: Ken Rollins

Date	Opponent	Site		
Nov. 28	Indiana Central	H	78	36
Nov. 30	Tulane	H	64	35
Dec. 2	Ft. Knox	H	68	31
Dec. 7	Cincinnati	A	80	49
Dec. 9	Idaho	H	65	35
Dec. 12	DePaul	N1	65	45
Dec. 14	Texas A & M	H	83	18
Dec. 16	Miami (Ohio) U.	H	62	49
Dec. 21	St. John's	N2	70	50
Dec. 23	Baylor	H	75	34
Dec. 28	Wabash	H	96	24
Sugar Bowl (New Orleans, La.)				
Dec. 30	**Oklahoma A & M**		**31**	**37**
Jan. 4	Ohio U.	H	46	36
Jan. 11	Dayton U.	H	70	29
Jan. 13	Vanderbilt	A	82	30
Jan. 18	Tennessee	A	54	39
Jan. 20	Georgia Tech	A	70	47
Jan. 21	Georgia	A	84	45
Jan. 25	Xavier	H	71	34
Jan. 27	Michigan State	H	86	36
Feb. 1	Notre Dame	N1	60	30
Feb. 3	Alabama	A	48	37
Feb. 8	**DePaul**	**A**	**47**	**53**
Feb. 10	Georgia	H	81	40
Feb. 15	Tennessee	H	61	46
Feb. 17	Alabama	H	63	33
Feb. 19	Xavier	A	58	31
Feb. 21	Vanderbilt	H	84	41
Feb. 22	Georgia Tech	H	83	46
SEC Tournament (Louisville, Ky.)				
Feb. 27	Vanderbilt		98	29
Feb. 28	Auburn		84	18
Mar. 1	Georgia Tech		75	53
Mar. 1	Tulane (finals)		55	38
Postseason Game (Louisville, Ky.)				
Mar. 8	Temple		68	29
National Invitation Tournament (New York, N.Y.)				
Mar. 17	Long Island		66	62
Mar. 19	North Carolina State		60	42
Mar. 24	**Utah[1]**		**45**	**49**
			2536	1416

(N1) Louisville, Ky.
(N2) New York, N.Y.

—Leading Scorers—

Ralph Beard (5-10 So. G)	10.9
Alex Groza (6-7 So. C-F)	10.6
Kenneth Rollins (6-0 Jr. G)	8.4
Joe Holland (6-4 So. F)	6.2
Wallace Jones (6-4 So. C)	5.9

[1] Madison Square Garden Record Crowd, 18,493

1947/48—Won 36, Lost 3
World Champions (Olympic Games)
National Champions (NCAA Tournament)
SEC Champions (Tournament)

Coach: Adolph Rupp
Captain: Kenneth Rollins

Date	Opponent	Site		
Nov. 29	Indiana Central	H	80	41
Dec. 1	Ft. Knox	H	80	41
Dec. 5	Tulsa U.	H	72	18
Dec. 6	Tulsa U.	H	71	22
Dec. 10	DePaul	N1	74	50
Dec. 13	Cincinnati	A	67	31
Dec. 17	Xavier	H	79	37
Dec. 20	**Temple**	**A**	**59**	**60**
Dec. 23	St. John's	A	52	40
Jan. 2	Creighton	A	65	23
Jan. 3	Western Ontario	H	98	41
Jan. 5	Miami (Ohio)	A	67	53
Jan. 10	Michigan State	A	47	45
Jan. 12	Ohio U.	A	79	57
Jan. 17	Tennessee	A	65	54
Jan. 19	Georgia Tech	A	71	56
Jan. 20	Georgia	A	88	51
Jan. 24	Cincinnati	H	70	43
Jan. 31	DePaul	A	68	51
Feb. 2	**Notre Dame**	**A**	**55**	**64**
Feb. 5	Alabama	A	41	31
Feb. 7	Washington U.	N2	69	39
Feb. 9	Vanderbilt	A	82	51
Feb. 14	Tennessee	H	69	42
Feb. 16	Alabama	H	63	33
Feb. 20	Vanderbilt	H	79	43
Feb. 21	Georgia Tech	H	78	54
Feb. 24	Temple	N1	58	38
Feb. 28	Xavier	A	59	37
SEC Tournament (Louisville, Ky.)				
Mar. 4	Florida		87	31
Mar. 5	Louisiana State		63	47
Mar. 6	Tennessee		70	47
Mar. 6	Georgia Tech (finals)		54	43
NCAA Tournament (New York, N.Y.)				
Mar. 18	Columbia		76	53

| Mar. 20 | Holy Cross | | 60 | 52 |
| Mar. 23 | Baylor (finals) | | 58 | 42 |

NCAA CHAMPIONS FOR FIRST TIME
Olympic Trials (New York)

| Mar. 27 | Louisville | | 91 | 57 |
| Mar. 29 | Baylor | | 77 | 59 |

(Championship Collegiate Bracket)

| **Mar. 31** | **Phillips Oilers (AAU Champs)** | | **49** | **53** |
| | | | 2690 | 1730 |

(N1) Louisville, Ky.
(N2) Memphis, Tenn.

Olympic Team Exhibition Games
Kentucky vs. Phillips Oilers

June 30	Tulsa, Okla.		**52**	**60**
July 2	Kansas City, Mo.		70	**69
July 7	Lexington, Ky.		**50**	**56**

@ Olympic Games (London, England)

July 30	Switzerland		86	21
Aug. 2	Czechoslovakia		53	28
Aug. 3	Argentina		59	57
Aug. 4	Egypt		66	28
Aug. 6	Peru		61	33
Aug. 9	Uruguay		63	28
Aug. 11	Mexico		71	40
Aug. 13	France (finals)		65	21

World Champions
—Leading Scorers—

Alex Groza (6-7 Jr. C) 12.5
(488 TP in 39 games)
Ralph Beard (5-10 Jr. G) 12.5
Wallace Jones (6-4 Jr. C-F) 9.3
James Line (6-2 So. F) 6.9
Kenneth Rollins (6-0 Sr. G) 6.6

1948/49—Won 32, Lost 2
National Champions (NCAA Tournament)
SEC Champions (Tournament)
Ranked First AP
Runner-Up Sugar Bowl
Loser NIT in attempted "Grand Slam"

Coach: Adolph Rupp
Captain:

Nov. 29	Indiana Central	H	74	38
Dec. 8	DePaul	N1	67	36
Dec. 10	Tulsa U.	H	81	27
Dec. 13	Arkansas	H	76	39
Dec. 16	Holy Cross	A	+É	48
DR . 18	St. John's	A	57	30
Dec. 22	Tulane	N1	51	47

Sugar Bowl (New Orleans, La.)

Dec. 9	Tulane		78	47
Dec. 30	**St. Louis**		**40**	**42**
Jan. 11	Bowling Green State	N2	63	61
Jan. 15	Tennessee	A	66	51
Jan. 17	Georgia Tech	A	56	45
Jan. 22	DePaul	A	56	45
Jan. 29	Notre Dame	N1	62	38
Jan. 31	Vanderbilt	A	72	50
Feb. 2	Alabama	A	56	40
Feb. 3	Mississippi	N3	75	45
Feb. 5	Bradley	N4	62	52
Feb. 8	Tennessee	H	71	56
Feb. 12	Xavier	H	96	50
Feb. 14	Alabama	H	74	32
Feb. 16	Mississippi	H	85	31
Feb. 19	Georgia Tech	H	78	32
Feb. 21	Georgia	H	95	40
Feb. 24	Xavier	A	51	40
Feb. 26	Vanderbilt	H	70	37

SEC Tournament (Louisville, Ky.)

Mar. 3	Florida		73	36
Mar. 4	Auburn		70	39
Mar. 5	Tennessee		83	44
Mar. 5	Tulane (finals)		68	52

National Invitation Tournament
(New York, N.Y.)

| **Mar. 14** | **Loyola of Chicago** | | **56** | **67** |

NCAA Tournament
Eastern Regional
(New York, N.Y.)

| Mar. 21 | Villanova | | 85 | 72 |
| Mar. 22 | Illinois | | 76 | 47 |

NCAA Finals
(Seattle, Wash.)

| Mar. 26 | Oklahoma A & M | | 46 | 36 |
| | | | 2320 | 1492 |

NCAA CHAMPIONS FOR SECOND TIME

(N1) Louisville, Ky.
(N2) Cleveland, Ohio
(N3) Memphis, Tenn.
(N4) Owensboro, Ky.

—Leading Scorers—

Alex Groza (6-7 Sr. C) 20.5
Ralph Beard (5-10 Sr. G) 10.8
Wallace Jones (6-4 Sr. F-C) 8.6
Cliff Barker (6-2 Sr. G-F) 7.3
Dale Barnstable (6-3 Jr. F-G) 6.1

1949/50—Won 25, Lost 5
SEC Champions (Tournament)
Sugar Bowl Champions
NIT Participant
Ranked 3rd AP

Coach: Adolph Rupp
Captain: Dale Barnstable

Dec. 3	Indiana Central	H	84	61
Dec. 10	Western Ontario	H	90	18
Dec. 15	**St. John's**	**A**	**58**	**69**
Dec. 21	DePaul	N1	49	47
Dec. 23	Purdue	A	60	54

Sugar Bowl (New Orleans, La.)

Dec. 29	Villanova		57	*56
Dec. 30	Bradley (finals)		71	66
Jan. 2	Arkansas	N2	57	53
Jan. 4	Mississippi State	N3	87	55
Jan. 9	N. Carolina U.	H	83	44
Jan. 14	**Tennessee**	**A**	**53**	**66**
Jan. 16	Georgia Tech	A	61	47
Jan. 17	**Georgia**	**A**	**60**	**71**
Jan. 21	DePaul	A	86	53
Jan. 23	**Notre Dame**	**A**	**51**	**64**
Jan. 26	Xavier	A	58	47
Jan. 28	Georgia	H	88	56
Jan. 30	Vanderbilt	A	58	54
Feb. 2	Alabama	A	66	64
Feb. 4	Mississippi	N4	61	55
Feb. 11	Tennessee	H	79	52
Feb. 13	Alabama	H	77	57
Feb. 15	Mississippi	H	90	50
Feb. 18	Georgia Tech	H	97	62
Feb. 23	Xavier	H	58	53
Feb. 25	Vanderbilt	H	70	66

SEC Tournament (Louisville, Ky.)

Mar. 3	Mississippi State		56	46
Mar. 4	Georgia		79	63
Mar. 4	Tennessee (finals)		95	58

National Invitation Tournament
(New York, N.Y.)

| **Mar. 14** | **City Col. of New York** | | **50** | **89** |
| | | | 2089 | 1696 |

(N1) Louisville, Ky.
(N2) Little Rock, Ark.
(N3) Owensboro, Ky.
(N4) Memphis, Tenn.

—Leading Scorers—

Bill Spivey (7-0 So. C) 19.3
Jim Line (6-2 Sr. F) 13.1
Walt Hirsch (6-4 Jr. F) 9.9
Bobby Watson (5-10 So. G) 7.5
Dale Barnstable (6-3 Sr. G) 5.9

MEMORIAL COLISEUM ERA

1950/51—Won 32, Lost 2
National Champions (NCAA Tournament)
SEC Champions (14-0)
Ranked 1st AP-UPI
Third Sugar Bowl Tournament

Coach: Adolph Rupp
Captain: Walt Hirsch
(Including exhibition games, Kentucky won 39 games and lost 2)

Dec. 1	W. Texas State	H	73	43
Dec. 9	Purdue	H	70	52
Dec. 12	Xavier	A	67	56
Dec. 14	Florida	H	85	37
Dec. 16	Kansas	H	68	39
Dec. 23	St. John's	A	43	37

Sugar Bowl (New Orleans, La.)

Dec. 29	**St. Louis**		**42**	***43**
Dec. 30	Syracuse (consolation)		69	59
Jan. 5	Auburn	H	79	35
Jan. 8	DePaul	H	63	55
Jan. 13	Alabama	H	65	48
Jan. 15	Notre Dame	H	69	44
Jan. 20	Tennessee	A	70	45
Jan. 22	Georgia Tech	A	82	61
Jan. 27	Vanderbilt	A	74	49
Jan. 29	Tulane	A	104	68
Jan. 31	Louisiana State	A	81	59
Feb. 2	Mississippi State	A	80	60
Feb. 3	Mississippi	N1	86	39
Feb. 9	Georgia Tech	H	75	42
Feb. 13	Xavier	H	78	51
Feb. 17	Tennessee	H	86	61
Feb. 19	DePaul	A	60	57
Feb. 23	Georgia	H	88	41
Feb. 24	Vanderbilt	H	89	57

SEC Tournament (Louisville, Ky.)

Mar. 1	Mississippi State		92	70
Mar. 2	Auburn		84	54
Mar. 3	Georgia Tech		82	56
Mar. 3	**Vanderbilt**		**57**	**61**

Postseason Game

| Mar. 13 | Loyola of Chicago | H | 97 | 61 |

NCAA Tournament
First Round
(Raleigh, N.C.)

| Mar. 20 | Louisville | | 79 | 68 |

Eastern Regional
(New York, N.Y.)

| Mar. 22 | St. John's | | 59 | 43 |
| Mar. 24 | Illinois | | 76 | 74 |

Finals
(Minneapolis, Minn.)

| Mar. 27 | Kansas State (finals) | | 68 | 58 |
| | | | 2540 | 1783 |

NCAA CHAMPIONS FOR THIRD TIME
Exhibition Game

| Apr. 27 | KY All-Stars | H | 92 | 49 |

Puerto Rico Exhibition Tour

Aug. 25	San German Ath.		86	38
Aug	Ponce Lions		83	43
Aug. 27	San Turce		93	40
Aug. 29	Univ. of Puerto Rice		91	44
Sept. 2	U.S. Navy		52	23

(Called at half on account of rain)

| Sep. 3 | Puerto Rico | | 75 | 46 |

(N1) Owensboro, Ky.

—Leading Scorers—

Bill Spivey (7-0 Jr. C) 19.2
Shelby Linville (6-5 Jr. F) 10.4
Bobby Watson (5-10 Jr. G) 10.4
Frank Ramsey (6-3 So. G) 10.1
Walt Hirsch (6-3 Sr. F) 9.1

1951/52—Won 29, Lost 3
Ranked 1st AP, UPI
SEC Champions (14-0)
NCAA Participant
Runner-Up Sugar Bowl

Coach: Adolph Rupp
Captain: Robert Watson

Dec. 8	Washington & Lee	H	96	46
Dec. 10	Xavier	A	97	72
Dec. 13	**Minnesota**	**A**	**57**	**61**
Dec. 17	St. John's	H	81	40
Dec. 20	DePaul	H	98	60
Dec. 26	UCLA	H	84	53

Sugar Bowl (New Orleans, La.)

Dec. 28	Brigham Young		84	64
Dec. 29	**St. Louis**		**60**	**61**
Jan. 2	Mississippi	N1	116	58
Jan. 5	Louisiana State	H	57	47
Jan. 7	Xavier	H	83	50
Jan. 12	Florida	A	99	52
Jan. 14	Georgia	N2	95	55
Jan. 19	Tennessee	A	65	56
Jan. 21	Georgia Tech	A	96	51
Jan. 26	Alabama	A	71	67
Jan. 28	Vanderbilt	A	88	51
Jan. 30	Auburn	A	88	48
Feb. 2	Notre Dame	N3	71	66
Feb. 4	Tulane	H	103	54
Feb. 6	Mississippi	H	81	61
Feb. 9	Georgia Tech	H	93	42
Feb. 11	Mississippi State	H	110	66
Feb. 16	Tennessee	H	95	40
Feb. 21	Vanderbilt	H	75	45
Feb. 23	DePaul	A	63	61

SEC Champions
SEC Tournament (Louisville, Ky.)

Feb. 28	Georgia Tech		80	59
Feb. 29	Tulane		85	61
Mar. 1	Tennessee		81	66
Mar. 1	Louisiana State (finals)		44	43

NCAA Tournament
Eastern Regional
(Raleigh, N.C.)

Mar. 21	Penn. State		82	54
Mar. 22	**St. John's**		**57**	**64**
			2635	1774

(N1) Owensboro, Ky.
(N2) Louisville, Ky.
(N3) Chicago, Ill.

—Leading Scorers—

Cliff Hagan (6-4 Jr. C)	21.6
Frank Ramsey (6-3 Jr. G)	15.9
Bobby Watson (5-10 Sr. G)	13.1
Lou Tsioropoulos (6-5 Jr. F)	7.9
Lucian Whitaker (6-0 Sr. F)	7.8

1952/53—No Schedule
(Under suspension by NCAA)
Intra Squad Scrimmage Result

Coach: Adolph Rupp
Co-Captains: Cliff Hagan and Frank Ramsey

Dec. 13	Varsity	76	Freshman	45
Jan. 19	Ramsey's	71	Hagan's	50
Feb. 4	Hagan's	68	Ramsey's	55
Feb. 28	Blues	49	Whites	47
		264		197

1953/54—Won 25, Lost 0
Ranked 1st AP, 2nd UPI
UKIT Champions
SEC Champions (14-0)
Declined NCAA Berth

Coach: Adolph Rupp
Co-Captains: Cliff Hagan and Frank Ramsey

Dec. 5	Temple	H	86	59
Dec. 12	Xavier	A	81	66
Dec. 14	Wake Forest	H	101	69

Dec. 18	St. Louis	A	71	59

UK Invitation Tournament

Dec. 21	Duke		85	69
Dec. 22	LaSalle (finals)		73	60
Dec. 28	Minnesota	H	74	59
Jan. 4	Xavier	H	77	71
Jan. 9	Georgia Tech	H	105	53
Jan. 11	DePaul	H	81	63
Jan. 16	Tulane	H	94	43
Jan. 23	Tennessee	A	97	71
Jan. 30	Vanderbilt	A	85	63
Feb. 2	Georgia Tech	N1	99	48
Feb. 4	Georgia	H	106	55
Feb. 6	Georgia	N2	100	68
Feb. 8	Florida	A	97	55
Feb. 13	Mississippi	H	88	62
Feb. 15	Mississippi State	H	81	49
Feb. 18	Tennessee	H	90	63
Feb. 20	DePaul	A	76	61
Feb. 22	Vanderbilt	H	100	64
Feb. 27	Auburn	N3	109	79
Mar. 1	Alabama	A	68	43

SEC Playoff
(Nashville, Tenn.)

(Playoff game to determine SEC Champion and representative in NCAA Tournament. Kentucky and LSU tied for league title due to a schedule disagreement. Kentucky won but declined NCAA.)

Mar. 9	Louisiana State		63	56
			2187	1508

(N1) Louisville, Ky.
(N2) Owensboro, Ky.
(N3) Montgomery, Ala.

—Leading Scorers—

Cliff Hagan (6-4 Sr. C)	24.0
Frank Ramsey (6-3 Sr. G)	19.6
Lou Tsioropoulos (6-5 Sr. F)	14.5
Billy Evans (6-1 Jr. F)	8.4
Gayle Rose (6-0 Jr. G)	6.7

1954/55—Won 23, Lost 3
NCAA Tournament Participant
UKIT Champions
SEC Champions (12-2)
Ranked 2nd AP, UPI

Coach: Adolph Rupp
Captain: Bill Evans

Dec. 4	Louisiana State	H	74	58
Dec. 11	Xavier	A	73	69
Dec. 18	Temple	H	79	61

UK Invitation Tournament

Dec. 21	Utah		70	65
Dec. 22	LaSalle (finals)		63	54
Dec. 30	St. Louis	H	82	65
Jan. 1	Temple	A	101	69
Jan. 8	**Georgia Tech**	**H**	**58**	**59**
Jan. 10	DePaul	H	92	59
Jan. 15	Tulane	A	58	44
Jan. 17	Louisiana State	A	64	62
Jan. 22	Tennessee	A	84	66
Jan. 29	Vanderbilt	A	75	71
Jan. 31	**Georgia Tech**	**A**	**59**	**65**
Feb. 3	Florida	H	87	63
Feb. 5	Mississippi	N1	84	66
Feb. 7	Mississippi State	A	61	56
Feb. 9	Georgia	H	86	40
Feb. 14	Xavier	H	66	55
Feb. 19	DePaul	A	76	72
Feb. 21	Vanderbilt	H	77	59
Feb. 26	Auburn	H	93	59
Feb. 28	Alabama	H	66	52
Mar. 5	Tennessee	H	104	61

NCAA Tournament
Eastern Regional
(Evanston, Ill.)

Mar. 11	**Marquette**		**71**	**79**
Mar. 12	Penn. State		84	59
			1987	1588

(N1) Memphis, Tenn.

—Leading Scorers—

Bob Burrow (6-7 Jr. C)	19.0
Billy Evans (6-1 Jr. F)	13.9
Jerry Bird (6-6 Jr. F)	10.7
Phil Grawemeyer[1] (6-7 Jr. F)	13.0
Gayle Rose (6-0 Sr. G)	7.4

[1] Grawemeyer ranked 4th in total points with 260 in 20 games. Broke leg against DePaul and missed last six games.

1955/56—Won 20, Lost 6
Ranked 9th AP
2nd SEC (12-2)
NCAA Tournament Participant
UKIT Runner-Up

Coach: Adolph Rupp
Captain: Phil Grawemeyer

Dec. 3	Louisiana State	A	62	52
Dec. 10	**Temple**	**H**	**61**	**73**
Dec. 12	DePaul	H	71	69
Dec. 15	Maryland	A	62	61
Dec. 17	Idaho	H	91	49

UK Invitation Tournament

Dec. 20	Minnesota		72	65
Dec. 21	**Dayton (finals)**		**74**	**89**
Dec. 28	St. Louis	A	101	80
Jan. 7	Georgia Tech	H	104	51
Jan. 12	Tulane	H	85	63
Jan. 14	Louisiana State	H	107	65
Jan. 21	Tennessee	A	95	68
Jan. 28	**Vanderbilt**	**A**	**73**	**81**
Jan. 30	Georgia Tech	A	84	62
Feb. 1	Duke	H	81	76
Feb. 4	Auburn	N1	82	81
Feb. 6	Florida	A	81	70
Feb. 11	Mississippi	H	88	49
Feb. 13	Mississippi State	H	86	65
Feb. 18	**DePaul**	**A**	**79**	**81**
Feb. 20	Vanderbilt	H	76	55
Feb. 25	**Alabama**	**N1**	**77**	**101**
Feb. 27	Georgia	N2	143	66
Mar. 3	Tennessee	H	101	77

NCAA Tournament
(Kentucky represented the SEC in NCAA when champion Alabama declined the bid.)

Eastern Regional
(Iowa City, Iowa)

Mar. 16	Wayne U.	A	84	64
Mar. 17	**Iowa**	**A**	**77**	**89**
			2197	1802

(N1) Montgomery, Ala.
(N2) Louisville, Ky.

—Leading Scorers—

Bob Burrow (6-7 Sr. C)	21.1
Jerry Bird (6-6 Sr. F)	16.2
Vernon Hatton (6-3 So. G)	13.3
Gerry Calvert (5-11 Jr. G)	11.2
Phil Grawemeyer (6-7 Sr. F)	8.4

1956/57—Won 23, Lost 5
Ranked 3rd AP, UPI
UKIT Champions
SEC Champions (12-2)
Sugar Bowl Champions
NCAA Tournament Participant

Coach: Adolph Rupp
Honorary Co-Captains: Ed Beck and Gerry Calvert

Dec. 1	Washington & Lee	H	94	66
Dec. 3	Miami (FL)	H	114	75
Dec. 8	Temple	A	73	58
Dec. 10	**St. Louis**	**H**	**70**	**71**
Dec. 15	Maryland	H	76	55
Dec. 18	**Duke**	**A**	**84**	**85**

UK Invitation Tournament

Dec. 21	Southern Methodist		73	67
Dec. 22	Illinois (finals)		91	70

Sugar Bowl
(New Orleans, La.)

Dec. 28	Virginia Tech		56	55

Dec. 29	Houston (finals)		111	76
Jan. 5	Georgia Tech	H	95	72
Jan. 7	Loyola (Chicago)	H	81	62
Jan. 12	Louisiana State	A	51	46
Jan. 14	**Tulane**	**A**	**60**	**68**
Jan. 19	Tennessee	A	97	72
Jan. 26	Vanderbilt	A	91	83
Jan. 28	Georgia Tech	A	76	65
Jan. 30	Georgia	H	84	53
Feb. 2	Florida	H	88	61
Feb. 8	Mississippi	N1	75	69
Feb. 11	**Mississippi State**	**A**	**81**	**89**
Feb. 15	Loyola (Chicago)	A	115	65
Feb. 18	Vanderbilt	H	80	78
Feb. 23	Alabama	H	79	60
Feb. 25	Auburn	H	103	85
Mar. 2	Tennessee	H	93	75

SEC Champions
NCAA Tournament
Midwest Regional
(Lexington, Ky.)

Mar. 15	Pittsburgh		98	92
Mar. 16	**Michigan State**		**68**	**80**
			2357	1953

(N1) Memphis, Tenn.

—Leading Scorers—

Johnny Cox (6-4 So. F)	19.4
Gerry Calvert (5-11 Sr. G)	15.2
Vernon Hatton (6-3 Jr. G)	14.8
John Crigler (6-3 Jr. F)	10.3
Ed Beck (6-7 Jr. C)	9.5

1957/58—Won 23, Lost 6
National Champions (NCAA Tournament)
SEC Champions (12-2)
Ranked 9th AP, 14th UPI
UKIT Participant

Coach: Adolph Rupp
Honorary Captain: Ed Beck

Dec. 2	Duke	H	78	74
Dec. 4	Ohio State	A	61	54
Dec. 7	Temple	H	85	***83
Dec. 9	**Maryland**	**A**	**62**	**71**
Dec. 14	St. Louis	A	73	60
Dec. 16	**Southern Methodist**	**A**	**64**	**65**

UK Invitation Tournament

Dec. 20	**West Virginia**		**70**	**77**
Dec. 21	Minnesota		78	58
Dec. 23	Utah State	H	92	64
Dec. 30	Loyola (Chicago)	H	75	42
Jan. 4	Georgia Tech	H	76	60
Jan. 6	Vanderbilt	A	86	81
Jan. 11	Louisiana State	H	97	52
Jan. 13	Tulane	H	86	50
Jan. 18	Tennessee	H	77	68
Jan. 27	**Georgia Tech**	**A**	**52**	**71**
Jan. 29	Georgia	N1	74	55
Jan. 31	Florida	A	78	54
Feb. 8	Mississippi	H	96	65
Feb. 10	Mississippi State	H	72	62
Feb. 15	**Loyola (Chicago)**	**A**	**56**	**57**
Feb. 17	Vanderbilt	H	65	61
Feb. 22	Alabama	N2	45	*43
Feb. 24	**Auburn**	**N3**	**63**	**64**
Mar. 1	Tennessee	A	77	66

NCAA Tournament
Mideast Regional
(Lexington, Ky.)

| Mar. 14 | Miami (Ohio) | | 94 | 70 |
| Mar. 15 | Notre Dame | | 89 | 56 |

Finals
(Louisville, Ky.)

Mar. 21	Temple		61	60
Mar. 22	Seattle (finals)		84	72
			2166	1817

NCAA CHAMPIONS FOR RECORD FOURTH TIME

(N1) Atlanta, Ga.
(N2) Montgomery, Ala.

(N3) Birmingham, Ala.

—Leading Scorers—

Vernon Hatton (6-3 Sr. G)	17.1
Johnny Cox (6-4 Jr. F)	14.9
John Crigler (6-3 Sr. F)	13.6
Adrian Smith (6-0 Sr. G)	12.4
Ed Beck (6-7 Sr. C)	5.6

1958/59—Won 24, Lost 3
NCAA Tournament Participant
UKIT Champions
2nd SEC (12-2)
Ranked 2nd in Polls

Coach: Adolph Rupp
Honorary Captain: Johnny Cox

Dec. 1	Florida State	H	91	68
Dec. 6	Temple	A	76	71
Dec. 8	Duke	A	78	64
Dec. 11	Southern Methodist	H	72	60
Dec. 13	St. Louis	H	76	57
Dec. 15	Maryland	H	58	*56

UK Invitation Tournament

Dec. 19	Ohio State		95	76
Dec. 20	West Virginia (finals)		97	91
Dec. 29	Navy	H	82	69
Dec. 30	Illinois	N1	76	75
Jan. 3	Georgia Tech	H	72	62
Jan. 6	**Vanderbilt**	**A**	**66**	**75**
Jan. 10	Louisiana State	A	76	61
Jan. 12	Tulane	A	85	68
Jan. 17	Tennessee	H	79	58
Jan. 26	Georgia Tech	A	94	70
Jan. 29	Georgia	H	108	55
Jan. 31	Florida	H	94	51
Feb. 7	Mississippi	N2	97	72
Feb. 9	**Mississippi State**	**A**	**58**	**66**
Feb. 14	Notre Dame	N3	71	52
Feb. 18	Vanderbilt	H	83	71
Feb. 21	Auburn	H	75	56
Feb. 23	Alabama	H	39	32
Feb. 28	Tennessee	A	69	56

NCAA Tournament
(Kentucky represented the SEC in NCAA when champion Mississippi State declined the bid.)
Mideast Regional
(Evanston, Ill.)

Mar. 13	**Louisville**		**61**	**76**
Mar. 14	Marquette		98	69
			2126	1737

(N1) Louisville, Ky.
(N2) Jackson, Miss.
(N3) Chicago, Ill.

—Leading Scorers—

Johnny Cox (6-4 Sr. F)	17.9
Billy Ray Lickert (6-3 So. G)	13.5
Bennie Coffman (6-0 Jr. G)	10.7
Don Mills (6-6 Jr. C)	10.5
Sid Cohen (6-1 Jr. G)	8.1
Dickie Parsons (5-10 So. G)	8.0

1959/60—Won 18, Lost 7
3rd SEC (10-4)
UKIT Runner Up

Coach: Adolph Rupp
Co-Captains: Bill Lickert and Don Mills

Dec. 1	Colorado State	H	106	73
Dec. 4	UCLA	A	68	66
Dec. 5	**Southern California**	**A**	**73**	**87**
Dec. 12	**St. Louis**	**A**	**61**	**73**
Dec. 14	Kansas	A	77	*72

UK Invitation Tournament

Dec. 18	North Carolina		76	70
Dec. 19	**West Virginia (finals)**		**70**	**79**
Dec. 20	Temple	N1	97	92
Dec. 28	Ohio State	H	96	93
Jan. 2	**Georgia Tech**	**H**	**54**	**62**
Jan. 5	Vanderbilt	A	76	59
Jan. 9	Louisiana State	H	77	45

Jan. 11	Tulane	H	68	42
Jan. 16	Tennessee	A	78	68
Jan. 25	**Georgia Tech**	**A**	**44**	**65**
Jan. 27	Georgia	N2	84	60
Jan. 29	Florida	A	75	62
Feb. 6	Mississippi	H	61	43
Feb. 8	Mississippi State	H	90	59
Feb. 13	Notre Dame	H	68	65
Feb. 16	Vanderbilt	H	68	60
Feb. 20	**Auburn**	**A**	**60**	**61**
Feb. 22	Alabama	N3	75	55
Feb. 27	**Tennessee**	**H**	**63**	**65**
Mar. 5	Pittsburgh	H	73	66
			1838	1642

(N1) Louisville, Ky.
(N2) Columbus, Ga.
(N3) Montgomery, Ala.

—Leading Scorers—

Billy Ray Lickert (6-3 Jr. f-G)	14.4
Don Mills (6-6 Sr. C-F)	12.7
Sid Cohen (6-1 Sr. G)	10.7
Bennie Coffman (6-0 Sr. G)	10.2
Ned Jennings (6-9 Jr. C)	8.8

1960/61—Won 19, Lost 9
NCAA Tournament Participant
UKIT Runner-Up
2nd SEC (10-4)
Ranked 18th UPI

Coach: Adolph Rupp
Captain: Dick Parsons

Dec. 1	Virginia Military Inst.	H	72	56
Dec. 3	**Florida State**	**H**	**58**	**63**
Dec. 7	Notre Dame	N1	68	62
Dec. 13	North Carolina	N2	70	65
Dec. 17	**Temple**	**A**	**58**	**66**

UK Invitation Tournament

Dec. 21	Illinois		83	78
Dec. 22	**St. Louis (finals)**		**72**	***74**
Dec. 31	Missouri	H	81	69
Jan. 2	Miami (Ohio)	H	70	58
Jan. 7	Georgia Tech	H	89	79
Jan. 9	**Vanderbilt**	**A**	**62**	**64**
Jan. 13	**Louisiana State**	**A**	**59**	**73**
Jan. 14	**Tulane**	**A**	**70**	**72**
Jan. 21	Tennessee	H	83	54
Jan. 30	**Georgia Tech**	**A**	**60**	**62**
Feb. 4	Florida	H	89	68
Feb. 7	Georgia	H	74	67
Feb. 11	Mississippi	N3	74	60
Feb. 13	Mississippi State	A	68	62
Feb. 17	UCLA	H	77	76
Feb. 21	Vanderbilt	H	60	59
Feb. 25	Alabama	H	80	53
Feb. 27	Auburn	H	77	51
Mar. 4	Tennessee	A	68	61

SEC Playoff
(Knoxville, Tenn.)

(To determine SEC representative in NCAA Tournament after champion Mississippi State declined bid. Second place Kentucky and Vanderbilt each had 10-4 records.)

| Mar. 9 | Vanderbilt | | 88 | 67 |
| **Mar. 11** | **Marquette** | **N4** | **72** | **88** |

NCAA Tournament
Mideast Regional
(Louisville, Ky.)

Mar. 17	Morehead		71	64
Mar. 18	**Ohio State**		**74**	**87**
			2027	1858

(N1) Louisville, Ky.
(N2) Greensboro, N.C.
(N3) Jackson, Miss.
(N4) Chicago, Ill.

—Leading Scorers—

Billy Ray Lickert (6-3 Sr. F-G)	16.0
Roger Newman (6-4 Sr. F-G)	14.1
Larry Pursiful (6-1 Jr. G)	13.4
Ned Jennings (6-9 Sr. C)	11.5
Carroll Burchett (6-4 Jr. F-C)	5.1

1961/62—Won 23, Lost 3

UKIT Champions
SEC Co-Champions (13-1)
NCAA Tournament Participant
Ranked 3rd AP, UPI

Coach: Adolph Rupp
Captain: Larry Pursiful

Dec. 2	Miami (Ohio)	H	93	61
Dec. 4	**Southern California**	**H**	**77**	**79**
Dec. 11	St. Louis	H	86	77
Dec. 16	Baylor	H	94	60
Dec. 18	Temple	H	78	55
	UK Invitation Tournament			
Dec. 22	Tennessee		96	69
Dec. 23	Kansas State (finals)		80	67
Dec. 27	Yale	H	79	58
Dec. 30	Notre Dame	N1	100	53
Jan. 2	Virginia	H	93	73
Jan. 6	Georgia Tech	H	89	70
Jan. 8	Vanderbilt	A	77	68
Jan. 12	Louisiana State	H	84	63
Jan. 15	Tennessee	A	95	82
Jan. 29	Georgia Tech	A	71	62
Jan. 31	Georgia	N2	86	59
Feb. 2	Florida	A	81	69
Feb. 10	Mississippi	H	83	60
Feb. 12	**Mississippi State**	**H**	**44**	**49**
Feb. 19	Vanderbilt	H	87	80
Feb. 24	Alabama	A	73	65
Feb. 26	Auburn	A	63	60
Mar. 5	Tulane	H	97	72
Mar. 10	Tennessee	H	90	59
	NCAA Tournament Mideast Regional (Iowa City, Iowa)			
Mar. 16	Butler		81	60
Mar. 17	**Ohio State**		**64**	**74**
			2141	1704

(N1) Freedom Hall, Louisville, Ky.
(N2) Georgia Tech Coliseum, Atlanta, Ga.

—Leading Scorers—

Cotton Nash (6-5 So. C-F) 23.4
Larry Pursiful (6-1 Sr. G) 19.1
Carroll Burchett (6-4 Sr. C-F) 11.2
Scotty Baesler (6-0 Jr. G) 10.9
Roy Roberts (6-4 Jr. F) 7.0

1962/63—Won 16, Lost 9

5th SEC (8-6)
UKIT Champions

Coach: Adolph Rupp
Captain: Scotty Baesler

Dec. 1	**Virginia Tech**	**H**	**77**	**80**
Dec. 8	Temple	A	56	52
Dec. 12	Florida State	H	83	54
Dec. 15	Northwestern	H	71	60
Dec. 17	**North Carolina**	**H**	**66**	**68**
	UK Invitation Tournament			
Dec. 21	Iowa		94	69
Dec. 22	West Virginia (finals)		79	75
Dec. 27	Dartmouth	H	95	49
Dec. 29	Notre Dame	N1	78	70
Dec. 31	**St. Louis**	**A**	**63**	**87**
Jan. 5	**Georgia Tech**	**H**	**85**	****86**
Jan. 7	Vanderbilt	A	106	82
Jan. 11	Louisiana State	A	63	56
Jan. 12	Tulane	A	81	72
Jan. 19	**Tennessee**	**H**	**69**	***78**
Jan. 26	Xavier	H	90	76
Jan. 28	**Georgia Tech**	**A**	**62**	**66**
Jan. 31	Georgia	H	74	67
Feb. 2	Florida	H	94	71
Feb. 9	Mississippi	N2	75	69
Feb. 11	**Mississippi State**	**A**	**52**	**56**
Feb. 18	**Vanderbilt**	**H**	**67**	**69**
Feb. 23	Auburn	H	78	59
Feb. 25	Alabama	H	80	63
Mar. 2	**Tennessee**	**A**	**55**	**63**
			1893	1697

(N1) Louisville, Ky.
(N2) Jackson, Miss.

—Leading Scorers—

Cotton Nash (6-5 Jr. F-C) 20.6
Charles Ishmael[1] (6-5 Jr. G) 11.1
Ted Deeken (6-3 Jr. F) 9.8
Scotty Baesler (6-0 Sr G) 9.7
Roy Roberts (6-4 Sr. F) 9.0

[1] Ineligible second semester

1963/64—Won 21, Lost 6

UKIT and Sugar Bowl Champions
SEC Champions (11-3)
Ranked 3rd UPI, 4th AP
NCAA Tournament Participant

Coach: Adolph Rupp
Co-Captains: Cotton Nash and Ted Deeken

Nov. 30	Virginia	H	75	64
Dec. 2	Texas Tech	H	107	91
Dec. 7	Northwestern	A	95	63
Dec. 9	North Carolina	H	100	80
Dec. 14	Baylor	H	101	65
	UK Invitation Tournament			
Dec. 20	Wisconsin		108	85
Dec. 21	Wake Forest (finals)		98	75
Dec. 28	Notre Dame	N1	101	81
	Sugar Bowl (New Orleans, La.)			
Dec. 30	Loyola (La.)		86	64
Dec. 31	Duke (finals)		81	79
Jan. 4	**Georgia Tech**	**A**	**67**	**76**
Jan. 6	**Vanderbilt**	**A**	**83**	**85**
Jan. 10	Louisiana State	H	103	84
Jan. 11	Tulane	H	105	63
Jan. 18	Tennessee	H	66	57
Jan. 25	Georgia Tech	H	79	62
Feb. 1	Florida	A	77	72
Feb. 3	Georgia	A	103	83
Feb. 8	Mississippi	H	102	59
Feb. 10	Mississippi State	H	65	59
Feb. 17	Vanderbilt	H	104	73
Feb. 23	Auburn	N2	99	79
Feb. 24	**Alabama**	**A**	**59**	**65**
Feb. 29	Tennessee	A	42	38
Mar. 2	**St. Louis**	**H**	**60**	**67**
	NCAA Tournament Mideast Regional (Minneapolis, Minn.)			
Mar. 13	**Ohio University**		**69**	**85**
Mar. 14	**Loyola (Chicago)**		**91**	**100**
			2326	1954

(N1) Louisville, Ky.
(N2) Montgomery, Ala.

—Leading Scorers—

Cotton Nash (6-5 Sr. C-F) 24.0
Ted Deeken (6-3 Sr. F) 18.5
Larry Conley (6-3 So. F-C) 12.2
Terry Mobley (6-2 Jr. G) 9.4
Randy Embry (5-11 Jr. G) 7.2

1964/65—Won 15, Lost 10

5th SEC (10-6)
UKIT Runner Up

Coach: Adolph Rupp
Captain: Randy Embry

Dec. 4	Iowa	H	85	77
Dec. 7	**North Carolina**	**N1**	**67**	**82**
Dec. 9	Iowa State	H	100	74
Dec. 12	Syracuse	H	110	77
	UK Invitation Tournament			
Dec. 18	West Virginia		102	78
Dec. 19	**Illinois (finals)**		**86**	**91**
Dec. 22	**St. Louis**	**A**	**75**	**80**
Dec. 29	**Notre Dame**	**N2**	**97**	**111**
Jan. 2	Dartmouth	H	107	67
Jan. 5	**Vanderbilt**	**H**	**79**	**97**
Jan. 9	Louisiana State	A	79	66
Jan. 11	Tulane	A	102	72
Jan. 16	**Tennessee**	**A**	**58**	**77**
Jan. 18	Auburn	H	73	67
Jan. 23	**Florida**	**A**	**68**	**84**
Jan. 25	Georgia	A	102	82
Jan. 30	Florida	H	78	61
Feb. 1	Georgia	H	96	64
Feb. 6	Mississippi	H	102	65
Feb. 8	Mississippi State	H	74	56
Feb. 16	**Vanderbilt**	**A**	**90**	**91**
Feb. 20	**Auburn**	**A**	**69**	**88**
Feb. 22	**Alabama**	**A**	**71**	**75**
Feb. 27	Tennessee	H	61	60
Mar. 1	Alabama	H	78	72
			2109	1914

(N1) Charlotte, N.C.
(N2) Louisville, Ky.

—Leading Scorers—

Louie Dampier (6-0 So. G) 17.0
Pat Riley (6-4 So. F) 15.0
Tommy Kron (6-5 Jr. G-F) 12.3
John Adams (6-7 Sr. C) 11.8
Larry Conley (6-3 Jr. F) 11.6

1965/66—Won 27, Lost 2

SEC Champions (15-1)
UKIT Champions
Ranked First in Polls
National Runner-Up in NCAA

Coach: Adolph Rupp
Honorary Captain:

Dec. 1	Hardin-Simmons	H	83	55
Dec. 4	Virginia	A	99	73
Dec. 8	Illinois	A	86	68
Dec. 11	Northwestern	H	86	75
	UK Invitation Tournament			
Dec. 17	Air Force		78	58
Dec. 18	Indiana (finals)		91	56
Dec. 22	Texas Tech	A	89	73
Dec. 29	Notre Dame	N1	103	69
Jan. 3	St. Louis	H	80	70
Jan. 8	Florida	A	78	64
Jan. 10	Georgia	A	69	**65
Jan. 15	Vanderbilt	H	96	83
Jan. 24	Louisiana State	H	111	85
Jan. 29	Auburn	H	115	78
Jan. 31	Alabama	H	82	62
Feb. 2	Vanderbilt	A	105	90
Feb. 5	Georgia	H	74	50
Feb. 7	Florida	H	85	75
Feb. 12	Auburn	A	77	64
Feb. 14	Alabama	A	90	67
Feb. 19	Mississippi State	A	73	69
Feb. 21	Mississippi	A	108	65
Feb. 26	Tennessee	H	78	64
Mar. 5	**Tennessee**	**A**	**62**	**69**
Mar. 7	Tulane	H	103	74
	NCAA Tournament Mideast Regional (Iowa City, Iowa)			
Mar. 11	Dayton[1]		86	79
Mar. 12	Michigan		84	77
	Finals (College Park, Md.)			
Mar. 18	Duke		83	79
Mar. 19	**Texas Western**		**65**	**72**
			2519	2028
	International Universities Tournament (Tel Aviv, Israel) (Not Counted in Won-Lost Record)			
Aug. 3	Warsaw University		67	58
Aug. 4	Cambridge University		104	45
Aug. 6	Salonika University		91	60
Aug. 10	Istanbul University		82	36
Aug. 11	Warsaw University		87	57

(N1) Louisville, Ky.

Pat Riley (6-4 Jr. F) 22.0
Louie Dampier (6-0 Jr. G) 21.1
Thad Jaracz (6-5 So. C) 13.2
Larry Conley (6-3 Sr. F) 11.5
Tommy Kron (6-5 Sr. G) 10.2

[1] Adolph Rupp wins his 747th game to pass Phog Allen of Kansas.

1966/67—Won 13, Lost 13
(Worst Record under Rupp)
Tied 5th SEC (8-10)
UKIT Champions

Coach: Adolph Rupp
Honorary Captain:

Dec. 3	Virginia	H	104	84
Dec. 5	**Illinois**	**H**	**97**	***98**
Dec. 10	Northwestern	A	118	116
Dec. 13	**North Carolina**	**H**	**55**	**64**
Dec. 17	**Florida**	**H**	**75**	**78**
UK Invitation Tournament				
Dec. 22	Oregon State		96	66
Dec. 23	Kansas State (finals)		83	79
Dec. 28	**Cornell**	**H**	**77**	**92**
Dec. 31	Notre Dame	N1	96	85
Jan. 5	**Vanderbilt**	**H**	**89**	***91**
Jan. 14	**Florida**	**A**	**72**	**89**
Jan. 16	**Georgia**	**A**	**40**	**49**
Jan. 21	Auburn	H	60	58
Jan. 23	**Tennessee**	**H**	**50**	****52**
Jan. 28	Louisiana State	H	102	72
Jan. 30	Mississippi	H	96	53
Feb. 4	Louisiana State	A	105	84
Feb. 6	Mississippi	A	79	70
Feb. 11	**Mississippi State**	**H**	**72**	***77**
Feb. 13	**Tennessee**	**A**	**57**	**76**
Feb. 18	Mississippi State [1]	A	103	74
Feb. 20	Georgia	H	101	76
Feb. 25	**Alabama**	**A**	**71**	**81**
Feb. 27	**Auburn**	**A**	**49**	**60**
Mar. 4	**Vanderbilt**	**A**	**94**	**110**
Mar. 6	Alabama	H	110	78
			2151	2012

(N1) Louisville, Ky.

—Leading Scorers—

Louie Dampier (6-0 Sr. G) 20.6
Pat Riley (6-4 Sr. F) 17.4
Thad Jaracz (6-5 Jr. C-F) 11.3
Cliff Berger (6-8 Jr. C) 11.3
Phil Argento (6-0 So. G) 5.2

[1] Coach Rupp passes Western Kentucky's E.A. Diddle to become the all-time winningest coach with 760 victories.

1967/68—Won 22, Lost 5
Ranked 4th in Polls
SEC Champions (15-3)
UKIT Champions

Coach: Adolph Rupp
Captain: Thad Jaracz

Dec. 2	Michigan	A	96	79
Dec. 4	Florida	H	99	76
Dec. 6	Xavier	H	111	76
Dec. 9	Pennsylvania	H	64	49
Dec. 12	**North Carolina**	**N1**	**77**	**84**
UK Invitation Tournament				
Dec. 22	Dayton		88	85
Dec. 23	South Carolina (finals)		76	66
Dec. 30	Notre Dame	N2	81	73
Jan. 6	Vanderbilt	A	94	78
Jan. 8	Alabama	A	84	76
Jan. 13	**Florida**	**A**	**78**	**96**
Jan. 15	Georgia	H	104	73
Jan. 20	**Auburn**	**A**	**73**	**74**
Jan. 22	**Tennessee**	**A**	**59**	**87**
Jan. 27	Louisiana State	A	121	95
Jan. 29	Mississippi	A	85	76
Feb. 3	Louisiana State	H	109	96
Feb. 5	Mississippi	H	78	62
Feb. 10	Mississippi State	A	92	84
Feb. 12	Tennessee	H	60	59
Feb. 17	Mississippi State	H	107	81
Feb. 19	Georgia	A	106	87
Feb. 24	Alabama	H	96	83
Feb. 26	Auburn	H	89	57
Mar. 2	Vanderbilt	H	85	80
NCAA Tournament				
Mideast Regional				
(Lexington, Ky.)				
Mar. 15	Marquette		107	89
Mar. 16	**Ohio State**		**81**	**82**
			2400	2103

(N1) Greensboro, N.C.
(N2) Louisville, Ky.

—Leading Scorers—

Mike Casey (6-4 So. G) 20.1
Dan Issel (6-8 So. C) 16.4
Mike Pratt (6-4 So. F) 14.1
Phil Argento (6-2 Jr. G) 12.3
Thad Jaracz (6-5 Sr. F) 11.3

1968/69—Won 23, Lost 5
Ranked 7th in Polls
SEC Champions (16-2)
UKIT Champions

Coach: Adolph Rupp
Captain: Phil Argento

Nov. 30	Xavier	H	115	77
Dec. 2	Miami	A	86	77
Dec. 7	**North Carolina**	**H**	**77**	**87**
Dec. 14	Pennsylvania	A	102	78
UK Invitation Tournament				
Dec. 20	Michigan		112	104
Dec. 21	Army (finals)		80	65
Dec. 28	Notre Dame	N1	110	90
Dec. 31	**Wisconsin**	**N2**	**65**	**69**
Jan. 4	Mississippi	H	69	59
Jan. 6	Mississippi State	A	91	72
Jan. 11	Florida	H	88	67
Jan. 13	Georgia	H	88	68
Jan. 18	Tennessee	A	69	66
Jan. 25	Louisiana State	A	108	96
Jan. 27	Alabama	A	83	*70
Feb. 1	Vanderbilt	H	103	89
Feb. 3	Auburn	H	105	93
Feb. 8	Mississippi	H	104	68
Feb. 10	Mississippi State	H	91	69
Feb. 15	**Florida**	**A**	**81**	**82**
Feb. 17	Georgia	A	85	77
Feb. 22	Louisiana State	H	103	89
Feb. 26	Alabama	H	108	79
Mar. 1	**Vanderbilt**	**A**	**99**	**101**
Mar. 3	Auburn	A	90	86
Mar. 8	Tennessee	H	84	69
NCAA Tournament				
Mideast Regional				
(Madison, Wisc.)				
Mar. 13	**Marquette**		**74**	**81**
Mar. 15	Miami		72	71
			2542	2199

(N1) Louisville, Ky.
(N2) Chicago, Ill.

—Leading Scorers—

Dan Issel (6-8 Jr. C) 26.6
Mike Casey (6-4 Jr. G) 19.1
Mike Pratt (6-4 Jr. F) 16.9
Phil Argento (6-2 Sr. G) 10.0
Larry Steele (6-5 So. F) 8.6

1969/70—Won 26, Lost 2
SEC Champions (17-1)
UKIT Champions
Ranked First in Polls

Coach: Adolph Rupp
Co-Captains: Dan Issel and Mike Pratt

Dec. 1	West Virginia	H	106	87
Dec. 6	Kansas	H	115	85
Dec. 8	North Carolina	N1	94	87
Dec. 13	Indiana	H	109	92
UK Invitation Tournament				
Dec. 19	Navy		73	59
Dec. 20	Duke (finals)		98	76
Dec. 27	Notre Dame	N2	102	100
Dec. 29	Miami (Ohio)	H	80	58
Jan. 3	Mississippi	H	95	73
Jan. 5	Mississippi State	H	111	76
Jan. 10	Florida	A	88	69
Jan. 12	Georgia	A	72	71
Jan. 17	Tennessee	H	68	52
Jan. 24	Louisiana State	H	109	96
Jan. 26	Alabama	H	86	71
Jan. 31	**Vanderbilt**	**A**	**81**	**89**
Feb. 2	Auburn	A	84	83
Feb. 7	Mississippi	A	120	85
Feb. 9	Mississippi State	A	86	57
Feb. 14	Florida	H	110	66
Feb. 16	Georgia	H	116	86
Feb. 21	Louisiana State	A	121	105
Feb. 23	Alabama	A	98	89
Feb. 28	Vanderbilt	H	90	86
Mar. 2	Auburn	H	102	81
Mar. 7	Tennessee	A	86	69
NCAA Tournament				
Mideast Regional				
(Columbus, Ohio)				
Mar. 12	Notre Dame		109	99
Mar. 14	**Jacksonville**		**100**	**106**
			2709	2253

—Leading Scorers—

Dan Issel (6-8 Sr. C) 33.9
Mike Pratt (6-4 Sr. F) 19.3
Tom Parker (6-6 So. F) 10.4
Larry Steele (6-5 Jr. F) 8.8
Terry Mills (6-2 Jr. G) 8.1

1970/71—Won 22, Lost 6
SEC Champions (16-2)
UKIT Runner Up
Ranked 10th AP

Coach: Adolph Rupp
Honorary Co-Captains: Mike Casey and Larry Steele

Dec. 1	Northwestern	A	115	100
Dec. 5	Michigan	H	104	93
Dec. 7	West Virginia	A	106	100
Dec. 12	Indiana	A	95	*93
UK Invitation Tournament				
Dec. 18	DePaul		106	85
Dec. 19	**Purdue (finals)**		**83**	**89**
Dec. 22	Oregon State	H	84	78
Dec. 29	**Notre Dame**	**N1**	**92**	**99**
Jan. 2	Mississippi	A	103	95
Jan. 4	Mississippi State	A	79	71
Jan. 9	Florida	H	101	75
Jan. 11	Georgia	H	79	66
Jan. 16	**Tennessee**	**A**	**71**	**75**
Jan. 23	Louisiana State	A	82	79
Jan. 25	Alabama	A	86	73
Jan. 30	Vanderbilt	H	102	92
Feb. 1	Auburn	H	114	76
Feb. 6	Mississippi	H	121	86
Feb. 8	Mississippi State	H	102	83
Feb. 13	**Florida**	**A**	**65**	**74**
Feb. 15	Georgia	A	107	95
Feb. 20	Louisiana State	H	110	73
Feb. 22	Alabama	H	101	74

Feb. 27	Vanderbilt	A	119	90
Mar. 1	Auburn	A	102	83
Mar. 6	Tennessee	H	84	78

NCAA Tournament
Mideast Regional
(Athens, Ga.)

Mar. 18	**Western Kentucky**		83	107
Mar. 20	**Marquette**		74	91
			2670	2373

(N1) Louisville, Ky.

—Leading Scorers—

Tom Parker (6-7 Jr. F)	17.6
Mike Casey (6-4 Sr. G)	17.0
Tom Payne (7-2 So. C)	16.9
Kent Hollenbeck (6-4 Jr. G)	14.0
Larry Steele (6-5 Sr. F)	13.1

1971/72—Won 21, Lost 7
SEC Champions (14-4)
UKIT Champions
Ranked 14th UPI and 18th AP

Coach: Adolph Rupp
Honorary Co-Captains: Stan Key and Tom Parker

Dec. 1	Northwestern	H	94	85
Dec. 4	Kansas	A	79	69
Dec. 6	Kansas State	A	71	64
Dec. 11	**Indiana**	**N1**	89	**90
Dec. 13	**Michigan State**	H	85	91

UK Invitation Tournament

Dec. 17	Missouri		83	79
Dec. 18	Princeton (finals)		96	82
Dec. 28	Notre Dame	N1	83	67
Jan. 8	Mississippi	H	93	82
Jan. 10	Mississippi State	H	104	76
Jan. 15	**Florida**	**A**	70	72
Jan. 17	**Georgia**	**A**	73	85
Jan. 22	Tennessee	H	72	70
Jan. 24	Vanderbilt	H	106	80
Jan. 29	Louisiana State	H	89	71
Jan. 31	Alabama	H	77	74
Feb. 5	Vanderbilt	A	85	*80
Feb. 7	Auburn	A	78	72
Feb. 12	Mississippi	A	90	82
Feb. 14	Mississippi State	A	63	55
Feb. 19	Florida	H	95	68
Feb. 21	Georgia	H	87	63
Feb. 26	**Louisiana State**	**A**	71	88
Feb. 28	**Alabama**	**A**	70	73
Mar. 6	Auburn	H	102	67
Mar. 9	Tennessee	A	67	66

(Earned NCAA bid by beating Tennessee twice.)
NCAA Tournament
Mideast Regional
(Dayton, Ohio)

Mar. 16	Marquette		85	69
Mar. 18	**Florida State**		54	73
			2311	2093

(N1) Louisville, Ky.

—Leading Scorers—

Jim Andrews (6-11 Jr. C)	21.5
Tom Parker (6-7 Sr. F)	18.0
Ronnie Lyons (5-10 So. G)	13.2
Stan Key (6-3 Sr. G)	12.5
Larry Stamper (6-6 Jr. F)	10.3

JOE B. HALL ERA

1972/73—Won 20, Lost 8
SEC Champions (14-4)
UKIT Champions
Ranked 15th UPI and 17th AP

Coach: Joe B. Hall
Honorary Captain: Jim Andrews

Dec. 2	Michigan State	A	75	66
Dec. 4	**Iowa**	**H**	66	79
Dec. 9	**Indiana**	**A**	58	64

| Dec. 11 | **North Carolina** | **N1** | **70** | **78** |

UK Invitation Tournament

Dec. 15	Nebraska		85	60
Dec. 16	Oregon (finals)		95	68
Dec. 23	Kansas	H	77	71
Dec. 30	Notre Dame	N1	65	63
Jan. 6	**Mississippi**	**A**	58	61
Jan. 8	Mississippi State	A	90	81
Jan. 13	Florida	H	95	65
Jan. 15	Georgia	H	89	68
Jan. 20	**Tennessee**	**A**	64	65
Jan. 22	**Vanderbilt**	**A**	75	76
Jan. 27	Louisiana State	A	86	71
Jan. 29	Alabama	A	95	93
Feb. 3	**Vanderbilt**	**H**	76	83
Feb. 5	Auburn	H	88	57
Feb. 10	Mississippi	H	88	70
Feb. 12	Mississippi State	H	100	*87
Feb. 17	Florida	A	94	83
Feb. 19	Georgia	A	99	86
Feb. 24	Louisiana State	H	94	76
Feb. 26	Alabama	H	111	95
Mar. 3	Auburn	A	91	79
Mar. 8	Tennessee	H	86	81

NCAA Tournament
Mideast Regional
(Nashville, Tenn.)

Mar. 15	Austin Peay		106	*100
Mar. 17	**Indiana**		65	72
			2341	2098

(N1) Louisville, Ky.

—Leading Scorers—

Jim Andrews (6-11 Sr. C)	20.1
Kevin Grevey (6-5 So. F)	18.7
Jimmy Dan Conner (6-4 So. G-F)	11.2
Ronnie Lyons (5-10 Jr. G)	9.2
Mike Flynn (6-3 So. G)	9.1

1973/74—Won 13, Lost 13
(Worst Under Hall)
UKIT Champions
Tied 4th SEC (9-9)

Coach: Joe B. Hall
Captain: Ronnie Lyons

Dec. 1	Miami (Ohio)	H	81	68
Dec. 3	**Kansas**	**A**	63	71
Dec. 8	**Indiana**	**N1**	68	77
Dec. 10	**North Carolina**	**N2**	84	101
Dec. 14	Iowa	A	88	80

UK Invitation Tournament

Dec. 21	Dartmouth		102	77
Dec. 22	Stanford (finals)		78	77
Dec. 29	**Notre Dame**	**N1**	79	94
Jan. 5	**Louisiana State**	**A**	84	95
Jan. 7	Georgia	H	80	74
Jan. 12	Auburn	H	79	58
Jan. 14	**Tennessee**	**A**	54	67
Jan. 19	Mississippi	H	93	64
Jan. 21	**Alabama**	**A**	77	81
Jan. 26	Florida	A	91	82
Jan. 28	**Vanderbilt**	**H**	65	82
Feb. 2	Mississippi State	A	82	70
Feb. 4	Louisiana State	H	73	70
Feb. 9	Georgia	A	86	72
Feb. 11	**Auburn**	**A**	97	*99
Feb. 16	Tennessee	H	61	58
Feb. 18	**Mississippi**	**A**	60	61
Feb. 23	**Alabama**	**H**	71	94
Feb. 25	**Florida**	**H**	65	75
Mar. 2	**Vanderbilt**	**A**	69	71
Mar. 4	Mississippi State	H	108	69
			2038	1987

(N1) Louisville, Ky.
(N2) Greensboro, N.C.

—Leading Scorers—

Kevin Grevey (6-5 Jr. F)	21.9
Bob Guyette (6-9 Jr. C)	12.7
Jimmy Dan Conner (6-4 Jr. F-G)	12.0
Mike Flynn (6-3 Jr. G)	11.5
Ronnie Lyons (5-10 Sr. G)	7.8

1974 Australian Exhibition Tour
(Not Counted in Won-Lost Record)

May 13	Tahitian National Team		116	62
May 17	**Australia**		87	97
May 18	Newcastle		90	78
May 19	N.S.W. All Stars		123	67
May 21	Illawaarra Hawks		115	57
May 22	N.S.W. All Stars		106	50
May 23	A.C.T.		96	69
May 25	Bulleen Heidelberg		88	83
May 26	St. Kilda Business House		80	67
May 27	Nunawading		99	82
May 28	**Melbourne**		79	86
May 30	Gippsland All Stars		127	74
May 31	Bulleen Heidelberg		72	71
June 1	Laker All Stars		111	83
June 3	South Australian All Stars		109	96
Jane 4	South Australian All Stars		110	81
June 5	South Australian All Stars		111	84
June 6	Coburg		108	82
June 7	St. Kilda Business House		96	85
			1923	1454

1974/75—Won 26, Lost 5
National Runner-Up (NCAA Tournament)
SEC Co-Champions (15-3)
UKIT Champions
Ranked 2nd AP and 4th UPI

Coach: Joe B. Hall
Captain: Jimmy Dan Conner

Nov. 30	Northwestern	H	97	70
Dec. 2	Miami (Ohio)	A	80	73
Dec. 7	**Indiana**	**A**	74	98
Dec. 9	North Carolina	N1	90	78

UK Invitation Tournament

Dec. 20	Washington State		97	75
Dec. 21	Oklahoma State (finals)		90	65
Dec. 23	Kansas	N1	100	63
Dec. 28	Notre Dame	N1	113	96
Jan. 4	Louisiana State	H	115	80
Jan. 6	Georgia	A	96	77
Jan. 11	**Auburn**	**A**	85	90
Jan. 13	Tennessee	H	88	82
Jan. 18	Mississippi	A	85	82
Jan. 20	Alabama	H	74	69
Jan. 25	Florida	H	87	65
Jan. 27	Vanderbilt	A	91	90
Feb. 1	Mississippi State	H	112	79
Feb. 3	Louisiana State	A	77	76
Feb. 8	Georgia	H	75	61
Feb. 10	Auburn	H	119	76
Feb. 15	**Tennessee**	**A**	98	103
Feb. 17	Mississippi	H	108	89
Feb. 22	Alabama	A	84	79
Feb. 24	**Florida**	**A**	58	66
Mar. 1	Vanderbilt	H	109	84
Mar. 8	Mississippi State	A	118	80

NCAA Tournament
(Mideast Regional)
(Tuscaloosa, Ala., and Dayton, Ohio)

Mar. 15	Marquette	N2	76	54
Mar. 20	Central Michigan	N3	90	73
Mar. 22	Indiana	N3	92	90

Finals (San Diego, Calif.)

Mar. 29	Syracuse	N4	95	79
Mar. 31	**UCLA**	**N4**	85	92
			2858	2434

(N1) Louisville, Ky.
(N2) Tuscaloosa, Ala.
(N3) Dayton, Ohio
(N4) San Diego, Calif.

—Leading Scorers—

Kevin Grevey (6-5 Sr. F)	23.6
Jimmy Dan Conner (6-4 Sr. G)	12.4
Rick Robey (6-10 Fr. C)	10.4
Jack Givens (6-4 Fr. F)	9.4
Mike Flynn (6-3 Sr. G)	9.0
Bob Guyette (6-9 Sr. F)	8.6

1975/76—Won 20, Lost 10
UKIT Champions
NIT Champions
Tied 4th SEC (11-7)

Coach: Joe B. Hall
Captain: Jack Givens

Dec. 1	Northwestern	A	77	89
Dec. 8	North Carolina	N1	77	90
Dec. 10	Miami	H	91	69
Dec. 13	Kansas	A	54	48
Dec. 15	Indiana	N2	68	*77
UK Invitation Tournament				
Dec. 19	Georgia Tech		66	64
Dec. 20	Oregon State (finals)		82	74
Dec. 30	Notre Dame	N2	79	77
Jan. 3	Mississippi State	A	73	77
Jan. 5	Alabama	A	63	76
Jan. 10	Tennessee	H	88	*90
Jan. 12	Georgia	H	92	76
Jan. 17	Vanderbilt	H	77	76
Jan. 24	Florida	A	89	82
Jan. 26	Auburn	A	84	*91
Jan. 31	Mississippi	H	89	81
Feb. 2	Louisiana State	H	85	71
Feb. 7	Tennessee	A	85	92
Feb. 9	Georgia	A	81	86
Feb. 14	Vanderbilt	A	65	69
Feb. 21	Florida	H	96	89
Feb. 23	Auburn	H	93	82
Feb. 28	Mississippi	A	94	87
Mar. 1	Louisiana State	A	85	70
Mar. 6	Alabama	H	90	85
Mar. 8	Mississippi State	H	94	*93
National Invitation Tournament				
(New York, N.Y.)				
Mar. 13	Niagara		67	61
Mar. 16	Kansas State		81	78
Mar. 18	Providence		79	78
Mar. 21	U.N.C. Charlotte (finals)		71	67
			2415	2345

(N1) Charlotte, N.C.
(N2) Louisville, Ky.

—Leading Scorers—

Jack Givens (6-4 So. F)	20.1
Mike Phillips (6-10 So. C)	15.6
Larry Johnson (6-2 Jr. G)	11.2
James Lee (6-5 So. F)	9.3
Rick Robey[1] (6-10 So. C-F)	15.6
Reggie Warford (6-1 Sr. G)	6.5

[1] Played in 12 games.

RUPP ARENA ERA

1976/77—Won 26, Lost 4
SEC Co-Champions (16-2)
Ranked 6th AP, 5th UPI

Coach: Joe B. Hall
Captains: Larry Johnson and Merion Haskins

Nov. 27	Wisconsin	H	72	64
Dec. 2	Texas Christian	H	103	53
Dec. 6	Indiana	A	66	51
Dec. 11	Kansas	H	90	63
Dec. 13	South Carolina	A	98	67
UK Invitation Tournament				
Dec. 17	Bowling Green State		77	59
Dec. 18	Utah (finals)		68	70
Dec. 30	Notre Dame	N2	102	78
Jan. 3	Georgia	H	64	*59

Jan. 8	Vanderbilt	A	64	62
Jan. 12	Tennessee	H	67	*71
Jan. 15	Auburn	A	75	68
Jan. 17	Florida	A	73	71
Jan. 22	Louisiana State	H	87	72
Jan. 24	Mississippi	H	100	73
Jan. 29	Alabama	A	87	85
Jan. 31	Mississippi State	A	92	85
Feb. 5	Vanderbilt	H	113	73
Feb. 7	Florida State	N2	97	57
Feb. 12	Auburn	H	89	82
Feb. 14	Florida	H	104	78
Feb. 19	Louisiana State	A	90	76
Feb. 21	Mississippi	A	81	69
Feb. 26	Alabama	H	85	70
Feb. 28	Mississippi State	H	77	64
Mar. 5	Tennessee	A	79	81
Mar. 1	Georgia	A	72	54
NCAA Tournament				
East Regional				
(Philadelphia, Pa., and College Park, Md.)				
Mar. 12	Princeton	N3	72	58
Mar. 17	VMI	N4	93	78
Mar. 19	North Carolina	N4	72	79
			2509	2070

(N1) Memorial Coliseum
(N2) Louisville, Ky.
(N3) Philadelphia, Pa.
(N4) College Park, Md.

—Leading Scorers—

Jack Givens (6-4 Jr. F)	18.9
Rick Robey (6-10 Jr. F)	14.2
Mike Phillips (6-10 Jr. C)	12.2
Larry Johnson (6-3 Sr. G)	10.7
James Lee (6-5 Jr. F)	9.8
Jay Shidler (6-1 Fr. G)	7.8
Truman Claytor (6-1 So. G)	6.6

1977/78—Won 30, Lost 2
National Champions (NCAA Tournament)
SEC Champions (16-2)
UKIT Champions
Ranked 1st AP and UPI

Coach: Joe B. Hall
Captains: Jack Givens and Rick Robey

Nov. 26	Southern Methodist	H	110	86
Dec. 5	Indiana	H	78	64
Dec. 10	Kansas	A	73	66
Dec. 12	South Carolina	H	84	65
UK Invitation Tournament				
Dec. 16	Portland State		114	88
Dec. 17	St. John's (finals)		102	72
Dec. 23	Iona	H	104	65
Dec. 31	Notre Dame	N2	73	68
Jan. 2	Vanderbilt	H	72	59
Jan. 7	Florida	A	86	67
Jan. 9	Auburn	A	101	77
Jan. 14	Louisiana State	H	96	76
Jan. 16	Mississippi	H	76	56
Jan. 21	Mississippi State	A	75	65
Jan. 23	Alabama	A	62	78
Jan. 30	Georgia	H	90	73
Feb. 4	Florida	H	88	61
Feb. 6	Auburn	H	104	81
Feb. 11	Louisiana State	A	94	*95
Feb. 13	Mississippi	A	64	52
Feb. 15	Tennessee	H	90	77
Feb. 18	Mississippi State	H	58	56
Feb. 20	Alabama	H	97	84
Feb. 25	Tennessee	A	68	57
Feb. 27	Georgia	A	78	67
Mar. 4	Nevada-Las Vegas	H	92	70
Mar. 6	Vanderbilt	A	78	68
NCAA Tournament				
Mideast Regional				
(Knoxville, Tenn., and Dayton, Ohio)				
Mar. 11	Florida State	N3	85	76

Mar. 16	Miami (Ohio)	N4	91	69
Mar. 18	Michigan State	N4	52	49
Finals				
(St. Louis, Mo.)				
Mar. 25	Arkansas		64	59
Mar. 27	Duke		94	88
			2693	2234

NCAA CHAMPIONS FOR FIFTH TIME

(N1) Memorial Coliseum
(N2) Louisville, Ky.
(N3) Knoxville, Tenn.
(N4) Dayton, Ohio

—Leading Scorers—

Jack Givens (6-4 Sr. F)	18.1
Rick Robey (6-10 Sr. F)	14.4
Kyle Macy (6-3 So. G)	12.5
James Lee (6-5 Sr. F)	11.3
Mike Phillips (6-10 Sr. C)	10.2
Truman Claytor (6-1 Jr. G)	6.9

1978 Japan Exhibition Tour
(All Games vs. Japan National Team)
(Not Counted in Won-Lost Record)

Jun. 13	at Tokyo		104	71
Jun. 15	at Niigata		102	89
June 18	at Nagoya		97	59
June 19	at Osaka		87	82
June 20	at Fukuoka		88	61
June 22	at Nagasaki		122	79
June 24	at Tokyo		125	57
			705	498

1978/79—Won 19, Lost 12
6th in SEC (10-8)
SEC Tournament Runner-Up

Coach: Joe B. Hall
Captains: Dwane Casey and Truman Claytor

Dec. 2	LaSalle	H	109	77
Dec. 4	West Texas	H	121	66
Dec. 9	Kansas	H	67	*66
Dec. 16	Indiana	A	67	*68
UK Invitation Tournament				
Dec. 22	Texas A & M		69	73
Dec. 23	Syracuse		94	87
Dec. 30	Notre Dame	N1	81	76
Jan. 3	Florida	A	65	76
Jan. 6	Louisiana State	H	89	93
Jan. 8	Mississippi	H	90	64
Jan. 13	Alabama	A	52	55
Jan. 15	Mississippi State	A	61	63
Jan. 20	Tennessee	H	55	66
Jan. 22	Georgia	H	73	64
Jan. 25	Auburn	A	86	*83
Jan. 27	Florida	H	87	81
Jan. 29	Auburn	H	66	59
Feb. 3	Louisiana State	A	61	70
Feb. 5	Mississippi	A	87	82
Feb. 7	Vanderbilt	A	58	68
Feb. 10	Alabama	H	80	71
Feb. 12	Mississippi State	H	80	65
Feb. 17	Tennessee	A	84	101
Feb. 19	Georgia	A	90	74
Feb. 23	Vanderbilt	H	96	70
Feb. 25	South Carolina	A	79	74
SEC Tournament				
(Birmingham, Ala.)				
Feb. 28	Mississippi		82	77
Mar. 1	Alabama		101	100
Mar. 2	Louisiana State		80	67
Mar. 3	Tennessee		69	*75
National Invitation Tournament				
(Lexington, Ky.)				
Mar. 7	Clemson		67	*68
			2446	2280

(N1) Louisville, Ky.

—Leading Scorers—
Kyle Macy (6-3 Jr. G) 15.2
Dwight Anderson (6-3 Fr. G) 13.3
LaVon Williams (6-6 So. F) 11.5
Fred Cowan (6-8 So. C-F) 9.4
Truman Claytor (6-1 Sr. G) 8.7

1979/80—Won 29, Lost 6
SEC Champions (15-3)
SEC Tournament Runner-Up
UKIT Champions
Great Alaska Shootout Champions
Ranked 4th AP, 3rd UPI

Coach: Joe B. Hall
Captain: Kyle Macy

Nov. 17	**Duke**	**N1**	**76**	***82**
Nov. 30	Bradley	N2	79	58
Dec. 1	Alaska	N2	97	68
Dec. 2	Iona	N2	57	50
Dec. 8	Baylor	H	80	46
Dec. 10	South Carolina	H	126	81
Dec. 12	Kansas	A	57	56
Dec. 15	Indiana	H	69	58
Dec. 17	Georgia	N3	95	69
	UK Invitation Tournament			
Dec. 21	California		78	52
Dec. 22	Purdue (finals)		61	60
Dec. 29	Notre Dame	N4	86	80
Jan. 2	Auburn	H	67	65
Jan. 5	**Tennessee**	**A**	**47**	**49**
Jan. 9	Mississippi	A	79	73
Jan. 12	**Alabama**	**H**	**64**	**78**
Jan. 17	Florida	A	76	63
Jan. 19	Vanderbilt	H	106	90
Jan. 23	Mississippi State	A	89	67
Jan. 26	Georgia	H	56	*49
Jan. 28	**Louisiana State**	**H**	**60**	**65**
Jan. 30	Auburn	A	64	62
Feb. 2	Tennessee	H	83	75
Feb. 6	Mississippi	H	86	72
Feb. 9	Alabama	A	72	63
Feb. 13	Florida	H	95	70
Feb. 15	Vanderbilt	A	91	73
Feb. 17	Nevada-Las Vegas	A	74	69
Feb. 20	Mississippi State	H	71	65
Feb. 24	Louisiana State	A	76	*74
	SEC Tournament **(Birmingham, Ala.)**			
Feb. 28	Auburn		69	61
Feb. 29	Mississippi		70	67
Mar. 1	**Louisiana State**		**78**	**80**
	NCAA Tournament **Mideast Regional** **(Bowling Green and Lexington, Ky.)**			
Mar. 8	Florida State	N5	97	78
Mar. 13	**Duke**	**H**	54	55
			2685	2323

(N1) Springfield, Mass.
(N2) Anchorage, Alaska
(N3) Atlanta, Ga.
(N4) Louisville, Ky.
(N5) Bowling Green, Ky.

—Leading Scorers—
Kyle Macy (6-3 Sr. G) 15.4
Sam Bowie (7-1 Fr. C) 12.9
Fred Cowan (6-8 Jr. F) 12.5
LaVon Williams (6-7 Sr. F) 7.5
Jay Shidler (6-1 Sr. G) 6.2

1980/81—Won 22, Lost 6
SEC Runner-Up (15-3)
UKIT Champions
Ranked 8th AP and UPI

Coach: Joe B. Hall
Captain: Chuck Verderber

Nov. 29	East Tennessee	H	62	57
Dec. 3	Ohio State	H	70	64
Dec. 6	Indiana	A	68	66
Dec. 13	Kansas	H	87	73
	UK Invitation Tournament			
Dec. 19	Alaska		91	56
Dec. 20	Alabama-Birmingham (finals)		61	53
Dec. 27	**Notre Dame**	**N1**	**61**	**67**
Dec. 30	Maine	H	100	54
Jan. 3	Georgia	H	76	62
Jan. 7	Auburn	A	79	66
Jan. 10	Tennessee	H	48	47
Jan. 14	Mississippi	H	64	55
Jan. 17	**Alabama**	**A**	**55**	**59**
Jan. 19	**Louisiana State**	**A**	**67**	**81**
Jan. 21	Florida	H	102	48
Jan. 24	Vanderbilt	A	78	64
Jan. 28	Mississippi State	H	71	64
Jan. 31	Georgia	A	71	**68
Feb. 4	Auburn	H	102	74
Feb. 7	**Tennessee**	**A**	**71**	**87**
Feb. 11	Mississippi	A	62	55
Feb. 14	Alabama	H	77	62
Feb. 18	Florida	A	69	56
Feb. 21	Vanderbilt	H	80	48
Feb. 25	Mississippi State	A	78	74
Mar. 1	Louisiana State	H	73	71
	SEC Tournament **(Birmingham, Ala.)**			
Mar. 5	**Vanderbilt**		**55**	**60**
	NCAA Tournament **Mideast Regional** **(Tuscaloosa, Ala.)**			
Mar. 15	**Alabama-Birmingham**		62	69
			2040	1760

(N1) Louisville, Ky.

—Leading Scorers—
Sam Bowie (7-1 So. C) 17.4
Dirk Minniefield (6-3 So. G) 10.4
Derrick Hord (6-6 So. G-F) 8.9
Fred Cowan (6-8 Sr. F) 8.2
Chuck Verderber (6-6 Jr. F) 7.5

1981/82—Won 22, Lost 8
SEC Co-Champions (13-5)
UKIT Champions
Ranked 8th AP, 9th UPI

Coach: Joe B. Hall
Captain: Chuck Verderber

Nov. 28	Akron	H	83	64
Dec. 5	Ohio State	A	78	62
Dec. 8	Indiana	H	85	69
Dec. 12	Kansas	A	77	*74
	UK Invitation Tournament			
Dec. 18	Jacksonville	H	107	91
Dec. 19	Seton Hall	H	98	74
Dec. 26	**North Carolina**	**N1**	**69**	**82**
Dec. 29	Notre Dame	N2	34	*28
Jan. 2	Georgia	A	68	66
Jan. 6	Auburn	H	83	71
Jan. 9	**Tennessee**	**A**	**66**	**70**
Jan. 13	**Mississippi**	**A**	**65**	**67**
Jan. 16	Alabama	H	86	69
Jan. 20	Florida	A	91	76
Jan. 23	Vanderbilt	H	67	58
Jan. 25	Louisiana State	H	76	65
Jan. 27	**Mississippi State**	**A**	**51**	**56**
Jan. 30	Georgia	H	82	73
Feb. 3	**Auburn**	**A**	**81**	***83**
Feb. 6	Tennessee	H	77	67
Feb. 10	Mississippi	H	56	49
Feb. 13	Alabama	A	72	62
Feb. 17	Florida	H	84	78
Feb. 20	Vanderbilt	A	73	69
Feb. 24	Mississippi State	H	71	54
Feb. 27	**Louisiana State**	**A**	**78**	**94**
	SEC Tournament **(Lexington, Ky.)**			
Mar. 4	Auburn		89	66
Mar. 5	Mississippi		62	58
Mar. 6	**Alabama**		**46**	**48**
	NCAA Mideast Regional **(Nashville, Tenn.)**			
Mar. 4	**Middle Tennessee**		44	50
			2199	1993

(N1) East Rutherford, N.J.
(N2) Louisville, Ky.

—Leading Scorers—
Derrick Hord (6-6 Jr. F) 16.3
Jim Master (6-5 So. G) 13.4
Melvin Turpin (6-10 So. C) 13.1
Dirk Minniefield (6-3 Jr. G) 11.3
Charles Hurt (6-6 Jr. F) 6.6

1982 Japan Exhibition Tour (Not Counted in Won-Lost Record)

July 1	W. Germany at Kariya	84	73
July 2	France at Kyotta	77	65
July 4	W. Germany at Sapporo	82	72
July 7	Japan Nat. at Akita	86	6
July 10	France at Moebashi	86	8
July 11	Japan at Tokyo	106	71

Note: The Wildcats also toured Taiwan and Hong Kong during the 1982 trip. The following are results of games played there:

July 12	China #2 at Taipei	86	63
July 15	China #1 at Hong Kong	119	48

1982/83—Won 23, Lost 8
SEC Champions (13-5)
UKIT Champions
Ranked 12th AP and UPI

Coach: Joe B. Hall
Captain: Charles Hurt

Nov. 27	Butler	H	90	53
Dec. 1	Notre Dame	A	58	45
Dec. 4	Villanova	H	93	79
Dec. 7	Detroit	H	83	46
Dec. 11	Illinois	H	76	57
	UK Invitation Tournament			
Dec. 17	Duquesne	H	55	42
Dec. 18	Tulane	H	80	61
Dec. 22	**Indiana**	**A**	**59**	**62**
Dec. 29	Kansas	N1	83	62
Jan. 3	Mississippi	H	72	60
Jan. 5	Louisiana State	H	52	50
Jan. 8	**Alabama**	**A**	**67**	**74**
Jan. 10	Mississippi State	A	59	*53
Jan. 15	**Auburn**	**H**	**67**	**75**
Jan. 17	Florida	H	70	63
Jan. 22	Vanderbilt	A	82	*77
Jan. 29	**Georgia**	**A**	**63**	**70**
Jan. 31	**Tennessee**	**A**	**63**	**65**
Feb. 5	Alabama	H	76	70
Feb. 8	Mississippi State	H	88	67
Feb. 12	Auburn	A	71	69
Feb. 14	Florida	A	73	61
Feb. 19	Vanderbilt	H	82	63
Feb. 26	Georgia	H	81	72
Feb. 27	Tennessee	H	69	61
Mar. 3	Mississippi	H	61	58
Mar. 5	**Louisiana State**	**A**	**60**	**74**
	SEC Tournament **(Birmingham, Ala.)**			
Mar. 11	**Alabama**	**N2**	**64**	**69**
	NCAA Mideast Regional **(First Round)**			
Mar. 19	Ohio	N3	57	40
	NCAA Mideast Region			
Mar. 24	Indiana	N4	64	59
Mar. 26	**Louisville**	**N4**	68	*80
			2186	1937

(N1) Louisville, Ky.
(N2) Birmingham, Ala.
(N3) Tampa, Fla.
(N4) Knoxville, Tenn.

—Leading Scorers—

Melvin Turpin (6-11 Jr. C)	15.1
Jim Master (6-5 Jr. G)	12.5
Derrick Hord (6-6 Sr. F)	8.9
Dirk Minniefield (6-3 Sr. G)	8.6
Charles Hurt (6-6 Sr. F)	8.2

1983/84—Won 29, Lost 5
NCAA Mideast Region Champions
SEC Tournament Champions
SEC Champions (14-4)
UKIT Champions
Ranked 3rd AP and UPI

Coach: Joe B. Hall
Captain: Dicky Beal

Date	Opponent			
Nov. 26	Louisville	H	65	44
Dec. 3	Indiana	H	59	54
Dec. 10	Kansas	A	72	50
	UK Invitation Tournament			
Dec. 16	Wyoming		66	40
Dec. 17	Brigham Young (finals)		93	59
Dec. 20	Cincinnati	A	24	11
Dec. 24	Illinois	A	56	54
Dec. 28	Purdue	N1	86	67
Jan. 2	Mississippi	A	68	55
Jan. 7	Louisiana State	A	96	80
Jan. 9	Alabama	H	76	66
Jan. 11	Mississippi State	H	51	42
Jan. 13	**Auburn**	**A**	**63**	**82**
Jan. 17	**Florida**	**A**	**57**	**69**
Jan. 20	Vanderbilt	H	67	46
Jan. 22	Houston	H	74	67
Jan. 28	Georgia	H	64	40
Jan. 30	Tennessee	H	93	74
Feb. 4	**Alabama**	**A**	**62**	**69**
Feb. 6	Mississippi State	A	77	58
Feb. 11	Auburn	H	84	64
Feb. 13	Florida	H	67	65
Feb. 19	Vanderbilt	A	58	54
Feb. 25	Georgia	A	66	64
Feb. 27	**Tennessee**	**A**	**58**	**63**
Mar. 1	Mississippi	H	76	57
Mar. 3	Louisiana State	H	90	68
	SEC Tournament			
	(Nashville, Tenn.)			
Mar. 8	Georgia	N2	92	79
Mar. 9	Alabama	N2	48	46
Mar. 10	Auburn (finals)	N2	51	49
	NCAA Mideast Regional			
	(First Round)			
Mar. 17	Brigham Young	N3	93	68
	NCAA Mideast Region			
	(Lexington, Ky.)			
Mar. 22	Louisville	H	72	67
Mar. 24	Illinois	H	54	51
	NCAA Final Four			
	(Seattle, Wash.)			
Mar. 31	**Georgetown**	**N4**	**40**	**53**
			2318	1975

(N1) Louisville, Ky.
(N2) Nashville, Tenn.
(N3) Birmingham, Ala.
(N4) Seattle, Wash.

—Leading Scorers—

Melvin Turpin (6-11 Sr. C)	15.2
Kenny Walker (6-8 So. F)	12.4
Sam Bowie (7-1 Sr. F)	10.5
Jim Master (6-5 Sr. G)	9.6
Winston Bennett (6-7 Fr. F)	6.5

1984/85—Won 18, Lost 13
NCAA "Final 16"
Tied for 3rd in SEC (11-7)
UKIT Champions

Coach: Joe B. Hall
Captains: Winston Bennett and Kenny Walker

Date	Opponent			
Nov. 27	Toledo	H	63	54
Dec. 1	**Purdue**	**A**	**56**	**66**
Dec. 4	Southern Methodist	H	54	56
Dec. 8	**Indiana**	**A**	**68**	**81**
Dec. 15	**Louisville**	**A**	**64**	**71**
	UK Invitation Tournament			
Dec. 21	East Tennessee State		69	54
Dec. 22	Cincinnati		66	55
Dec. 31	Kansas	N1	92	89
Jan. 2	Auburn	H	68	61
Jan. 5	North Carolina State	H	78	62
Jan. 7	Vanderbilt	H	75	58
Jan. 9	Mississippi	A	57	45
Jan. 12	**Alabama**	**A**	**58**	**60**
Jan. 16	Mississippi State	H	58	57
Jan. 19	**Florida**	**H**	**55**	**67**
Jan. 23	**Georgia**	**A**	**73**	**81**
Jan. 27	**Tennessee**	**A**	**65**	**81**
Jan. 31	Louisiana State	H	53	43
Feb. 2	Auburn	A	49	*47
Feb. 7	Vanderbilt	A	68	62
Feb. 9	Mississippi	H	67	52
Feb. 13	Alabama	H	51	48
Feb. 16	**Mississippi State**	**A**	**69**	**82**
Feb. 20	Florida	A	76	68
Feb. 24	**Georgia**	**H**	**77**	**79**
Feb. 28	Tennessee	H	92	67
Mar. 2	**Louisiana State**	**A**	**61**	**67**
	SEC Tournament			
	(Birmingham, Ala.)			
Mar. 7	**Florida**	**N2**	**55**	**58**
	NCAA West Regional			
	First Round			
	(Salt Lake City, Utah)			
Mar. 14	Washington	N3	66	58
Mar. 16	Nevada-Las Vegas	N3	64	61
	NCAA West Regional			
	(Denver, Colo.)			
Mar. 22	**St. John's**	**N4**	**70**	**86**
			2037	1976

(N1) Louisville, Ky.
(N2) Birmingham, Ala.
(N3) Salt Lake City, Utah
(N4) Denver, Colo.

—Leading Scorers—

Kenny Walker (6-8 Jr. F)	22.9
Ed Davender (6-1 Fr. G)	8.5
Winston Bennett (6-7 So. F)	7.2
Bret Bearup (6-9 Sr. C)	6.3
James Blackmon (6-2 So. G)	5.4
Roger Harden (6-1 Jr. G)	5.3

EDDIE SUTTON ERA

1985/86—Won 32, Lost 4
NCAA "Final 8"
SEC Champions (17-1)
SEC Tournament Champions
Ranked 3rd AP and UPI

Coach: Eddie Sutton
Captains: Kenny Walker, Roger Harden and Leroy Byrd

Date	Opponent			
Nov. 22	Northwestern (LA) State	H	77	58
Nov. 26	Chaminade	A	89	57
Nov. 27	Hawaii	A	98	65
Dec. 3	Cincinnati	H	84	54
Dec. 7	Indiana	H	63	58
Dec. 14	**Kansas**	**A**	**66**	**83**
	UK Invitation Tournament			
Dec. 20	East Carolina	H	86	52
Dec. 21	Pepperdine (finals)	H	88	56
Dec. 28	Louisville	H	69	64
Dec. 30	Va. Military Institute	N1	93	55
Jan. 4	Vanderbilt	A	80	71
Jan. 6	**Auburn**	**A**	**56**	**60**
Jan. 8	Mississippi	H	75	58
Jan. 11	Alabama	H	76	52
Jan. 15	Mississippi State	A	64	52
Jan. 18	Florida	H	72	55
Jan. 23	Georgia	H	74	69
Jan. 25	Tennessee	H	74	57
Jan. 29	LSU	A	54	52
Jan. 31	Auburn	H	81	71
Feb. 2	**North Carolina State**	**A**	**51**	**54**
Feb. 5	Vanderbilt	H	73	65
Feb. 8	Mississippi	A	62	58
Feb. 13	Alabama	A	73	71
Feb. 15	Mississippi State	H	88	62
Feb. 19	Florida	H	80	69
Feb. 22	Georgia	A	80	75
Feb. 27	Tennessee	A	62	60
Mar. 1	LSU	H	68	57
	SEC Tournament			
	(Lexington, Ky.)			
Mar. 6	Mississippi		95	69
Mar. 7	Louisiana State		61	58
Mar. 8	Alabama		83	72
	NCAA Southeast Regional			
	First/Second Round			
	(Charlotte, N.C.)			
Mar. 14	Davidson	N2	75	55
Mar. 16	Western Kentucky	N2	71	64
	NCAA Southeast Regional			
	(Atlanta, Ga.)			
Mar. 20	Alabama	N3	68	63
Mar. 22	**Louisiana State**	**N3**	**57**	**59**
			2666	2210

(N1) Louisville, Ky.
(N2) Charlotte, N.C.
(N3) Atlanta, Ga.

—Leading Scorers—

Kenny Walker (6-8 Sr. F)	20.0
Winston Bennett (6-7 Jr. F)	12.7
Ed Davender (6-2 So. G)	11.5
James Blackmon (6-3 Jr. G)	9.4
Roger Harden (6-1 Sr. G)	6.8

1986 Japan Tour
(Not Counted in Won-Lost Record)

Date	Opponent		
June 21[1]	Japan at Tokyo	80	55
June 22[1]	Finland at Tokyo	87	67
June 24	Japan at Sendai	82	65
June 26	Japan at Niigata	79	73
June 28	Finland at Ohtsu	80	56
June 29	**Czechoslovakia at Sapporo**	**74**	**80**
July 2	S. China	87	45

[1] Kirin World Tournament Hong Kong Game

1986/87—Won 18, Lost 11
NCAA Tournament Participant
UKIT Champions
SEC 3rd Place (10-8)

Coach: Eddie Sutton
Captains: James Blackmon and Paul Andrews

Date	Opponent			
Nov. 29	Austin Peay	H	71	69
Dec. 2	Texas Tech	H	66	60
Dec. 6	**Indiana**	**A**	**66**	**71**
Dec. 13	Lamar	H	71	56
	UK Invitation Tournament			
Dec. 19	Iona		75	59
Dec. 20	Boston U. (finals)		81	69
Dec. 27	Louisville	A	85	51
Dec. 30	**Georgia**	**N1**	**65**	**69**
Jan. 3	Auburn	A	63	60
Jan. 7	**Alabama**	**H**	**55**	**69**
Jan. 10	**Tennessee**	**A**	**68**	**75**
Jan. 12	Mississippi State	A	57	49
Jan. 14	Florida	H	67	62
Jan. 18	**LSU**	**H**	**41**	**76**
Jan. 21	Vanderbilt	A	71	65
Jan. 25	Navy	H	80	69
Jan. 29	**Ole Miss**	**A**	**65**	**76**
Jan. 31	Mississippi State	H	50	36
Feb. 4	Auburn	H	75	71
Feb. 7	Alabama	A	70	69
Feb. 11	Tennessee	H	91	*84
Feb. 14	**Florida**	**A**	**56**	**74**
Feb. 19	Vanderbilt	H	65	54
Feb. 21	**LSU**	**A**	**52**	**65**

Feb. 25	Georgia	A	71	79
Feb. 28	Ole Miss	H	64	63
Feb. 29	Oklahoma	H	75	74
SEC Tournament (Atlanta, Ga.)				
Mar. 6	Auburn	N2	72	79
NCAA Southeast Regional First/Second Round (Atlanta, Ga.)				
Mar. 13	Ohio State	N2	77	91
			1965	1944

(N1) Freedom Hall, Louisville, Ky.
(N2) The Omni, Atlanta, Ga.

—Leading Scorers—

Rex Chapman (6-4 Fr. G)	16.0
Ed Davender (6-3 Jr. G)	15.2
Richard Madison (6-7 Jr. F)	9.1
James Blackmon (6-3 Sr. G)	8.4
Robert Lock(6-11 Jr. C)	7.5

1987/88—Won 25, Lost 5[1]
UKIT Champions
Best SEC Record (13-5)
Ranked 6th AP and UPI

Coach: Eddie Sutton
Captains: Winston Bennett, Ed Davender, Cedric Jenkins, Rob Lock, and Richard Madison

Nov. 28	Hawaii	H	86	59
Dec. 1	Cincinnati	H	101	77
Dec. 5	Indiana	N1	82	*76
Dec. 12	Louisville	H	76	75
UK Invitation Tournament				
Dec. 18	Miami (Ohio)		85	71
Dec. 19	N.C. Charlotte (finals)		84	81
Dec. 28	Alaska	H	100	58
Dec. 31	Vanderbilt	H	81	74
Jan. 2	Georgia	A	84	77
Jan. 6	Mississippi State	H	93	52
Jan. 9	**Auburn**	**H**	**52**	**53**
Jan. 13	Alabama	A	63	55
Jan. 16	Tennessee	H	83	65
Jan. 20	**Florida**	**H**	**56**	**58**
Jan. 23	LSU	A	76	61
Jan. 27	**Vanderbilt**	**A**	**66**	**83**
Jan. 31	Notre Dame	N2	78	69
Feb. 3	Ole Miss	H	94	65
Feb. 6	Mississippi State	A	83	59
Feb. 10	Auburn	A	69	62
Feb. 13	Alabama	H	82	68
Feb. 17	**Tennessee**	**A**	**70**	**72**
Feb. 20	**Florida**	**A**	**76**	**83**
Feb. 24	LSU	H	95	69
Feb. 28	Syracuse	H	62	58
Mar. 2	Georgia	H	80	72
Mar. 5	Ole Miss	A	78	71
SEC Tournament[2] (Baton Rouge, La.)				
Mar. 11	Ole Miss	N3	82	64
Mar. 12	LSU	N3	86	80
Mar. 13	Georgia	N3	62	57
			2365	2024

(N1) Indianapolis, Ind.
(N2) Louisville, Ky.
(N3) Baton Rouge, La.

—Leading Scorers—

Rex Chapman (6-4 So. G)	19.0
Ed Davender (6-3 Sr. G)	15.7
Winston Bennett (6-7 Sr. F)	15.3
Rob Lock (6-11 Sr. C)	10.9
Eric Manuel (6-6 Fr. F)	7.1

[1] As part of sanctions imposed upon the UK basketball program in 1989, the National Collegiate Athletic Association ordered Kentucky to erase from the record three NCAA tournament games from the 1987/88 season. Kentucky's 99-84 win over Southern, a 90-81 win over Maryland, and an 80-74 loss to Villanova have been deleted from the records, thus changing the 1987/88 season record from 27-6 to 25-5.

[2] The presidents of the Southeastern Conference institutions voted to strip Kentucky of the 1987/88 SEC regular season and SEC tournament championships. Kentucky was not forced to forfeit any of those regular season or tournament games.

1988/89—Won 13, Lost 19
Tied for 6th in SEC (8-10)

Coach: Eddie Sutton
Captain: Mike Scott

Nov. 19	**Duke**	**N1**	**55**	**80**
Nov. 25	Iona	N2	56	54
Nov. 26	**Seton Hall**	**N2**	**60**	**63**
Nov. 28	California	N2	89	71
Dec. 3	**Notre Dame**	**N3**	**65**	**81**
Dec. 7	**Northwestern State**	**H**	**82**	**85**
Dec. 10	Western Carolina	H	78	60
UK Invitation Tournament				
Dec. 16	**Bowling Green State**	**H**	**54**	**56**
Dec. 17	Marshall	H	91	78
Dec. 20	**Indiana**	**H**	**52**	**75**
Dec. 27	Austin Peay	N4	85	77
Dec. 31	**Louisville**	**A**	**75**	**97**
Jan. 4	Georgia	H	76	65
Jan. 7	Vanderbilt	H	70	61
Jan. 12	Florida	A	69	56
Jan. 14	**LSU**	**H**	**62**	**64**
Jan. 18	**Alabama**	**A**	**64**	**76**
Jan. 21	Tennessee	A	66	65
Jan. 25	Auburn	H	86	76
Jan. 28	**Ole Miss**	**A**	**65**	**70**
Feb. 1	Mississippi State	H	73	61
Feb. 5	**Georgia**	**A**	**72**	**84**
Feb. 8	**Vanderbilt**	**A**	**51**	**81**
Feb. 11	**Florida**	**H**	**53**	**59**
Feb. 15	**LSU**	**A**	**80**	**99**
Feb. 18	**Alabama**	**H**	**67**	**71**
Feb. 20	**Auburn**	**A**	**75**	**77**
Feb. 22	Tennessee	H	76	71
Feb. 26	**Syracuse**	**A**	**73**	**89**
Mar. 1	Ole Miss	H	70	69
Mar. 4	**Mississippi State**	**A**	**67**	**68**
SEC Tournament (Knoxville, Tenn.)				
Mar. 10	Vanderbilt		63	77
			2220	2316

(N1) Springfield, Mass.
(N2) Anchorage, Alaska
(N3) Indianapolis, Ind.
(N4) Louisville, Ky.

—Leading Scorers—

LeRon Ellis (6-10 So. C)	16.0
Chris Mills (6-7 Fr. F)	14.3
Derrick Miller (6-5 Jr. G)	13.9
Reggie Hanson (6-7 So. F)	9.8
Sean Sutton (6-1 So. G)	5.9

RICK PITINO ERA

1989/90—Won 14, Lost 14
SEC Record (10-8)

Coach: Rick Pitino
Captain: Derrick Miller

Nov. 28	Ohio	H	76	73
Dec. 2	**Indiana**	**N1**	**69**	**71**
Dec. 4	Mississippi State	H	102	97
Dec. 6	Tennessee Tech	H	111	75
Dec. 9	**Kansas**	**A**	**95**	**150**
Dec. 19	Furman	H	104	73
UK Invitation Tournament				
Dec. 22	Portland		88	71
Dec. 23	**Southwestern La. (finals)**		**113**	***116**
Dec. 27	**North Carolina**	**N2**	**110**	**121**
Dec. 30	**Louisville**	**H**	**79**	**86**
Jan. 3	**Georgia**	**A**	**91**	**106**
Jan. 6	**Vanderbilt**	**A**	**85**	**92**
Jan. 10	Florida	H	89	81
Jan. 13	**LSU**	**A**	**81**	**94**
Jan. 17	Alabama	H	82	65

Jan. 20	Tennessee	H	95	83
Jan. 24	**Auburn**	**A**	**70**	**74**
Jan. 27	Ole Miss	H	98	79
Jan. 31	**Mississippi State**	**A**	**86**	**87**
Feb. 3	Georgia	H	88	77
Feb. 7	Vanderbilt	H	100	73
Feb. 12	Florida	A	78	74
Feb. 15	LSU	H	100	95
Feb. 17	**Alabama**	**A**	**58**	**83**
Feb. 21	**Tennessee**	**A**	**100**	**102**
Feb. 24	Auburn	H	98	95
Feb. 28	**Ole Miss**	**A**	**74**	**88**
Mar. 5	**Notre Dame**	**A**	**67**	**80**
			2487	2461

(N1) Indianapolis, Ind.
(N2) Louisville, Ky.

—Leading Scorers—

Derrick Miller (6-5 Sr. G)	19.2
Reggie Hanson (6-7 Jr. C)	16.4
Deron Feldhaus (6-7 So. F)	14.4
John Pelphrey (6-7 So. F)	13.0
Sean Woods (6-2 So. G)	9.1

1990/91—Won 22, Lost 6
Best Record in SEC (14-4)
Ranked 9th AP

Coach: Rick Pitino
Captains: Deron Feldhaus, Reggie Hanson, and John Pelphrey

Nov. 24	Pennsylvania	H	85	62
Nov. 28	Cincinnati	A	75	71
Dec. 1	Notre Dame	N1	98	90
Dec. 8	Kansas	H	88	71
Dec. 10	**North Carolina**	**A**	**81**	**84**
Dec. 15	Tennessee-Chattanooga	H	86	70
Dec. 18	**Indiana**	**A**	**84**	**87**
Dec. 21	Western Kentucky	N2	84	70
Dec. 27	Eastern Kentucky	H	74	60
Dec. 29	Louisville	A	93	85
Jan. 2	Georgia	A	81	80
Jan. 5	LSU	H	93	80
Jan. 9	Mississippi State	H	89	70
Jan. 12	Tennessee	A	78	74
Jan. 16	Ole Miss	A	95	85
Jan. 19	Vanderbilt	H	58	50
Jan. 23	Florida	H	81	65
Jan. 26	**Alabama**	**A**	**83**	**88**
Jan. 29	Auburn	A	89	81
Feb. 3	Georgia	H	96	84
Feb. 5	**LSU**	**A**	**88**	**107**
Feb. 9	**Mississippi State**	**A**	**82**	**83**
Feb. 13	Tennessee	H	85	74
Feb. 16	Ole Miss	H	89	77
Feb. 20	**Vanderbilt**	**A**	**87**	**98**
Feb. 23	Florida	A	90	74
Feb. 28	Alabama	H	79	73
Mar. 2	Auburn	H	114	93
			2405	2186

(N1) Indianapolis, Ind.
(N2) Louisville, Ky.

—Leading Scorers—

John Pelphrey (6-7 Jr. F)	14.4
Reggie Hanson (6-8 Sr. C)	14.4
Jamal Mashburn (6-9 Fr. F)	12.9
Deron Feldhaus (6-7 Jr. F)	10.8
Richie Farmer (6-0 Jr. G)	10.1

1991/92—Won 29, Lost 7
NCAA "Final 8"
SEC East Champions (12-4)
SEC Tournament Champions
Ranked 6th AP and CNN/USA Today

Coach: Rick Pitino
Captains: Richie Farmer, Deron Feldhaus, John Pelphrey, and Sean Woods

Preseason NIT

Nov. 20	West Virginia	H	106	80
Nov. 22	**Pittsburgh**	**H**	**67**	**85**

Dec. 4	Massachusetts	H	90	69
Dec. 7	Indiana	N1	76	74
Dec. 10	SW Texas State	H	82	36
Dec. 12	Morehead State	N2	101	84
Dec. 14	Arizona State	H	94	68
Dec. 21	**Georgia Tech**	**A**	**80**	**81**
Dec. 23	Ohio	N3	73	63
Dec. 28	Louisville	H	103	89
Jan. 2	Notre Dame	H	91	70
Jan. 4	South Carolina	A	80	63
Jan. 7	Georgia	H	78	66
Jan. 11	Florida	H	81	60
Jan. 15	Vanderbilt	A	84	71
Jan. 18	Eastern Kentucky	H	85	55
Jan. 21	**Tennessee**	**A**	**85**	**107**
Jan. 25	**Arkansas**	**H**	**88**	**105**
Jan. 29	Ole Miss	H	96	78
Feb. 2	**LSU**	**A**	**53**	**74**
Feb. 8	Auburn	A	85	67
Feb. 12	Alabama	H	107	83
Feb. 15	Western Kentucky	H	93	83
Feb. 19	Mississippi State	A	89	84
Feb. 23	Georgia	A	84	73
Feb. 26	South Carolina	H	74	56
Mar. 1	**Vanderbilt**	**H**	**80**	**56**
Mar. 4	**Florida**	**A**	**62**	**79**
Mar. 7	Tennessee	H	99	88

SEC Tournament
(Birmingham, Ala.)

Mar. 13	Vanderbilt	N4	76	57
Mar. 14	LSU	N4	80	74
Mar. 15	Alabama	N4	80	54

NCAA East Regional
First/Second Rounds
(Worcester, Mass.)

Mar. 20	Old Dominion	N5	88	69
Mar. 22	Iowa State	N5	106	98

NCAA East Regional
(Philadelphia, Pa.)

Mar. 26	Massachusetts	N6	87	77
Mar. 28	**Duke**	**N6**	**103**	***104**
			3086	2680

(N1) Indianapolis, Ind.
(N2) Louisville, Ky.
(N3) Cincinnati, Ohio
(N4) Birmingham, Ala.
(N5) Worcester, Mass.
(N6) Philadelphia, Pa.

—Leading Scorers—
Jamal Mashburn (6-8 So. F) 21.3
John Pelphrey (6-7 Sr. F) 12.5
Deron Feldhaus (6-7 Sr. F) 11.4
Richie Farmer (6-0 Sr. G) 9.6
Sean Woods (6-2 Sr. G) 7.7

1992/93—Won 30, Lost 4
NCAA "Final 4"
SEC Tournament Champions
2nd SEC East (13-3)
Ranked 6th AP, 3rd CNN/USA Today

Coach: Rick Pitino
Captains: Junior Braddy and Dale Brown

Dec. 2	Wright State	H	81	65
Dec. 5	Georgia Tech	H	96	87
Dec. 8	Eastern Kentucky	H	82	73
Dec. 12	Louisville	A	88	68
Dec. 19	Morehead State	H	108	65
Dec. 22	Miami (Ohio)	H	65	49

ECAC Holiday Festival
(New York, N.Y.)

Dec. 28	Rutgers	N1	89	67
Dec. 30	St. John's (finals)	N1	86	77
Jan. 3	Indiana	N2	81	78
Jan. 5	Georgia	A	74	59
Jan. 9	Tennessee	H	84	70
Jan. 13	**Vanderbilt**	**A**	**86**	**101**
Jan. 19	Alabama	A	73	59
Jan. 23	South Carolina	A	108	82

Jan. 26	LSU	H	105	67
Jan. 30	Florida	H	71	48
Feb. 3	Mississippi State	H	87	63
Feb. 6	Vanderbilt	H	82	67
Feb. 10	**Arkansas**	**A**	**94**	**101**
Feb. 13	Notre Dame	A	81	62
Feb. 17	South Carolina	H	87	66
Feb. 20	Georgia	H	86	70
Feb. 24	**Tennessee**	**A**	**77**	**78**
Feb. 27	Auburn	H	80	78
Mar. 3	Mississippi	A	98	66
Mar. 9	Florida	A	85	77

SEC Tournament
(Lexington, Ky.)

Mar. 12	Tennessee	N3	101	40
Mar. 13	Arkansas	N3	92	81
Mar. 14	LSU	N3	82	65

NCAA Southeast Regional
First/Second Rounds
(Nashville, Tenn.)

Mar. 19	Rider College	N4	96	52
Mar. 21	Utah	N4	83	62

NCAA Southeast Regional
(Charlotte, N.C.)

Mar. 25	Wake Forest	N5	103	69
Mar. 27	Florida State	N5	106	81

NCAA Final Four
(New Orleans, La.)

April 3	Michigan	N6	78	*81
			2975	2374

(N1) New York, N.Y.
(N2) Louisville, Ky.
(N3) Lexington, Ky.
(N4) Nashville, Tenn.
(N5) Charlotte, N.C.
(N6) New Orleans, La.

—Leading Scorers—
Jamal Mashburn (6-8 Jr. F) 21.0
Travis Ford (5-9 Jr. G) 13.6
Dale Brown (6-2 Sr. G) 9.4
Rodrick Rhodes (6-6 Fr. F) 9.1
Rodney Dent (6-10 Jr. C) 6.4

1993/94—Won 27, Lost 7
NCAA Second Round
SEC Tournament Champions
Tied for 1st SEC East (12-4)
Ranked 7th AP

Coach: Rick Pitino
Captains: Travis Ford, Gimel Martinez, and Jeff Brassow

Nov. 27	Louisville	H	78	70
Dec. 1	Tennessee Tech	H	115	77
Dec. 4	**Indiana**	**N1**	**84**	**96**
Dec. 8	Eastern Kentucky	H	107	78
Dec. 17	Morehead State	H	97	61

Maui Invitational

Dec. 21	Texas	N2	86	61
Dec. 22	Ohio State	N2	100	88
Dec. 23	Arizona (finals)	N2	93	92
Dec. 28	San Francisco	H	110	83
Dec. 30	Robert Morris	H	92	67
Jan. 4	Vanderbilt	H	107	82
Jan. 6	Notre Dame	H	84	59
Jan. 8	**Georgia**	**A**	**90**	***94**
Jan. 12	Mississippi	N3	98	64
Jan. 15	Tennessee	H	93	74
Jan. 18	**Florida**	**A**	**57**	**59**
Jan. 22	Mississippi State	A	86	70
Jan. 26	South Carolina	H	79	67
Jan. 30	Auburn	A	91	74
Feb. 2	Alabama	H	82	67
Feb. 6	Massachusetts	N4	67	64
Feb. 9	**Arkansas**	**H**	**82**	**90**
Feb. 12	**Syracuse**	**A**	**85**	**93**
Feb. 15	LSU	A	99	95
Feb. 19	Vanderbilt	A	77	69
Feb. 23	Tennessee	A	77	73
Feb. 27	Georgia	H	80	59

Mar. 2	Florida	H	80	77
Mar. 5	**South Carolina**	**A**	**74**	**75**

SEC Tournament
(Memphis, Tenn.)

Mar. 11	Mississippi State	N5	95	76
Mar. 12	Arkansas	N5	90	78
Mar. 13	Florida	N5	73	60

NCAA Southeast Regional
First/Second Rounds
(St. Petersburg, Fla)

Mar. 18	Tennessee State	N6	83	70
Mar. 20	**Marquette**	**N6**	**63**	**75**
			2954	2537

(N1) Indianapolis, Ind.
(N2) Maui, Hawaii
(N3) Louisville, Ky.
(N4) East Rutherford, N.J.
(N5) Memphis, Tenn.
(N6) St. Petersburg, Fla.

—Leading Scorers—
Tony Delk (6-1 So. G) 16.6
Rodrick Rhodes (6-7 So., F) 14.6
Travis Ford (5-9 Sr. G) 11.3
Jared Prickett (6-9 So. F) 8.2
Andre Riddick (6-9 Jr. C) 7.9

1994/95—Won 28, Lost 5
SEC Champions (14-2)
SEC East Champions
SEC Tournament Champions
Ranked 2nd AP, 5th CNN/USA Today

Coach: Rick Pitino
Captains: Tony Delk, Mark Pope, and Rodrick Rhodes

Nov. 26	Tennessee-Martin	H	124	50
Nov. 30	Ohio	H	79	74
Dec. 3	**UCLA**	**N1**	**81**	**82**
Dec. 7	Indiana	N2	73	70
Dec. 10	Boston University	H	90	49
Dec. 17	Texas Tech	N3	83	68
Dec. 27	Marshall	H	116	75
Jan. 1	**Louisville**	**A**	**86**	**88**
Jan. 4	Auburn	H	98	64
Jan. 7	South Carolina	A	80	55
Jan. 10	Florida	A	83	67
Jan. 14	Georgia	H	83	71
Jan. 18	Mississippi	N4	82	65
Jan. 21	Vanderbilt	H	81	68
Jan. 25	Tennessee	H	69	50
Jan. 29	**Arkansas**	**A**	**92**	**94**
Feb. 1	South Carolina	H	90	72
Feb. 5	Syracuse	H	77	71
Feb. 8	Tennessee	A	68	48
Feb. 12	Notre Dame	A	97	58
Feb. 14	**Mississippi State**	**H**	**71**	**76**
Feb. 18	Florida	H	87	77
Feb. 21	Alabama	A	72	52
Feb. 25	Vanderbilt	A	71	60
Mar. 1	Georgia	A	97	74
Mar. 4	LSU	H	127	80

SEC Tournament
(Atlanta, Ga.)

Mar. 10	Auburn	N5	93	81
Mar. 11	Florida	N5	86	72
Mar. 12	Arkansas	N5	95	*93

NCAA Southeast Regional
First/Second Rounds
(Memphis, Tenn.)

Mar. 16	Mount St. Mary's	N6	113	67
Mar. 18	Tulane	N6	82	60

NCAA Southeast Regional
(Birmingham, Ala.)

Mar. 23	Arizona State	N7	97	73
Mar. 25	**North Carolina**	**N7**	**61**	**74**
			2884	2278

(N1) Anaheim, Calif.
(N2) Louisville, Ky.
(N3) Cincinnati, Ohio
(N4) Memphis, Tenn.

(N5) Atlanta, Ga.
(N6) Memphis, Tenn.
(N7) Birmingham, Ala.

—Leading Scorers—
Tony Delk (6-1 Jr. G) 16.7
Rodrick Rhodes (6-7 Jr. F) 12.9
Walter McCarty (6-9 Jr. F) 10.5
Jeff Sheppard (6-4 So. G) 8.3
Mark Pope (6-10 Jr. C) 8.2

1995 Italy Tour
(Not Counted in Won-Lost Record)

Aug. 14	Cagiva Varese	A	123	114
Aug. 16	Venice Reyer	A	113	78
Aug. 17	Russia Dinamo	N8	116	81
Aug. 18	**Montecatini**	**A**	**115**	**123**
Aug. 21	Siena	N9	115	86

(N8) Venice, Italy
(N9) Scauri, Italy

1995/96—Won 34, Lost 2
National Champions (NCAA Tournament)
SEC Champions (16-0)
SEC East Champions
ECAC Holiday Festival Champions
Ranked 1st CNN/USA Today, 2nd AP

Coach: Rick Pitino
Captains: Tony Delk, Walter McCarty, and Mark Pope

Nov. 24	Maryland	N1	96	84
Nov. 28	**Massachusetts**	**N2**	**82**	**92**
Dec. 2	Indiana	N3	89	82
Dec. 6	Wisconsin-Green Bay	H	74	62
Dec. 9	Georgia Tech	H	83	60
Dec. 16	Morehead State	H	96	32
Dec. 19	Marshall	N4	118	99
Dec. 23	Louisville	H	89	66

ECAC Holiday Festival
(New York, N.Y.)

Dec. 27	Rider	N5	90	65
Dec. 29	Iona (finals)	N5	106	79
Jan. 3	South Carolina	A	89	60
Jan. 6	Ole Miss	H	90	60
Jan. 9	Mississippi State	A	74	56
Jan. 13	Tennessee	H	61	44
Jan. 16	LSU	A	129	97
Jan. 20	Texas Christian	H	124	80
Jan. 24	Georgia	A	82	77
Jan. 27	South Carolina	H	89	57
Feb. 3	Florida	H	77	63
Feb. 7	Vanderbilt	A	120	81
Feb. 11	Arkansas	H	88	73
Feb. 14	Georgia	H	86	73
Feb. 17	Tennessee	A	90	50
Feb. 20	Alabama	H	84	65
Feb. 24	Florida	A	94	63
Feb. 27	Auburn	A	88	73
Mar. 2	Vanderbilt	H	101	63

SEC Tournament
(New Orleans, La.)

Mar. 8	Florida	N6	100	76
Mar. 9	Arkansas	N6	95	75
Mar. 10	**Miss. State (finals)**	**N6**	**73**	**84**

NCAA Midwest Regional
First/Second Rounds
(Dallas, Texas)

Mar. 14	San Jose State	N7	110	72
Mar. 16	Virginia Tech	N7	84	60

NCAA Midwest Regional
(Minneapolis, Minn.)

Mar. 21	Utah	N8	101	70
Mar. 23	Wake Forest	N8	83	63

NCAA Final Four
(East Rutherford, N.J.)

Mar. 30	Massachusetts	N9	81	74
Apr. 1	Syracuse (finals)	N9	76	67
			3292	2497

NCAA CHAMPIONS FOR SIXTH TIME

(N1) Springfield, Mass.
(N2) Auburn Hills, Mich.
(N3) Indianapolis, Ind.

(N4) Louisville, Ky.
(N5) New York, N.Y.
(N6) New Orleans, La.
(N7) Dallas, Texas
(N8) Minneapolis, Minn.
(N9) East Rutherford, N.J.

—Leading Scorers—
Tony Delk (6-1 Sr. G) 17.8
Antoine Walker (6-8 So. F) 15.2
Walter McCarty (6-10 Sr. F) 11.3
Derek Anderson (6-4 Jr. G-F) 9.4
Ron Mercer (6-7 Fr. F) 8.0

1996/97—Won 35, Lost 5
NCAA Runner-up (NCAA Tournament)
SEC Tournament Champions
2nd SEC East (13-3)
Great Alaska Shootout Champions
Ranked 2nd CNN/USA Today, 5th AP

Coach: Rick Pitino
Captains: Derek Anderson, Anthony Epps, and Jared Prickett

Nov. 15	**Clemson**	**N1**	**71**	***79**

Great Alaska Shootout

Nov. 28	Syracuse	N2	87	53
Nov. 29	Alaska Anchorage	N2	104	72
Nov. 30	Col/Charleston (final)	N2	92	65
Dec. 3	Purdue	N3	101	87
Dec. 7	Indiana	N4	99	65
Dec. 9	Wright State	H	90	62
Dec. 14	Notre Dame	H	80	56
Dec. 21	Georgia Tech	N5	88	59
Dec. 23	UNC Asheville	H	105	51
Dec. 28	Ohio State	N6	81	65
Dec. 31	Louisville	A	74	54
Jan. 4	Tennessee	H	74	40
Jan. 7	Mississippi State	H	90	61
Jan. 9	Canisius	H	68	45
Jan. 11	**Ole Miss**	**A**	**69**	**73**
Jan. 14	Georgia	A	86	65
Jan. 18	Auburn	H	77	53
Jan. 22	Vanderbilt	N7	58	46
Jan. 26	Arkansas	A	83	73
Jan. 29	Florida	A	92	65
Feb. 1	Georgia	H	82	57
Feb. 4	**South Carolina**	**A**	**79**	***84**
Feb. 6	Western Carolina	H	82	55
Feb. 9	Villanova	H	93	56
Feb. 12	LSU	H	84	48
Feb. 15	Florida	H	85	56
Feb. 19	Alabama	A	75	61
Feb. 22	Vanderbilt	A	82	79
Feb. 25	Tennessee	A	74	64
Mar. 2	**South Carolina**	**H**	**66**	**72**

SEC Tournament
(Memphis, Tenn.)

Mar. 7	Auburn	N8	92	50
Mar. 8	Ole Miss	N8	88	70
Mar. 9	Georgia (finals)	N8	95	68

NCAA West Regional
First/Second Rounds
(Salt Lake City, Utah)

Mar. 13	Montana	N9	92	54
Mar. 15	Iowa	N9	75	69

NCAA West Regional
(San Jose, Calif.)

Mar. 20	St. Joseph's	N10	83	68
Mar. 22	Utah	N10	72	59

NCAA Final Four
(Indianapolis, Ind.)

Mar. 29	Minnesota	N1	78	69
Mar. 31	**Arizona (finals)**	**N1**	**79**	***84**
			3325	2512

(N1) Indianapolis, Ind.
(N2) Anchorage, Alaska
(N3) Chicago, Ill.
(N4) Louisville, Ky.
(N5) Atlanta, Ga.
(N6) Cleveland, Ohio
(N7) Cincinnati, Ohio

(N8) Memphis, Tenn.
(N9) Salt Lake City, Utah
(N10) San Jose, Calif.

—Leading Scorers—
Ron Mercer (6-7 So. G-F) 18.1
Derek Anderson (6-5 Sr. G) 17.7
Scott Padgett (6-9 So. F) 9.6
Anthony Epps (6-2 Sr. G) 8.9
Allen Edwards (6-5 Jr. F) 8.6

TUBBY SMITH ERA

1997/98—Won 35, Lost 4
National Champions (NCAA Tournament)
SEC Tournament Champions
SEC Champions (14-2)
SEC East Champions
Ranked 1st CNN/USA Today, 5th AP

Coach: Orlando "Tubby" Smith
Captains: Allen Edwards, Cameron Mills, and Jeff Sheppard

Nov. 20	Morehead State	H	88	49

Maui Invitational

Nov. 24	George Washington	N1	70	55
Nov. 25	**Arizona**	**N1**	**74**	**89**
Nov. 26	Missouri	N1	77	55
Nov. 29	Clemson	N2	76	61
Dec. 3	Purdue	N3	89	75
Dec. 6	Indiana	A	75	72
Dec. 10	Canisius	A	81	54
Dec. 13	Georgia Tech	H	85	71
Dec. 20	Tulsa	H	74	53
Dec. 23	American	H	75	52
Dec. 27	**Louisville**	**H**	**76**	**79**
Dec. 30	Ohio U.	A	95	58
Jan. 3	Vanderbilt	H	71	62
Jan. 6	Georgia	A	90	79
Jan. 10	Miss. State	A	77	71
Jan. 13	South Carolina	H	91	70
Jan. 17	Arkansas	H	80	*77
Jan. 21	Alabama	N4	70	67
Jan. 24	Tennessee	A	85	67
Jan. 27	Vanderbilt	A	63	61
Feb. 1	**Florida**	**H**	**78**	**86**
Feb. 4	LSU	A	63	61
Feb. 8	Villanova	A	79	63
Feb. 11	Tennessee	H	80	74
Feb. 14	**Ole Miss**	**H**	**64**	**73**
Feb. 18	Florida	A	79	54
Feb. 22	Georgia	H	85	74
Feb. 25	Auburn	A	83	58
Feb. 28	South Carolina	A	69	57

SEC Tournament
(Atlanta, Ga.)

Mar. 6	Alabama	N5	82	71
Mar. 7	Arkansas	N5	99	74
Mar. 8	South Carolina	N5	86	56

NCAA Southeast Regional
First/Second Rounds
(Atlanta, Ga.)

Mar. 13	South Carolina State	N5	82	67
Mar. 15	St. Louis	N5	88	61

NCAA Southeast Regional
(St. Petersburg, Fla.)

Mar. 20	UCLA	N6	94	68
Mar. 22	Duke	N6	86	84

NCAA Final Four
(San Antonio, Texas)

Mar. 28	Stanford	N7	86	*85
Mar. 30	Utah	N7	78	69
			3032	2557

NCAA CHAMPIONS FOR SEVENTH TIME

(N1) Maui, Hawaii
(N2) Phoenix, Ariz.
(N3) Chicago, Ill.
(N4) Louisville, Ky.
(N5) Atlanta, Ga.
(N6) St. Petersburg, Fla.
(N7) San Antonio, Texas

Bibliographic Note

The primary sources available for the study of sports in the twentieth century are rich, varied, and abundant. They include manuscript materials, published sources, and oral history. Oral interviews proved to be a particularly valuable source in the preparation of this study. With the help of the University of Kentucky Alumni Association we were able to locate and interview the following current or former players, some living as far away as Florida, California, or the state of Washington.

The athletes interviewed were John Adams, Marvin Akers, Jim Andrews, Scotty Baesler, Cliff Barker, Dicky Beal, Ralph Beard, Cecil Bell, Winston Bennett, Gerry Calvert, Ralph Carlisle, Dwane Casey, Truman Claytor, Ray Edelman, Elmer (Baldy) Gilb, Jack Givens, Phil Grawemeyer, Alex Groza, Bob Guyette, Cliff Hagan, Joe Hall, Roger Harden, Basil Hayden, Derrick Hord, Lee Huber, Charles Hurt, Dan Issel, Ned Jennings, Phil Johnson, Wallace Jones, William Kleiser, Ed Lander, Bo Lanter, Dave Lawrence, James Lee, Jim LeMaster, Bill Lickert, Steve Lochmueller, Paul McBrayer, James McFarland, Lawrence McGinnis, Louis McGinnis, Kyle Macy, Cameron Mills, Don Mills, Dirk Minniefield, Terry Mobley, Cotton Nash, C.M. Newton, Bernie Opper, J. Ed (Buddy) Parker, Tom Parker, Dick Parsons, Linville Puckett, Sam Ridgeway, Ken Rollins, Forest (Aggie) Sale, James Sharpe, Carey Spicer, Bill Spivey, Guy Strong, Lou Tsioropoulos, Lovell Underwood, Kenny Walker, Reggie Warford, Bob Watson, and LaVon Williams.

In addition to players we also interviewed UK Athletics Board members, athletics directors, coaches, and others connected with the basketball program as well as sportswriters, television sportscasters, and fans. Among the more than one hundred interviewees were Mark Bradley, Robert Bradley, A.B. (Happy) Chandler, Thomas D. Clark, Oscar Combs, Brad Davis, Joe Dean, James Dickey, Pat Etcheberry, D.G. FitzMaurice, Leonard Hamilton, Lake Kelly, Harry Lancaster, Ray Mears, Mickey Patterson, Rick Pitino, Billy Reed, Russell Rice, Tubby Smith, Eddie Sutton, Jerry Tipton, Denny Trease, and J. Richard Whitt. Winston Bennett, Dwane Casey, Baldy Gilb, Cliff Hagan, Joe Hall, Paul McBrayer, and C.M. Newton have already been listed among the team players.

Our research was greatly facilitated by the availability of scrapbooks and photographs from players or their relatives. We found these, like oral interviews, to be virtually untapped sources. Several players or relatives (as in the case of Bill King and Wilbur Schu, who are deceased) lent us their scrapbooks and photos. In addition, we made extensive use of the clippings files maintained on current and former players by the UK Media Relations Office as well as their large collection of individual and team photographs.

For information on former Wildcat coaches and players we used the clipping files maintained in the University Archives. We also examined and made extensive use of the other material in the archives, including copies of the university yearbook, the *Kentuckian* (whose title varies), minutes of the Board of Trustees meetings, and other university records for the years from 1903 to the present. The UK Alumni Office files also contained information and photos which we found useful in the preparation of this study.

The sports pages of several newspapers were read in

search of information on individuals, games, and other components of the UK basketball tradition. Most of the reading was in the *Louisville Courier-Journal* and the *Lexington Herald* and *Lexington Leader* (now the *Lexington Herald-Leader*), as well as the campus newspaper, the *Kentucky Kernel* (title varies). Copies of the *Kernel* are on file in the newspaper office. In addition to these papers we read selected issues of the *New York Times, Chicago Tribune, Chicago Sun-Times, Boston Globe, Los Angeles Times, Atlanta Constitution, Atlanta Journal, New Orleans Times-Picayune, Washington Post, Kansas City Star, Miami Herald, New York Post, New York Daily News, Cincinnati Post, Wall Street Journal,* and *USA Today*. Also used in the preparation of this study were selected issues of *Sports Illustrated, Chronicle of Higher Education, The Cats' Pause,* and other periodicals.

Our discussion of the basketball scandal of 1951 is based in large part on an extensive file on that event made available to us on condition that we not divulge the name of the person who provided it. The file contains, among other things, a typescript copy of Judge Saul Streit's statement on the UK athletic program, a photostatic copy of the indictments of Ralph Beard, Alex Groza, Dale Bamstable, Walt Hirsch, and Jim Line on bribery charges, as well as the perjury indictment of Bill Spivey and the sentencing of Beard, Groza, and Barnstable.

Among other valuable primary sources we used are: *University of Kentucky Basketball Facts* (title varies), a press guide prepared annually since 1944 by the UK Sports Information Office (now called Media Relations); Adolph F. Rupp, *An Outline of Basketball* (Lexington, 1948) and *Championship Basketball for Player, Coach, Fan* (Englewood Cliffs, N.J., 1948); Harry Lancaster as told to Cawood Ledford, *Adolph Rupp as I Knew Him* (Lexington, 1979), a reminiscence by the longtime assistant basketball coach and later athletics director at UK; Rick Pitino with Dick Weiss, *Full-Court Pressure: A Year in Kentucky Basketball* (New York, 1992); Jack Givens as told to Bert Nelli, "Goose" (an unpublished autobiography); and *The Official Southeastern Conference Sports Record Book, 1933-1959* (Birmingham, 1959).

The history of the University of Kentucky down to the mid-1960s is traced by James F. Hopkins, *The University of Kentucky: Origins and Early Years* (Lexington, 1951); and Charles G. Talbert, *The University of Kentucky: The Maturing Years* (Lexington, 1965).

Among the books written in recent years about basketball at UK and in the state of Kentucky are Lonnie Wheeler, *Blue Yonder* (Wilmington, Oh., 1998); Rick Bozich et al., *A Legacy of Champions* (Indianapolis,

1997); Dr. V.A. Jackson, team physician, *Beyond the Baron: A Personal Glance at Coach Adolph Rupp* (Kuttawa, Ky., 1998); Cawood Ledford, *Six Roads to Glory* (Lexington, 1997); *The Cats' Pause 1997-98 Basketball Yearbook* (Lexington, 1997); *Courier-Journal, Comeback Cats* (Louisville, 1998); *Courier-Journal, A Journey to Greatness: The 1995-96 Kentucky Wildcats' National Championship Season* (Louisville, 1996); *Herald-Leader, Out of the Blue* (Lexington, 1998), *Blue Grit* (Lexington, 1997), and *Bravo Blue* (Lexington, 1996); Brian Weinberg, *Portrait of the Writer as a Young Fan* (Louisville, 1997); Alexander Wolff and Armen Keteyian, *Raw Recruits* (New York, 1990); Jamie Vaught, *Crazy about the Cats* (Kuttawa, Ky., 1992) and *Still Crazy about the Cats* (Kuttawa, Ky., 1996); Cawood Ledford, as told to Billy Reed, *Hello Everybody, This Is Cawood Ledford* (Lexington, 1992); Russell Rice, *Kentucky Basketball's Big Blue Machine* (Huntsville, Ala., 1978), as well as his biography of Joe B. Hall and Adolph Rupp; Tev Laudeman, *The Rupp Years* (Louisville, 1972); Luke Walton, *Basketball's Fabulous Five* (New York, 1950); Oscar Combs, *Kentucky Basketball: A New Beginning* (Lexington, 1979); Dave Kindred, *Basketball: The Dream Game in Kentucky* (Louisville, 1975); and John McGill, *Kentucky Sports* (Lexington, 1978).

We have also used the following more general treatments of basketball in America: Neil D. Isaacs, *All the Moves: A History of College Basketball* (Philadelphia, 1975), the best treatment available on the subject; Larry Fox, *Illustrated History of Basketball* (New York, 1974); James Naismith, *Basketball: Its Origins and Development* (New York, 1941); Al Hershberg, *Basketball's Greatest Teams* (New York, 1966); Sandy Padwe, *Basketball's Hall of Fame* (Englewood Cliffs, N. J., 1970); Billy Packer with Roland Lazenby, *50 Years of the Final Four* (Dallas, 1987); Bill Russell and Taylor Branch, *Second Wind: The Memoirs of an Opinionated Man* (New York, 1979); John Wooden as told to Jack Tobin, *They Call Me Coach* (New York, 1973); John Feinstein, *A Season on the Brink: A Year with Bob Knight and the Indiana Hoosiers* (New York, 1986); Mike Recht, "Basketball," in *A Century of Sports,* Associated Press Sports Staff (Maplewood, N. J., 1971); Charles Rosen, *Scandals of '51: How the Gamblers Almost Killed College Basketball* (New York, 1978); Pete Axthelm, *The City Game* (New York, 1970); Alexander M. Weyland, *The Cavalcade of Basketball* (New York, 1960); Zander Hollander, ed., *The Modern Encyclopedia of Basketball* (New York, 1969), and *Basketball's Greatest Games* (Englewood Cliffs, N. J., 1970).

Index

Note: Italic numbers refer to photographs.